Complex Systems and Sustainability in the Global Auditing, Consulting, and Credit Rating Agency Industries

Michael I. C. Nwogugu
Independent Researcher, Nigeria

IGI Global
PUBLISHER of TIMELY KNOWLEDGE

A volume in the Advances in E-Business Research (AEBR) Book Series

Published in the United States of America by
IGI Global
Business Science Reference (an imprint of IGI Global)
701 E. Chocolate Avenue
Hershey PA, USA 17033
Tel: 717-533-8845
Fax: 717-533-8661
E-mail: cust@igi-global.com
Web site: http://www.igi-global.com

Library of Congress Cataloging-in-Publication Data

Names: Nwogugu, Michael C. I., author.
Title: Complex systems and sustainability in the global auditing, consulting, and credit rating agency industries / by Michael C. Nwogugu.

Description: Hershey, PA : Business Science Reference, [2021] | Includes bibliographical references and index. | Summary: "This book focuses on aspects of Complex Systems (including Networks), Mechanism-Design and Behavioral Game Theory, introducing new models and "informal" algorithms that solve social-choice problems (using behavioral Game Theory, Complex Systems Theory and Mechanism Design) and presents new mathematical proofs"-- Provided by publisher.
Identifiers: LCCN 2020048944 (print) | LCCN 2020048945 (ebook) | ISBN 9781799874188 (hardcover) | ISBN 9781799874195 (paperback) | ISBN 9781799874201 (ebook)
Subjects: LCSH: Credit bureaus. | Credit ratings. | Accounting firms. | Consulting firms.
Classification: LCC HG3751.5 .N96 2021 (print) | LCC HG3751.5 (ebook) | DDC 332.701/1--dc23
LC record available at https://lccn.loc.gov/2020048944
LC ebook record available at https://lccn.loc.gov/2020048945

This book is published in the IGI Global book series Advances in Finance, Accounting, and Economics (AFAE) (ISSN: 2327-5677; eISSN: 2327-5685)

British Cataloguing in Publication Data
A Cataloguing in Publication record for this book is available from the British Library.

For electronic access to this publication, please contact: eresources@igi-global.com.

Advances in Finance, Accounting, and Economics (AFAE) Book Series

Ahmed Driouchi
Al Akhawayn University, Morocco

ISSN:2327-5677
EISSN:2327-5685

Mission

In our changing economic and business environment, it is important to consider the financial changes occurring internationally as well as within individual organizations and business environments. Understanding these changes as well as the factors that influence them is crucial in preparing for our financial future and ensuring economic sustainability and growth.

The **Advances in Finance, Accounting, and Economics (AFAE)** book series aims to publish comprehensive and informative titles in all areas of economics and economic theory, finance, and accounting to assist in advancing the available knowledge and providing for further research development in these dynamic fields.

Coverage

- Economic Downturn
- Economic Policy
- Managerial Accounting
- Economic Theory
- Fiscal Policy
- Behavioral Economics
- Theoretical Issues in Economics, Finance, and Accounting
- Entrepreneurship in Accounting and Finance
- Microeconomics
- Taxes

IGI Global is currently accepting manuscripts for publication within this series. To submit a proposal for a volume in this series, please contact our Acquisition Editors at acquisitions@igi-global.com or visit: https://www.igi-global.com/publish/.

The Advances in Finance, Accounting, and Economics (AFAE) Book Series (ISSN 2327-5677) is published by IGI Global, 701 E. Chocolate Avenue, Hershey, PA 17033-1240, USA, www.igi-global.com. This series is composed of titles available for purchase individually; each title is edited to be contextually exclusive from any other title within the series. For pricing and ordering information please visit https://www.igi-global.com/book-series/advances-finance-accounting-economics/73685. Postmaster: Send all address changes to above address.

Titles in this Series

For a list of additional titles in this series, please visit:
https://www.igi-global.com/book-series/advances-finance-accounting-economics/73685

Money Laundering and Terrorism Financing in Global Financial Systems
Abdul Rafay (University of Management and Technology, Pakistan)
Business Science Reference • © 2021 • 374pp • H/C (ISBN: 9781799887584) • US $215.00

Financial Management and Risk Analysis Strategies for Business Sustainability
Joaquín Enríquez-Díaz (University of A Coruña, Spain) Laura Castro-Santos (University of A Coruña, Spain) and Félix Puime-Guillén (University of A Coruña, Spain)
Business Science Reference • © 2021 • 320pp • H/C (ISBN: 9781799876342) • US $215.00

Theory of Shocks, COVID-19, and Normative Fundamentals for Policy Responses
Olga Ivanovna Pilipenko (The Russian Presidential Academy of National Economy and Public Administration, Russia) Zoya Andreevna Pilipenko (Bank of Russia, Russia) and Andrey Igorevich Pilipenko (The Russian Presidential Academy of National Economy and Public Administration, Russia)
Business Science Reference • © 2021 • 300pp • H/C (ISBN: 9781799843092) • US $195.00

Handbook of Research on Theory and Practice of Financial Crimes
Abdul Rafay (University of Management and Technology, Pakistan)
Business Science Reference • © 2021 • 650pp • H/C (ISBN: 9781799855675) • US $345.00

Comparative Research on Earnings Management, Corporate Governance, and Economic Value
Elisabete S. Vieira (University of Aveiro, Portugal) Mara Madaleno (University of Aveiro, Portugal) and Graça Azevedo (University of Aveiro, Portugal)
Business Science Reference • © 2021 • 433pp • H/C (ISBN: 9781799875963) • US $215.00

Examining the Intersection of Circular Economy, Forestry, and International Trade
Badri Narayanan Gopalakrishnan (University of Washington, USA) Taranjeet Duggal (Amity University, India) and Tavishi Tewary (Jaipuria Institute of Management Noida, India)
Business Science Reference • © 2021 • 266pp • H/C (ISBN: 9781799849902) • US $195.00

Influence of FinTech on Management Transformation
Amira Sghari (Faculty of Economics and Management, University of Sfax, Tunisia) and Karim Mezghani (Al Imam Mohammad Ibn Saud Islamic University, Saudi Arabia & University of Sfax, Tunisia)
Business Science Reference • © 2021 • 273pp • H/C (ISBN: 9781799871101) • US $215.00

IGI Global
PUBLISHER of TIMELY KNOWLEDGE

701 East Chocolate Avenue, Hershey, PA 17033, USA
Tel: 717-533-8845 x100 • Fax: 717-533-8661
E-Mail: cust@igi-global.com • www.igi-global.com

Table of Contents

Preface

BACKGROUND

The global services industry and the global capital markets continues to undergo significant changes and increasing harmonization and standardization due to internet penetration, the sub-prime loan problems, the Global Financial Crisis of 2007-2014 and the enactment of new financial regulations in many countries. Antitrust/competition has not been fully addressed even though it's pervasive in capital markets transactions. Nwogugu (2009) critiqued Antitrust detection models, and introduced new Antitrust detection models. The antitrust and legal analysis in this book is based on US laws and standards. Given that the US has probably the most advanced antitrust laws, real estate industry and capital markets in the world (and that many countries have copied US laws and business processes), the issues and theories discussed in the book are applicable in other countries.

CRAs have been a central and critical element of global debt capital markets and real estate markets, of financial institution regulation, and monetary/fiscal policy in most developed countries. Credit ratings have direct impact on the borrowing costs of companies and government agencies, and indirectly on that of individuals. Globally, top-three rating agencies affect more than the equivalent of seventy Trillion euros of corporate debt, government municipal debt, and securitized debt (in the public markets, the Rule-144A market, the Regulation-D market, and commercial paper market), and trillions of euros of swaps/derivatives. However, as evidenced by investigations and prosecutions of rating agencies during 2008-2018 by government agencies in many countries (e.g. the Attorney General of New York State), there are significant legal, psychological, and economic problems in the regulation and functioning of rating agencies, much to the detriment of investors, issuers and the government. The structure of the rating agency industry has evolved into an oligopoly, and regulation has resulted in redundancy, increased collusion (or opportunities for collusion), and reduced competition. The securitization of trillions of dollars of mortgages and real estate leases in the US and other countries (and thus capital-formation, liquidity and pricing in both real estate and corporate loan markets) during 1990-2008 were heavily dependent on the functioning and regulation of CRAs (both of which failed as confirmed by the Global Financial Crisis of 2008-2014). This book explains these problems, analyzes economic and liability issues, and introduces solutions and new Mechanism Design based models for the compensation and operations of CRAs. The issues analyzed are also relevant to developing and under-developed countries, many of whom are now trying to develop their capital markets.

One major issue that is often overlooked is that NPLs (non-performing loans), LRCs and CRAs are significantly affected by both business processes and the nature and tenure of human computer interactions (HCI) of the financial markets ecosystem (e.g. bankers, traders, research analysts, investors; accounting firms, CRAs, regulators, etc.). In most countries, all or significant portions of lending, loan servicing, NPL management and CRA operations and bond/stock trading are now automated. Unlike other HCI or business process books, this book does not focus on the direct short-term individual-level interactions between humans and computers, but rather, develops theories about business processes and the long-term impact of the use of computers on individuals and groups within the context of corporate strategy, and vice versa (the long term impact of corporate strategy on individuals and groups that pervasively communicate, research and make decisions using computers and networks). Unlike other HCI books, this book analyzes and develops theories about public policy and "inter-business" business processes that are designed and executed within the context of computer networks.

Similarly, Accounting firms are critical elements of global capital markets and have or can have significant effects on Monetary Policy (earnings management, market-volatility, market-crash-risk; etc.), Fiscal Policy (tax liability; tax evasion), Climate Policy (documentation; compliance; financial reporting) and Social welfare Policy.

The Business Opportunities industry coves at least an estimated forty percent of economic activity in many countries, but remains substantially under-regulated and quasi-informal in many developed countries and Emerging Markets countries. Nwogugu (2019a;b) analyzed various aspects of franchising and Quasi-Franchising, critiqued models of Franchising and introduced new models of Franchising, Quasi-Franchising and online Services.

Nwogugu (2019c;d;e) introduced three new *Theories-of-The-Firm* that unify Entrepreneurship Theory, Bankruptcy Theory, Complex Systems Theory, Macroeconomic Theory and Financial Stability.

Hence, economic phenomena such as the Global Financial Crisis, excessive systemic risk; the sub-prime crisis, corporate bankruptcy and financial distress can be partly explained within the framework of industry dynamics in the global accounting/consulting industry and the evolution of firms therein.

The issues raised in this book are critical in the portfolio management, organizational studies, legal and accounting fields, and are also relevant to countries that are developing their economies and capital markets. The book analyzes Industrial Organization, Mechanism Design, Political Economy and Complex Systems issues in the global accounting/consulting industry, the "Quasi-franchising industry" and the global Credit Rating Agency (CRA) industry which are currently some of the most international of all services industries, and have or can have substantial effects on international trade and international capital flows. During 2000-2020, the Global Services sector in general expanded in many countries and especially in emerging markets countries. From the Industrial Organization, Mechanism Design, Political Economy and Complex Systems perspectives, the objectives and achievements of this book are as follows:

1. Explain the macroeconomic, behavioral operations research and political economy issues that affect and the evolution of accounting/auditing firms, CRAs, management consulting firms and environmental auditing firms.
2. Introduces some human behavioral biases, and analyzes the types of intra-company decisions and group dynamics and auditor-decisions that can have significant effects on innovation and competition within the accounting/consulting industry and (on clients' industries) and on overall economic growth in nations.
3. Analyze structural changes and antitrust problems in the global accounting/consulting industry and the CRA industry; and explains how these issues have worsened Climate Change and corporate compliance with environmental regulations.

4. Critique of the business and compensation models of CRAs. Critiques regulatory frameworks that were proposed by governments and individual researchers. Proposes new solutions and regulatory frameworks for Credit Rating Agencies which are based in part on economic psychology and complex systems considerations and theories. Includes theories of economic psychology and behavioral biases – such as critique of the "Tie-Breaker" phenomenon; "Stability" in ratings; perceived "roles" of CRAs; reliance on ratings; Social Capital; etc..
5. The book can help regulators, economic psychologists, lawyers and economists to gain a better understanding of: a) how antitrust laws can affect transactions, outcomes (occupancy rates, quality of life, investment, etc.) and market dynamics (prices, demand/supply, etc.); and b) how antitrust laws can be modified to improve markets; c) the symbiotic relationships among antitrust, loan markets and the effectiveness of CRAs.
6. Identifies the issues that affect contracting between auditing/consulting firms and their auditee-clients and also affect industry structure and evolution.
7. Identifies the issues that affect contracting between CRAs and issuers (and their investment banks) and also affect industry structure and evolution.
8. Critique various existing and proposed CRA business models and compensation models.
9. Introduces new mathematical models and "learning algorithms" (new "*learning business models*" and compensation contracts) for CRAs and Accounting firms that can solve the conflicts of interest, antitrust, greed, Regret, deadweight losses, complexity and industrial organization problems inherent both industries; and also contravenes various "Impossibility Theorems" including the *Myerson-Satterthwaite Impossibility Theorem* and *Arrow's Impossibility Theorem.*
10. Introduces new and testable theories/hypothesis of complex systems, organizational psychology and group dynamics, group behavior and risk within firms as they react to external and internal forces and regulation. The group-behavior theories introduced in the chapters are tied directly to firms' profitability and competitive advantages.
11. Introduces new concepts and theories in behavioral game theory, HCI and complex systems theory, Industrial Organization, Sustainability (social, economic, urban and environmental sustainability), Climate Change and Environmental Compliance.
12. The book analyzes the relationship between economic growth and risk regulation institutions; and relates business processes, operations and organizational psychology to economic growth, sustainability and political economy trends.
13. The book includes reference materials and the scope is international; and the book can be helpful in building macro-economic and political economy models of interactions of firms; and models of how intra-firm interactions affect economic growth.

From *Mechanism Design, Dynamical Systems, Sustainability* and *Complex Systems Theory* perspectives, this book addresses the following classes of issues:

1. *Multi-sided Incentives* that can reduce or increase earnings management, asset-quality management, sustainability and incentive-effects management.
2. "*Many-person re-generative institutions*" such as legal processes; etc..
3. "*Many-person Mechanisms*" that can reduce or increase harmful group collusion, and the incentives for transparency and truthfulness.
4. The elicitation of: i) "best" preferences for organizations; ii) preferences of groups in organizations.

5. Complex adaptive systems.

In some chapters in this book, "conditions" (represented by mathematical equations, derivatives and inequalities) are introduced, under which some hypothesis or event will exist. These "conditions" are in the nature of:

1. *Mechanism Design* elements.
2. *Game Theory strategies* – similar to the mathematical of representation of *Supermodularity* and *Complementarity* by the inequality $\partial^2 f/\partial z_i \partial z_j \geq 0$; for all $i \neq j$; where and z_i and z_j are strategies of participants in the action space and each action is chosen from an interval z_i, z_j ε [a,b]; and the payoff function (f(.)) depends on actions/strategies of two or more types of participants z_i and z_j in the action space (i = 1……..n; j=1………n).
3. *Invariants* – which are used to characterize key elements of *Groups.*
4. *Decision elements* – wherein groups of these "conditions" can also be weighted and converted into decision-scores for decision making.
5. *Dynamical Systems* elements.

With regards to public policy and affected populations, the theories introduced and issues analyzed in this book collectively (and directly or indirectly) affect more than two billion people in several continents; and more than €310 trillion (three hundred and ten trillion euros) of corporate, government and household assets; and more than €5 trillion (five trillion euros) of daily transactions around the world (e.g. loans/bonds/notes; money-markets; stock markets; swaps/derivatives; asset securitizations; commodities; credit transactions; executive compensation; employee incentives; International-Trade, performance benchmarking; etc.).

This book is an academic monograph about Industrial Organization, Complex Systems and Mechanism Design, (and is not a literature review) and the book doesn't cover the automation of CRAs' and auditing firms' daily research operations. Such automation (e.g. AI and data-mining) has been adopted across both the CRA and auditing industries (such that it hasn't been a major competition differentiator). The main target audience for this book is as follows:

1. University Professors – in Behavioral Operations Research, Risk Management, Industrial Organization, Applied Mathematics and Complex Systems, Behavioral Political Economy, Accounting, Law & Economics, Mathematical Psychology and Organizational Psychology.
2. PHD-degree-holders who work in industry, think-tanks, consulting firms, financial services companies and government agencies.
3. PHD students – in Behavioral Operations Research, Risk Management, Industrial Organization, Applied Mathematics and Complex Systems, Behavioral Political Economy, Accounting, Law & Economics, Mathematical Psychology and Organizational Psychology.

Many of the chapters in this book are revised excerpts from my articles Nwogugu (2008) [1], Nwogugu (2016)[2] and Nwogugu (2010/2015)[3] (collectively, the "Original Materials"), which have been cited in various academic journals and PHD thesis.

RESEARCH METHODS

This section explains the various research methods that were used in this book – and especially in Chapters 3, 4, 5, 6, 8 and 9. The approach in this book is entirely theoretical and the book uses and introduces concepts and theories in Behavioral Game Theory, Mechanism-Design, HCI and Complex Systems theory.

Except for technological advances in CRAs' and auditing firms' process automation, both the contexts and subject matters of the book haven't changed much in the last ten years (many of the "new" post-2015 articles rehash and discuss and reframe the same issues and use the same/similar research methods as the "old" pre-2016 articles).

Method-#1: Critical Theory

Critical Theory was developed by the "*Frankfurt School*" of social sciences in Germany in the 1930s, and essentially adopts a multi-faceted critical approach to relationships, political influences, entities and institutions. Earlier focus was on the critical methods of Karl Marx and Sigmund Freud; and later influences propagated pragmatism and idealism, and incorporated historical contexts and political dynamics.

Method-#2: Capital Dynamics Theory

Capital Dynamics Theory was developed by the Author Michael C. Nwogugu. "*Capital Dynamics Theory*" relates corporate financial policies, Behavioral Operations Research, Game-Theory type analysis of Managerial Risk Preferences, *Contract Theory*, "*Accounting Biases*" and earnings management on one hand, to Sustainable Growth, *Fintech-Gaps*, AI, Financial Stability, *Complex Systems Theory* and capital markets. *Fintech-Gaps* consists of the psychological effects of Fintech and associated Artificial Intelligence, inefficiencies inherent in the use of Fintech/AI, "*Fintech/AI Externalities*", and *Externalities* that can affect Fintech.

Capital Dynamics Theory can help improve Computer Science, Physics, Decision Sciences and Artificial Intelligence models that are used to identify or predict financial statement fraud, securities fraud and or *Non-Compliance* (as a physical and evolutionary phenomenon); and to model Portfolio Management, Public Policy, Financial Instability, Stock-market Fluctuations, Financial Distress, Household Dynamics, Consumer Behavior, Retailing Trends, Organizational Psychology trends, *International Contagion* (of Culture, market-volatility, Corporate Governance; Usage-of-Trade, enforcement patterns; etc.), "Personal Growth", and or Asset Pricing.

Method-#3: Complexity Theory and Complex Adaptive Systems Theory

Both terms collectively focus on complex, emergent and macroscopic properties of systems and systems-of-systems; and refer to the identification and analysis of following:

1. Nonlinearity in relationships of firms and regulators.
2. Nonlinearity in the causes of evolutions of firms and industries.
3. Nonlinearity in the Rule-of-Law.
4. "Emergent" phenomena in firms and industries as systems and systems-of-systems.
5. Anomalies in established theories, transactions and patterns of behavior.

6. Chaos and Chaotic Systems.
7. Existence and dynamics of various types of Networks.
8. Various types of evolution and associated causal factors.

The underlying premise is that firms, industries, groups, transactions, processes and the economy are or can be systems and systems-of-systems that consists of interacting parts whose collective interactions may produce different dynamics from the whole.

Method-#4: Value-And-Evolution Factors Analysis

This methodological approach involves the identification and factor-by-factor analysis of all or most of the following points/issues that are likely to be Value-Drivers and the fulcrum or trigger-points for evolution/change in companies, industries, regulation, risk-perception, value-creation, relationships and transactions:

1. Motivation And Literature Summary.
2. Did The Firm's Operations Comply With Or Contradict Academic Theories In Finance, Business Economics, Management Science, Decision Sciences And Or Operations Research ?.
3. Complexity And The Rule Of Law.
4. Sustainability.
5. Summary of Financial Statement Analysis.
6. Corporate Governance Issues.
7. Financial Distress And Insolvency.
8. Boundaries Of The Firm - Strategic Alliances, Joint Ventures And Growth/Expansion.
9. Expansion By Mergers/Acquisitions (And Or Reactions To Competitors' M&A Transactions).
10. The Impact Of Technology And Innovation – By The Firm And On The Firm.
11. Effects Of Specific Regulations/Statutes And Enforcement.
12. The Impact Of the Firm On Industry Structures And Vice Versa (Industrial Organization).
13. Structural Changes.
14. Globalization.
15. Financial Stability And Systemic Risk.
16. New Theories Of Managerial Behavior, Organizational Behavior, Behavioral Economics And Or Behavioral Finance.
17. Regulatory Failure And Or Regulatory Fragmentation.
18. Regulatory Capture.

INVALIDITY OF IMPOSSIBILITY THEOREMS: THE MYERSON-SATTERTHWAITE IMPOSSIBILITY THEOREM, ARROW'S IMPOSSIBILITY THEOREM, SEN'S IMPOSSIBILITY THEOREM, GIBBARD'S THEOREM, THE GIBBARD-SATTERTHWAITE IMPOSSIBILITY THEOREM, AND THE GREEN-LAFFONT IMPOSSIBILITY THEOREM

In several chapters, this book introduces new *"Informal" Algorithms4* (business/compensation models, Work-allocation, Penalty-Allocation, etc.) which prove that the *Myerson-Satterthwaite Impossibility Theorem5* and *Arrow's Impossibility Theorem6* and *Sen's Impossibility Theorem7*, the *Gibbard-Satterthwaite Impossibility Theorem*8 [1973;1975], *Gibbard's Theorem9*, and the *Green-Laffont Impossibility Theorem*10 are wrong or inapplicable in some circumstances. These foregoing *Impossibility Theorems* have been and remain major Foundation Theorems in various branches of Computer Science, Artificial Intelligence, Operations Research, Economic Theory and Applied Math.

This book introduces the following *"Informal" Algorithms"*: i) new "*learning business models*" and compensation contracts for CRAs that can solve the conflicts of interest, antitrust, greed, Regret, deadweight losses, complexity and industrial organization problems inherent in the credit rating agency industry; ii) new "*business models*", work-allocation models, liability-allocation models and compensation contracts for Accounting firms that can solve the conflicts of interest, antitrust, greed, Regret, deadweight losses, complexity and industrial organization problems inherent in the Accounting industry. These said Mechanism Design and Complex Systems based models have desirable properties such as the following:

1. *Individual Rationality* (*Myerson-Satterthwaite Impossibility Theorem*).
2. *Exact And Approximate Welfare Maximization* (*Myerson-Satterthwaite Impossibility Theorem*).
3. *Strong Budget Balance* (*Myerson-Satterthwaite Impossibility Theorem*).
4. *Dominant-Strategy Incentive Compatibility* of sellers and buyers (*Myerson-Satterthwaite Impossibility Theorem*).
5. *Pareto Optimality* (*Myerson-Satterthwaite Impossibility Theorem*).
6. *Feasibility* (*Myerson-Satterthwaite Impossibility Theorem*).
7. *No-Dictatorship* (*Arrow's Impossibility Theorem; Gibbard-Satterthwaite Impossibility Theorem*).
8. *Pareto-Efficiency* (*Arrow's Impossibility Theorem*).
9. *Independence of Irrelevant Alternatives* (*Arrow's Impossibility Theorem*).
10. *Non-dictatorial* (*Gibbard's Theorem*; the *Gibbard-Satterthwaite Impossibility Theorem*) - there isn't any distinguished agent who can impose the outcome.
11. *No Two-Option Limit* (*Gibbard's Theorem*; the *Gibbard-Satterthwaite Impossibility Theorem*) - the process doesn't limit the possible outcomes to only two options.
12. *No Strategic-Voting* (*Gibbard's Theorem*, the *Gibbard-Satterthwaite Impossibility Theorem*) - the process isn't open to Strategic-Voting (once an agent has identified their preferences, it isnt possible that they have no action at their disposal that best protects such preferences regardless of the other agents' actions).

Thus, each of those models (introduced in this book) contravene the *Myerson-Satterthwaite Impossibility Theorem* and *Arrow's Impossibility Theorem, Sen's Impossibility Theorem, Gibbard's Theorem*, The *Gibbard-Satterthwaite Impossibility Theorem*, and the *Green-Laffont Impossibility Theorem*.

INFORMAL ALGORITHMS AND ALGORITHMIC CONTRACTS

Informal Algorithms are relatively new in the literature and its definitions vary across authors and subject-areas. On *Informal Algorithms*, see the comments in: Burke (2019), Dourish (2016), Seaver (2017), US Executive Office of the President (2016), Yeung (2018), Žliobaitė (2017), Australian Competition and Consumer Commission (2018), and Devendorf & Goodman (2014).

On *Algorithmic Contracts*, see Scholz (2016), Surden (2014), Calo (2015), Cifrino (2014), Hoffman (2016), and Yadav (2016).

THE "REPLICABILITY AND REPRODUCIBILITY CRISIS" IN ACADEMIC RESEARCH: UNRELIABILITY OF EMPIRICAL RESEARCH IN PSYCHOLOGY (INCLUDING MATHEMATICAL PSYCHOLOGY), COMPLEX SYSTEMS, BEHAVIORAL POLITICAL ECONOMY AND BEHAVIORAL OPERATIONS RESEARCH

The ongoing "*Replicability And Reproducibility Crisis*" in academic research (significant un-reliability and distortion of empirical research in Behavioral Operations Research, Behavioral Political Economy, Psychology, Mathematical Psychology; etc.) was addressed in the first chapters in Nwogugu (2019). Also see: Zeng, Shen & Zhou (2017); Cairney & Geyer (2017); Świątkowski & Dompnier (2017); Loken & Gelman (2017); Aguinis, Cascio & Ramani (2017); Cristea & Ioannidis (2018); and BEC Crew (August 28, 2015)11.

THE CHAPTERS

The section summarizes the other chapters in this book.

Chapter 1 surveys elements of decision patterns, group interactions, political economy factors and macroeconomic factors that affect or can affect the structure and evolution of the global accounting/consulting industry and the global Credit Rating Agency industry.

Chapter 2 analyzes the "*Business Opportunity Industry*", Sustainability And Systemic Risk. In the US and some countries/jurisdictions, there are statutory differences between franchises and "*Business Opportunities*", and the use of either business-type require specific disclosures/filings and compliance at the state and federal government levels. The concept of "*Business Opportunities*" refers to traditional service industry business-relationships that are very similar (functionally and operationally but not always legally or contractually) to franchises but are not regulated as, and are not perceived as such. Thus, *Business Opportunities* is a relatively new industry and encompasses segments of many traditional service industry sectors. These include but are not limited to correspondence banking; affiliate marketing systems; Insurance brokerages; mortgage brokers; one-to-many Auto dealership agreements (with and without warehouse lines); auto finance companies (with or without warehouse lines); Mutual Fund families (including mutual funds created by strategic alliances and joint ventures); medical and dental practices; manufacturing cooperatives; some types of agriculture cooperatives; Manufacturing Licenses; one-to-many Distribution Agreements; one-to-many Strategic Alliances; one-to-many Joint Ventures (ie. for distribution or some types of manufacturing); one-to-many Strategic Alliances by auditing/accounting firms; one-to-many hotel management agreements by hotel chains and hotel management companies; one-to-many Outsourcing Agreements; multi-customer loan/card processing; etc.. Given this definition, *Business Opportunities* cover or affect more than an estimated forty percent of the economic activity in all developed countries, and most Emerging Markets countries. This chapter: i) discusses various types of *Business Opportunities* within the context of systemic risk; ii) introduces models of Business-Opportunity/Quasi-Franchising contracts.

Chapter 3: i) analyzes the failure of, and Unconstitutionality of the Sarbanes-Oxley Act (SOX) and the Dodd-Frank Act, and their Impact on Accounting Firms and Credit Rating Agencies; and ii) introduces models of *Willingness-To-Comply* with SOX and similar statutes. SOX directly/indirectly governs internal controls, and some aspects of disclosure at exchange-traded companies in the US, and the practice of Accounting in the US. The US has the world's largest economy and the largest securities markets and US statutes (including SOX) affect foreign companies that are listed on US stock exchanges, and exchange-traded US multinational corporations that operate in many foreign countries, and thus SOX has significant *Multiplier Effects* on the Global Economy. SOX was the first legislation in the world that simultaneously attempted to address corporate governance, securities law issues, the practice of accounting, internal controls, accounting fraud and enforcement and was long overdue given prior corporate scandals. Many countries (e.g. Canada, France; UK; Japan; South Africa; China; Australia; India; etc.) subsequently followed the US and enacted laws that were conceptually similar to, and had the same objectives as SOX. Furthermore, SOX has affected and is likely to continue to affect and influence legislation and adjudication in many countries because many such countrys' constitutions are based on the US constitution (and were either enacted or amended within the last twenty years). Under US laws (and generally accepted common-law principles), many elements of SOX are un-constitutional; and SOX is inefficient and has caused many companies to de-list from exchanges. Limiting SOX to only publicly traded companies is not meaningful given the large number of medium and large non-listed companies. This chapter explains why SOX has failed and sections of SOX are un-constitutional. The chapter also develops new models of *Willingness-To-Comply* with SOX – which can be used for Internal Audits, enforcement, portfolio management and stock-selection. The theories and models in this chapter can be extended to similar statutes in other countries. The Dodd Frank Act applies to accounting firms and CRAs in the US; and to US companies (many of which have vast global operations and international suppliers) and to non-US companies whose stocks or bonds are listed in US financial exchanges; and thus, the Dodd Frank Act's reach and "*Multiplier Effects*" are indeed global. The Dodd Frank Act continues to have significant effects on the structure and evolution of the CRA industry and the global accounting/consulting industry (https://www.journalofaccountancy.com/issues/2010/sep/20103108.html) in various ways. However, the Dodd Frank Act and similar statutes in many countries/jurisdictions are inefficient, and have failed to address the fundamental problems in financial systems; and parts of the Dodd Frank Act are un-constitutional. Other countries/jurisdictions have enacted statutes that are similar to the Dodd Frank Act [12]. Canada, Brazil and Asia countries have also introduced similar statutes. The United Kingdom introduced the Vickers Report, which is similar to the Volcker Rule (the Vickers Report has the same purpose of the Volcker Rule but it has different methods, and is based on the ring fence and not on the separation of commercial and investment banks). The EU also released the Report of the European Commission's High-level Expert Group on Bank Structural Reform" (aka *Liikanen Group Report*) which addresses such differences. The European Union enacted the European Market Infrastructure Regulation ("EMIR"),[13] the Markets in Financial Instruments Directive II and related Regulation ("MiFID II" and "MIFIR"),[14] the new Capital Requirements Directive and Regulation ("CRD IV"),[15] and other statutes.

Chapter 4: i) compares CRAs (Credit Rating Agencies), Management Consulting Firms, Environmental Auditing Firms, Tax Consulting Firms and Auditing/Accounting Firms with the purpose of providing a better understanding of the current and possible regulatory, Mechanism Design and Industrial Organization factors that can affect the global accounting/auditing industry and the global CRA industry; ii) analyzes banks, credit rating agencies (CRAs) and investors as joint tortfeasors and co-conspirators (in litigation against accounting/auditing firms).

Chapter 5: analyzes Structural Change and Antitrust in the Global Auditing/Consulting Industry and Environmental-Pollution/Climate-Change issues. During 1990-2020, the global auditing/accounting and management consulting industry sectors experienced significant structural changes which have had un-even effects among large, medium and small auditing firms. The first section of this chapter summarizes the structural changes and compares accounting firms, management-consulting firms, tax-consulting firms and credit rating agencies. The second section summarizes the antitrust problems. The third section discusses some of the resultant climate-change and environmental pollution problems and introduces new solutions. In many countries, accounting firms have primary responsibility for auditing compliance with mechanisms such as carbon credits, environmental/sustainability accounting and compliance with environmental regulations. The topics of the three sections (structural change, antitrust and the auditing/consulting firm's role in pollution audits/management) are linked and have or can have symbiotic effects on each other.

Chapter 6: analyzes Networks, Complex Systems and International Trade and introduces new *Allocation Mechanisms* for Accounting/Consulting Firms. The "Big-Four" accounting firms dominate the global accounting/auditing industry, and the big-seven consulting firms (Bain; McKinsey; Booz; Deloitte; PwC; KPMG and E&Y) dominate the global business/management consulting industry and stifle competition. During 1990-2017, the global auditing/accounting industry and the global management consulting industry experienced significant structural changes that have implications for Financial Stability, systemic risk and the proper functioning of capital markets. Some of the results included the collapses of stock prices and bond prices of firms suspected of earnings management; and substantial litigation against auditing firms, CRAs and board of directors. Accounting/audit firms and consulting firms have always been key elements in the fight against earnings management, securities fraud, corruption and asset quality management because of their unique position as external auditors and advisors. Clearly, auditor fees and consulting fees affect auditor/consultant independence which in turn affects investors, investment professionals, the investment decision processes of companies and funds, and capital allocation processes by governments. This chapter: i) analyzes liability-allocation within the context of the adverse effects of oligopoly and auditor-independence in the audit/accounting industry, traditional liability and non-compliance with Climate Finance disclosure requirements; iv) introduces some properties of efficient *Auditor-Work Allocation Mechanisms* ("AAM"), *Audit-Fee Allocation Mechanisms* ("AFM"); *Audit Liability-allocation Mechanisms* (ALAM); and *Audit Penalty-Allocation Mechanisms* (APAM) for both audit and consulting firms, to which concepts of *Group Theory*, *Complex Systems Theory* and *Algorithmic Mechanism Design* can be applied – these proposed models represent structural changes that can reform competition in both industries; v) introduces some efficient models of Auditor-Compensation Mechanisms. These models have desirable properties such as *individual rationality*; *exact and approximate welfare maximization*; *strong budget balance*; *dominant-strategy incentive compatibility* of sellers and buyers; *pareto optimality*, *feasibility*, *No-Dictatorship* and *Pareto-Efficiency* – and thus, each model contravenes both Arrow's Impossibility Theorem and the *Myerson-Satterthwaite Impossibility Theorem*. These issues have implications for international trade and international capital flows given the prevalence of Accounting firms, Quasi-Franchising and management consulting firms in almost all aspects of modern business. An earlier (pre-2015) version of this chapter is available in www.ssrn.com.

Chapter 7: explains why existing and proposed Credit Rating Agency (CRA) Business Models and Compensation Models are inefficient. This chapter explains why existing and proposed CRA business models and compensation models are inefficient and result in *Deadweight Losses*, fraud and Antitrust violations. These models are those that are either currently in use, or have been proposed by academic researchers or government agencies. This chapter is an excerpt (and subsequently updated material) from my (pre-2014) article about CRAs which is available in www.ssrn.com.

Chapter 8: analyzes Complex Systems, Competition/Antitrust and Legal Problems In The Credit Rating Agency Industry. This chapter: i) analyzes antitrust and legal problems in the global CRA industry; ii) explains systemic risk problems inherent in the CRA industry; iii) analyzes the *Tie-Breaker phenomenon* and introduces new definitions of "*Equilibrium*" in the CRA ratings processes; iv) discusses the effects of CRAs on international capital flows, international asset allocation, systemic risk and financial stability; v) discusses *Reputational Capital* as a sub-set of *Influence*. This chapter is an excerpt (and subsequently updated material) from my (pre-2014) article about CRAs which is available in www.ssrn.com.

Chapter 9: introduces new "*Learning*" Business Models for the Global Credit Rating Agency industry. Credit Ratings Agencies ("CRAs") are prone to various antitrust and conflict-of-interest problems that arise from their regulation and their business and compensation models. CRAs have played a critical role in global capital markets for the last few decades, and the inefficiencies inherent in the compensation contracts for, and business models of CRA were clearly illustrated during the Global Financial Crisis of 2007-2011, during which ABS Trusts and some large companies suddenly defaulted without prior downgrades of their ratings – its well known that markets often price in potential defaults or down-grades before CRAs revise their ratings downwards. Given significant dependence on CRAs by investors and regulators, CRA can be a substantial source of systemic risk; and thus, the challenge is not only to develop optimal CRA contracts, but also to develop and implement CRA business-models that facilitate such contracts such that social welfare is maximized, and the issuer-CRA relationship cannot be re-characterized as a joint venture, strategic alliance or a franchise. This chapter adopts agent-based and complexity approaches and: i) introduces new game theoretic "*learning business models*" and compensation contracts for CRAs that can solve the conflicts of interest, antitrust, greed, Regret, deadweight losses, complexity and industrial organization problems inherent in the credit rating agency industry; and have desirable properties such as *individual rationality*; *exact and approximate welfare maximization*; *strong budget balance*; *dominant-strategy incentive compatibility* of sellers and buyers; *pareto optimality*, *feasibility*, *No-Dictatorship* and *Pareto-Efficiency* – and thus, each model contravenes both Arrow's Impossibility Theorem and the *Myerson-Satterthwaite Impossibility Theorem*. The pricing models include "quasi multi-sided auctions" wherein at any time t, several auctions can simultaneously occur, and the payoff functions of any buyer-seller pair in any auction depends on the bidding done by at least another buyer-seller pair either at the same time, or at a different time (this "*long-memory*" bias of buyers and sellers is new in the literature). This chapter is an updated excerpt (and subsequently updated material) from my (pre-2014) article about CRAs which is available in www.ssrn.com.

NEW BEHAVIORAL-BIAS INDICATORS

When aggregated at the national economy level, human behavioral biases such as those introduced in Chapters 4, 5, 6, 9 & 10 in this book combine to create a class of Complex-Systems, Behavioral Operations Research, Macroeconomic and IPE (International Political Economy) indicators which are hereby referred to as the "*Behavioral Bias Indicators*". These indicators have not been properly recognized in the economics/finance, IPE, Behavioral Operations Research or Psychology literatures and are not tracked. Niamir, Filatova, et. al. (2018); Nakagawa, Oiwa & Takeda (2012); Korniotis & Kumar (1993); Acquier, Daudigeos & Pinkse (2017); Schnellenbach & Schubert (2015); Pennings & Wansink (2004); and Rosenbaum, Billinger, et. al. (2012) concluded or implied that human biases can affect national economies, although the links they established or theorized were indirect and they didn't discuss the issue of *Behavioral Bias Indicators*.

REFERENCES

Akcay, E., Meirowitz, A., & Ramsay, K. (2018, February). Two-sided Unobservable Investment, Bargaining, and Efficiency. *Review of Economic Design*, *22*(3), 123–147. doi:10.100710058-018-0213-4

Arrow, K. (2014). The Origins of the Impossibility Theorem. In The Arrow Impossibility Theorem. New York: Columbia University Press.

Australian Competition & Consumer Commission. (2018). *Digital Platforms Inquiry: Preliminary Report*. Australian Competition and Consumer Commission.

Banks, G., Kepes, S., & McDaniel, M. (2015). Publication bias: Understand the myths concerning threats to the advancement of science. In C. E. Lance & R. J. Vandenberg (Eds.), *More Statistical and methodological myths and urban legends* (pp. 36–64). Routledge.

Banks, G., O'Boyle, E. Jr, Pollack, J. M., White, C. D., Batchelor, J. H., Whelpley, C. E., Abston, K. A., Bennett, A. A., & Adkins, C. L. (2016). Questions about questionable research practices in the field of management: A guest commentary. *Journal of Management*, *42*(1), 5–20. doi:10.1177/0149206315619011

Beltrame, B., & Mattos, L. (2017). Amartya Sen's criticism of Kenneth Arrow's social choice theory. *Nova Economia*, *1*, 65–88. doi:10.1590/0103-6351/2790

Benoit, J. (2000). The Gibbard–Satterthwaite theorem: A simple proof. *Economics Letters*, *69*(3), 319–322. doi:10.1016/S0165-1765(00)00312-8

Blumrosen, L., Nisan, N., & Segal, I. (2007). Auctions with severely bounded communication. *Journal of Artificial Intelligence Research*, *28*, 233–266. doi:10.1613/jair.2081

Bosco, F., Aguinis, H., Field, J., Pierce, C. A., & Dalton, D. R. (2016). Harking's threat to organizational research: Evidence from primary and meta-analytic sources. *Personnel Psychology*, *69*(3), 709–750. doi:10.1111/peps.12111

Bruss, F., Louchard, G., & Ward, M. (2009). Inverse auctions: Injecting unique minima into random sets. *ACM Transactions on Algorithms*, *6*(1), 21. doi:10.1145/1644015.1644036

Burke, A. (2019). Occluded algorithms. *Big Data & Society*, *6*(2).

Cairney, P., & Geyer, R. (2017). A critical discussion of complexity theory: How does 'complexity thinking' improve our understanding of politics and policymaking? *Complexity. Governance and Networks*, *3*(2), 1–11. doi:10.20377/cgn-56

Calo, R. (2015). Robotics and the Lessons of Cyberlaw. *California Law Review*, *103*, 513–532.

Calvano, E., & Calzolari, G. (2018). *Artificial Intelligence, Algorithmic Pricing And Collusion*. CEPR Discussion Paper 13405.

Charoontham, K. (2019). Compensation Contract Impact on Credit Rating Agencies' Decision Toward Disclosing Accurate Credit Ratings. *Academic Conference Proceedings*. https://www.dpublication.com/wp-content/uploads/2019/04/icarbme-2-112.pdf

Charoontham, K., & Amornpetchkul, T. (2018). Impact of Pay-for-Performance on Rating Accuracy. In Contemporary Trends in Accounting, Finance and Financial Institutions. Springer. doi:10.1007/978-3-319-72862-9_7

Cifrino, C. (2014). Virtual Property, Virtual Rights: Why Contract Law, Not Property Law, Must Be the Governing Paradigm in the Law of Virtual Worlds. *Boston College Law Review. Boston College. Law School*, *55*, 235–264.

Colignatus, T. (2008). *Review of Howard DeLong (1991), 'A refutation of Arrow's theorem', with a reaction, also on its relevance in 2008 for the European Union*. MPRA working paper. https://mpra.ub.uni-muenchen.de/9661/1/MPRA_paper_9661.pdf

DeLong, H. (1991). *A Refutation of Arrow's Theorem*. University Press of America.

Deng, X., Goldberg, P., Tang, B., & Zhang, J. (2014). Revenue Maximization In A Bayesian Double Auction Market. *Theoretical Computer Science*, *539*(1), 1–12. doi:10.1016/j.tcs.2014.04.013

Devendorf, L., & Goodman, E. (2014). *The Algorithm Multiple, the Algorithm Material. Contours of Algorithmic Life*. UC Davis.

Dourish, P. (2016). Algorithms and their others: Algorithmic culture in context. *Big Data & Society*, *3*(2), 1–11. doi:10.1177/2053951716665128

Genc, E., & Basar, O. (2019). Comparison Of Country Ratings Of Credit Rating Agencies With MOORA Method. *Business & Economics Research Journal*, *10*(2), 391–404. doi:10.20409/berj.2019.175

Gendin, S. (1994). Why Arrow's Impossibility Theorem Is Invalid. *Journal of Social Philosophy*, *25*(1), 144–159. doi:10.1111/j.1467-9833.1994.tb00311.x

Gibbard, A. (1973). Manipulation of voting schemes. *Econometrica*, *41*(4), 587–602. doi:10.2307/1914083

Green, J., & Laffont, J. (1977). Characterization of satisfactory mechanisms for the revelation of preferences for public goods. *Econometrica*, *45*(2), 427–438. doi:10.2307/1911219

Hermalin, B. (2013). Unobserved investment, endogenous quality, and trade. *The RAND Journal of Economics*, *44*(1), 33–55. doi:10.1111/1756-2171.12009

Hoffman, D. (2016). From Promise to Form: How Contracting Online Changes Consumers. *NYU Law Review*, *91*, 1595–1605. doi:10.2139srn.2724661

István, B. (2016). Empirical Research and Practice-oriented Physics for the Humanities and Sciences. *Comparative Literature & Culture*, *18*(2).

Jain, S., Gujar, S., Bhat, S., Zoeter, O., & Narahari, Y. (2018). A quality assuring, cost optimal multi-armed bandit mechanism for expert-sourcing. *Artificial Intelligence*, *254*, 44–63. doi:10.1016/j.artint.2017.10.001

John, L. K., Loewenstein, G., & Prelec, D. (2012). Measuring the prevalence of questionable research practices with incentives for truth telling. *Psychological Science*, *23*(5), 524–532. doi:10.1177/0956797611430953 PMID:22508865

Kisgen, D., Nickerson, J., Osborn, M., & Reuter, J. (2019). Analyst Promotions Within Credit Rating Agencies: Accuracy Or Bias? *Journal of Financial and Quantitative Analysis*, *55*(3), 869–896. doi:10.1017/S0022109019000243

Korniotis, V., & Kumar, A. (1993). Do behavioral Biases Adversely Affect The Economy? *Review of Financial Studies*, *24*(5), 1513–1559. doi:10.1093/rfs/hhq110

Krishnan, K., Basu, S., & Thampy, A. (2019). The Financial Crisis and Corporate Credit Ratings. *Review of Quantitative Finance and Accounting*, *54*(4), 1163–1193.

Kwasnioka, F. (2018). Detecting, anticipating, and predicting critical transitions in spatially extended systems. *Chaos (Woodbury, N.Y.)*, *28*(3), 033614. doi:10.1063/1.5022189 PMID:29604649

Lau, S. (2011). Investment incentives in bilateral trading. *Games and Economic Behavior*, *73*(2), 538–552. doi:10.1016/j.geb.2011.02.006

Liu, S., Zhu, Y., & Hu, Q. (2016). Dynamic procurement management by reverse auctions with fixed setup costs and sales levers. *Applied Mathematical Modelling*, *40*(4), 3049–3061. doi:10.1016/j.apm.2015.10.008

Makowski, L., & Mezzetti, C. (1993). The Possibility of Efficient Mechanisms for Trading an Indivisible Object. *Journal of Economic Theory*, *59*(2), 451–465. doi:10.1006/jeth.1993.1029

Masicampo, E., & Lalande, D. (2012). A peculiar prevalence of *p* values just below. 05. *The Quarterly Journal of Experimental Psychology. A, Human Experimental Psychology*, *65*(11), 2271–2279. doi:10.1080/17470218.2012.711335 PMID:22853650

Miglionico, A. (2019). *The Governance Of Credit Rating Agencies: Regulatory Regimes And Liability Issues*. Edward Elgar. doi:10.4337/9781786439949

Myerson, R., & Satterthwaite, M. (1983). Efficient mechanisms for bilateral trading. *Journal of Economic Theory*, *28*(2), 265–281. doi:10.1016/0022-0531(83)90048-0

Nwogugu, M. (2008). The Efficiency Of Sarbanes-Oxley Act: Willingness To Comply And Agency Problems. *Corporate Control & Ownership*, *5*(1), 449–454. doi:10.22495/cocv5i1c3p5

Nwogugu, M. (2009). Some New Antitrust Models. *International Journal of Mathematics. Game Theory & Algebra*, *17*(5/6), 241–254.

NwoguguM. (2010/2015). *Complex Systems, International Capital Flows and New 'Learning' Business Models for the Credit Rating Agency Industry*. Working paper. https://ssrn.com/abstract=2373373 doi:10.2139srn.2373373

Nwogugu, M. (2016). *Complexity, Climate-Finance And International Trade: Credit Rating Agencies (CRAs) And Allocation Mechanisms For Accounting Firms*. Working paper.

Nwogugu, M. (2019). Complex Systems, Multi-sided Incentives And Risk Perception. In *Companies*. Palgrave MacMillan. doi:10.1057/978-1-137-44704-3

Nwogugu, M. (2019a). Knowledge Representation And Network Decisions. In *Franchising And Online Retailing Under Combined MN-Transferable Utility*. WTAL, Perception And Regret Minimization Regimes.

Nwogugu, M. (2019b). On Franchise Royalty Rates, Franchise Fees And Incentive Effects. In *Complex Systems, Multi-sided Incentives And Risk Perception*. Palgrave MacMillan.

Nwogugu, M. (2019c). Complex Systems, International Political Economy And The Externalities/Governmental-Influence Theory Of The Firm. In *Complex Systems, Multi-sided Incentives And Risk Perception*. Palgrave MacMillan.

Nwogugu, M. (2019d). Complex Systems, International Political Economy And The behavioral/Contracts Theory Of The Firm. In *Complex Systems, Multi-sided Incentives And Risk Perception*. Palgrave MacMillan.

Nwogugu, M. (2019e). Complex Systems, International Political Economy And Communications/Information-Differential Theory Of The Firm. In *Complex Systems, Multi-sided Incentives And Risk Perception*. Palgrave MacMillan.

Nwogugu, M. I. C. (2019f). Perception-Based Decisions, Strategic Alliances and Optimal Financial Contracting: Auctions, Strategic Alliances and a Critique of Third-Generation Prospect Theory and Related Approaches. In Complex Systems, Multi-Sided Incentives and Risk Perception in Companies. Palgrave Macmillan. doi:10.1057/978-1-137-44704-3_4

Nwogugu, M. I. C. (2019g). Economic Policy, Complex Adaptive Systems, Human-Computer-Interaction and Managerial Psychology: Popular-Index Ecosystems. In Indices, Index Funds And ETFs. Palgrave Macmillan. doi:10.1057/978-1-137-44701-2_12

O'Boyle, E., Banks, G., & Gonzalez-Mule, E. (2017). The chrysalis effect: How ugly initial results metamorphoze into beautiful articles. *Journal of Management*, *43*(2), 376–399.

Open Science Collaboration. (2015). Estimating the reproducibility of psychological science. *Science*, *349*(6251), 4716. doi:10.1126cience.aac4716 PMID:26315443

Othman, A., & Sandholm, T. (2009). How Pervasive is the Myerson-Satterthwaite Impossibility? In *Proceedings of the International Joint Conference on Artificial Intelligence (IJCAI). Working paper.* Computer Science Department, Carnegie Mellon University. https://www.cs.cmu.edu/~sandholm/myersat.ijcai09.pdf

Resende, A. (2020). *Qualidade Da Auditoria Externa E Sua Relação Com Nível De Investimento De Companhias Abertas.* Doctorate Thesis. Tese (doutorado). Universidade de Brasília, Faculdade de Economia, Administração, Contabilidade e Gestão de Políticas Públicas, Brazil.

Sarkar, S. (2017). Mechanism design for land acquisition. *International Journal of Game Theory*, *46*(3), 783–812. doi:10.100700182-016-0556-4

Satterthwaite, M. (1975). Strategyproofness and Arrow's conditions: Existence and correspondence theorems for voting procedures and social welfare functions. *Journal of Economic Theory*, *10*(2), 187–217. doi:10.1016/0022-0531(75)90050-2

Schmidt, F., & Hunter, J. (2015). *Methods of meta-analysis: Correcting error and bias in research findings* (3rd ed.). Sage. doi:10.4135/9781483398105

Schnellenbach, J., & Schubert, C. (2015). Behavioral political economy: A survey. *European Journal of Political Economy*, *40B*, 395–417. doi:10.1016/j.ejpoleco.2015.05.002

Scholz, L. (2016). Algorithmic Contracts. *Stanford Technology Law Review: STLR: An Online High-Technology Law Journal from Stanford Law School*, *20*(2), 128–133.

Seaver, N. (2017). Algorithms as culture: Some tactics for the ethnography of algorithmic systems. *Big Data & Society*, *4*(2), 1–12. doi:10.1177/2053951717738104

Sen, A. (2014). Arrow's Impossibility Theorem. In The Arrow Impossibility Theorem. New York: Columbia University Press.

Sham, H., Sing, T., & Tsai, I. (2009). Are there efficiency gains for larger Asian REITs? *Journal of Financial Management of Property and Construction*, *14*(3), 231–247. doi:10.1108/13664380911000459

Smyth, S., Cole, I., & Fields, D. (2020). From Gatekeepers To Gateway Constructors: Credit Rating Agencies And The Financialisation Of Housing Associations. *Critical Perspectives on Accounting*, *71*, 71. doi:10.1016/j.cpa.2019.102093

Sun, W. (2015). *Expectations And Performance of Chinese Credit Rating Agencies* (PHD Thesis). University of the West of Scotland, UK. https://www.academia.edu/34199903/Expectations_and_Performance_of_Chinese_Credit_Rating_Agencies

Surden, H. (2014). Machine Learning and Law. *Washington Law Review (Seattle, Wash.)*, *89*, 87–97.

Suzumura, K. (2011). Chapter Twenty-Three - Welfarism, Individual Rights, and Procedural Fairness. In *Handbook of Social Choice and Welfare* (Vol. 2, pp. 605–685). Elsevier. doi:10.1016/S0169-7218(10)00023-7

Thevenot, M. (2012). The factors affecting illegal insider trading in firms with violations of GAAP. *Journal of Accounting and Economics*, *53*(1-2), 375–390. doi:10.1016/j.jacceco.2011.08.002

Tuzel, S. (2010). Corporate Real Estate Holdings and the Cross-Section of Stock Returns. *Review of Financial Studies*, *23*(6), 2268–2302. doi:10.1093/rfs/hhq006

US Executive Office of the President. (2016). *Big Data: A Report on Algorithmic Systems, Opportunity, and Civil Rights*. US Executive Office of the President.

Usher, D. (2017). *Interpreting Arrow's Impossibility Theorem*. Queen's Economics Department Working Paper No. 1384. Queen's University, Canada.

Wang, G., Xu, H., & Lai, Y. (2018). Emergence, evolution, and control of multistability in a hybrid topological quantum/classical system. *Chaos (Woodbury, N.Y.)*, *28*(3), 033601. doi:10.1063/1.4998244 PMID:29604629

White, L. (2010). Markets: The Credit Rating Agencies. *The Journal of Economic Perspectives*, *24*(2), 211–226. doi:10.1257/jep.24.2.211

Wilson, R. (1972). Social Choice Theory without the Pareto principle. *Journal of Economic Theory*, *5*(3), 478–486. doi:10.1016/0022-0531(72)90051-8

Yadav, Y. (2016). The Failure of Liability in Modern Markets. *Virginia Law Review*, *102*, 1031–1036.

Yeung, K. (2018). Algorithmic regulation: A critical interrogation. *Regulation & Governance*, *12*(4), 505–523. doi:10.1111/rego.12158

Zeng, A., Shen, Z., Zhou, J., Wu, J., Fan, Y., Wang, Y., & Stanley, H. E. (2017). The science of science: From the perspective of complex systems. *Physics Reports*, *714–715*, 1–73. doi:10.1016/j.physrep.2017.10.001

Žliobaitė, I. (2017). Measuring discrimination in algorithmic decision making. *Data Mining and Knowledge Discovery*, *31*(4), 1060–1089. doi:10.100710618-017-0506-1

ENDNOTES

[1] *Cited in*: Resende (2020) and Nwogugu (2019f; 2019g).

[2] *Cited in*: Krishnan, Basu & Thampy (2019).

[3] *Cited in*: Smyth, Cole & Fields (2020), Kisgen, Nickerson, et. al. (2019), Miglionico (2019), Genc & Basar (2019), Charoontham & Amornpetchkul (2018), Charoontham (2019), White (2010), and Sun (2015).

[4] *See*: Chatterjee, S. & Ravindran, S. (2019). There Is Need For A Legal, Organizational Framework To Regulate Bias In Algorithms. *The Indian Express*, February 28, 2019. Available at: https://indianexpress.com/article/opinion/columns/rules-for-the-machine-algorithm-artificial-intelligence-5603795/.

[5] Myerson & Satterthwaite (1983) developed the *Myerson-Satterthwaite Impossibility Theorem*. Othman & Sandholm (2009), Akcay, Meirowitz & Ramsay (2018), Sarkar (2017), Makowski & Mezzetti (1993), Hermalin (2013) and Lau (2011) directly or indirectly critiqued (and or proved the invalidity of) the *Myerson-Satterthwaite Impossibility Theorem*. Blumrosen, Nisan & Segal (2007), Liu, Zhu & Hu (2016), Calvano, Calzolari, et. al. (2018), Wang, Xu & Lai (2018), Deng, Goldberg, Tang & Zhang (2014), Bruss, Louchard & Ward (2009), Jain, Gujar, et. al. (2018) and Kwasnioka (2018) all discussed applications of the *Myerson-Satterthwaite Impossibility Theorem* in different contexts.

[6] Arrow (2014) explained the origins of the *Arrow Impossibility Theorem.* Sen (2014), Usher (2017), DeLong (1991), Colignatus (July 2008), Wilson (1972), Beltrame & Mattos (2017) and Gendin (1994) all critiqued (and or discussed criticisms of) *Arrow's Impossibility Theorem.*

[7] *Sen's Impossibility Theorem* consists of a group of three theorems that were developed by Sen in 1976/1982, and are summarized in Appendices (Theorems 21, 22 & 23) in Suzumura (2011).

[8] Satterthwaite (1975) and Gibbard (1973) developed the *Gibbard-Satterthwaite Impossibility Theorem.* Also see: Benoit (2000).

[9] Gibbard (1973) developed the *Gibbard Theorem.*

[10] Green & Laffont (1977) developed the *Green-Laffont Impossibility Theorem.*

[11] This article stated in part "..........A landmark study involving one hundred scientists from around the world has tried to replicate the findings of 270 recent findings from highly ranked psychology journals and by one measure, only 36 percent turned up the same results. That means that for over half the studies, when scientists used the same methodology, they could not come up with the same results........ And earlier this year, a separate study found that the prevalence of irreproducible pre-clinical research exceeds fifty percent, "resulting in approximately US$28,000,000,000/year spent on pre-clinical research that is not reproducible - in the United States alone".........."

[12] *See*: Shearman & Sterling, *Dodd-Frank, UK, EU & Other Regulatory Reforms* (2013) at http://www.shearman.com/dodd-frank/[Accessed July 1, 2013].

[13] *See*: Regulation 648/2012 on OTC derivatives, central counterparties and trade repositories [2012] OJ L201/1.

[14] *See*: FSA (UK) (2012), Review of The *Markets in Financial Instruments Directive II. Available at:* http://www.fsa.gov.uk/about/what/international/mifid.

See: DIRECTIVE 2008/10/EC OF THE EUROPEAN PARLIAMENT AND OF THE COUNCIL of 11 March 2008. Available at: http://eur-lex.europa.eu/LexUriServ/LexUriServ.do?uri=OJ:L:2008:076:0033:0036:EN:PDF.

[15] Directive 2006/48 relating to the taking up and pursuit of the business of credit institutions [2006] OJ L177/1.

Chapter 1
Enforcement Theory, ESG, and Geopolitical Issues:
A Review of Auditors', Auditees' and Investors' Group-Decisions, Environmental-Remediation Systems, and IPE Factors

ABSTRACT

The objective of this chapter is to review some of the complex systems and institutional factors that can influence the evolution of professional services companies (accounting/auditing firms, CRAs, and management consulting firms), compliance (as a physical phenomenon), enforcement, allocation of resources, risk perceptions, and sustainable growth (within the context of investors' decisions, sustainable growth, and geopolitical factors).

INTRODUCTION

The global consensus is that both Accounting/Derivatives Standards Organizations and associated Standards-Setting processes have been and remain heavily politicized in most countries. The different interest groups include but are not limited to the following:

1. MNCs (multinational corporations).
2. Accounting/Auditing firms.
3. Industry Trade Associations.
4. Labor unions.
5. Pension funds.
6. Financial Services companies (banks; insurance companies; asset management companies; etc.).

DOI: 10.4018/978-1-7998-7418-8.ch001

7. Government agencies (including state governments).
8. Trade Associations.
9. Political-Lobbying firms and law firms.

The following research method was used for this chapter:

1. Searched major academic research databases (including Springer and Sciencedirect.com) using relevant keywords.
2. Gathered relevant academic-journal articles that were published during 2010-2020; with a focus on articles that were published during 2015-2020.
3. Further narrowed the choice of articles to those that analyzed issues in a broad range of countries.
4. Further narrowed the choice of articles to mostly empirical research that used interesting, "practical" or relatively medium/large data-sets. These choices were made with the caveat (as stated in Chapoter-1 in this book) that there is an ongoing and significant *Reproducibility & Replicability Crisis* in academic research wherein less than fifty percent of worldwide empirical academic research can be replicated using the procedures stated in the subject articles.
5. Further narrowed the choice of articles to those whose empirical findings could be easily generalized to other countries/regions or related issues.

EXISTING LITERATURE

On the politicization of both Accounting/Derivatives Standards Organizations and associated Standards-Setting processes, see the comments in: Camfferman (2020), Botzem (2012), Gäumann & Dobler (2019), Giner & Mora (2019), Jorissen, Lybaert, Orens & Van der Tas (2013), Sokolov (2016), Walton (2020), Li X. & Soobaroyen (2020), Temiz & Gulec (2017), Rehman & Shahzad (2014), Melgarejo (2017), and Dima, Dima, et. al. (2014). The IASB's IFRS standards, the SASB/PCAF sustainability disclosure standards and the ISDA/ICMA derivatives standards have been widely adopted or copied in many Emerging Markets countries and thus the politicization of IASB standards-setting directly affects Emerging Markets countries.

During the last fifteen years, the Auditing, Management Consulting and CRA Industries went through digital transformation in their operations in mainly in the form of automation (Artificial Intelligence; and IoT) of their research processes and "internal" operations. As mentioned in Chapter-1, this book doesn't cover such trends which have been well researched in the literature - see the comments in Rudge (2021), Mithas, Murugesan & Seetharaman (2020), Fagella (April 2020), Nissen, Nissen & Rauscher (2019), Boneva (2018), Stark (2020), Bensberg, Buscher & Czarnecki (2019), Nissen (2018), Marques, Santos & Inácio (2019), Ozturk (2019) and Marques (2021).

The remainder of this chapter surveys the relevant literature on Auditors', Auditees' and Investors' Group-Decisions, Environmental-Regulations Enforcement and IPE Factors.

EARNINGS MANAGEMENT, ASSET QUALITY MANAGEMENT AND "INCENTIVE-EFFECTS MANAGEMENT" AROUND THE WORLD: A SURVEY OF INTERNATIONAL POLITICAL ECONOMY AND MACROECONOMIC FACTORS

Two troubling inconsistencies in the global accounting/consulting and CRA industries are as follows:

1. the dichotomy in the accounting regulations for Intangible Assets (including some Climate Finance Instruments such as Carbon-emissions permits; etc.) and Swaps/Derivatives, both of which have overlapping definitions. Under IFRS/IASB accounting regulations, US GAAP and the accounting regulations of most countries, there are very different and perhaps conflicting accounting regulations for Intangible assets and Swaps/Derivatives even though many types of Swaps/Derivatives can be construed as Intangible assets (more specifically, as contract rights) and some types of Intangible assets are derivatives (such as employee stock options; contract rights; some Climate Finance Instruments; etc.) as explained herein and above.
2. the dichotomy in bankruptcy court adjudication/rules for Intangible Assets and for Swaps/Derivatives. Furthermore in many countries, Intangibles and Swaps/Derivatives are treated very differently in bankruptcy proceedings – for example in the US, there is an automatic "bankruptcy-stay" for some types of Swaps/Derivatives which is not applied to most intangible assets.

These two types of dichotomy are increasingly critical because:

1. Both the worldwide volume of Intangible assets and the global Swaps/Derivatives markets are large and growing rapidly and affect both the real and financial sectors of economies;
2. They create significant opportunities for earnings management, asset-quality management and incentive-effects management (defined in Nwogugu (2020)), and thus reduces the comparability of financial statements;
3. They increase the probability of divergent risk perceptions among investors (which can increase market volatility);
4. They have significant implications for economic growth, financial stability, Climate/Sustaibaility Policy, systemic risk and public policy.

Chen, Lee & Li (2008) analyzed how local governments in China helped listed firms perpetrate earnings management to circumvent the central government's regulation, and found that Chinese local governments provide subsidies to help firms boost their earnings above the regulatory threshold of rights offering and delisting; and such collusion between government and listed firms in earnings management exists mainly in firms controlled by local governments. Chen, Lee & Li (2008) also noted that the relatively new *semi-market economy* in China has created many conflicts of interests and collusion between firms and different layers of governments wherein the central government in China sets capital markets regulations (including accounting quality), while local governments engage in inter-jurisdictional competition for more capital, and their interests are aligned with listed firms through the stringent IPO quota system.

Using data from the industrial census of China, Li, Selover & Stein (2011) analyzed the institutional patterns of earnings management by manufacturing firms in china, and found that earnings management is more pervasive in China than in mature market economies such as the U.S., and that Chinese firms appear to follow a "*keep silent, make money*" strategy by managing their reported earnings to zero; and that increased earnings management is associated with state-owned firms, firms reporting to higher levels of government, and firms in more commercialized regions of China.

Chen, Li, et. al. (2011) noted that Chinese firms are affected by macroeconomic policies and thus have faced high political costs during China's economic transition; and that political costs are negatively related to earnings management in listed real estate firms. Chen, Li, et. al. (2011) found that non-state-owned enterprises used more income-decreasing accruals during China's economic transition period; all of which are consistent with the *political costs hypothesis*.

Using a sample of politically affiliated private firms in China, Jacoby, Li & Liu (2016) found that financially distressed firms were more likely to report small positive earnings than to financially healthy firms; and political affiliation weakens the association between financial distress and small positive earnings management; and the moderating effect of political affiliation is influenced by regional development.

Chen, Jiang, et. al. (2011) found empirical evidence of selective enforcement of securities laws in China, and specifically that the China Securities Regulatory Commission (CSRC) takes into account whether companies violating the rules have a state-owned background and the strength of that background when investigating and punishing non-compliance. After controlling for the degree of violation, Chen, Jiang, et. al. (2011) also found that state-owned-enterprises (SOEs) were punished less severely than private companies; and the higher the hierarchy of the SOE in question, the less severe the punishment; and it takes longer for SOEs to be punished.

Martinez (2013) reviewed the academic literature on earnings management (EM) in Brazil.

Attia, Lassoued & Attia (2016) conducted empirical analysis and noted that:

1. executives' political connection is not directly related to earnings management;
2. the interaction between executives' political connection and the state control affects the firm's sensitivity to political pressure and its earnings management practices;
3. non-connected firms and state-controlled firms attempt to use accounting policies to decrease their earnings especially during periods of the former government when they had to face high political costs;
4. private firms with political connection enjoy a significantly lower insurance right, tax and donations and grants compared to other firms.

Galligan (1997) tested the *Political Costs Theory* and found that: i) earnings management is consistent with managerial incentives to mitigate the effects of political scrutiny and potential industry reregulation; ii) firms for which proposed regulations are expected to be more harmful have greater income-decreasing accruals, and for some tests, firms for which cable television operations are more important have greater income-decreasing accruals (the test results were robust to the inclusion of control variables for firm performance and size).

Using a unique panel data set of 5,493 publicly traded firms in thirty countries, Braam, Nandy, et. al. (2015) found that politically connected firms are more likely to substitute real earnings management strategies for accrual-based earnings management strategies than non-connected firms; and that when the risk of detection increases, politically connected firms are more likely to resort to less detectable real earnings management strategies. Thus, focusing only on accrual-based measurements underestimates the total earnings management activities of politically connected firms.

Using Indonesian data, Habib, Muhammadi & Jiang (2017) found that politically connected firms use related party loans as a tunneling mechanism which is more pronounced for firms with government connections; and that politically connected firms perpetrate earnings management to hide their tunneling activities.

Using a dataset of 493 PCON and non-PCON from 2002-to-2016 in Malaysia (a country characterized by relationship-capitalism), Wong & Hooy (2018) categorized politically connected firms (PCON) into four different types which are government-linked, board of directors, businessman, and family members; and noted that only PCON with a more stable connection (government-linked companies and board of directors) have a positive relationship with firm performance and that such a relationship does not exist in less-stable-connections PCON (businessman and family members).

Elnahass, Izzeldin & Steele (2018) found evidence that unlike islamic banks, conventional banks engaged in capital and earnings management through loan loss provisions – which was more common for large and loss-generating banks. The difference can be attributed to ethical orientation, the constrained business model of Islamic banking and strict governance.

Using data for Chinese firms that did IPOs and SEOs, He (2016) noted that firms that get more preferential tax treatment or more financial subsidies from local governments have a lower level of earnings management prior to the offerings; and that earnings management can be a costly tool for a firm to achieve its earnings targets.

Trombetta & Imperatore (2014) noted that the literature is inconclusive about the direction of the relationship between earnings quality and economic downturn; and that corporate survival as an objective of earnings manipulation likely change as crisis becomes worse; and the relationship between financial crises and earnings management is non-monotonic; and earnings management decreases when the intensity of the crisis is low, while it increases when the crisis is acute.

Ze-To (2012) noted that earnings management exists in both "*Up*" and "*Down*" market states, but management effort is less effective and short-lived in the *Down* state; and that accrual profits are consistently positive across both "*Up*" and "*Down*" market states and significantly higher in DOWN markets; and the *Accrual Effect* exists but varies across industries; and accruals mispricing cannot be fully captured by returns predicted by macroeconomic models.

Cheng & Leung (2016) noted that in order to protect its national and economic interests Mainland Chinese government grants government protection to specific industries and maintains political-linkage with certain firms (the "strategic firms"); and that strategic firms with economic and national interests recover faster from financial distress than non-strategic firms; and strategic firms perform better and have higher management turnovers, but management turnovers are less frequent if the chairpersons and CEOs are politically-connected.

Belz, von Hagen & Steffens (2019) noted that: i) Accounting literature offers two competing theories on the relation between effective tax rate (ETR) and firm size: the *Political Cost Theory* (which suggests a positive size-ETR relation), and the *Political Power Theory* (which suggests a negative size-ETR relation); ii) using a unique data set of 56 studies that do not show a clear tendency towards either of the two theories, there was evidence supporting the political cost theory; iii) using a cross-country meta-data set, Hofstede's cultural dimensions theory, a transparency index and a corruption index explain variation in the size-ETR relation; iii) independent of the *Political Cost Theory* and the *Political Power Theory*, tax planning aspects potentially affect the size-ETR relation.

Using a sample of 219 cross-border mergers conducted by Chinese listed companies from 2000 to 2013 Zhang & Mauck (2018) noted that:

1. in target-nations that have relatively low political risk, the interaction between government-affiliation and change in political relations is positively related to longer-term bidder performance and government-affiliation can be value enhancing in some circumstances;
2. longer-term post-merger bidder abnormal returns are lower for government-affiliated bidders, consistent with the general inefficiency associated with government-affiliation;
3. improving bilateral political relations between China and target nations are positively associated with both short and long-term bidder performance (thus economic nationalism in firm outcomes is an issue);
4. a government-affiliated bidder's (i.e., those with political connections and/or government ownership) abnormal returns do not differ from non-affiliated bidders in the announcement period after controlling for deal characteristics;
5. the interaction between government-affiliation and change in political relations is generally unrelated to bidder performance.

He (2016) noted that firms tend to manipulate earnings before IPO (initial public offerings) and SEO (seasoned equity offerings) and using data for Chinese IPO and SEO firms, they found that pre-offering earnings management is lower when the firm has more preferential tax treatment or more financial subsidies from local governments; and thus firms that receive stronger fiscal support have smaller demand for earnings management, which is a costly tool.

Anderson, Chi & Wang (2017) found: i) a positive relationship between political ties (PTs) and successful venture capital (VC) exits in China wherein PTs are crucial for VCs to exit via Chinese mainland stock markets and M&As; ii) VCs with management-level PTs enjoy greater success than those with ownership-level PTs, whereas no significant difference between central and local government PTs on VC exits; iii) the empirical results remained stable after controlling for selection bias, alternative measures for VC exits, and legal and institutional differences across regions.

Using a large sample over the period of 2001-to-2015, Jiang, Habib & Wang (2018) found: i) that current-period real activities manipulation (hereafter REM) is positively associated with future performance; ii) that the *Positive Performance Effect* is caused by firms operating in countries with strong institutional environments; iii) that future operating performance improves when REM is undertaken by firms in strong institutional environments only during a non-economic crisis period, but not during an economic crisis period.

Bushman & Piotroski (2006) noted that a country's legal/judicial system, securities laws, and political economy create incentives that influence the behavior of corporate executives, investors, regulators and other market participants; and such incentives affect accounting disclosure (ie. Earnings management; incentive-effects management and asset-quality management).

Using a sample period from 2001 to 2009, Jiang & Habib (2012) analyzed the impact of split-share (A and B shares) structure reform (and the mandatory conversion of non-tradable shares into tradable shares from 2006 onwards) on earnings management in China and the incentives for earnings management during the reform-transition period. The split-share reform requires non-tradable share (NTS) holders to compensate the tradable share (TS) holders. During the Chinese privatization process, when a company lists on the stock market for the first time, about 64% of its shares were retained by the founders, typically, the state owned enterprises (SOEs); while the remaining 36% of the shares were offered to the public as TS. The NTS were not tradable on either the Shanghai or the Shenzhen Stock Exchange, but could be transferred off-market to other government agencies, legal entities, and foreign investing firms on a State Asset Management Bureau (SAMB) approved price normally higher than the book value per share. TS include A-shares, B-shares, and H-shares. Jiang & Habib (2012) used absolute discretionary accruals (DACCR) as a proxy for earnings management, and found that NTS holding is positively associated with DACCR implying the presence of earnings manipulation in the pre-reform period.

Wei & Geng (2008) noted that because of the co-existence of non-tradable share (NTS) and tradable share (TS) in listed SOEs and the absolute controlling shares held by non-tradable share (NTS) holders, management and NTS holders tend to collude through related party transactions or insider trading detrimental to the TS holders interest and firm value. Wei & Geng (2008) implied that China's Two-tier share structure distorts managerial incentives for shareholder value maximization because managers of the state and legal person-controlled firms have greater incentives to act in the best interest of state or legal persons/institutions because of their political appointments.

Building on research on why some national financial systems are based on banks and others on markets, Lavezzolo, Rodríguez-Lluesma & Elvira (2018) concluded that: i) culturally-based social preferences regarding uncertainty avoidance help explain cross-national differences in financial system configuration - national culture is a good predictor of financial systems as long as "constrained" governments are able to credibly commit to not interfering in the functioning of banks and markets; ii) political institutions condition this relationship; iii) when political institutions limit governmental action, culturally-driven preferences for uncertainty avoidance affect significantly financial configuration.

Using a unique dataset of 350 privatized firms from forty-five countries, Ben-Nasr, Boubakri & Cosset (2015) found that:

1. state ownership is associated with lower earnings quality while foreign ownership is associated with higher earnings quality; and
2. that the impact of foreign ownership on earnings quality varies with the country's institutional environment;
3. foreign ownership is associated with higher earnings quality in countries with higher government stability and lower risk of government expropriation.

Using a large sample of firms from forty-six countries, Boubakri, El Ghoul & Saffar (2015) concluded that:

1. tighter political constraints stimulate firm growth and that effect is more pronounced in weak legal environments; ii) the results of such empirical studies are significant and robust to a number of sensitivity tests, such as alternative proxies for political institutions, alternative measures of firm growth, additional controls, firm- versus country-level regressions, and the endogeneity of political constraints;
2. reforms aimed at improving a country's political institutions can significantly impact firm growth, and firms are incentivized to invest in profitable projects as a result of improved political institutions.

Using an international sample of banks from ninety-eight countries over the period 1998–2007, Ashraf (2017) noted that:

1. political and legal institutions complement each other to influence bank risk-taking behavior;

2. sound political institutions encourage higher bank risk-taking - consistent with the hypotheses that better political institutions increase banks' risk by boosting the credit market competition from alternative sources of finance and generating the moral hazard problems due to the expectation of government bailouts in worst economic conditions;
3. that is contrary to the hypotheses that better political institutions decrease banks' risk by lowering the government expropriation risk and the information asymmetries between banks and borrowers;
4. the results of the empirical tests are robust to sensitivity tests, including alternative proxies of bank risk-taking and political institutions, cross-sectional bank- and country-level regressions, endogeneity concerns of political institutions, country income levels, explicit deposit insurance schemes and sample extension from 1998 to 2014.

Gungoraydinoglu, Çolak & Öztekin (2017) noted that:

1. the political environment is a critical determinant of financial intermediation costs, which affects the external financing patterns of firms;
2. political changes create policy uncertainty which increases information risk, weakens the investor demand, and reduces the sizes of securities offerings – and the financial intermediaries pass on the increased costs to the issuing firms in the form of higher underwriter spreads;
3. as a result the issuance costs for new equity and debt capital increase, leading to lower leverage;
4. this channel is distinct from previously documented effects of policy uncertainty on corporate outcomes.

Using two Finnish MNCs with operations in Russia as samples, Salmi & Heikkilä (2015) noted that relationships between business firms and public sector actors are critical for business in the emerging markets; firms maintain several simultaneous relationships with public officials, firms also rely on intermediaries and may build indirect relationships to create some distance to public officials; and the relationships are mainly used for mutual information exchange.

Huskey (2010) noted that Russia has a peculiar form of authoritarianism that exhibits pronounced technocratic features.

Using a unique dataset of joint-stock companies in Russia (a 2005 survey of managers of more than 800 firms in Russia), Frye & Iwasaki (2011):

1. introduced three ideal types of business–state relations in a transition economy and explore the impact of government directors on corporate boards for firm behavior;
2. noted that the presence of government directors on corporate boards is more consistent with a "collusion" ideal type of relations between firms and the state than with a managerial discipline or rent-extraction ideal type;
3. the government sends directors to firms that both extract resources from the state and also provide important benefits and services to the state.

Using the FIBEN database, Bruneau, et. al. (2012) analyzed the relationships between macroeconomic shocks and companies' financial fragility (between firms' bankruptcies and macroeconomic variables and the business cycle) and found that:

1. there was evidence of reciprocal links between the bankruptcy rate and the output gap;
2. there was evidence of "second round effects" of shocks to the output gap on bankruptcies (between macroeconomic cycles and changes in financial fragility, as measured at the microeconomic level by corporate bankruptcies);
3. the dynamic transmission of macroeconomic shocks matters in stress testing exercises;
4. there are a few trade-offs associated with the approach, regarding endogenous defaults, the use of accounting data, the relevance of financial market variables, the identification assumptions in VAR models.

Using a dataset of merger and acquisition events from thirty countries for the period 2004–2015, Karim, Sarkar & Zhang (2016) analyzed accruals based earnings management by acquiring firms and found that:

1. the acquiring firms do manage earnings surrounding mergers when the method of payment is acquirer's stock, but there is no such evidence when the method of payment is cash;
2. acquirers' accrual manipulation differs based on the level of economic development, country-specific institutional characteristics and other institutional variables.

Using a dataset of the financial statements of 77 companies listed in Tehran stock exchange in five industry levels over the time period 2002-2011, Kordestani & Mohammadi (2016) analyzed the relationship between intense competition in the product market and earnings management; and noted that: i) entry cost and industry concentration have a significant relationship with earnings management; ii) contrary to existing literature, the relationship between market size and earnings management is not confirmed.

Riahi-Belkaoui (2004) found evidence that supports both a "*diversion hypothesis*" where earnings management is decreasing in economic freedom, and a "*penalty hypothesis*" where earnings management is increasing in human development.

Agarwal, Chomsisengphet, Liu & Rhee (2007) studied 78 Japanese banks' earnings management behavior under three distinct economic environments: (1) high-growth with asset price bubble economy (1985–1990); (2) stagnant growth with financial distress economy (1991–1996); and (3) severe recession with credit crunch economy (1997–1999). Agarwal, Chomsisengphet, Liu & Rhee (2007) found that:

1. earnings management behavior by Japanese banks differ considerably across the three periods and banks used security trading gains for earnings management during all three periods;
2. banks used loan loss provisions to manage earnings primarily during the first two periods;
3. consistent with previous studies, Japanese banks significantly lowered their lending when there was increased loan-loss provisions.

Using a sample of firms from twenty-six countries and drawing from institutional theory, Lewellyn & Bao (2017) concluded that institutional forces that influence earnings management; and corruption (an informal institution) is a major factor in explaining cross-national variation in earnings management. Using a sample of firms from 26 countries, we find support for both direct and interactive effects of these important informal aspects of the institutional context.

Based on institutional theory and using a unique data-set of manufacturing companies in Brazil and Germany, Brandau, Endenich, et. al. (2013) found that:

1. Management accounting structures and practices in both countries were converging towards international standards under the pressure of coercive, mimetic and normative isomorphism;
2. While firms generally adopt Anglo-American practices, German management accounting concepts have a strong influence in Brazil;
3. There are the pressures created by the adoption of the International Financial Reporting Standards and the pursuit of legitimacy via adherence to social expectations.

Samsonova (2009) analyzed three episodes of audit policy making in Russia (relevant to the development of the Russian audit law and auditing standards) and how international policy templates affect the local audit environment and found that globalisation doesn't reflect the increasingly transnational nature of the present-day world order where cross-border activities of various private and public actors and "transnational" organizations increasingly shape national audit practices.

Fung, Raman & Zhu (2017) analyzed whether the Public Company Accounting Oversight Board (PCAOB) international inspection program improves audit quality for a sample of non-US-listed foreign public client companies from fifty-five countries audited by foreign (i.e., non-US) auditors; and found that initial PCAOB inspections improved audit quality, over and above the threat of such inspections, for foreign auditors' non-US-listed foreign clients.

Dye (2002) studied the selection and evolution of accounting standards in the context of Classifications Manipulation and noted that the possibility of classifications manipulation creates a distinction between the official classification described in the statement of the accounting standard and the de facto classification, determined by the "shadow standard" actually adopted by preparers.

A SURVEY OF AUDITORS' GROUP DECISIONS IN VARIOUS COUNTRIES

LaSalle (2006) questioned whether a disclaimer of an opinion is any indication of audit quality or professionalism; discussed three alternative explanations for the empirical regularities; and discussed the *Gatekeeper Story* (auditors are simply not willing to risk reducing their reputational capital by acquiescing to clients that are not likely to survive their own financial distress), the *Herding Story* (when auditors are faced with uncertainties or a gap in the authoritative literature, auditors will herd together to form a common response that mimic one-another) and the *Value of Incumbency Story* (as the value of incumbency declines with the client's inability to survive, auditors will have fewer incentives to incur the incremental costs to gather sufficient competent evidential matter necessary to support an unqualified opinion).

Lam & Mensah (2006) critiqued the LaSalle (2006) conclusions.

In a 13-country study of the specialist auditor premium, Srinidhi, Lim & Hossain (2009) found that: i) country-level institutional strength increases average audit fees, but reduces the incremental demand for specialist auditors; ii) strong institutions and the demand for specialist knowledge are substitutes in providing assurance of financial statements.

Andiola & Bedard (2018) noted that:

1. regulatory risk has made audit reviews more critical, and audit supervisors are struggling with how to effectively deliver the "tough message";

2. there are both adverse and beneficial reactions to more negative feedback, including worse attitudes toward coaching relationships, more attempts to manage supervisors' impressions, but greater performance improvement efforts;
3. these reactions are moderated by the subordinate auditor's feedback orientation (i.e., receptivity), and sometimes by the supervisor's goal framing (i.e., emphasis on learning versus performance);
4. participants in a study more often chose engagement over workpaper reviews to represent their most salient experiences, and some results differ between these review contexts.

Quick & Schmidt (2018) analyzed whether perceptions of auditor independence and audit quality are influenced by audit firm rotation, auditor retention and joint audits, and they found:

1. a negative main effect for joint audits on perceived auditor independence, and that a rotation cycle of 24 years marginally significantly impairs participant perceptions of audit quality, compared to a rotation cycle of only ten years;
2. that planned contrast tests suggest a negative interaction between rotation and joint audit on participant perceptions of auditor independence;
3. a negative interaction effect is revealed between rotation after 24 years and retention on perceptions of audit quality;
4. there wasn't a positive impact of the regulatory measures taken or supported by the European Commission on perceptions of auditor independence and audit quality.

Booker (2018) used a nationwide random selection of 111 lenders in a 2 × 2 between-subjects experiment to study whether an auditor's economic dependence on a client and type of auditor rotation affect lenders' independence and reliability perceptions and decisions to lend money to a potential borrower, and found that:

1. prior studies indicate that financial statement users use client importance as a measure of audit quality when revenue streams are not equal across clients and that can negatively affect perceptions of independence and financial statement reliability;
2. lenders view the financial statements of auditee-clients of economically dependent auditors (CEDA) as less reliable than those of auditee-clients without a dependent auditor (non-CEDA);
3. Lenders are less likely to grant a loan to CEDA;
4. under audit-firm rotation, there both an increase in lenders' perceptions of reliability of CEDA financials, and no difference in perceptions of reliability of CEDA and non-CEDA financials.

Using UK data, Wu, Hsu & Haslam (2016) analyzed whether the effect of auditor-provided non-audit services (NAS) on auditors' reporting decisions is mediated by audit committee characteristics in failed firms, and found that:

1. failed firms with higher proportions of independent non-executive directors (NEDs) and financial experts on the audit committee were more likely to receive auditor going-concern modifications prior to their failure;
2. there is no significant relationship between NAS fees and the probability of a modification of a going-concern report by the auditor;

3. the relationship between NAS and auditors' reporting decisions can be affected by audit committee characteristics;
4. where the audit committee is more "independent" and includes a greater proportion of financial experts, auditors providing the client with NAS are less likely to issue a standard unmodified going-concern report prior to failure;
5. the study results support corporate governance regulators' concerns about the monitoring benefits of audit committee independence and the presence of board members with financial expertise on the audit committee for auditors' reporting decisions.

Trotman, Bauer & Humphreys (2015) reviewed the judgment and decision-making research literature on audit groups/teams (the hierarchical review process; brainstorming as part of the fraud detection planning process, and consultation within firms).

Lennox & Li (2012) analyzed the audit firm's decision to protect its partners' personal assets by becoming a limited liability partnership (LLP), and found that:

1. the likelihood of an audit firm switching from unlimited to limited liability entity is increasing in its size and exposure to litigation risk;
2. audit firms dont supply lower audit quality, lose market share, or charge lower audit fees after they become LLPs;
3. audit firms shift toward riskier publicly traded companies after they switch to limited liability;
4. large audit-firms that have riskier clients are more likely to become LLPs;
5. Clients do not prefer to be audited by partners that have unlimited liability.

Windsor (2017) analyzed China's transition from command economy toward a market economy within a theory of comparative political economy; and interpretation of China's model for business which combines a dynamically evolving combination of state-owned and privately owned enterprises within a process of marketization and privatization directed by a one-party regime

Using a cross-sectional survey design and 146 responses from among 800 surveyed experienced Swedish auditors, Svanberg, Öhman & Neidermeyer (2018) analyzed whether auditor *negotiation self-efficacy* (an auditor's perceived ability to negotiate discretionary accounting issues with clients) is related to *auditor-objectivity*, and whether an auditor's *negotiation self-efficacy* has a greater impact on his/her objectivity when the auditor's accuracy motive (*professional identity*) is strong rather than weak; and they found that:

1. auditors with higher negotiation self-efficacy were more likely to make decisions on a material and discretionary accounting issue contrary to their clients' desires compared to auditors with lower self-efficacy;
2. the relationship between *negotiation self-efficacy* and *auditor objectivity* was not moderated by *professional-identity* strength;
3. recruiting and training auditors to increase their negotiation self-efficacy may be an effective method to enhance auditor objectivity without the problems inherent in other methods, such as auditor rotation;
4. the effect of auditor negotiation self-efficacy may not be generalizable to countries that limit auditor-tenure through regulation.

Erdogan & Uludag (2014) analyzed auditor decision making. Read & Yezegel (2018):

1. noted that Geiger, Raghunandan & Rama (2005) examined auditor going-concern decisions prior to client bankruptcy in the periods surrounding the enactment of the Sarbanes-Oxley Act (2002) at the start of this century and found evidence of improved conservatism;
2. Feldmann & Read (2010) extended Geiger, et. al. (2005) and found that the proportion of *going-concern opinions* (GCOs) increases sharply in the post-SOX period (2002 – 2003) relative to the pre-SOX period (2000 – 2001) and that the improvement in conservatism is largely transitory and that the GCO ratio quickly declines over time;
3. Analyzed a sample of 340 U.S. public companies that filed for bankruptcy during the years 2006–2015, and found that auditors were significantly more likely to issue GCOs to subsequently bankrupt clients after the onset of the GR; and after controlling for confounding factors, there was no significant change in the propensity of auditors to issue a GCO during the two post-GR recovery periods compared to going-concern decisions during the GR.

Based on a sample that consisted of fifty-nine (59) US and sixty-one (61) Hong Kong auditors employed by the Big-4 accounting firms, Hwang & Chang (2010) found that:

1. litigation environment has a significant effect on auditors' decisions;
2. Auditors who practice in more litigious environments are less willing to agree to clients' aggressive reporting than those who practice in less litigious environments;
3. there is a significant interactive effect between litigation environment, client business risk, and client retention pressure on auditors' decisions to accept clients' aggressive reporting choices.

Using a sample that consisted of bank directors and institutional investors in Germany, Quick & Schmidt (2018) and found that:

1. there was a negative main effect for joint audits on perceived auditor independence, and that a rotation cycle of 24 years marginally significantly impairs participant perceptions of audit quality, compared to a rotation cycle of only ten years;
2. apart from the main effects, planned contrast tests suggest a negative interaction between rotation and joint audit on participant perceptions of auditor independence;
3. there was a negative interaction effect between rotation after 24 years and retention on perceptions of audit quality.

Kaspina (2015) noted that Compliance with continuing professional educational requirements by the auditors and accountants can enhance their accuracy and reliability.

Based on World Bank data on 114 countries, Nikbakht, Sarkar & Spieler (2017) and found that: i) there isn't a single set of "universal" factors that affect firms' decision to engage external auditors; ii) such factors differ across the various categories of economic development.

Gul, Fung & Jaggi (2009) noted that: i) although prior studies concluded that auditors with short tenure are associated with lower earnings quality because of the lack of client-specific knowledge and/or low balling; there isn't any evidence for the low-balling explanation; and ii) the relationship between shorter auditor tenure and lower earnings quality is weaker for firms audited by industry specialists compared to non-specialists.

Based on a sample of 171 senior corporate managers, Chen, Kelly & Salterio (2012) found that:

1. compared to the condition where the audit processes were similar to the prior years' processes, managers anticipate less earnings management when the collected evidence has increased probative value; and when the auditor does more critical inquiry combined with either an increase in the evidence extent (increased sample size) or the nature of the evidence;
2. the reduction in anticipated earnings management is not found with either the increased extent of evidence collected alone or more critical inquiry alone, suggesting that a combination of action and attitude changes compared to a change in either action alone or attitude alone better signals to managers the heightened scepticism that enhances the effectiveness of auditor deterrence;
3. after controlling for the underlying ethical disposition of managers, that the different audit procedures and attitudes conveyed to management affect managers' perceptions of the ethicality of anticipated earnings management;
4. the conditions that facilitate increased earnings management also paradoxically increase managers' perceived unethicality of the anticipated earnings management.

Using a sample of 114 experienced auditors, Segovia, Arnold & Sutton (2009), and found that: i) auditors are more willing to allow clients to manage earnings under rules-based standards even under external pressure; and ii) more experienced auditors are less willing to allow clients who exert high pressure to report earnings aggressively, while SEC pressure has more effect on less experienced auditors.

Kleinman & Palmon (2009) developed a four stage model of group decision-making, during which the differing assets and liabilities (cognitive, ability, expertise) of audit group members are combined (the four stages are diversity, controversy, insight and resolution); and Kleinman & Palmon (2009) noted that:

1. auditor judgment prowess and resultant decision-making success has been an important topic in the behavioral auditing area but little literature exists on how differences in individual group member cognitive heuristics (fallibility) and ability impact the group process, and are impacted upon by the group process; and thus
2. understanding circumstances that give rise to either more flawed ('process losses'), or better ('process gains'), group decision-making outcomes are important.

Moroney & Simnett (2009) noted that auditors working in a complex industry have a greater comparative ability to identify business risks, information sources, and evidence-gathering processes in their industry than auditors working in a generic industry.

Palmon & Sudit (_____) proposed a system of commercial insurance of financial disclosures (CIFD), wherein users of financial information (such as investors and potential owners of business enterprises) and providers of financial information (managers of business enterprises) can purchase insurance policies from private insurers (commercial insurance companies).

Using a sample of 181 auditors, Robertson, Stefaniak & Curtis (2011) studied the effects of auditor-wrongdoer *Reputations* for performance and likeability on fellow auditors' intentions in response to a questionable audit act, and they found that:

1. *Likeability Reputation* is a significant determinant of intention to take action, while *Performance Reputation* is marginally significant;
2. auditors have the greatest intention to take action against less likeable, poor performers;
3. intention to take action against a more likeable, good performer is no lower than the mixed conditions; and the effects of the two dimensions of reputation is complex;
4. auditors are more likely to whistle-blow internally than externally, and through non-anonymous outlets than anonymous outlets.

Robertson (2010) noted that the literature suggest that clients can influence auditor judgment using *Ingratiation*, and found that:

1. when the client *ingratiates,* auditors are more likely to comply with the requests of clients with low incentive to influence the auditor than those with high incentive; and ingratiation amplifies the effect of client incentive on auditor judgment;
2. auditors experience stronger positive affect toward both ingratiating clients and clients with low incentive relative to non-ingratiating clients and clients with high incentive;
3. auditors were more likely to comply with client requests as positive affect toward the client increases; iv) clients can influence auditor judgment through ingratiation under certain circumstances, and clients can strategically induce positive affect to influence auditor judgment.

Iatridis (2012) analyzed the relationships among IFRS implementation, hedging and earnings management and found that:

1. The transition to IFRS standards affected the equity, earnings, leverage and liquidity of hedgers in a significantly positive manner inn contrast to non-hedgers, who the opposite effects;
2. Hedgers are usually larger sized entities that have higher profitability, growth, leverage and liquidity; and they have foreign revenues, are cross-listed in foreign stock markets and are audited by a Big-4 auditor;
3. Hedging and earnings management inversely related;
4. Firm value is positively related to hedging and negatively related to discretionary accruals and managerial opportunism;
5. Effective corporate governance mechanisms are negatively related to discretionary accruals and are positively related to firm value.

A SURVEY OF AUDITEE-COMPANIES' DECISIONS ABOUT AUDITS AND AUDITORS

Kelly (2010) analyzed the effects of different compensation contracts (flat wage, group incentive, and noncompetitive individual incentive) on decision quality when information is distributed among different individuals. Kelly (2010) found that information exchange and decision quality are better under the group incentive regime than the individual incentive regime, even when both incentives provide an economic motivation for information exchange; and that information exchange and decision quality are also better under the flat wage than the individual incentive, despite the stronger economic motivation for information exchange under the individual incentive. Kelly (2010) showed that the effect of compensation contracts on decision quality is partially mediated through information exchange between group members. The results are consistent with higher group membership saliency under the group incentive and the flat wage than the individual incentive, and group membership saliency promoting information exchange between group members. Kelly (2010) concluded that in a group decision-making context, differences in decision quality across compensation contracts may be better explained by psychological factors rather than economic factors.

Peng, Wei & Yang (2011) used connected transaction data from China to test the Friedman, et al. (2003) model in which, in equilibrium, controlling shareholders may choose either *tunneling* or *propping* of their listed companies depending on the magnitude of an adverse shock and the magnitude of the private benefits of control. Peng, Wei & Yang (2011) found that: i) when listed companies are financially healthy (in financial distress), their controlling shareholders are more likely to conduct connected transactions to *tunnel* (*prop up*) their listed companies and the market reacts unfavorably (favorably) to the announcement of these transactions; and ii) all of the transaction types in their sample could be used for tunneling or propping depending on different financial situations of the firms; iii) political connections is negatively associated with the *announcement effect*; and there was evidence that *propping* and *tunneling* could occur in the same company but at different times. Liu & Zhou (2007) studied the relationship between earnings management and corporate governance in China within the context of tunneling; and found that: i) there were systematic differences in earnings management across the universe of China's listed companies during 1999–2005, and ii) firms that had better corporate governance had lower levels of earnings management; iii) where listed firms have strong incentives to manage earnings in order to meet certain return on equity (ROE) thresholds, and earnings management has been shown to be the most conspicuous, here was evidence of *tunneling*; iv) agency conflicts between controlling shareholders and minority investors account for a significant portion of earnings management in China's listed firms.

Based on a questionnaire completed by sixty-five auditors in India and analyzed using descriptive statistics and factor analysis methods, Divya (2014) found that most of the auditee-firms indulge in earnings management even in the presence of regulatory frameworks; and that firms' management tries to interpret and modify the law provisions to suit their purposes and to manipulate the financial results.

Using a sample of five hundred (500) large companies in India over a two-year period, Sarkar, Sarkar & Sen (2008) studied the impact of board characteristics on opportunistic earnings management (where business organizations differ from those in "developed" countries), and how characteristics that proxy for the 'quality' of inside and outside directors affect the role of boards in curbing earnings management; and they found that:

1. board quality was more relevant for earnings management than board independence;
2. diligent boards were associated with lower earnings management, while boards that had directors with multiple appointments had greater earnings management; and
3. chief executive officer (CEO) duality and the presence of controlling shareholders on the board increased earnings management;
4. domestic institutional owners were a compensating control mechanism to mitigate the detrimental influence of controlling shareholders on earnings management.

Using 1,353 observations for a period of eleven years (2000-2010) from a sample of 123 (one hundred and twenty three) Brazilian companies listed on BM&F Bovespa, Almeida-Santos, Dani, Machado &

Krespi (2013) analyzed whether the open family-controlled Brazilian companies engaged in earnings management, and if this influence reduces reported firm performance (ie. whether family control is positively related to discretionary accruals of Brazilian companies, and the influence of family ownership on the production of negative accruals). Almeida-Santos, Dani, Machado & Krespi (2013) found that family-controlled companies generated lower profits than profits earned by non-family-controlled companies; and that that family-owned businesses have negative discretionary accruals higher than those reported by non-family owned firms, and that family control had a positive influence on this type of earnings management.

Using a sample of firms listed on the BMF& Bovespa during 2008-2012, Cardoso, Martinez & Teixeira (2014) analyzed whether in Brazilian firms that had excess free cash flow (FCF) and low growth perspectives (Jensen. 1986), managers have incentives to camouflage the impact of investments in projects with negative net present value (NPV) by presenting inflated profits when there is excess FCF and limited growth prospect. Cardoso, Martinez & Teixeira (2014) estimated Discretionary accruals (DA) by the modified *Jones Model* and then the relationship between FCF and DA was ascertained by multiple regression. Cardoso, Martinez & Teixeira (2014) found that firms that had low growth perspectives and excess FCF were more likely to manage earnings to increase profits, but that *Shareholding Concentration* and adoption of IFRS moderates that relationship.

Siregar & Utama (2008) studied whether companies listed on the Jakarta Stock Exchange (JSE) perpetrate *efficient* or *opportunistic Earnings Management* and the effect of ownership structure, firm size, and corporate-governance practices on such behavior; and the found that:

1. JSE listed firms tended to use *efficient earnings management*, but that was inconsistent with the common view that earnings management in Indonesia is opportunistic;
2. family ownership had a significant effect on the type of earnings management selected; and firms with a high proportion of family ownership and non-business groups were more inclined to choose efficient earnings management than other types of firms;
3. there was inconsistent evidence about the impact of institutional ownership, firm size, and corporate-governance practices on type of earnings management.

Iatridis & Kadorinis (2009) studied the motives for and characteristics of UK firms that engage in earnings management activities, with a focus on the provision of voluntary accounting disclosures, the violation of debt covenants, management compensation, and on the equity and debt capital needs of firms and their relation with the use of earnings management; and the earnings management inclination of firms that seek to meet or exceed financial analysts' forecasts; and they found that:

1. firms that had low profitability and high leverage measures were likely to use earnings management;
2. firms needed equity and or debt capital and were close to debt covenant violation were more likely engage in earnings management practices; and
3. firms tended to use earnings management to improve their financial performance and subsequently reinforce their compensation and meet and/or exceed financial analysts' earnings forecasts;
4. firms that provide voluntary accounting disclosures were less likely to perpetrate earnings management.

Rosman, Biggs & Hoskin (2012) noted that archival and behavioral research suggests that discretionary accruals are managed to increase bonuses when the risk of being discovered is lowest; and investigated whether knowledge of how to manage earnings strategically is learned tacitly over time through experience in a series of three studies – and they found that more experienced study participants appear to recognize the potential benefit of upward earnings management, but only in the no monitoring condition where the potential risk of getting caught is low.

Elitzur (2011) found that:

1. bounded rationality and the ethical compass play an important role in the managers' decisions;
2. earnings management has multi-period dynamic properties, while the effort and insider trading decisions are made independently each period;
3. earnings manipulation can only occur in a world with ethically diverse managers;
4. contrary to common beliefs, shareholders have a vested interest in eliciting income management because it boosts their wealth – and thus expected market losses to shareholders' value, in response to detected accounting manipulations, are necessary to mitigate shareholders' preferences for earnings management;
5. shareholders' preferences for earnings management (balanced by the expected market losses) imply that they would not necessarily prefer to hire the most ethical and least 'bounded rationality' decision-making managers.

Wang & Esqueda (2014) analyzed corporate leverage decisions in the context of national culture during 1996–2010 and they found that:

1. cultural characteristics can explain capital structure decisions from emerging-markets cross-listings;
2. firms from countries with high *Individualism* and *Indulgence* use more debt;
3. Firms located in countries with high *Power Distance*, *Masculinity*, *Uncertainty Avoidance*, and *Long-term Orientation* were less leveraged;
4. exchange-traded and capital-raising ADR-companies (companies that issued ADRs) were more likely to be from countries with weaker corporate governance;
5. Univariate tests showed that capital-raising ADR-companies used less debt compared to non-capital-raising ADR-companies, and notably, in the post-cross-listing period;
6. the home country's cultural characteristics of capital-raising and exchange-traded ADRs exerted less influence on their capital structure decisions;
7. there was a value discount associated with increased firm leverage.

Using a unique dataset obtained from large-scale panel enterprise surveys conducted in 2005 and 2009, Iwasaki (2014) analyzed the survival status of Russian industrial firms before and after the global financial crisis and they noted that: i) the estimation of the *Cox proportional hazard model* provided evidence that the independence of a company's governance bodies, their human resource abundance, and influence over corporate management were statistically significant factors that affected the survival probability of the surveyed firms; ii) the board of directors and the audit committee are likely to play a vital role in reducing the potential exit risk; iii) there is a significant difference in the viewpoints of economic logic for firm survival held by independent firms and group companies.

Using a large sample of change-of-auditor by companies during 2001–2012, Li, Sun & Ettredge (2017) analyzed the influences of peer firms' prior choices on whether or not an audit client chooses to affiliate with a "social norm" audit office in its metropolitan area after auditor turnover; and they found that: i) peer firms used four alternative dimensions of similarity: client geographic location, industry affiliation, client size (filing status), and departing auditor type (Big N versus non-Big N); ii) for every dimension of similarity, the propensity of a client to select a norm (as opposed to a non-norm) audit office as the succeeding auditor is positively associated with 1) the proportion of its peers audited by the "norm" office in the prior year (i.e., social norm evidence) and 2) the proportion of its auditor-switching peers selecting a "norm" audit office in the prior year (i.e. social learning evidence); iii) Social norm and social learning evidence provided by "more similar" peers had greater effect than evidence provided by "less similar" peers across all four dimensions of peer similarity; iv) social norm and learning evidence has incremental power (beyond each other) in explaining auditor selection, with norm evidence exhibiting a larger effect than learning evidence; v) an analysis of the implementation of SOX 404(b) mandatory internal control audits in 2004 indicated that clients' tendency to choose pre-existing social norm audit offices can be disrupted by exogenous events.

Using a nationwide random selection of 111 lenders in the US and in a 2 × 2 between-subjects experiment, Booker (2018) analyzed whether the level of an auditor's economic dependence on a client and type of auditor rotation affect lenders' independence and reliability perceptions and decisions to lend money to a potential borrower; and they found that: i) lenders view clients of economically dependent auditors (CEDA) as less independent from its auditor and perceive its financials as less reliable than clients without a dependent auditor (non-CEDA); ii) Lenders are less likely to grant a loan to CEDA; iii) under audit-firm rotation, there is both an increase in lenders' perceptions of reliability of CEDA financials, and also no difference in perceptions of reliability of CEDA and non-CEDA financials.

Using 7,258 firm-year observations in China from 1998 to 2005, Wong (2018) analyzed whether the percentage of asset write-downs by state-controlled firms differs from those of non-state-controlled firms, conditional upon more conservative financial reporting rules, and whether local auditors supported managerial decisions on asset write-downs; and they noted that: i) state-controlled entities tended to have lower asset write-downs; and ii) local auditors supported managerial decisions on asset write-downs, especially when the companies were controlled by local governments.

Boghean, F. (2015) analyzed the implementation of risk management systems in entities through relevant international standards, in order to identify the issues that organizations are facing in implementing the Standard 11 "Risk Management" and in outlining a model of risk assessment.

Using a cross-sectional sample of 142,193 firm-year observations from 46 countries over 1998–2007, Houqe, Monem & van Zijl (2012) showed that: i) the *government quality* of a country has a significant positive effect on the likelihood of choosing Big-4 auditors by firms in that country; ii) that firms in countries with strong governments that have adopted IFRS were more likely to choose Big-4 than non-Big-4 auditors; iii) Choice of a Big 4 auditor may be regarded as a proxy for the demand for high quality financial reporting.

Using a sample of 132,853 firm-year observations from forty-six countries during 1998-2007 and controlling for a number of firm- and country-level factors, Houqe, van Zijl, et. al. (2015) studied whether firms' auditor choice reflected the strength of corporate ethics, and they found that: i) firms in countries where "high corporate ethical values" prevailed were more likely to hire a Big-4 auditor; ii) the positive effect of home country corporate ethical values on the likelihood of hiring a high-quality auditor was reinforced by the extent of the firm's board size; iii) there is an indirect link between corporate ethics and financial reporting quality through the firms' choice of auditor.

Anderlini, Gerardi & Lagunoff (2016) analyzed the relative performance of disclosure and auditing in decentralized institutions, and the *Information Transmission Problem* between two decision makers who take actions in sequence at two decision dates where the first decision maker has private information about a state of nature that is relevant for both decisions, and sends a message to the second decision maker who can commit to only observe the message (disclosure), or can retain the option to observe the action of the first decision maker (auditing) or, at some cost, to verify the state. Anderlini, Gerardi & Lagunoff (2016) noted that: i) in equilibrium, state verification will never occur and the second decision maker effectively chooses between auditing and disclosure; ii) when the misalignment in preferences reflects an agency bias (a bias in a decision maker's own action relative to that of the other) then the second decision maker chooses to audit in equilibrium; iii) when the misalignment in preferences reflects an ideological bias (one decision maker prefers all actions to be biased relative to the other decision maker) then, for a large enough misalignment, the second decision maker chooses disclosure in equilibrium; iv) the ability to commit to forego the audit has value in the latter case.

Wang & Xin (2011) studied the relationship between *auditor choice* and the accruals patterns of Chinese listed firms that cross-list in Hong Kong, and they found that: i) the clients of Big-4 auditors reported lower unsigned discretionary accruals relative to the clients of non-Big-4 auditors; ii) cross-listed firms with non-Big-4 auditors were more likely to understate their earnings and experience larger reversals of accruals in the future than cross-listed firms with Big-4 auditors; iii) Big-4 auditors play a meaningful role in improving earnings quality for cross-listed firms, which helps to explain why cross-listed firms have higher earnings quality than their domestic counterparts, as documented in the previous literature.

Zhang, Uchida & Bu (2013) found that: i) the introduction of IFRS-convergent new accounting standards (NAS) significantly increased earnings management in China; ii) although there wasn't evidence that split share structure reform (SSSR) in China directly decreased earnings management of the average firm, the increase in earnings management surrounding the introduction of NAS is negatively related to the reduction in non-tradable shares; iii) accounting standards are the more important factor associated with the level of earnings management; iv) insiders' incentives affect earnings management given a specific set of accounting standards.

A SURVEY OF INVESTORS' DECISIONS AND REACTIONS TO ACCOUNTING DISCLOSURES

Dai, Kong & Wang (2013) noted that: (1) reducing information asymmetry improves firms' earnings management behavior; (2) relative to short-term mutual funds, long-term mutual funds promote earnings quality by adopting a monitoring role; and (3) the information environment significantly increases the effect of long-term mutual funds on firms' earnings management. In this paper, we provide new evidence for the role that institutional investors play in a typical emerging capital market; 4) to increase earnings quality, it is essential to improve information transparency and develop long-term institutional investors. Chi, Yang & Young (2014) found that: i) Long- or short-term funds impact different earnings management measures differently and such impact is stronger in non-state-controlled firms; ii) Chinese long-term mutual funds' holdings have an insignificant impact on accruals; while Chinese short-term funds' holdings encourage an increase in earnings management.

Using a sample of 892 (eight hundred and ninety-two) block acquisitions across forty-two countries during 1990-2008 and using earnings management as a proxy for corporate governance outcome, Dai, Dharwadkar, et. al. (2017) analyzed the *Governance Transfer Effect* of corporate blockholders and they found that: i) target firms' earnings management was aligned with that of block acquirers after acquisitions, which implys that blockholders transfer their own governance quality to investee firms; ii) there were three economic mechanisms that drive the *Governance Transfer Effect*, which are *Monitoring Effectiveness*, *Monitoring Cost*, and *Monitoring Environment*.

Using Hong Kong listed firms subject to increase the extent of disclosure, Bazrafshan, Kandelousi & Hooy (2016) critiqued the notion that seeking to increase disclosure may not necessarily improve firm performance; and they concluded that: i) the net benefit of disclosure is contingent on conditions such as the quality and integrity of a firm's information; ii) during 2006-2013, there was a nonlinear relation between disclosure and firm performance when measured performance is adjusted for the impact of earnings management; iii) corporate disclosure is likely to result in benefits, but after an *optimum level*, increasing disclosure reduces true firm performance – and this *optimum level* also declines when differences between other firm's monitoring environments (e.g., independent boards) are in place; iv) intense monitoring of CEOs offsets the advantage of additional corporate disclosure.

Using quarterly institutional holding data of 1,591 Indian firms during 2001-2015 (a total of 95,460 firm-quarters), Deb (2018) analyzed the temporal variation of domestic institutional investors' (DII) and foreign institutional investors (FIIs) dynamic preferences towards firm characteristics in an Indian context and across varying market swings. We use quarterly institutional holding data of 1591 Indian firms between 2001 and 2015 (amounting to a total of 95460 firm-quarters) and found that: i) common preferences are manifested towards firms with existing institutional investment, higher dividend-yield, more liquidity, higher earnings-margins, existing international exposure and longer survival history in industry; ii) common strong dislike is visible for high leverage and high price-book stocks and for stocks with high variability in earnings; iii) preferences varied across different classes of institutions with respect to some firm attributes - FIIs exhibited preferences towards 'index-stocks' and large stocks while both these traits are not preferred by MFs and DIIs; iv) there was also evidence of temporal variation of these patterns across bull and bear cycles.

Using a sample of exchange traded firms from thirty-seven countries, and regressions that control for country, industry, and year fixed effects as well as other firm-level determinants, El Ghoul, Guedhami & Pittman (2016) found that: i) corporate equity financing worldwide was cheaper when Big-Four auditors monitored the financial reporting process, although this relation is weaker outside the U.S.; ii) U.S. and non-U.S. public firms' cost of equity capital fell by, on average, 55 and 23 basis points, respectively, when a Big Four auditor was involved; iii) there was empirical support for the predictions that the equity pricing role of Big Four auditors was stronger in countries with better institutions governing investor protection and disclosure standards.

Schneider (2018) reviewed studies that examined how accounting information impacts commercial lending judgments – ie. the usefulness of accounting data in lending decisions, effects of different accounting methods on lenders' judgments, bankruptcy and default judgments, and decision processes about the use of accounting information in lending decisions.

Chugh, Fargher & Wright (2014) studied factors that affect international firms' decisions to cross-list as Global Depository Receipts (GDRs); and found that: i) the home country is an important factor and reflects trade ties; ii) higher US regulation and governance requirements affected emerging markets firms' decision to issue GDRs rather than ADRs on a US exchange; iii) using local GAAP or IFRS deters firms from listing as an ADR (the cost of US GAAP reconciliation is an important factor).

Schneider (2015) analyzed the effect of auditor dismissals and resignations on investing decisions (ie. whether these decisions differ due to a reason given for the dismissal or resignation) and they found that: i) auditor switches produce higher investment risk assessments and marginally lower amounts invested than without auditor switches; ii) the effects of resignations were not significantly different from the effects of dismissals; iii) disclosure of a disagreement as a reason for an auditor switch had no impact.

In four experiments, which are consistent with *affect theory* from psychology, Tan & Koonce (2011) noted that retratcions and corrections of corporate accounting disclosures have unexpected effects on investor judgment; and they noted that: i) when a company provides a retraction of a previous erroneous voluntary disclosure, investors' judgments continue to reflect the implications of the initial erroneous information – ie. investors under-adjust; ii)on the contrary, when a company provides a correction (alone or with a prior retraction) with an opposite earnings implication, investors tend to over-adjust; iii) if investors do not form a strong initial affective reaction to the initial erroneous forecast, they are less prone to over-adjustment when the correction is later received.

Lander & Auger (2008) discussed several ways in which companies manipulate off-balance sheet transactions to satisfy personal and business objectives as well as the impact of such manipulations; and they noted that: i) Off-balance-sheet amounts are substantial and in the trillions of dollars, not including all transactions with off-balance-sheet implications; ii) financial managers and consultants intentionally structure transactions that are contravene and abuse off-balance sheet accounting rules, which leads to opaque financial reporting.

Using participants from eight countries who evaluated thirteen vignettes that described various earnings management practices (Merchant & Rockness, 1994), Geiger & O'Connell, et. al. (2006) analyzed whether national culture influences perceptions of the acceptability of earnings management; and they found that; i) there was substantial variation in perceptions across nations to the earnings management scenarios; ii) using *Hofstede's (1991) cultural indices*, the differences in aggregate perceptions across countries were not closely associated with any of the cultural dimensions examined; iii) perceptions of earnings manipulations that involve the timing of operating decisions were associated with both the *Power Distance Index* and the *Masculinity Index.*

ENFORCEMENT THEORY AND COMPLIANCE: A SURVEY OF GOVERNMENTS' ENVIRONMENTAL ENFORCEMENT POLICIES; AND AUDITEE-COMPANIES' DECISIONS ABOUT CLIMATE FINANCE AND COMPLIANCE WITH ENVIRONMENTAL REGULATIONS

As of 2021, most existing and proposed systems of environmental management and Climate Policy around the world (e.g. environmental regulations; carbon trading; emissions permits; etc.): i) are substantially based on, and or evaluated using accounting processes and accounting data/disclosures; and ii) have failed, have been circumvented or will fail. Environmental pollution and illegal cross border dumping of waste have been increasing around the world. The failure or refusal of companies or government agencies to comply with environmental regulations/statutes, requirements/standards for Climate Finance instruments, and compliance with requirements for carbon credits/permits and emissions-permits trading often has direct and beneficial effects on their financial statements and by extension on the values of their Equity-based Incentives and cash incentives and thus, constitutes types of earnings management, asset quality management and incentive-effects management.

Audit/accounting firms and management consulting firms (collectively and in this context, "audit firms") are critical players in the global systems of environmental management because they serve or can serve as external monitors that verify firms' compliance with environmental/waste regulations and statutes, requirements/standards for Climate Finance instruments, and compliance with requirements for carbon credits/permits and emissions-permits trading.

Relying on interviews, Sabonis-Helf (2003) analyzed the evolution of climate policy in Russia, Ukraine and Kazakhstan each of which participated actively in the UN Framework Convention on Climate Change (UNFCCC) Conferences of the Parties, and is developing domestic rules and institutions to address UN obligations under the treaties.

Ruban & Rydén (2019) discussed the introduction, development and practice of environmental auditing in Ukraine and how it was affected by the EU-Ukraine integration process, and noted that:

1. environmental auditing in Ukraine has combined features of both command-and-control and marked-based policy tools, which reflects a complex combination of influences from its Soviet past and international practices adopted as part of its transition to a market economy;
2. there are two types of environmental auditing: mandatory and voluntary, which, although based on different normative documents, largely rely on the same practitioners - environmental auditors. Ruban & Rydén (2019) developed a theoretical framework that consists of: 1) *'Shift Of Policy Paradigms'* theory, 2) *'Collective Action'* theory and 3) *'Community Of Practice'* theory. Several qualitative methods were used for data collection: literature review, semi-structure open-ended interviews, and participant/non-participant observations.

Tulaeva (2013) analyzed "trust" in the international system of forest certification promoted by transnational non-governmental organizations (NGOs); and noted that:

1. on an international level, the degree of trust in the system is affected by its design features (management structure and organization of the certification process) as well as the expert activities of a number of transnational NGOs and certification bodies;
2. at the local level, trust in the new system is constructed on interpersonal relationships between the local community and the certified company;
3. the initial foundation of this process is the rational interest of the local community in the new opportunities and resources offered by the system;
4. using the new rights, residents gradually begin to adopt new rules and values which results in further development of institutional trust and its transformation from the instrumental to the social, based on common shared values;
5. the communities and of the factors involved in local trust formation are diverse in variety of different cases.

Hultman, Pulver, et. al. (2012) conducted firm-level interviews covering 82 CDM (clean development mechanism) plants in the sugar and cement sectors in Brazil and India, about managers' perceptions of CDM, and they found that:

1. in practice, CDM operates in more complex ways than that of simply adding a marginal increment to a project's internal rate of return;
2. although anticipated revenue played a central role in most managers' decisions to pursue CDM investments, there was no standard practice to account for financial benefits of CDM investments;
3. some managers identified non-financial reputational factors as their primary motivation for pursuing CDM projects;
4. under changing regulatory regimes with real immediate costs and uncertain CDM revenue, managers chose projects that often did not require carbon revenue to be viable;
5. the post-2012 CDM architecture can benefit from incorporating these insights, and in particular reassess goals for strict additionality and mechanisms for achieving them.

Orazalin & Mahmood (2018) analyzed the nature of sustainability reporting practices of the largest public oil and gas companies in Russia and found that: i) standalone sustainability reporting, firm age, and auditor type are the main factors in the dissemination of sustainability information in the Russian context; ii) Foreign ownership has a positive impact on sustainability reporting; iii) companies that prepare sustainability reports only in Russian provide more valuable sustainability information than companies that publish reports in both English and Russian.

Yang, Guo, et.al. (2018) tested the consistence of the Pollution Haven Hypothesis (PHH) and examined china-based firms' location choice in response to the environmental regulations, and found that: i) different measures of environmental regulation lead to different conclusions of the PHH; ii) firms' relocation patterns are common and consistent; iii) this pattern is consistent with the industrial planning of the Jiangsu province, suggesting that local government may use environmental regulations to achieve economic objectives.

Telle (2013) analyzed the effects of self-reporting, audit frequency and specific deterrence; and found that: i) there was evidence of under-reporting of violations in firms' self-audits, as more violations are detected in on-site audits than in self-audits; ii) announcing the increased audit frequency had no effect on firms' compliance, but an audit raises subsequent compliance substantially.

Using datasets from Italy, D'Amato, Mazzanti, et. al. (2018) analyzed how environmental and enforcement policies impact environmental non-compliance; and they found that:

1. environmental non-compliance is affected by the decentralized shaping of environmental policy by local governments and enforcement actions by public bodies;
2. commitment to a more stringent waste policy tends to increase illegal disposal of waste;
3. a nonlinear bell shaped relationship exists between the number of inspections and the quantity of illegal disposal;
4. deterrence might only result after a relatively high level of controls is implemented.

Using data from 87 countries during 2004-2010 and within the Environmental Kuznets Curve (EKC) framework, Aşici & Acar (2018) studied how the location of non-carbon ecological footprint (home or abroad) changes with environmental regulation (Ecological footprint measures the amount of biocapacity required to sustain the consumption patterns of human beings); and they found that:

1. an EKC relationship cannot be validated for income (GDP per capita) and non-carbon footprints of production and of imports;

2. countries reach the turning points for import footprint at lower levels of income once stringency of environmental regulation and enforcement of environmental regulation are accounted for;
3. environmental regulations push the economic structure towards a cleaner transformation by which resources can be exploited more effectively, and short run losses in economic growth can be avoided in the medium and long run, conditional on a successful transformation toward higher value-added and cleaner production processes.

Using a unique firm-level Chinese Environmental Statistics dataset and a regression discontinuity design to assess the impact of central supervision through the NSMF program on an industrial firm's chemical oxygen demand (COD) emissions, Zhang, Chen & Guo (2018) found that central supervision significantly reduces industrial COD emissions by at least 26.8%; and also noted that a more flexible environmental decentralization regime and comprehensive central supervision are thus recommended for future.

Sjöberg (2016) noted that mismatch of local and national incentives is a potential problem with local enforcement of national legislation and using a dataset of environmental fines issued in each of Sweden's 290 municipalities, they also found that:

1. the Green Party values the tradeoff between business friendliness and environmental concerns differently from other parties;
2. using both a difference-in-differences approach and IV, there was evidence that municipalities with the Green Party in the ruling coalition issued more fines than other municipalities – which is problematic from an efficiency and equality perspective;
3. politicians do not only affect environmental policy, but also that for a given policy, they can affect the outcome through implementation and enforcement.

Shen, Liao, et. al. (2019) used the Metafrontier Malmquist-Luenberger (MML) method to analyze the influence of technology gaps and pollution emissions on the total factor productivity (TFP) of Chinese industry during 2000–2016 and found that:

1. due to the presence of industry heterogeneity, the different types of environmental regulations exerted heterogeneous influences on the environmental total factor productivity (ETFP) in different industries;
2. in heavy-pollution industries, an excessively high intensity of environmental regulation weakened the technological innovation of these enterprises;
3. in moderate-pollution industries, there was medium intensity of environmental regulation, with the command-and-control and market-based types of environmental regulation being quite well coordinated;
4. among slightly polluting industries, there was a significant "N-shaped" characteristic between the market-based type of environmental regulation and the ETFP;
5. the outcomes imply that given industry heterogeneity, environmental regulations should avoid both the unified adoption of static standards and the blind increase of regulation intensity.

Earnhart & Glicksman (2015) compared the effects of two different approaches to enforcement of environmental regulations: the coercive approach (which emphasizes the deterrence of noncompliance through inflexibly imposed sanctions), and the cooperative approach (which emphasizes the inducement of compliance through flexibility and assistance), and their empirical studies found that a more cooperative relationship induces better environmental management.

Galinato & Chouinard (2018) developed a framework that links the impacts of own and neighboring measures of institutional quality as well as neighboring country environmental regulations on environmental regulation stringency in own country; and they estimated a Spatial Panel Durbin model to identify significant determinants of environmental regulations for several European countries; and they found that:

1. there was no evidence of strategic interaction as the environmental regulations implemented by a neighbor have no significant impact on environmental regulations implemented in the own country;
2. the higher the quality of government institutions in a country, the more stringent the implementation of environmental regulations;
3. some institutional quality variables significantly positively affect the stringency of environmental regulations in neighboring countries.

Fang, Hipel & Kilgour (1997) developed Game-theoretic models for formally studying enforcement of environmental laws and regulations – the key questions and associated issues were how variations in the severity of penalties affect violation levels and frequencies; methods for measuring the effectiveness of enforcement, improving the efficiency of monitoring, and optimizing the design of regulations.

Oestreich (2017) analyzed the auditing problem of an environmental enforcement agency with fixed audit resources which is how to decide which firms to audit after having observed the firms' taxable emissions reports; and they derived an optimal audit mechanism capable of implementing the socially efficient emissions level. In the context of a market where firms with different characteristics decide upon both the level of emissions and their reports, Macho-Stadler & Perez-Castrillo (2006) analyzed the optimal audit policy for an enforcement agency whose objective is to minimize the level of emissions, and they found that: i) it is optimal to devote the resources primarily to the easiest-to-monitor firms and to those firms that value pollution the less; ii) unless the budget for monitoring is very large, there are always firms that do not comply with the environmental objective and others that do comply; but all of them evade the environmental taxes.

Stranlund, Chávez & Villena (2009) studied the pricing of a uniformly mixed pollutant with a model of optimal, possibly firm-specific emissions taxes and their enforcement under incomplete information about firms' abatement costs, enforcement costs, and pollution damage; and they noted that: i) optimality requires an enforcement strategy that induces full compliance by every firm, except possibly when a regulator can base the probabilities of detecting individual violations on observable correlates of violators' actual emissions; ii) optimality requires discriminatory taxes, except when a regulator is unable to use observable firm-level characteristics to gain some information about the variation in firms' abatement costs or monitoring costs.

Gilpatric, Vossler & McKee (2011) developed and tested two endogenous audit mechanisms that use contemporaneous relative comparisons, based on disclosed information or imperfect signals of compliance effort, to generate a compliance competition among agents; and they noted that: i) this type of audit mechanism has some advantages over the more widely studied dynamic audit mechanisms that condition an agent's audit probability on past compliance, and ii) this audit mechanism provides an alternative explanation for the stylized fact, in many settings, that most agents are compliant most of the time even though audit rates and expected penalties are low.

Akpalu, Eggert & Vondolia (2009) noted that many resource users are not directly involved in the formulation and enforcement of resource management rules in developing countries; and they developed a model of interactions among users and enforcement officers in the context of bribery.

Benchekroun & Van Long (1998) developed externality-aware "corrective tax rules" in dynamic Cournot games for situations when firms are oligopolists whose production processes generate emissions that add to a stock of pollution that accumulates over time; and they noted that:

1. there exists a time-independent tax rule that guides the oligopolists to achieve the socially optimum production path;
2. the optimal tax per unit of output is dependent on the current level of pollution stock, and it may be negative (implying a subsidy) when the pollution stock is low;
3. in some cases, the optimal tax rule gives firms a subsidy for an initial time interval even though under laissez-faire their output exceeds the socially optimal output at each point of time;
4. that subsidy induces firms to produce less than they would under laissez-faire, because they know that if they produce more then the subsidy will be reduced in the future and/or will soon turn into a tax.

Oestreich (2015) compared the incentives on firms' emissions and self-reporting behavior under the random audit mechanism to the incentives under competitive audit mechanisms (CAMs); and observed that:

1. many environmental tax systems rely on self-reported emissions by firms which are verified through costly auditing efforts by regulatory agencies that are constrained in their auditing budgets;
2. the typical assumption in the literature is that the agencies allocate audit efforts randomly among otherwise identical firms (random audit mechanism);
3. under CAMs, higher reported emissions by a firm relative to other firms result in a lower audit intensity; and that creates a reporting contest between the firms;
4. the two CAMs under investigation apply different degrees of competitiveness in the reporting contest; and both CAMs lead to more truthful reporting, which is in line with the previous literature;
5. some competition in reporting may induce fewer emissions compared with random auditing, while too much competition in reporting may induce comparatively higher emissions caused by firms (that was novel to the literature).

Mata, Fialho & Eugénio (2018) surveyed the literature environmental reports and environmental accounting based on papers published in twenty accounting journals between 2006 and 2015 (most were published in journals, such as Accounting, Auditing & Accountability Journal; Accounting Forum; Critical Perspectives on Accounting; and Accounting, Organizations and Society).

Imoniana, Soares & Domingos (2018) studied the sustainability accounting for *Emission Reduction Credit* (ERC) and compliance with emission rules through the discourse analysis; and they found that:

1. preparers of financial statement will continue to take advantage of the existing loophole of the variability of accounting treatments if the regulating bodies did not institute the classifications that should uphold in every case of ERC transactions;
2. the treatment of ERC aims at recording additional wealth for the entity and could be bookkept as other receivables;

3. in the context of sustainability, the then current concerns was compliance.

Using data from the U.S. chemical manufacturing sector during 1999-2001, Earnhart & Harrington (2014) studied the effect of environmental self-audits ("audits") on the extent of facilities' compliance with wastewater discharge limits; and they noted that theoretically, audits may: (1) improve compliance by enhancing the effectiveness of treatment technologies and pollution prevention methods, (2) undermine compliance by distracting facilities' personnel with audit-related administrative burdens, or (3) not influence compliance because these effects neutralize each other.

Evans & Gilpatric (2017) analyzed compliance with environmental regulations, pollution abatement, and care spending by firms facing two sources of insolvency risk (poor profit or a liability); and noted that:

1. the behavioral implications of this survival motive vary across firms;
2. firms for whom the principal insolvency risk is liability-related now choose precaution above the level chosen by the solvent firm;
3. for firms whose primary insolvency risk is profit-related, the survival motive reinforces incentives for care below the solvent benchmark arising from the familiar judgment-proof effect;
4. insolvency risks affect incentives to conceal adverse events linked to these choices, such as an accident or a regulatory violation.

Phillips (2014) generalized the classical evasion theory to account for the endogeneity of audit and payment rates, and noted that: i) taxpayers with large amounts of non-third-party-reported income usually self-report at least a portion of it, which is inconsistent with common theories of compliance; ii) taxpayers refrain from more evasion not due to deterrence, but to tilt the odds and payoffs of the evasion gamble and that incentive helps explain many empirical findings that seemingly contradict a more restrictive and unrealistic version of the "deterrence paradigm."

Earnhart & Leonard (2016) analyzed the effects of firm-level organizational structure on facility-level environmental management practices and the extent of environmental management practiced by U.S. chemical manufacturing facilities around 2001, as measured by the number of environmental internal audits conducted by facilities annually; and their empirical results indicated a difference in auditing behavior based on whether facilities were owned by firms operating within a single state or multiple states.

Using a unique facility-level dataset from Michigan (USA), Evans, Liu, et. al. (2011) analyzed the effect of environmental auditing on manufacturing facilities' long-term compliance with U.S. hazardous waste regulations and they accounted for the potential endogeneity of the audit measure and the censoring of the compliance measure using a censored trivariate probit; and they found that: i) larger facilities and those subject to more stringent regulations are more likely to audit; while facilities with poor compliance records are less likely to audit; ii) there were no significant long-run effects of auditing on the probability of a regulatory inspection or compliance among these Michigan manufacturing facilities.

Emergy Analysis (which provides a systematic approach in identifying the balance between socio-economic development and natural environment) was used by He, Yang, et. al. (2017) to developed a ternary *emergetic* environmental performance auditing framework to evaluate the behavior (preliminary work), ecological-economic efficiency (Level 1), environmental impact (Level 2), and mitigation effect (Level 3) of a typical industrial park in Beijing; and they found that: i) the concerned industrial park mainly depended on labor and service inputs and had a relatively high economic efficiency; ii) the large dependence on purchased *emergy* exerted great pressure on the resource and environment, and affected the stability of the industrial park.

Elnaboulsi, Daher & Sağlam (2018) analyzed the potential asymmetry-reducing role of disclosure and its impact on setting environmental taxes, and noted that: i) disclosure with verifiable reports is a valuable public good, provides greater transparency in the market, and is generally efficiency enhancing; ii) access to publicly disclosed information enables the fine-tuning of the tax rules towards specific environmental circumstances and improves the ability of the regulator to levy firm-specific environmental taxes; iii) despite its advantages, exogenously disclosed information can also produce anticompetitive effects by facilitating collusive behavior; iv) information sharing among firms may occur and thus result in a superior outcome in terms of industry output and emissions, which undermines environmental policy performance.

Based on a survey of 2,076 United Kingdom firms, Demirel, Iatridis & Kesidou (2018) analyzed how direct and indirect state regulation and its stringency influence both non-certified in-house and externally certified adoption of EMS (environmental management systems) and they found that: i) effective environmental protection involves collaboration between environmental state regulation and in-house adoption of EMS; ii) externally certified EMS substitute for state environmental regulation, filling the void that results from weakening state regulation in the context of neoliberalism.

Using a firm-level dataset on the adoption of a voluntary environmental auditing program, Evans, Liu & Stafford (2015) developed and tested a theoretical model to examine the conditions under which a multi-facility firm chooses to employ a standardized adoption policy for a voluntary program and found that: i) consistent with the theoretical model, a standardized auditing outcome is less likely among firms with more heterogeneous portfolios of facilities; ii) the effect of environmental auditing on facility compliance (using both firm-level and facility-level controls) depends on whether or not measures that proxy for firm incentives for standardization are included in the analysis; iii) these findings question the effectiveness of voluntary programs in improving compliance based on analyses that assume standardization on the part of the firm.

Wang, Zhang & Chen (2011) reviewed the development history of China's environmental audit, and analyzed the then current situation and main challenges that China's environmental audit faces.

Using Policy Cycle Analysis and a review of national implementation documents and thirty semi-structured interviews with stakeholders involved in the process of EU's Article 8 EED, Nabitz & Hirzel (2019) analyzed differences and communalities in the national requirements for the statute; and they found that: i) the transposition of Article 8 EED was delayed in more than half of the EU-28 MS; ii) the inter-linkages of the policy cycles are important for a smooth policy process; iii) almost all countries involved maneuvered during the transposition process.

Tai, Lai & Yang (2018) studied the effects of corporate governance on corporate risk-management activities in S&P 500 firms during 2004–2010 by measuring the characteristics of the board directors and audit committee; and they found that the board of directors, especially the audit committee, plays an important role in the firm's hedging decisions, including whether to hedge and to what extent (especially for high-leveraged firms with large risk-shifting incentives).

Alola (2019) analyzed the effects of trade policy, monetary policy, and migration index on carbon emissions over the period 1990:Q1–2018: Q2 in the USA, and found that: i) uncertainty in policy changes in trade, monetary and immigration cause harmful environment degradation; ii) such impact of the migration index on the carbon dioxide emissions is barely significant in the long-run and at the immediate time; iii) there is both significant long-run and the short-run nexus of CO2, trade policy, monetary policy and migration index; iv) suboptimal US government policies on trade, monetary policies and immigration makes it harder to achieve the Sustainable Development Goals 2030 and also reduces the environmental sustainability of the United States.

Tang, Li, et.al. (2020) discussed the transition from command-and-control to market-based environmental policies in China.

Asante-Appiah (2020) studied whether an audit-client's negative/low ESG Reputation affects audit effort and audit quality, and noted that: i) ESG risk can affect business processes and controls and can increase a firm's financial/operational risk; ii) auditors manage the higher expected engagement risk implicit in low ESG-Reputation by applying higher audit effort; which in turn is associated with auditors likely detecting and requiring adjustments for material misstatements; iii) low ESG-Reputation is associated with fewer misstatements (i.e., reduces poor audit quality) and low ESG Reputation is positively associated with audit effort and reduces poor audit quality for up to three years (the *audit effort and audit quality effect*); iv) the relationship between low ESG reputation and audit quality (*audit effort and audit quality effect*) is driven primarily by increased audit report lag, not by increased audit fees; and the *audit effort and audit quality effect* varies across the three components of ESG.

CONCLUSION

Clearly, the issues/topics surveyed in this chapter are critical for worldwide enforcement, sustainability programs, regulation, and policy-formulation.

REFERENCES

Agarwal, S., Chomsisengphet, S., Liu, C., & Rhee, G. (2007). Earnings management behaviors under different economic environments: Evidence from Japanese banks. *International Review of Economics & Finance, 16*(3), 429–443. doi:10.1016/j.iref.2005.08.003

Akpalu, W., Eggert, H., & Vondolia, G. (2009). Enforcement of exogenous environmental regulation, social disapproval and bribery. *Journal of Socio-Economics, 38*(6), 940–945. doi:10.1016/j.socec.2009.06.002

Alola, A. (2019). The trilemma of trade, monetary and immigration policies in the United States: Accounting for environmental sustainability. *The Science of the Total Environment, 658*, 260–267. doi:10.1016/j.scitotenv.2018.12.212 PMID:30577021

Anderlini, L., Gerardi, D., & Lagunoff, R. (2016). Auditing, disclosure, and verification in decentralized decision problems. *Journal of Economic Behavior & Organization, 131A*, 393–408. doi:10.1016/j.jebo.2016.09.002

Anderson, H., Chi, J., & Wang, Q. (2017). Political ties and VC exits: Evidence from China. *China Economic Review, 44*, 48–66. doi:10.1016/j.chieco.2017.03.007

Andiola, L., & Bedard, J. (2018). Delivering the "tough message": Moderators of subordinate auditors' reactions to feedback. *Accounting, Organizations and Society, 70*, 52–68. doi:10.1016/j.aos.2018.02.002

Asante-Appiah, B. (2020). Does the severity of a client's negative environmental, social and governance reputation affect audit effort and audit quality? *Journal of Accounting and Public Policy, 39*(3), 106713. doi:10.1016/j.jaccpubpol.2019.106713

Ashraf, B. (2017). Political institutions and bank risk-taking behavior. *Journal of Financial Stability, 29*, 13–35. doi:10.1016/j.jfs.2017.01.004

Aşıcı, A., & Acar, S. (2018). How does environmental regulation affect production location of non-carbon ecological footprint? *Journal of Cleaner Production, 178*, 927–936. doi:10.1016/j.jclepro.2018.01.030

Attia, M., Lassoued, N., & Attia, A. (2016). Political costs and earnings management: Evidence from Tunisia. *Journal of Accounting in Emerging Economies, 6*(4), 388–407. doi:10.1108/JAEE-05-2013-0022

Bayer, R., & Cowell, F. (2009). Tax compliance and firms' strategic interdependence. *Journal of Public Economics, 93*(11-12), 1131–1143. doi:10.1016/j.jpubeco.2009.07.007

Bazrafshan, E., Kandelousi, A., & Hooy, C. (2016). The impact of earnings management on the extent of disclosure and true financial performance: Evidence from listed firms in Hong Kong. *The British Accounting Review, 48*(2), 206–219. doi:10.1016/j.bar.2015.09.001

Belz, T., von Hagen, D., & Steffens, C. (2019). Taxes and firm size: Political cost or political power? *Journal of Accounting Literature, 42*, 1–28. doi:10.1016/j.acclit.2018.12.001

Ben-Nasr, H., Boubakri, N., & Cosset, J. (2015). Earnings quality in privatized firms: The role of state and foreign owners. *Journal of Accounting and Public Policy, 34*(4), 392–416. doi:10.1016/j.jaccpubpol.2014.12.003

Benchekroun, H., & Van Long, N. (1998). Efficiency inducing taxation for polluting oligopolists. *Journal of Public Economics, 70*(2), 325–342. doi:10.1016/S0047-2727(98)00038-3

Bensberg, F., Buscher, G., & Czarnecki, C. (2019). Digital transformation and IT topics in the consulting industry: A labor market perspective. In *Advances in consulting research* (pp. 341–357). Springer. doi:10.1007/978-3-319-95999-3_16

Boghean, F. (2015). Risk Management in the Decision-making of Romanian Entities. *Procedia Economics and Finance, 32*, 1066–1074. doi:10.1016/S2212-5671(15)01569-5

Boneva, M. (2018). Challenges related to the digital transformation of business companies. In Innovation Management, Entrepreneurship and Sustainability (IMES 2018) (pp. 101-114). Vysoká škola ekonomická v Praze.

Booker, K. (2018). Can clients of economically dependent auditors benefit from voluntary audit firm rotation? An experiment with lenders. *Research in Accounting Regulation, 30*(1), 63–67. doi:10.1016/j.racreg.2018.03.008

Botzem, S. (2012). The Politics Of Accounting Regulation: Organizing Transnational Standard Setting. In *Financial Reporting*. Edward Elgar.

Boubakri, N., El Ghoul, S., & Saffar, W. (2015). Firm growth and political institutions. *Journal of Multinational Financial Management, 31*, 104–125. doi:10.1016/j.mulfin.2015.05.003

Braam, G., Nandy, M., Weitzel, U., & Lodh, S. (2015). Accrual-based and real earnings management and political connections. *The International Journal of Accounting*, *50*(2), 111–141. doi:10.1016/j.intacc.2013.10.009

Brandau, M., Endenich, C., Trapp, R., & Hoffjan, A. (2013). Institutional drivers of conformity – Evidence for management accounting from Brazil and Germany. *International Business Review*, *22*(2), 466–479. doi:10.1016/j.ibusrev.2012.07.001

Bruneau, C., de Bandt, O., & El Amri, W. (2012). Macroeconomic fluctuations and corporate financial fragility. *Journal of Financial Stability*, *8*(4), 219–235. doi:10.1016/j.jfs.2012.02.002

Bushman, R., & Piotroski, J. (2006). Financial reporting incentives for conservative accounting: The influence of legal and political institutions. *Journal of Accounting and Economics*, *42*(1-2), 107–148. doi:10.1016/j.jacceco.2005.10.005

Camfferman, K. (2020). International Accounting Standard Setting and Geopolitics. *Accounting in Europe*, *17*(3), 243–263. doi:10.1080/17449480.2020.1795214

Chen, D., Jiang, D., Liang, S., & Wang, F. (2011). Selective enforcement of regulation. *China Journal of Accounting Research*, *4*(1–2), 9–27. doi:10.1016/j.cjar.2011.04.002

Chen, D., Li, J., Liang, S., & Wang, G. (2011). Macroeconomic control, political costs and earnings management: Evidence from Chinese listed real estate companies. *China Journal of Accounting Research*, *4*(3), 91–106. doi:10.1016/j.cjar.2011.06.002

Chen, Q., Kelly, K., & Salterio, S. (2012). Do changes in audit actions and attitudes consistent with increased auditor scepticism deter aggressive earnings management? An experimental investigation. *Accounting, Organizations and Society*, *37*(2), 95–115. doi:10.1016/j.aos.2011.11.001

Cheng, L., & Leung, T. (2016). Government protection, political connection and management turnover in China. *International Review of Economics & Finance*, *45*, 160–176. doi:10.1016/j.iref.2016.03.010

Chi, J., Yang, J., & Young, M. (2014). Mutual funds' holdings and listed firms' earnings management: Evidence from China. *Journal of Multinational Financial Management*, *28*, 62–78. doi:10.1016/j.mulfin.2014.10.002

Chugh, S., Fargher, N., & Wright, S. (2014). Cross-listing as a Global Depository Receipt: The influence of emerging markets, regulation, and accounting regime. *Journal of Contemporary Accounting & Economics*, *10*(3), 262–276. doi:10.1016/j.jcae.2014.10.004

Cornett, M., Marcus, A., & Tehranian, H. (2008). Corporate governance and pay-for-performance: The impact of earnings management. *Journal of Financial Economics*, *87*(2), 357–373. doi:10.1016/j.jfineco.2007.03.003

D'Amato, A., Mazzanti, M., Nicolli, F., & Zoli, M. (2018). Illegal waste disposal: Enforcement actions and decentralized environmental policy. *Socio-Economic Planning Sciences*, *64*, 56–65. doi:10.1016/j.seps.2017.12.006

Dai, L., Dharwadkar, R., Shi, L., & Zhang, B. (2017). The governance transfer of blockholders: Evidence from block acquisitions and earnings management around the world. *Journal of Corporate Finance*, *45*, 586–607. doi:10.1016/j.jcorpfin.2017.06.004

Dai, Y., Kong, D., & Wang, L. (2013). Information asymmetry, mutual funds and earnings management: Evidence from China. *China Journal of Accounting Research*, *6*(3), 187–209. doi:10.1016/j.cjar.2013.03.001

Deb, S. (2018). Institutional Investors and firm characteristics: New evidence from India. *Research in International Business and Finance*, *46*, 30–42. doi:10.1016/j.ribaf.2017.09.005

Demirel, P., Iatridis, K., & Kesidou, E. (2018). The impact of regulatory complexity upon self-regulation: Evidence from the adoption and certification of environmental management systems. *Journal of Environmental Management*, *207*, 80–91. doi:10.1016/j.jenvman.2017.11.019 PMID:29154011

Dima, S., Dima, B., & … . (2014). A discussion over IFRS' adoption in Islamic countries. *Accounting and Management Information*, *13*(1), 35–49.

Dimitras, A., Kyriakou, M., & Iatridis, G. (2015). Financial crisis, GDP variation and earnings management in Europe. *Research in International Business and Finance*, *34*, 338–354. doi:10.1016/j.ribaf.2015.02.017

Dou, Y., Khan, M., & Zou, Y. (2016). Labor unemployment insurance and earnings management. *Journal of Accounting and Economics*, *61*(1), 166–184. doi:10.1016/j.jacceco.2015.06.001

Dye, R. (2002). Classifications Manipulation and Nash Accounting Standards. *Journal of Accounting Research*, *40*(4), 1125–1162. doi:10.1111/1475-679X.00084

Earnhart, D., & Glicksman, R. (2015). Coercive vs. cooperative enforcement: Effect of enforcement approach on environmental management. *International Review of Law and Economics*, *42*, 135–146. doi:10.1016/j.irle.2015.02.003

Earnhart, D., & Harrington, D. (2014). Effect of audits on the extent of compliance with wastewater discharge limits. *Journal of Environmental Economics and Management*, *68*(2), 243–261. doi:10.1016/j.jeem.2014.06.004

Earnhart, D., & Leonard, M. (2016). Environmental audits and signaling: The role of firm organizational structure. *Resource and Energy Economics*, *44*, 1–22. doi:10.1016/j.reseneeco.2016.01.002

El Ghoul, S., Guedhami, O., & Pittman, J. (2016). Cross-country evidence on the importance of Big Four auditors to equity pricing: The mediating role of legal institutions. *Accounting, Organizations and Society*, *54*, 60–81. doi:10.1016/j.aos.2016.03.002

Elitzur, R. (2011). The accounting art of war: Bounded rationality, earnings management and insider trading. *Journal of Accounting and Public Policy*, *30*(3), 203–216. doi:10.1016/j.jaccpubpol.2010.11.002

Elnaboulsi, J., Daher, W., & Sağlam, Y. (2018). On the social value of publicly disclosed information and environmental regulation. *Resource and Energy Economics*, *54*, 1–22. doi:10.1016/j.reseneeco.2018.05.003

Elnahass, M., Izzeldin, M., & Steele, G. (2018). Capital and Earnings Management: Evidence from Alternative Banking Business Models. *The International Journal of Accounting*, *53*(1), 20–32. doi:10.1016/j.intacc.2018.02.002

Erdogan, N., & Uludag, E. (2014). Comparison of Analysis Performed by Classical Approach and Bayesian Approach in Auditors' Decision Making Process. *Procedia: Social and Behavioral Sciences*, *150*(15), 668–677. doi:10.1016/j.sbspro.2014.09.086

Evans, M., & Gilpatric, S. (2017). Abatement, Care, and Compliance by Firms in Financial Distress. *Environmental and Resource Economics*, *66*(4), 765–794. doi:10.100710640-015-9972-3

Evans, M., Liu, L., & Stafford, S. (2015). Standardization and the impacts of voluntary program participation: Evidence from environmental auditing. *International Review of Law and Economics*, *43*, 10–21. doi:10.1016/j.irle.2015.04.003

Evans, M., Liu, L., & Stafford, S. L. (2011). Do environmental audits improve long-term compliance? Evidence from manufacturing facilities in Michigan. *Journal of Regulatory Economics*, *40*(3), 279–302. doi:10.100711149-011-9163-2

Fagella, D. (2020). *AI in the Accounting Big Four – Comparing Deloitte, PwC, KPMG, and EY*. https://emerj.com/ai-sector-overviews/ai-in-the-accounting-big-four-comparing-deloitte-pwc-kpmg-and-ey/

Fang, L., Hipel, K., & Kilgour, M. (1997). How penalty affects enforcement of environmental regulations. *Applied Mathematics and Computation*, *83*(2-3), 281–301. doi:10.1016/S0096-3003(96)00189-0

Friesen, L. (2003). Targeting enforcement to improve compliance with environmental regulations. *Journal of Environmental Economics and Management*, *46*(1), 72–85. doi:10.1016/S0095-0696(02)00033-5

Frye, T., & Iwasaki, I. (2011). Government directors and business–state relations in Russia. *European Journal of Political Economy*, *27*(4), 642–658. doi:10.1016/j.ejpoleco.2011.06.003

Fung, s., Raman, K., & Zhu, X. (2017). Does the PCAOB international inspection program improve audit quality for non-US-listed foreign clients? *Journal of Accounting and Economics*, *64*(1), 15-36.

Galinato, G., & Chouinard, H. (2018). Strategic interaction and institutional quality determinants of environmental regulations. *Resource and Energy Economics*, *53*, 114–132. doi:10.1016/j.reseneeco.2018.04.001

Galligan, K. (1997). Political cost incentives for earnings management in the cable television industry. *Journal of Accounting and Economics*, *23*(3), 309–337. doi:10.1016/S0165-4101(97)00012-8

Gäumann, M., & Dobler, M. (2019). Formal participation in the EFRAG's consultation processes: The role of European national standard-setters. *Accounting in Europe*, *16*(1), 44–81. doi:10.1080/17449480.2018.1514124

Geiger, M., O'Connell, B., Clikeman, P. M., Ochoa, E., Witkowski, K., & Basioudis, I. (2006). Perceptions of Earnings Management: The Effects of National Culture. *Advances in International Accounting*, *19*, 175–199. doi:10.1016/S0897-3660(06)19007-8

Gilpatric, S., Vossler, C., & McKee, M. (2011). Regulatory enforcement with competitive endogenous audit mechanisms. *The RAND Journal of Economics*, *42*(2), 292–312. doi:10.1111/j.1756-2171.2011.00134.x

Giner, B., & Mora, A. (2019). *Political Interference In Financial Reporting In The Financial Industry: Evidence From Spain.* Available at www.ssrn.com

Gul, F., Fung, S., & Jaggi, B. (2009). Earnings quality: Some evidence on the role of auditor tenure and auditors' industry expertise. *Journal of Accounting and Economics*, *47*(3), 265–287. doi:10.1016/j.jacceco.2009.03.001

Gul, F., & Tsui, J. (1992). An empirical analysis of Hong Kong bankers' perceptions of auditor ability to resist management pressure in an audit conflict situation. *Journal of International Accounting, Auditing & Taxation*, *1*(2), 177–190. doi:10.1016/1061-9518(92)90015-8

Gungoraydinoglu, A., Çolak, G., & Öztekin, O. (2017). Political environment, financial intermediation costs, and financing patterns. *Journal of Corporate Finance*, *44*, 167–192. doi:10.1016/j.jcorpfin.2017.03.007

Habib, A., Muhammadi, A., & Jiang, H. (2017). Political Connections and Related Party Transactions: Evidence from Indonesia. *The International Journal of Accounting*, *52*(1), 45–63. doi:10.1016/j.intacc.2017.01.004

He, G. (2016). Fiscal Support and Earnings Management. *The International Journal of Accounting*, *51*(1), 57–84. doi:10.1016/j.intacc.2016.01.009

He, G. (2016). Fiscal Support and Earnings Management. *The International Journal of Accounting*, *51*(1), 57–84. doi:10.1016/j.intacc.2016.01.009

He, G., Yang, J., Lu, Y., Wang, S., Chen, B., Hayat, T., Alsaedi, A., & Ahmad, B. (2017). Ternary emergetic environmental performance auditing of a typical industrial park in Beijing. *Journal of Cleaner Production*, *163*, 128–135. doi:10.1016/j.jclepro.2015.03.040

Houqe, M., Monem, R., & van Zijl, T. (2012). Government quality, auditor choice and adoption of IFRS: A cross country analysis. *Advances in Accounting*, *28*(2), 307–316. doi:10.1016/j.adiac.2012.09.013

Houqe, M., van Zijl, T., Dunstan, K., & Karim, A. K. M. W. (2015). Corporate ethics and auditor choice – international evidence. *Research in Accounting Regulation*, *27*(1), 57–65. doi:10.1016/j.racreg.2015.03.007

Hultman, N., & Pulver, S. (2012). Carbon market risks and rewards: Firm perceptions of CDM investment decisions in Brazil and India. *Energy Policy*, *40*, 90–102.

Huskey, E. (2010). Elite recruitment and state-society relations in technocratic authoritarian regimes: The Russian case. *Communist and Post-Communist Studies*, *43*(4), 363–372. doi:10.1016/j.postcomstud.2010.10.004

Hwang, N., & Chang, J. (2010). Litigation environment and auditors' decisions to accept clients' aggressive reporting. *Journal of Accounting and Public Policy*, *29*(3), 281–295. doi:10.1016/j.jaccpubpol.2010.02.002

Iatridis, G. (2012). Hedging and earnings management in the light of IFRS implementation: Evidence from the UK stock market. *The British Accounting Review*, *44*(1), 21–35. doi:10.1016/j.bar.2011.12.002

Imoniana, J., Soares, R., & Domingos, L. (2018). A review of sustainability accounting for emission reduction credit and compliance with emission rules in Brazil: A discourse analysis. *Journal of Cleaner Production*, *172*, 2045–2057. doi:10.1016/j.jclepro.2017.11.217

Iwasaki, I. (2014). Global financial crisis, corporate governance, and firm survival: The Russian experience. *Journal of Comparative Economics*, *42*(1), 178–211. doi:10.1016/j.jce.2013.03.015

Jacoby, J., Li, J., & Liu, M. (2016). Financial distress, political affiliation and earnings management: The case of politically affiliated private firms. *European Journal of Finance*, *25*(6), 508–523. doi:10.1080/1351847X.2016.1233126

Jiang, H., Habib, A., & Wang, S. (2018). Real Earnings Management, Institutional Environment, and Future Operating Performance: An International Study. *The International Journal of Accounting*, *53*(1), 33–53. doi:10.1016/j.intacc.2018.02.004

Jorissen, A., Lybaert, N., Orens, R., & Van der Tas, L. (2013). A geographic analysis of constituents' formal participation in the process of international accounting standard setting: Do we have a level playing field? *Journal of Accounting and Public Policy*, *32*(4), 237–270. doi:10.1016/j.jaccpubpol.2013.04.005

Karim, M., Sarkar, S., & Zhang, S. (2016). Earnings management surrounding M&A: Role of economic development and investor protection. *Advances in Accounting*, *35*, 207–215. doi:10.1016/j.adiac.2016.10.002

Kaspina, R. (2015). Continuing Professional Development of Accounting and Auditing: Russian Experience and Challenges. *Procedia: Social and Behavioral Sciences*, *191*, 550–553. doi:10.1016/j.sbspro.2015.05.110

Kleinman, G., & Palmon, D. (2009). Procedural Instrumentality and Audit Group Judgment: An Exploration of the Impact of Cognitive Fallibility and Ability Differences. *Group Decision and Negotiation*, *18*(2), 147–168. doi:10.100710726-008-9116-z

Kordestani, G., & Mohammadi, M. (2016). A Study of the Relationship between Product Market Competition and Earnings Management. *Procedia Economics and Finance*, *36*, 266–273. doi:10.1016/S2212-5671(16)30037-5

Lam, K., & Mensah, Y. (2006). A reply to Randall E. LaSalle: "The civil justice system and going-concern audit reports: Comments on 'Auditors' decision-making under going-concern uncertainties in low litigation-risk environments: Evidence from Hong Kong'. *Journal of Accounting and Public Policy*, *25*(6), 746–754. doi:10.1016/j.jaccpubpol.2006.09.006

Lander, G., & Auger, K. (2008). The Economic Impact of the Lack of Transparency in Financial Reporting. *Atlantic Economic Journal*, *36*(1), 105–116. doi:10.100711293-007-9107-5

LaSalle, R. (2006). The civil justice system and going concern audit reports: Comments on "Auditors' decision-making under going concern uncertainties in low litigation risk environments: Evidence from Hong Kong". *Journal of Accounting and Public Policy*, *25*(6), 740–745. doi:10.1016/j.jaccpubpol.2006.09.005

Lavezzolo, S., Rodríguez-Lluesma, C., & Elvira, M. (2018). National culture and financial systems: The conditioning role of political context. *Journal of Business Research, 85*, 60–72. doi:10.1016/j.jbusres.2017.12.021

Lennox, C., & Li, B. (2012). The consequences of protecting audit partners' personal assets from the threat of liability. *Journal of Accounting and Economics, 54*(2-3), 154–173. doi:10.1016/j.jacceco.2012.06.002

Lewellyn, K., & Bao, S. (2017). The role of national culture and corruption on managing earnings around the world. *Journal of World Business, 52*(6), 798–808. doi:10.1016/j.jwb.2017.07.002

Li, S., Selover, D., & Stein, M. (2011). "Keep silent and make money": Institutional patterns of earnings management in China. *Journal of Asian Economics, 22*(5), 369–382. doi:10.1016/j.asieco.2011.06.003

Li, T., & Zaiats, N. (2017). Information environment and earnings management of dual class firms around the world. *Journal of Banking & Finance, 74*, 1–23. doi:10.1016/j.jbankfin.2016.09.009

Li, X., & Soobaroyen, T. (2020). Accounting, Ideological and Political Work and Chinese multinational operations: A neo-Gramscian perspective. *Critical Perspectives on Accounting*, (102160). Advance online publication. doi:10.1016/j.cpa.2020.102160

Li, X., Sun, L., & Ettredge, M. (2017). Auditor selection following auditor turnover: Do peers' choices matter? *Accounting, Organizations and Society, 57*, 73–87. doi:10.1016/j.aos.2017.03.001

Lima, L., & Magrini, A. (2010). The Brazilian Audit Tribunal's role in improving the federal environmental licensing process. *Environmental Impact Assessment Review, 30*(2), 108–115. doi:10.1016/j.eiar.2009.08.005

Macho-Stadler, I., & Perez-Castrillo, D. (2006). Optimal enforcement policy and firms' emissions and compliance with environmental taxes. *Journal of Environmental Economics and Management, 51*(1), 110–131. doi:10.1016/j.jeem.2005.06.001

Marques, R. (2021). Continuous Assurance as Digital Transformation Enabler of Audit, Risk Management, and Business Compliance. In *Encyclopedia of Organizational Knowledge, Administration, and Technology* (pp. 392–406). IGI Global. doi:10.4018/978-1-7998-3473-1.ch030

Marques, R., Santos, C., & Inácio, H. (2019). *Organizational Auditing and Assurance in the Digital Age*. IGI Global. doi:10.4018/978-1-5225-7356-2

Martins, F., & Fonseca, L. (2018). Comparison between eco-management and audit scheme and ISO 14001:2015. *Energy Procedia, 153*, 450–454. doi:10.1016/j.egypro.2018.10.023

Mata, C., Fialho, A., & Eugénio, T. (2018). A decade of environmental accounting reporting: What we know? *Journal of Cleaner Production, 198*, 1198–1209. doi:10.1016/j.jclepro.2018.07.087

Melgarejo, M. (2017). Additional evidence on the impact of the International Financial Reporting Standards on earnings quality: evidence from Latin America. *Journal of Applied Business and Economics*.

Mithas, S., Murugesan, S., & Seetharaman, P. (2020). What is your artificial intelligence strategy? *IEEE Annals of the History of Computing, 22*(02), 4–9.

Moroney, R., & Simnett, R. (2009). Differences in Industry Specialist Knowledge and Business Risk Identification and Evaluation. *Behavioral Research in Accounting*, *21*(2), 73–89. doi:10.2308/bria.2009.21.2.73

Nabitz, L., & Hirzel, S. (2019). Transposing The Requirements of the Energy Efficiency Directive on Mandatory Energy Audits for Large Companies: A Policy-Cycle-based review of the National Implementation in the EU-28 Member States. *Energy Policy*, *125*, 548–561. doi:10.1016/j.enpol.2017.12.016

Nikbakht, E., Sarkar, S., & Spieler, A. (2017). External monitoring of private firms: A cross-country empirical analysis. *Global Finance Journal*, *32*, 113–127. doi:10.1016/j.gfj.2016.05.003

Nissen, V. (2018). Digital transformation of the consulting industry—introduction and overview. In *Digital Transformation of the Consulting Industry* (pp. 1–58). Springer. doi:10.1007/978-3-319-70491-3_1

Nissen, V., Nissen, V., & Rauscher. (2019). *Advances in consulting research.* Springer International Publishing.

Oestreich, A. (2015). Firms' Emissions and Self-Reporting Under Competitive Audit Mechanisms. *Environmental and Resource Economics*, *62*(4), 949–978. doi:10.100710640-014-9855-z

Oestreich, A. (2017). On optimal audit mechanisms for environmental taxes. *Journal of Environmental Economics and Management*, *84*, 62–83. doi:10.1016/j.jeem.2017.02.005

Orazalin, N., & Mahmood, M. (2018). Economic, environmental, and social performance indicators of sustainability reporting: Evidence from the Russian oil and gas industry. *Energy Policy*, *121*, 70–79. doi:10.1016/j.enpol.2018.06.015

Ozturk, M. S. (2019). Emerging Auditing Perspectives in the Age of the Fourth Industrial Revolution. *Organizational Auditing and Assurance in the Digital Age*, 172-187.

Palmon, D., & Sudit, E. (2009). Commercial Insurance of Financial Disclosure: Auditors' Independence, and Investors' Protection. *Group Decision and Negotiation*, *18*(1), 27–40. doi:10.100710726-008-9120-3

Phillips, M. (2014). Deterrence vs. gamesmanship: Taxpayer response to targeted audits and endogenous penalties. *Journal of Economic Behavior & Organization*, *100*(C), 81–98. doi:10.1016/j.jebo.2014.01.018

Quick, R., & Schmidt, F. (2018). Do audit firm rotation, auditor retention, and joint audits matter? – An experimental investigation of bank directors' and institutional investors' perceptions. *Journal of Accounting Literature*, *41*, 1–21. doi:10.1016/j.acclit.2018.01.003

Read, W., & Yezegel, A. (2018). Going-concern opinion decisions on bankrupt clients: Evidence of long-lasting auditor conservatism? *Advances in Accounting*, *40*, 20–26. doi:10.1016/j.adiac.2017.12.004

Rehman, I., & Shahzad, F. (2014). The economic consequences of mandatory IFRS reporting: Emerging market perspective. *The Engineering Economist*, *25*(4).

Riahi-Belkaoui, A. (2004). Is Earnings Management Affected by Human Development and Economic Freedom? *Review of Accounting and Finance*, *3*(1), 115–127. doi:10.1108/eb043398

Robertson, J. (2010). The Effects of Ingratiation and Client Incentive on Auditor Judgment. *Behavioral Research in Accounting*, *22*(2), 69–86. doi:10.2308/bria.2010.22.2.69

Robertson, J., Stefaniak, C., & Curtis, M. (2011). Does Wrongdoer Reputation Matter? Impact of Auditor-Wrongdoer Performance and Likeability Reputations on Fellow Auditors' Intention to Take Action and Choice of Reporting Outlet. *Behavioral Research in Accounting*, *23*(2), 207–234. doi:10.2308/bria-50022

Rongbing, H. (2011). Environmental Auditing: An Informationized Regulatory Tool of Carbon Emission Reduction. *Energy Procedia*, *5*, 6–14. doi:10.1016/j.egypro.2011.03.002

Rose, A., Rose, J., & Dibben, M. (2010). The Effects of Trust and Management Incentives on Audit Committee Judgments. *Behavioral Research in Accounting*, *22*(2), 87–103. doi:10.2308/bria.2010.22.2.87

Rosman, A., Biggs, S., & Hoskin, R. (2012). The Effects of Tacit Knowledge on Earnings Management Behavior in the Presence and Absence of Monitoring at Different Levels of Firm Performance. *Behavioral Research in Accounting*, *24*(1), 109–130. doi:10.2308/bria-10120

Ruban, A., & Rydén, L. (2019). Introducing environmental auditing as a tool of environmental governance in Ukraine. *Journal of Cleaner Production*, *212*, 505–514. doi:10.1016/j.jclepro.2018.11.059

Sabonis-Helf, T. (2003). Catching air? Climate change policy in Russia, Ukraine and Kazakhstan. *Climate Policy*, *3*(2), 159–170. doi:10.3763/cpol.2003.0319

Salmi, A., & Heikkilä, K. (2015). Managing relationships with public officials - A case of foreign MNCs in Russia. *Industrial Marketing Management*, *49*, 22–31. doi:10.1016/j.indmarman.2015.05.026

Samsonova, A. (2009). Local sites of globalisation: A look at the development of a legislative framework for auditing in Russia. *Critical Perspectives on Accounting*, *20*(4), 528–552. doi:10.1016/j.cpa.2008.08.003

Sawers, K., Wright, A., & Zamora, V. (2011). Does Greater Risk-Bearing in Stock Option Compensation Reduce the Influence of Problem Framing On Managerial Risk-Taking Behavior? *Behavioral Research in Accounting*, *23*(1), 185–201. doi:10.2308/bria.2011.23.1.185

Schneider, A. (2015). Does information about auditor switches affect investing decisions? *Research in Accounting Regulation*, *27*(1), 39–44. doi:10.1016/j.racreg.2015.03.004

Schneider, A. (2018). Studies on the impact of accounting information and assurance on commercial lending judgments. *Journal of Accounting Literature*, *41*, 63–74. doi:10.1016/j.acclit.2018.03.005

Shen, N., Liao, H., Deng, R., & Wang, Q. (2019). Different types of environmental regulations and the heterogeneous influence on the environmental total factor productivity: Empirical analysis of China's industry. *Journal of Cleaner Production*, *211*, 171–184. doi:10.1016/j.jclepro.2018.11.170

Sjöberg, E. (2016). An empirical study of federal law versus local environmental enforcement. *Journal of Environmental Economics and Management*, *76*, 14–31. doi:10.1016/j.jeem.2015.11.007

Sokolov, V. (2016). *Russia: Can IFRS Be Considered Accounting*? Chapter. In D. Bensadon & N. Praquin (Eds.), *IFRS In A Global World* (pp. 187–200). Springer. doi:10.1007/978-3-319-28225-1_14

Srinidhi, B., Lim, C., & Hossain, M. (2009). Effects of country-level legal, extra-legal and political institutions on auditing: A cross-country analysis of the auditor specialization premium. *Journal of Contemporary Accounting & Economics*, *5*(1), 34–46. doi:10.1016/j.jcae.2009.03.001

Stark, J. (2020). *Digital Transformation of Industry*. Springer International Publishing. doi:10.1007/978-3-030-41001-8

Stranlund, J., Chávez, C., & Villena, M. (2009). The optimal pricing of pollution when enforcement is costly. *Journal of Environmental Economics and Management*, *58*(2), 183–191. doi:10.1016/j.jeem.2008.12.002

Svanberg, J., Öhman, P., & Neidermeyer, P. (2018). (in press). Auditor objectivity as a function of auditor negotiation self-efficacy beliefs. *Advances in Accounting*.

Tai, V., Lai, Y., & Yang, T. (2020). (in press). The role of the board and the audit committee in corporate risk management. *The North American Journal of Economics and Finance*, *54*(C).

Tan, S., & Koonce, L. (2011). Investors' reactions to retractions and corrections of management earnings forecasts. *Accounting, Organizations and Society*, *36*(3), 382–397. doi:10.1016/j.aos.2011.06.004

Tang, M., Li, X., Zhang, Y., Wu, Y., & Wu, B. (2020). From command-and-control to market-based environmental policies: Optimal transition timing and China's heterogeneous environmental effectiveness. *Economic Modelling*, *90*, 1–10. doi:10.1016/j.econmod.2020.04.021

Telle, K. (2013). Monitoring and enforcement of environmental regulations: Lessons from a natural field experiment in Norway. *Journal of Public Economics*, *99*, 24–34. doi:10.1016/j.jpubeco.2013.01.001

Temiz, H., & Gulec, O. (2017). Mandatory Adoption of IFRS in Emerging Markets: The Case of Turkey. *Journal of Accounting and Management Information Systems*, *16*(4), 560–580. doi:10.24818/jamis.2017.04007

Trombetta, M., & Imperatore, C. (2014). The dynamic of financial crises and its non-monotonic effects on earnings quality. *Journal of Accounting and Public Policy*, *33*(3), 205–232. doi:10.1016/j.jaccpubpol.2014.02.002

Trotman, K., Bauer, T., & Humphreys, K. (2015). Group judgment and decision making in auditing: Past and future research. *Accounting, Organizations and Society*, *47*, 56–72. doi:10.1016/j.aos.2015.09.004

Tulaeva, S. (2013). Institutional trust: The process of trust formation in Russian forest villages in accordance with the international system of forest certification. *Forest Policy and Economics*, *31*, 20–27. doi:10.1016/j.forpol.2012.03.006

Walton, P. (2020). Accounting and Politics in Europe: Influencing the Standard. *Accounting in Europe*.

Wang, B., & Xin, Q. (2011). Auditor choice and accruals patterns of cross-listed firm. *China Journal of Accounting Research*, *4*(4), 233–251. doi:10.1016/j.cjar.2011.09.002

Wang, D., & Esqueda, O. (2014). National cultural effects on leverage decisions: Evidence from emerging-market ADRs. *Research in International Business and Finance*, *31*, 152–177. doi:10.1016/j.ribaf.2013.06.006

Wang, J., Zhang, B., & Chen, T. (2011). The case study of China's environmental audit: Taking the Taihu Lake as an example. *Energy Procedia*, *5*, 2108–2113. doi:10.1016/j.egypro.2011.03.364

Windsor, D. (2017). *Interpreting China's Model for Business: Roles of Corruption, Favoritism, Reliability, and Responsibility*. Chapter-3. In E. Paulet & C. Rowley (Eds.), *The China Business Model: Originality and Limits* (pp. 41–69). Chandos Publishing. doi:10.1016/B978-0-08-100750-1.00003-6

Wong, P. (2018). Are state ownership and auditors' locality determinants of asset write-downs? Evidence from China. *China Journal of Accounting Research, 11*(4), 385–405. doi:10.1016/j.cjar.2018.07.002

Wong, W., & Hooy, C. (2018). Do types of political connection affect firm performance differently? *Pacific-Basin Finance Journal, 51*, 297–317. doi:10.1016/j.pacfin.2018.08.009

Wu, C., Hsu, H., & Haslam, J. (2016). Audit committees, non-audit services, and auditor reporting decisions prior to failure. *The British Accounting Review, 48*(2), 240–256. doi:10.1016/j.bar.2015.03.001

Yang, J., Guo, H., Liu, B., Shi, R., Zhang, B., & Ye, W. (2018). Environmental regulation and the Pollution Haven Hypothesis: Do environmental regulation measures matter? *Journal of Cleaner Production, 202*, 993–1000. doi:10.1016/j.jclepro.2018.08.144

Ze-To, S. (2012). Earnings management and accrual anomaly across market states and business cycles. *Advances in Accounting, 28*(2), 344–352. doi:10.1016/j.adiac.2012.09.011

Zhang, B., Chen, X., & Guo, H. (2018). Does central supervision enhance local environmental enforcement? Quasi-experimental evidence from China. *Journal of Public Economics, 164*, 70–90. doi:10.1016/j.jpubeco.2018.05.009

Zhang, W., & Mauck, N. (2018). Government-affiliation, bilateral political relations and cross-border mergers: Evidence from China. *Pacific-Basin Finance Journal, 51*, 220–250. doi:10.1016/j.pacfin.2018.07.003

Zhang, Y., Uchida, K., & Bu, H. (2013). How do accounting standards and insiders' incentives affect earnings management? Evidence from China. *Emerging Markets Review, 16*, 78–99. doi:10.1016/j.ememar.2013.04.002

Chapter 2
Financial Stability, Sustainable Growth, and the Global Quasi-Franchising/Business-Opportunity Industry

ABSTRACT

Franchising, Quasi-Franchising and Business-Opportunities have become major business models (particularly in the retailing and hospitality industries), and have substantial effects on company strategy, growth and survival Business Opportunities (regulated in some developed countries) and Quasi-Franchising (often un-regulated in many countries) are milder types of Franchising. There are at least 1,500 operating franchising networks in the U.S. that represent more than 760,000 franchisees and more than 18 million employees, and provide more than US$506 billion of payroll (or about 11% of the U.S. private sector payroll) and generating a total annual economic output that exceeds US$1.5 trillion (about ten percent of the U.S. private-sector economy). This chapter: i) critiques existing theoretical and empirical studies on franchise contracts, Business Opportunity contracts and incentives; ii) critiques the use of game theory in franchising studies; iii) introduces new mathematical models of Business Opportunities and Quasi-Franchising; iv) compares Business Opportunities, Franchising and Quasi Franchising.

INTRODUCTION

In the US and some countries/jurisdictions, there are statutory differences between franchises and "Business Opportunities", and both business types requires specific mandatory disclosures and compliance at the state and federal government levels. The concept of "Business Opportunities" refers to traditional service industry business-relationships that are very similar (functionally and operationally but not always legally or contractually) to franchises but are not regulated as, and are not perceived as such. Thus, Business Opportunities is a relatively new industry and encompasses segments of many traditional service industry sectors. These include but are not limited to correspondence banking; affiliate market-

DOI: 10.4018/978-1-7998-7418-8.ch002

ing systems; Insurance brokerages; mortgage brokers; one-to-many Auto dealership agreements (with and without warehouse lines); auto finance companies (with or without warehouse lines); Mutual Fund families (including mutual funds creates by strategic alliances and join ventures); medical and dental practices; manufacturing cooperatives; some types of agriculture cooperatives; Manufacturing Licenses; one-to-many Distribution Agreements; one-to-many Strategic Alliances; one-to-many Joint Ventures (ie. for distribution or some types of manufacturing); one-to-many Strategic Alliances by auditing/accounting firms; one-to-many hotel management agreements by hotel chains and hotel management companies; one-to-many Outsourcing Agreements; multi-customer loan/card processing; etc.. Given this definition, Business Opportunities cover or affect more than forty percent of the economic activity in all developed countries, and most "emerging" countries.

EXISTING LITERATURE

Nwogugu (2019a;b) and Nwogugu (2009) analyzed various aspects of franchising. Nwogugu (2019c;d;e) introduced new Theories-of-The-Firm.

Contract Theory and *Mechanism Design Theory* have been jointly studied from various perspectives including Economics/Finance, Operations Research, Mathematical Psychology, Computer Science, Game Theory and Applied Math - see: Hoppe & Schmitz (2018); Niederhoff & Kouvelis (2019); Hong, Wernz & Stillinger (2016); Wu, Zhao & Tang (2014); Li, Liu & Chen (2018); Lin & Chou (1990); Park & Kim (2014); Goetz, Yatsenko, et. al. (2019); Fang & Yuan (2018); Madureira, Pereira, et. al. (2014); Meneguzzi, Modgil, et. al. (2012); Meneguzzi, Modgil, Oren, et. al. (2011); Zohar & Rosenschein (2008); Terán, Aguilar & Cerrada (2017); Eenmaa-Dimitrieva & Schmidt-Kessen (2019); Drozd & Serrano-Padia (2018), and Wei, Wang, et.al. (2018). However, the models in most of these foregoing articles and literature are static, don't incorporate relevant variables; don't consider varying "states" and often complex "joint" effects of variables; and they don't consider Industrial Organization effects of contracts/ mechanisms – for example, see Nwogugu (2007;b), Nwogugu (2019f;g) and Nwogugu (2006).

Standardization of contracts can affect economic growth, Sustainability, Inequality and Economic Growth as noted by various academic researchers - see Sussman (1999), Van Assche & Schwartz (2013), Patterson (2010), Engert & Hornuf (2018), Aguirre (2017), Ayotte & Bolton (2011), Baffi (2007; 2012), He, Xue & Zhou (2019), Vo, Nguyen, et.al. (2019), Sheng (2019), Eenmaa-Dimitrieva & Schmidt-Kessen (2019), Dekker, Kawai & Sakaguchi (2018), Iossa & Martimort (2018) and Sprinkle, Williamson & Upton (2008).

Sussman (1999) noted that "The main implications of contract standardization are that (i) "financial history matters in the growth process,(ii) early formation of the system may create a drag on economic growth and (iii) the effect may be non-monotonic because the system may be modernized at some point." In the realm of CRAs (credit rating agencies), CRAs have developed their own standardized contracts for ratings projects and the Big-Three CRAs are dominant.

A COMPARISON OF BUSINESS OPPORTUNITIES AND QUASI-FRANCHISING[1]

The main differences between franchise systems and *Business opportunities* are explained in Table-1 below.

FINANCIAL STABILITY, SYSTEMIC RISK, AND SUSTAINABLE GROWTH

De Jong, Jiang & Verwijmeren (2011), and Gonzalez-Diaz & Solis-Rodriguez (2012) analyzed franchising as a financing tool. De Jong, Jiang & Verwijmeren (2011), analyzed franchisee's and franchisors' capital structures, and limits imposed on borrowing by franchisees, and found that the franchisor's leverage is significantly related to the maximum leverage allowed for the franchisee. Gonzalez-Diaz & Solis-Rodriguez (2012) found that once the agency argument is controlled for, the higher the cost of alternative funds for the franchisor, the more the franchisor will rely on expansion through franchising as opposed to company-ownership. Gonzalez-Diaz & Solis-Rodriguez (2012) also argued that contrary to the existing literature, franchisees are not such an expensive source of capital, because their compensation is more efficiently designed, and directly depends on variables which are under franchisees' control.

Unfortunately and as of 2020, most of these types of Quasi-Franchising contracts and Business Opportunity contracts (especially in industry sectors discussed in this section) don't: i) contain any provisions about energy-use reduction, waste management, environmental pollution limits, environmental audits, compliance with specific local ordinances (that pertain to waste management and pollution) and building codes; etc.. This trend hampers or can hamper sustainability efforts in various dimensions- e.g. allocation of legal liability; clean up costs; pollution; conduct and accuracy of environmental audits; climate change; efficiency of carbon-trading systems (and similar systems); etc..

Furthermore, many franchisees in Business Opportunities and Quasi-Franchises are SMEs (small and medium enterprises) that use substantial debt (ie. working capital loans, mortgages, equipment leases, long term real estate leases, Trade-Credit; etc.) to finance their operations. That often hides structural weaknesses in the business models of Business Opportunity systems and Quasi-Franchise systems and reduces the franchisee's ability to react to changes in the economy and to economic/regulatory/sustainability shocks. That trend can also cause *Domino-Effects* wherein:

1. the operational/financial distress or failure of a franchisee triggers additional failures of franchisees in the same city or neighborhood;
2. the operational/financial distress or failure of a franchisee causes local banks and finance companies to either increase loan interest rates for, and or reduce the volume of new loans to franchisees, which in turn causes additional franchisee failures (and personal bankruptcies; loss of household savings; job losses; store-closings; etc.);
3. the operational/financial distress or failure of a franchisee causes suppliers to change their payment and or delivery terms which in turn causes additional franchisee failures (and personal bankruptcies; loss of household savings; job losses; store-closings; etc.);
4. the operational/financial distress or failure of a franchisee causes the franchisor to change or reduce its advertising/marketing efforts in that Trade-Area and or payment terms for supplied products in that Trade-Area, which in turn causes additional franchisee failures (and personal bankruptcies; loss of household savings; job losses; store-closings; etc.).

More specifically and in the following industries, Business Opportunities and Quasi-Franchising can affect Financial Stability, Systemic Risk and Sustainable Growth in the following ways.

Table 1. The main differences between franchise systems, Quasi-Franchising and Business opportunities

	Business Opportunity (Type-1)	Business Opportunity (Type-2) (Quasi-Franchising)	Franchise
Set-up/Startup Costs	Much less expensive than a Franchise Right. Set-up/Startup costs can be negotiated.	Much less expensive than a Franchise Right. Set-up/Startup costs can be negotiated. Most require ongoing payments by one or both parties.	Much higher startup costs (typically more than US$70,000 in many countries) than Business Opportunities. Typically, Set-up/Startup costs cannot be negotiated. Usually, prospective Franchisees have to borrow and use up their life-savings to pay the startup costs.
Asset Types	Mostly services businesses that don't require substantial tangible assets.	Mostly services businesses that don't require substantial tangible assets.	Typically requires substantial long term investment in tangible assets – (real estate, equipment and machinery) and Intangible Assets (contract rights; signage; advertising/marketing; staff training; etc.).
System Structure	Relatively un-structured. The seller (of the Business Opportunity Right) may provide minimal guidelines. The buyer (of the Business Opportunity Right) has substantial flexibility to customize operations.	Relatively un-structured. The buyer (of the Business Opportunity Right) has substantial flexibility to customize operations.	Franchising systems are highly structured and have little flexibility in operational processes, store-layout requirements, equipment, signage, etc.. Franchise systems usually have one of three structures: the Business-format franchise, the Personal-Services Franchise and the Manufacturing Cooperative Franchise.
Fees	Typically, there is only a one-time fee at inception of the Business Opportunity Contract. Most contracts don't require royalty payments or other ongoing payments.	The buyer or seller (of the Business Opportunity Right) may or may not pay a fee at inception; but usually one or both parties pay ongoing fees/ commissions to the other during the life of the contract.	The Franchisee typically pays various types of fees to the franchisor - royalty fees, initial one-time franchise fees; group marketing fees, etc.. Some Franchisors also require that franchisees must purchase products/services from only the Franchisor.
Ongoing Support	There is usually substantial contact between the seller and buyer of the Business Opportunity Right after the contract is signed.	Minimal contact between the seller and purchaser of the business opportunity after the contract is signed. Any support is usually informal and not based upon a contract.	Franchisors typically provide ongoing guidance, inspections, training, marketing-support, inventory and other items to Franchisees as a requirement of the Franchise Agreement.
Legal Regulation	Varies in various jurisdictions, and is un-regulated in some countries. Usually the licensor (seller of Contract Right) must provide some sort of disclosure to the purchaser. The US Federal Trade Commission (FTC) and some US states have Business Opportunity statutes.	The Business Opportunity Right is un-regulated in most countries.	Varies in various jurisdictions, but is regulated in most developed countries and many developing countries. In most countries, Franchisors must provide a full Disclosure Statement to the franchisee before any agreement is signed/finalized.
Marketing	Buyer of the Contract Right usually does its own marketing.	Buyer of the Contract Right usually does its own marketing. Both parties may agree to do joint or separate marketing.	Usually, Franchisors do the group marketing but Franchisees can also market locally. Some Franchise Systems require Franchisee to contribute cash towards group marketing efforts.
Transferability of Contract Rights	Usually a personal services contract and contract right is typically not transferable. Assignment of the contract right may be permitted.	Usually a personal services contract and contract right is typically not transferable. Assignment of the contract right may be permitted.	Franchisor may contractually limit the Franchisee's ability to sell, encumber or mortgage the Franchising Right. Franchisors typically require that prospective buyers of the Franchise Right must also be trained and approved by the Franchisor.

Source: Michael C. I. Nwogugu

Mortgage Brokers

Many banks, insurance companies and pension funds enter into agreements with mortgage brokers and business loans brokers wherein such financial institutions: i) provide lines of credit to these brokers who then provide loans to consumers, or ii) the banks effectively outsource their credit analysis functions to these brokers, and underwrite any loans that the brokers approve. These relationships are in the nature of franchising or business opportunities. These relationships effectively outsource all or part of the lenders' credit analysis and risk management functions to brokers whose interest are usually not aligned with those of financial institutions, and whose focus is on loan volume rather than quality or risk reduction. These quasi-franchises were a major cause of the subprime crisis in the US, and can have substantial effects on systemic risk. mortgage brokers usually use two types of business models: i) they conduct the initial screening, gather information from the borrower, and then find a lender who provides the loan and pays a commission to the mortgage broker – the mortgage broker servs as an agent and does not carry the loan on its books and the lender relies on the mortgage brokers assessment of the borrower; ii) the mortgage broker obtains a warehouse loan from a lender (and typically agrees to conform to the lender's criteria), conducts the initial screening, gathers information from the borrower, and then provides the loan (which is carried on the mortgage broker's balance sheet) and the soon thereafter, the mortgage broker sells the loans to a third party. In both cases, the relationship is quasi-franchising. Most of these mortgage brokers are not as regulated as financial institutions and are not subject to education requirements although the brokers have substantial influence on the loan origination process and loan quality. Where such mortgage brokers circumvent the lenders' criteria, and or implement weak controls, they can exacerbate systemic risk, primarily because of the automation and standardization inherent in modern mortgage brokerage. Systemic risk arises where: i) the standard contract between the mortgage broker and the lender is inefficient and causes operating losses for the lender(s) and or the mortgage brokers; ii) the standard loan agreement between the mortgage broker and the borrower causes losses for the borrower and or the mortgage broker; iii) one or both of the aforementioned contracts increases the government's costs of monitoring, enforcement and adjudication; or reduces the credibility of monetary policies; or reduces transparency in markets; or increases transaction costs or reduces social welfare; iv) one or more mortgage broker(s) facilitates or participates in fraud (ie. mortgage fraud; title fraud; use of forged documents in the loan application process; fraudulent misrepresentation of the characteristics of the mortgage or the building/property; etc.) which results in a transaction that should not have occurred; v) the mortgage broker recommends an inappropriate lender or title insurance company or real estate lawyer to the prospective property buyer/seller; vi) the lenders rely on the mortgage broker for initial due diligence; but the mortgage broker's internal controls, risk management systems and due diligence are weak; vii) the mortgage broker originates loans primarily for re-sale, and as a result has little incentive to ensure the long term viability of such loans; viii) the mortgage broker does not comply with state and federal lending statutes (such as RESPA and TILA in the USA).

Government Small-Business Loan Programs

Government small-business loan programs (such as the SBA program in the US) also involve a quasi-franchise relationship with the firms who are selected to disburse the loans. Systemic risk arises where: a) the standard contract between the intermediary and the SBA is inefficient and causes operating losses for the lender(s) and or the SBA; b) the standard loan agreement between the intermediary and the borrower causes losses for the borrower and or the intermediary; c) the intermediary's due diligence and monitoring procedures are inefficient; d) the intermediary's operating processes, and one or both of the aforementioned contracts increases the government's costs of monitoring, enforcement and adjudication; or reduces the credibility of monetary policies; or reduces transparency in markets; or increases transaction costs and default-rates; or reduces social welfare. The failures of the government sponsored small-business loan programs in the Obama Administration's HAMP program, and the Trump Administration's COVID-19 bailout package of 2020 (and the associated prosecution of criminal "borrowers") are well documented in the literature.

"Credit Chains"[2]

Credit Chains are another form of quasi-franchising that have substantial implications for systemic risk. Credit chains are inherent in commercial real estate leases, distribution agreements, traditional franchise agreements, strategic alliances and traditional trade-credit. Credit Chains are prevalent in many industries and are an un-regulated form of business opportunity or franchising because of the following reasons: a) by extending credit, one party (the Initial Lender) provides the "first sub lender", the right to sell credit; and similarly, by extending credit, the first-sub-lender provides one or more second-sub-lenders, the right to sell credit to one or more third-sub-lenders; and so on. Systemic risk arises where: a) the standard loan agreement between the any lender-borrower pair in the Credit-Chain is inefficient and causes operating losses for the lender and or the borrower(s); or b) there is a high probability that any default by a borrower in the Credit Chain will result in defaults by other lender-borrower pairs in the same or related Credit Chains; c) the lenders' due diligence and monitoring procedures are inefficient; d) the bank/franchisor's policies and operating processes, and the franchisees' compliance rate and operations; and one or both of the aforementioned standard loan contracts increases the government's costs of monitoring, enforcement and adjudication; or reduces the credibility of monetary policies; or reduces transparency in markets; or increases transaction costs and default-rates; or reduces social welfare.

Bank Branches

In some countries, bank branches are being franchised to entrepreneurs[3]. That can create the possibility of substantial systemic risk, even where the franchisees are properly trained and comply with the franchise-system operating procedures. Systemic risk arises where: a) the standard contract between the intermediary and the SBA is inefficient and causes operating losses for the lender(s) and or the SBA; b) the standard loan agreement between the intermediary and the borrower causes losses for the borrower and or the intermediary; c) the intermediary's due diligence and monitoring procedures are inefficient; d) the bank/franchisor's policies and operating processes, and the franchisees' compliance rate and operations; and one or both of the aforementioned contracts increases the government's costs of monitoring, enforcement and adjudication; or reduces the credibility of monetary policies; or reduces transparency in markets; or increases transaction costs and default-rates; or reduces social welfare.

Traditional Franchising

Traditional franchising in retailing accounts for more than 35% (thirty five percent) of the retail industry revenues and expenses in most developed countries. Because most franchise systems use a specific business format, any weaknesses and or inefficiencies in the operations of such franchise formats/systems can cause wide spread business failure and operating losses, and thus exacerbate systemic risk. Most franchisees finance their purchase of franchise rights and associated operating expenses with debt. Hence, the failure or inefficiency of a large or medium franchise system can adversely affect many lenders, many credit chains, capital formation, and the rate of new business formation in regions and countries. More specifically, the failure of an individual franchisee affects the following persons: i) the suppliers (franchisees are usually contractually required to purchase supplies from designated suppliers); ii) the franchisee's lenders and the suppliers' lenders; iii) the franchisee's employees; d) the franchisor (loss of royalties.

Systemic risk arises and can have substantial multiplier effects where: i) the standard franchise agreement (between the franchisor and the franchisee) is inefficient and causes operating losses for either party; or iiii) the standard supplier agreement between the franchisee and any designated supplier causes losses/Regret for either party; iii) one or both of the aforementioned contracts increases the government's costs of monitoring, enforcement and adjudication; or reduces the credibility of monetary policies; or reduces transparency in markets; or increases transaction costs or reduces social welfare; iv) the franchisee or franchisor does not comply with the franchise agreement; v) the franchisor recommends an inappropriate product supplier to the franchisee.

Insurance Companies

Insurance companies typically rely on independent insurance brokers for retail and some commercial business. These brokers act as the primary contact, and collect information from prospective borrowers including supporting documentation (which is where and when most fraud occurs). The insurance brokers also often offer advice to clients on business conditions and on managing risk; and thus, can have substantial effects on systemic risk.

Real Estate Brokerage Companies

these companies often operate as part of large franchise networks (e.g. NAI, Cushman & Wakefield, CBRE; Sotheby's International; etc.); or where they are able to obtain exemptions from franchise statutes, they operate as a network through a series of joint venture agreements and strategic alliance agreement which constitute quasi-franchising. Increasingly and in many countries, individual franchisee real estate brokers exert substantial influence on property buyers, and typically recommend lenders and or mortgage companies from which buyers (new loans) or property owners (refinance) obtain loans. In such circumstances, the real estate brokers act as the primary contact, and collect information from prospective borrowers including supporting loan application documentation (which is where and when most mortgage fraud occurs). Real estate brokers often offer informal advice about property values and local/regional market prospects even though most brokers are not trainer appraisers. Hence, these franchisees continue to have substantial impact on systemic risk and on risk perception in most countries. Systemic risk arises and can have multiplier effects where: i) the standard broker contract between the real estate broker and the franchisor (franchise system) or network-sponsor (network of alliances and joint ventures) is inefficient and causes operating losses for both parties; or ii) the standard brokerage agreement between the franchisee broker and the customer causes losses/Regret for the customer or the franchisee/broker; iii) one or both of the aforementioned contracts increases the government's costs of monitoring, enforcement and adjudication; or reduces the credibility of monetary policies; or reduces transparency in markets; or increases transaction costs or reduces social welfare; iv) the one or more real estate broker(s) facilitates or participates in fraud (mortgage fraud; title fraud; fraudulent misrepresentation of the characteristics of the building/property) which results in a transaction that should not have occurred; v) the real estate broker recommends an inappropriate mortgage broker or title insurance company or real estate lawyer to the prospective property buyer/seller.

Independent Finance Companies (Including Auto Finance Companies)

Insurance companies and pension funds and other institutions often provide "warehouse lines" to independent finance companies that then use such capital to provide loans to consumers and companies. Although often overlooked and relatively lightly-regulated or un-regulated, these relationships are essentially quasi-franchise relationships and quasi-banking. In some instances, the staff of these finance companies are not well trained and the finance companies don't face the same regulatory burdens as financial institutions. Systemic risk arises and can have multiplier effects where: i) the standard contract between the insurance company and the finance company is inefficient and causes operating losses for the insurance company and or the finance company; ii) the standard loan agreement between the finance company and the borrower causes losses for the borrower and or the finance company; iii) one or both of the aforementioned contracts increases the government's costs of monitoring, enforcement and adjudication; or reduces the credibility of monetary policies; or reduces transparency in markets; or increases transaction costs or reduces social welfare; iv) one or more finance companies facilitates or participates in fraud (ie. loan fraud; title fraud; use of forged documents in the loan application process; fraudulent misrepresentation of the characteristics of the loan or the collateral; etc.) which results in a transaction that should not have occurred; v) the finance company recommends an inappropriate lender or title insurance company or lawyer to the prospective property buyer/seller; vi) the finance company's internal controls, risk management systems and due diligence are weak; vii) the finance company originates loans primarily for re-sale, and as a result has little incentive to ensure the long term viability of such loans; h) the finance company does not comply with state and federal real estate statutes (such as RESPA and TILA in the USA).

Auto Dealerships (With and Without Warehouse Lines)

Auto dealerships enter into either franchise agreements or distribution agreements with auto manufacturers; and such contracts are essentially quasi-franchise contracts. Auto dealerships often provide on-site auto loans. The auto dealer typically uses three auto financing business models: i) the auto dealer obtains a warehouse line from a lender, and then originates auto loans which it re-sells or keeps on its books; ii) the auto dealer serves only as a loan broker, and processes loan applications in exchange for a commission; and the loans are funded directly by the lender. Auto dealerships also finance their purchase of vehicles with loans. Systemic Risk arises where: i) the standard contract between the auto-dealer and the manufacturers is inefficient and causes operating losses for the auto manufacturer and or the auto-dealers; ii) the standard contract between the auto-dealers and the consumer-buyer is inefficient and causes operating losses for the auto manufacturer and or the consumer-buyers; iii) the standard loan agreement between the lender and the auto dealer is inefficient and causes operating losses for either party; iv) one or both of the aforementioned contracts increases the government's costs of monitoring, enforcement and adjudication; or reduces the credibility of monetary policies; or reduces transparency in markets; or increases transaction costs or reduces social welfare; v) the auto dealership facilitates or participates in fraud (ie. title fraud; use of forged documents in the loan application process; fraudulent misrepresentation of the characteristics of the auto loan or the vehicle; etc.) which results in a transaction that should not have occurred; vi) the auto dealership recommends an inappropriate lender or title insurance company to the prospective auto buyer/seller; vii) the lenders rely on the auto dealer for initial due diligence; but the auto dealer's internal controls, risk management systems and due diligence are weak; h) the auto dealer originates auto loans primarily fo re-sale, and as a result has little incentive to ensure the long term viability of such loans; h) the auto dealer does not comply with state and federal real estate statutes (such as RESPA and TILA in the USA).

Mutual Fund "Families"

Mutual fund families are another type of quasi-franchise system because even though each fund in the "family" may have its own objectives/policies/criteria, such funds typically have similar operating procedures, technology platforms and the same compliance infrastructure, and are typically sponsored/ originated by one quasi-franchisor. Systemic Risk arises where: i) the standard management contract between the fund sponsor and each fund, is inefficient and causes operating losses for either the fund or the fund-sponsor; ii) the standard contract between the fund, and each investor is inefficient and causes operating losses for the fund or the investors; iii) the fund "family" manages substantial amounts of capital, and the operations policies and compliance infrastructure of the fund sponsor are inefficient; iv) one or both of the aforementioned contracts or the aforementioned operations policies and compliance infrastructure increases the government's costs of monitoring, enforcement and adjudication; or reduces the credibility of monetary policies; or reduces transparency in markets; or increases transaction costs or reduces social welfare.

Medical and Dental Practices

These professional companies are essentially quasi franchises because the government grants them limited practice rights with some exclusivity. Systemic Risk arises where: i) the standard contract between the physicians and the patient is inefficient and causes operating losses for the physician and or the patient; ii) the standard contract between the physician and the third-party payor (ie. insurance company, HMO; PPO; Medicare/Medicaid, etc.) is inefficient, encourages wasteful procedures and causes operating losses for the payor and or the patient, and or the government; iii) one or both of the aforementioned contracts increases the government's costs of monitoring, enforcement and adjudication; or reduces the credibility of fiscal policies; or reduces transparency in markets; or increases transaction costs or reduces social welfare.

Manufacturing Licenses

These licenses grant third parties the right to manufacture specific products in specific geographical regions, and sometimes under specific conditions. Systemic Risk arises where: i) the standard contract between the auto-dealers and the manufacturers is inefficient and causes operating losses for the auto manufacturer and or the auto-dealers; ii) the standard contract between the auto-dealers and the consumer-buyer is inefficient and causes operating losses for the auto manufacturer and or the consumer-buyers; iii) one or both of the aforementioned contracts increases the government's costs of monitoring, enforcement and adjudication; or reduces the credibility of monetary policies; or reduces transparency in markets; or increases transaction costs or reduces social welfare.

Distribution Agreements

In these agreements a source-grantor company grants third parties the exclusive or non-exclusive rights to distribute the grantor's products. Distribution companies often fund their operations with bank loans and trade credit; and thus, are very much part of several Credit Chains at any point in time. Systemic Risk arises where: i) the standard distribution contract is inefficient and causes operating losses for the grantee-distributor and or the grantor-company; ii) the standard contract between the grantee-distributor and the retailer inefficient and causes operating losses for the auto manufacturer and or the consumer-buyers; iii) one or both of the aforementioned contracts increases the government's costs of monitoring, enforcement and adjudication; or reduces the credibility of monetary policies; or reduces transparency in markets; or increases transaction costs or reduces social welfare.

Joint Ventures and Strategic Alliances (for Distribution or Some Types of Manufacturing)

In these agreements, two or more companies agree to share costs and profits in one or more business ventures. JV Entities often fund their operations with bank loans and trade credit; and thus, are very much part of several Credit Chains at any point in time. Some companies that routinely enter into JV or strategic alliance agreements use standard-form agreements for such transactions. Systemic Risk arises where: i) the standard JV/Alliance Agreement is inefficient and causes operating losses for one or more of the parties; or causes an inefficient allocation of risk, costs or profits; ii) the standard JV/alliance Agreement create tax issues; iii) the standard JV/Alliance Agreement increases the government's costs of monitoring, enforcement and adjudication; or reduces the credibility of monetary/fiscal policies; or reduces transparency in markets; or increases transaction costs or reduces social welfare; iv) the JV/Alliance Agreement essentially transmits systemic risk between the real side and the financial side of the national economy (this typically occurs where the operating results of the JV Agreement are publicly disclosed in whole or part and securities analysts and credit analyses use such information to evaluate/value the parties to the JV/Alliance Agreement).

Manufacturing Cooperatives

In such arrangements a manufacturer creates a marketing cooperative with two or more retailers; wherein the manufacturer is the "leader" and supplies products to the retailers for subsequent re-sale. The manufacturers also provide trade credit to the coop members. Systemic Risk arises where: i) the standard Cooperative Agreement is inefficient and causes operating losses for one or more of the parties; or causes an inefficient allocation of risk, costs or profits; ii) the standard Cooperative Agreement create tax issues; iii) the standard Cooperative Agreement increases the government's costs of monitoring, enforcement and adjudication; or reduces the credibility of the government's monetary/fiscal policies; or reduces transparency in markets; or increases transaction costs or reduces social welfare; iv) the Cooperative

Agreement essentially transmits (two-way) systemic risk between the real economy and the financial sector of the national economy (this typically occurs where the operating results of the cooperative and or its members are publicly disclosed in whole or part and securities analysts and credit analysts use such information to evaluate/value the Cooperative's members).

Hotel Management Agreements and Property Management Agreements

In these agreements a landlord or lessee grants a third-party manager, the exclusive non-exclusive rights to manage the subject property/building. Distribution companies often fund their operations with bank loans and trade credit; and thus, are very much part of several Credit Chains at any point in time. Systemic Risk arises where: i) the standard distribution contract is inefficient and causes operating losses for the grantee-distributor and or the grantor-company; ii) the standard contract between the grantee-distributor and the retailer inefficient and causes operating losses for the auto manufacturer and or the consumer-buyers; iii) one or both of the aforementioned contracts increases the government's costs of monitoring, enforcement and adjudication; or reduces the credibility of monetary policies; or reduces transparency in markets; or increases transaction costs or reduces social welfare.

Outsourcing Agreements

Such agreements contractually assign specific tasks to another company/person based on specific in a written agreement. The corporate outsourcing customer typically makes periodic service payments to the outsourcing provider, and the arrangement may also involve sharing of costs. The corporate client may outsource similar tasks to several companies. Systemic Risk arises where: i) the standard outsourcing contract is inefficient and causes operating losses for the corporate client or the service provider; ii) the aforementioned contracts increases the government's costs of monitoring, enforcement and adjudication; or reduces the credibility of monetary policies; or reduces transparency in markets; or increases transaction costs or reduces social welfare; iii) the Outsourcing Agreement essentially transmits (two-way) systemic risk between the real economy and the financial sector of the national economy (this typically occurs where the operating results of the corporate client and or the service provider are publicly disclosed in whole or part and securities analysts and credit analysts use such information to evaluate/value these companies).

CHARACTERIZATION OF THE STANDARD BUSINESS OPPORTUNITY CONTRACT AND QUASI-FRANCHISING CONTRACT

The standard quasi-franchise agreement and Business Opportunity agreement has the following characteristics:

1. *Scale Variance* – the franchisee's payoff and the franchisors's payoff from the quasi-franchise agreement varies drastically depending on the magnitude of franchisee's sales volume, estimated local demand, franchisee's cash position; etc..

2. *Incentive Variance* - the incentive effects of the quasi-franchise agreement varies drastically depending on the magnitude of franchisee's sales volume, estimated local demand, franchisee's cash position; etc.
3. *Time dependency.*
4. *Asymmetrical Risk Allocation.*
5. *Asymmetrical Cost Allocation.*
6. Monitoring Negative – (mechanisms for bilateral monitoring by both parties are weak).
7. *Brand Variance.*
8. *Non-Coalition proof* – the franchisee can collude with third parties or with other franchisees to circumvent elements and requirements of the quasi-franchise agreement; and similarly, the franchisor can collude with their parties to circumvent the quasi-franchise agreement and to .
9. *Transmission Positive inconsistency*[4] – the quasi-franchise agreement transmits systemic risk between the real economy and the financial sector of the national economy in a manner that is not consistent or appropriate over time. A contract is said be *Transmission Positive* if it satisfies the following conditions:
    a. The contract is standard or near-standard and is widely used.
    b. Any change in compliance with the contract affects the enterprise values of both parties.
    c. The financial impact of the contract is disclosed in the financial statements of parties to the contract.
    d. Changes in the key operating metrics (sales revenues; operating cash flow; operating expenses; etc.) of both parties affects the value and efficiency of the contract.
10. *Monotonic Function.*
11. *Strategic Non-Complementarity and Non-modularity* – the franchisee's payoff is not always complimentary to the franchisor's payoff function; and the best strategy implemented by one party (franchisee; franchisor) to maximize his/her payoff, does not always or necessarily increase the marginal returns of the other party (franchisor; franchisee) and vice versa.
12. *Bankruptcy Inefficiency* – the contract decreases the franchisor's and franchisee's payoffs drastically, if franchisee or franchisor enters voluntary/involuntary bankruptcy.
13. *Manipulation Positive* – manipulation of costs and revenues by franchisee and franchisor.
14. Additive or Super-Additive Aggregate Risk – an increase in the number of this type of quasi-franchise contract in the franchise system creates a greater than proportional increase in the risk of the franchise system and in overall systemic risk.
15. *Increasing Recursion* – the Franchisor's and franchisee's payoffs are increasingly a function of prior returns/payoffs.
16. *Increasing Opportunity Cost.*
17. Non-Continuous Payoffs – franchisee/franchisor's payoffs are no-continuous in time and space, and can be interrupted by inadequate capital (and maybe other factors).

Given the foregoing, most or all of the models and theories in the following articles are wrong: Barthelemy (2011); Etro (2011); Guan & Zhao (2010); Hempelmann (2006); Hendrikse & Jiang (2011); Huang (1997); Kaya (2011); Klein (1995); Kunter (2012); Li (1997); Li, Huang, Zhu & Chau (2002); Martin-Herran, Sigue & Zaccour (2011); Krishnan & Winter (2011); Reuer, Arino & Mellewigt (2006); Tan, Yang & Guo (2010); Basu & Nair (2012); Aksin, de Vericourt & Karaesmen (2008); Levin (2002);

Sloof & Sonnemans (2011); Burkle & Posselt (2008); Liang, Lee, Huang & Lei (2013); and Yan & Wang (2012). That is partly because of the following reasons:

1. The models don't capture the entire scope of the quasi-franchise contract (in terms of relevant rights, obligations, real options, intangibles and allocation of costs).
2. The models erroneously define "optimality" of franchise contracts almost solely within the framework of the traditional franchise contract – ie. within the framework of royalty rates, franchisee fees, transfer prices and retail prices. As explained above, this traditional quasi-franchising model and framework is inefficient.
3. The models don't account for litigation costs and the costs of resolving disputes.
4. The models implicitly assume constant causal elements and levels of activity.
5. The models don't account for *Shirking* and *non-compliance* by the franchisee/member or the franchisor/sponsor.

NEW MODELS OF THE STANDARD BUSINESS OPPORTUNITY CONTRACT AND THE STANDARD QUASI-FRANCHISING CONTRACT

Given the above-mentioned summaries of various types of quasi-franchise contracts, and properties of quasi-Franchising contracts, the commonalities are that: i) in these contracts, one party (the sponsor or franchisor) provides the other party (franchisee or network-member) with the right to perform a service, or produce a product or sell a product/service; ii) the contract effectively expands the boundaries of the franchisor's/sponsor's firm; iii) the contract represents a form of outsourcing. Hence, there is a general class of quasi-franchise contracts (which includes Business Opportunity contracts) that can be characterized.

In the models below, the terms franchisor and sponsor, franchisee and member and franchise and network are used inter-changeably for franchise systems and networks (ie. distribution networks; licensing; etc.).

The typical quasi-franchise contract has the following form:

$$\text{Max } Q_e=(U_e+U_{hce}+U_{sce})^{(1-(\theta-\Psi))}+[\{A_e+R_e-F_f-F_s-F_{ex}-F_r-F_{oe}-(P_e*\Omega)+\text{Max}(0,(F_y-F_{ep}))+(J_e-(L_b*P_l)+M_e-\varepsilon_b)^{(1-(\theta-\Psi))}+M_t-C_b-\kappa_b-\Phi_s\}*(1-P_d)*$$

$$\text{Max}(\Pi_f>x;0)]+[P_d*D_e]-\gamma_e$$

$$\text{Max } Q_f=(U_f+U_{hce}+U_{scf})^{(\theta-\Psi)}+[\{A_f+\mu_f+F_f+F_r-\varepsilon_f-F_{of}-\text{Max}(0,(F_y-F_{ep}))+(P_e*\Omega)+(J_f-(L_f*P_l)+M_f)^{(\theta-\Psi)}-M_t-C_f-\kappa_f+\Phi_s\}*(1-Pd_e)*$$

$$\text{Max}(\Pi_f>x;0)]+[(P_d*D_f)-D_o]-\gamma_f$$

Where:

Max Q_e= the value of the quasi-franchise contract to the franchisee.

Max Q_f = the value of the quasi-franchise contract to the franchisor company.

U_e = the non-monetary utility that the franchisee/member gains from the quasi-franchise agreement and quasi-franchise relationship. $-\infty<U_e<+\infty$.

U_f = the non-monetary utility that the franchisor gains from the franchise agreement and franchise relationship. $-\infty<U_e<+\infty$.

V_e = the value of the franchise contract to the franchisee/member during time t

V_f = the value of the franchise contract to the franchisor during time t.

Q_e = the payoff of the quasi-franchise contract to the franchisee/member during time t

Q_f = the payoff of the quasi-franchise contract to the franchisor during time t.

P_d = the probability of default by either franchisee/member or franchisor/sponsor.

D_e = the sum of amount gained, if any (ie. greater of liquidated damages or court awards) by franchisee/member upon default, less litigation/settlement costs incurred by franchisee/member upon default.

D_f = the sum of amount gained, if any (ie. greater of liquidated damages or court awards) by franchisor/sponsor upon default, less litigation/settlement costs incurred by franchisor/sponsor upon default.

D_o = the franchisor's cost of replacing the Franchisee upon default that is not cured.

J_e = the value of the renegotiation option inherent in the contract, to the franchisee/member. This real option is low in traditional retailing franchise agreements and distributions agreements because of standardization; but can be high or substantial in licensing agreements and strategic alliances.

J_f = the value of the Renegotiation-Option inherent in the contract, to the franchisor/sponsor. This real option is low in traditional retailing franchise agreements and distributions agreements because of standardization; but can be high or substantial in licensing agreements and strategic alliances.

M_e = the value of the Strategic Default Option inherent in the contract, to the franchisee/membe during time t.

M_f = the value of the Strategic Default Option inherent in the contract, to the franchisor/sponsor during timet.

M_t = the value of the trade credit granted by franchisor/sponsor to franchisee/member in time t.

U_{hce} = the value of the Human Capital gained from the contract, by the franchisee/member.

U_{hcf} = the value of the Human Capital gained from the contract, by the franchisor/sponsor.

Φ_s = opportunity cost of mandatory supplier relations. In the typical quasi-franchise agreement, the quasi-franchisor typically requires that the franchisee purchase supplies and equipment from the franchisor and or designated suppliers. However, the franchisee may be able to purchase these items at lower costs and better terms from other suppliers. Φ_s is the difference between the price charged by the designated suppliers, and the non-designated suppliers. Thus,

1. $\Phi_s > 0$, if the franchisee can purchase supplies/equipment at lower costs from non-designated suppliers;
2. $\Phi_s < 0$, if the franchisee achieves substantial cost savings from buying suppliers from the designated suppliers; and
3. $\Phi_s = 0$, of the franchisee is indifferent between the designated and non-designated suppliers (costs are same), or if the agreement is an outsourcing agreement or licensing agreement or distribution agreement or JV/alliance agreement.

O_c = opportunity cost of mandatory supplier relations. In the typical franchise agreement, the franchisor typically requires that the franchisee purchase supplies and equipment from designated suppliers. However, the franchisee may be able to purchase these items at lower costs and better terms from other suppliers. O_s is the difference between the price charged by the designated suppliers, and the non-designated suppliers. Thus,

a) O_s >0, if the franchisee can purchase supplies/equipment at lower costs from non-designated suppliers;
b) O_s<0, if the franchisee achieves substantial cost savings from buying suppliers from the designated suppliers; and
c) O_s=0, of the franchisee is indifferent between the designated and non-designated suppliers (costs are same), or if the agreement is an outsourcing agreement or licensing agreement or distribution agreement or JV/alliance agreement.

A_e = the intangible value of the franchise right to the franchisee during time t.

A_f = the intangible value of the franchise right to the franchisor during time t.

R_e = Franchisee's/member's revenues that were generated from the franchise/distribution/licensing/outsourcing Agreement. $R_e = (R_a*n)$, where R_a is the average price per product unit and n is the number of sales transactions.

μ_f = the franchisor's non-royalty revenues that are generated as a result of the quasi franchisee agreement – such as product sales, commissions for referral of suppliers; sponsorships, etc.

Ω = this is either: a) the initial good faith deposit that is paid by the franchisee, licensor, or outsourcing vendor or distributor or strategic alliance partner; or b) in a securities brokerage or real estate brokerage it's the amount that the trainer agrees to pay to the firm, if the trainee's employment is terminated or if the trainee breaches the employment agreement.

P_e = this is the probability that: a) the franchisee, licensee, or outsourcing vendor or distributor or strategic alliance partner will breach the agreement and thus, forfeit the good faith deposit; or b) the trainee real estate broker or securities broker will resign from, or cause his/her employment agreement to be terminated.

F_f = the initial upfront franchisee/member fee paid by franchisee/member to franchisor/sponsor. F_f is negative for outsourcing contracts, licensing agreements, alliance agreements and distribution agreements.

F_g = the guaranteed profit if any, that the franchisor provides to the franchisee for the period t. Thus, F_g will be zero if the franchisee's Operating Profit (F_{ep}) is equal to or greater than a certain threshold (F_y), and $F_g = (F_y - F_{ep})$, if otherwise.

F_s = franchisee's/member's amortized startup costs other than the initial upfront franchisee fee paid by franchisee to franchisor – this includes training costs; and the costs of buying inventory, FF&E and other items; leases; the cost of hiring advisors (legal and accounting); etc..

F_r = the franchisee's or licensee's periodic royalty fee payment. F_r is negative for outsourcing agreements; and F_r is zero for distribution agreements, outsourcing agreement and some strategic alliances.

F_{ex} = franchisee's operating expenses other than the franchisee's periodic royalty fee payment (includes the franchise royalty rate; the cost of the goods purchased from franchisor/sponsor by franchisee/member; etc.).

ε_b = franchisee's/member's effort towards the contract.

ε_f = franchisor's/sponsor's effort towards the contract. This includes intangible efforts, and all direct costs and allocated portion of overhead costs, that the franchisor/sponsor incurs as a result of the franchise agreement during time t.

L_b = litigation costs incurred by the franchisee/member.

L_f = litigation costs incurred by the franchisor/sponsor.

P_l = probability of litigation in time t.

C_b = the franchisee's/member's compliance costs in time t.

C_f= the franchisor's/sponsor's compliance costs in time t.

κ_b = the costs and losses incurred by franchisee/member as a result of shirking and non-compliance (with contractual terms) by franchisor/sponsor. In all types of quasi-franchise agreements, this cost is generally inversely related to the franchisor's/sponsor's compliance costs, but the strength of the inverse relationship also depends on the franchisor's/sponsor's effort.

κ_f = the costs and losses incurred by franchisor/sponsor as a result of shirking and non-compliance (with contractual terms) by the franchisee/member. In all types of quasi-franchise agreements, this cost is generally inversely related to the franchisee's/member's compliance costs, but the strength of the inverse relationship also depends on the franchisee/member's effort.

F_{oe} = the franchisee's other costs incurred to work such as professional licensing, continuing education; transportation; personal marketing costs; employee related taxes and payments; out-of-office business development expenses; etc.. This cost is usually substantial in licensing agreements, distribution agreements and strategic alliances.

F_{of} = the franchisor/sponsor's other costs incurred to enable the franchisee work - such as professional licensing, continuing education; office space; utilities; marketing and business development costs; etc.. This cost is usually relatively small in licensing agreements and distribution agreements.

U_{sce} = the franchisee/member's social capital that is obtained and built primarily as a result of the franchise/distribution/licensing/outsourcing Agreement.

U_{scf}= the franchisor/sponsor's social capital that is obtained and built primarily as a result of the franchise/distribution/licensing/outsourcing Agreement.

Π_f = the franchisor's/sponsor's compliance index which has a value of between zero and one, and is zero (if the franchisor/sponsor or the franchisee/member are not in compliance, and thus cannot operate) or one (if the franchisor/sponsor and the franchisee/member are in full compliance and can operate). Π_f is necessarily scale-variant (the difference in impact/effect between any two contiguous equal intervals in (0,1) is not equal) such that as Π_f tends to one, each successive equal interval in (0,1) indicates successively lower compliance – this is because of the nature of perceived and actual compliance. If Π_f is below a specific level (x), then the firm will not be able to operate due to non-compliance; and for firms that operate in non-regulated industries (firms that are not regulated by either trade/industry associations or government agencies), Π_f is always equal to one.

θ = an index that represents the marginal rate of substitution of labor, which indicates the extent to which labor (franchisee's and franchisor's workers' efforts or outsourcing) can be replaced by automation or other workers (ie. by having other workers work harder and for longer hours); or by incentives (which can increase workers' productivity while maintaining the same number of work hours). $0<\theta<1$. H tends to one as the marginal rate of labor-substitution increases. θ is necessarily scale-variant (the difference in impact/effect between any two contiguous equal intervals in (0,1) is not equal) such that as θ tends to one, each successive equal interval in (0,1) indicates successively lower labor substitution – this is because of the nature of perceived and actual labor-substitution. From the point of view of the franchisor/sponsor, θ should be a great as possible because greater labor substitution reduces or eliminate quality problems, renegotiation, strategic default and litigation associated with human workers.

Ψ = an index that measures the cost of replacing labor with other factors such as automation, incentives and other workers. $0<\Psi<1$. W tends to one as the marginal cost of labor-substitution increases. H is necessarily scale-variant (the difference in impact/effect between any two contiguous equal intervals in (0,1) is not equal) such that as Ψ tends to one, each successive equal interval in (0,1) indicates successively greater cost of labor substitution – this is because of the nature of perceived and actual labor-substitution.

From the point of view of the franchisor/sponsor, Ψ should be a low as possible because lower cost of labor substitution reduces the cost of implementing more efficient alternatives to human labor.

γ_e= the franchisee's/member's opportunity cost (for entering into the quasi-franchising agreement) during time *t*.

γ_f= the franchisor's/sponsor's opportunity cost (for entering into the quasi-franchising agreement) during time t.

ζ_e= the franchisee/member's coefficient of risk aversion.

ζ_f =the frscnhosr's/sponsor's coefficient of risk aversion.

Yan & Wang (2012) noted that the franchisor's payoff model is a variation of the *Newsboy Problem* model (in Operations Research and Applied Mathematics). See: Agrawal & Seshadri (2000); Petruzzi & Dada (1999); and Porteus (1990).

THE STANDARD FRANCHISING AND BUSINESS-OPPORTUNITY MODELS ARE FLAWED AND CAN IMPOSE COSTS AND EXTERNALITIES ON SOCIETY

These costs can include but are not limited to the following:

1. The risks of "Domino Effects" and Financial Stability problems – among different franchising networks.
2. Built-in (and replicated) inefficiencies due to standardization in franchising networks.
3. Conflicts of interest (especially among franchisors).
4. Inefficient and or unfair cost-shifting between franchisor, suppliers and franchisees.
5. Inadequate marketing and support by Franchisors.
6. Inadequate risk-sharing among franchisor, franchisees and suppliers.

REDUCING THE RISKS INHERENT IN AND/OR CREATED BY BUSINESS OPPORTUNITY SYSTEMS AND QUASI-FRANCHISE SYSTEMS

That can be achieved by implementing the following:

1. The taxation Of Business Opportunity sponsors and Franchisors should be changed.
2. Disclosure Is Not enough – Testing, Profitability Analysis, Reporting Of Franchisee performance And Franchisee Solvency. The standard disclosure models for Franchising and Business Opportunity networks in many countries are inadequate.
3. There should be minimum capital requirements for Business Opportunity sponsors and quasi-Franchisors. Thatcan ensure that such entities: 1) have enough capital to provide marketing, sales and administrative support to franchisees and business opportunity operators; 2) such entities don't have significant incentives to shift costs and or risk to franchisees and suppliers in unfair ways that endanger the entire network.
4. National governments should consider enacting statutory re-Allocation of franchise Risk to Business Opportunity Sponsors and Quasi-Franchisors; or in the alternative, grant annual tax Credits to Business Opportunity Sponsors and Quasi-Franchisors that voluntarily and formally reallocate

such risks in their system-wide standard Master Franchise Agreements and by-laws which every unit-operator is required to sign.

5. National governments should consider granting Tax Credits to companies that use statutorily-determined new and non-traditional Franchising and Business Opportunity Models because both industry segments are in dire need of process-innovation. The global use of a few business models incurs Systemic Risk and the risks of Fraud and Collusion (in the Supply Chain). The GVCs of many medium and large Franchising, Business Opportunity And Quasi-Franchise Systems are now global and can have substantial effects on foreign companies and on immigrants (ie. Global Remittances, FDI, foreign investment; international capital flows; etc.).
6. National governments should consider limiting the sizes of Business Opportunity And Quasi-Franchise Systems (e.g. limits based on the nature of the industry, system-wide profitability record/history, franchisee-success-rate, and the number of years of operation of the entire system). There have been many instances in which large percentages of unit-operators in a system/network are unprofitable or are only marginally profitable; or a system's franchisees' failures-rates are significant (e.g. above 10%). Such systems/networks perpetrate "*Inefficient Continuance*", increase cost-of-funds and reduce access to capital for other systems/networks and unit-operators; and can cause *Domino Effects*. Such suggested statutory limitations will help ensure that only proven and truly profitable Franchising, Business Opportunity and Quasi-Franchise networks/systems are allowed to expand without reducing Social Welfare.
7. In countries that have dual/bi-cameral Business-Opportunity/Franchise Laws (ie. both state and federal statutes), the national government should consider eliminating the state Franchising, Business-Opportunity and quasi-Franchise Laws. By their nature, Business-Opportunity, Franchising and quasi-Franchising systems are large scale systems whose direct and indirect operations often cross state and national borders. Thus having multiple levels of regulations (especially where the industry processes/contracts are heavily standardized) increases transaction costs, uncertainty, Costly Regulatory Fragmentation and risk.

CONCLUSION

This chapter has introduced more accurate mathematical models for and key properties of efficient Business Opportunity systems and Quasi-Franchising Systems. These mathematical models can be used in optimization models in order to: i) develop better economic policies and Sustainability policies; ii) optimize operations; and iii) determine the relative importance of various factors.

The foregoing discussion directly/indirectly explains how Business Opportunities and

Quasi-Franchising Systems can cause and or increase Financial Instability, Systemic Risk and Inequality, and can reduce Sustainable Growth.

REFERENCES

Aguirre, A. (2017). Contracting institutions and economic growth. *Review of Economic Dynamics*, *24*, 192–217. doi:10.1016/j.red.2017.01.009

Aksin, O., de Vericourt, F., & Karaesmen, F. (2008). Call Center Outsourcing Contract Analysis And Choice. *Management Science*, *54*(2), 354–368. doi:10.1287/mnsc.1070.0823

Ayotte, K., & Bolton, P. (2011). *Covenant lite lending, liquidity, and standardization of financial contracts*. Chapter. In P. Bolon (Ed.), *Research Handbook on the Economics of Property Law* (pp. 174–189). Edward Elgar Publishing Ltd. doi:10.4337/9781849808972.00013

Baffi, E. (2000). *Some Characteristic Features of Mass Contracting*. Working Paper. Università degli Studi "Roma Tre" – Faculty of Law.

Baffi, E. (2007). *The Economics of Standard Form Contracts*. Working Paper. Università degli Studi "Guglielmo Marconi".

Baffi, E. (2012). Contracting in modern world. *Aperta Contrada*. https://www.apertacontrada.it/2012/11/13/contracting-in-modern-world/

Barthelemy, J. (2011). Agency and institutional influences on franchising decisions. *Journal of Business Venturing*, *26*(1), 93–103. doi:10.1016/j.jbusvent.2009.05.002

Basu, P., & Nair, S. (2012). Analysis of back-office outsourcing contracts for financial services operations. *The Journal of the Operational Research Society*, *63*(12), 1679–1692. doi:10.1057/jors.2012.5

Boissay, F. (2006). *Credit Chains And The Propagation Of Financial Distress*. Working paper, European Central Bank. https://www.ecb.int/pub/pdf/scpwps/ecbwp573.pdf

Boissay, F., & Monnet, C. (2003). *Bankruptcy in Credit Chains*. European Central Bank, D.G. Research. https://www.clevelandfed.org/research/conferences/2003/july2/credit_chain.pdf

Burkle, T., & Posselt, T. (2008). Franchising as a plural system: A risk-based explanation. *Journal of Retailing*, *84*(1), 39–47. doi:10.1016/j.jretai.2008.01.004

Dekker, H., Kawai, T., & Sakaguchi, J. (2018). Contracting abroad: A comparative analysis of contract design in host and home country outsourcing relations. *Management Accounting Research*, *40*, 47–61. doi:10.1016/j.mar.2017.09.003

Drozd, L., & Serrano-Padia, R. (2018). Financial contracting with enforcement externalities. *Journal of Economic Theory*, *178*, 153–189. doi:10.1016/j.jet.2018.09.002

Eenmaa-Dimitrieva, H., & Schmidt-Kessen, M. (2019). Creating markets in no-trust environments: The law and economics of smart contracts. *Computer Law & Security Review*, *35*(1), 69–88. doi:10.1016/j.clsr.2018.09.003

Etro, F. (2011). Endogenous market structures and contract theory: Delegation, principal-agent contracts, screening, franchising and tying. *European Economic Review*, *55*(4), 463–479. doi:10.1016/j.euroecorev.2010.08.001

Fang, X., & Yuan, F. (2018). The Coordination and Preference of Supply Chain Contracts Based on Time-Sensitivity Promotional Mechanism. *Journal of Management Science and Engineering*, *3*(3), 158–178. doi:10.3724/SP.J.1383.303009

Goetz, R., Yatsenko, Y., Hritonenko, N., Xabadia, A., & Abdulai, A. (2019). The dynamics of productive assets, contract duration and holdup. *Mathematical Social Sciences*, *97*, 24–37. doi:10.1016/j.mathsocsci.2018.10.004

Gonzalez-Diaz, M., & Solis-Rodriguez, V. (2012). Why do entrepreneurs use franchising as a financial tool?: An agency explanation. *Journal of Business Venturing*, *27*(3), 325–341. doi:10.1016/j.jbusvent.2011.03.001

Guan, R., & Zhao, X. (2010). On contracts for VMI program with continuous review (r,Q) policy. *European Journal of Operational Research*, *207*(2), 656–667. doi:10.1016/j.ejor.2010.04.037

He, Q., Xue, C., & Zhou, S. (2019). Does contracting institution affect the patterns of industrial specialization in China? *China Economic Review*, *54*, 191–203. doi:10.1016/j.chieco.2018.11.003

Hempelmann, B. (2006). Optimal franchise contracts with private cost information. *International Journal of Industrial Organization*, *24*(2), 449–465. doi:10.1016/j.ijindorg.2005.07.008

Hendrikse, G., & Jiang, T. (2011). An Incomplete Contracting Model of Dual Distribution in Franchising. *Journal of Retailing*, *87*(3), 332–344. doi:10.1016/j.jretai.2011.01.003

Hong, S., Wernz, C., & Stillinger, J. (2016). Optimizing maintenance service contracts through mechanism design theory. *Applied Mathematical Modelling*, *40*(21-22), 8849–8861. doi:10.1016/j.apm.2015.07.009

Hoppe, E., & Schmitz, P. (2018). Hidden action and outcome contractibility: An experimental test of moral hazard theory. *Games and Economic Behavior*, *109*, 544–564. doi:10.1016/j.geb.2018.02.006

Huang, Z. (1996). Bargaining, Risk And Franchising Coordination. *Computers & Operations Research*, 24(1), 73-83. (ng Iossa, E., & Martimort, D. (2018). Corruption in PPPs, incentives and contract incompleteness. *International Journal of Industrial Organization*, *44*, 85–100.

Kaya, O. (2011). Outsourcing vs. in-house production: A comparison of supply chain contracts with effort dependent demand. *Omega*, *39*(2), 168–178. doi:10.1016/j.omega.2010.06.002

Klein, B (1995). Economics Of Franchise Contracts. *Journal of Corporate Finance*, *2*, 9-27.

Krishnan, H., & Winter, R. (2011). On the role of revenue-sharing contracts in supply chains. *Operations Research Letters*, *39*(1), 28–31. doi:10.1016/j.orl.2010.10.007

Kuner, M. (2012). Coordination via cost and revenue sharing in manufacturer–retailer channels. *European Journal of Operational Research*, *216*(2), 477–486. doi:10.1016/j.ejor.2011.07.001

Levin, J. (2002). Multilateral Contracting And The Employment Relationship. *The Quarterly Journal of Economics*, *117*(3), 1075–1103. doi:10.1162/003355302760193968

Li, S. (1997). Transaction Efficiency Analysis of Franchising Arrangements Through Chance Constrained Game Theory. *Computers & Operations Research*, *24*(10), 919–929. doi:10.1016/S0305-0548(97)00015-4

Li, W., Liu, Y., & Chen, Y. (2018). Modeling a two-stage supply contract problem in a hybrid uncertain environment. *Computers & Industrial Engineering, 123*, 289–302. doi:10.1016/j.cie.2018.06.031

Lia, S., & Huang, Z. (2002). Cooperative advertising, game theory and manufacturer–retailer Supply chains. *Omega, 30*(5), 347–357. doi:10.1016/S0305-0483(02)00051-8

Liang, H., Lee, K., Huang, C., & Lei, H. (2013). The optimal decisions in franchising under profit uncertainty. *Economic Modelling, 31*, 128–137. doi:10.1016/j.econmod.2012.11.044

Lin, E., & Chou, M. (1990). Optimal contracts. *Applied Mathematics Letters, 3*(2), 65–68. doi:10.1016/0893-9659(90)90016-5

Madureira, A., Pereira, I., Pereira, P., & Abraham, A. (2014). Negotiation mechanism for self-organized scheduling system with collective intelligence. *Neurocomputing, 132*, 97–110. doi:10.1016/j.neucom.2013.10.032

Martin-Herran, G., Sigue, S., & Zaccour, G. (2011). Strategic interactions in traditional franchise systems: Are franchisors always better off? *European Journal of Operational Research, 213*(3), 526–537. doi:10.1016/j.ejor.2011.03.015

Meneguzzi, F., Modgil, S., Oren, N., Miles, S., Luck, M., & Faci, N. (2012). Applying electronic contracting to the aerospace aftercare domain. *Engineering Applications of Artificial Intelligence, 25*(7), 1471–1487. doi:10.1016/j.engappai.2012.06.004

Meneguzzi, F., Modgil, S., & Oren, N. (2011). Algorithms and mechanisms for procuring services with uncertain durations using redundancy. *Artificial Intelligence, 175*(14–15), 2021–2060.

Niederhoff, J., & Kouvelis, P. (2019). Effective and necessary: Individual supplier behavior in revenue sharing and wholesale contracts. *European Journal of Operational Research, 277*(3), 1060–1071. doi:10.1016/j.ejor.2019.03.038

Nwogugu, M. (2007a). Issues In Disintermediation In The Real Estate Brokerage Industry. *Applied Mathematics and Computation, 186*(2), 1054–1064. doi:10.1016/j.amc.2006.08.053

Nwogugu, M. (2007b). Some Issues In Securitization And Disintermediation. *Applied Mathematics and Computation, 186*(2), 1031–1039. doi:10.1016/j.amc.2006.08.052

Nwogugu, M. (2006). Employee Stock Options, Production Functions And Game Theory. *Applied Mathematics and Computation, 181*(1), 552–562. doi:10.1016/j.amc.2005.12.067

Nwogugu, M. (2019f). *Human Computer Interaction, Incentive Conflicts And Methods For Eliminating Index Arbitrage, Index-Related Mutual Fund Arbitrage And ETF Arbitrage. In Indices, Index Funds And ETFs HCI: Exploring HCI, Nonlinear Risk And Homomorphisms*. Palgrave MacMillan.

Nwogugu, M. (2019g). Economic Policy, Complex Adaptive Systems, Human-Computer Interaction And Managerial Psychology: Popular-Index Ecosystems. In Indices, Index Funds And ETFs HCI: Exploring HCI, Nonlinear Risk And Homomorphisms. New York: Palgrave MacMillan.

Nwogugu, M. (2009). Franchise Royalty Rates, Franchise Fees And Incentive Effects. *International Journal Of Mathematics. Game Theory & Algebra, 17*(5/6), 303–316.

Nwogugu, M. (2019c). Complex Systems, International Political Economy And The Externalities/Governmental-Influence Theory Of The Firm. In Complex Systems, Multi-sided Incentives And Risk Perception In Companies. New York: Palgrave MacMillan.

Nwogugu, M. (2019d). Complex Systems, International Political Economy And The behavioral/Contracts Theory Of The Firm. In Complex Systems, Multi-sided Incentives And Risk Perception In Companies. New York: Palgrave MacMillan.

Nwogugu, M. (2019e). Complex Systems, International Political Economy And Communications/Information-Differential Theory Of The Firm. In Complex Systems, Multi-sided Incentives And Risk Perception In Companies. New York: Palgrave MacMillan.

Nwogugu, M. (2019a). Knowledge Representation And Network Decisions In Franchising And Online Retailing Under Combined MN-Transferable Utility, WTAL, Perception And Regret Minimization Regimes. In Complex Systems, Multi-sided Incentives And Risk Perception In Companies. New York: Palgrave MacMillan.

Nwogugu, M. (2019b). On Franchise Royalty Rates, Franchise Fees And Incentive Effects. In Complex Systems, Multi-sided Incentives And Risk Perception In Companies. New York: Palgrave MacMillan. doi:10.1057/978-1-137-44704-3_8

Park, S., & Kim, J. (2014). A mathematical model for a capacity reservation contract. *Applied Mathematical Modelling, 38*(5-6), 1866–1880. doi:10.1016/j.apm.2013.10.005

Patterson, M. (2010). Standardization Of Standard-Form Contracts: Competition And Contract Implications. *William and Mary Law Review, 52*(2), 327–340.

Reuer, J., Arin, A., & Mellewigt, T. (2006). Entrepreneurial alliances as contractual forms. *Journal of Business Venturing, 21*(3), 306–325. doi:10.1016/j.jbusvent.2004.09.003

Sheng, J. (2019). Neoliberal environmentality and incentive-coordinated REDD+ contracts. *Land Use Policy, 81*, 400–407. doi:10.1016/j.landusepol.2018.10.055

Sloof, R., & Sonnemans, J. (2011). The interaction between explicit and relational incentives: An experiment. *Games and Economic Behavior, 73*(2), 573–594. doi:10.1016/j.geb.2011.03.006

Sprinkle, G., Williamson, M., & Upton, D. (2008). The effort and risk-taking effects of budget-based contracts. *Accounting, Organizations and Society, 33*(4-5), 436–452. doi:10.1016/j.aos.2007.11.001

Sussman, O. (1999). Economic growth with standardized contracts. *European Economic Review, 43*(9), 1797–1818. doi:10.1016/S0014-2921(98)00040-3

Tan, Z., Yang, H., & Guo, X. (2010). Properties of Pareto-efficient contracts and regulations for road franchising. *Transportation Research Part B: Methodological, 44*(4), 415–433. doi:10.1016/j.trb.2009.10.002

Terán, J., Aguilar, J., & Cerrada, M. (2017). Integration in industrial automation based on multi-agent systems using cultural algorithms for optimizing the coordination mechanisms. *Computers in Industry, 91*, 11–23. doi:10.1016/j.compind.2017.05.002

Van Assche, A., & Schwartz, G. (2013). Contracting institutions and ownership structure in international joint ventures. *Journal of Development Economics*, *103*, 124–132. doi:10.1016/j.jdeveco.2013.02.008

Wei, W., Wang, J., Chen, X., Yang, J., & Min, X. (2018). Psychological contract model for knowledge collaboration in virtual community of practice: An analysis based on the game theory. *Applied Mathematics and Computation*, *329*, 175–187. doi:10.1016/j.amc.2018.01.053

Wu, Z., Zhao, R., & Tang, W. (2014). Optimal contracts for the agency problem with multiple uncertain information. *Knowledge-Based Systems*, *59*, 161–172. doi:10.1016/j.knosys.2014.01.009

Zohar, A., & Rosenschein, J. (2008). Mechanisms for information elicitation. *Artificial Intelligence*, *172*(16–17), 1917–1939. doi:10.1016/j.artint.2008.08.005

ENDNOTES

1 *See*: Terry, A. (2011). *Quasi-Franchising: A New Model for Strategic Business Cooperation*. Paper presented at EMNet 2011Conference, December 1-3, 2011, Limassol, Cyprus. (http://emnet.univie.ac.at/). *See*: Holmes, D. (2003). *The Advantages And Disadvantages of Franchising*. http://www.holmeslofstrom.com/z_pdf/articles/franchisors/Fran%20Advantages.pdf *See*: DLA Piper (2007). *Expanding A Business By Franchising*. http://www.franchise.org/uploadedFiles/Franchise_Industry/Resources/Education_Foundation/Expanding%20a%20Business%20by%20Franchising%20full%20article.pdf

2 *See*: Boissay (Jan. 2006) and Boissay & Monnet (2003).

3 *See*: *Promising Perspective for Franchised Bank Branches*. http://www.zeb.de/en/press/press-archive/press-detail.html&detailid=75. See: Abbey National launches franchise scheme to boost branch network. See: Commonwealth Banks to be Franchised?. http://www.mrmortgage.com.au/commonwealth-bank.htm. See: UniCredit Bank opens first franchise. http://www.czech-marketplace.cz/en/3227.unicredit-bank-opens-first-franchise.

4 *See*: Basel Committee on Banking Supervision (2011). *The Transmission Channels Between The Financial And Real Sectors: A Critical Survey Of The Literature*. Working Paper No. 18. http://www.bis.org/publ/bcbs_wp18.pdf. *See*: Kambhu, J. & Mosser, P. (May 2006). *Systemic Risk and the Financial System*. Background Paper - NAS-FRBNY Conference on New Directions in Understanding Systemic Risk, Federal Reserve Bank of New York. https://www.newyorkfed.org/registration/research/risk/background.pdf.

Chapter 3
Models of Willingness-to-Comply:
Internal-Controls and the Failures of Sarbanes-Oxley Act, the Dodd-Frank Act, and the PCAOB (USA) and Similar Institutions

ABSTRACT

Sarbanes Oxley Act ("SOX"; USA), the PCAOB, and the Dodd Frank Act (USA statute) and similar institutions in other countries have become major macroeconomic, sustainability, and IPE (international political economy) policies because of their significant domestic and cross-border multiplier effects across countries and industries via US multinational corporations (MNCs) and foreign companies that do business in the US and or list their shares/debts on US financial exchanges. SOX, the PCAOB and the Dodd Frank Act have had pervasive effects on accounting firms, consulting firms, and credit rating agencies (CRAs) in the US (e.g., disclosures, professional standards, regulation/compliance, standard-of-care, legal liability, internal controls, daily operations processes, etc.), but SOX, the Dodd Frank Act, and the PCAOB have failed.

INTRODUCTION

The Dodd Frank Act was enacted by the US Congress in 2010 in response to the GFC – and other countries have since enacted similar statutes. Some of the cross-border *Multiplier Effects* of Dodd Frank Act are analyzed in Nwogugu (2021b). As explained in this chapter, Dodd Frank Act affects the structures and efficiency of both the global CRA industry and the global accounting/consulting industry.

SOX was enacted by the US Congress in 2002 in response to the series of corporate scandals in the US and the perceived urgent need for better corporate Governance, disclosures, Internal-Controls and

DOI: 10.4018/978-1-7998-7418-8.ch003

accountability – and other countries have since enacted similar statutes. As explained in this chapter, SOX affects the structures and efficiency of both the global CRA industry and the global accounting/consulting industry, and directly regulates the accounting industry in the US and indirectly regulates that global accounting industr.

Some of the cross-border *Multiplier Effects* of Dodd Frank Act and SOX are analyzed in Nwogugu (2021a) and Nwogugu (2021b) respectively.

Japan, the European Union, Canada, and Israel and other countries have enacted regulations that are very similar to SOX (collectively, the "World SOX"). Since SOX was enacted in the US, most industrialized countries have announced and adopted purported "higher standards" for dealing with accounting fraud, but those have been ineffective. The main issue is that World SOX is very similar to SOX, and has been equally or more inefficient, and creates similar Constitutional Political Economy problems.

Other countries and jurisdictions have enacted statutes that are very similar to SOX such as the following:

1. The United Kingdom's Companies (Audit, Investigations and Community Enterprise) Act of 2004.
2. The EU enacted the Financial Services Action Plan (www.financial-services-action-plan.com); and the European Union's 8th Company Law Directive on Statutory Audit (Directive 2006/43/EC) (www.8th-company-law-directive.com).
3. India enacted *Clause-49.*
4. The China Securities Regulatory Commission (CSRC) passed the *Company Law* and the *Securities Law*, both of which became effective in May 2006.
5. Japan's *Financial Instruments and Exchange Act* was enacted on June 14th, 2006, and became effective in April 2008.
6. The Canadian government enacted "*Policy 52-109*"; and Ontario (Canada) enacted "*Keeping The Promise For A Strong Economy Act (Budget Measures) of 2002*".
7. Australia's government enacted the "*CLERP-9*".

Collectively, these and other SOX-type statutes/regulations that were enacted by non-US countries are hereafter referred to as "*World SOX*".

EXISTING LITERATURE

With regards to the existing literature: i) the majority of academic research on SOX was published during 2002-2006, and since then the annual number of published academic journal articles on SOX has substantially declined; ii) most of the post-2006 journal articles on SOX focus on the same SOX-related issues/topics and use the same or very similar research/empirical methods, and focus on the US. Thus, many of the academic articles cited in tis chapter were published during 2003-2008.

Internal Controls, SOX and PCAOB regulations and similar statutes in other countries have had and can continue to have significant effects on a broad range of issues pertaining to Sustainable Growth, Climate Policy, Financial Stability and Systemic Risk:

1. On the relationships between Internal Controls and various dimensions of company operations (in the context of SOX and PCAOB regulations and similar statutes in other countries), see: Chang, Chen, Cheng, & Chi (2019), Kim & Kim (2017) and Schroeder & Shepardson (2016).
2. On Internal Controls and market crash-risk (in the context of SOX and PCAOB regulations and similar statutes in other countries), see: Chen, Chan, Dong & Zhang (2017), Kim, Yeung & Zhou (2019), Chen, Li, et. al. (2019), Cheng, Felix & Indjejikian (2019), Baker, Biddle, Lowry & O'Connor (2018), Ashfaq & Rui (2019) and Chen, Li, Shao & Zheng (2019).
3. On Internal Controls, Innovation and R&D (in the context of SOX and PCAOB regulations and similar statutes in other countries), see: Li, Han & He (2019a), Li, Shu, Tang & Zheng (2019b), and Gao & Zhang (2019).
4. On Internal Controls and Tax Avoidance (in the context of SOX and PCAOB regulations and similar statutes in other countries), see: Bauer (2016), and Ashfaq & Rui (2019).
5. On Internal Controls in the post-GFC (global financial crisis) global banking industry, see: Cheng, Felix & Indjejikian (2019), Wilford (2016), Lentner, Vasa, Kolozsi & Zeman (2019), Bhaskar, Schroeder & Shepardson (2019), and Chen, Li, Shao & Zheng (2019).
6. On Institutional factors and the implementation of SOX and PCAOB regulations (and similar statutes in other countries), see: Henk (2020), Wang, Xu, Zhang & Shu (2018), Defond & Lennox (2017), Cheng, Felix & Indjejikian (2019), Wilford (2016), Bauer (2016), Ashfaq & Rui (2019), Bhaskar, Schroeder & Shepardson (2019).
7. On the relationships between Internal Controls and various dimensions of Sustainability (in the context SOX and PCAOB regulations and similar statutes in other countries), see: Henk (2020) and Litan (July 2019).
8. On the relationships between Internal Controls and various dimensions of executive compensation, see: Paletta & Alimehmeti (2018).

Nwogugu (2021) explains why many parts of SOX are unconstitutional. Baker, Bédard & Hauret (2014), Gordon & Nazari (2018), Hoffman & Nagy (2016), Bhabra, Hossain & Karmakar (2019), Bhabra & Hossain (2018), Chang & Choy (2016) and Loehlein (2017) discussed various important *Multiplier Effects* of SOX. Many authors have documented many weaknesses inherent in the *Sarbanes Oxley Act* ("SOX")[1].

Bather & Burnaby (2006), Huang & Chong (2016), Chiu, Chien & Lin (2013), Loehlein (2017), Baker, Bédard & Hauret (2014) and Udeh (2017) analyzed various important *Multiplier Effects* of PCAOB and its regulatory functions. The PCAOB's interpretation of the portions of SOX that pertain to internal controls has imposed substantial additional costs on exchange-traded companies (both foreign and domestic) in the USA[2].

Nwogugu (2015a;b) explained why the *Dodd Frank Act* failed and is unconstitutional – however, this chapter discusses the *Dodd Frank Act* only with respect to the accounting/auditing industry and the credit-rating agency industry. Nwogugu (2008) developed new models of *Willingness-To-Comply* and critiqued SOX.

Some researchers have found that the bailouts of financial institutions in the US during 2008-2010 were unconstitutional. Some researchers have analyzed the trade implications of accounting regulations and government bailouts – see the comments in Trujillo (2010); Poretti (2009); Delimatsis (2012) and International Institute For Sustainable Development (March 2009).

The literature on associated institutional law & economics issues is well developed. Kunst & Wagner (2011) discussed the concept of constitutional framework and its role in ordering society. Metelska-Szaniawska (2010) found substantial positive correlations between constitutional rules and the economic reform process in post-socialist countries of Europe and Asia after 1989. Metelska-Szaniawska (2010) is among many studies that have confirmed similar relationships in developed countries. Doring & Schnellenbach (2010) compared federalism in Germany and the US, and concluded that a constitutional framework of competitive federalism does not prevent the long-term centralization of competencies; and that formal institutions affect the pathways of government centralization; and that informal political institutions may have a substantial effect on the preservation of state and local autonomy. These informal political institutions include trade associations, standards organizations (such as PCAOB), specific statutes (such as Sarbanes Oxley Act and the Dodd Frank Act), quasi-government agencies, etc.. Witt & Schubert (2009) argued that constitutional interests of individuals are often improperly or insufficiently defined, and that within the context of innovative activities with pecuniary and technological externalities, the citizens' constitutional interests vary with their risk preferences, and thus, the nature of the appropriate social contract depends on the risk preferences of individuals.

THE FAILURE OF SARBANES OXLEY ACT OF 2002 ("SOX") (AND "WORLD-SOX")

The Sarbanes Oxley Act (SOX) governs internal controls and some aspects of disclosure at exchange-traded companies in the US. The US has the world's largest economy and the largest securities markets and US statutes (including SOX) affect foreign companies that are listed on US stock exchanges, and exchange-traded US multinational corporations that operate in many foreign countries, and thus SOX has significant effects on the global economy. SOX was the first legislation in the world that simultaneously attempted to address corporate governance, securities law issues, the practice of accounting, internal controls, accounting fraud and enforcement and was long overdue given prior corporate scandals.

Furthermore, SOX and World SOX have affected and is likely to continue to affect and influence legislation and adjudication in many countries because many such countrys' constitutions are based on the US constitution (and were either enacted or amended within the last twenty years). Under US laws (and generally accepted common-law principles), many elements of SOX are un-constitutional; and SOX is inefficient and has caused many companies to de-list from exchanges. Limiting SOX to only publicly traded companies is not meaningful given the large number of medium and large non-listed companies.

On the effectiveness of regulations, see: Jain, Kim & Rezaee (March 2004), Cunningham (2003), Rezaee & Jain (2004), Stiglitz & Uy (1996), Stiglitz (1994), and Liu (2005). The effectiveness of SOX and World SOX should be measured in terms of:

- Reduction of costs of compliance.
- Companys' and employee Willingness-To-Comply with regulations.
- Maximization of deterrence-effect of sanctions implicit in regulations.
- Reduction of investigation and prosecution costs.
- Reduction/elimination of divergencies in interpretation of information presented to users of financial statements.

Hence, the methods used in Linciano (2003) to evaluate the effectiveness and economics of a new laws/regulations are inappropriate in this, and most instances. Granted that one of the aims of SOX and World SOX is to reduce information asymmetry, that is not the primary objective of SOX and World SOX. The wording and intent of SOX and World SOX is geared towards reducing fraud and illegal wealth transfers, but without much consideration for transaction costs inherent in implementation (as is evidenced in current compliance costs).

Statutes like SOX and World SOX and securities regulations should be designed to protect not only shareholders but also persons/entities that either contract with or can be adversely affected by operations of companies. Large and medium-sized private companies enter into contracts with numerous suppliers and customers all over the world, and provide critical services to thousands (or millions) of customers worldwide and thus can substantially affect systemic risk. Hence, the key criteria for applicability of SOX and World SOX should not be whether or not the company's shares are traded on a stock exchange, but rather, should be the nature, scope and the potentially adverse economic influence of the company's operations.

The sub-prime crisis and Global Financial Crisis began in the US during 2006-2007 despite the fact that the US Congress enacted SOX in 2002.

See the comments in: Gupta & Leech (2005); Palter, Munck & Leverette (Jan./Feb. 2006); Karmel (____);Rouse, Weirich & Hambleton (May/June 2005); Tackett, Wolf & Claypool (2006); Linsley (2003); Ribstein (Oct. 2003); Kamar & Karaca-Mandic (2006).

Gao & Zhang (2019) noted that SOX Section-404 reduces or can reduce Corporate Innovation.

Baker, Bédard & Hauret (2014); Gordon & Nazari (2018); Hoffman & Nagy (2016); Bhabra, Hossain & Karmakar (2019); Bhabra & Hossain (2018); Chang & Choy (2016) and Loehlein (2017) discussed various important *Multiplier Effects* of SOX. Many authors have documented many weaknesses inherent in the Sarbanes Oxley Act ("SOX")[3] and World SOX.

The possible reasons for the ineffectiveness of SOX are explained as follows.

Inadequate Penalties for External Auditors

SOX and World SOX don't provide sufficient penalties for external auditors.

Inadequate Penalties for Mid-Level Managers

- SOX heavily penalizes top-level officers (CFO, CEO) who are somewhat removed from daily operations of companies. SOX does not penalize mid-level managers who are directly responsible for daily operations, internal controls and risk management. Mid-level managers are often not subject to reputational penalties (unlike top officers), and are not "hedged" (most mid-level managers don't have professional liability insurance, or substantial savings or asset protection schemes), and have more to loose in terms of career advancement (they have not reached the apex of their careers) compared to top officers, and thus, the deterrence effect of SOX is more likely to function and prevail among mid-level managers than top officers. By essentially allocating liability for fraud and mis-statements to CEOs and CFOs before the crimes are committed, SOX provides huge incentives for mid-level managers to commit crimes. *See*: Nwogugu (2008).

Collusion

SOX does not provide sufficient penalties for *Collusion* at all levels in the firm (ie. between staff and auditors; or between staff and suppliers). *Collusion* is perhaps the dominant type of misconduct that causes or amplifies earning management, asset quality management, corporate governance deficiencies and antitrust problems.

Constitutional Political Economy Problems and the Un-Constitutionality of SOX

SOX (and by extension, World SOX) creates and amplifies *Constitutional Political Economy* problems because of the following reasons:

1. SOX doesn't sufficiently regulate or limit Political Lobbying by ordinary companies, financial services companies and accounting firms. Lobbying has become a significant problem (especially in developed countries) that has shaped disclosure requirements, compliance, regulation and the evolution of industries. SOX increases the need for political lobbying by companies and accounting firms.
2. As explained herein, SOX creates Separation-of-Powers problems.
3. SOX doesn't sufficiently delineate enforcement responsibilities which creates uncertainty.
4. The Dodd Frank Act required many studies and additional legislation which haven't been completed, and some pertain to areas covered by SOX – that creates "Regulatory Gaps".
5. Private rights-of-action (enforcement rights of companies and individuals) is severely and un-necessarily limited in SOX, and that compounds Constitutional Law problems created by SOX.

The un-constitutionality of SOX was discussed in Nwogugu (2021a) – and parts of SOX are unconstitutional.

Ineffective Tests

The Internal Controls and Control Environment tests/checks mandated by SOX are inefficient and insufficient. Earnings management, asset-quality management and corporate governance deficiencies remain significant problem in companies in the USA. The sub-prime crisis and Global Financial Crisis began in the US during 2006-2007 despite the fact that the US Congress enacted SOX in 2002.

Stability Assumption

SOX erroneously and implicitly assumes that markets remain "stable" and there are no "extreme" events – the collapse of Bear Stearns and Lehman Brothers was partly attributable to sharp changes in market conditions that affected their actual and perceived liquidity.

Duplication of Work

SOX is inefficient mainly because the processes that it requires create opportunities for duplication of effort, un-necessary work and

SOX Should be Extended to Non-Listed Companies

Limiting SOX to only publicly traded companies is not meaningful given the large number and economic influence of medium and large non-listed companies. In the US, listed companies constitute less than 2% of all companies. The critical issue is the economic, social, psychological and political impact of firms, and these cannot be measured only by whether a company is listed. Non-listed companies whose annual revenues and or assets exceed specific benchmarks should be made subject to SOX. Most importantly, the FSA (Dodd Frank Act) fails to extend and apply SOX to large private companies and medium-sized private companies that have the same (or greater) magnitude of economic activity and influence on the US economy as publicly traded companies.

Regulatory Fragmentation

The Dodd Frank Act (USA) and SOX itself did not fully integrate SOX into the US federal securities law framework. The result has been suboptimal duplication of effort, conflicts-of-laws, jurisdictional/regulatory overlap, and *Regulatory Fragmentation.*

Scope

Statutes like SOX and securities regulations should be designed to protect not only shareholders but also persons/entities that either contract with or can be adversely affected by operations of companies. Large and medium-sized private companies enter into contracts with numerous suppliers and customers all over the world, and provide critical services to thousands (or millions) of customers worldwide and thus can substantially affect systemic risk. Hence, the key criteria for applicability of SOX should not be whether or not the company's shares are traded on a stock exchange, but rather, should be the nature, scope and the potentially adverse economic influence of the company's operations.

The SOX Requirement for Certification of Financial Statements by Top Managers (Section 906) Has Not Been Very Effective

The SOX requirement for certification of financial statements by top managers (Section 906) has not been very effective. The certification requirement should not be completely eliminated, but most of the associated liability should be shifted downwards to mid-level managers. Top-managers (CFOs, CEOs and Presidents) can afford fines/penalties, and are often "prepared" (they have substantial savings; and they purchase professional liability insurance; and they have personal "protective trusts" and asset-protection schemes that are insulated from penalties; and top officers have social networks, all of which blunt the deterrence effects of SOX). Most top officers that are targeted by SOX have reached the apex of their careers, and don't have anything to lose in terms of career advancement or personal aspirations. SOX targets and victimizes top officers/managers who are subject to substantial reputational penalties because of their positions. SOX provides significant incentives for top officers to hide misconduct and fraud. On the contrary, these top officers (CFO, CEO, COO) should become the government's "internal enforcement partners" because they have the authority to: 1) facilitate investigations, 2) improve monitoring, 3) implement corrective actions, 4) facilitate the accurate allocation of causation and liability among managers.

Inadequate Incentives for Whistle-Blowers

SOX does not provide sufficient incentives for whistle-blowers who are often fired and ostracized for reporting misconduct. There should be statutory prohibitions on the termination of employments of whistleblowers for six months to one-year after such reports are made to the government (to enable government agencies to determine if there are sufficient reasons for further investigation).

Over-Emphasis on Routine Report-Writing and Data Collection Instead of Problem Identification and Resolution

SOX and World SOX over-emphasizes report-writing and filings instead of problem identification and solutions.

Inadequate Regulation of Executive Compensation and Incentive Compensation

SOX and World SOX don't provide sufficient regulation of Employee incentives. The structure and open-ended nature of stock options and other equity based incentives contribute to risk taking and systemic risk.

SOX Erroneously and Implicitly Assumes That Markets Remain "Stable" and There Are No "Extreme" Events

For example, the collapse of Bear Stearns and Lehman Brothers was partly attributable to sharp changes in market conditions that affected their actual and perceived liquidity.

SOX and World-SOX Are Costly and SOX Compliance and Analysis Has Substantial Opportunity Costs

SOX is inefficient and has caused many companies to de-list from exchanges. Limiting SOX to only publicly traded companies is not meaningful given the large number of medium and large non-listed companies.

SOX imposes substantial economic and psychological burdens on micro-cap and small publicly-traded companies (which constitute more than Seventy Percent of the publicly traded companies in the US). SOX violates the US Constitution in various ways and the "State Actions" are as follows: a) the enactment of SOX, b) SOX's delegation of rule-making and adjudication powers to the SEC, and c) the requirement for mandatory compliance with SOX, d) SOX's delegation of powers (search; reports, etc.) to external accounting firms and law firms, and e) the creation and powers of the PCAOB. The following are summaries of various violations of the US Constitution.

The immediately obvious opportunity costs of SOX include: **a**) additional auditing costs, **b**) distraction of management and employees that now have to spend more time on compliance and controls matters. Braddock (2006: 194-196). The other opportunity cost attributable to SOX compliance include the following: **a**) reduced capital formation opportunities – companies that would have otherwise become public, remain in the private markets; **b**) reduced transparency – as more companies remain in the private market, there less overall transparency since less information is in the public domain; **c**) increased volatility – due to more market-changing information; **d)** increased transaction costs which are distinct from compliance costs – with SOX, the costs of executing corporate transactions.

During 2002-2020, the costs of complying with SOX were greater than expected. See: Braddock (2006); Leech (Nov. 2003); Leung & Cooper (2003); Jain & Rezaee (2004); Gupta & Leech (2005); Teles (2004); Leech (April 2003); Leuz (2007); Akerblad, Johansson & Jangvik (2007). Only public companies with market capitalization of $75 million or more were required to comply with the Sarbanes-Oxley rules in 2005, but smaller publicly-traded companies were required to comply by 2006. A 2005 study estimated that the annual cost of SOX implementation at US companies was about $1.4 trillion. The SOX burden is heavy for small and medium sized companies. Some reports have estimated that compliance with SOX in 2005 incurred about $35 billion of additional costs for American companies in 2005 — this about twenty times more than the US SEC originally estimated.

On November 8, 2007, the U.S. Chamber of Commerce Center for Capital Markets Competitiveness (with IMA® and the American Stock Exchange), released results from the "*Cost of SOX*" survey. The report confirms that Sarbanes-Oxley (SOX) Section-404 disproportionately burdens small businesses. [4] The survey shows that more than half of the responding companies with less than $75 million in market value spent more than 3% of their net income on SOX 404(a). According to the report, Sixty-three percent of respondents anticipate a cost increase in the next year due to compliance with SOX 404(a) and 404(b); and more than 58% of the respondents believe that SOX 404 will not help detect and prevent fraud. The U.S. Chamber of Commerce's Commission on the Regulation of U.S. Capital Markets in the 21st Century issued a report on March 14, 2007, which made several recommendations on how the U.S. Capital Markets can be improved and better aligned with the global marketplace, in a cost-effective and timely manner. [5] This report specifically recommends that SOX be made part of the US Securities & Exchange Act of 1934.

Although Sarbanes-Oxley has introduced some beneficial reforms, much of the benefits of SOX is outweighed by the unexpected negative consequences of SOX's Section 404. According to a July 2004 report by Financial Executives International (FEI), the total cost of Section 404 compliance per company was estimated at $3.14 million. Publicly-traded companies expect to spend an average of 25,667 internal hours and 5,037 external hours for compliance with Section 404. Companies also expect to spend an additional $1,037,100 on software and IT consulting. Furthermore, with SOX, the external public auditing firms that cause many of the corporate fraud scandals (arising from inadequate disclosure) now have more power than before, and effectively regulate the information technology operations of publicly-traded US companies. The crux of the problem is that under SOX, while revenues of public accounting firms have increased, their role as a balance against executive malfeasance and corporate crime has not changed substantially. This is directly attributable to the drafting and specifications of SOX. SOX focuses on micro-operational details of companies, and (Section 404) does not adequately regulate the high-level fraud and deception perpetrated by top management (such as reserves, capitalization instead of expensing some items, asset values, etc.).

Unfortunately, SOX has the most impact on small publicly traded companies and emerging growth companies that want to list their shares on stock exchanges; both of which generate a significant percentage of new jobs in the United States. Because of SOX, many start-ups have been hesitant to execute IPOs; and approximately one-fifth of all small publicly-traded companies in the US have considered going private because of the costs of complying with SOX (source: Thomson Venture Economics, and the National Venture Capital Association). In addition, and for the first time in the history of US capital markets, during 2004-2006, many US companies were considering de-listing from traditional stock exchanges to pink-sheets, or to go private. This exodus also involves foreign-domiciled companies who must comply with Sarbanes-Oxley because of being listed on one of the U.S. stock exchanges.

Expectations for Profits

Table 1. Costs of Compliance With Sarbanes-Oxley Act (including internal costs and auditing).

Company revenue	Average cost
• Less than $100 million	$800,000
• $100 million to $499 million	$1 million
• $500 million to $999 million	$1.3 million
• $1 billion to $4.9 billion	$2.4 million
• Over $5 billion	$8 million

Source: Financial Executives International (2006)

Expectations for profits is the primary motivation for fraud. The wording and legislative history and legislative intent of SOX does not show any attempt to curtail expectations of legal and illegal profits from disclosure, fraud, manipulation or other misconduct – SOX's focus is on obvious disclosure issues. See: Blanton & Christie (2003); Arlen & Kraakman (1997); Cialdini & Goldstein (2004); Engelen (2004). Byam (1982) has argued that corporate criminal liability is inefficient – in a world with transaction costs, information asymmetry and information costs, this contention is reasonable. SOX focuses on placing liability on corporate entities - although sections of SOX require penalties for offending individuals (monetary fines and jail sentences): a) the required standard of proof for finding individual liability under SOX is high and probably expensive to achieve, and such costs of evidence and discovery discourages prosecution and civil lawsuits, b) the percentage of possible offenses/violations/non-compliances for which SOX mandates individual liability is relatively small, c) since SOX expressly incorporates SEC rules (1934 Act), courts are very likely to (formally or informally) use the same sentencing guidelines for both 1934 Act and SOX offenses, d)

Insufficient Statutory Definitions

Apparently, given the ESR case, there should be more statutory definitions of matters that should be put to a vote of shareholders and those that should be decided by the boards of directors, because shareholders would probably have reacted much differently than decisions made by BOSS's, GMAC's and ESR's boards of directors.

SOX Does Not Address Discovery Issues Sufficiently

SOX does not address pre-litigation and post-conviction discovery issues properly. See: Hughes (1994). This results in high expected litigation costs (discovery and evidence) which discourages investigation and prosecution.

SOX Does Not Address Excessive Management Discretion in Disclosure

The ESR transactions shows that management typically has a lot of discretion in highly leveraged transactions and situations of financial distress, and that such discretion can and is often abused. SOX does not address this excessive discretion. SOX does not distinguish between: a) regimes of company growth, stabilization and decline, b) regimes of profitability, financial distress, bankruptcy and post-bankruptcy recovery, c) regimes of turbulence or relative calm in financial markets (equity markets, etc.). In all these regimes, the information disclosures mandated by SOX have substantial information content that creates un-necessary volatility. See: Bergstrom, Eisenberg & Sundgren (2001). The SEC has rejected several proposals to exempt small companies from SOX compliance on the basis of excessive compliance costs. costs.

The Substantial Information Content of SOX Requirements

Most of the disclosures and certifications required by SOX carry valuable information content. Jain & Rezaee (2004). Jain, Kim & Rezaee (March 2004) have analyzed the effect of SOX on stock markets. SOX requires disclosure of a stream of information by the firm, almost continuously and at various times during the year. Furthermore, the disclosure required by SOX is now more relevant to a company's suppliers and customers, than previously required disclosures. Hence, apart from its accounting impact, SOX has substantial financial and information effects, and effects on the company's supply chain. The net effect is increased volatility of share prices, and more information asymmetry among a larger group of entities. SOX fails to distinguish between compliance, corporate privacy and efficient disclosure. Because of potentially substantial information effects and the advent of the Internet (which ensures rapid information diffusion), SOX should have made some disclosures restricted from public view, while being accessible only to regulators – that will reduce adverse selection and moral hazard inherent in the company's, auditor's choices of the amount and quality of information to disclose. See the comments in Richardson & Welker (2001).

SOX Does Not State Minimum Standards for Internal Audits

See: James (2003). While SOX states internal control requirements, SOX does not state minimum standards for the organization of internal audits - in this instance, audit organization is just as important as, and determines the quality of internal audit reports.

SOX Does Not Address Major Accounting Issues

To the extent that SOX did not expressly or impliedly resolve or even address existing major accounting standards issues (intangibles, goodwill, employee stock options, pensions accounting and leases), disclosures made by SOX don't have a meaningful effect in terms of reducing information asymmetry – instead, additional disclosures simply magnify information asymmetry problems.

SOX Does Not Address the Role of Bond Trustees and US Securities and Exchange Commission's Approval Processes Although SOX Expressly Incorporates SEC Rules (the 1934 Act)

The ESR transactions involved the sale of publicly traded bonds. In the case of publicly traded bonds, the role of the bond trustee should be mandatorily expanded to include periodic certifications that the issuer is solvent, and such reports should be made mandatory SEC filings. The second issue is whether bond indentures should contain specific language about bondholders' recourse if the issuer is deemed insolvent – bank loans and private debt often contain such terms and conditions. The inaction of the bond trustee in the ESR case illustrates why the SEC should improve their processes for pre-transaction and post transaction due diligence in leveraged transactions. The very essence of disclosure filings at the SEC is the protection of holders of public securities. The SEC has an implied duty to the holders of publicly traded bonds to monitor filings for the types of problems that arose in the BOSS, GMAC and ESR filings. The Sarbanes-Oxley Act requires certification by CEOs and CFO as to accuracy of financial statements; but does not explicitly require tests for solvency, or certification as to solvency, and does not require solvency certification from external auditors, internal auditors and lawyers.

SOX Does Not Address Moral Hazard, Information Asymmetry, and Adverse Selection Inherent in Relationships Between Banks/Lenders and Corporate Clients

See the comments in Chen & Daley (1996). The Encompass Services case (discussed herein) illustrates the importance and consequences of transparency, disclosure and monitoring in these relationships.

SOX Does Not Sufficiently Address the Role of the Audit Committee (of the Board of Directors)

SOX does not address the role of the audit committee adequately in a manner that compels pro-active over-sight and coordination. The ESR transactions also indicates that the audit committees of the boards of directors of banks must be statutorily required to: a) Establish and ensure conformance with standards for loan reviews and monitoring of portfolio companies; b) Become very familiar with risk management procedures as they pertain to capital adequacy and default risk; c) Establish and ensure conformance to standards and procedures for dealing with non-performing loans; d) Establish and regularly review standards for loan originations and related-party transactions; e) Establish and regularly review standards purchasing of syndicated loans; f) Establish and regularly review standards for compliance with regulations; g) Monitor and assess activities and quality of external auditors. In essence the audit committees now have a broader implied mandate with respect to risk management, risk reduction and compliance issues at banks. In particular, the ESR transactions indicate that the audit committees of the boards of directors of technology companies must now be required to become more involved in the activities of the internal audit team, and must closely monitor the quality/performance of external auditors and third-party consultants (that are retained to assess intangible assets). The audit committee's implied and actual mandate now includes bringing critical issues before the full board of directors, and constantly identifying issues, legal/regulatory problems and potential liabilities that may affect firm value. Given that many technology companies have substantial intangible assets, the audit committee must be statutorily required to develop acceptable and defensible standards for accounting, impairment of, and valuation of intangible assets. The audit committee now has a justifiably broader implied mandate with regard to the operations of technology companies.

SOX Does Not Address Inherent Conflict Between Corporate Strategy and Corporate Disclosure Requirements

In the ESR case (Nwogugu (2003)), execution of BOSS's and GMAC's corporate strategy was more important to them than compliance with GAAP and SEC rules, and this choice eventually led to the collapse/bankruptcy of ESR. In many instances, there is often inherent conflict between corporate strategy and corporate disclosure requirements, primarily because: a) disclosure has information effects that may complicate or deter corporate strategy, b) disclosure requirements and execution of corporate strategy can have opposing/conflicting and simultaneous effects on incentive compensation schemes. These issues are not addressed by SOX. There should be specific and express rules that mandate approval of corporate strategy by the audit committee of the board of directors, and certification by senior executives without public disclosure (much like SOX requires certification of financial statements.

SOX and World-SOX Do Not Address Group Decision Processes at Banks and at Investment Firms

These entities have access to as much information, and sometimes have as much influence on company management as law firms and accounting firms, but are not subject to the same expectations/standards/rules pertaining to due diligence and disclosure.

SOX and World-SOX Do Not Sufficiently Address Moral Hazard and Adverse Selection in External Auditors

There should have been mechanisms/statutes that would have triggered the removal of BOSS's and GMAC's external auditors during their industry consolidation acquisitions.

SOX and World-SOX Can Complicate the Agency Problems Inherent in Hiring External Auditors

SOX does not address, and complicates the principal-agent problems inherent in hiring external auditors. Under SOX, the external auditor's role has become much more prominent, and the external auditor's compensation has increased. Under SOX, the external auditor's incentives to report fraud to regulators are much lower, because: a) the external auditor is likely to loose both SOX and traditional audit work, if the relationship deteriorates – loss of SOX engagements at one client is likely to substantially affect the accounting firm's probability of getting other audit or SOX engagements; b) SOX has shifted more responsibility for accuracy of disclosure to company management (via certifications); c) SOX has broadened the potential pool of claimants that can sue external auditors.

These principal-agent problems are compounded by the fact that under SOX, external auditors effectively serve as the agents of various parties – the public, investors/shareholders, regulators and the company's management. The external auditor's role as an agent of shareholders directly conflicts with the external auditor's duty to the public and to regulators. With regard to external auditors, there are substantial moral hazard problems and principal-agent problems in implementation of SOX - accounting firms have an inherent incentive to delay the reporting of negative financial information about clients. Cialdini & Goldstein (2004); Lai-Yee & Leung (2005); Street & Gray (2001); Lerner & Tetlock (1999); Verrecchia (2001). These moral hazard problems can be solved or reduced by statutory restrictions and guidelines which are lacking in many national jurisdictions. SOX has only worsened the moral hazard problems by effectively granting more control over companys' internal controls to public accounting firms.

SOX's Requirement That CEOs and CFOs Certify Financial Statements Increases Principal-Agent Problems and Provides More Incentives for Fraud

This requirement places undue psychological burdens on executives who are already burdened with management responsibilities, accountability to shareholders, etc.. The certification requirement does not help in terms of apportioning liability (for misconduct) among employees, because many of the documents that require certification are large complex documents, produced from many departments by many people over time. These people may have different departmental cultures, incentive/compensation systems, performance measurement systems, departmental internal controls and education. Essentially holding one person criminally responsible for internal controls of the firm is not reasonable, logical or appropriate.

These points raise the issue of the role of internal auditors in large multinational technology companies. Most of the problems at BOSS and GMAC could have been identified by effective internal audits conducted by independent internal audit teams that report only to the board of directors, coordinate with external auditors and have proper incentive compensation – that, the hiring criteria, performance criteria and incentive compensation for internal audit professionals are tied directly to the quality of external audits, incidences of fraud, improvement in operations, quality of recommendations, reduction of business risk, and reduction/elimination of existing/potential/contingent liabilities. The internal audit function must now go beyond traditional analysis of operations, marketing and finance functions, and mandatorily include legal, regulatory, political, labor and environmental analysis.

Similarly, at banks, the internal audit function has become more relevant and has to be changed. The hiring criteria, performance criteria and incentive compensation for internal audit professionals should be directly linked to abilities pertaining to the quality of external audits, incidences of fraud, improvement in operations, quality of recommendations, reduction of business risk, and reduction/elimination of existing/potential/contingent liabilities.

THE CASE OF ENCOMPASS SERVICES, INC. (NWOGUGU, 2003): SARBANES-OXLEY ACT AND THE ROLE OF INTERNAL AUDITORS IN TECHNOLOGY COMPANIES AND IN BANKS

Using the events that occurred in a series of "roll-up" corporate transactions in the US (Nwogugu (2003)), this section analyzes the efficiency of the Sarbanes-Oxley Act of 2002. See: Nwogugu (2003), and Leung & Cooper (2003). Encompass Services Corp. ("ESR") was formed in 2000 by the two-phase restructuring and merger of Building One Services Corp. ("BOSS"), and Group Maintenance America ("GMAC") which was announced on November 3, 1999 and approved by shareholders of both companies on February 22, 2000. ESR provided maintenance and electrical/mechanical services and installation of building equipment at various types of facilities in many industries and residential buildings. ESR, formerly a Fortune–500 was subsequently de-listed from the New York Stock Exchange and as of 2002/2003 was trading on the NASDAQ Pink sheets (symbol was "ESVN"). Shortly after the merger, a confluence of events resulted in ESR's financial distress. On October 18, 2002, some of ESR's creditors proposed a restructuring and a pre-packed bankruptcy filing, but there was no agreement among the creditors and ESR. On or around November 19, 2002, ESR filed for Chapter Eleven bankruptcy protection in the Federal Bankruptcy Court in Texas, USA. While under bankruptcy protection, ESR's 25,000 employees in 200+ offices, provide mechanical services, electrical services, cleaning systems/services and network technologies to commercial and residential buildings in the US.

As of September 2002, ESR had about $1.2 billion of indebtedness ($589 million Secured Credit Facility; $339 million of unsecured bonds and note obligations; $309 million of outstanding mandatorily redeemable convertible preferred stock; and trade obligations).

ESR's roll-up transactions and subsequent bankruptcy were partly attributable to its management's failure to manage knowledge creation and knowledge delivery. ESR's main assets were its human capital. ESR's business was providing expert services and advisory services in building/facilities engineering. The merger resulted in BOSS providing services in new segments where it was not previously active. The combination of inadequate union involvement in critical decisions, and failure to adequately manage knowledge-based work teams, and also customers' negative perceptions of ESR's ability to deliver adequate services eventually resulted in ESR's inability to win enough profitable service contracts. This phenomenon occurred even though immediately after the merger in April 2000, ESR was the industry leader, and had the most resources (in the industry) to provide such services – but customers actually choose to hire smaller competitors with presumably less knowledge and geographical coverage. ESR apparently failed to develop marketable and well-defined internal systems of knowledge creation, or knowledge management or knowledge storage, that prospective clients could rely on for adequate service. Any additional skills that BOSS/GMAC did not have could have been developed in-house or obtained using strategic alliances and joint ventures. Nwogugu (2004). Several principles can be derived from the ESR transactions:

- Management's ability to manage knowledge is a direct function of worker cohesion and status of labor unions.
- Management's ability to manage knowledge across partner organizations (strategic alliances) or recently merged companies is a direct function of integration of information systems, ability to assess customer needs, strength of client relations, and assessment of workers' skills.

Similarly, that ESR's advisors allowed the transactions to occur, is also attributable to knowledge management problems. Human capital is the key distinguishing factor at banks, accounting firms, law firms and consultants that worked on BOSS's, GMAC's and ESR's roll-up transactions. These entities were apparently not able to manage knowledge networks within their organizations and outside their organizations. The loan origination function, the credit function, the risk management function and advisory function of banks (and accounting firms) are all knowledge- intensive processes. The modern bank and financial institution are essentially technology companies that rely heavily on information management in their daily operations. Thus, senior management and the boards of directors at banks must emphasize and implement knowledge creation and knowledge management processes in order to reduce risk and increase shareholder value. Government regulators should also develop and implement supervision rules that require financial institutions to develop better knowledge creation and knowledge management systems, and to file periodic reports about the configurations and performance of such knowledge management systems.

Knowledge management must be coordinated with internal audit and corporate governance efforts. Unfortunately, SOX does not address or establish standards for integrating knowledge management and internal audit systems. Its worth noting that in its present form, SOX" would not have prevented any of the following:

- The internal control problems and string of fraudulent conveyances at BOSS, and GMAC.
- The internal control problems and fraud implicit in the ESR transactions.
- The inaction of banks – ie. inadequate due diligence and improper monitoring of existing loans;
- Inaction of bond trustees. Sarbanes-Oxley Act applies only to companies that meet the definition of 'issuer'.
- Inaction of external auditors – moral hazard.

The key aspects of Sarbanes-Oxley Act[6] that could have been applicable to BOSS, GMAC and ESR before April 2000 (ie. if SOX were enacted before 2000) are as follows:

- ***Section 302***: Corporate Responsibility For Financial Reports - requires certification of information by company CEOs and CFOs. The maximum penalties for willful and knowing violations of this section are a fine of not more than $500,000 and/or imprisonment of up to five years. However, this isnt adequate incentive for CEOs and CFOs to comply, where as in the ESR case, substantial amounts of money and potentially unlimited incentive compensation were at stake.
- Empowerment of audit committees to engage and approve the services provided by independent auditors.
- Auditor independence standards.
- ***Section 404*** *– reports on internal controls.* Most of the internal control reports would have missed financing-related problems. Senior management of BOSS and GMAC, and Apollo were intent on consummating the series of mergers, and had a history of M&A transactions involving bankrupt entities. Most internal control reports focus on operational issues as opposed to loan covenants. & Pierre-Mari (2005).
- ***Section 303***: *Improper Influence on Conduct of Audits* (by officers or directors of the company). ESR, BOSS and GMAC's senior management clearly had substantial influence on the conduct of audits of BOSS and GMAC – which resulted in non-disclosure of the bankruptcy/insolvency of BOSS and GMAC for many years. Execution of both GMAC's and BOSS's industry consolidation strategies depended on good audit reports regardless of compliance with loan covenants.
- ***Section 204***: Auditor Reports to Audit Committees - the external auditor must report to the audit committee all "critical accounting policies and practices to be used all alternative treatments of financial information within [GAAP] that have been discussed with management ramifications of the use of such alternative disclosures and treatments, and the treatment preferred" by the firm. A close review of BOSS's and GMAC's SEC filings will reveal that their external auditors did not reveal obvious problems related to their insolvencies. Doing so would probably have cost the accounting firms substantial business from the industry consolidation transactions.

- ***Section 305***: Officer And Director Bars And Penalties.
- ***Section 401(a):*** *Disclosures In Periodic Reports*; Disclosures Required. The periodic disclosures made by BOSS, GMAC and ESR were grossly insufficient.
- ***Section 409***: *Real Time Disclosure* - Issuers must disclose information on material changes in the financial condition or operations of the issuer on a rapid and current basis. BOSS, ESR and GMAC omitted required disclosures.
- **The Sarbanes-Oxley Act incorporates the SEC Act of 1934** - a violation of Rules of the Public Company Accounting Oversight Board is considered as a violation of the 1934 Act, and results in the same penalties that may be imposed for violations of the 1934 Act.

THE FAILURE AND UN-CONSTITUTIONALITY OF THE PCAOB (USA)

The PCAOB is a US non-profit entity that was incorporated (pursuant to the Sarbanes Oxley Act of 2002 ("SOX") in Washington D. C., USA. Other countries have created similar accounting regulatory agencies – see Baker, Bédard & Hauret (2014) and Loehlein (2017). PCAOB monitors and regulates the accounting firms that conduct external audits of companies that operate in, and or whose shares are listed on stock exchanges in the US – and indirectly affects foreign companies and international operations of such accounting firms. Thus, PCAOB has a significant effect on reported risk, regulation of risk and Risk-Perception in global markets. PCAOB oversees auditing firms and the audits of public companies, other issuers and broker-dealers (including compliance reports). All PCAOB rules and standards, and its annual budget must be approved by the U.S. Securities and Exchange Commission (the "SEC"). The PCAOB is funded with fees paid by the companies and broker-dealers who rely on the audit/accounting firms that are managed by PCAOB. PCAOB is managed by a Board of Directors which has five Board members, all of whom are appointed by the US SEC. The PCAOB must consult with the US Secretary of the Treasury and the Chairman of the Board of Governors of the Federal Reserve System before each Board Member is appointed. No more than two Board members may be Certified Public Accountants.

The PCAOB and similar oversight entities in other countries are a huge improvement compared to self-regulation of the accounting/auditing industry. The PCAOB (USA) is among a class of very powerful non-governmental organizations/associations that have "*quasi-executive powers*" (similar to powers of the executive branch of the federal government) even though they are not part of the government (but are implicitly supported and encouraged by governments). The diffusion of power inherent in PCAOB-type organizations/associations creates or can create a diffusion of accountability and lack of appropriate oversight, which effectively subverts the powers of the executive branch of the federal government in many countries. Through its rule-making functions, the PCAOB (USA) has "quasi-executive powers" even though they are not part of the government (but are implicitly supported and encouraged by governments). PCAOB (USA) receives substantial input on accounting regulations from, and are lobbied by the private sector. Thus, PCAOB (USA) has '*federal-government type*' power and control over capital markets, securities brokers and disclosure patterns, and such power is essentially the same as government control and or 'state-action' required to prove violations of the US Constitution.

As explained in Nwogugu (2021), the existence and current operations of the Public Company Accountability Oversight Board (the "PCAOB" in the US) is un-constitutional[7]; and some of the US Supreme Court's rulings in *Free Enterprise Fund vs. PCAOB* were error. Bader & Berlau (Competitive Enterprise Institute) (Oct. 2005)[8], Russell (June 28, 2010)[9], Salky & Rosman (2004), Shapiro & Cushman (Dec.

2009) and other authors[10] explain how the existence and operations of PCAOB are un-constitutional (for reasons different from those mentioned in Nwogugu [2021]).

PCAOB and similar institutions in other countries have wide-ranging international *Multiplier Effects* some of which are negative – see: Bather & Burnaby (2006), Loehlein (2017), and Huang & Chong (2016). Researchers have noted that the PCAOB affects audit quality and disclosure quality – see: Chiu, Chien & Lin (2013), and Udeh (2017).

PCAOB and similar institutions in other countries are not really sufficiently independent – see: Loehlein (2017).

PCAOB and similar institutions in other countries have sometimes increased audit costs in other countries – see: Huang & Chong (2016).

While PCAOB oversees the audits of public/listed companies, other issuers and broker-dealers (including compliance reports), PCAOB's jurisdiction should have been extended to audits of: i) large franchising networks; ii) non-listed companies that are "systemically important"; iii) state and federal government agencies that provide services to large numbers of consumers; iv)

Bather & Burnaby (2006); Huang & Chong (2016); Chiu, Chien & Lin (2013); Loehlein (2017); Baker, Bédard & Hauret (2014) and Udeh (2017) analyzed various important *Multiplier Effects* of PCAOB and its regulatory functions – and some of those *Multiplier Effects* can be harmful and or costly.

Flasher & Schenck (2019) analyzed the use of PCAOB reports on audit firms headquartered outside of the United States (US) to measure audit quality, and they focused on five different categories of auditing firm arrangements – which are Big Four network affiliates; BDO and Grant Thornton network affiliates; firms with other network affiliations; firms with associations and alliances; and other (unknown or no stated affiliation). Flasher & Schenck (2019) found that: i) non-US firms that don't have formal agreements with other audit firms have lower audit-quality compared to the other four arrangement types; i) audit firms that have more formal connections (i.e., networks and larger associations/alliances arrangements) have similar levels of audit quality; iii) network audit-firms that primarily do work referred to them by US audit firms have better results on PCAOB inspections; however, this relationship doesn't hold for associations and alliances; iv) there is a need for a more nuanced understanding of global audit quality. Prasad & Webster (2020) analyzed the recurring nature of audit deficiencies both within and across U.S. and non-U.S. auditing firms (PCAOB Part I audit deficiencies) based on three categories which are Generally Accepted Accounting Principles (GAAP), *Generally Accepted Auditing Standards* (GAAS), and *Internal Controls over Financial Reporting* (ICFR). Using 1,551 inspections conducted during 2003–2017, Prasad & Webster (2020) analyzed found that: i) 67% of Part I audit deficiencies pertained to GAAP and triennially-inspected audit firms had the highest occurrence of these deficiencies; ii) 22% of audit deficiencies pertained to GAAS and occurred most frequently in annually-inspected audit firms; iii) ICFR has the least audit deficiencies (11%), but such deficiencies have been increasing since 2009; iv) there were no significant differences in the mean number of GAAP, GAAS, and ICFR audit deficiencies between first- and second-round inspections, but there was a significant increase in the mean number of ICFR audit deficiencies between the third- to fifth-round inspections; v) most importantly, the most frequent audit deficiencies identified by the PCAOB reports were the audit areas of "*revenue recognition*", "*inventory,*" and "*fair value measurements*" (all of which require significant auditor-judgment and for which GAAP permits significant audit-client discretion in interpretation) – thus measures of. The PCAOB reports inadvertently penalizes auditors for using their judgement, whereas the real issue is that GAAS and GAAP should be revised to eliminate more auditor-discretion and audit-client discretion in interpretation. The Flasher & Schenck (2019) and Prasad & Webster (2020) studies indicate or imply that: i) PCAOB reports may be biased and or politicized to favor non-US network audit firms that focus on work referred by US audit firms – such audit firms have significant incentives to pressure the PCAOB or to influence the PCAOB reports and or to falsify documents, compared to the other types of auditing firms; ii) PCAOB may not be using accurate or practical measures of audit-quality; and there is a need for more accurate measures of audit-quality that account for differences in auditor-judgement and amounts of information that audit-clients provide to auditors; iii) the frequency of PCAOB inspections may affect PCAOB-reported audit-quality; iv) PCAOB inspection access may affect PCAOB-reported audit quality. These foregoing observations/conclusions are highly probable given the global standardization of audit processes and existence of generally accepted measures of audit-quality.

Abernathy, Barnes & Stefaniak (2013) reviewed prior studies on the four primary functions of PCAOB (registration, standard-setting, inspections, and enforcement) – ie. effects of PCAOB's standards and inspection process on auditor behavior, the auditing profession and audit quality; reactions of markets react to information disseminated by the PCAOB; etc.. Acito, Hogan & Mergenthaler (2018), Aobdia (2018), Aobdia & Shroff (2017), DeFond & Lennox (2017), and Kleinman, Lin & Palmon (2020) analyzed various effects of PCAOB.

The Dodd-Frank Act of *2010* (USA) did not amend SOX to eliminate the constitutional violations inherent in the existence of PCAOB (e.g. the Separation of Powers Clause).

PCAOB maybe deemed redundant or duplicative (and thus amplifies *Regulatory Fragmentation*) because it performs and duplicates functions that are either currently being performed by, or are best performed by the US SEC (and state securities agencies) and state accounting boards, and FINRA. The PCAOB does not have any powers that the US SEC does not already have either fully or in a form/amount that can be rapidly expanded. It was error to designate PCAOB as a self-regulatory organization[11] – PCAOB should rightfully be a US government agency (PCAOB should be a division/subsidiary of the US SEC), given the nature of its functions. PCAOB should not be a self-regulatory organization[12], given the nature, scope, intensity and economic/political/social effects of its functions.

PCAOB is un-constitutional because its a non-governmental monopoly that has been inadvertently (or even intentionally) granted regulatory and taxing powers[13] by the US Congress.

The SOX enabling statutes that created PCAOB also violate both the procedural and substantive due process clauses of the US Constitution for other reasons. PCAOB has extensive powers to interpret the portions of SOX such as those that pertain to Section-404 (internal controls), and such powers can conflict with those of the US SEC. Such conflict can produce different results for different classes of exchange-traded companies and auditing-firms, and which can burden interstate commerce by increasing compliance costs and or audit costs.

PCAOB's interpretation of the portions of SOX that pertain to internal controls has imposed substantial additional costs on publicly traded US companies (ie. by requiring audits, etc.) - see: Skouvakis (2005), Grundfest & Bochner (2007), Backer (2004), Gupta & Leech (2005), Engel, Hayes & Wang (2007), Bartlett (April 2008), Kamar & Karaca-Mandic (2006), Tackett, Wolf & Claypool (2006), and Rose (2005).

Its conjectured here that PCAOB's regulations may have increased Industry-Concentration and reduced competition in the accounting/auditing industry because the costs of its regulations have caused many small accounting firms to stop auditing publicly traded companies.

SOX prohibits accounting/auditing firms from providing eight designated types of consulting for their audit clients; and SOX authorized PCAOB to "........prohibit any other service that the Board determines, by regulation, is impermissible.....". This provision provides significant incentives for political lobbying, detrimental *Collusion* and *Regulatory Capture*.

The un-constitutionality of the EESA and PCAOB are an example of the far-reaching effects of state and federal constitutions on risk regulation. The *Financial Stability Act of 2010* ("FSA"; which is part of the Dodd-Frank Act) did not amend the Sarbanes Oxley Act ("SOX") to eliminate the inherent violations of the Separation of Powers Clause – e.g. pertaining to the existence and functions of PCAOB.

FAILURE OF THE DODD-FRANK ACT WITH RESPECT TO THE ACCOUNTING/ CONSULTING INDUSTRY, THE CREDIT RATING AGENCY (CRA) INDUSTRY AND THE QUASI-FRANCHISING/BUSINESS-OPPORTUNITY INDUSTRY

The section explains why the Dodd Frank Act is inefficient, has failed, and doesn't inadequately address Sustainable Growth, Systemic Risk and Financial Stability. Many countries copied the objectives and methods of the Dodd Frank Act and enacted their own statutes which were similar and have also failed. "Restoring American Financial Stability Act" of 2010 ("*RAFSA*" or the "Dodd-Frank Act") was the first set of statutes in any country, that attempted to simultaneously address the Global Financial Crisis, financial stability, systemic risk, consumer protection, sustainable growth, the national securities law framework, the structure of the executive branch of the federal government, and delegation of powers to federal government agencies (to the detriment of state governments). However, the Dodd Frank Act and similar statutes in many countries/jurisdictions are inefficient, and have failed to address the fundamental problems in financial systems; and parts of the Dodd Frank Act are un-constitutional. Other countries/ jurisdictions have enacted statutes that are similar to the Dodd Frank Act [14]. Canada, Brazil and Asia countries have also introduced similar statutes.

The United Kingdom introduced the Vickers Report, which is similar to the Volcker Rule (the Vickers Report has the same purpose of the Volcker Rule but it has different methods, and is based on the ring fence and not on the separation of commercial and investment banks). The EU also released the Report of the European Commission's High-level Expert Group on Bank Structural Reform" (aka *Liikanen Group Report*) which addresses such differences. The European Union enacted the European Market Infrastructure Regulation ("EMIR"),[15] the Markets in Financial Instruments Directive II and related Regulation ("MiFID II" and "MIFIR"),[16] the new Capital Requirements Directive and Regulation ("CRD IV"),[17] and other statutes.

Nwogugu (2015a) detailed the many failures of the Dodd Frank Act, many of which apply directly to the Accounting/Consulting industry, the Quasi-Franchising/Business-Opportunity industry and the CRA industry. Nwogugu (2015b) explained why many aspects of the Dodd Frank Act are un-constitutional.

The Dodd Frank Act (USA) did not fully integrate SOX into the federal securities law framework. Most importantly, the Dodd Frank Act fails to extend and apply SOX to large private companies and medium-sized private companies that have the same (or greater) magnitude of economic activity and influence on the US economy as publicly traded companies.

The Dodd Frank Act applies to accounting firms and CRAs in the US; and to US companies (many of which have vast global operations and international suppliers) and to non-US companies whose stocks or bonds are listed in US financial exchanges; and thus, the Dodd Frank Act's reach and "*Multiplier Effects*" are indeed global.

The Dodd Frank Act continues to have significant effects on the structure and evolution of the global accounting/consulting industry (https://www.journalofaccountancy.com/issues/2010/sep/20103108.html) in various ways including but not limited to the following:

1. The Dodd-Frank Act authorized the Public Company Accounting Oversight Board (PCAOB) to monitor auditors of nonpublic broker-dealers; and PCAOB can share its inspection and investigative reports with non-U.S. regulators. The Dodd-Frank Act provides the PCAOB with standard-setting, inspection and disciplinary authority regarding broker-dealer audits.
2. Under the Dodd-Frank Act: 1) auditing firms (employees and non-CPA partners) are exempt from being regulated by US Consumer Financial Protection Bureau (CFPB) provided the services they provide are considered customary and usual; 2) auditing firms and or consulting firms (e.g. tax consulting; environmental consulting) may be made parties to disputes adjudicated or prosecuted by the CFPB; 3) audited financial statements and audited account statements for investment/brokerage accounts will probably be used as evidence and auditing firms and or consulting firms may be used as witnesses.
3. The Dodd Frank Act gives the US *Financial Stability Oversight Council* (FSOC) the duty to monitor domestic and international financial regulatory proposals and developments, including insurance and accounting issues, and to advise the US Congress and make recommendations in such areas that will enhance the integrity, efficiency, competitiveness and stability of the U.S. financial markets.
4. The Dodd Frank Act grants the FSOC the power to submit comments to the US SEC and any standard-setting body with respect to an existing or proposed accounting principle, standard or procedure.
5. The Dodd Frank Act gives the FSOC the statutory power to takeover any company in the US (after obtaining permission from a US federal district court) that is deemed a financial stability risk (including accounting/auditing firms and CRAs). Much of this assessment and exercise may be based on the target company's financial statements and or credit ratings – that exposes auditing firms, CRAs and some types of consulting firms to costly litigation.
6. The Dodd Frank Act provides a permanent funding mechanism for GASB by authorizing the US SEC to require a national securities association to levy an "accounting support fee," the proceeds from which would be remitted to the Financial Accounting Foundation.
7. The Dodd Frank Act's amendments to the Sarbanes Oxley Act (SOX): 1) eliminates some filing/compliance requirements for smaller companies (e.g. listed companies whose market-caps are below $250 million) and thus reduces business volume of accounting/consulting firms; 2) increases the audit-liability risk of auditing firms; 3) places more "personal audit risk" on CEOs and CFOs which in turn affects audit-quality and the nature of contracting between auditing firms and their auditee-clients.
8. The Dodd Frank Act doesn't sufficiently address the many inconsistencies in the judgments of US bankruptcy court judges. That affects auditing firms, CRAs and consulting firms.
9. The Dodd Frank Act doesn't address the un-constitutionality of accounting standards setting bodies such as PCAOB, GASB and FASB in the US.
10. The Dodd Frank Act doesn't address the *Separation-Of-Powers Doctrine* problems inherent in the concurrent investigatory, adjudication and enforcement activities of the US SEC and the US CFPB, all of which directly affect accounting/auditing firms and consulting firms.

11. Many of the statutes in, and reports required by the Dodd Frank Act directly or indirectly depend on audited financial statements and or external consultant's reports – all of which expose auditing firms and consulting firms to regulation and liability.

Similarly, the Dodd Frank Act continues to have significant effects on the structure and evolution of the global CRA[18] industry in various ways including but not limited to the following:

1. The Dodd Frank Act changed the requirements for regulation of CRAs by the US SEC – and especially the big-three CRAs (Fitch, Moodys and S&P) which collectively have more than 80% (eighty percent) market-share in the global CRA industry.
2. The *Dodd-Frank Act of 2010* (USA) expressly imposed liability on CRAs for their erroneous ratings – and that has far-reaching worldwide *Multiplier Effects* because it applies to S&P and Moodys ratings businesses around the world, and to Fitch's ratings of US companies.
3. The Dodd Frank Act provisions are grossly insufficient for solving problems in the CRA industry. The Dodd Frank Act will probably increase the cost of obtaining credit ratings.
4. Many disputes that will be litigated at or by the US CFPB and the US SEC and that pertain to fixed income instruments will directly or indirectly involve credit ratings but the Dodd Frank does not establish any efficient framework for that.
5. The Dodd Frank Act greatly reduced the dependence and inclusion of credit ratings in government policy documents and statutes; but without providing viable substitutes for credit ratings.
6. The Dodd Frank Act doesn't sufficiently address the many inconsistencies in credit ratings; and in the judgments of US bankruptcy court judges. That affects CRAs.
7. The Dodd Frank Act doesn't address the constitutional law problems of credit ratings and the issue of the acceptable scope of legal liabilities of CRAs.
8. The Dodd Frank Act doesn't address the *Separation-Of-Powers Doctrine* problems inherent in the concurrent investigatory, adjudication and enforcement activities of the US SEC and the US CFPB, all of which directly affect CRAs.
9. The Dodd Frank Act doesn't address the un-constitutionality of accounting standards setting bodies such as PCAOB, GASB, SASB, PCAF and FASB in the US, which directly and indirectly affects CRAs.
10. Many of the statutes in, and reports required by the Dodd Frank Act directly or indirectly depend on audited financial statements and or external consultant's reports and or credit ratings– all of which expose CRAs to regulation and legal liability.

MODELS OF WILLINGNESS-TO-COMPLY (WTC) WITH SOX, THE DODD-FRANK ACT, SUSTAINABILITY STANDARDS/REGULATIONS, AND SIMILAR STATUTES

SOX, Sustainability Standards/Regulations and Dodd-Frank Act raises the issue of employees' *Willingness-To-Comply* (WTC) with those laws/regulations, which in this instance, is intertwined with the *Willingness-to-disclose* (WTD) financial information. See: Arora & Gangopadhyay (1995); Zheng (2002); Tackett (2004); Teles (2004); Kyung & In-Gyu (2001); Lai-Yee & Leung (2005), Van Der Torre & Tan (____), Jackson (2004), Camras & Witherington (2005), Fogel, Nwokah, Dedo & Messinger (1992), Thelen (2005); Thelen (2005), and Van Geert & Steenbeek (2005). SOX has both civil and criminal penalties for non-compliance. The deterrence effect of SOX has not been proven or analyzed in detail – indeed, even after its implementation, companies are still reporting problems with internal controls. The ideal level of deterrence is complete deterrence (ie. Complete-compliance, which is different from over-compliance). Hence, the sanction must be sufficient to prevent recurrence by sufficiently reducing perpetrators' resources and providing a deterrence effect (or sufficiently reduce the probability of recurrence).

These WTC models can also be used as stock-selection and bond-selection models because they address investment criteria used by some portfolio managers (such as ESG).

Let:

P_{pn} = probability of prosecution under non-compliance. $P_{pn} \in (0, 1)$.
P_{pc} = probability of prosecution under complete-compliance. $P_{pc} \in (0, 1)$.
$\mathbf{P_{ta}}$ = probability of corporate tax audit. $P_{ta} \in (0,1)$.
F_c = estimated/statutory fine/penalty for company if convicted – lost wages, monetary fines, etc. $\mathbf{F_c} \in (0, \infty)$.
F_e = estimated/statutory total fines/penalties for top ten managers if convicted. $F_e \in (0, \infty)$.
C_c = company's compliance costs required to achieve complete compliance with SOX.
G_c = present value of potential benefits to company from falsifications in reporting period t. more ESO awards, higher repricing, etc.. $\mathbf{G_c} \in (-\infty, \infty)$.
G_e = present value of potential benefits to employee from falsifications in reporting period t. $\mathbf{G_e} \in (-\infty, \infty)$.
M = average employee propensity to commit fraud. $M \in (0, 1)$. $M \rightarrow 1$, as the employee becomes more likely to commit fraud.
CE = control environment – company size, culture, geographic scope of operations, centralized/decentralized operations, manager's ability to coordinate fraud, etc.. $CE \in (0, 1)$. $CE \rightarrow 1$, as the Control Environment becomes stricter, and management has more control over procedures/processes.
S = savings from complete compliance with SOX – absence of investigations, fraud, etc.
$\mathbf{L_e}$ = percentage of total liability imposed on employee, upon conviction.
$\mathbf{L_c}$ = percentage of total liability imposed on company, upon conviction.
R = company's/employee's Regret. $R \in (-1,1)$. $R \rightarrow 1$, as the employee/company becomes more likely to regret any misconduct, due to prior penalties, financial position or fear of consequences.
H = horizon of influence/falsification (time in years/months/week). $H \in (0, \infty)$.
$\mathbf{T_{cr}}$ = transaction costs involved in falsifying corporate records. $\mathbf{T_{cr}} \in (-\infty, \infty)$.
$\mathbf{T_p}$ = company's transaction costs for prosecuting falsification. $\mathbf{T_p} \in (-\infty, \infty)$.
$\mathbf{T_i}$ = company's transaction costs for investigating falsification. $\mathbf{T_i} \in (-\infty, \infty)$.
$\mathbf{T_{pg}}$ = government's transaction costs for prosecuting falsification. $\mathbf{T_{pg}} \in (0, \infty)$.
$\mathbf{T_{ig}}$ = government's transaction costs for investigating falsification. $\mathbf{T_{ig}} \in (0, \infty)$.
EM = employee collusion-motivation index. $0 < EM < 1$. This factor refers as to the degree of estimated and feasible collusion among employees, and between employees and external auditors. $EM \rightarrow 1$, as the employee becomes more likely to collude with other employees and external audit staff, suppliers and vendors
SR = expected stock market reaction from any major change in reporting. $SR \in (-1,1)$. $SR \rightarrow 1$, as the stock market reacts more positively to any change (positive or negative) in ESO reporting, and vice versa.

EP = employee's propensity to falsify records. EP = *f*(P, T,I,C,K,PI,IR,D,E). EP $\in (0,1)$. EP is different from EM because EM pertains to collusion with internal staff and auditors, while EP pertains to possibility of actual fraud by the employee. EP $\rightarrow 1$, as the employee's propensity to falsify records increases.

Where:

P = personality; T = amount of company's tax burden before falsification, I = intensity of enforcement efforts; C = complexity of the tax system; K = employee's knowledge and skills in law and accounting; PI = peer influence; IR = influence of reference groups; DE = employee's direct experience with the government's tax system. P,T,I,C,K,PI,IR,D,E $\in (0,1)$

IN = perceived inequity index – which reflects the average employee's perceptions about inequity of the tax system/regime and internal controls. IN $\in (0,1)$. IN $\rightarrow 1$, as the average employee's perception of the tax system as inequitable increases.

$$\mathbf{WTC_1} = [LN\{((1 - P_{pc})*(S-C_c)) /(((1-P_{pn})*(G_c+ G_e)) - ((F_c+F_e)*P_{pn}))\}]*M*CE^{-1}$$

$$\mathbf{WTC_2} = \{{}_0\int^H ([(P_{pn}\text{ú } P_{ta})*(L_e)] / [(SR*(L_c)*(1- (P_{pn}\text{ú}P_{ta}))]) \partial H\}$$

$$\mathbf{WTC_3} = \{{}_0\int^H ([(P_{pn}\text{ú } P_{ta})*(L_e)] / [(SR*(L_c)*(1- (P_{pn}\text{ú } P_{ta}))]) \partial H\} * \{\partial(T_p+T_i)/\partial(T_{pg}+T_{ig})\}*(\partial CE/\partial EM) * (\partial EP/\partial IN)*(\partial(T_{pg}+T_{ig})/\partial EM)$$

$$\mathbf{WTC_4} = [(L_c/L_e)*\{(T_p+T_i)/(T_{eg}+T_{ig})\}*(CE/EM)*(EP/IN)*(SR/CE)*(EP/EM)*(IN/(CE*SR*EM))]$$

WTC $\in (-\infty, +\infty)$.

WTC $\rightarrow 1$, as the company becomes more likely to comply with SOX standards.

The models are self explanatory. There are different formulas for *Spatio-Temporal-Cognition WTC* because industries differ substantially; and companies differ; employee knowledge and incentives differ across companies; and most important, the formation and maintenance of groups/coalitions in companies also differ.

Activist/ESG Investing: Generating Alternative Risk Premia by Using WTC

As mentioned above, these WTC models can also be used as stock-selection and bond-selection models because they address investment criteria used by some portfolio managers (such as ESG and "Activist" investors). Around the world, ESG and socially-responsible investing is growing and many institutional investors have invested directly or indirectly (through index funds, ETFs and equity swaps) in companies that are subject to SOX, the Dodd Frank Act and or climate regulations – and the penalties for non-compliance can be substantial. Thus, corporate compliance with statutes that pertain SOX, PCAOB, the Dodd Frank Act and or climate regulations can be a major indicator of the future prospects and opportunity set, profitability, solvency and share-price performance of company. This is because such compliance touches and is partly based on many critical aspects of a company's operations, culture, controls, financing and structure – such as corporate governance, organizational structure; internal controls; liquidity and financing; capital structure; opportunity set; managerial capacity; human capital; public relations; reputation and social capital; etc.. See the comments in Tang, Tian & Yan (2015); Braddock (2006); Linciano (2003); Richardson & Welker (2001); Wallace (2009); Sullivan & Gouldson (2017);

Tang & Demmeritt (2018)[19]; and Asia Investor Group On Climate Change (2017). Thus, its possible to generate *alternative risk premia* by investing in companies that have high WTC, and or by shorting (or buying listed put options on) companies that have low WTC. Nwogugu (2008) developed a *WTC* model for the Sarbanes Oxley Act (hereafter "SOX"; a US statute). However, several academic studies have concluded that the degree of compliance with SOX is an indicator of the future prospects, opportunity-set and stock-price performance of a company.

CONCLUSION

The ESR/BOSS/GMAC transactions, the Global Financial Crisis of 2007-2014 and the COVID-19 Pandemic of 2020-present illustrate some of the inadequacies of the Sarbanes-Oxley Act. The implementation and enforcement of the Sarbanes-Oxley Act, PCAOB regulations and Dodd Frank Act within the Accounting/Consulting, Business-Opportunity/Quasi-Franchising and CRA industries often results in excessive compliance costs, over-compliance, agency problems, regulatory friction, misallocation of liability, inadequate/improper penalties, inefficiency and information asymmetry. The cross-border Multiplier Effects of SOX (and similar statutes in other countries) are or can be significant but haven't been studied sufficiently in the literature.

WTC can be a useful measure of Compliance (as a physical phenomena), and can also be used to generate *alternative risk premia.*

REFERENCES

Abernathy, J., Barnes, M., & Stefaniak, C. (2013). A summary of ten years of PCAOB research: What have we learned? *Journal of Accounting Literature*, *32*(1), 30–60. doi:10.1016/j.acclit.2013.10.002

Acito, A., Hogan, C., & Mergenthaler, R. (2018). The effects of PCAOB inspections on auditor-client relationships. *The Accounting Review*, *93*(2), 1–35. doi:10.2308/accr-51811

Akerblad, P., Johansson, M., & Jangvik, E. (2007). *Implementation Of Section 404 Of The Sarbanes-Oxley Act In A Swedish Environment.* Working paper.

Aobdia, D. (2018). The impact of the PCAOB individual engagement inspection process: Preliminary evidence. *The Accounting Review*, *93*(4), 53–80. doi:10.2308/accr-51948

Aobdia, D., & Shroff, N. (2017). Regulatory oversight and auditor market share. *Journal of Accounting and Economics*, *63*(2), 262–287. doi:10.1016/j.jacceco.2017.03.001

Aprill, E. (2009). What Critiques Of Sarbanes-Oxley Can Teach About Regulation Of Non-profit Governance. *Fordham Law Review*, *76*, 765–775.

Arora, S., & Gangopadhyay, S. (1995). Toward A Theoretical Model Of Voluntary Overcompliance. *Journal of Economic Behavior & Organization*, *28*(3), 289–299. doi:10.1016/0167-2681(95)00037-2

Ashfaq, K., & Rui, Z. (2019). The effect of board and audit committee effectiveness on internal control disclosure under different regulatory environments in South Asia. *Journal of Financial Reporting and Accounting*, *17*(2), 170–200. doi:10.1108/JFRA-09-2017-0086

Asia Investor Group On Climate Change. (2017). *Connecting Commodities, Investors, Climate, And The Land - A Toolkit For Institutional Investors*. http://aigcc.net/wp-content/uploads/2017/10/IGCC-Sustainable-Land-Use.pdf

Backer, L. (2004). Surveillance And Control: Privatizing And Nationalizing Corporate Monitoring After Sarbanes Oxley Act. *Detroit College of Law at Michigan State University Law Review*, *2004*, 327–370.

Bader, H., & Berlau, J. (2005). *The Public Company Accounting Oversight Board: An Unconstitutional Assault on Government Accountability*. http://cei.org/pdf/4873.pdf

Bainbridge, S., & Johnson, C. (2004). Managerialism, Legal Ethics And Sarbanes-Oxley Section 307. *Detroit College of Law at Michigan State University Law Review*, *2004*, 299–316.

Baker, R., Bédard, J., & Hauret, C. (2014). The regulation of statutory auditing: An institutional theory approach. *Managerial Auditing Journal*, *29*(5), 371–394. doi:10.1108/MAJ-09-2013-0931

Baker, R. R., Biddle, G. C., Lowry, M. R., & O'Connor, N. G. (2018). Shades of gray: Internal control reporting by Chinese US-listed firms. *Accounting Horizons*, *32*(4), 1–30. doi:10.2308/acch-52300

Bargeron, L., Lehn, K., & Zutter, C. (2010). Sarbanes-Oxley and corporate risk-taking. *Journal of Accounting and Economics*, *49*(1-2), 34–52. doi:10.1016/j.jacceco.2009.05.001

Bartlett, R. (2008). *Going Private But Staying Public: Reexamining the Effect of Sarbanes-Oxley on Firms' Going-Private Decisions*. American Law & Economics Association Annual Meetings. http://law.bepress.com/cgi/viewcontent.cgi?article=2521&context=alea

Bather, A., & Burnaby, P. (2006). The Public Company Accounting Oversight Board: National and international implications. *Managerial Auditing Journal*, *21*(6), 657–669. doi:10.1108/02686900610674915

Bauer, A. M. (2016). Tax avoidance and the implications of weak internal controls. *Contemporary Accounting Research*, *33*(2), 449–486. doi:10.1111/1911-3846.12151

Baynes, L. (2002). Just Pucker And Blow? An Analysis Of Corporate Whistleblowers, The Duty of Care, The Duty Of Loyalty And The Sarbanes-Oxley Act. *St. John's Law Review*, *76*, 875–895.

Berlau, J. (2006). *Sarbanes-Oxley vs. the Free Press: How the government used business regulations to strong-arm the media*. Reason.com. https://reason.com/archives/2006/01/01/sarbanes-oxley-vs-the-free-pre

Bhaskar, L. S., Schroeder, J. H., & Shepardson, M. L. (2019). Integration of internal control and financial statement audits: Are two audits better than one? *The Accounting Review*, *94*(2), 53–81. doi:10.2308/accr-52197

Birg, E. (2003). *Is the Public Company Accounting Oversight Board Constitutional?* Academic Press.

Braddock, C. (2006). Pennywise And Pound Foolish: Why Investors Would Be Foolish To Pay A Penny Or A Pound For The Protections Provided By Sarbanes-Oxley. *Brigham Young University Law Review, 2006*, 175–185.

Brown, J. (2006). Criticizing The Critics: Sarbanes Oxley And Quack Corporate Governance. *Marquette Law Review, 90*, 309–319.

Burks, J. (2010). Disciplinary measures in response to restatements after Sarbanes–Oxley. *Journal of Accounting and Public Policy, 29*(3), 195–225. doi:10.1016/j.jaccpubpol.2010.03.002

Butler, H., & Ribstein, L. (1994). Corporate Governance Speech and the First Amendment. *Kansas Law Review, 42*, 163–173.

Butler, H., & Ribstein, L. (2006). The Sarbanes Oxley Debacle: What We've Learned; How To Fix It. AEI Press.

Camras, L., & Witherington, D. (2005). Dynamical Systems Approaches To Emotional Development. *Developmental Review, 25*(3-4), 328–350. doi:10.1016/j.dr.2005.10.002

Carrillo, D. (2008). Disgorgement Plans under the Fair Funds Provision of the Sarbanes-Oxley Act of 2002: Are Creditors and Investors Truly Being Protected. *DePaul Business & Commercial Law, 6*, 315–325.

Chang, H., & Choy, H. (2016). The effect of the Sarbanes–Oxley Act on firm productivity. *Journal of Centrum Cathedra, 9*(2), 120–142. doi:10.1108/JCC-09-2016-0012

Chang, J., & Sun, H. (2009). Crossed-listed foreign firms' earnings informativeness, earnings management and disclosures of corporate governance information under SOX. *The International Journal of Accounting, 44*(1), 1–32. doi:10.1016/j.intacc.2008.12.004

Chang, Y. T., Chen, H. C., Cheng, R. K., & Chi, W. C. (2019). The impact of internal audit attributes on the effectiveness of internal control over operations and compliance. *Journal of Contemporary Accounting & Economics, 15*(1), 1–19. doi:10.1016/j.jcae.2018.11.002

Chen, C. H., Li, T. Z., Shao, R. Q., & Zheng, S. X. (2019). Dynamics of deterioration in internal control reported under SOX 404. *International Review of Economics & Finance, 61*, 228–240. doi:10.1016/j.iref.2019.02.009

Chen, J., Chan, K. C., Dong, W., & Zhang, F. (2017). Internal control and stock price crash risk: Evidence from China. *European Accounting Review, 26*(1), 125–152. doi:10.1080/09638180.2015.1117008

Cheng, S. J., Felix, R., & Indjejikian, R. (2019). Spillover effects of internal control weakness disclosures: The role of audit committees and board connections. *Contemporary Accounting Research, 36*(2), 934–957. doi:10.1111/1911-3846.12448

Choi, H., Frye, M., & Yang, M. (2008). Shareholder Rights And The Market Reaction To Sarbanes Oxley. *The Quarterly Review of Economics and Finance, 48*(4), 756–771. doi:10.1016/j.qref.2007.01.001

Cialdini, R., & Goldstein, N. (2004). Social Influence: Compliance And Conformity. *Annual Review of Psychology, 55*(1), 591–621. doi:10.1146/annurev.psych.55.090902.142015 PMID:14744228

Coates, J. IV. (2007). The Goals and Promise of the Sarbanes-Oxley Act. *The Journal of Economic Perspectives*, *21*(1), 91–116. doi:10.1257/jep.21.1.91

Cowart, K. (2004). Sarbanes-Oxley Act: How a Current Model in the Law of Unintended Consequences May Affect Securities Litigation. *Duquesne Law Review*, *42*, 293–303.

Cremers, M., & Nair, V. B. (2005). Governance Mechanisms And Equity Prices. *The Journal of Finance*, *60*(6), 2859–2869. doi:10.1111/j.1540-6261.2005.00819.x

Cunningham, L. (2003). The Sarbanes-Oxley Yawn: Heavy Rhetoric, Light Reform (And It Just Might Work). *Connecticut Law Review*, *35*(3), 915–988.

Cutler, C. (2010). *Despite Ruling on Constitutionality, PCAOB (and SoX) Wins at Supreme Court.* https://www.subjecttoinquiry.com/pcaob/news/the-us-supreme-court-today/

Daub, F. (2007). *New Whistleblowing Regulations in the USA: How Sarbanes-Oxley failed to implement a working concept.* VDM Verlag Dr. Müller.

DeFond, M., & Lennox, C. (2017). Do PCAOB inspections improve the quality of internal control audits? *Journal of Accounting Research*, *55*(3), 591–627. doi:10.1111/1475-679X.12151

Delimatsis, P. (2012). *Of Bailouts and Rescue Measures: Subsidies in Financial Services.* Working Paper No 2012/24. Swiss National Center of Competence In Research. http://www20.iadb.org/intal/catalogo/PE/2012/12020.pdf

Dey, A. (2010). The chilling effect of Sarbanes–Oxley: A discussion of Sarbanes–Oxley and corporate risk-taking. *Journal of Accounting and Economics*, *49*(1-2), 53–57. doi:10.1016/j.jacceco.2009.06.003

Doring, T., & Schnellenbach, J. (2010). A tale of two federalisms: Germany, the United States and the ubiquity of centralization. *Constitutional Political Economy*, *22*(1), 83–102. doi:10.100710602-010-9096-2

Engelen, J. (2004). Criminal Behavior: A Real Option Approach With an Application to Restricting Illegal Insider Trading. *European Journal of Law and Economics*, *17*(3), 329–352. doi:10.1023/B:EJLE.0000028640.24757.5d

Flasher, R., & Schenck, K. (2019). Exploring PCAOB inspection results for audit firms headquartered outside of the US. [in-press.]. *Journal of International Accounting, Auditing & Taxation*, *37*, 37. doi:10.1016/j.intaccaudtax.2019.100287

Fogel, A., Nwokah, E., Dedo, J., Messinger, D., Dickson, K. L., Matusov, E., & Holt, S. A. (1992). Social Process Theory of Emotion: A Dynamic Systems Approach. *Social Development*, *1*(2), 122–142. doi:10.1111/j.1467-9507.1992.tb00116.x

Foley & Lardner LLP. (2007). *The Cost of Being Public in the Era of Sarbanes-Oxley.* Available at: http://www.foley.com/files/tbl_s31Publications/Fstudy The Cost of Being Public in the Era of Sarbanes-Oxley.ileUpload137/3736/Foley2007SOXstudy.pdf

Freeman, J. (2009). *The Supreme Case Against Sarbanes-Oxley.* Available at: http://online.wsj.com/article/NA_WSJ_PUB:SB10001424052748704431804574539921864252380.html

FSA (UK). (2012). *Review of The Markets in Financial Instruments Directive II.* Available at: http://www.fsa.gov.uk/about/what/international/mifid

Gao, H., & Zhang, J. (2019). SOX Section 404 and Corporate Innovation. *Journal of Financial and Quantitative Analysis*, *54*(2), 759–787. doi:10.1017/S0022109018000844

Gifford, R., & Howe, H. (2009). Regulation and Unintended Consequences: Thoughts on Sarbanes-Oxley. *The CPA Journal*. http://www.nysscpa.org/cpajournal/2004/604/perspectives/p6.htm

Gordon, I., & Nazari, J. (2018). Review of SOX in the business ethics literature. *Managerial Auditing Journal*, *33*(5), 470–502. doi:10.1108/MAJ-08-2017-1629

Greene, E., & Pierre-Mari, E. (2005). Post Sarbanes Oxley Corporate Governance In Europe And The USA: Americanization Or Convergence? *International Journal of Disclosure and Governance*, *1*(1), 21–34. doi:10.1057/palgrave.jdg.2040011

Grundfest, J., & Bochner, S. (2007). Fixing 404. *Michigan Law Review*, *105*, 1643–1666.

Gupta, P., & Leech, T. (2005). Making Sarbanes Oxley 404 Work: Reducing Cost, Increasing Effectiveness. *International Journal of Disclosure and Governance*, *3*(1), 27–48. doi:10.1057/palgrave.jdg.2040063

Harrison, J., Oler, D., & Allen, M. (2005). *Event Studies And The Importance Of Longer-Term Measures In Assessing The Performance Outcomes Of Complex Events*. Working paper.

Harshbarger, S., & Jois, G. (2007). Looking Back And Looking Forward: Sarbanes-Oxley And The Future Of Corporate Governance. *Akron Law Review*, *40*(1), 8–20.

Henk, O. (2020). Internal control through the lens of institutional work: A systematic literature review. *Journal Of Management Control*, *31*(3), 239–273. doi:10.100700187-020-00301-4

Hoffman, B., & Nagy, A. (2016). SOX 404(b) exemption effects on auditor changes. *Managerial Auditing Journal*, *31*(4/5), 387–402. doi:10.1108/MAJ-05-2015-1189

Huang, H., & Chong, G. (2016). Audit and legal implications of PCAOB's inspections among BRIC. *International Journal of Law and Management*, *58*(2), 231–244. doi:10.1108/IJLMA-03-2015-0012

Hughes, G. (1994). Administrative Subpeonas And The Grand Jury: Converging Streams Of Criminal And Civil Process. *Vanderbilt Law Review*, *47*, 573–583.

Hunter, B. (2007). *Punishing the Innocent: The Sarbanes-Oxley Act: The Law Has Inflicted Endless Losses on Businesses in Time and Money*. Available at: http://www.thefreemanonline.org/featured/punishing-the-innocent-the-sarbanes-oxley-act/#

IlievP. (2007). *The Effect of the Sarbanes-Oxley Act (Section 404) Management's Report on Audit Fees, Accruals and Stock Returns* (Brown University Working Paper). Available at: http://ssrn.com/abstract=983772

Institute of management Accountants. (2007). *Testimony On Application of Sarbanes Oxley Act In Small Companies*. Testimony to the Small Business Committee of the US House of Representatives Committee.

International Institute For Sustainable Development. (2009). *Will government bailouts lead to trade wars?* https://www.iisd.org/gsi/news/will-government-bailouts-lead-trade-wars

Jackson, C., Furnham, A., & Willen, K. (2000). Employer Willingness To Comply With The Disability Discrimination Act Regarding Staff Selection In The UK. *Journal of Occupational and Organizational Psychology*, *73*(1), 119–129. doi:10.1348/096317900166912

Jackson, J. (2004). The Effect Of Legal Culture And Proof In Decisions To prosecute. *Law Probability and Risk*, *3*(2), 109–121. doi:10.1093/lpr/3.2.109

Jahangar, A., Kamran, A., & Henry, D. (2004). Disclosure Compliance With National Accounting Standards By Listed Companies In South Asia. *Accounting and Business Research*, *34*(3), 183–199. doi:10.1080/00014788.2004.9729963

Jain, K., & Rezaee, Z. (2004). Industry-wide Effects Of The Sarbanes Oxley Act Of 2002. *Journal Of Forensic Accounting*, *6*, 147–162.

Jain, P., Kim, J., & Rezaee, Z. (2004). *The Effect Of The Sarbanes Oxley Act Of 2002 On Market Liquidity*. Presented at the *14th Annual Conference In Financial Economics and Accounting*.

Jain, P., Kim, J., & Rezaee, Z. (2006). Trends and Determinants Of Market Liquidity In The Pre- And Post Sarbanes Oxley Act Periods. Presented at the *14th Annual Conference In Financial Economics and Accounting*.

James, K. (2003). The Effects Of Internal Audit Structure On Perceive Financial Statement Fraud Prevention. *Accounting Horizons*, *17*(4), 315–327. doi:10.2308/acch.2003.17.4.315

John, D., & Marano, N. (2007). *The Sarbanes-Oxley Act: Do We Need a Regulatory or Legislative Fix*? Heritage Foundation. Available at: https://www.heritage.org/Research/Reports/2007/05/The-Sarbanes-Oxley-Act-Do-We-Need-a-Regulatory-or-Legislative-Fix; or http://s3.amazonaws.com/thf_media/2007/pdf/bg2035.pdf

Kamar, E., Karaca-Mandic, P., & Talley, E. (2007). *Sarbanes-Oxley and Small Firms: What is the Evidence?* USC CLEO Research Paper No. C07-9. USC Law Legal Studies Paper No. 07-8. Harvard Law & Economics Discussion Paper No. 588 (2007).

Kamar, E., Karaca-Mandic, P., & Talley, E. (2009). Going-Private Decisions and the Sarbanes-Oxley Act of 2002: A Cross-Country Analysis. *Journal of Law Economics and Organization*, *25*(1), 107–114. doi:10.1093/jleo/ewn019

Kang, Q., Liu, Q., & Qi, R. (2010). The Sarbanes-Oxley act and corporate investment: A structural assessment. *Journal of Financial Economics*, *96*(2), 291–305. doi:10.1016/j.jfineco.2010.02.002

Kim, B. (2003). Sarbanes-Oxley Act. *Harvard Journal on Legislation*, *40*, 235–248.

Kim, J. B., Yeung, I., & Zhou, J. (2019). Stock price crash risk and internal control weakness: Presence vs. disclosure effect. *Accounting and Finance*, *59*(2), 1197–1233. doi:10.1111/acfi.12273

Kim, S. M., & Kim, Y. (2017). Product market competition on the effectiveness of internal control. *Asia-Pacific Journal of Accounting & Economics*, *24*(1–2), 163–182. doi:10.1080/16081625.2015.1090323

Kingston, J., Schafer, B., & Vandenberghe, W. (2004). Towards A Financial Fraud Ontology: A Legal Modelling Approach. *Artificial Intelligence and Law, 12*(4), 419–446. doi:10.100710506-005-4163-0

Kleinman, G., Lin, B., & Palmon, D. (2020). Audit quality: A cross-national comparison of audit regulatory regimes. *Journal of Accounting, Auditing & Finance, 29*(1), 61–87. doi:10.1177/0148558X13516127

Kunst, P., & Wagner, R. (2011). Choice, emergence, and constitutional process: A framework for positive analysis. *Journal of Institutional Economics, 7*(1), 131–145. doi:10.1017/S1744137410000287

Langevoort, D. (2006). Internal Controls After Sarbanes–Oxley: Revisiting Corporate Law's "Duty Of Care As Responsibility For Systems". *The Journal of Corporation Law, 31*(3), 949–974.

Leech, T. (2003). *Sarbanes Oxley Sections 302 & 404: A White Paper Proposing Practical Cost Effective Compliance Strategies*. Working Paper.

Lentner, C., Vasa, L., Kolozsi, P. P., & Zeman, Z. (2019). New dimensions of internal controls in banking after the GFC. *Economic Annals-Xxi, 176*(3–4), 38–48. doi:10.21003/ea.V176-04

Leuz, C. (2007). Was the Sarbanes–Oxley Act of 2002 really this costly? A discussion Of Evidence From Event Returns And Going-private decisions. *Journal of Accounting and Economics, 44*(1-2), 146–165. doi:10.1016/j.jacceco.2007.06.001

Li, P., Shu, W., Tang, Q. Q., & Zheng, Y. (2019b). Internal control and corporate innovation: Evidence from China. *Asia-Pacific Journal of Accounting & Economics, 26*(5), 622–642. doi:10.1080/16081625.2017.1370380

Li, W., Han, Y., & He, J. (2019a). How does the heterogeneity of internal control weakness affect R&D investment? *Emerging Markets Finance and Trade*.

Linck, J., Netter, J., & Yang, T. (2009). The Effects And Unintended Consequences Of The Sarbanes Oxley Act On Corporate Boards. *Review of Financial Studies, 22*(8), 3287–3328. doi:10.1093/rfs/hhn084

Linsley, C. (2003). Auditing, Risk Management And A Post-Sarbanes Oxley World. *Review of Business, 24*(3), 21–25.

Litan, S. (2019). The COSO Internal Control Framework and Sustainability Reporting: The Benefits of Good Governance and Internal Controls. *The CPA Journal*. https://www.cpajournal.com/2019/07/29/the-coso-internal-control-framework-and-sustainability-reporting/

Litvak, K. (2007). The Effect of the Sarbanes-Oxley Act on Non-US Companies Cross-Listed in the US. *Michigan Law Review, 105*, 1857–1867.

Liu, S. (2005). Corporate Governance & Development: The Case Of China. *Managerial and Decision Economics, 26*(7), 445–449. doi:10.1002/mde.1257

Loehlein, L. (2017). Measuring the independence of audit oversight entities: a comparative empirical analysis. *Accounting Research Journal, 30*(2).

MacKinley, A. (1997). Event Studies In Economics & Finance. *Journal of Economic Literature, 35*(10), 13–39.

McWilliams, A., Siegel, D., & Teoh, S. H. (1999). Issues In The Use Of The Event Study Methodology: A Critical Analysis Of Corporate Social Responsibility Studies. *Organizational Research Methods, 2*(4), 340–365. doi:10.1177/109442819924002

Metelska-Szaniawska, K. (2010). Constitutions and economic reforms in transition: An empirical study. *Constitutional Political Economy, 20*(1), 1–41. doi:10.100710602-008-9049-1

Moberl, R. (2006). Sarbanes Oxley Structural Model To Encourage Whistleblowers. *Brigham Young University Law Review, 2006*(5), 1107–1180.

Mulligan, L. (2007). What's Good for the Goose Is Not Good for the Gander: Sarbanes-Oxley-Style Nonprofit Reforms. *Michigan Law Review, 105*, 1981–1991.

Muth, K. (2009). Sarbanes-Oxley Writ Large: Sarbanes-Oxley and the Foreign Commerce Clause. *Journal of International Business & Law, 8*, 29–39. http://www.karlmuth.com/uploads/Sarbanes-Oxley.pdf

Nagy, D. (2005). Playing Peekaboo with Constitutional Law: The PCAOB and Its Public/Private Status. *The Notre Dame Law Review, 80*, 975–1053.

Nielsen, P., & Main, C. (2004, October). Company Liability After The Sarbanes Oxley Act. *Insight: The Corporate & Securities Law Advisor, 18*(1), 1–10.

Niskanen, W. (2006). *Congress Should Repeal the Sarbanes-Oxley Act*. Cato Institute. Available at https://www.cato.org/pub_display.php?pub_id=6624

Nwogugu, M. (2004). Corporate Governance, Legal Reasoning And Credit Risk: The Case Of Encompass Services Inc. *Managerial Auditing Journal, 18*(4), 270–291. doi:10.1108/02686900310474299

Nwogugu, M. (2008). The Efficiency Of Sarbanes-Oxley Act: Willingness To Comply And Agency Problems. *Corporate Control & Ownership, 5*(1), 449–454. doi:10.22495/cocv5i1c3p5

Nwogugu, M. (2010/2013). *Problems Inherent In The Compensation And Business Models Of Credit Rating Agencies*. Working Paper.

Nwogugu, M. (2015a). Failure Of The Dodd-Frank Act. *Journal of Financial Crime, 22*(4), 520–572. doi:10.1108/JFC-11-2014-0053

Nwogugu, M. (2015b). Un-Constitutionality of The Dodd-Frank Act. *European Journal of Law Reform, 17*(1), 185–190. doi:10.5553/EJLR/138723702015017001007

Paletta, A., & Alimehmeti, G. (2018). SOX Disclosure and the Effect of Internal Controls on Executive Compensation. *Journal of Accounting, Auditing & Finance, 33*(2), 277–295. doi:10.1177/0148558X16630445

Pautz, M., & Washington, C. P. (2009). Sarbanes-Oxley and the Relentless Pursuit of Government Accountability: The Perils of 21st-Century Reform. *Administration & Society, 41*(6), 651–673. doi:10.1177/0095399709339011

Perino, M. (2004). American Corporate Reform Abroad: Sarbanes-Oxley and the Foreign Private Issuer. *European Business Organization Law Review, 4*(2), 213–244. doi:10.1017/S1566752903002131

Pollock, A. (2007). *Reforming Sarbanes-Oxley*. AEI (American Enterprise Institute). https://www.aei.org/speech/25803

Poretti, P. (2009). *The Regulation of Subsidies within the General Agreement on Trade in Services - Problems and Perspective*. Kluwer Law International.

Power, R., & Forte, D. (2005). Sarbanes-Oxley: Maybe A Blessing, Maybe A Curse. *Computer Fraud & Security*, *9*(9), 4–7. doi:10.1016/S1361-3723(05)70250-5

Prasad, A., & Webster, J. (2020). What Are the Trends in PCAOB Inspections and the Reported Audit Deficiencies? *Journal of Accounting, Auditing & Finance*.

Prentice, R., & Spence, D. (2005). Sarbanes-Oxley As Quack Corporate Governance: How Wise is the Received Wisdom? *The Yale Law Journal*, *114*, 1521–1611.

Public Company Accounting Oversight Board (PCAOB). (n.d.). https://www.sec.gov/answers/pcaob.htm. https://pcaobus.org/Pages/default.aspx

Recine, J. (2002). Examination Of The White Collar Crime Penalty Enhancements In The Sarbanes Oxley Act. *The American Criminal Law Review*, *39*, 1535–1570.

Reiser, D. (2004). *Enron.org: Why Sarbanes-Oxley Will Not Ensure Comprehensive Nonprofit Accountability*. Brooklyn Law School, Public Law Research Paper No. 6.

Rezzy, O. (2007). Sarbanes-Oxley: Progressive Punishment for Regressive Victimization. *Houston Law Review*, *44*(1), 95–105.

Ribstein, L. (2002). Market vs. Regulatory Responses to Corporate Fraud: A Critique of the Sarbanes-Oxley Act of 2002. *The Journal of Corporation Law*, *28*, 18–47. doi:10.2139srn.332681

Ribstein, L. (2003). International Implications Of Sarbanes Oxley: Raising The Rent On US Law. *Journal of Corporate Law Studies*, 299-309.

Richardson, A., & Welker, M. (2001). Social Disclosure, Financial Disclosure And The Cost OF Equity Capital. *Accounting, Organizations and Society*, *26*(7), 597–616. doi:10.1016/S0361-3682(01)00025-3

Romano, R. (2004). The Sarbanes-Oxley Act And The Making Of Quack Corporate Governance. *The Yale Law Journal*, *114*, 1521–1531.

Rose, P. (2005). Balancing Public Market Benefits and Burdens for Smaller Public Companies Post Sarbanes-Oxley. *Willamette Law Review*, *41*, 707–736.

Rouse, R., Weirich, T., & Hambleton, W. (2005, May/June). Sarbanes Oxley Update: Where Are We Today? *Journal of Corporate Accounting & Finance*, *16*(4), 61–65. doi:10.1002/jcaf.20120

Russell, K. (2010). *Provision Of Sarbanes-Oxley Un-Constitutionally Interferes With Presidential Authority*. https://www.scotusblog.com/2010/06/provision-of-sarbanes-oxley-unconstitutionally-interferes-with-presidential-authority/

Salky, S., & Rosman, B. (2004). *Is Sarbanes Oxley Vulnerable To Constitutional Challenge*? https://www.zuckerman.com/files/Publication/375468a3-d518-43e5-a6da-63474799822c/Presentation/PublicationAttachment/50441453-cd29-4d49-8dae-b030df75c042/media.88.pdf

Schaumann, N. (2004). The Sarbanes Oxley Act: Bird's Eye View. *William Mitchell Law Review*, *30*(4), 1316–1336. http://www.wmitchell.edu/lawreview/Volume30/Issue4/5Schaumann.pdf

Schiller, J. (2008). Deterring Obstruction of Justice Efficiently: The Impact of Arthur Andersen and the Sarbanes-Oxley Act. *NYU Annual Survey Of American Law*, *63*, 267–277.

Schroeder, J. H., & Shepardson, M. L. (2016). Do SOX 404 control audits and management assessments improve overall internal control system quality? *The Accounting Review*, *91*(5), 1513–1541. doi:10.2308/accr-51360

Shapiro, I., & Cushman, T. (2009). *Peekaboo, I See a Constitutional Violation*. Cato Institute. https://www.cato.org/pub_display.php?pub_id=11033

Shearman & Sterling. (2013). *Dodd-Frank, UK, EU & Other Regulatory Reforms*. https://www.shearman.com/dodd-frank/

Skouvakis, A. (2005). Note: Exiting the Public Markets - A difficult Choice for Small Public Companies Struggling with Sarbanes-Oxley. *Penn State Law Review*, *109*, 1279–1289.

Soederberg, S. (2008). A Critique of the Diagnosis and Cure for 'Enronitis': The Sarbanes-Oxley Act and Neo-Liberal Governance of Corporate America. *Critical Sociology*, *34*(5), 657–680. doi:10.1177/0896920508093362

Stiglitz, J. (1994). The Role Of The State In Financial Markets. In *Proceedings Of The World Bank Annual Conference On Development Economics*. Washington DC: World Bank.

Stiglitz, J., & Uy, M. (1996). Financial Markets, Public Policy And The East Asian Miracle. *The World Bank Research Observer*, *11*(2), 249–276. doi:10.1093/wbro/11.2.249

Sullivan, R., & Gouldson, A. (2017). The Governance of Corporate Responses to Climate Change: An International Comparison. *Business Strategy and the Environment*, *26*(4), 413–425. doi:10.1002/bse.1925

Tackett, J., Wolf, F., & Claypool, G. (2004). Sarbanes-Oxley And Audit Failure. *Managerial Auditing Journal*, *19*(3), 340–350. doi:10.1108/02686900410524355

Tackett, J., Wolf, F., & Claypool, G. (2006). Internal Control Under Sarbanes Oxley: A Critical Examination. *Managerial Auditing Journal*, *21*(3), 317–323. doi:10.1108/02686900610653044

Tang, S., & Demmeritt, D. (2018). Climate Change and Mandatory Carbon Reporting: Impacts on Business Process and Performance. *Business Strategy and the Environment*, *27*(4), 437–455. doi:10.1002/bse.1985

Taylor, C. (2006). Breaking the Bank: Reconsidering Central Bank of Denver after Enron And Sarbanes-Oxley. *Missouri Law Review*, *71*, 368–388.

Teles, V. (2004). The Effects Of Macroeconomic Policies On Crime. *Economic Bulletin*, *11*(1), 1–9.

Thelen, E. (2005). Dynamic Systems Theory And Complexity of Change. *Psychoanalytic Dialogues, 15*(2), 255–283. doi:10.1080/10481881509348831

Trujillo, E. (2010). International Trade and the Financial Crisis. [American Society of International Law]. *Proceedings of the Annual Meeting (American Association of University Teachers of Insurance), 104*, 438–443.

Udeh, I. (2017). Disclosure effects of the PCAOB part II reports. *Journal of Accounting & Organizational Change, 13*(4), 568–580. doi:10.1108/JAOC-11-2016-0070

Unger, C. (2007). Section 1103 of the Sarbanes-Oxley Act. *Western New England Law Review, 29*, 231–241.

US Chamber of Commerce's Commission On The Regulation of U.S. Capital Markets in the 21st Century. (n.d.). *March 2007 Report On US Capital Markets.* https://www.imanet.org/pdf/CMS.pdf

Valenti, A. (2007). The Sarbanes-Oxley Act of 2002: Has It Brought About Changes in the Boards of Large U. S. Corporations? *Journal of Business Ethics, 50*, 177–186.

Van Der Torre, L., & Tan, Y. (1994). Diagnosis And Decision Making In Normative Reasoning. *Artificial Intelligence and Law, 7*(1), 51–67. doi:10.1023/A:1008359312576

Van Geert, P. (1998). We Almost Has A Great Future Behind Us: The Contribution Of Non-Linear Dynamics To Developmental-Science-In-The-Making. *Developmental Science, 1*(1), 143–159. doi:10.1111/1467-7687.00020

Van Geert, P., & Steenbeek, H. (2005). Explaining After By Before: Basic Aspects Of A Dynamics Systems Approach To The Study Of Development. *Developmental Review, 25*(3-4), 408–442. doi:10.1016/j.dr.2005.10.003

Vancea, M. (2005). Exporting US Corporate Governance Standards Through The Sarbanes Oxley Act: Unilateralism Or Cooperation? *Duke Law Journal, 53*, 833–844.

Wade, C. (2008). The Sarbanes-Oxley Act and Ethical Corporate Climates: What the Media Reports; What the General Public Knows. *Brooklyn Journal of Corporate And Commercial Law, 2*, 421–431.

Wallace, P. (2009). Climate Change, Corporate Strategy, and Corporate Law Duties. *Wake Forest Law Review, 44*(3), 757–776.

Wang, F., Xu, L., Zhang, J., & Shu, W. (2018). Political connections, internal control and firm value: Evidence from China's anti-corruption campaign. *Journal of Business Research, 86*, 53–67. doi:10.1016/j.jbusres.2018.01.045

Wang, X. (2010). Increased Disclosure Requirements and Corporate Governance Decisions: Evidence from Chief Financial Officers in the Pre- and Post-Sarbanes-Oxley Periods. *Journal of Accounting Research, 48*(4), 885–920. doi:10.1111/j.1475-679X.2010.00378.x

Watnick, V. (2006). *Whistleblower Protections Under The Sarbanes-Oxley Act: A Primer And A Critique.* BE Press Legal Series Paper 1822. Working Paper, Baruch College, CUNY.

Wilford, A. L. (2016). Internal control reporting and accounting standards: A cross-country comparison. *Journal of Accounting and Public Policy*, *35*(3), 276–302. doi:10.1016/j.jaccpubpol.2015.12.006

Wilson, R., La See, A., & Choo, K. (2004). An Accountant's Defining Moments: Questionable Corporate Practices Before And After The Sarbanes-Oxley Act of 2002. *Journal of Economic Crime Management*, *2*(2), 1–7.

Witt, U., & Schubert, C. (2009). Constitutional interests in the face of innovations: How much do we need to know about risk preferences? *Constitutional Political Economy*, *9*(3), 203–225. doi:10.100710602-008-9044-6

Yakhou, M., & Dorweiler, V. (2005). Corporate Governance Reform: Impact On Accounting And Auditing. *Corporate Governance*, *5*(1), 39–44. doi:10.1108/14720700510583458

Zhang, I. (2007). Economic consequences of the Sarbanes–Oxley Act of 2002. *Journal of Accounting and Economics*, *44*(1-2), 74–115. doi:10.1016/j.jacceco.2007.02.002

ENDNOTES

1 *See*: Sarbanes-Oxley Act of 2002, Pub. L. No. 107-204, 116 Stat. 745 (codified at various sections of 11, 15,18, 28, and 29 U.S.C. (Supp. III 2003)). *See*: Nwogugu (2008), Butler & Ribstein (2006), Ribstein (2002), Iliev (2007), Litvak (2007) (compliance with SOX has had a net negative effect on the share prices of cross-listed foreign companies), Romano (2004), Bainbridge & Johnson (2004), Baynes (2002), Braddock (2006), Jain, Kim & Rezaee (2006), Kamar, Karaca-Mandic & Talley (2008), Zhang (2007), Burks (2010), Dey (2010), Chang & Sun (2009), Kang, Liu & Qi (2010), Bargeron, Lehn & Zutter (2010), Wang (2010), Leech (Nov. 2003), Linck, Netter & Yang (2009), Linsley (2003), McTamaney (august 2002), Nielsen & Main (Oct. 2004), Perin (October 2002), Recine (2002), Cunningham (2002), Coates (2007), Carrillo (2008), Unger (2007), Wade (2008), Tackett, Wolf & Claypool (2004), Soederberg (2008), Taylor (2006), Cowart (2004), Schiller (2008), and Pautz (2009). *See*: *FEI Survey: Management Drives Sarbanes-Oxley Compliance Costs Down by 23%, But Auditor Fees Virtually Unchanged.* Financial Executive International, May 16, 2007. A*vailable at:* http://fei.mediaroom.com/index.php?s=press_releases&item=187.

2 *See*: Skouvakis (2005), Grundfest & Bochner (2007), Backer (2004), Carney (2006), Gupta & Leech (2005), Engel, Hayes & Wang (2007), Bartlett (April 2008), Kamar & Karaca-Mandic (2006), Tackett, Wolf & Claypool (2006), and Rose (2005).

3 *See*: Nwogugu (2008); Ribstein (2002), Butler & Ribstein (2006), Iliev (2007), Litvak (2007), Ribstein (Oct. 2003), Romano (2004), Bainbridge & Johnson (2004), Baynes (2002), Braddock (2006), Jain, Kim & Rezaee (2006), Jain & Rezaee (2004), Kamar, Karaca-Mandic & Talley (2008), Zhang (2007), Burks (2010), Dey (2010), Chang & Sun (2009), Kang, Liu & Qi (2010), Bargeron, Lehn & Zutter (2010), Wang (2010), Coates (2007), Carrillo (2008), Unger (2007), Wade (2008), Tackett, Wolf & Claypool (2004), Soederberg (2008), Taylor (2006), Cowart (2004), Schiller (2008), and Pautz (2009). *See*: Sarbanes-Oxley Act of 2002, Pub. L. No. 107-204, 116 Stat. 745 (codified at various sections of 11, 15,18, 28, and 29 U.S.C. (Supp. III 2003)). *See*: *FEI Survey: Management Drives Sarbanes-Oxley Compliance Costs Down by 23%, But Auditor Fees Virtually Unchanged.*

Financial Executive International, May 16, 2007. *Available at:* http://fei.mediaroom.com/index.php?s=press_releases&item=187.

4 See: US Chamber Of Commerce, Center For Capital Markets Competitiveness (November 2007). "*Cost Of Sox 404 Survey*". See: Institute of management Accountants (June 5, 2007). *Testimony On Application of Sarbanes Oxley Act In Small Companies.* Testimony to the Small Business Committee of the US House of Representatives Committee.

5 See: The US Chamber of Commerce's Commission On The Regulation of U.S. Capital Markets in the 21st Century - *March 2007 Report On US Capital Markets.* http://www.imanet.org/pdf/CMS.pdf.

6 See the comments in: Tackett (2004); Duke (2003); Greene & Pierre-Marie (2005); Jahangar, Kamran & Henry (2004); Ge & McVay (2004); James (2003); Rezaee & Jain (2004); Cunningham (2003); Jain, Kim & Rezaee (March 2004); Klein (2003); Romano (2004); Carney (Feb. 2005) Nielsen & Main (Oct. 2004); Yakhou & Dorweiler (2005); Leung & Cooper (2003); Leech (Nov. 2003); Braddock (2006); Perino (October 2002); Moberly (2006); Cunningham (2004); Darley (2005); Linck et al (August 2005); Murphy (2003); Zhang (2007); Leuz (2007); Choi, Frye & Yang (2007/2008); Power & Forte (2005); Langevoort (2006); Brown (2006); Watnick (2006); Valenti (2007); Akerblad, Johansson & Jangvik (2007); Harshbarger & Jois (2007); Daub (2007); Prentice & Spence (2005); Taylor (2006); Hill (2005).

7 See: Free Enterprise Fund v. PCAOB, _____ *US ____ (2010; US Supreme Court case).* http://www.supremecourt.gov/opinions/09pdf/08-861.pdf. Justice Roberts delivered the, 5-4 opinion of the Court which stated in part: "The Board's existence does not violate the *separation of powers*, but the substantive removal restrictions imposed do. Concluding that the removal restrictions here are invalid leaves the Board removable by the Commission at will. The consequence is that the Board may continue to function as before, but its members may be removed at will by the [Securities and Exchange] Commission.". See: AccountingWeb (2010). Update: Supreme Court Rules PCAOB Violates Constitution's Separation of Powers Principle. http://www.accountingweb.com/topic/accounting-auditing/supreme-court-rules-pcaob-unconstitutional. See: Cutler, C. (June 10, 2010). Despite Ruling on Constitutionality, PCAOB (and SoX) Wins at Supreme Court. http://www.subjecttoinquiry.com/pcaob/news/the-us-supreme-court-today/. *See*: *Memorandum Of Proposed Intervenor United States In Opposition to Plaintiffs' Motion For Summary Judgment And In Support Of United States' Cross-Motion For Summary Judgment.* http://www.sec.gov/news/extra/2006/2006-147_brief.pdf. *See:* King, R. (Oct. 2009). *The PCAOB Meets the Constitution: The Supreme Court to Decide on PCAOB's Conformity with the Separation of Powers Doctrine and Appointments Clause.* http://www.olin.wustl.edu/docs/Faculty/KingCommentaryPCAOB-Submission.pdf. See: Public Company Accounting Oversight Board (PCAOB). http://www.sec.gov/answers/pcaob.htm. http://pcaobus.org/Pages/default.aspx. See: PCAOB (USA) (Nov. 2009). Board Approves Its 2010 Budget And Related Strategic Plan. http://pcaobus.org/News/Releases/Pages/11302009_Approves_Budget.aspx.

8 *See*: Bader, H. & Berlau, J. (Competitve Enterprise Institute) (Oct. 2005). *The Public Company Accounting Oversight Board: An Unconstitutional Assault on Government Accountability.* http://cei.org/pdf/4873.pdf.

9 See: Russell, K. (June 28, 2010). *Provision Of Sarbanes-Oxley Un-Constitutionally Interferes With Presidential Authority.* http://www.scotusblog.com/2010/06/provision-of-sarbanes-oxley-unconstitutionally-interferes-with-presidential-authority/.

10 *See*: Shapiro, I. & Cushman, T. (Dec. 5, 2009). *Peekaboo, I See a Constitutional Violation.* http://www.cato.org/pub_display.php?pub_id=11033. *See:* Birg, E. (2003). *Is the Public Company Accounting Oversight Board Constitutional?*, at pg. 6 Federalist Society for Law and Public Policy Studies, Corporate Responsibility Practice Group, 2003. http://www.fed-soc.org/Publications/Corpresp/ApptClauseFinal.pdf. (noting that: "Board members . . . are appointed by the SEC as a whole"). *See*: Wallison, ___ (May 12 2003). Rein In the Public Company Accounting Oversight Board; PCAOB Constitutionality Questioned. *Corporate Financing Week*, May 12, 2003, 29(19), 2003 WLNR 6489089. *See*: Nagy (2005) (noting that the PCAOB may violate the *Appointments Clause* and the constitutional *separation of powers*).

11 *See:* Schaumann (2004: 1319).

12 *See:* Schaumann (2004: 1319) which states in part "Formally, the Public Company Accounting Oversight Board (the "Board") is not an agency of the U.S. government; it is a nonprofit corporation organized under the District of Columbia Nonprofit Corporation Act. The Board comprises five members, of which two must—and only two may—be certified public accountants".

13 *See*: Niskanen, W. (2006). *Congress Should Repeal the Sarbanes-Oxley Act.* Cato Institute. Available at: http://www.cato.org/pub_display.php?pub_id=6624.

14 *See*: Shearman & Sterling (2013). *Dodd-Frank, UK, EU & Other Regulatory Reforms.* http://www.shearman.com/dodd-frank/.

15 *See*: Regulation 648/2012 on OTC derivatives, central counterparties and trade repositories [2012] OJ L201/1.

16 *See*: FSA (UK) (2012), Review of The *Markets in Financial Instruments Directive II. Available at:* http://www.fsa.gov.uk/about/what/international/mifid. *See*: DIRECTIVE 2008/10/EC OF THE EUROPEAN PARLIAMENT AND OF THE COUNCIL of 11 March 2008. Available at: http://eurlex.europa.eu/LexUriServ/LexUriServ.do?uri=OJ:L:2008:076:0033:0036:EN:PDF.

17 Directive 2006/48 relating to the taking up and pursuit of the business of credit institutions [2006] OJ L177/1.

18 *See:* "*China rating agency condemns rivals*" (2010) at http://www.ft.com/cms/s/0/5632a0b8-94b7-11df-b90e-00144feab49a.html [Accessed July 1, 2013] ("... the head of China's largest credit rating agency has slammed his western counterparts for causing the global financial crisis and said that as the world's largest creditor nation, China should have a bigger say in how governments and their debt are rated. 'The western rating agencies are politicized and highly ideological and they do not adhere to objective standards,' Last week, privately-owned Dagong published its own sovereign credit ranking in what it said was a first for a non-western credit rating agency. The results were very different from those published by Moody's, Standard & Poor's and Fitch, with China ranking higher than the United States, Britain, Japan, France and most other major economies, reflecting Dagong's belief that China is more politically and economically stable than all of these countries. 'The US is insolvent and faces bankruptcy as a pure debtor nation but the rating agencies still give it high rankings,' Mr Guan said. 'Actually, the huge military expenditure of the US is not created by themselves but comes from borrowed money, which is not sustainable.' A wildly enthusiastic editorial published by Xinhua, China's official state newswire, lauded Dagong's report as a significant step toward breaking the monopoly of western rating agencies of which it said China has long been a 'victim'. "Compared with the US's conquest of the world by means of force, Moody's has controlled the world through its dominance in credit rating" the editorial said First established in 1994, Dagong signed a three-year 'technology co-operation' agreement in 1999 with Moody's,

which provided the Chinese company with its 'core knowledge' and its first 'systemic understanding'"). *See*: Nwogugu M. (2010/2013). *Problems Inherent In The Compensation And Business Models Of Credit Rating Agencies*. Working Paper – available at www.ssrn.com.

19 Tang & Demmeritt (2018) noted that "Scholars and business analysts have offered a number of competing explanations for this expansion of corporate social responsibility (CSR) reporting about carbon, ranging from rational pursuit of cost savings (Kolk & Pinkse [2004]; Hoffman [2007]), brand differentiation (Delmas, et. al. [2006]; Matisoff, et. al. [2013]) or reputational gains (Hoffman [2005]) to coercive pressures from regulators (Levy & Egan [2003]; Lyon & Maxwell [2004]; Jones & Levy [2007]), institutional investors (Pfeifer & Sullivan [2008]; Knox-Hayes& Levy [2011]; Sullivan and Gouldson [2012]; Cotter and Najah [2012]) or environmental pressure groups (Stanny and Ely [2008]; Hahn, et. al. [2015]) and mimetic pressures to follow the latest corporate fashions in CSR (Sullivan [2008]; Ihlen [2009]). Some scholars argue that CSR practices such as carbon reporting not only minimize pollution and environmental harm, but also promote profitability, technological innovation, and wider economic competitiveness (Hajer [1995]; Mol, et. al. [2009]). Such ecological modernization promises to reconcile the imperatives of economic growth and profit with environmental protection, delivering win–win outcomes (Boiral, et al. [2012]; Gouldson & Sullivan [2012])".

Chapter 4
A Comparison of CRAs (Credit Rating Agencies), Management Consulting Firms, Environmental Auditing Firms, Tax Consulting Firms, and Auditing/Accounting Firms

ABSTRACT

This chapter compares CRAs (credit rating agencies), management consulting firms, environmental auditing firms, tax consulting firms, and auditing/accounting firms with the purpose of providing a better understanding of the current and possible regulatory, mechanism design, and industrial organization factors that can affect the global accounting/auditing industry and the global CRA industry. It also analyzes banks, credit rating agencies (CRAs), and investors as joint tortfeasors and co-conspirators (in litigation against accounting/auditing firms).

INTRODUCTION

The comparison of CRAs, audit-firms and consulting firms often revolves around the nature/structure of their contracts (employee contracts, client contracts, government relations; etc.).

Most of the theoretical and empirical studies on CRAs have completely omitted analysis of the nature of the relationship between the selected CRA(s) and the issuer's accounting/CPA firm ("CPA") that performs annual audits; as well as the reputational competition between CRAs and accounting firms. The CRA typically relies heavily on the issuer's audited financial statements. The CPA-firm and the CRA face reputation risk and potential legal liability when an issuer suddenly becomes financially distressed or files for bankruptcy or experiences other adverse shocks that are not reflected in its credit ratings

DOI: 10.4018/978-1-7998-7418-8.ch004

or audited financial statements. CPA firms face somewhat different competitive threats, regulation, cost structure and demand-curves compared to CRAs. First, the CPA industry is larger and much more fragmented than the CRA industry. The big-four accounting firms are much less dominant in the CPA industry than the top-four CRAs are in the CRA industry. Regional and local CPA firms account for a substantial portion of CPA industry revenues. Unlike credit ratings, there are almost no substitutes for annual audited financial statements. Unlike CRAs, CPAs' Human Capital is more diffused - ie. there is less focus on individual employees in CPA firms, than there is on ratings analysts in CRAs. CPA firms face much more regulation at the state and federal levels than CRA firms; and CPA firms often serve as active client advocates (at the US SEC and in Tax courts). CPA firms have more flexible cost structures than CRA firms (CPA firms can make a larger percentage of their costs to be variable costs), and unlike CRAs, CPA firms can outsource a significant amount of their audit work to other firms.

However, there are differences in the frequency and uses of credit ratings and audited financial statements. The audited financial statements are usually prepared annually and are used extensively in many aspects of the issuer's business. The CRA's credit ratings are prepared only on an as-needed basis and is used primarily in investment related matters. The level of verification required from the CPA is often greater than that of the CRA, but CRA accuracy requirements are greater than that of the CPA. However, while the CRA has a narrow range of classification (the ratings scales), the CPA has a much wider range of classification of companies. CPA switching costs are much greater than costs of switching CRAs.

Hence, the CRA and the CPA can either collude to prop up a failing company by issuing unjustified favorable reports, or to reduce the prospects (and Opportunity Set) of an otherwise healthy company. For any one issuer, the effort levels and commitment of the CPA and the CRA may also vary drastically. While it may be prudent to use a clearinghouse to select a CPA firm for an issuer, its impractical to do so for a CRA simply because the CPA firm and the CRA have very different *Information-Supply Curves* (the amount of information provided by the issuer), demand curves (the demand for the audited financial statement differs from demand for credit-ratings), cost structures, public-reliance, etc.

Given that the CRA often relies on the CPA's audited financial statements, the CRA can drag the CPA into court as a co-defendant or third-party defendant. Given these commonalities and somewhat symbiotic relationship between the CPA and the CRA, in many jurisdictions, there should be adequate regulations that govern: i) the relationship and flow of information between the CPA and the CRA of an issuer; ii) the allocation of liability between the CPA and CRA for inaccurate ratings and or fraud; iii) the allocation of liability between the CPA and CRA for collusion between them or among them and third parties; iv)

Thus, the optimal CRA contract should: i) reduce or eliminate illegal collusion between the CPA and CRA; ii) reward the CRA for low reliance on audited financial statements; iii) ensure that the issuer's decision to rate a financial instrument or to select a CRA is not influenced by the "type" of its CPA; iv) ensure that that CRA can obtain sufficient information from the CPA, including the audit work-papers; v) limit or modify the CRA's liability where it relies on the CPA's audited financial statement.

EXISTING LITERATURE

Contract Theory and *Mechanism Design Theory* have been jointly studied from various perspectives including Economics/Finance, Operations Research, Mathematical Psychology, Computer Science, Game Theory and Applied Math - see: Hoppe & Schmitz (2018), Niederhoff & Kouvelis (2019), Hong,

Wernz & Stillinger (2016), Wu, Zhao & Tang (2014), Li, Liu & Chen (2018), Lin & Chou (1990), Park & Kim (2014), Goetz, Yatsenko, et. al. (2019), Fang & Yuan (2018), Madureira, Pereira, et. al. (2014), Meneguzzi, Modgil, et. al. (2012), Meneguzzi, Modgil, Oren, et. al. (2011), Zohar & Rosenschein (2008), Terán, Aguilar & Cerrada (2017), Eenmaa-Dimitrieva & Schmidt-Kessen (2019), Drozd & Serrano-Padia (2018) and Wei, Wang, et.al. (2018). However, the models in most of these foregoing articles and literature are static, don't incorporate relevant variables; don't consider varying "states" and often complex "joint" effects of variables; and they don't consider Industrial Organization effects of contracts/mechanisms - see Nwogugu (2007;b), Nwogugu (2019a;b) and Nwogugu (2006).

Standardization of contracts can affect economic growth, Sustainability, Inequality and Economic Growth as noted by various academic researchers - see Sussman (1999), Van Assche & Schwartz (2013), Patterson (2010), Engert & Hornuf (2018), Aguirre (2017), Ayotte & Bolton (2011), Baffi (2007; 2012), He, Xue & Zhou (2019), Vo, Nguyen, et.al. (2019), Sheng (2019), Eenmaa-Dimitrieva & Schmidt-Kessen (2019), Dekker, Kawai & Sakaguchi (2018), Iossa & Martimort (2018) and Sprinkle, Williamson & Upton (2008). Sussman (1999) noted that "The main implications of contract standardization are that: (i) "financial history matters in the growth process; (ii) early formation of the system may create a drag on economic growth; and (iii) the effect may be non-monotonic because the system may be modernized at some point". In the realm of Accounting/Consulting firms, they have developed their own standardized contracts for ratings projects and the Big-Four accounting firms and the Big-even consulting firms are dominant.

A COMPARISON OF CRAS (CREDIT RATING AGENCIES), MANAGEMENT CONSULTING FIRMS, TAX CONSULTING FIRMS, ENVIRONMENTAL AUDITING FIRMS AND AUDITING/ACCOUNTING FIRMS.

The intent is to explain some the factors that affect the evolution, adaptation and structural changes in these four sectors of the global auditing/consulting industry. See Table-3 below. The nature and structure of the CRA industry makes it imperative that their *Fee-allocation Mechanism* be combined with their *Work-allocation Mechanism* – specifically for the following reasons:

1. Companies seek multiple ratings in variable period, whereas companies seek only one audit per audit year.
2. The useful-life of a credit rating is shorter and more variable than that of an annual audit report.
3. Ratings fees are smaller and can be more variable than audit fees.
4. The CRA industry is highly concentrated and is an oligopoly, whereas the audit industry is more fragmented.
5. Audit firms tend to maintain exclusive client relationships for longer periods; whereas each issuer-companies typically maintains active contractual relationships with several CRAs.

In the CRA industry, the *Fee-allocation system* (compensation model) and the *Work-allocation system* (business model) can and should be combined for the foregoing reasons and the following reasons:

1. Companies seek multiple ratings in variable period, whereas companies seek only one audit per audit year.

2. The useful-life of a credit rating is shorter and more variable than that of an annual audit report.
3. Credit ratings fees are smaller and can be more variable than audit fees.
4. The CRA industry is highly concentrated and is an oligopoly, whereas the audit industry is more fragmented.
5. Audit firms tend to maintain exclusive client relationships for longer periods; whereas each issuer-company typically maintains active contractual relationships with several CRAs.
6. The internal politics of Audits firms are or can be more intense and disruptive than that of CRAs. Audit firm partners often run fiefdoms.
7. The differences between CRAs and Audit-firms described in the table below (that compares Audit reports and credit ratings) also support the separation of auditors' Fee-allocation Mechanism from their Work-allocation Mechanism.
8. Companies seek multiple ratings in variable period, whereas companies seek only one audit per audit year.
9. The useful-life of a credit rating is shorter and more variable than that of an annual audit report.
10. Ratings fees are smaller and can be more variable than audit fees.
11. The CRA industry is highly concentrated and is an oligopoly, whereas the audit industry is more fragmented.
12. Audit firms tend to maintain exclusive client relationships for longer periods; whereas each issuer-companies typically maintains active contractual relationships with several CRAs.

The table below compares credit ratings with audited financial statements; and also compares CPA firms, CRAs, Management Consulting firms, independent Environmental-Auditing firms (especially those that are not affiliated with Accounting/Auditing firms) and Tax Consulting firms.

There is generally much greater Advisor-Entrenchment in the CPA/audit industry that in the CRA industry because of the above-mentioned reasons and also because of the costs that issuers face when then switch CPA firms. The type of Advisor-Entrenchment in the CPA/auditing industry is more pervasive and much more damaging than that in the CRA industry. Table-1 clearly shows that unlike CPA-Issuer relationships, it will be inefficient to use third-party platforms to match CRAs to issuers in both the short term and the long-term. Such matching can substantially reduce CRA effort and competition; and also create significant Producer Surpluses in the CRA industry.

Platform-Matching by random assignment, rotation of rating agencies, or performance-based metrics all reduce competition among CRAs because each such method does not enable the CRAs to compete based on quality/accuracy and free of monetary and profit concerns. Platform Matching is likely to increase collusion among CRAs – either by compelling them to migrate towards the same analytical models; or to synchronize their ratings. Having issuers select rating agencies is beneficial and stimulates competition only if all or a substantial portion of the ratings fees are not paid by such issuers – in such circumstances, CRAs will have incentives to compete based on quality.

Section-939F of the Dodd Frank Act expressly requires that the US SEC study the feasibility of a system wherein a board will assign CRAs to issuers; and to implement such system unless the US SEC can develop a better system. In December 2012, the US SEC[1] released the study requested by Section 939F, and in May 2013, the SEC sought public opinions about the CRA industry. The American Securitization Forum's[2] May 13, 2013 Letter to the US SEC opposed Platform Matching. Given Table-1 above, the Dodd Frank Act's proposed Platform-Matching system will not be feasible (and thus Section 15E(w) of the Exchange Act of 1934 should be repealed).

Table 1. Comparison Of Credit Ratings And CRAs On One Hand, With Audited Financial Statements And Auditing Firms, And Management Consulting Firms, Environmental-Auditing Firms And Tax Consulting Firms

Factor	Audited Financial Statements Prepared By CPA Firm	Credit Ratings Issued By CRA	Consulting Reports/ Recommendations Issued By Management Consulting Firms	Consulting Reports/ Recommendations Issued By Tax Consulting Firms	Reports Issued By Independent Environmental Auditing Firms
Location Of External Advisor	CPA firms' Staff typically work on-site at issuer's offices	Most of CRA's work is done within the CRA's offices.	Consulting firms' Staff typically work both at their own offices and on-site at clients' offices.	Consulting firms' Staff typically work both at their own offices and on-site at clients' offices.	Consulting firms' Staff typically work both at their own offices and on-site at clients' offices.
Duration of project	The annual audit usually takes 4-7 weeks, and is done around the end of the issuer's fiscal year	Each ratings project takes 2-4 weeks when ratings are requested by the issuer (solicited ratings); or when scheduled by the CRA (unsolicited ratings)	Each consulting project typically takes 2-26 weeks (and sometimes longer), depending on the subject matter	Each consulting project typically takes 2-26 weeks (and sometimes longer), depending on the subject matter	Each auditing project typically takes 2-26 weeks (and sometimes longer), depending on the subject matter
Information production by issuer/client	Issuer provides detailed confidential information to CPA firm - including its General ledger; contracts; legal opinions; correspondence/emails; receipts and invoices; etc.	Issuer provides limited information to the CRA including audited annual reports (solicited ratings); or for unsolicited ratings, the issuer may choose not to cooperate with the CRA, in which case the CRA will rely on only publicly available materials. Current proposals recommend that any CRA that works on a solicited rating will disseminate all information gathered from the issuer to other licensed CRAs.	The client company provides detailed confidential information to the consulting firm - including its board resolutions, financial data; marketing data; operations data; etc.	The client company provides detailed confidential information to the tax consulting firm - including its General ledger; contracts; legal opinions; financial data; correspondence/ emails; receipts and invoices; etc.	The client company provides detailed confidential information to the auditing firm - including its production processes; waste management processes; compliance records; financial data; correspondence/emails; receipts and invoices; etc.
"Useful-Life" of External Advisor's report	The audited annual financial statement has a useful life of 1-3 years; and very rare and limited revisions	The useful life of a CRA rating is generally until the CRA issues an updated report or ratings; or until another CRA issues a substantially different credit rating for the same issuer.	The useful life of a management consulting report varies drastically. The client may not re-hire the consulting firm, and may choose to ignore the recommendations.	The useful life of a tax filing is for the regulatory period and it may be amended by the client company or the consultant. The useful life of a tax opinion varies drastically depending on the situation and the client may not use the tax opinion.	The useful life of an environmental audit is for the regulatory period and it may be amended only by the auditing firm.
Substitutes for Class of Advisor report	None	Some substitutes include: i) the use of unlicensed CRAs; ii) the use of credit spreads; iii) use of reports from independent research companies; iv) use of probabilities-of-bankruptcy; v) leasing/ strategic-alliances/ Joint-Ventures; vi) use of in-house research analysts at institutional investors; etc.	Some substitutes include: i) the use of other consulting firms; ii) the use of in-house consulting teams, in-house internal audit teams and in-house strategic planning teams.	There are no substitutes for tax opinions. Some companies choose to do their own tax filings. Some substitutes tax consulting include: i) expanding the traditional annual audit to include tax questions; ii) the use of in-house internal audit teams.	"Self-auditing" is statutorily permitted in some jurisdictions/ countries, but otherwise, there are no substitutes.
Number of External Advisors' Reports per year	The annual audit report is typically produced only once per year by one CPA Firm.	Typically, 1-3 CRAs may provide one or more un-solicited ratings per financial instrument per year; and when necessary, the issuer typically requests for "solicited" ratings from 2-3 CRAs at the same time, and for each debt offering (the issuer may effect more than one debt offering in each year).	Theoretically, there is no limit.	Theoretically, there is no limit.	Theoretically, there is no limit. Some jurisdictions require a minimum number of audits in each regulatory period.
Issuer's Switching Costs	Very High - and switching CPA firms may affect the issuer's reputation and perceived solvency over the long term.	Very low - but the issuer faces the risk of a Big-Three CRA issuing a downgrade in retaliation. Any effect of switching on the issuer's reputation and perceived solvency are usually short-term.	Low to moderate - but the client faces reputation risk when it changes consulting firms. Some firms simultaneously use more than one consulting firm.	Low to moderate - but the client faces reputation risk when it changes consulting firms. Some firms simultaneously use more than one consulting firm.	Very high - but the client faces reputation risk when it changes auditing firms.

continued on following page

Table 1. Continued

Factor	Audited Financial Statements Prepared By CPA Firm	Credit Ratings Issued By CRA	Consulting Reports/ Recommendations Issued By Management Consulting Firms	Consulting Reports/ Recommendations Issued By Tax Consulting Firms	Reports Issued By Independent Environmental Auditing Firms
Level of Entrenchment by External Advisor	Very high; many client relationships are long term and are exclusive (i.e. all other auditing firms are excluded)	Medium; and client relationships are non-exclusive because for each debt offering, the issuer usually simultaneously requests for ratings from 2-3 of the Big-Three CRAs.	Low-to-Medium; and client relationships are non-exclusive and the client can simultaneously retain more than one consulting firm.	Medium; and client relationships are non-exclusive and the client can simultaneously retain more than one consulting firm.	Medium-to-high; and client relationships are usually exclusive.
Level of Governance in the Issuer-Advisor relationship	High level of governance of issuer-advisor relationship; and the CPA firm is highly regulated by the US SEC, the IRS; state government regulatory agencies; and professional associations.	Medium level of governance of issuer-advisor relationship; and the CRA is moderately regulated by only the US SEC.	Medium level of governance of issuer-advisor relationship; and the CRA is moderately regulated by only the US SEC.	Medium level of governance of issuer-advisor relationship; and the CRA is moderately regulated by only the US SEC.	Medium level of governance of issuer-advisor relationship; and in most jurisdictions, auditing firms are not regulated as environmental auditing firms although their principals/owners typically hold professional licenses such as engineering licenses.
Barriers To Entry	Moderate - requires government licensing at both the firm level and employee level. CPA firms have relatively moderate fixed costs and can outsource parts of the audit work.	High - requires government licensing at the firm level; and continuing education at employee level. CRA's have very high fixed costs and semi-fixed costs (compensation of analysts and support staff; general/administrative costs; marketing; IT infrastructure; etc.). CRAs typically don't outsource ratings analysis. The Big-Three CRAs have significant Reputational Capital and control more than 80% market-share. CRA Reputation also affects the pricing of fixed-income instruments; and clients of the Big-three CRAs that attempt to switch to other CRAs face the risk of downgrades in retaliation.	Low-to-moderate - doesn't require government licensing at the firm level; and doesn't require continuing education at employee level. Some management consulting firms outsource analysis. The Big-seven consulting firms have significant Reputational Capital and control more than 40% market-share. Consultant reputation also affects the pricing of consulting projects.	Low-to-moderate - some types of tax opinions and tax consulting (e.g. practice before government taxation agencies) require government licensing at the firm level; and require continuing education at employee level. Some tax consulting firms outsource analysis. The Big-seven consulting firms have significant Reputational Capital and control more than 40% market-share. Consultant reputation also affects the pricing of consulting projects.	Low-to-moderate - in some jurisdictions, state/ local governments require that principals/owners of environmental auditing firms hold professional licenses.
Advisor's Fees	Audit Fees are paid once a year; and audit fees cannot be contingent; and audit fees are negotiated between the CPA firm and the issuer. Fees are not regulated in most jurisdictions.	Issuers usually don't pay for unsolicited ratings. Issuers pay fees for solicited ratings. Most CRAs also earn subscription-fees from investors and non-issuers. Some researchers and the US GAO have recommended that part of CRA fees should be contingent (but that creates conflicts of interest). Fees are not regulated in most jurisdictions.	Management consulting Fees are usually paid in stages as the work is performed; and some consulting fees can be contingent. Consulting fees are negotiated between the consulting firm and the client. Fees are not regulated in most jurisdictions.	Tax Consulting Fees are usually paid in stages as the work is performed or once the project is completed. Some tax consulting fees can be contingent (e.g., a share of tax savings identified by the consultant, or a share of overpaid taxes that are recovered). Consulting fees are negotiated between the consulting firm and the client. Fees are not regulated in most jurisdictions.	Audit Fees are paid during or upon completion of environmental audit. Audit fees are negotiated between the client and the environmental auditing firm. Fees are not regulated in most jurisdictions.
Independence of External Advisor	Government statutes and trade association rules require Independence	Most of the current and proposed CRA compensation models create obvious conflicts-of-interest; and or significant incentives for CRAs to be biased.	Independence not statutorily required	Independence is required for some types of tax practices (e.g. practice before a government agency).	Independence is usually not regulated or required.
Any time limits on issuer-advisor relationship?	None	None	None	None	None

continued on following page

Table 1. Continued

Factor	Audited Financial Statements Prepared By CPA Firm	Credit Ratings Issued By CRA	Consulting Reports/ Recommendations Issued By Management Consulting Firms	Consulting Reports/ Recommendations Issued By Tax Consulting Firms	Reports Issued By Independent Environmental Auditing Firms
Does Platform Matching increase or reduce the ratio of the Marginal Reputation (MR) to Marginal Advisor Effort (MAE)? - i.e., MR/ MAE (ideally, MR/MAE should be between zero and one).	Platform Matching reduces the MR/MAE ratio.	Platform Matching reduces the MR/MAE ratio.	Platform Matching reduces the MR/MAE ratio.	Platform Matching reduces the MR/MAE ratio.	Platform Matching reduces the MR/MAE ratio.
Magnitude of differences in analytical procedures/ standards used by External Advisors	Very high uniformity -In the audit industry, the analytical methods used by audit firms are the same or very similar, and the minimum auditing standards are specified by state regulations and by industry trade associations such as the AICPA and state CPA associations. Thus, use of Platform Matching/Allocation is likely to have minimal effects on uniformity of analytical standards/ methods.	Very low uniformity - In the CRA industry, different CRAs use widely divergent analytical models. Industry trade associations don't specify analytical standards. Thus, using Platform Matching/ Allocation will not result in greater uniformity of analytical standards/ methods.	low-to-medium uniformity which is increasing - consulting firms use increasingly similar methods and analytical models. Industry trade associations don't specify analytical standards. Thus, using Platform Matching/ Allocation will not result in greater uniformity of analytical standards/methods.	Medium-to-high uniformity which is increasing - tax consulting firms use tax codes, practice standards and increasingly similar methods and analytical models for practice at government tax agencies. Thus, using Platform Matching/ Allocation will not result in greater uniformity of analytical standards/methods.	Medium-to-high uniformity which is increasing. Thus, using Platform Matching/ Allocation will not result in greater uniformity of analytical standards/ methods.
Importance of Client relationships to External Advisors	Client relationships are extremely important to CPA/auditing firms. There are many CPA firms; and the Big-4 CPA firms are less dominant in the CPA industry, than the Big-3 CRA firms are in the CRA industry.	Client relationships are or can be of low importance to the Big-three CRA firms - because of their Reputational Capital and because there are relatively very few CRAs. Issuers typically simultaneously request for ratings from 2-3 of Big-3 CRAs; and issuers that don't cooperate face ratings downgrades by the CRAs.	Client relationships are extremely important to management consulting firms. It's an oligopoly and there are many consulting firms; and the Big-7 consulting firms are less dominant in the management consulting industry, than the Big-3 CRA firms are in the CRA industry.	Client relationships are extremely important to tax consulting firms. It's an oligopoly and there are many tax consulting firms; and the Big-7 consulting firms are less dominant in the tax consulting industry, than the Big-3 CRA firms are in the CRA industry.	Client relationships are extremely important to environmental auditing firms. It's a very fragmented sector and there are many firms.
Are revenues from the Advisor's clients concentrated?	Yes - one single audit client can account for a significant portion of the CPA firm's total annual revenues. Thus, Platform Matching can help reduce such revenue concentration which breeds collusion, fraud and low-quality.	No - Client revenues are dispersed. Each Big-three CRA rates hundreds or thousands of securities and financial-instruments in each year. For each of the Big-three CRAs, no issuer or issuer-group accounts for more than 3% (three percent) of the CRA's gross annual revenues from the ratings business. Thus, Platform Matching will have minimal effects on revenue concentration in each of the Big-three CRAs, and small CRAs.	Yes - one single management consulting client can account for a significant portion of the consulting firm's total annual revenues. Thus, Platform Matching can help reduce such revenue concentration which breeds collusion, fraud and low-quality.	Yes - one single tax consulting client can account for a significant portion of the consulting firm's total annual revenues. Thus, Platform Matching can help reduce such revenue concentration which breeds collusion, fraud and low-quality.	Yes - one single auditing client can account for a significant portion of the environmental auditing firm's total annual revenues. Thus, Platform Matching can help reduce such revenue concentration which breeds collusion, fraud and low-quality.
Audience for Advisor's reports	Large audience - that covers almost all aspects of the issuer's business operations.	Large audience that consists of investors, regulators, suppliers, customers, competitors and some business partners.	The client's senior executives and board members. The audience is smaller and the impact of their work is less perceptible than those of audit firms and CRAs.	The client's senior executives and board members. The audience is smaller and the impact of their work is less perceptible than those of audit firms and CRAs.	The client's senior executives and board members; government agencies; shareholders and organizations that report on CSR and environmental management practices and compliance. The economic effects of the audit report can be significant.

continued on following page

Table 1. Continued

Factor	Audited Financial Statements Prepared By CPA Firm	Credit Ratings Issued By CRA	Consulting Reports/ Recommendations Issued By Management Consulting Firms	Consulting Reports/ Recommendations Issued By Tax Consulting Firms	Reports Issued By Independent Environmental Auditing Firms
Does Platform Matching/Allocation reduce collusion	Yes - because it reduces Entrenchment (and thus creates a type of quasi per-review system wherein the replacement CPA firm reviews the work of the prior CPA firm); and the issuer hires only one CPA firm for each annual audit or review. State CPA regulations limit opportunities for collusion. Also, the fee/risk tradeoff is very high - any colluding CPA firm takes a lot of risk (revocation of license and the loss of audit-type fees) for relatively substantial one-time annual fees.	No - even after Platform Matching, the CRA can still collude (with other CRAs, the issuer, the securitization sponsor, the investment bank or investors) at the same or higher rate than without Platform Matching. The issuer typically hires 2-3 CRAs simultaneously for each debt offering and apart from the matched-CRA (licensed CRA), the issuer can also simultaneously hire an un-licensed CRA. The fee/ risk tradeoff is low - any colluding CRA takes low risk (loss of CRA license) for relatively substantial fees (fees for many ratings).	Yes - because it reduces Entrenchment (and thus creates a type of quasi per-review system wherein the replacement consulting firm reviews the work of the prior consulting firm). Also, the fee/risk tradeoff is very high - any colluding consulting firm takes a lot of risk (the loss of reputation and consulting fees).	Yes - because it reduces Entrenchment (and thus creates a type of quasi per-review system wherein the replacement CPA firm reviews the work of the prior CPA firm). Tax consultants can still collude with the client's executives and suppliers. Government tax agency regulations can limit opportunities for collusion. Also, the fee/risk tradeoff is very high - any colluding consulting firm takes a lot of risk (revocation of license and the loss of tax consulting fees).	Yes - because it reduces Entrenchment (and thus creates a type of quasi per-review system wherein the replacement auditing firm reviews the work of the prior auditing firm). Auditing firms can still collude with the client's executives and suppliers. "Self-auditing" remains a problem. Government regulations can limit opportunities for collusion. Also, the fee/risk tradeoff is very high - any colluding auditing-firm takes a lot of risk (revocation of contract; blacklisting by government agencies, and the loss of fees).
Does Platform Matching/Allocation increase competition among External Advisors ?	Yes - because there are many CPA firms, and each issuer typically requests for only one annual audit from one CPA, and audit fees are much higher than ratings fees, Platform Matching typically reduces entrenchment and can foster competition among CPA firms.	No. Since there are relatively few CRAs (and the Big-three CRAs have substantial Reputational Capital) and each issuer typically requests for ratings from 2-3 CRAs at a time, most recommended Platform Matching models will increase the probability that each participating CRA will achieve a minimum amount of revenues in each year while reducing competition among CRAs; which in turn reduces, or can reduce CRAs' effort.	Yes - because there are many management consulting firms, and each client can simultaneously retain more than one management consulting firm. Platform Matching can reduce entrenchment and can foster competition among consulting firms.	Yes - because there are many tax consulting firms, and each client can simultaneously retain more than one management consulting firm. Platform Matching can reduce entrenchment and can foster competition among consulting firms.	Yes. Platform Matching can reduce entrenchment and can foster competition among auditing firms.
Does Platform Matching reduce the mobility of the External Advisor's employees ?	Yes - the partners and senior managers of CPA firms are subject to state CPA practice rules, and trade-association rules that limit their ability to work at other CPA firms; or to collude with other CPA firms.	No - employees of CRAs can move freely to work at other CRAs and other firms. This increases the potential for illegal collusion among CRAs.	No - employees of management consulting firms can move freely to work at other firms. That can increase the potential for illegal collusion among consulting firms and between a consulting firm and its clients.	No - employees of tax consulting firms can move freely to work at other firms. That can increase the potential for illegal collusion among consulting firms and between a consulting firm and its clients.	No - employees of auditing firms can move freely to work at other firms. That can increase the potential for illegal collusion among auditing firms and between an auditing firm and its clients.
Does Platform Matching/allocation increase the actual and perceived Fairness of External Advisors' Fees ?	Yes - if the Platform has accurate information about the cost structure of the CPA firms; and even more probable if the Platform also sets CPA fees.	Yes, only if the Platform has accurate information about the cost structure of the licensed CRAs and also sets ratings fees; and the Platform also regulates or limits or sets the separate Subscription fees that the CRA charges to users of its data (note that the cost structure of CRAs are more likely to vary widely that those of CPA firm, because CRAs use more diverse methods and procedures).	Yes - if the Platform has accurate information about the cost structure of the management consulting firms; and even more probable if the Platform also sets consulting fees.	Yes - if the Platform has accurate information about the cost structure of the tax consulting firms; and even more probable if the Platform also sets tax consulting fees.	Yes - if the Platform has accurate information about the cost structure of the auditing firms; and even more probable if the Platform also sets audit fees.

continued on following page

Table 1. Continued

Factor	Audited Financial Statements Prepared By CPA Firm	Credit Ratings Issued By CRA	Consulting Reports/ Recommendations Issued By Management Consulting Firms	Consulting Reports/ Recommendations Issued By Tax Consulting Firms	Reports Issued By Independent Environmental Auditing Firms
Does Platform Matching reduce Consumer Surplus or Producer Surplus ?	Yes; Platform Matching reduces both Consumer Surplus or Producer Surplus, particularly where the Platform obtains accurate information about the cost structure of CPA firms, and or the Platform also determines/limits the CPA firm's fees.	Where the Platform sets the ratings fees (in addition to Matching), it can reduce Consumer Surplus and Producer Surplus, but only if the Platform has access to information about the cost structure of many CRAs.	Where the Platform sets the fees (in addition to Matching), it can reduce Consumer Surplus and Producer Surplus, but only if the Platform has access to information about the cost structure of many participating firms.	Where the Platform sets the fees (in addition to Matching), it can reduce Consumer Surplus and Producer Surplus, but only if the Platform has access to information about the cost structure of many participating firms.	Where the Platform sets the fees (in addition to Matching), it can reduce Consumer Surplus and Producer Surplus, but only if the Platform has access to information about the cost structure of many participating firms.
Does Platform Matching change or increase Strategic Complementarity?	Yes - Platform Matching can change or substantially increase Strategic Complementarity because of the nature of the relationships among the relatively few players (issuer; one CPA firm; regulators).	It's much less likely that Platform Matching will change or increase Strategic Complementarity because there are relatively many active players (issuer; several CRAs that issue solicited and un-solicited ratings; CPA firm; investment bank; securitization sponsor; investors; government regulators) who often have divergent interests, and whose payoff functions are often partially or substantially dependent on un-related parties (thus, multiple equilibria is possible). Stability is low/weak because their incentives to deviate from any equilibrium are or can be significant and often cannot be changed by other active participants.	It's much less likely that Platform Matching will change or increase Strategic Complementarity because there are relatively many active players (issuer; several consulting firms; CPA firm; investment bank; securitization sponsor; investors; government regulators) who often have divergent interests, and whose payoff functions are often partially or substantially dependent on un-related parties (thus, multiple equilibria is possible). Stability is low/weak because their incentives to deviate from any equilibrium are or can be significant and often cannot be changed by other active participants.	It's much less likely that Platform Matching will change or increase Strategic Complementarity because there are relatively many active players (issuer; several consulting firms; CPA firms; investment bank; investors; government regulators) who often have divergent interests, and whose payoff functions are often partially or substantially dependent on un-related parties (thus, multiple equilibria is possible). Stability is low/weak because their incentives to deviate from any equilibrium are or can be significant and often cannot be changed by other active participants.	It's much less likely that Platform Matching will change or increase Strategic Complementarity because there are relatively many active players (issuer; several auditing firms; investors; government regulators) who often have divergent interests, and whose payoff functions are often partially or substantially dependent on un-related parties (thus, multiple equilibria is possible). Stability is low/weak because their incentives to deviate from any equilibrium are or can be significant and often cannot be changed by other active participants.
Can the External Advisor outsource its workload?	Yes. Audit procedures are standardized and the value of the audit report is not heavily dependent on the Reputation of individual CPA partner or senior managers.	No - CRA contracts are typically specific to the CRA. The value of the ratings heavily depends on the reputation of individual ratings analysts.	Yes, but sometimes the value of the advice heavily depends on the reputation of the consulting firm.	Yes, but sometimes the value of the advice heavily depends on the reputation of the consulting firm.	Yes, but sometimes the value of the audit report heavily depends on the reputation of the auditing firm.

continued on following page

Table 1. Continued

Factor	Audited Financial Statements Prepared By CPA Firm	Credit Ratings Issued By CRA	Consulting Reports/ Recommendations Issued By Management Consulting Firms	Consulting Reports/ Recommendations Issued By Tax Consulting Firms	Reports Issued By Independent Environmental Auditing Firms
Any Tie-breaker Effect ? And if so, the value of Tie-Breaker Effect	Not applicable (the client hires only one CPA firm for the annual audit).	Potential for Tie-breaker Effect - Most types of Platform Matching will prevent issuers from obtaining "Tie-Breaker" ratings; unless the Platform-Matching system allows each issuer to obtain ratings from more than one CRA for each debt offering; or if regulations permit a matched-issuer to also obtain a rating from an unlicensed CRA. Platform Matching will probably compel issuers to retain non-certified ratings companies. Thus, Platform Matching amplifies the demand for Tie-Breaker Ratings which in turn increases the likelihood of fraud and collusion in the ratings process. The demand for Tie-Breaker ratings can be reduced or eliminated only by making it economically feasible/profitable for all or most of the certified CRAs to provide ratings for each debt offering - in the long run (and perhaps even in the short run), this approach can reduce the regulation-driven and market-power-driven reputational disparities between the Big-three CRAs and the smaller CRAs.	Potential for Tie-breaker Effect - Most types of Platform Matching will prevent issuers from obtaining "Tie-Breaker" ratings; unless the Platform-Matching system allows each issuer to obtain ratings from more than one CRA for each debt offering; or if regulations permit a matched-issuer to also obtain a rating from an unlicensed CRA. Platform Matching will probably compel issuers to retain non-certified ratings companies. Thus, Platform Matching amplifies the demand for Tie-Breaker Ratings which in turn increases the likelihood of fraud and collusion in the ratings process. The demand for Tie-Breaker ratings can be reduced or eliminated only by making it economically feasible/profitable for all or most of the certified CRAs to provide ratings for each debt offering - in the long run (and perhaps even in the short run), this approach can reduce the regulation-driven and market-power-driven reputational disparities between the Big-three CRAs and the smaller CRAs.	Potential for Tie-breaker Effect - Most types of Platform Matching will prevent issuers from obtaining "Tie-Breaker" ratings; unless the Platform-Matching system allows each issuer to obtain ratings from more than one CRA for each debt offering; or if regulations permit a matched-issuer to also obtain a rating from an unlicensed CRA. Platform Matching will probably compel issuers to retain non-certified ratings companies. Thus, Platform Matching amplifies the demand for Tie-Breaker Ratings which in turn increases the likelihood of fraud and collusion in the ratings process. The demand for Tie-Breaker ratings can be reduced or eliminated only by making it economically feasible/profitable for all or most of the certified CRAs to provide ratings for each debt offering - in the long run (and perhaps even in the short run), this approach can reduce the regulation-driven and market-power-driven reputational disparities between the Big-three CRAs and the smaller CRAs.	Not applicable.
Can Platform Matching reduce *Deadweight Losses* ?	Yes.	No.	No.	No.	Yes
Can Platform-Matching increase Advisors' accuracy and or effort ?	Yes - by reducing CPA Entrenchment (which in turn, provides incentives for CPA firms to increase their efforts); and by instituting a type of sequential peer-review system (succeeding CPA firm reviews the work of the prior CPA firm); and by providing more CPA firms with access to a broader range of clients.	No - not necessarily because CRAs can issue un-solicited ratings; and issuers can migrate downwards to unlicensed CRAs.	Yes	Yes	Yes - by reducing Entrenchment (which in turn, provides incentives for advisor firms to increase their efforts); and by instituting a type of sequential peer-review system (succeeding auditing firm reviews the work of the prior auditing firm); and by providing more auditing firms with access to a broader range of clients.
Can Platform-Matching reduce the Advisor's Marginal Cost of providing services ?	Yes - by reducing CPA Entrenchment; and by increasing the probability of generating revenues, and by providing more CPA firms with access to a broader range of clients, the CPA firm has a better chance of achieving knowledge effects (which reduces marginal costs), and can reduce its client-acquisition expenses.	No - not necessarily because CRAs can and do issue un-solicited ratings; and issuers can migrate downwards to unlicensed CRAs.	Yes - by reducing advisor Entrenchment; and by increasing the probability of generating revenues, and by providing more advisor firms with access to a broader range of clients, the advisor firm has a better chance of achieving knowledge effects (which reduces marginal costs), and can reduce its client-acquisition expenses.	Yes - by reducing advisor Entrenchment; and by increasing the probability of generating revenues, and by providing more advisor firms with access to a broader range of clients, the advisor firm has a better chance of achieving knowledge effects (which reduces marginal costs), and can reduce its client-acquisition expenses.	Yes - by reducing advisor Entrenchment; and by increasing the probability of generating revenues, and by providing more advisor firms with access to a broader range of clients, the advisor firm has a better chance of achieving knowledge effects (which reduces marginal costs), and can reduce its client-acquisition expenses.

continued on following page

Table 1. Continued

Factor	Audited Financial Statements Prepared By CPA Firm	Credit Ratings Issued By CRA	Consulting Reports/ Recommendations Issued By Management Consulting Firms	Consulting Reports/ Recommendations Issued By Tax Consulting Firms	Reports Issued By Independent Environmental Auditing Firms
Can Platform-Matching reduce the Advisor's Fixed Cost of providing services ? And or the variability of such fixed costs ?	Yes - where revenues are more predictable and more stable, the CPA firm can reduce its fixed costs. Also, because Platform Matching reduces excessive reliance on client relationships, the CPA firm can outsource more of its work and reduce its fixed costs.	No - even where revenues are more predictable and more stable, since the client can choose to migrate downwards to unlicensed CRAs or choose not to rate the security/ instrument, the CRA still incurs marketing/ advertising costs and other costs and may have to increase its fixed costs. Also, the CRA's reputation is linked to the personal Reputations of its individual Industry Research Analysts, and so the CRA cannot or does not outsource a substantial portion of its fixed labor costs. The low standardization of ratings methodology which reduces the possibility of outsourcing or reducing fixed costs.	Yes - where revenues are more predictable and more stable, the advisor firm can reduce its fixed costs. Also, because Platform Matching reduces excessive reliance on client relationships, the advisor firm can outsource more of its work and reduce its fixed costs.	Yes - where revenues are more predictable and more stable, the advisor firm can reduce its fixed costs. Also, because Platform Matching reduces excessive reliance on client relationships, the advisor firm can outsource more of its work and reduce its fixed costs.	Yes - where revenues are more predictable and more stable, the advisor firm can reduce its fixed costs. Also, because Platform Matching reduces excessive reliance on client relationships, the advisor firm can outsource more of its work and reduce its fixed costs.
Can Platform Matching affect the Advisor's variable costs of providing other services (such as tax services and valuation services by CPA firms; and in the case of CRAs, research reports, Index services and securities valuation services) ?	Yes - Platform Matching increases the knowledge of the average CPA firm and with or without outsourcing, can reduce the CPA firm's variable costs.	No. Platform-Matching does not reduce the CRA's variable costs of providing research reports, Index services and or valuation services.	Yes - Platform Matching can increase the knowledge of the average advisor firm and with or without outsourcing, can reduce the advisor firm's variable costs.	Yes - Platform Matching can increase the knowledge of the average advisor firm and with or without outsourcing, can reduce the advisor firm's variable costs.	Yes - Platform Matching can increase the knowledge of the average advisor firm and with or without outsourcing, can reduce the advisor firm's variable costs.
Can Platform Matching reduce the probability of *Multiple Equilibria* in the services sub-market ?	Yes - Platform Matching can increase the knowledge of the average advisor firm and with or without outsourcing, can reduce the advisor firm's variable costs.	No - because CRAs can and do issue un-solicited ratings; and an issuer can obtain ratings simultaneously from two or more CRAs; and issuers can migrate downwards to unlicensed CRAs.	Yes, in some cases - particularly where the Platform also sets the maximum consulting fees; and Side-payments and collusion are statutorily banned.	Yes, in some cases - particularly where the Platform also sets the maximum consulting fees; and Side-payments and collusion are statutorily banned.	Yes, in some cases - particularly where the Platform also sets the maximum fees; and Side-payments and collusion are statutorily banned.
Can Platform Matching reduce the probability of *Multiple Equilibria* in the investment markets ?	Yes - particularly where the Platform also sets the CPA firm's maximum fees. There is only one annual audited financial statement, and to the extent Platform Matching increases the CPA firm's effort and accuracy, the probability of Multiple Equilibria can be reduced.	Yes in most cases because it reduces Entrenchment. However, CRAs can and do issue un-solicited ratings; and issuers can migrate downwards to unlicensed CRAs. Even where the Matching System allocates 2-3 licensed CRAs to an issuer for a rating, the issuer can still migrate downwards to unlicensed CRAs. Ratings are not the only investment consideration, and most institutional investors employ in-house research analysts that provide similar credit evaluations. Independent non-CRA research companies provide credit research reports.	Yes	Yes	Yes - particularly where the Platform also sets the advisor firm's maximum fees. To the extent Platform Matching increases the advisor firm's effort and accuracy, the probability of Multiple Equilibria can be reduced.

continued on following page

Table 1. Continued

Factor	Audited Financial Statements Prepared By CPA Firm	Credit Ratings Issued By CRA	Consulting Reports/ Recommendations Issued By Management Consulting Firms	Consulting Reports/ Recommendations Issued By Tax Consulting Firms	Reports Issued By Independent Environmental Auditing Firms
Can Platform Matching Increase Social Welfare ?	Yes - the benefits of reducing Entrenchment of CPA firms far outweighs any reduction of competition that arises from implementation of any Platform-Matching system. Platform Matching can increase the probability that each CPA firm will gain exposure to more clients, and that increases competition for non-audit services.	No - CRAs can issue unsolicited ratings; and issuers can choose not to obtain any ratings; and issuers can migrate downwards to unlicensed CRAs. There are substitutes for ratings.	Yes - the benefits of reducing Entrenchment of advisor firms far outweighs any reduction of competition that arises from implementation of any Platform-Matching system. Platform Matching can increase the probability that each advisor firm will gain exposure to more clients, and that increases competition.	Yes - the benefits of reducing Entrenchment of advisor firms far outweighs any reduction of competition that arises from implementation of any Platform-Matching system. Platform Matching can increase the probability that each advisor firm will gain exposure to more clients, and that increases competition.	Yes - the benefits of reducing Entrenchment of advisor firms far outweighs any reduction of competition that arises from implementation of any Platform-Matching system. Platform Matching can increase the probability that each advisor firm will gain exposure to more clients, and that increases competition.

Source: Michael I. C. Nwogugu (author).

BANKS, CRAs, AND INVESTORS AS JOINT TORTFEASORS AND CO-CONSPIRATORS IN LITIGATION/CLAIMS AGAINST AUDITING FIRMS AND CONSULTING FIRMS

Banks and Credit Rating Agencies (CRAs) also function as quasi-auditors because they also receive confidential documents from, and perform due diligence on prospective borrowers. Banks and the top CRAs (Moody's, S&P and Fitch) are regulated entities, and are statutorily required to report earnings management and inadequate disclosures by their customers to government agencies. More importantly, the public and regulators formally and informally rely on the judgment and lending decisions of banks and CRAs as indicators of existence of earning management and or asset-quality management and or inadequate disclosures (note that liability for inaccurate credit ratings differs substantially for liability for earnings management and inadequate disclosures).

From a tort theory perspective, the following factors are notable. *First*, imposing liability on Banks, CRAs and "Sophisticated Investors" improves social welfare, and will compel such persons to conduct more thorough due diligence and monitor their investee-companies. *Second*, the benefits of compelling banks, CRAs and "Sophisticated Investors" to monitor companies for earnings management and fraud far outweigh the costs of resolving earnings management disputes or prosecuting perpetrators. *Third*, the costs of eliminating the possibility of imposing liability on Banks and CRAs far outweighs the cost of imposing liability on them. *Fourth*, banks and CRAs can become joint tortfeasors and criminal conspirators if the companies provide sufficient incentives. *Fifth*, banks and CRAs have a moral and statutory duty to identify and report inaccurate/inadequate disclosures, earnings management and asset quality management. *Sixth*, failure to impose liability on banks and CRAs may trigger Constitutional-Tort liability for governments. *Seventh*, Strict-Liability applies. *Eighth*, public welfare considerations should be priority (ie. bank failures due to inaccurate disclosures; wrong credit ratings which cause contagion in debt markets; inability of companies and governments to raise capital due to investors' fears; etc.). *Ninth*, the compensation structure of CRAs and their analysts combined with the low customer-switching costs and plurality of ratings (most customers simultaneously obtain more than one rating) provides sufficient incentives for CRAs to cover-up earnings management and fraud in order to retain clients. Furthermore, CRAs face significant Reputation Costs if a rated company is subsequently found to have engaged in earnings management – this also provides additional incentives for CRAs to collude in earnings management and fraud. Note that CRAs' liability for inaccurate credit ratings differs substantially from CRAs' liability for earning management and or asset-quality management. In most jurisdictions, CRAs cannot be held liable for inaccurate credit ratings. *Tenth*, the compensation structure of banks and their credit officers provides sufficient incentives for banks to cover-up earnings management and fraud in order to retain clients. Banks and their credit officers face significant *Reputation Costs*, NPL-reporting costs (ie. Non-performing loans) and restructuring costs if a borrower company is subsequently found to have engaged in earnings management – this also provides additional incentives for banks to collude in earnings management and fraud. *Eleventh*, some Sophisticated Investors can also intentionally collude in, or fail to report earnings management, in order to: 1) maintain the values of their investments (same, related or similar investments); 2) profit from shorting the stock; 3) retain current management (who may be more disposed to paying dividends than another group of new managers). Investors can be segmented into passive investors (mostly small individual investors), Sophisticated Investors (funds; insurance companies; pension funds; etc.), and operator-investors (such as senior executives). Sophisticated investors such as institutional investors are often required by statutes (e.g. insurance companies), or regulations (e.g. pension funds) or their own internal rules or by contracts to conduct formal due diligence before making investments. Third-parties often rely on such due diligence for their own investment decisions, and "Herding" is an empirically established fact in Behavioral Finance. Thus, there is a case (however weak) for imposing liability and penalties for earnings management and fraud on institutional "Sophisticated Investors" based partly on their knowledge of accounting and finance, and the degree of their knowledge of, and participation in such misconduct.

CONCLUSION

The differences among CRAs, audit firms and various types of consulting firms can be substantial and revolves around their "*Contracts Opportunity Sets*". Understanding the implications and effects of such differences on industry-structure and cross-industry "pollination" (spillovers and market-integration) can help policymakers to develop better regulations and sustainability/economic policies.

REFERENCES

Aguirre, A. (2017). Contracting institutions and economic growth. *Review of Economic Dynamics*, *24*, 192–217. doi:10.1016/j.red.2017.01.009

Ayotte, K., & Bolton, P. (2011). *Covenant lite lending, liquidity, and standardization of financial contracts*. Chapter. In P. Bolon (Ed.), *Research Handbook on the Economics of Property Law* (pp. 174–189). Edward Elgar Publishing Ltd. doi:10.4337/9781849808972.00013

Baffi, E. (2007). The Economics of Standard Form Contracts. Università degli Studi "Guglielmo Marconi".

Baffi, E. (2012). Contracting in modern world. *Aperta Contrada*. https://www.apertacontrada.it/2012/11/13/contracting-in-modern-world/

Baffi, E. (2000). *Some Characteristic Features of Mass Contracting*. Università degli Studi "Roma Tre" – Faculty of Law".

Dekker, H., Kawai, T., & Sakaguchi, J. (2018). Contracting abroad: A comparative analysis of contract design in host and home country outsourcing relations. *Management Accounting Research*, *40*, 47–61. doi:10.1016/j.mar.2017.09.003

Drozd, L., & Serrano-Padia, R. (2018). Financial contracting with enforcement externalities. *Journal of Economic Theory*, *178*, 153–189. doi:10.1016/j.jet.2018.09.002

Eenmaa-Dimitrieva, H., & Schmidt-Kessen, M. (2019). Creating markets in no-trust environments: The law and economics of smart contracts. *Computer Law & Security Review*, *35*(1), 69–88. doi:10.1016/j.clsr.2018.09.003

Fang, X., & Yuan, F. (2018). The Coordination and Preference of Supply Chain Contracts Based on Time-Sensitivity Promotional Mechanism. *Journal of Management Science and Engineering*, *3*(3), 158–178. doi:10.3724/SP.J.1383.303009

Goetz, R., Yatsenko, Y., Hritonenko, N., Xabadia, A., & Abdulai, A. (2019). The dynamics of productive assets, contract duration and holdup. *Mathematical Social Sciences*, *97*, 24–37. doi:10.1016/j.mathsocsci.2018.10.004

He, Q., Xue, C., & Zhou, S. (2019). Does contracting institution affect the patterns of industrial specialization in China? *China Economic Review*, *54*, 191–203. doi:10.1016/j.chieco.2018.11.003

Hong, S., Wernz, C., & Stillinger, J. (2016). Optimizing maintenance service contracts through mechanism design theory. *Applied Mathematical Modelling*, *40*(21-22), 8849–8861. doi:10.1016/j.apm.2015.07.009

Hoppe, E., & Schmitz, P. (2018). Hidden action and outcome contractibility: An experimental test of moral hazard theory. *Games and Economic Behavior*, *109*, 544–564. doi:10.1016/j.geb.2018.02.006

Iossa, E., & Martimort, D. (2018). Corruption in PPPs, incentives and contract incompleteness. *International Journal of Industrial Organization*, *44*, 85–100. doi:10.1016/j.ijindorg.2015.10.007

Li, W., Liu, Y., & Chen, Y. (2018). Modeling a two-stage supply contract problem in a hybrid uncertain environment. *Computers & Industrial Engineering*, *123*, 289–302. doi:10.1016/j.cie.2018.06.031

Lin, E., & Chou, M. (1990). Optimal contracts. *Applied Mathematics Letters*, *3*(2), 65–68. doi:10.1016/0893-9659(90)90016-5

Madureira, A., Pereira, I., Pereira, P., & Abraham, A. (2014). Negotiation mechanism for self-organized scheduling system with collective intelligence. *Neurocomputing*, *132*, 97–110. doi:10.1016/j.neucom.2013.10.032

Meneguzzi, F., Modgil, S., & Oren, N. (2011). Algorithms and mechanisms for procuring services with uncertain durations using redundancy. *Artificial Intelligence*, *175*(14–15), 2021–2060.

Meneguzzi, F., Modgil, S., Oren, N., Miles, S., Luck, M., & Faci, N. (2012). Applying electronic contracting to the aerospace aftercare domain. *Engineering Applications of Artificial Intelligence*, *25*(7), 1471–1487. doi:10.1016/j.engappai.2012.06.004

Niederhoff, J., & Kouvelis, P. (2019). Effective and necessary: Individual supplier behavior in revenue sharing and wholesale contracts. *European Journal of Operational Research*, *277*(3), 1060–1071. doi:10.1016/j.ejor.2019.03.038

Nwogugu, M. (2006). Employee Stock Options, Production Functions And Game Theory. *Applied Mathematics and Computation, 181*(1), 552–562. doi:10.1016/j.amc.2005.12.067

Nwogugu, M. (2007a). Issues In Disintermediation In The Real Estate Brokerage Industry. *Applied Mathematics and Computation, 186*(2), 1054–1064. doi:10.1016/j.amc.2006.08.053

Nwogugu, M. (2007b). Some Issues In Securitization And Disintermediation. *Applied Mathematics and Computation, 186*(2), 1031–1039. doi:10.1016/j.amc.2006.08.052

Nwogugu, M. (2019a). *Human Computer Interaction, Incentive Conflicts And Methods For Eliminating Index Arbitrage, Index-Related Mutual Fund Arbitrage And ETF Arbitrage. In Indices, Index Funds And ETFs HCI: Exploring HCI, Nonlinear Risk And Homomorphisms.* Palgrave MacMillan.

Nwogugu, M. (2019b). Economic Policy, Complex Adaptive Systems, Human-Computer Interaction And Managerial Psychology: Popular-Index Ecosystems. In Indices, Index Funds And ETFs HCI: Exploring HCI, Nonlinear Risk And Homomorphisms. Palgrave MacMillan.

Park, S., & Kim, J. (2014). A mathematical model for a capacity reservation contract. *Applied Mathematical Modelling, 38*(5-6), 1866–1880. doi:10.1016/j.apm.2013.10.005

Patterson, M. (2010). Standardization Of Standard-Form Contracts: Competition And Contract Implications. *William and Mary Law Review, 52*(2), 327–340.

Sheng, J. (2019). Neoliberal environmentality and incentive-coordinated REDD+ contracts. *Land Use Policy, 81*, 400–407. doi:10.1016/j.landusepol.2018.10.055

Sprinkle, G., Williamson, M., & Upton, D. (2008). The effort and risk-taking effects of budget-based contracts. *Accounting, Organizations and Society, 33*(4-5), 436–452. doi:10.1016/j.aos.2007.11.001

Sussman, O. (1999). Economic growth with standardized contracts. *European Economic Review, 43*(9), 1797–1818. doi:10.1016/S0014-2921(98)00040-3

Terán, J., Aguilar, J., & Cerrada, M. (2017). Integration in industrial automation based on multi-agent systems using cultural algorithms for optimizing the coordination mechanisms. *Computers in Industry, 91*, 11–23. doi:10.1016/j.compind.2017.05.002

Van Assche, A., & Schwartz, G. (2013). Contracting institutions and ownership structure in international joint ventures. *Journal of Development Economics, 103*, 124–132. doi:10.1016/j.jdeveco.2013.02.008

Wei, W., Wang, J., Chen, X., Yang, J., & Min, X. (2018). Psychological contract model for knowledge collaboration in virtual community of practice: An analysis based on the game theory. *Applied Mathematics and Computation, 329*, 175–187. doi:10.1016/j.amc.2018.01.053

Wu, Z., Zhao, R., & Tang, W. (2014). Optimal contracts for the agency problem with multiple uncertain information. *Knowledge-Based Systems, 59*, 161–172. doi:10.1016/j.knosys.2014.01.009

Zohar, A., & Rosenschein, J. (2008). Mechanisms for information elicitation. *Artificial Intelligence, 172*(16–17), 1917–1939. doi:10.1016/j.artint.2008.08.005

ENDNOTES

1 *See:* US SEC (December 2012). *Report to Congress on Assigned Credit Ratings - As Required by Section 939F of the Dodd-Frank Wall Street Reform and Consumer Protection Act.* https://www.sec.gov/news/studies/2012/assigned-credit-ratings-study.pdf.

2 *See*: *American Securitization Forum's May 13, 2013 Letter to the US SEC, Re: Release No. 34-69433;* File No. 4-661. https://www.sec.gov/comments/4-661/4661-14.pdf. This article states in part "Section 939F was included in the Dodd-Frank Act in lieu of Section 939D of H.R. 4173 (111th Congress) ("Section 939D"), as passed by the Senate on May 20, 2010 (the "Senate Bill"), which would have added Section 15E(w) to the Exchange Act ("Section-15E(w)"). In place of Section 939D, Section 939F requires that the Commission implement the system described in Section 15E(w) unless the Commission determines that an alternative system would better serve the public interest and the protection of investors. Section 15E(w) would have established an SRO in the form of a board responsible for assigning a qualified NRSRO to provide the initial credit ratings on structured finance products. Section-15E(w) would have precluded issuers of structured finance products from requesting an initial credit rating directly from an NRSRO but would not have precluded an issuer from obtaining other ratings from an NRSRO if the initial credit rating was provided in accordance with the board assignment provisions. The Rule 17g-5 Program precludes an NRSRO from rating structured finance products where an issuer-pay conflict exists unless it complies with certain requirements, including the requirement that it obtain from the transaction issuer, underwriter or sponsor (the arranger) a representation that the arranger will post all of the information provided to a hired NRSRO on a website that is available to other NRSROs. Ultimately, and as further discussed below, the structure of Section-15E(w) raises the potential for new conflicts of interest and moral hazards that make the assignment system unworkable. These same concerns do not arise under Rule 17g-5. In light of this, ASF believes that a revamped Rule-17g-5 Program would ultimately be more beneficial than the implementation of a Section 15E(w) system. We are concerned that creation of a board will further encourage overreliance by investors on credit ratings through the implication that the board has endorsed the ratings of the NRSROs it qualifies, thus conferring an implicit stamp of government approval. By creating a government-sanctioned special category of NRSROs that are the only NRSROs permitted to issue initial credit ratings to issuers, Section 15E(w) would further entrench certain NRSROs into the system; this is in direct conflict with Section-939A of Dodd-Frank, which aimed to remove ratings from regulations to eliminate what then Senator George LeMieux (R-FL) referred to as a "sanctioned monopoly."

Chapter 5
Structural Change and Antitrust in the Global Auditing/Consulting Industry and Associated Environmental-Pollution/Climate-Change Issues

ABSTRACT

During 1990-2020, the global auditing/accounting and management consulting industry sectors experienced significant structural changes which have had un-even effects among large, medium and small auditing firms. The first section of this chapter summarizes the structural changes. The second section summarizes the antitrust problems. The third section discusses some of the climate-change and environmental pollution problems that are significantly affected by regulation of accounting firms and consulting firms; and introduces new solutions. In many countries, accounting firms have the primary responsibility for auditing firms' compliance with mechanisms such as emissions credits, environmental/sustainability accounting and compliance with environmental regulations; and consulting firms (by advising boards-of-directors and senior executives) informally and substantially influence firms' policies and procedures pertaining to waste/pollution and climate-change. The topics of the three sections (structural change, antitrust and the auditing/consulting firms' role in external audits and strategy pertaining to pollution, climate change and waste-management) are linked and or can have symbiotic effects on each other.

DOI: 10.4018/978-1-7998-7418-8.ch005

INTRODUCTION

Accounting and management consulting are the most global/international of all professional services, and critically affect how international trade is conducted, recorded and its disputes resolved; and also affect the efficiency of emissions-management systems and corporate compliance with pollution/emissions policies and regulation. The World Trade Organization (WTO) *Working Party on Professional Services* and the *General Agreement on Trade in Services* (GATS) has made the global accounting sector a priority; and WTO's deliberations also cover Sarbanes-Oxley Act (SOX) and similar statutes in other countries (which often apply to companies involved in cross-border finance and or business). The standardization/harmonization of accounting and auditing regulations and management consulting practices across countries, and market-access for foreign accounting and consulting firms remain important elements of International Trade negotiations and Sustainability management systems around the world. See the comments in White (2001), WTO (2017) and Cattaneo, Engman, Saez & Stern (2010). Thus, issues that pertain to audit-fees, management consulting fees, *auditor/consultant-work-allocation Mechanisms* and *Auditor-liability-allocation Mechanisms* can have significant direct effects on international trade and international capital flows, and compliance with environmental/climate policies and regulations; and can have indirect effects on international capital flows (mostly of auditee-companies and consulting clients). Some of the structural changes in the accounting and management consulting sectors are driven or affected by International Trade.

Accounting Biases is relatively new line of research and has been studied from Behavioural Accounting, Management Science[2] and Operations Research[3] perspectives. Chen & Jorgensen (2018) noted that accounting Biases can affect competition and Industry Structure in various non-accounting industries (which in turn, affects auditing and consulting processes). Marquardt & Zur (2015) found evidence that financial accounting quality is positively related to the efficient capital/resource allocation in economies.

EXISTING LITERATURE

The literature on the relationship between complexity and structural change is developed and includes Robert & Yoguel (2016), Cimoli, Pereima & Porcile (2016), Dosi & Virgillito (2017), Comim (2000), Heinrich & Dai (2016), Ciaschini, Pretaroli & Socci (2011), Brida, Anyul & Punzo (2003) and Cantwell & Santangelo (2006).

Ozturk (2019) and Marques, Santos & Inácio (2019) discussed issues in organizational auditing.

Nissen (2018) and Bensberg, Buscher & Czarnecki (2019) discussed *Digital Transformation* in the consulting industry; and Boneva (2018) and Stark (2020) analyzed *Digital Transformation* in other industries.

On pollution and Climate Change, see the comments in Sikka & Hampton (2005), Konrad Adeneaur Stiftung (2017), Condon & Sinha (2013), Asia Investor Group On Climate Change (2017) and Tang & Demmeritt (2018)[4].

Many researchers have critiqued Climate-Change/environmental policies and various types of emissions-trading/emissions-permit systems around the world – see: Lu, Fang, et. al. (2020), Jin, Liu, et. al. (2020), Rojas-Vallejos & Lastuk (2020), Driver, Parsons & Fisher (2018), Felli (2019), Kama (2014), Bowman, Enion, et. al. (2011), Helm (2009), Hinterman (2016), Interpol (June 2013), Frondel, Schmidt & Vance (2012), Pang & Duan (2016), Brisson (2014), Schneider, Kollmuss & Lazarus (2015), Tanaka

& Chen (2012), Tanuro (2008), Tang & Demmeritt (2018), Vlachou & Pantelias (2017), Wang, Teng, Zhou & Cai (2017), Weishaar (2014), Zeng, Weishaar & Vedder (2018), Sales (2017), Miller & Facanha (2016), Gambhir, Napp, et. al. (2014), Dubash, Khosla, et. al. (2014) and Van der Hoff & Rajão (2020).

COMPLEXITY AND STRUCTURAL CHANGES IN THE GLOBAL AUDITING/ACCOUNTING AND CONSULTING INDUSTRY

In this context, elements of complexity arise in various ways including but not limited to the following:

1. The self organization of industries, regional economies and national economies.
2. The self organization of Multinational Corporations (MNCs) – ie. trade associations; their operations strategies; their internal and external contracting; etc..
3. The self organization of auditing firm, tax consulting firms and management consulting firms – ie. IASB/IFRS; FASB/GASB; trade associations; their operations strategies; their internal and external contracting; etc..
4. Complex networks in economies – ie. networks that consist of large/small/medium firms; audit firms; consulting firms; individuals, households, intermediaries, regulators and institutions.
5. Nonlinearity in the decline/growth of MNCs and their relationships with auditing and consulting firms – ie. the influence of the growth/decline of MNCs on regional and national economies; etc..
6. Nonlinearity in the decline/growth of audit firms and management consulting firms – ie. the influence of the growth/decline of such firms on regional and national economies; etc..
7. Non-linearity in the growth/decline of economic development factors such as human capital, wealth, technological advancement, etc..
8. Nonlinear structural changes in industries, regional economies and national economies.
9. MNCs, regional economies and national economies as adaptive systems.
10. Large and medium sized auditing/accounting firms and management consulting firms as adaptive systems.

The structural changes in the global auditing/consulting industry include but are not limited to the following:

1. Industry consolidation and the emergence of the *big-four oligopoly* in accounting/auditing and the *big-seven oligopoly* in management consulting. In both the auditing/accounting and management consulting sectors[5], industry consolidation continues with larger firms and regional firm acquiring smaller and local/regional competitors (the acquire-companies often have narrower practices or limited geographic scope).
2. There is increasing use of joint ventures and strategic alliances among auditing firms and consulting firms in some countries (e.g. China) – which has become problematic. There has been increased intra-firm cross-border collaboration within audit firms and consulting firms.
3. The enactment of new regulations in many countries such as the US, EU, UK, China, Canada, India and Japan (e.g. the Sarbanes-Oxley Act and the Dodd Frank Act in the US.

4. There has been *Regulatory Convergence* such as the increasing adoption of IASB/IFRS standards and harmonization of accounting regulations and auditing standards across many countries; and the harmonization of auditing methods and management consulting tools/methods across countries.
5. In many developed countries and some developing countries, an increasing number of large/medium companies in industry have been creating their own in-house management consulting groups (different from their internal audit teams), which are usually partly staffed by former management consultants that worked at the top consulting firms.
6. There has been technological progress and the increased use of technology in audits, quality control and consulting projects (combined with increased automation of finance/accounting functions within audit-clients). Accounting firms and management consulting firms have been investing in technology for in-house uses.
7. The emergence and regulatory powers of regulatory agencies such as the *Public Company Accounting Oversight Board* (PCAOB) in the US; the *Financial Reporting Council* in the UK; the *Financial Reporting Council of Nigeria*; and the *Chinese Accounting Standards Committee* (within the Ministry of Finance in China) which develops all accounting standards in China.
8. There have been changes in accounting education and management consulting education at the undergraduate degree level and in the continuing professional education requirements in some countries (including data science; computers and statistical/mathematical methods).
9. In the management consulting sector, low-cost specialized boutique firms and freelancers with little or no overhead costs are successfully competing with more established firms.
10. A few countries are implementing regulations for mandatory *auditor-rotation*.
11. In some specialized industries or for some specialized services (e.g. environmental audits), non-accounting firms are doing a substantial and increasing volume of audits; even though their work is ultimately tied to, and reflected in financial statements that are audited by traditional accounting firms. That can create dichotomies and conflicts.
12. Collusion in setting audit fees remains a problem in some countries.
13. The financial regulations of some countries (e.g. the Sarbanes-Oxley Act and the Dodd Frank Act in the US) have had significant effects on: 1) the auditing of the foreign operations of their MNCs, and on foreign cross-listed companies; and 2) accounting practice.
14. The financial regulations of some countries (e.g. the Sarbanes-Oxley Act and similar statutes in other countries) have had significant effects on the practice of accounting/auditing and requirements for auditing firms.
15. Outsourcing is growing in management consulting.
16. Traditional auditing, Management Consulting and tax Consulting are being disrupted by automation and data science (new ways of data gathering and analysis; cognitive computing; visualization, and the cloud).
17. In management consulting and tax consulting, the Billable Time-based business model is the dominant model, but the use of Value-Pricing (where consultants' fees are directly tied to results and tangible benefits from their work) is increasing.
18. In general, the global services industry expanded during 2010-2020. The implications and results include increased firm diversification, strategic alliances and cross-pollination – for example digital marketing is emerging as a major type/element of consulting, and large management consulting firms have been acquiring digital marketing companies. Accounting firms and Information Technology

firms are diversifying into management consultancy services. Bai, Chen, Song & Wang (2019) noted recent growth in China's services sector.

19. Many researchers have noted risks in the financial systems of some large-GDP countries – See: Song & Xiong (2018) and Bai, Hsieh & Qian (2006; 2016; 2019) which discussed risks in China's financial system. Such risks obviously have psychological effects on managers and auditors.
20. There has been increasing *political Interference* in auditing in some countries such as China, wherein the central government or local governments actively or implicitly support earnings management, asset quality management and incentive effects management at companies and government entities (mostly for political and economic gains). Some researchers have reported that the Chinese government has severally refused to hand over the audit workpapers for Chinese companies that were cross-listed in US stock exchanges and were being investigated by the US SEC for securities fraud[6].
21. In many developed and developing countries, many (if not most) environmental audits are done by government employees or relatively small non-accounting firms (some are engineering firms) that are not subjected to the professional standards, penalties and discipline of the auditing/accounting profession. That causes or can cause *political interference* (wherein governments under-report environmental pollution for political gains), lapses in judgment and lax reporting, collusion and bribery. Small consulting firms typically have fewer revenue sources and are more susceptible to bribery and collusion especially for repeated consulting projects. In many (if not most) countries, these government auditors and non-accounting environmental auditors are not subject to *Auditor-Rotation, Auditor Work Allocation Mechanisms* or *Auditor Liability-Allocation Mechanisms.* Also, the professional liability standards and penalties for auditing/accounting firms are more comprehensive and severe, and have been more litigated than those of engineering professions (ie. civil, chemical and environmental engineering).
22. Some countries deliberately produce false/misleading economic data – which: 1) affects estimates used in traditional auditing and environmental auditing; and 2) has or can have negative psychological effects on managers and auditors; 3) encourages collusion between corporate/government managers and auditors. Many Chinese and non-Chinese researchers have noted fraud and errors in the calculation of China's statistical data (national accounting data). See: Orlik (2014), Lyu, Wang, et. al. (2018), Ma, Song, et. al. (2014), Liu, Zhang & Zhu (2016), Holz (2014) and Gao (2016). In 2019, Chen, Chen, Hsieh & Song (2019), a Brookings Institute research paper (paper's analysis covered 2008 to 2016), stated that the annual Chinese GDP was overstated by as much as 12% (twelve percent) and that China's real growth has been overstated by about two percentage points annually in recent years, and Chinese statisticians don't have the power correct China's inflated GDP figures. Chen, Chen, Hsieh & Song (2019) contains important economic data for China such as *Aggregate TFP Growth*; *Debt-to-GDP*; *Aggregate Returns to Capital*; *Official and Adjusted Investment Rates*; *Fixed Asset Investment (FAI) vs. Fixed Capital Formation (FCF)*; *Sectoral GDP and Corporate Income Tax Revenue Growth*; *Corporate Income Tax Revenue/GDP*; *Wholesale and Retail GDP: Micro-Data/National Accounts*; *Growth in Value-Added Tax Revenues and GDP*; *Gap between Local and Aggregate GDP by Expenditure*; and the *Gap between Local and Aggregate GDP by Sector*; many of which are negative (declining economy). Chen, Chen, Hsieh & Song (2019) noted that:
    a. In China, local governments are rewarded for meeting growth and investment targets, thus they have substantial incentives to falsify local statistics.

b. For many years, the sum of China's provincial GDP exceeded the national GDP number which is clear evidence of statistical inflation at the local level.
c. In China, the National Bureau of Statistics (NBS) has acknowledged that some local statistics are falsified and in 2017 the central Chinese government accused three provinces in China's north-east rust belt of fabricating economic data.
d. Chinese government data overstated growth of nominal GDP by an average of 1.7% per year during 2008-2016, and thus the Chinese economy was 12% smaller in 2016 than official figures indicated.

See the comments in Englund, Gerdin & Abrahamsson (2013), Abbott, Parker & Peters (2011), Abidin, Beattie & Goodacre (2010), Nwogugu (2013/2015), Nwogugu (2010/2015), Abbott, Parker & Peters (2011), Carson, Soo & Wright (2012), Gillis (2014), Ferguson, Pinnuck & Skinner (April 2014), Ramanna & Sletten (2014) and Payne (Aug. 2016). Some of those structural changes can have significant and negative collateral effects on international trade, capital markets and the banking/securities, CRA (credit rating agency) and insurance industries. Some of the structural changes in the auditing industry and the consulting industry may have affected the practice of management accounting within firms in industries; and certainly created some antitrust problems in the auditing industry.

ANTITRUST PROBLEMS IN THE GLOBAL AUDITING/ACCOUNTING AND MANAGEMENT CONSULTING INDUSTRY

There are significant antitrust/competition and structural problems in the global audit/accounting and management consulting industry which have not been adequately addressed in the literature or by regulators, but which can be solved by the introduction of *Auditor-Work Allocation Mechanisms* ("AAM"), and *Audit-Fee Allocation Mechanisms* ("AFM")[7]. In this instance, the collusion implicates the theory-of-the firm – see the comments in Tirole (1992).

Specific Antitrust Problems

General Antitrust principles were discussed in Economides (2012a;b) and Economides (1998). Market concentration was addressed in Huang, Chang & Chiou (2016); Ferguson, Pinnuck & Skinner (April 2014); Dunn, Kohlbeck & Mayhew (2011); Liu & Simunic (2005); Carson, Soo & Wright (2012); and Ballas & Fafalliou (Nov. 2008). One of the biggest difficulties is that the antitrust problems and violations in the global auditing/consulting industry have been manifested and effected in *non-price anti-competitive conduct*. These antitrust and structural problems include but are not limited to the following:

1. *Market-Concentration* – ie. the big-four audit firms and the big-seven consulting firms are dominant and in some local/regional markets one big-4 or big-seven firm may maintain a near-monopoly in one or more industries. One major result has been "*Adverse Reputation Effects*" wherein the Big-four and big-seven firms have larger-than-justified reputations in the audit market or consulting market which can interfere with the quality of services they provide – ie. such reputation enables them to provide lower QoS (quality of services) to the detriment of investors and regulators that rely on their services and reports. Many academic empirical studies have debated the effects of

market-concentration in the auditing industry (especially on audit fees) but their evidence is mixed – see Singh (2013).

2. Actual, apparent or threatened *Tying* by auditing firms and consulting firms (tying of audit and non-audit services). See: Economides (2012a).
3. Actual, apparent or threatened *Foreclosure* (by auditing and consulting firms partly because of their strong client relationships; limit-pricing; exclusive dealing and auditing contracts; division of territories; etc.).
4. There can be the following types of *Collusion*: 1) *Collusion* (e.g. to divide territories; set prices; determine scope-of-work; to control disclosure and or compliance levels; to deny services to prospective clients; to hide fraud; etc.) and or *price-fixing* among auditing and consulting firms; 2) Collusion between auditing/consulting firms and CRAs; 3) *Collusion* between audit/consulting firms and their clients (ie. to determine the scope-of-work; to control disclosure and or compliance levels; to deny services to the audit-client's competitors; to hide fraud; etc.).
5. Inability of foreign regulators (such as the US SEC) to conduct investigations of audit/consulting firms and their clients in other countries (such as China, which in several cases, did not allow the US SEC to access the working papers of some Chinese accounting firms that audited Chinese firms that were cross-listed in US stock exchanges and were being investigated for fraud).
6. Actual, apparent or threatened *Rebate-Pricing* by audit/consulting firms - ie. the audit/consulting firm offers rebates to some but not all of its clients in order to gain market-share, and or influence and or to preclude market-entry by other firms.
7. Actual, apparent or threatened *Predatory-Pricing* by audit/consulting firms – 1) the audit/consulting firm offers a low total audit-fee at the beginning to entice the audit client, but as the audit progresses, the audit firm increases the fees; and 2) the auditing firm charges hidden-fees; and or 3) the auditing firm charges fees that it knows that the client cannot afford and then forces the client to issue debt and or equity to it; 4) the audit/consulting firm charges fees that are partly or wholly based on "discovered items" which can vastly increase the scope of the audit.
8. Actual, apparent or threatened *Extortion* by audit/consulting firms and or audit/consulting staff that can threaten to report audit problems to regulators; and or Bribery of external auditors/consultants by the staff/executives of audit-clients.
9. "*Regulatory Fragmentation*" by audit/consulting firms (who perpetrate it by lobbying, improper advice; forum-shopping; etc.).
10. "*Regulatory Capture*" by audit/consulting firms (who assist their audit and consulting clients to avoid or to weaken regulations/statutes).
11. Actual, apparent or threatened "*Refusal-To-Deal*" by audit/consulting firms (wherein an auditing or consulting firm refuses to provide services to a client).
12. Actual, apparent or threatened *Conflicts-Of-Interest* among accounting/consulting staff that change jobs between audit/consulting firms one hand, and the CFO/finance groups within companies.
13. Actual, apparent or threatened *Price-Discrimination* by auditing and consulting firms.
14. Actual, apparent or threatened *Audit-Quality Discrimination* by auditing and or consulting firms (wherein an audit/consulting firm provides different levels of *quality-of-service* to similarly situated auditing consulting clients that pay the same or similar fees).
15. As mentioned herein and above, in many developed and developing countries, many (if not most) environmental audits are done by government-agency employees or relatively small non-accounting firms (some are engineering firms) that are not subjected to the professional standards, penalties and

discipline of the auditing/accounting profession (see the survey of environmental auditing trends in Chapter-2 in this book). That causes or can cause *political interference* (wherein governments under-report environmental pollution for political gains), lapses in judgment and lax reporting, *Collusion*, *Price-fixing* (in the global markets for emissions permits, emissions credits, Green Bonds; climate derivatives; environmental auditing; etc.) and bribery. In some countries, these non-accounting environmental auditors are not subject to *Mandatory Auditor-Rotation*, *Auditor Fee-Allocation Mechanisms*, *Auditor Work-Allocation Mechanisms* or *Auditor Liability-Allocation Mechanisms*. Also, in some countries, the professional liability standards and penalties for auditing/accounting firms are more comprehensive and severe, have more public policy impact and have been more litigated than those of engineering professions (ie. civil, chemical and environmental engineering).

16. In environmental auditing, "*Self-Auditing*" has or can have significant financial statement and accounting-audit implications; and can also affect the prices and trading of *Environmental Management Instruments* (EMIs) and *Climate Finance Instruments* (CFIs) (such as emissions credits; emissions permits; Green Bonds; etc.). The prices and trading of CFIs and EMIs partly depend on both aggregate pollution and each specific firm's pollution levels. Permitting *Self-Auditing* is like allowing the CFO of a company to prepare its quarterly/annual audited financial statements and hoping that the CFO will always be truthful (the actual un-reported monetary liabilities for non-compliance with environmental regulations and climate change regulations that is attributable to Self-Auditing may be in the trillions of Euros). It's now clear that the inefficient systems of "*Self-Auditing*" of environmental pollution (by polluting companies and government agencies) have woefully failed in many countries given increasing pollution and climate change around the world. There should be mandatory and independent environmental audits done by "independent" firms that are subject to penalties and regulations. Companies that pollute should bear the costs of such environmental audits. *Self-auditing* causes or can cause substantial Antitrust problems such as the following:
    a. Actual, apparent or threatened *Price-Fixing* in the global markets for *emissions-permits* and *emissions-credits*.
    b. Actual, apparent or threatened *Collusion* in the global markets for *emissions-permits* and *emissions-credits*.
    c. Actual, apparent or threatened *Collusion* – among employees of polluting companies; and between such employees and government agencies.
    d. Actual, apparent or threatened *Price-Fixing* for environmental audit fees.
    e. Actual, apparent or threatened *Conflicts-Of-Interest* in polluting firms.
    f. Actual, apparent or threatened "*Regulatory Capture*" by polluting firms (who avoid or weaken regulations/statutes, sometimes in connivance with government employees).
    g. Actual, apparent or threatened *Extortion* by government agency employees.
17. Other problems that may arise from *Self-Auditing* (in environmental auditing) are as follows:
    a. *Deadweight Losses* - in environmental auditing; and in the prices and the global markets for CFIs and EMIs.
    b. *Truth-Telling Problems* - polluting-company managers and in some cases, government auditors have no or minimal incentives to tell the truth.
    c. *Political Costs* (- un-reported environmental pollution increases government's remediation expenditures, and or reduces amounts allocated by the government to social welfare programs). Under the current regulatory regimes in some countries, each of these foregoing problems

can be very difficult to resolve because polluting-entitys' managers' compensation, incentives and career advancement (and the fact that under *Self Auditing* regulations in some countries, managers don't face any personal losses) compel them to lie, distort information and or collude. Also, some governments gain political capital by suppressing environmental pollution and avoiding remediation costs. As of 2019, the U.S. Environmental Protection Agency (EPA) was operating a *Self-Auditing*[8] program which has been heavily criticized by various stakeholders. The US EPA, environmental groups, and other industry players have critiqued Self-Auditing and noted that: 1) Self-auditing laws and associated secrecy protections result in polluters violating environmental statutes without suffering any penalties; and 2) Self-Auditing secrecy protections can cause decreased visibility of environmental practices and decisions which will result in increased complacency in compliance.

18. Non-uniform application of IASB/IFRS accounting standards by auditing and or consulting firms.

Other quasi-Antitrust problems in the global auditing/consulting industry are as follows:

1. Intense lobbying by auditing/accounting and consulting firms and their MNC clients – e.g. lobbying of the national/regional legislatures, FASB, IASB, GASB, ICMA, securities regulators; etc..
2. The significant and perhaps unjustified increases in auditing and consulting fees because of implementation of statutes such as Sarbanes Oxley Act (US).
3. The lack of true independence of the audit committees of the boards of directors of companies.
4. Auditors and consultants have significant discretion in the types and amounts of misconduct that they are statutorily required to report to government agencies.
5. Under-investment in knowledge, training and technology by auditing/consulting firms – which enables them to increase their profits with little or no corresponding increases in effort and or costs.
6. Harmful "*External Control/Influence*" exerted by auditing/consulting firms over boards of directors and or senior executives of companies.
7. *Conflicts-Of-Interest* wherein auditing/consulting clients pay professional fees to auditing/consulting firms even when there is a conflict-of-interest.
8. *Regulatory Capture.*
9. Movement of professionals (jobs) between auditing firms, regulatory agencies (e.g. US SEC) and standards-setting organizations (e.g. FASB; IASB; GASB; ICMA).

The "Big-Four" accounting firms dominate the global auditing/accounting sector, and the "big-seven" consulting firms (Bain; McKinsey; Booz; Deloitte; PwC; KPMG and E&Y) are dominate the global business/management consulting sector and often stifle competition. It's clear from the many corporate scandals of the last two decades that this oligopoly reduces the quality of audits, financial statements and corporate decisions; limits innovation and diffusion of knowledge, and negatively affects the functioning of capital markets. Long term relationships between accounting firm and their clients breeds complacency and fosters inertia. The Big-Four audit firms have developed an aura of accuracy and stability which investors have come to depend on. Companies often seek the stamp of approval of Big-Four firms, and are willing to pay excessive fees to get such implicit approval regardless of the quality of the audits. The Dodd Frank Act and Sarbanes Oxley Act (SOX) and similar statutes that were enacted in many countries (such as UK, south Africa; China; France; Canada; Japan; India; etc.) during 2002-2015 did not solve the primary structural problems in the global accounting/auditing industry which have increased and contributed to both systemic risk and financial instability. The issues of oligopoly, auditor-independence, competition for audit fees and liability-allocation in the global accounting/auditing industry have not been adequately addressed in the literature or by regulators and their evolution represents structural changes in the industry.

The UK Government's July 2020 New Regulations for the Quasi-Ring-Fencing[9] of the Big-Four Accounting/Consulting Firms

During July 2020, the UK Financial Reporting Council (FRC)[10] enacted a set of guidelines for the break-up of the Big-4 accounting/consulting firms) which are to be implemented by 2024 (the big-four accounting firms are to complete their plans by October 2020). The UK FRC's Principles (2020) are listed in Appendix-1 herein and below.

However, the FRC's 2020 directives doesn't go far enough to solve Structural Antitrust problems, and requires only an "*Internal Separation of Functions and Ring-Fencing*" and not an actual break-up of each Big-four accounting/consulting firm (into legally distinct and operationally separate entities).

Each of the Big-4 accounting/consulting firm can still engage in anti-competitive practices.

The Obstacles That Can Hamper the Efficiency of Break-Up of Any or All of the Big Four Auditing Firms (or the Big-Seven Consulting Firms) in Any Country: The Break-Ups Won't Solve Many Antitrust Problems

Breaking up each of the big-four audit firms or big-seven consulting firms won't solve the antitrust problems in both industry-sectors because the problems include "*transactional antitrust*" and "*behavioral antitrust*" that goes beyond oligopoly and are defined as follows:

1. "*Transactional antitrust*" – refers to antitrust violations that arise primarily from specific one-time or repeated transactions, and either before, during or after such transaction(s).
2. "*Behavioral antitrust*" – refers to antitrust violations that arise from or are implicit in usage-of-trade, and the expectations, conduct and or omissions of employees/agents of big-4 or big-7 firms and or their clients.

These two types of antitrust are often embedded in conduct, regulations, expectations, usage-of-trade, personal relationships and perceptions and in ways that cannot be readily recorded as evidence (for litigation purposes), and certainly is very difficult to identify and prove in a court-of-law under current antitrust statutes in various countries. Antitrust problems such as *Audit-quality Discrimination, Price Discrimination, Rebate-Pricing, Refusal-to-Deal, collusion, illegal splitting/sharing of local audit markets*, etc., cannot be completely resolved by only breaking-up the big-four auditing firms or the big-seven consulting firms. Thus, any such break-ups (either voluntary or involuntary) must be combined with structural reforms of the global accounting/consulting industry and new statutes (e.g. mandatory *Auditor-Rotation*; *Audit Work Allocation Mechanisms*; *Audit Liability Allocation Mechanism*; new antitrust laws; new "business opportunity" laws; etc.).

Climate Finance, Environmental Pollution[11] And Climate Change[12]

Environmental pollution and Climate Change have become critical issues around the world and in most countries. The potential criminal acts, Non-Compliance (with statutes; and as a physical phenomena), environmental damage (flooding; rising tides in coasts; droughts; untreated waste/garbage in oceans and in communities; etc.), diseases/health-problems, reduced productivity, reduced retirement-assets (amplifies the Global Pension Crisis), famines and mass hysteria (and other mental health problems) that can arise from Climate Change and pollution are vastly understated and not yet fully understood.

Because of their unique position as advisors and external-assurance-services providers, accounting/auditing firms and consulting firms have the statutory and or moral responsibility to report and ensure compliance with various Sustainability, Climate Policy and Pollution standards/regulations.

Hook & Reed (Oct. 24, 2018) noted that the G7 countries produce most of the plastic/paper waste in the world, a large percentage of which was shipped to China until 2018, after which a significant percentage is being shipped to southeast Asian counties, where many illegal waste dumps and waste-processing factories operate (see the figures/chards herein and below). It's conjectured here that the *Structural Changes* and Antitrust problems in the global auditing/consulting industry contributed to an increase in environmental pollution and adverse climate change in various ways including but not limited to the following:

1. Given their position as external auditors/advisors (that owe duties to the general public, shareholders of their audit/consulting clients and government regulators), accounting/audit firms and consulting firms have the primary responsibility for verifying their audit/consulting clients' compliance, non-compliance or under-compliance with regulatory climate-change disclosures, environmental management disclosures and associated accounting disclosure and other requirements for *Environmental Management Instruments* (EMIs) and *Climate Finance Instruments* (CFIs). CFIs and EMIs include emissions permits, climate derivatives, climate-linked bonds, emissions credits; Green Bonds; etc.). CFIs and EMIs are traded both locally and globally and have or can have significant financial statement and disclosure requirements and implications. However, the antitrust problems explained herein and above hamper these critical functions of auditing/consulting firms. As of 2020, accounting firms could collude with their clients to circumvent the requirements of international Climate-Change and emissions-control agreements, emissions trading systems, standards and "global initiatives". See the comments in Sikka & Hampton (2005), Konrad Adeneaur Stiftung (2017), Condon & Sinha (2013), Asia Investor Group On Climate Change (2017), and Tang & Demmeritt (2018)[13], all of which noted some problems inherent in implementation of environmental/climate/pollution reduction programs.
2. Accounting/audit firms and consulting firms can and should be allocated some liability for their audit/consulting clients' non-compliance or under-compliance with regulatory climate-change disclosures, and accounting disclosure and other requirements for CFIs and EMIs – but such liability-allocation hasn't been done in many countries.
3. Improper or inadequate accounting disclosures for CFIs and EMIs can result in price-fixing and collusion in the global markets for CFIs and EMIs.
4. In some countries, the lack of mandatory *auditor rotation* and the "*entrenchment*" and dominance of the Big-four audit firms and Big-7 consulting firms breeds complacency among auditors and collusion among auditors and their clients. *Audit-fee Allocation Mechanisms, Auditor-work-allocation*

Mechanisms and *Auditor-liability-allocation Mechanisms* can have significant effects on compliance with environmental regulations, climate change and climate finance instruments; but the necessary changes have not been implemented in many countries.

5. There has been increasing and significant governmental interference in the auditing process in some countries such as China (ie. the Chinese government's implicit and explicit support of earnings management). Some researchers have also reported that the Chinese government has on several occasions, refused to hand-over the audit work papers for audits of Chinese companies (that are cross-listed in the US) that were being investigated for potential securities fraud in the US. In some countries such as China, complacency and encouragement of earnings management by local government and federal government agencies (which has been confirmed by both Chinese and foreign researchers) distorts the work of audit/accounting firms and environmental auditors and encourages (or doesn't sufficiently punish) environmental pollution and non-compliance. Such governments and their staff often manipulate environmental compliance (and associated accounting disclosures) for political gains, economic gains and for bargaining advantages in international trade negotiations.
6. During the last fifteen years, some of the main catalysts for the external use, perception and quality of sustainability reports issued by companies were based on, or affected by the structure of, and Antitrust in the global auditing/consulting industry.
7. In companies and government agencies that pollute and or are non-compliant, Managers' Incentives and managers' "*Incentive-effects Management*" are critical and are affected by audits and audit-firms.
8. As mentioned herein and above, in many developed and developing countries, many (if not most) environmental audits are done by government employees or relatively small non-accounting firms (some are engineering firms) that are not subjected to the professional standards, penalties and discipline of the auditing/accounting profession. That causes or can cause *political interference* (wherein governments under-report environmental pollution for political gains), lapses in judgment and lax reporting, collusion and bribery. In any countries, these non-accounting environmental auditors are not subject to *Auditor-Rotation, Auditor Work Allocation Mechanisms* or *Auditor Liability-Allocation Mechanisms*. Also, the professional liability standards and penalties for auditing/accounting firms are more comprehensive and severe, and have been more litigated than those of engineering professions (ie. civil, chemical and environmental engineering).
9. As mentioned herein and above, it's now clear that the inefficient systems of "*Self-auditing*" (by polluting companies and government agencies) has woefully failed given increasing pollution and climate change around the world. *Self-auditing* creates substantial Antitrust problems (e.g. *Collusion; Price-fixing* for EMIs and CFIs; etc.) and *Truth-Telling Problems* which are very difficult to resolve partly because corporate manager's compensation, incentives and career advancement compel (and the fact under *Self Auditing* regulations in most countries, managers don't face any personal losses) them to lie. *Self-Auditing* is the functional equivalent of permitting the CFO (chief financial officer) or President of an exchange-traded company to prepare its annual audited financial statements and hoping that he/she won't tell lies (in harsh and competitive capital markets were stock markets punish companies for missing their quarterly/annual earnings targets). As of 2019, the U.S. Environmental Protection Agency (EPA) operated a Self-Auditing[14] program which has been heavily criticized by various stakeholders.
10. The critical issues are that: 1) environmental-audits, EMIs and CFIs can have significant financial statement effects (assets, liabilities and Income Statement items) and may mean the difference between reporting profitability and operating losses in an operating quarter in an environment where

exchange traded firms are harshly punished for missing earnings targets; 2) environmental audits can create significant liabilities for polluting companies – which means they may have to purchase more EMIs or make more payments under CFI contracts; 3) the values and market-prices of EMIs and CFIs to any company/person directly depend on the aggregate volume of pollution and also pollution by that company and specific companies. Thus, *Self-auditing* is an actual or potential Antitrust issue and can cause the following problems:

a. *Collusion* (between self-auditing firms; and among staff of self-auditing firms).
b. *Price-Fixing* for EMI/CFI prices (between self-auditing firms; and between self-auditing firms and government agency staff; and between self-auditing firms and non-self-auditing firms).
c. *Deadweight Losses* in the prices of CMIs/EMIs.
d. *Deadweight Losses* in the demand/supply of environmental-audits and environmental regulations. Similarly, environmental audits by government auditors is an actual or potential antitrust problem and can cause *Collusion* (between auditee-firms and government staff; and between/among auditee-firms; and among staff of self-auditing firms).
e. *Price-Fixing* for EMI/CFI prices (between auditee-firms; and between auditee-firms and government agency staff).

During the last fifteen years, some of the main catalysts for the external use, perception and quality of Sustainability Reports issued by companies were as follows:

1. Sustainability rankings, emissions-rankings and environmental pollution rankings (of companies) that were published by various companies, non-profit entities and governments.
2. The investment/selection criteria of various "social impact funds", "green funds", "green-indices" and "sustainability indices" which have been rapidly growing in popularity.
3. The Non-Financial Reporting and CSR Resource Centre (https://docs.com/jernej-zavrl).
4. The guidelines of the Global Reporting Initiative's (GRI) GRI Sustainability Reporting Guidelines.
5. The International Integrated Reporting Council (IIRC).
6. Award schemes and international conferences.
7. International agreements and "commitments" such as the United Nations Global Compact Initiative (https://www.unglobalcompact.org/what-is-gc/participants).
8. Publicly available and widely circulated reports and surveys such as KPMG's "*Currents of change: The KPMG Survey of Corporate Responsibility Reporting – 2015*" (2015; https://assets.kpmg.com/content/dam/kpmg/pdf/2015/11/kpmg-international-survey-of-corporate-responsibility-reporting-2015.pdf) have highlighted issues of CSR and sustainability disclosures.

Given the substantial participation in, and subscriptions to these foregoing factors by many different players around the world, they seem to have affected the risk-perceptions of investors, regulators and corporate executives. As of 2018, many Multinational Corporations (MNCs) (such as Apple, Alibaba, TMobile, AT&T; etc.) were not members of the United Nations Global Compact Initiative; and the sustainability (economic; environmental, urban and social sustainability) disclosures and initiatives of many MNCs during 2010-2018 were woefully deficient and much below standards expected of MNCs.

Many MNCs (such as Facebook; Oracle; Alphabet/Google; Deutsche Telecomm; Apple; Samsung; Lenovo; Airbnb, Uber, Alibaba, Ebay, WeChat; Snap; Baidu; Amazon; Mitsubishi; Microsoft; IBM; telecomm companies; large international banks; automobile and aeroplane manufacturers; electronics manufacturers; etc.) market, sell and cause the annual purchases of millions of cellphones, computers, hand-held devices, electronic parts, automobiles and auto-parts, plastic products and accessories around the world, many of which are made of non-biodegradable and or highly toxic (or potentially toxic) plastics/synthetics/materials and are manufactured under very questionable circumstances[15] in developing countries. All or most of these developing countries (such as China, India, Indonesia, Thailand, Mexico, Brazil; etc.) have much weaker enforcement regimes and environmental laws compared to developed countries (such as USA, EU, Japan, etc.). Some MNC-affiliated foreign factories in emerging markets countries have reported suicides, and have been fined for improper waste-management and labor law violations; and MNCs have been fined in several countries for the same and other violations/misconduct. Many MNCs outsource production of goods and or service-delivery to services-contractors and manufacturers that are located in LCLRLELCHP Countries – and those companies violate such laws. As of 2018, many of such MNCs didn't have any comprehensive and effective waste disposal, labor or environmental remediation policies/practices for those products (e.g. waste management for the computers, hand-held devices, batteries, car-parts; inks; metals; printer-cartridges and plastic products and other non-biodegradable products that are implicated in the use of their services/products).

Many MNCs (such as Facebook; Oracle; Lenovo; Samsung; Alphabet/Google; Airbnb, Uber, Alibaba, Ebay, WeChat; Snap; Apple; Baidu; Amazon; IBM; large international banks; Microsoft; automobile manufacturers; etc.) cause or facilitate the sales and use of products and equipment that consume significant amounts of energy that was generated from fossil fuels (the MNCs significantly increased the *emissions footprints* and *toxic-waste-production footprints* of households, companies and governments). Also, the emissions footprints and *toxic-waste-production footprints* of many MNCs and their suppliers are significant and growing. As of December 2018, most of those MNCs didn't have any programs to generate clean energy for mass consumption, or to significantly reduce energy consumed by their operations and the products/service that they sell, or caused the purchases of (including ancillary and complementary products that are manufactured and sold by other companies).

MNCs' earnings management and asset-quality management and their other corporate governance problems (see Nwogugu (2020)) have or had or could have had "*Governance Contagion Effects*" both in their industries and in other industries which in turn, can cause or increase systemic risk and financial instability (and also increase firms' cost-of-capital and perceived risk), all of which reduces economic/financial sustainability. The corporate governance, strategy, operations research and corporate finance literatures indicate that in many countries, many large and medium sized companies hire senior executives and board members from, and copy the corporate governance policies and operational strategies of their competitors.

Thus legally, those MNCs may be partly liable for the foregoing environmental pollution problems under tort law (e.g. Contribution; product liability) and or criminal law – because the relevant elements exist (ie. knowledge or *mens rea*; intent or omission; result; actual or proximate causation; and injury). Ironically, given that the statutes-of-limitations for legal claims against such offending companies have not expired, in some instances the monetary amount of such legal liabilities may exceed the total assets (and sometimes the equity market values) of such companies, which renders them technically insolvent. Companies that don't generate enough clean energy that exceeds the sum of their own direct energy consumption plus the energy consumption of their customers plus the allocated energy consumption of their regulators and suppliers, are henceforth referred to as "*Energy-Negative Companies*"; and companies that do the opposite are "*Energy Positive Companies*". Similarly, companies that don't have processes to adequately manage and dispose of waste that arise or are derived from their products/services are henceforth referred to as "*Waste-Negative Companies*"; and companies that do the opposite are "*Waste-Positive Companies*. Incorporating the foregoing portfolio selection criteria and equity/debt valuation factors into credit analysis and financial analysis can compel companies (and government agencies) to better manage their product development, energy consumption and "*energy-impact*".

Emissions Taxes and emissions trading systems (tradable pollution permits/credits and subsidies) around the world have failed as indicated by rising CO2, global warming and increasing pollution. The existing and most proposed Emissions Taxes and Emissions Trading systems[16] around the world are greatly inefficient and harmful because of the following reasons:

1. They don't provide any meaningful incentives for government agencies, companies and households to transition to clean energy. Without such incentives, sufficient capital and effort won't be allocated to producing cheap clean energy and managing waste. They create and amplify a destructive "*Pollute-As-Long-As-You-Can-Pay*" mentality (in companies, households and government agencies) which doesn't provide effective incentives to eliminate (not just reduce) pollution.
2. In Most countries the taxation of employee/executive compensation and employee retirement benefits don't provide specific and sufficient incentives for managers and employee to reduce pollution and waste.
3. They sometimes don't accurately allocate the Emissions Taxes and Emissions Permits based on the true "energy impact" and pollution loads of polluters.
4. They disproportionately over-burden poor/low-income households and smaller companies (who are disproportionately affected by the resultant price increases, environmental damage and health problems).
5. Most existing (and proposed) emissions-trading systems have been or can be circumvented, and many cases of fraud and other misconduct (in inaccuracy of disclosures, under-reporting of environmental-liabilities, bribery, trading, side-payments, inefficient "self-auditing"; etc.) in many countries such as Russia, India, China and Ukraine have been reported in journal articles and the popular media. Such misconduct should be statutorily criminalized. While much of the Emissions Trading systems are based on voluntary reporting by companies and government agencies, there are significant *verification* and "*Truth-Telling*" problems (by polluters) and "*political interference*" problems (etc. political lobbying; "Gerry-mandering"; etc.) in the current systems of global regulation of pollution and climate change. Such problems can be resolved by using external auditing firms, consulting firms and government auditors. Emissions Trading Systems have the following disadvantages:
    a. The Emissions Permits/Credits and Emissions Trading can be easily manipulated - e.g. by using *Side-Payments*; by intentionally colluding to bid low prices for Emissions Credits/Permits or colluding to buy Emissions Permits at very low prices; by hoarding Emissions Permits; by concentrating production activity in an industry in a few companies; by false disclosures; by concentrating their production/factories in Low-cost Low-regulation Low-Enforcement Low-Compliance High-Pollution countries ("LCLRLELCHP Countries") in Latin America, Central/Eastern Europe and Asia; by concentrating production activities among fewer companies that have higher "caps" (in the industry) and are in fewer locations; by outsourcing production; etc..
    b. Emissions Trading is based on voluntary disclosure which is very inefficient because pollutants have significant incentives to under-report their emissions/pollution liabilities.

c. The Emissions Permits are typically not priced accurately (prices have been extremely low) – otherwise global pollution and waste would have declined significantly during the last decade.

6. The "prices" for pollution that are implicit in emissions taxes, emissions permits and emissions trading systems are clearly inaccurate because they haven't been enough to reduce pollution and use of fossil-fuel based energy. Researchers have also noted that more than half of the sixty-five existing global emissions trading systems (as of 2020) had a carbon-price of less than $10 (ten US dollars) per metric ton, which was far less than the then current $50 (fifty US dollars) minimum-actual-cost of removing one metric ton of carbon from the earth's atmosphere. Low emissions-prices and current Emission-Trading Systems don't provide sufficient incentives for polluting-companies and their financiers and insurers to reduce their pollution. The entire (current and proposed) carbon/emissions taxes and emissions-trading frameworks encourage a very destructive *Pollute-As-Long-As-You-Can-Pay* (and *Pollute-As-Long-As-You-Can-Shift-Costs-To-Others*) mentality wherein polluters can shift costs (emissions permits, fines/penalties and emissions taxes) to their end-customers, and or outsource production/services to low-cost countries, and can obtain concessions (e.g. reduction of employees' salaries and or employee-benefits; reduction of permissible Labor Union activities; government tax credits; supplier-discounts; trade-credit; etc.) from their employees and suppliers and government agencies; and can use tax/legal advisors to avoid corporate taxes and to park cash in foreign low-tax jurisdictions. This *Cost-Shifting Phenomenon* is dangerous and can dampen associated "*Cost Remediation Policies*". *Cost Remediation Policies* refers to government policies that are designed to protect affected persons (such as low-income persons and small businesses) from the direct/indirect effects of taxation/penalties imposed on polluters and the resulting increases in prices. Such *Cost Remediation Policies* are often not fully transmitted through the economy (e.g. Banks sometimes refuse to provide government guaranteed loans that are part of stimulus packages and *Cost Remediation Policies*; moderate/high income persons/businesses sometimes fraudulently apply for loans and benefits designated for low-income persons/businesses; there may be low price-stability wherein increases in prices for goods/services vary widely across the economy/regions and product types; low-income recipients of government aid sometimes use the funds for other purposes such as gambling/entertainment; illicit drugs, leisure/recreation, etc.). Thus, *Emissions Taxes* and new (recomended herein) *Statutory Minimum Prices* of *Emissions permits* should be set high enough to: 1) eliminate all possible *Cost-Shifting*; 2) compel customers to abandon polluting products/services; 3) cover the actual short-term cost of environmental remediation (e.g. cost-per-ton to remove harmful emissions from the atmosphere); 4) cover government's current and future administrative/monitoring/enforcement costs; 5) cover part of "*Legacy Emissions-Capture*" ("*Legacy Emissions*" refers to harmful emissions that have accumulated in the earth's atmosphere during the last three hundred years).

7. Thus, there is an issue of "*Inefficient Receipts Allocation*" wherein governments don't use the proceeds of Emissions Taxes and Emissions Permits to efficiently reduce pollution and increase waste management, and to provide subsidies to persons affected by *Externalities*. Such cash proceeds are often subject to *Political Interference* and may not be adequately allocated to required R&D that will provide better clean energy and biodegradable materials. Thus, it's necessary to strictly limit or eliminate *Political Interference* (e.g. Political Lobbying, campaign contributions; advertising and fundraising by PACs; etc.) and to develop a tax system that forces or provides substantial incentives for pollutants to reduce their pollution and increase waste management.

8. Emissions Taxes are an indirect tax on transactions and products/services (not a direct tax, which taxes income) and so when transaction volumes or product volumes don't match actual pollution, there is inefficiency (hereafter, the "*Transaction-Inefficiency Gap*"). Pollution and associated waste management and consumption are intricately intertwined with income-generation of companies and government agencies, and it maybe more efficient to tax polluters' gross revenues (not their "Net Income" or "income") rather than impose Indirect Taxes. Furthermore, emissions taxes and emissions trading systems often don't align with the wishes and preferences of consumers and thus are inequitable. For example, an emissions-conscious and recycling household that wants to purchase electricity from one of five local electric utilities will typically not know the exact percentage of energy from each of the five utilities that is clean energy, and that can affect its choices and decisions, and ultimately will affect the utilitys' incentives to produce clean energy. Similarly, an individual that purchases fuel at a gas station cannot compare the emissions content of fuel sold at each gas station (and must buy fuel for their car even if they are against fossil fuel energy) and thus don't have any real choice (which provides "artificial price-and-demand support" and substantial incentives for continued pollution).
9. As of 2020, there were *Deadweight Losses* in the prices of Emissions Credits/Permits; and there were also *Deadweight Losses* in the demand and supply for Enforcement of Environmental/Climate-control programs and regulations.
10. The current and proposed Emissions Taxation/Permits systems and Emissions Trading Systems address the results but not the root causes of pollution and climate change. For example, around the world, most emissions-remediation and emissions-trading systems focus on harmful emissions that are produced from factories and automobiles/planes/ships/homes/offices in the form of gases, but omit emissions from "open" and untreated waste (e.g. gutters, municipal waste dumps, illegal waste-dumps; garbage in oceans; un-collected refuse; etc.) which can be more harmful. Researchers have noted that as of 2020, at least eighty percent of global emissions were not covered by any carbon/emissions pricing system.
11. As mentioned herein and above, it's now clear that the inefficient systems of "*self-auditing*" (by polluting companies and government agencies) have woefully failed given increasing pollution and climate change around the world. Self-auditing creates significant *Truth-Telling Problems* which are almost impossible to resolve because corporate manager's compensation, incentives and career advancement compel (and the fact under Self Auditing regulations in most countries, managers don't face any personal losses) them to lie and to distort data. The U.S. Environmental Protection Agency (EPA) operates a Self-Auditing program which has been heavily criticized by various stakeholders[17].
12. The *Border-Adjustments* for Emissions Taxes (implemented by some countries such as the European Union, and also being considered by other countries) can be manipulated in the following ways:
    a. Bribery and Corruption at seaports, airports and land borders.
    b. Shipping full-knockdown-parts from LCLRLELCHP Countries to "intermediate-level countries" and then to developed countries.
    c. Hiding the origins of products (ie. false declarations).
    d. Obtaining Import-Waivers from regional/central governments.
13. Sarbanes Oxley Act, the Dodd Frank Act and similar statutes in other countries didn't sufficiently address pollution, waste management and Climate Change - and these regulations may have created

effects/biases that make it more difficult and expensive for companies to comply with environmental/waste-management regulations and standards.

14. In many countries, securities regulators (such as the US SEC) haven't been adequately enforcing mandatory disclosure regulations and haven't developed specific and clear mandatory disclosure guidelines for Climate-Change and environmental pollution.
15. In any countries, there are no clear legal-liability standards for external auditors and external consultants that advise corporate boards and management. These advisors have or should be made to have statutory and or moral duty to monitor and report on their clients that are polluters.
16. In most countries, Climate-change/environmental policy and emissions-trading systems have almost completely omitted land-title systems (ie. structure/rights; development-controls; economic efficiency; *Multiplier-Effects*; etc.) which govern land-use and property-rights, and thus are central elements of environmental/pollution management. Ideally, municipal land development plans and zoning-plans should include waste-generation and emissions limits/caps, based on which violators should be statutorily required to participate in emissions/pollution/waste remediation programs.
17. In most countries, Climate-change/environmental and emissions-trading systems have almost completely omitted insurance (insurance regulations; structures of insurance policies; insurance industry networks; reinsurance and Financial Stability; economic efficiency; *Multiplier-Effects*; etc.) which is a core element of waste/pollution/climate-change management. In many developed and developing countries where some critical industries (such as automobiles, housing/real-estate, healthcare, telecommunications, etc.) won't work well without insurance policies, insurers essentially insure, encourage and provide a ready market for imported goods/services that are made in Low-cost Low-regulation Low-Enforcement Low-Compliance High-Pollution countries ("LCLRLELCHP Countries") in Latin America, Central/Eastern Europe and Asia (and similar domestic products), and thereby directly/indirectly reinforce and promote pollution and environmental damage. Thus, there is a pressing need to change regulations, risk-exposure documentation (e.g. exposure to LCLRLELCHP Countries) and mandatory disclosures (e.g. sources/origin of insured items; estimated direct/indirect pollution-impact of insured items; government classification/ranking of countries based on regulation, compliance, Enforcement, Pollution, etc.) for the global insurance industry. Under Tort Law, Criminal Law and causality principles, Insurance companies are a major *actual* and "*But-For*" cause of pollution/waste and are liable for "*Contribution*". In most instances, without the insurance, guarantees and other financial services that they provide, the polluting goods/services won't be produced. The following relevant legal elements exist: 1) knowledge or duty; 2) breach of actual or implied duty; 3) intent; 4) causation (proximate and but-for causation); 5) result; 6) harm to humans; 7) mens rea (driven by profits, greed, expectations; status-seeking; mental-health problems; etc.). Therefore, Insurance companies that insure "*Moderate/High Pollution Goods/Services*" and associated activities should be treated like polluting/waste-generating companies, and should mandatorily participate in emissions/waste reduction programs/systems (ie. they should made to purchase Carbon Permits, etc.); and in addition, they should be taxed for essentially insuring pollution/waste-production (ie. as recommended in this book and in Nwogugu (2020; 2019)). There should be criminal statutes that penalize insurance companies and their senior executives for insuring the production, storage/transportation or purchase of "high-pollution" goods/services are produced domestically or in LCLRLELCHP Regions (in countries). Directly or indirectly polluting the air/environment (or aiding/abetting pollution, or conspiracy to pollute) is more dangerous to human health and Social Welfare than the minor violations of automobile traffic-statute and the

illegal online filesharing that are already statutorily criminalized in many developed and emerging markets countries.

18. In most countries, Climate-change/environmental and emissions-trading systems have almost completely omitted banks, finance-companies and investment funds which finance most pollution-generating assets. Banks and investment funds finance, provide loan-guarantees for, encourage and help provide a ready market for both domestic pollutants and imported goods/services that are made in LCLRLELCHP Countries in Latin America, Central/Eastern Europe and Asia, and thereby directly and indirectly reinforce and promote pollution and environmental damage. Thus, there is a pressing need to change regulations, risk-exposure documentation (e.g. exposure to LCLRLELCHP Countries) and mandatory disclosures (e.g. sources/origin of financed items; estimated direct/indirect pollution-impact of financed items; government classification/ranking of countries based on regulation, compliance, Enforcement, Pollution, etc.) for the global banking/finance and asset management industry. Under Tort Law, Criminal Law and causality principles, banks, finance-companies and investment funds are a major *actual* and "*But-For*" cause of pollution/waste and are liable for "*Contribution*". In most instances, without the funds, guarantees and other financial services that they provide, the polluting goods/services won't be produced. The following relevant legal elements exist: 1) knowledge or duty; 2) breach of actual or implied duty; 3) intent; 4) causation (proximate and but-for causation); 5) result; 6) harm to humans; 7) mens rea (driven by profits, greed, expectations; status-seeking; mental-health problems; etc.). Therefore, Banks, finance companies and investment funds that finance "*Moderate/High Pollution Goods/Services*" and associated activities should be treated like polluting companies, and should mandatorily participate in emissions/waste reduction programs/systems (ie. they should be made to purchase Carbon Permits, etc.); and in addition, they should be taxed for essentially financing pollution/waste-production (ie. as recommended in this book and in Nwogugu (2020; 2019)). There should also be criminal statutes that penalize banks, finance-companies and investment funds and their senior executives for financing the production, storage/transportation or purchase of "high-pollution" goods/services that are produced domestically or in LCLRLELCHP Regions (in countries).

19. Most economists and policy-makers consider environmental pollution and waste to be "*Stand-alone Negative Externalities*", when in fact, environmental pollution and waste are "*Networked Negative Externalities*" that are intricately intertwined with consumption, corporate income, stock market values, executive compensation, status, human aspirations, household economics/dynamics, social-networks, and other externalities. Thus, these other externalities should also be regulated and taxed accordingly in a coordinated manner in order to elicit proper behaviors, create incentives and reduce pollution. Contrary to generally accepted economic theory, a tax on a *Negative Externality* (such as pollution) should substantially exceed (not just equal) the marginal damage costs in order to provide sufficient deterrence effects and the incentive to seek clean energy. The current systems merely penalize the use of fossil fuels but don't provide sufficient incentives to switch to clean energy (some or most of the penalties are passed on to consumers).

20. In most countries, Climate-change/environmental taxes and *Emissions-Trading* systems have almost completely *Legacy Emissions* and *Emissions-Capture*[18]. Ideally, a portion of Emissions Prices should be statutorily allocated towards reducing *Legacy Emissions* and perhaps to *Emissions Capture*. However, some problems inherent in *Emissions Capture* are as follows:

a. *Emissions Capture* technologies are costly, require the use of fossils fuels, and haven't been proven to be efficient at scale.
b. Current and planned *Emissions Capture* technologies by themselves won't be sufficient to eliminate 100% of *Legacy Emissions*.

21. Most of the comments in Nwogugu (2019b) about *Risk-Perception* and *Nonlinear Risk*, were confirmed by the failures of *Emissions Trading* systems, *Emissions Taxes* and *Emissions Capture* policies implemented by federal and state governments around the world. Secondly, Nwogugu (2019b) stated that: "………One of the implications of the theories introduced in this book is that macroeconomic policy-making should consist of at least six strands which should be simultaneously analyzed and which are *monetary and fiscal policies*; "*trade policies*", "*firm-structure policies*" (which will seek to manage macroeconomic issues that arise from the structure/nature/powers of organizations), "*regulatory-response and anti-regulatory-capture policies*" (which will manage responses to regulations, antitrust and regulatory-capture) and "*behavioral-effects policies*" (which will seek to manage behavioral biases and psychological responses and also develop and track indices of same). Indeed in most developed, developing and under-developed economies there are or can be distinct "sub-markets" for "*regulatory responses*", "*behavioral effects*" and "*firm-structure effects*". Although the discussions in Hosek (1975) are somewhat outdated, the book aptly made an observation which remains valid today, when it stated in part: "…….*Unfortunately, many textbooks discuss macroeconomic policy in the context of only the product market (the "Keynesian Cross") or only the product and money markets (the IS-LM model). The labor market and the determinants of aggregate supply are usually treated separately and are not integrated in the full model…Moreover, the linkages among the all three markets become important in transmitting policy changes…The fiscalist versus monetarist controversy is not the only controversy over policy method. The economics profession has been confronted by a radical challenge. The challenge is radical because traditional economists, in conducting their analysis and disagreeing with each other, have done so under the assumption of given institutions and given behavior patterns. However, the new challengers are unwilling to accept these assumptions. The basis of their policy recommendations is to change institutions and behavior patterns and thereby deal with problems of unemployment and inflation. Macroeconomic theory is therefore in a state of flux, and it's likely to continue in that state for years to come*…….". Clearly, in their responses to worldwide pollution and Climate Change, most governments haven't sufficiently addressed "*sub-markets*" for "*regulatory responses*", "*behavioral effects*" and "*firm-structure effects*". In the foregoing Nwogugu (2019b) suggested framework for macroeconomic policy-making, Labor issues and Environmental/Climate-Change issues are addressed under "*Trade Policies*". One more policy-making element is "*Healthcare Policies*", for which there are distinct submarkets in many countries (and especially in Emerging Markets countries) where the majority of the population don't have access to affordable and reliable healthcare services.

Like emissions permits and emissions taxes, the tax credits and *similar subsidies* granted to companies and households (for implementing "energy efficiency measures") don't address the primary causes and sources of pollution; they encourage targeted and unaffordable consumption and import-substitution (many such products are imported and their consumption is often financed with debt); and are limited by the company's or household's own cash-expenditure/wealth; and many governments cannot afford to provide such tax-credits in sufficient amounts to create sustainable change. Under current regulatory systems (emissions-permits-trading[19]; emissions taxes; subsidies; etc.), it's reasonably inferable that the implied prices of pollution, emissions permits and emissions-credits are relatively cheap and can be collusively manipulated downwards by polluting industries – for example, by the different methods explained herein and above. Without a steady and high-enough price for Emissions credits, polluters don't have sufficient incentives to develop clean energy solutions or to reduce their pollution. Speculators often participate in auctions for, and purchase emissions-credits and emissions-permits and also do "consignment auctioning" of emissions permits, all of which distorts the market. It's been shown that emissions-trading provides windfalls for polluting industries. On the contrary, the policy objectives should include complete elimination of pollution and waste (and not "caps") and introduction of "clean technologies" rather than economic gimmicks. See the comments in: Tanaka & Chen (2012), Hinterman (2016), Bowman, Enion, et. al. (2011), Interpol (June 2013), and Brisson (2014).

Governments (e.g. government interventions; bail-outs/bail-ins; environmental remediation costs; healthcare costs; increased government debt; reduced productivity; etc.), companies (e.g. higher taxes; higher employee costs; increased debt; reduced employee-productivity and profits; etc.) and households (e.g. higher taxes; unemployment; health problems; reduced productivity; reduced savings and purchasing power; consumer debt; investment losses; mortgage foreclosures; greater volatility and uncertainty in markets; etc.) typically bear the costs of environmental pollution and climate change problems[20]. At this time, it's reasonably inferable that national/state governments around the world provide an implied "*Governmental Pollution And Climate-Change Subsidy*" to, and households provide a "*Household Pollution And Climate-Change Subsidy*" to such offending companies and government agencies. Given the foregoing, most economic models of climate change and pollution (and inherent Complex Systems) are mis-specified and inaccurate[21].

Governments should consider creating "*National Sustainability Funds*" that will be financed by levies/fines/taxes on such MNCs, large companies and large institutional investors (e.g. mutual funds; hedge funds; ETFs; insurance companies; pension funds; banks; finance companies; etc.) and will be used to solve sustainability problems. See the proposals in Nwogugu (2019; 2020). Such taxes/levies can be pro-rated according to the magnitude of misconduct. For example, in the case of companies and government agencies:

1. Entities that are *Energy Negative* and or *Waste Negative* and whose annual gross revenues or total assets exceeds a designated amount (e.g. at least US$20 million of gross revenues or US$15 million of total assets) should pay a sustainability levy/tax that is a percentage of their annual gross revenues or total assets. Companies and government agencies whose annual gross revenues or total assets exceeds a designated amount (e.g. at least US$70 million of gross revenues or US$50 million of total assets) must have an external environmental audit every six months to determine their liability. Such external audit can be performed by a "*fully independent*" accounting/auditing firm, or a management consulting firm or a government agency. *Full Independence* means that the third-party company doesn't have any prior or current business relationship with, or interest (e.g. debt; equity; options/warrants; contracts; etc.) in, or conflict-of-interests with the subject entity.
2. For purposes of illustration, an entity that is *40% Energy Negative* is one that generates clean energy that covers only 60% (sixty percent) of its *Total Energy Impact* (the energy needs of its own operations plus the pro-rata share of its suppliers', customers' and regulator's energy needs). An entity that is *90% Waste Negative* is one that has verified and active programs to dispose of only 10% (ten percent) of its *Total Waste Impact* (the toxicity-weighted volume of physical waste generated

by its own operations plus the pro-rata share of its suppliers', customers' and regulator's wastes). Thus, for any period, an entity's *Energy Deficit* is its *Energy Negative* percentage multiplied by its *Total Energy Impact*; and its *Waste Deficit* is its *Waste Negative* percentage multiplied by its *Total Waste Impact*. "Waste Disposal" means that the physical waste is treated and managed in ways that have zero impact on the environment at any time.

3. For example, the proposed levy/tax can be pro-rated based on the severity of misconduct as follows:
   a. A *1%-19.99% Energy Negative* entity will pay the greater of S_{e1}% (e.g. 4%) of its Gross Quarterly Sales Revenues, or A_{e1}% (e.g. 2%) of its total assets at the end of each calendar quarter; or the equivalent of US$$X_1$ per unit of its *Energy Deficit* for the calendar quarter; or a stated mandatory minimum amount.
   b. A *20%-39.99% Energy Negative* entity will pay the greater of S_{e2}% (e.g. 5%) of its Gross Quarterly Sales Revenues, or A_{e2}% (e.g. 2.75%) of its total assets at the end of each calendar quarter; or the equivalent of US$$X_2$ per unit of its *Energy Deficit* for the calendar quarter (where $X_2>X_1$); or a stated mandatory minimum amount.
   c. A *40%-59.99% Energy Negative* entity will pay the greater of S_{e3}% (e.g. 6%) of its Gross Quarterly Sales Revenues, or A_{e3}% (e.g. 3.5%) of its total assets at the end of each calendar quarter; or the equivalent of US$$X_3$ per unit of its *Energy Deficit* for the calendar quarter (where $X_3>X_2$); or a stated mandatory minimum amount.
   d. A *60%-79.99% Energy Negative* entity will pay the greater of S_{e4}% (e.g. 7%) of its Gross Quarterly Sales Revenues, or A_{e4}% (e.g. 4.5%) of its total assets at the end of each calendar quarter; or the equivalent of US$$X_4$ per unit of its *Energy Deficit* for the calendar quarter (where $X_4>X_3$); or a stated mandatory minimum amount.
   e. A *80%-100% Energy Negative* entity will pay the greater of S_{e5}% (e.g. 9%) of its Gross Quarterly Sales Revenues, or A_{e5}% (e.g. 6%) of its total assets at the end of each calendar quarter; or the equivalent of US$$X_5$ per unit of its *Energy Deficit* (where $X_5>X_4$) for the calendar quarter; or a stated mandatory minimum amount.
   f. An entity that is both Energy Negative and Waste Negative will pay both the Energy Negative and Waste Negative taxes/levys; or two stated mandatory minimum amounts.
   g. A *1%-19.99% Waste Negative* entity will pay the greater of S_{w1}% (e.g. 5%) of its Gross Quarterly Sales Revenues, or A_{w1}% (e.g. 1%) of its total assets at the end of each calendar quarter; or the equivalent of US$$Y_1$ per unit of its *Waste Deficit* for the calendar quarter; or a stated mandatory minimum amount.
   h. A *20%-39.99% Waste Negative* entity will pay the greater of S_{w2}% (e.g. 5%) of its Gross Quarterly Sales Revenues, or A_{w2}% (e.g. 1.75%) of its total assets at the end of each calendar quarter; or the equivalent of US$$Y_2$ per unit of its *Waste Deficit* (where $Y_2>Y_1$) for the calendar quarter; or a stated mandatory minimum amount
   i. A *40%-59.99% Waste Negative* entity will pay the greater of S_{w3}% (e.g. 7%) of its Gross Quarterly Sales Revenues, or A_{w3}% (e.g. 2%) of its total assets at the end of each calendar quarter; or the equivalent of US$$Y_3$ per unit of its *Waste Deficit* (where $Y_3>Y_2$) for the calendar quarter; or a stated mandatory minimum amount.
   j. A *60%-79.99% Waste Negative* entity will pay the greater of S_{w4}% (e.g. 8%) of its Gross Quarterly Sales Revenues, or A_{w4}% (e.g. 2.75%) of its total assets at the end of each calendar quarter; or the equivalent of US$$Y_4$ per unit of its *Waste Deficit* (where $Y_4>Y_3$) for the calendar quarter; or a stated mandatory minimum amount.

k. A *80%-100% Waste Negative* entity will pay the greater of S_{w5}% (e.g. 9%) of its Gross Quarterly Sales Revenues, or A_{w5}% (e.g. 3%) of its total assets at the end of each calendar quarter; or the equivalent of US\$$Y_5$ per unit of its *Waste Deficit* (where $Y_5 > Y_4$) for the calendar quarter; or a stated mandatory minimum amount.

l. The Waste Tax and the Energy Tax can be phased in after a two-year grace-period. Each foregoing "*mandatory minimum amount*" will increase annually and will be payable only by small companies (e.g. those that have no more than US$70 million of gross revenues or US$50 million of total assets) and companies in few exempted industries where it is extremely difficult to calculate the exact energy-impact of companies.

m. Countries will grant reciprocal credit for similar/same taxes paid by each entity in a foreign country. The per-unit amounts \$$X_i$ and \$$Y_i$ will increase in each calendar year.

n. Entities can reduce their *Energy Deficits* by generating clean energy for their own use and or by contributing free clean energy to the national or regional grid. Entities can generate the clean energy by themselves, or buy verified units of clean energy during each calendar quarter from companies that generate clean energy. Entities can reduce their *Waste Deficits* by collecting and treating waste by themselves or outsourcing that.

o. Each entity's board of directors, CEO, COO and CFO will be made statutorily liable (both civil and criminal liability) for improper/misleading disclosures/reporting for such taxes; and the government will have powers to place liens on an entity's assets for non-payment of the taxes. Such taxes will not be voidable in any bankruptcy proceedings.

Some of the potential consequences of the above-mentioned taxation mechanism are as follows:

1. The Energy Tax and Waste Tax are likely to "displace" traditional corporate taxes. That is, one possible result is that the *Effective Corporate Tax Rates* for companies will probably decline in many countries.
2. Corporate tax evasion and tax avoidance will probably decline because there will be much less incentive and "capacity" to do that and because firms' pre-tax income will generally be lower.
3. Companies that park cash abroad in low-tax havens will be forced to repatriate such cash to fund their operations and to pay the Energy Tax and Waste Tax.
4. Corporate debt levels will increase for some companies that are either marginally profitable or are in high-competition industries.
5. Mergers/Acquisitions and industry consolidation will probably increase drastically because: 1) companies will want to reduce their costs in order to maintain profitability; 2) companies will want to reduce or eliminate the obvious duplication of Energy Taxes and Waste Taxes along their Global Value-Chains – through forward-integration and backward-integration; 3) marginally profitable or un-profitable companies will find it increasingly harder to operate and compete; 4) companies may not be able to quickly or sufficiently raise prices.
6. The number of distribution ("middle-men") companies will decline rapidly because: 1) they will pay the same Energy Tax and Waste Tax as their original equipment manufacturers; and 2) their margins will shrink or become negative. vi) As a result, manufacturers will likely take on more distribution and sales/marketing, and there may be emergence of "Manufacturers' Distribution Joint Ventures" wherein several manufacturers jointly distribute their products.

7. Entities will have a significant incentive to reduce their Energy Impact and Waste Impact because the taxes have a direct effect on valuation and credit analysis metrics which are regularly reviewed by investors, lenders and regulators; and also have a direct impact on their capital structures, perceived risk, solvency, opportunity-set and equity valuations.
8. Managerial compensation in many companies will likely decline and will be drastically revised to reflect the impact of the Waste Tax and Energy Tax (ie. to provide more incentives for managers to comply).
9. Companies may purchase insurance policies to hedge against their not being able to reduce their *Energy Impact* and or *Waste Impact.*
10. Auditing firms and management consulting firms will hire more professionals in Urban/Regional Planning, environmental science and environmental engineering. The same Independence, Fee-Allocation, Work-Allocation and Liability-Allocation problems discussed in this chapter will arise.
11. New loan covenants and bond indentures will incorporate the Waste Tax and the Energy Tax.
12. There will generally be drastic increases in R&D spending, and emphasis on bio-degradable materials. Many companies will be forced to change their product development and or service delivery processes. For example, cloud computing and SaaS/PaaS/IaaS models may become more prevalent.
13. Many national governments may have to create a new national electric utility company that will distribute the free clean energy that will be contributed by companies in their country. Existing electric utility companies will probably not want to reduce their prices even if they are given such free energy to distribute. Some electric utility companies may have to liquidate their operations.

These foregoing proposed taxes and levies will be collected by the applicable intermediaries (banks; etc.) and government agencies. It's clear that taxation/levies alone won't solve environmental pollution and waste problems, because: i) some companies and government agencies will always pass-on the increased costs to their customers and or to the government; ii) some companies can afford to operate while generating losses; iii) companies can afford to manipulate government tax-credits and subsidies, and can use offshore tax havens to drastically reduce or eliminate their tax burdens. Thus, these foregoing proposed taxes/levies should be supplemented by the following measures:

1. Annual or semi-annual "*Pollution Audits*", "*Emissions-Credit Audits*" and "*Climate Change Audits*" of all polluting companies and all companies whose annual revenues exceed a specific amount by government agencies and or independent auditors. There are definitely "*truth-telling*" problems (by polluters) and "*political interference*" problems (etc. political lobbying; "Gerry-mandering"; etc.) in the current systems of global regulation of pollution and climate change.
2. Increased penalties, monetary fines and jail sentences for fraud or misrepresentation by persons/ companies and government employees that participate in environmental audits, emissions control programs and Climate Change enforcement programs.
3. A "*Constitutionally-Credible Shut-Down Operations*" program wherein: 1) the federal government will set annual limits for environmental pollution (the entity's harmful emissions must not exceed a specified volume) and waste management (a specific minimum volume of the company's direct and indirect waste must be managed) for each company and government agency that cause environmental pollution or produces large amounts of waste; 2) such annual limits will be reduced each year; 3) any company or government agency that exceeds its environmental pollution or waste management limit during any specified time period (e.g. three consecutive years) will be

shut down by the government. This will require new laws that will give a specified government agency the statutory powers to shut down such entities – similar to how the US FSOC (USA) has the statutory powers to take-over any company that poses significant financial stability threats in the USA - but Nwogugu (2015) noted that parts of the US FSOC's "*Orderly Liquidation*" powers are un-constitutional.

4. Many academic researchers and government officials have proposed imposing "*emissions taxes*" on polluting companies and consumers even though such taxes address the results but not the root causes of pollution and climate change. If emissions taxes are used, then:
    a. Such taxes should be imposed on the annual worldwide revenues and total assets of polluting companies with adjustments for their actual pollution volumes; and similar taxes paid in foreign countries.
    b. Such taxes should also be imposed as "value added" sales taxes on consumers wherein consumers pay taxes only on value added by the use of fossil fuels.
    c. Polluting companies should be required to file annual audited financial statements at government regulatory agencies.
    d. There should be annual or semi-annual "*Pollution Audits*", "*Emissions-Credit Audits*" and "*Climate Change Audits*" of all polluting companies and all companies whose annual revenues exceed a specific amount by government agencies and or independent auditors.
    e. There should be statutory limits on political interference such as: a) lobbying by interest groups and polluting companies and trade associations; etc.; b) arbitrary and or frequent changes to enacted legislation; etc..
5. If "*cap-and-trade*" systems must be used, then the following adjustments should be made:
    a. The "cap" for each company must be reduced in each calendar year.
    b. speculators/arbitragers and other "non-primary users" of emissions-permits (who can distort the markets) must be barred from emissions trading markets and shouldn't be allowed to purchase emissions-permits ("primary users" are polluting companies and government agencies).
    c. The federal, state and local emissions trading markets and regulations in each country should be combined and shouldn't conflict.
    d. Governments should ensure that there are enough emissions permits at all times; and ideally, should reserve a minimum number of emissions permits for each actual or prospective polluting company.
    e. In each country, the government should establish a "*Semi-Annual Minimum Floor Price*" (the minimum price at which any emissions-permit can be bought or sold in the country) for emissions permits and that price should be generally adjusted upwards annually or semi-annually to account for inflation, increased consumption of energy, increased volumes of commodity futures contracts, Index Products and spot-market transactions; and opportunity costs (generally, as Clean Energy becomes more commercially available, the *Semi-Annual Minimum Floor Price* of emissions-permits should be increased to create deterrence effects). This minimum-price should also be adjusted annually to cover the sum of the actual then-current cost of removing pollutants from the atmosphere, plus government's actual direct monitoring and administrative costs, plus a "reserve cost" (which a probability-weighted cost of future pollution by the same company/entity).

f. There should be annual or semi-annual "*Pollution Audits*", "*Emissions-Credit Audits*" and "*Climate Change Audits*" of all polluting companies and all companies whose annual revenues exceed a specific amount by government agencies and or independent auditors.

g. *Cap-and-trade* regulations should be applied to the worldwide operations of multinational corporations (MNCs) and not just their domestic operations; and reciprocal credits/adjustments made for emissions-permits that are purchased in foreign countries and reported to the home-country government.

h. There should be statutory limits on political interference such as: a) lobbying by interest groups, polluting companies and trade associations; etc.; b) arbitrary and or frequent changes to enacted legislation; c) donations to political parties; d) any type of "*Side Payments*"; etc..

i. Governments should ban and criminalize "*Side Payments*" by buyers and sellers of emissions-permits, and their advisers and disclosed/undisclosed agents.

Figure 1. Changes in disposals of plastic waste around the world (2018)
Source: https://www.ft.com/content/360e2524-d71a-11e8-a854-33d6f82e62f8.

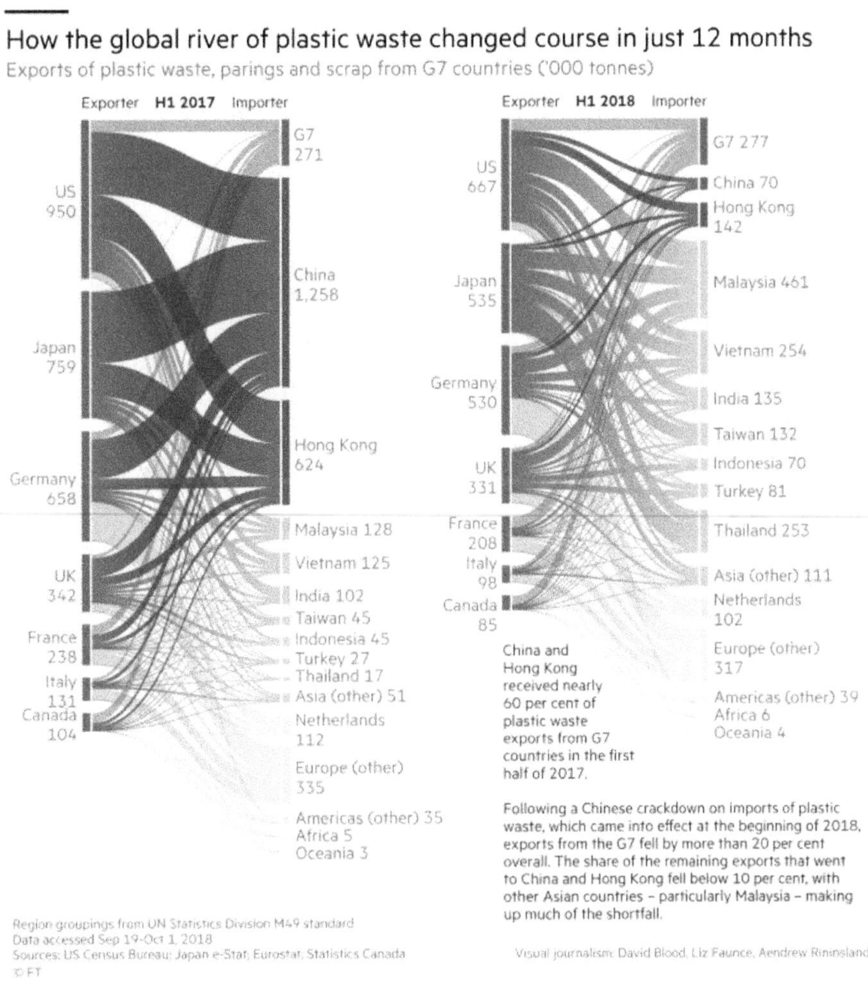

j. Governments should provide built-in incentives for companies that substantially reduce their emissions (many existing cap-and-trade systems around the world lack such built-in incentive mechanisms.

Figure 2. Decline of plastic waste from G7 countries after China's import ban
Source: https://www.ft.com/content/360e2524-d71a-11e8-a854-33d6f82e62f8.

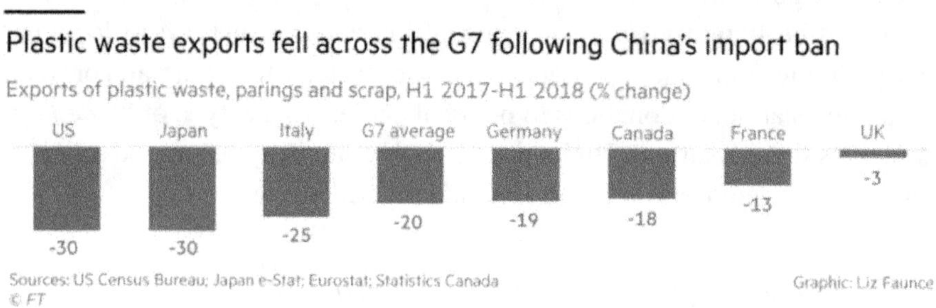

Figure 3. Other Asian Countries have collectively become the main importers of paper waste
Source: https://www.ft.com/content/360e2524-d71a-11e8-a854-33d6f82e62f8.

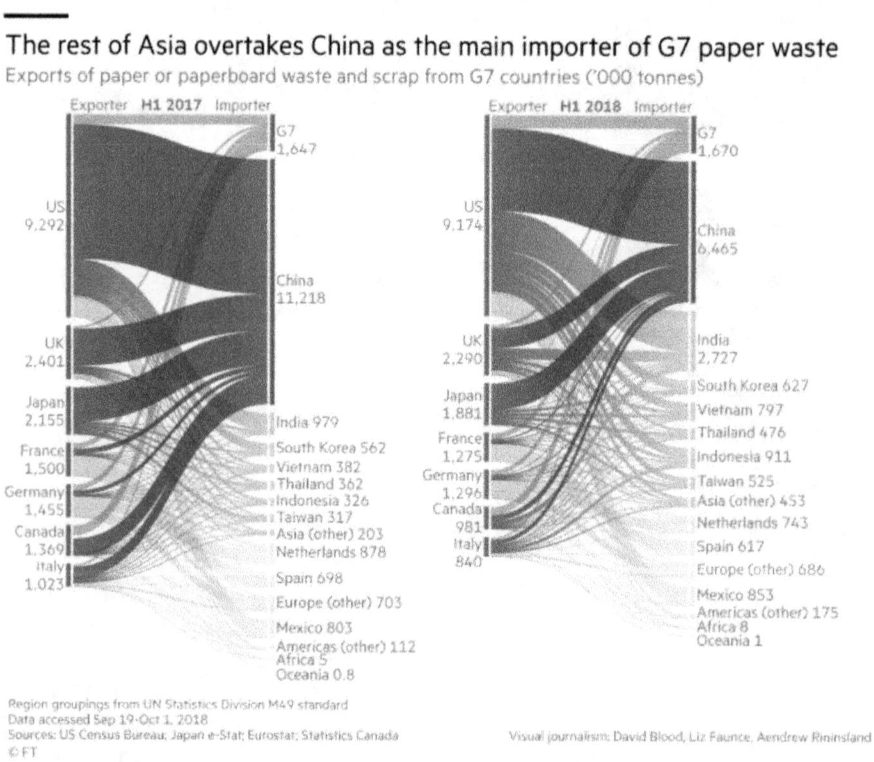

Figure 4. G7 countries generate most of the plastic and paper waste in the world (2017)
Source: https://www.ft.com/content/360e2524-d71a-11e8-a854-33d6f82e62f8.

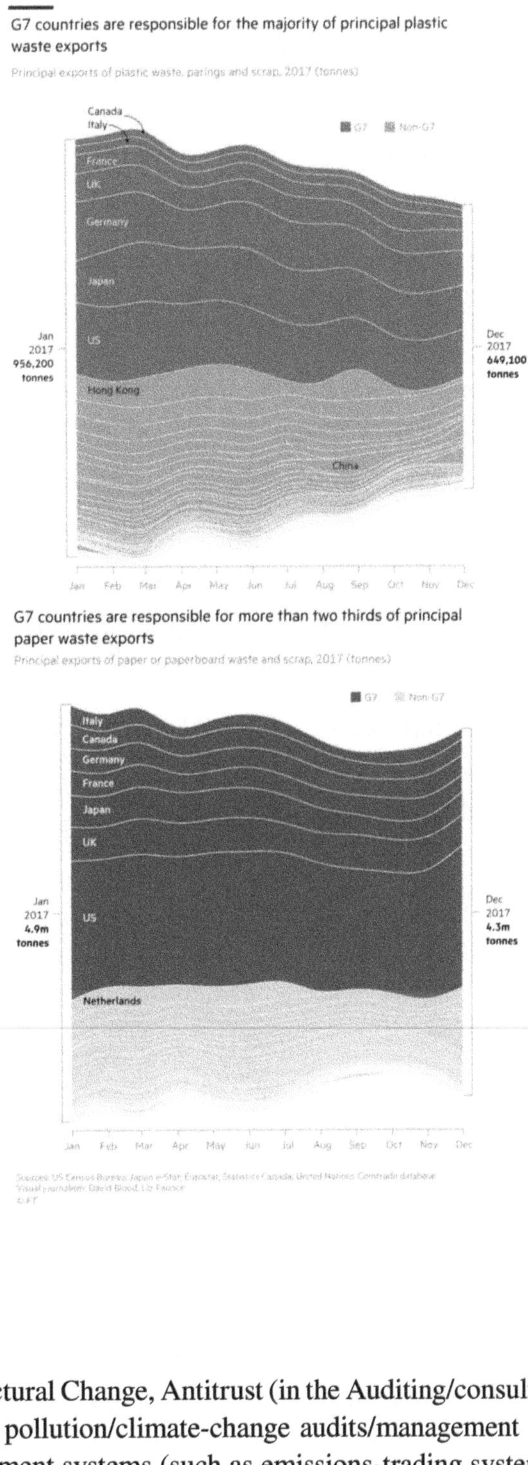

CONCLUSION

It's now evident that Structural Change, Antitrust (in the Auditing/consulting Industry) and the auditing/consulting firms' role in pollution/climate-change audits/management and the efficiency of climate-change/pollution management systems (such as emissions-trading systems) are linked and have or can have symbiotic effects on each other; and each by itself, can have significant effects on perceived and actual economic activity, Sustainability and Climate Change. Thus, structural reforms and new regulations are required in many countries.

REFERENCES

Abbott, L., Parker, S., & Peters, G. (2011). Does Mandated Disclosure Induce a Structural Change in the Determinants of Non-audit Service Purchases? *Auditing*, *30*(2), 51–76. doi:10.2308/ajpt-50001

Abidin, S., Beattie, V., & Goodacre, A. (2010). Audit market structure, fees and choice in a period of structural change: Evidence from the UK – 1998–2003. *The British Accounting Review*, *42*(3), 187–206. doi:10.1016/j.bar.2010.04.002

Antimiani, A., Costantini, V., Martini, C., Salvatici, L., & Tommasino, M. (2013). Assessing alternative solutions to emissions leakage. *Energy Economics*, *36*, 299–311. doi:10.1016/j.eneco.2012.08.042

Bai, C., Chen, X., Song, Z., & Wang, X. (2019). *The Rise of China's Service Sector*. Working Paper.

Bai, C., Hsieh, C., & Qian, Y. (2006). The Return to Capital in China. *Brookings Papers on Economic Activity*, *2006*(Fall), 61–101. doi:10.1353/eca.2007.0000

Bai, C., Hsieh, C., & Song, Z. (2016). The Long Shadow of China's Fiscal Expansion. *Brookings Papers on Economic Activity*, *2016*(Fall), 129–181. doi:10.1353/eca.2016.0027

Bai, C., Hsieh, C., & Song, Z. (2019). (forthcoming). Special Deals with Chinese Characteristics. *NBER Macroeconomics Annual.*

Ballas, A., & Fafalliou, I. (2008, November). Market Shares And Concentration In The EU Auditing Industry: The Effects Of Andersen's Demise. *International Advances in Economic Research*, *14*(4), 485–497. doi:10.100711294-008-9167-6

Bensberg, F., Buscher, G., & Czarnecki, C. (2019). Digital transformation and IT topics in the consulting industry: A labor market perspective. In *Advances in consulting research* (pp. 341–357). Springer, Cham. doi:10.1007/978-3-319-95999-3_16

Berthe, A., & Elie, L. (2015). Mechanisms Explaining The Impact Of Economic Inequality On Environmental Deterioration. *Ecological Economics*, *116*, 191–200. doi:10.1016/j.ecolecon.2015.04.026

Boneva, M. (2018). Challenges related to the digital transformation of business companies. In Innovation Management, Entrepreneurship and Sustainability (IMES 2018) (pp. 101-114). Vysoká škola ekonomická v Praze.

Bowman, B., & Enion, R. (2011). *Rules Of The Game: Examining Market Manipulation, Gaming and Enforcement in California's Cap-and-Trade Program*. Working Paper, UCLA School of Law.

Brida, J., Anyul, M., & Punzo, L. (2003). Coding Economic Dynamics To Represent Regime Dynamics. A teach-yourself exercise. *Structural Change and Economic Dynamics*, *14*(2), 133–157. doi:10.1016/S0954-349X(03)00003-1

Brisson, J. (2014). Outstanding Design Flaws. In *California's Cap-and-Trade Program*. Latham & Watkins, LLP.

Cantwell, J., & Santangelo, G. (2006). The boundaries of firms in the new economy: M&As as a strategic tool toward corporate technological diversification. *Structural Change and Economic Dynamics*, *17*(2), 174–199. doi:10.1016/j.strueco.2005.06.001

Carson, E., Soo, S., & Wright, A. (2012). Changes in Audit Market Competition and the Big N Premium. *Auditing*, *31*(3), 47–73. doi:10.2308/ajpt-10295

Cattaneo, O., Engman, M., Saez, S., & Stern, R. (Eds.). (2010). *International Trade in Services: New Trends and Opportunities for Developing Countries*. World Bank. doi:10.1596/978-0-8213-8353-7

Chan, J., Pun, N., & Selden, M. (2013). The politics of global production: Apple, Foxconn and China's new working class. *New Technology, Work and Employment*, *28*(2), 104–105. doi:10.1111/ntwe.12008

Chen, H., & Jorgensen, B. (2018). Market Exit Through Divestment— The Effect of Accounting Bias on Competition. *Management Science*, *64*(1), 1–493. doi:10.1287/mnsc.2016.2578

Ciaschini, M., Pretaroli, R., & Socci, C. (2011). Balance, Manhattan norm and Euclidean distance of industrial policies for the US. *Structural Change and Economic Dynamics*, *22*(3), 204–226. doi:10.1016/j.strueco.2011.03.002

Cimoli, M., Pereima, J., & Porcile, G. (2016). Introduction To The Special Issue SCED: *Complexity* And Economic Development. *Structural Change and Economic Dynamics*, *38*, 1–2. doi:10.1016/j.strueco.2016.04.004

Condon, B., & Sinha, T. (2013). *The Role of Climate Change in Global Economic Governance*. Oxford University Press. doi:10.1093/acprof:oso/9780199654550.001.0001

Dosi, G., & Virgillito, M. (2017). In Order To Stand Up You Must Keep Cycling: Change And Coordination In Complex Evolving Economies. Structural Change And Economic Dynamics.

Driver, E., Parsons, M., & Fisher, K. (2018). Technically political: The post-politics(?) of the New Zealand Emissions Trading Scheme. *Geoforum*, *97*, 253–267. doi:10.1016/j.geoforum.2018.09.023

Dubash, N., & Khosla, R. (2014). India's energy and emissions future: an interpretive analysis of model scenarios. *Environmental Research Letters*, *13*(7).

Dunn, K., Kohlbeck, M., & Mayhew, B. (2011). The impact of the Big-4 consolidation on audit market share equality. *Auditing*, *30*(1), 49–73. doi:10.2308/aud.2011.30.1.49

Economides, N. (1998). The incentive for non-price discrimination by an input Monopolist. *International Journal of Industrial Organization*, *16*(3), 271–284. doi:10.1016/S0167-7187(98)00005-8

Economides, N. (2012a). *Tying, bundling, and loyalty/requirement Rebates*. Book chapter. In E. Elhauge (Ed.), *Research Handbook of The Economics Of Antitrust Law*. Edward Elgar. doi:10.4337/9780857938091.00013

Economides, N. (2012b). Antitrust Issues In Network Industries. In I. Kokkoris & I. Lianos (Eds.), *The Reform of EC Competition Law*. Kluwer. https://www.stern.nyu.edu/networks/Economides_Antitrust_in_Network_Industries.pdf

Englund, H., Gerdin, J., & Abrahamsson, G. (2013). Accounting ambiguity and structural change. *Accounting, Auditing & Accountability Journal*, *26*(3), 423–448. doi:10.1108/09513571311311883

Felli, R. (2019). Beyond the critique of carbon markets: The real utopia of a democratic Climate Protection Agency. *Geoforum*, *98*, 236–243. doi:10.1016/j.geoforum.2018.02.031

Frondel, M., Schmidt, C., & Vance, C. (2012). Emissions trading: Impact on electricity prices and energy-intensive industries. *Inter Economics*, *47*(2), 104–111. doi:10.100710272-012-0410-2

Furceri, D., Loungani, P., & Zdzienicka, A. (2018). The effects of monetary policy shocks on inequality. *Journal of International Money and Finance*, *85*, 168–186. doi:10.1016/j.jimonfin.2017.11.004

Gambhir, A., Napp, T., Emmott, C. J. M., & Anandarajah, G. (2014). India's CO2 emissions pathways to 2050: Energy system, economic and fossil fuel impacts with and without carbon permit trading. *Energy*, *77*, 791–801. doi:10.1016/j.energy.2014.09.055

Gao, J. (2016). Bypass the Lying Mouths: How Does the CCP Tackle Information Distortion at Local Levels? *The China Quarterly*, *228*, 950–969. doi:10.1017/S0305741016001491

Gillis, P. (2014). *The Big Four and the Development of the Accounting Profession in China*. Emerald Group.

Goulder, L., & Stavins, R. (2011). Interactions between state and federal climate change policies. In *The design and implementation of US climate policy* (pp. 109–121). University of Chicago Press.

Grubb, M., Sha, F., Spencer, T., Hughes, N., Zhang, Z., & Agnolucci, P. (2015). A review of Chinese CO2 emission projections to 2030: The role of economic structure and policy. *Climate Policy*, *15*(1), S7–S39. doi:10.1080/14693062.2015.1101307

Helm, D. (2009). EU Climate-change Policy—A Critique. In D. Helm & C. Hepburn (Eds.), *The Economics and Politics of Climate Change*. Oxford University Press. doi:10.1093/acprof:osobl/9780199573288.003.0011

Hinterman, B. (2016). *Emissions Trading and Market Manipulation*. Chapter-5. In S. Weishar (Ed.), *Research Handbook on Emissions Trading". Research Handbooks in Climate Law series*. Edward Elgar. doi:10.4337/9781784710620.00014

Holz, C. (2014). The Quality of China's GDP Statistics. *China Economic Review*, *30*, 309–338. doi:10.1016/j.chieco.2014.06.009

Hook, L., & Reed, J. (2018). Why The World's Recycling System Stopped Working - China's Refusal To become The West's Dumping Ground Is Forcing The World To Face Up To A Waste Crisis. *Financial Times*. https://www.ft.com/content/360e2524-d71a-11e8-a854-33d6f82e62f8

Huang, T., Chang, H., & Chiou, J. (2016). Audit Market Concentration, Audit Fees, and Audit Quality: Evidence from China. *Auditing*, *35*(2), 121–145. doi:10.2308/ajpt-51299

Interpol. (2013). *Guide to Carbon Trading Crime*. www.Interpol.int

Jin, Y., Liu, X., Chen, X., & Dai, H. (2020). Allowance allocation matters in China's carbon emissions trading system. *Energy Economics*, *92*, 92. doi:10.1016/j.eneco.2020.105012

Kama, K. (2014). On the borders of the market: EU emissions trading, energy security, and the technopolitics of 'carbon leakage'. *Geoforum*, *51*, 202–212. doi:10.1016/j.geoforum.2013.11.010

Kerr, S., & Duscha, V. (2014). Going to the Source: Using an Upstream Point of Regulation for Energy in a National Chinese Emissions Trading System. *Energy & Environment*, *25*(3-4), 593–611. doi:10.1260/0958-305X.25.3-4.593

Khan, U., & Lo, A. (2018). Bank Lending Standards and Borrower Accounting Conservatism. *Management Science*.

Konrad Adeneaur Stiftung. (2017). *Climate Report 2017 - Private Sector And Climate Finance In The G20 Countries*. Http://Www.Kas.De/Wf/Doc/Kas_49589-544-2-30.Pdf?170719090813

Kwon, Y. (2005). Accounting Conservatism and Managerial Incentives. *Management Science*, *51*(11), 1593–1732. doi:10.1287/mnsc.1050.0417

Liu, X., & Simunic, D. (2005). Profit Sharing in an Auditing Oligopoly. *The Accounting Review*, *80*(2), 677–682. doi:10.2308/accr.2005.80.2.677

Lu, Q., & Fang, K. (2020). Imbalance and drivers of carbon emissions embodied in trade along the Belt and Road Initiative. *Applied Energy*, 280.

Ma, B., Song, G., Zhang, L., & Sonnenfeld, D. A. (2014). Explaining Sectoral Discrepancies between National and Provincial Statistics in China. *China Economic Review*, *30*, 353–369. doi:10.1016/j.chieco.2014.07.004

Marquardt, C., & Zur, E. (2015). The Role of Accounting Quality in the M&A Market. *Management Science*, *61*(3), 487–705. doi:10.1287/mnsc.2013.1873

Marques, R., Santos, C., & Inácio, H. (2019). *Organizational Auditing and Assurance in the Digital Age*. IGI Global. doi:10.4018/978-1-5225-7356-2

Miller, J., & Facanha, C. (2016). *Cost-benefit analysis of Brazil's heavy-duty emission standards (P-8)*. White paper.

Nan, L., & Wen, X. (2014). Financing and Investment Efficiency, Information Quality, and Accounting Biases. *Operations Research*, *60*(9), 2111–2380.

Nordhaus, W. (1974). Markets and Appropriable Resources. In Energy, Demand, Conservation, and Institutional Problems. Cambridge, MA: MIT Press.

Nordhaus, W. (1977). Economic Growth and Climate: The Case of Carbon Dioxide. *The American Economic Review*, *67*(1), 341–346.

Nordhaus, W. (1980). The Energy Crisis and Macroeconomic Policy. *Energy Journal*, *1*(1), 11–19. doi:10.5547/ISSN0195-6574-EJ-Vol1-No1-2

Nordhaus, W. (1981). Tax-Based Incomes Policies: A Better Mousetrap? In M. Clandon & R. Cornwall (Eds.), *An Incomes Policy for the United States: New Approaches*. Martinus Mijhoff. doi:10.1007/978-94-009-8763-0_7

Nordhaus, W. (1992). An Optimal Transition Path for Controlling Greenhouse Gases. *Science*, *258*(5086), 1315–1317. doi:10.1126cience.258.5086.1315 PMID:17778354

Nordhaus, W. (1994). Managing the Global Commons: The Economics of Climate Change. Cambridge, MA: MIT Press.

Nordhaus, W. (1995). Integrative Assessment of Mitigation, Impacts, and Adaptation to Climate Change. *Energy Policy*, *23*(4/5), 251–479.

Nordhaus, W. (Ed.). (1998). *Economic and Policy Issues in Climate Change*. Resources for the Future Press.

Nordhaus, W. (1998). *New Estimates of the Economic Impacts of Climate Change*. Yale University Press.

Nordhaus, W. (2006a). Geography and Macroeconomics: New Data and New Findings. [US]. *Proceedings of the National Academy of Sciences of the United States of America*, *103*(10), 3510–3517. doi:10.1073/pnas.0509842103 PMID:16473945

Nordhaus, W. (2006b). After Kyoto: Alternative Mechanisms to Control Global Warming. *The American Economic Review*, *96*(2), 31–34. doi:10.1257/000282806777211964

Nordhaus, W. (2007a). To Tax or Not to Tax: Alternative Approaches to Slowing Global Warming. *Review of Environmental Economics and Policy*, *1*(1), 26–44. doi:10.1093/reep/rem008

Nordhaus, W. (2007b). Critical Assumptions in the Stern Review on Climate Change. *Science*, *317*(5835), 201–202. doi:10.1126cience.1137316 PMID:17626869

Nordhaus, W. (2007c). Alternative Measures of Output in Global Economic-Environmental Models: Purchasing Power Parity or Market Exchange Rates? *Energy Economics*, *29*(3), 349–372. doi:10.1016/j.eneco.2006.02.003

Nordhaus, W., & Moffat, A. (2017). *Evolution of Modeling of the Economics of Global Warming: Changes in the DICE model, 1992-2017. Cowles Foundation Discussion Papers 2096, Cowles Foundation for Research in Economics*. Yale University.

Nwogugu, M. (2010/2015). *Economic Policy, Structural Changes And Systemic Risk: The Un-Constitutionality Of Accounting And Derivatives Standards-Setting Organizations; SOX; Government Bail-Out Programs For Financial Institutions; And Healthcare Reform In The US*. Working paper. Available in www.ssrn.com

Nwogugu, M. (2015). Un-Constitutionality of The Dodd-Frank Act. *European Journal of Law Reform*, *17*(1), 185–190. doi:10.5553/EJLR/138723702015017001007

Nwogugu, M. (2019a). Implications For Decision Theory, Enforcement, Financial Stability And Systemic Risk. In Indices, Index Funds And ETFs: Exploring HCI, Nonlinear Risk And Homomorphisms. New York: Palgrave Macmillan.

Nwogugu, M. (2019b). *Introduction*. In M. Nwogugu, (Ed.), *Complex Systems, Multi-Sided Incentives and Risk Perception in Companies*. New York: Palgrave MacMillan.

Nwogugu, M. (2020). *Earning Management, Fintech-Driven Incentives And Sustainable Growth: On Complex Systems, Legal And Mechanism Design Factors*. Routledge.

Orlik, T. (2014). Reform at China's National Bureau of Statistics under Ma Jiantang 2008-2013. *China Economic Review*, *30*, 304–308. doi:10.1016/j.chieco.2014.04.006

Pang, T., & Duan, M. (2016). Cap setting and allowance allocation in China's emissions trading pilot programmes: Special issues and innovative solutions. *Climate Policy*, *16*(7), 815–835. doi:10.1080/14693062.2015.1052956

Payne, R. (2016). *Structural Change in the US CPA Industry – Small Firm Challenges*. http://theconsultingaccountant.com/structural-change-in-the-us-cpa-industry-small-firm-challenges/

Ramanna, K., & Sletten, E. (2014). Network Effects in Countries' Adoption of IFRS. *The Accounting Review*, *89*(4), 1517–1543. doi:10.2308/accr-50717

Robert, V., & Yoguel, G. (2016). *Complexity* Paths In Neo-Schumpeterian Evolutionary Economics, *Structural Change* And Development Policies. *Structural Change and Economic Dynamics*, *38*, 3–14. doi:10.1016/j.strueco.2015.11.004

Rojas-Vallejos, J., & Lastuk, A. (2020). The income inequality and carbon emissions trade-off revisited. *Energy Policy*, *139*, 139. doi:10.1016/j.enpol.2020.111302

Romer, P. (1983). *Dynamic Competitive Equilibria With Externalities, Increasing Returns And Unbounded Growth* (Ph.D. Thesis). University of Chicago.

Sales, R. (2017). *A Brazilian Emissions Trading Scheme: modelling a legal framework to secure its environmental integrity and ensuring effective reduction of greenhouse gas emissions* (PhD Thesis). Faculty of law, UNSW.

Schneider, L., Kollmuss, A., & Lazarus, M. (2015). Addressing the risk of double counting emission reductions under the UNFCCC. *Climatic Change*, *131*(4), 473–486. doi:10.100710584-015-1398-y

Sijm, J., Neuhoff, K., & Chen, Y. (2006). CO^2 cost pass-through and windfall profits in the power sector. *Climate Policy*, *6*(1), 49–72. doi:10.1080/14693062.2006.9685588

Sikka, P., & Hampton, M. P. (2005). The Role Of Accountancy Firms In Tax Avoidance: Some Evidence And Issues. *Accounting Forum*, *29*(3), 325–343. doi:10.1016/j.accfor.2005.03.008

Song, Z., & Xiong, W. (2018). Risks in China's Financial System. *Annual Review of Financial Economics*, *10*(1), 261–286. doi:10.1146/annurev-financial-110716-032402

Stark, J. (2020). *Digital Transformation of Industry*. Springer International Publishing. doi:10.1007/978-3-030-41001-8

Tanaka, M., & Chen, Y. (2012). Market power in emissions trading: Strategically manipulating permit price through fringe firms. *Applied Energy*, *96*, 203–211. doi:10.1016/j.apenergy.2011.08.049

Tang, S., & Demmeritt, D. (2018). Climate Change and Mandatory Carbon Reporting: Impacts on Business Process and Performance. *Business Strategy and the Environment*, *27*(4), 437–455. doi:10.1002/bse.1985

Tanuro, D. (2008). *Fundamental Inadequacies of Carbon Trading for the Struggle Against Climate Change*. https://climateandcapitalism.com/2008/03/23/carbon-trading-an-ecosocialist-critique/

Tirole, J. (1992). Collusion and the Theory of Organizations. In *Advances in Economic Theory: The Sixth World Congress*. Cambridge University Press.

Tynkkynen, N. (2014). *Russia And Global Climate Governance*. IFRI - Russia/NIS Center. www.ifri.org

Van der Hoff, R., & Rajão, R. (2020). The politics of environmental market instruments: Coalition building and knowledge filtering in the regulation of forest certificates trading in Brazil. *Land Use Policy*, 96.

Vlachou, A., & Pantelias, G. (2017). The EU's Emissions Trading System, Part-2: A Political Economy Critique. *Capitalism, Nature, Socialism*, *28*(3), 108–127. doi:10.1080/10455752.2016.1234027

Wang, X., Teng, F., Zhou, S., & Cai, B. (2017). Identifying the industrial sectors at risk of carbon leakage in China. *Climate Policy*, *17*(4), 443–457. doi:10.1080/14693062.2015.1104497

Weishaar, S. E. (2014). *Linking Emissions Trading Schemes, Emissions Trading Design – A Critical Overview*. Edward Elgar.

White, L. (2001). *Reducing The Barriers To International Trade In Accounting Services*. AEI Press. https://www.aei.org/press/reducing-the-barriers-to-international-trade-in-accounting-services/

Zeng, Y., Weishaar, S., & Vedder, H. (2018). Electricity regulation in the Chinese national emissions trading scheme (ETS): Lessons for carbon leakage and linkage with the EU ETS. *Climate Policy*, *18*(10), 1246–1259. doi:10.1080/14693062.2018.1426553

ENDNOTES

1 This chapter contains excerpts from the following article: Nwogugu, M. (2010; Revised 2017). *Structural Changes, Competition And Complexity: Credit Rating Agencies (CRAs) And Allocation Mechanisms For Accounting Firms*. Available at SSRN: https://ssrn.com/abstract=1762560 or http://dx.doi.org/10.2139/ssrn.1762560

2 *See*: Khan & Lo (2018), Chen & Jorgensen (2018), Kwon (2005) and Marquardt & Zur (2015).

3 *See*: Nan & Wen (2014).

4 Tang & Demmeritt (2018) noted that "……..Scholars and business analysts have offered a number of competing explanations for this expansion of corporate social responsibility (CSR) reporting about carbon, ranging from rational pursuit of cost savings (Kolk & Pinkse (2004); Hoffman (2007)), brand differentiation (Delmas, et. al., 2006; Matisoff, et. al. (2013)) or reputational gains (Hoffman (2005)) to coercive pressures from regulators (Levy & Egan (2003); Lyon & Maxwell (2004); Jones & Levy (2007)), institutional investors (Pfeifer & Sullivan (2008); Knox-Hayes & Levy (2011); Sullivan& Gouldson (2012); and Cotter & Najah (2012)) or environmental pressure groups (Stanny & Ely (2008); Hahn, et. al.(2015)) and mimetic pressures to follow the latest corporate fashions in CSR (Sullivan, 2008; Ihlen (2009))…….Some scholars argue that CSR practices

such as carbon reporting not only minimize pollution and environmental harm, but also promote profitability, technological innovation, and wider economic competitiveness (Hajer (1995); Mol, et. al. (2009)). Such ecological modernization promises to reconcile the imperatives of economic growth and profit with environmental protection, delivering win–win outcomes (Boiral, et. al. (2012); Gouldson & Sullivan (2012))……In the hope that disclosure will incentivize business innovation and improved environmental performance, the UK government recently became the first jurisdiction in the world to require publicly listed firms to account for their greenhouse gas emissions as part of their annual financial reporting. Other jurisdictions, such as Norway, Singapore, and Hong Kong are now following the British lead in requiring companies to report on their GHG emissions……….".

5 *See*: Carroll, J. (2018). *The Management Consulting Industry in 2019 and Beyond.* https://www.business2community.com/strategy/the-management-consulting-industry-in-2019-and-beyond-02127403. *See*: Christensen, C., Wang, D. & Van Bever, D. (Oct. 2013). Consulting on the Cusp of Disruption. *Harvard Business Review*. https://hbr.org/2013/10/consulting-on-the-cusp-of-disruption. *See*: Naden, C. (May 2016). *Taking Management Consultancy Services To Another Level.* https://www.iso.org/news/2016/05/Ref2080.html.

6 *See*: Gillis, P. (______). *Longtop Financial Technologies Case Study - Accounting fraud in China.* Peking University's Guanghua School of Management. Available at: http://www.paulgillis.org/longtop_financial_technolog.pdf.

See: Gillis, P. (________). *Auditing cash in China.* Available at: http://www.chinaaccountingblog.com/weblog/auditing-cash-in-china.html. Peking University's Guanghua School of Management.

See: Norris, F. (May 26, 2011). *The Audacity of Chinese Frauds.* Available at: http://www.nytimes.com/2011/05/27/business/27norris.html?pagewanted=all&_r=0.

1 *See*: https://en.wikipedia.org/wiki/Apple_Pay; and https://www.apple.com/apple-pay/.

See: *Citron reports on Longtop Financial* (NYSE:LFT). Available at: http://www.paulgillis.org/citronresearchcom__citron.pdf.

See: Hempton, J. (Bronte Capital) (May 20, 2011). *Longtop Financial: Lessons In The Morphology Of Sin, Loss Of Virginity, And Your 17 Year Old Daughter.* http://www.businessinsider.com/john-hempton-longtop-financial-2011-5. Also see http://www.brontecapital.com/files/sma/Client_Letter_201105.pdf.

See: *SEC Charges China-Based Longtop Financial Technologies for Deficient Filings - For Immediate Release - 2011-241.* Washington, D.C., Nov. 10, 2011.

7 *See*: "Carillion's Demise Spurs Call For Action Against Big Four - MPs' Report On Collapse Asks For Possible Break-Up Of 'Cosy' Auditors". *Financial Times* (UK); May 16, 2018. This article stated in part "………British MPs have demanded the UK's big four accountancy firms be referred to competition authorities for potential break-up following the collapse of government contractor Carillion, calling them a "…..cosy club incapable of providing the degree of independent challenge needed……". The recommendation by members of two powerful parliamentary committees was contained in a damning 100-page report on Carillion's failure, which also accused the government, regulators and Carillion board members of failing in their responsibilities, often because they acted "entirely in line with their own personal incentives". Carillion, which went into liquidation in January with liabilities of £7 billion and just £29 million in cash, was "a giant and unsustainable time bomb", the report found. Its failure, one of the biggest in the UK in recent times, exposed "systemic flaws" in corporate Britain and its "toothless" and "feeble" regulators. Although Deloitte was Carillion's

sole internal auditor, all three of the other big-four did work for the group, with KPMG serving as external auditor, Ernst & Young providing turnaround advice and PriceWaterhouse advising the company, its pension schemes and the government. KPMG is already under investigation by the UK's accountancy regulator for its role…….The report also said that the government's Insolvency Service, which is handling the company's winding-up, should "carefully consider" whether Carillion's former directors, including Richard Howson, the chief executive, Philip Green, chairman, and Richard Adams, finance director, breached their duties under the *Companies Act* and should be recommended to the Secretary of State for disqualification……..".

See: United Kingdom Parliament (House of Commons - Business, Energy and Industrial Strategy and Work and Pensions Committees) (May 2018). *Carillion - Second Joint report from the Business, Energy and Industrial Strategy and Work and Pensions Committees of Session 2017–19.* https://publications.parliament.uk/pa/cm201719/cmselect/cmworpen/769/769.pdf.

See: United Kingdom Parliament (Work and Pensions Committee and Business, Energy and Industrial Strategy Committee) (March 2018). *Oral evidence: Carillion, HC 769 (Wednesday 21, March 2018) - Evidence given by Rt. Hon. Greg Clark MP, Secretary of State for Business, Energy and Industrial Strategy; and Rt. Hon Esther McVey MP, Secretary of State for Work and Pensions; Marissa Thomas, Partner, Head of Deals; David Kelly, Partner and Special Manager; and Gavin Stoner, Partner, Restructuring and Pensions, PwC.* http://data.parliament.uk/writtenevidence/committeeevidence.svc/evidencedocument/work-and-pensions-committee/carillion/oral/80775.pdf; https://www.parliament.uk/business/committees/committees-a-z/commons-select/work-and-pensions-committee/inquiries/parliament-2017/carillion-inquiry-17-19/.

8 *See*: "*Environmental Auditing*". https://www.inc.com/encyclopedia/environmental-audit.html.

9 *See*: "Big Four told to outline plans for audit split by October: UK regulator orders the largest shake-up of the industry in decades". *Financial Times.* Tabby Kinder. July 6, 2020. This article states in part: "………The UK's Big Four accounting firms have until 2024 to separate their audit practices following a severe edict from the accounting regulator that marks the largest shake-up of the industry in decades. The Financial Reporting Council has issued principles for the operational separation of the audit units of PwC, Deloitte, KPMG and EY. The firms must outline their plans to implement all 22 of its principles by the end of October, and have completed the measures by June 2024. It is the first structural overhaul of the way the firms operate since a string of reviews prompted by the failure of British outsourcer Carillion. Audit reform has been thrown into sharp focus in recent years by high-profile corporate collapses such as at BHS, Thomas Cook, and most recently, Wirecard. The FRC's new principles require that the firms pay auditors in line with the profits of their audits, ringfence the finances of the audit division with a separate profit and loss account, and introduce an independent audit board to oversee the practice. The Big Four generate around a fifth of revenues from their audit practices, which have been dwarfed by the rapid expansion of their advisory divisions in recent years……….".

10 *See*: Financial Reporting Council (July 2020). *Objectives, Outcomes And Regulation.* https://www.frc.org.uk/getattachment/281a7d7e-74fe-43f7-854a-e52158bc6ae2/Operational-separation-principles-published-July-2020.pdf. The UK FRC's Principles (2020) are listed in **Appendix-1** herein and below.

11 *See*: Hook, L. & Reed, J. (Oct. 24, 2018). "Why The World's Recycling System Stopped Working - China's Refusal To Become The West's Dumping Ground Is Forcing The World To Face Up To

A Waste Crisis". *Financial Times* (UK). https://www.ft.com/content/360e2524-d71a-11e8-a854-33d6f82e62f8.

12 *See*: Ross, S. (March 1, 2021). *The Role of Accounting and Auditing in Addressing Climate Change*. Washington D.C., USA. https://www.americanprogress.org/issues/economy/reports/2021/03/01/496290/role-accounting-auditing-addressing-climate-change/. This article stated in part: "………The stated purpose of the U.S. Securities and Exchange Commission's (SEC) disclosure regime is "to foster uniform and integrated disclosure" by companies that issue or trade securities in U.S. markets. When it comes to climate, though, the SEC has mostly discouraged uniformity and integration by resisting calls for consistent, mandatory disclosures that would give investors a basis to judge the impact of the climate crisis on a company's business model. Diversified investors, concerned about systematic risk, also want to know how a company is contributing to, or mitigating, climate risk. Instead, the SEC relies predominantly on the general principle that companies should disclose information that a reasonable investor would consider important or helpful………the SEC has recognized the sizable investor demand for climate-related information and has acknowledged that climate-related effects can be financially relevant—and thus, in each case, material to an investor. Yet it has not enforced its disclosure rules, either in financial statements, as required, or elsewhere (such as through mandated risk disclosures), effectively signaling that whether and what to disclose is up to a company's board and management. For all intents and purposes, investors are left to their own devices………Not surprisingly, most companies that voluntarily issue climate reports present them in a way that makes it difficult to assess the company's performance over time or to compare it to other companies. Moreover, it is often impossible for investors to discern how a company's climate report relates to its financial statements. ………The current approach to climate disclosure is instead costly and ineffectual, and it thwarts investors' ability to hold managers accountable for reducing emissions and managing climate-related risks..……In practical terms, investors have no way to discern what portion of earnings is attributable to good management of the company's assets as opposed to an unbounded opportunity to push costs off corporate accounts and onto society. The United States' sophisticated market, regulatory, and governance institutions can do better.………Climate-related risks are anticipated to impose costs that are so large they are difficult to measure but are likely to be in the trillions of dollars worldwide. An all-economy approach is needed to reduce emissions and in turn the risks associated with climate change. The financial system affects the flow of money away from harmful activities and toward sustainable, climate-friendly investments. But it can only function effectively with reliable information that is accessible to investors……….".

See: Sarbanes Oxley Act of 2002, Section 108, Accounting Standards, Public Law 204, 107th Cong., 2nd sess. (July 30, 2002). https://www.govinfo.gov/content/pkg/COMPS-1883/pdf/COMPS-1883.pdf.

See: Letter from David Batker and Ed Harrington of Earth Economics to the Financial Accounting Standards Board, August 31, 2018. https://www.fasb.org/cs/BlobServer?blobkey=id&blobnocache=true&blobwhere=1175835931830&blobheader=application%2Fpdf&blobheadername2=Content-Length&blobheadername1=Content-Disposition&blobheadervalue2=2358156&blobheadervalue1=filename%3DAR-2018.UNS.017.EARTH_ECONOMICS_DAVID_BATKER_ED_HARRINGTON.pdf&blobcol=urldata&blobtable=MungoBlobs. The letter states in part: "……...Carbon cap-and-trade systems operate in ten states (these states account for 29% of US GDP), and their impacts extend to thousands of manufacturing and utility firms. Firms in US cap-and-trade systems spent more than $4.2 billion in carbon allowance auctions in 2017. For many firms operating in cap-and-trade systems, emissions liabilities comprise between 1-3% of the total financial liabilities on their balance sheet, and this proportion is growing…….".

See: Yahoo! Finance, "*Investors can benefit from climate-related opportunities before they are priced in: JPM Asset Management Rpt*. https://money.yahoo.com/investors-benefit-climate-related-opportunities-170532898.html?guccounter=1. This reported noted that: i) eighty percent of global emissions are not covered by any carbon/emissions pricing system; ii) more than half of the sixty-five existing global pricing systems have a carbon price of less than $10 per metric ton, which is less than the current $50 actual cost of removing a metric ton of carbon from the atmosphere.

See: Partnership for Carbon Accounting Financials, "*The Global GHG Accounting and Reporting Standard for the Financial Industry*".

See: Partnership for Carbon Accounting Financials, "*Financial institutions taking action*. Available at https://carbonaccountingfinancials.com/financial-institutions-taking-action#overview-of-institutions.

See: U.N. Framework Convention on Climate Change, "*Commitments to Net Zero Double in Less Than a Year*," Press release, September 21, 2020. https://unfccc.int/news/commitments-to-net-zero-double-in-less-than-a-year.

See: Energy Innovation: Policy and Technology LLC (2020). "*The Costs of Delay*". San Francisco: 2021. Available at https://energyinnovation.org/wp-content/uploads/2021/01/Cost_of_Delay.pdf. (discussion of costs of climate-change to the United States - noted costs of US$750 billion per year by 2035 and more than US$900 billion per year by the 2040s).

See: Kahn, M. et.al. (2019). "Long-Term Macroeconomic Effects of Climate Change: A Cross-Country Analysis". Cambridge, MA: National Bureau of Economic Research. https://www.nber.org/papers/w26167.

See: Freedman, A. (2019). Climate change could cost the U.S. up to 10.5 percent of its GDP by 2100, study finds. *The Washington Post*, August 19, 2019. https://www.washingtonpost.com/weather/2019/08/19/climate-change-could-cost-us-up-percent-its-gdp-by-study-finds/.

See: Anderson, A. (2019). *IFRS Standards and Climate-related Disclosures*. London: International Financial Reporting Standards Foundation. https://cdn.ifrs.org/-/media/feature/news/2019/november/in-brief-climate-change-nick-anderson.pdf?la=en.

See: IFRS Foundation (Nov.2020). "*Educational material: the effects of climate-related matters on financial statements prepared applying IFRS Standards*". https://www.ifrs.org/news-and-events/2020/11/educational-material-on-the-effects-of-climate-related-matters/.

See: Livsey, A. (Feb. 4,2020). "Lex in Depth: the $900bn cost of 'stranded energy assets'". *Financial Times*. https://www.ft.com/content/95efca74-4299-11ea-a43a-c4b328d9061c.

See: U.S. Government Accountability Office (2018). *Climate-related Risks: SEC Has Taken Steps to Clarify Disclosure Requirements*. Washington D.C., USA. Available at https://www.gao.gov/assets/700/690197.pdf.

See: U.S. Government Accountability Office (2020). *Disclosure of Environmental, Social, and Governance Factors and Options to Enhance Them*. Washington D.C., USA. Available at https://www.gao.gov/assets/710/707949.pdf.

See: U.S. Securities and Exchange Commission (2010). "Commission Guidance Regarding Disclosure Related to Climate Change". Washington. D.C.. https://www.sec.gov/rules/interp/2010/33-9106.pdf.

See: U.S. Securities and Exchange Commission (Nov. 2020). *Testimony on 'Oversight of Securities and Exchange Commission': Chairman Jay Clayton before the U.S. Senate Committee on Banking, Housing, and Urban Affairs*. November 17, 2020. https://www.sec.gov/news/testimony/clayton-sec-oversight-2020-11-17.

See: U.S. Securities and Exchange Commission, "Testimony on 'Oversight of Securities and Exchange Commission': Chairman Jay Clayton before the U.S. Senate Committee on Banking, Housing, and Urban Affairs." *See*: U.S. Securities and Exchange Commission, "*Release Nos 33-8040; 34-45149, Cautionary Advice Regarding Disclosure About Critical Accounting Policies*". https://www.sec.gov/rules/other/33-8040.htm

See: U.S. Securities and Exchange Commission, "*Release Nos. 33-8350; 34-48960, Interpretation: Commission Guidance Regarding Management's Discussion and Analysis of Financial Condition and Results of Operations*". https://www.sec.gov/rules/interp/33-8350.htm.

See: U.S. Securities and Exchange Commission (2019). *Modernization of Regulation S-K Items 101, 103 and 105*. (Washington: 2019). https://www.sec.gov/rules/proposed/2019/33-10668.pdf.

See: Lee, A. (Feb. 2021). *Statement on the Review of Climate-Related Disclosure*. U.S. Securities and Exchange Commission. https://www.sec.gov/news/public-statement/lee-statement-review-climate-related-disclosure.

See: Public Company Accounting Oversight Board (2021). *Auditing Accounting Estimates, Including Fair Value Measurements*. Available at https://pcaobus.org/oversight/standards/implementation-resources-PCAOB-standards-rules/auditing-accounting-estimates-fair-value-measurements.

See: Coburn, J. & Cook, J. (2014). *Cool Response: The SEC & Corporate Climate Reporting*. Boston: Ceres. https://www.ceres.org/sites/default/files/reports/2017-03/Ceres_SECguidance-append_020414_web.pdf.

See: Task Force on Climate-related Financial Disclosures (2018). "*Task force on Climate-related Financial Disclosures: Status Report*". https://assets.bbhub.io/company/sites/60/2020/10/FINAL-2018-TCFD-Status-Report-092518.pdf.

See: Market Risk Advisory Committee of the U.S. Commodity Futures Trading Commission (September 9, 2020). "*Managing Climate Risk in the U.S. Financial System*". Press release, September 9, 2020. https://www.cftc.gov/PressRoom/PressReleases/8234-20.

See: Thornton, A., & Green, A. (2021). *The SEC's Time to Act: A New Strategy for U.S. Corporate Climate Disclosures*. Washington D.C.: Center for American Progress. https://www.american-progress.org/issues/economy/reports/2021/02/19/496015/secs-time-act/.

See: SYSTEMIQ (2020). *The Paris Effect: How the Climate Agreement Is Reshaping the Global Economy*. London, UK. https://www.systemiq.earth/wp-content/uploads/2020/12/The-Paris-Effect_SYSTEMIQ_Full-Report_December-2020.pdf.

See: Task Force on Climate-related Financial Disclosures (2017). *Final Report: Recommendations of the Task Force on Climate-related Financial Disclosures*. https://assets.bbhub.io/company/sites/60/2020/10/FINAL-2017-TCFD-Report-11052018.pdf.

See: BlackRock (2021). *Climate risk and the transition to a low-carbon economy*. New York: BlackRock. https://www.blackrock.com/corporate/literature/publication/blk-commentary-climate-risk-and-energy-transition.pdf. This article stated in part: "........Companies in carbon-intensive industries should also disclose scope-3 emissions. A significant portion of the transition to a low-carbon economy hinges on the eventual retirement of fossil fuels, and it is particularly important

for investors to understand the scope-3 emissions profile of oil, gas, and coal companies as the primary source of fuel transitions from carbon-intensive solutions to cleaner alternatives.........".
See: Report of Independent Registered Public Accounting Firm, "Form 20-F: BP p.l.c.". filed March 18, 2020. https://www.sec.gov/Archives/edgar/data/313807/000162828020003753/a31122019b-p20fdoc.htm.
See: Public Company Accounting Oversight Board, "*AS 2710: Other Information in Documents Containing Audited Financial Statements*". https://pcaobus.org/oversight/standards/auditing-standards/details/AS2710.
See: Market Risk Advisory Committee of the U.S. Commodity Futures Trading Commission, "*Managing Climate Risk in the U.S. Financial System.*"
See: Kraten, M. (July 2019). Sustainability Reports and the Limitations of 'Limited' Assurance. *CPA Journal*. https://www.cpajournal.com/2019/07/26/sustainability-reports-and-the-limitations-of-limited-assurance/.
See: Environmental Defense Fund (2020). Hitting the Mark: Improving the Credibility of Industry Methane Data. New York, USA. https://storage.googleapis.com/edfbiz_website/Oil%20Gas%20 Methane/Hitting-the-Mark.pdf.
See: Nasralla, S. (Dec. 8, 2020). *Big carbon? Oil majors turn to nature to help plug revenue gap.* Reuters. https://www.reuters.com/article/us-climate-change-oil-carboncredits-focu/big-carbon-oil-majors-turn-to-nature-to-help-plug-revenue-gap-idUSKBN28I0HM.
See: Elgin, B. (December 9, 2020). *These Trees Are Not What They Seem.* Bloomberg. https://www.bloomberg.com/features/2020-nature-conservancy-carbon-offsets-trees/.
See: International Financial Reporting Standards Foundation (2020). "*Consultation Paper on Sustainability Reporting*". London, UK. https://cdn.ifrs.org/-/media/project/sustainability-reporting/consultation-paper-on-sustainability-reporting.pdf.
See: Whieldon, E. (January 29, 2021). "*Why just transition, environmental justice are key to any climate plan*". S&P Global Market Intelligence. https://www.spglobal.com/marketintelligence/en/news-insights/latest-news-headlines/why-just-transition-environmental-justice-are-key-to-any-climate-plan-62330412.
See: Total S.A., "*Universal Registration Document 2019*" (Courbevoie: 2020). at https://www.total.com/sites/g/files/nytnzq111/files/atoms/files/2019_total_universal_registration_document.pdf.
See: Total S.A. (July 29, 2020). "*Short Term Price Revision And Climate Ambition: Total Announces Exceptional $8B Asset Impairments Including $7B In Canadian Oil Sands*". Press release. Available at: https://www.total.com/media/news/short-term-price-revision-and-climate-ambition-total-announces-exceptional-8-b-asset.
See: BP, "*Progressing strategy development, bp revises long-term price assumptions, reviews intangible assets and, as a result, expects non-cash impairments and write-offs*," Press release, June 15, 2020, available at https://www.bp.com/en/global/corporate/news-and-insights/press-releases/bp-revises-long-term-price-assumptions.html.
See: Parry, I. (March 10,2021). *A New Vision for the US Climate Agenda*. IMF. Washington D.C., USA. https://blogs.imf.org/2021/03/10/a-new-vision-for-the-us-climate-agenda/.

13 Tang & Demmeritt (2018) noted that "......Scholars and business analysts have offered a number of competing explanations for this expansion of corporate social responsibility (CSR) reporting about carbon, ranging from rational pursuit of cost savings (Kolk & Pinkse (2004); Hoffman (2007)), brand differentiation (Delmas, et. al., 2006; Matisoff, et. al. (2013)) or reputational gains

(Hoffman (2005)) to coercive pressures from regulators (Levy & Egan (2003); Lyon & Maxwell (2004); Jones & Levy (2007)), institutional investors (Pfeifer & Sullivan (2008); Knox-Hayes & Levy (2011); Sullivan& Gouldson (2012); and Cotter & Najah (2012)) or environmental pressure groups (Stanny & Ely (2008); Hahn, et. al. (2015)) and mimetic pressures to follow the latest corporate fashions in CSR (Sullivan, 2008; Ihlen (2009))…….Some scholars argue that CSR practices such as carbon reporting not only minimize pollution and environmental harm, but also promote profitability, technological innovation, and wider economic competitiveness (Hajer (1995); Mol, et. al.(2009)). Such ecological modernization promises to reconcile the imperatives of economic growth and profit with environmental protection, delivering win–win outcomes (Boiral, et. al. (2012); Gouldson & Sullivan (2012))……..In the hope that disclosure will incentivize business innovation and improved environmental performance, the UK government recently became the first jurisdiction in the world to require publicly listed firms to account for their greenhouse gas emissions as part of their annual financial reporting. Other jurisdictions, such as Norway, Singapore, and Hong Kong are now following the British lead in requiring companies to report on their GHG emissions……….".

14 *See*: "*Environmental Auditing*". https://www.inc.com/encyclopedia/environmental-audit.html.

15 *See*: Chan, Pun & Selden (2013).

See: *The Other Side Of Apple II: Pollution Spreads Through Apple's Supply Chain.* Institute of Public and Environmental Affairs, August 31, 2011. http://www.ipe.org.cn/Upload/Report-IT-V-Apple-II.pdf.

See: Barboza, D. (2012). Apple Cited as Adding to Pollution in China. *The New York Times*, September 1, 2011. Accessed March 26, 2012. https://www.nytimes.com/2011/09/02/technology/apple-suppliers-causing-environmental-problems-chinese-group-says.html?_r=1.

See: Watts, J. (January 19, 2011). Apple secretive about 'polluting and poisoning' supply chain, says report. *The Guardian*. https://www.theguardian.com/environment/2011/jan/20/apple-pollution-supply-chain.

See: Jobs, S., *A Greener Apple. Apple, Inc.*. https://www.apple.com/hotnews/agreenerapple/.

See: Greenpeace. *"Hazardous Materials Found in Apple's iPhone: Chemicals Include those Banned in Children's Toys in EU". Greenpeace International. Greenpeace.* http://www.greenpeace.org/usa/en/media-center/news-releases/hazardous-materials-found-in-a/.

See: Chen, B. (May 14, 2010), *"Workers Plan to Sue iPhone Contractor Over Poisoning", Wired.* https://www.wired.com/gadgetlab/2010/05/wintek-employees-sue/.

See: Greenpeace. "Toxins in your TV, poisons in your PC?". Greenpeace International. Greenpeace. http://www.greenpeace.org/international/en/news/features/toxins-in-your-tv-poisons-in/.

See: Appleinsider Staff. "Steve Jobs unveils Apple's environmental policy". Appleinsider.com. Appleinsider.com. http://appleinsider.com/articles/07/05/02/steve_jobs_unveils_changes_to_apples_environmental_policy.

See: Greenpeace. "*Apple: 6th position, 4.5/10*". Greenpeace. http://www.greenpeace.org/international/Global/international/publications/climate/2012/GuideGreenerElectronics/APPLE.pdf.

See: Benoit, D. (2018-01-08). "iPhones and Children Are a Toxic Pair, Say Two Big Apple Investors". *Wall Street Journal.* https://www.wsj.com/articles/iphones-and-children-are-a-toxic-pair-say-two-big-apple-investors-1515358834.

See: Carlson, N. (April 7, 2010). "*What It's Like To Work In China's Gadget Sweatshops Where Your iPhones And iPads Are Made*". *Business Insider.* Available at: http://www.businessinsider.

com/what-its-like-to-work-if-chinas-gadget-sweatshops-where-your-iphones-and-ipads-are-made-2010-4?utm_source=Daily+Buzz&utm_campaign=81432d578c-nl_emv_db_04082010_a&utm_medium=email.

See: "Apple's 2019 supplier report shows progress on labor and health issues". Jeremy Horwitz. March 6, 2019. https://venturebeat.com/2019/03/06/apples-2019-supplier-report-shows-progress-on-labor-and-health-issues/.

See: "*Apple and Foxconn broke Chinese Labour law to build new iPhones - US tech group and manufacturing partner admit using too many temporary workers*". Louise Lucas. September 9, 2019. https://www.ft.com/content/19fefd86-d2c3-11e9-8367-807ebd53ab77.

See: *"Apple - Supplier Responsibility" (PDF). Apple.* https://images.apple.com/supplierresponsibility/pdf/L418102A_SR_2010Report_FF.pdf

See: *"Apple under fire again for working conditions at Chinese factories". The Guardian.* December 19, 2014. https://www.theguardian.com/technology/2014/dec/19/apple-under-fire-again-for-working-conditions-at-chinese-factories?CMP=EMCNEWEML6619I2.

See: *"Poor Working Conditions Persist at Apple Supplier Pegatron". China Labor Watch.* October 22, 2015. http://www.chinalaborwatch.org/report/109.

See: "*Apple suppliers maintain tight security to avoid leaks: Foxconn said to have 'special status' in China*". MacNN, February 17, 2010. Available at: http://www.macnn.com/articles/10/02/17/foxconn.said.to.have.special.status.in.china/.

16 *See*: Parry, I. (March 10,2021). *A New Vision for the US Climate Agenda.* IMF. Washington D.C., USA. https://blogs.imf.org/2021/03/10/a-new-vision-for-the-us-climate-agenda/.

17 *See*: "*Environmental Audit*". https://www.inc.com/encyclopedia/environmental-audit.html.

18 *See*: IPCC (2018). *Special Report: Global Warming of 1.5 °C: Summary for Policymakers.* https://www.ipcc.ch/sr15/chapter/spm/?ftag=YHF4eb9d17.

See: *Carbon Capture And "Dimming" The Sun Pose Dilemmas For Climate.* By Jeff Berardelli. April 23, 2021. https://www.yahoo.com/news/carbon-capture-dimming-sun-pose-142027804.html. This article stated in part: "..........The climate crisis is arguably the biggest challenge humanity has ever faced, and to limit warming to manageable levels, time is our biggest opponent. While the transition from fossil fuels to cleaner renewable energy is now gaining steam, the pace is simply not fast enough to head off the harmful impacts that are already being felt throughout the world. The Intergovernmental Panel on Climate Change (IPCC) "*Special Report: Global Warming of 1.5°C*" — the international community's benchmark guide to averting climate disaster — says to reach the goal of staying below 1.5°C of warming requires "rapid and far-reaching transitions" in our energy, industrial and other systems that would be "unprecedented in scale." In other words, the task is herculean.........Since the Industrial Revolution, the burning of fossil fuels has released 1.6 trillion tons of heat-trapping greenhouse gases into the atmosphere. Carbon dioxide (CO_2) has increased by 50% — at a pace 100 times faster than it naturally should. As a result, our planet is now warming 10 times faster than it has in 65 million years. The scale and speed is unprecedented. Despite advances in clean energy like wind and solar, the world still gets 80% of its energy from fossil fuels..........A 2017 research paper, led by the Nature Conservancy, found that natural climate solutions like restoring forests, wetlands and grasslands can, in a best-case scenario, provide 37% of the CO_2 mitigation needed to keep humanity below the upper goal (2°C of warming) of the Paris Agreement. That's significant, but not enough........Collectively, all these CCUS and DAC facilities have the capacity to capture about forty million tons of carbon dioxide yearly. It sounds like a lot, until you consider that each year humans emit almost forty billion tons of carbon dioxide into the atmosphere —1,000 times more than we can capture — to say nothing about all the CO2 that is already up there as a result of the Industrial Revolution. To put it bluntly, critics say CCUS and DAC are not ready for prime-time and may never be. The processes are very expensive, they consume copious amounts of energy themselves — often, ironically, produced by burning fossil fuels — and their capacity is just a tiny fraction of what's needed. Frischmann said, "They will never scale to the level necessary to offset fossil fuel emissions, and will take twenty years of 20% annual growth to even start making a dent in the atmosphere. Highly unlikely rate of growth."......... Peter Kalmus (@ClimateHuman), a NASA climate scientist, says he supports the concept of carbon capture and thinks we should keep researching it, but he is "extremely skeptical it will ever be possible or helpful." He thinks it should not be included in planning until we know it can be done at scale. Kalmus puts it colorfully: "I feel the IPCC stepped way out of bounds in normalizing it in greenhouse gas budgets and scenarios. They may as well have included genies, fairies, and pixies in their scenarios." Kalmus shares a concern with many others in the climate community that focusing on carbon capture will distract us from the real work of getting off fossil fuels.........".

See: Griscom, B., Adams, J., et. al. (2017). Natural climate solutions. *PNAS*, 114 (44) 11645-11650.

19 *See*: Clemente, J. (Oct. 1, 2015). "Cap-And-Trade Is Fraught With Fraud". *Forbes*. https://www.forbes.com/sites/judeclemente/2015/10/01/cap-and-trade-green-climate-fund-are-fraught-with-fraud/#5efb15f54940.

See: Haley, B. (March 13, 2017). "Political Manipulation Could Derail Nova Scotia's Cap-and-Trade System". *Halifax Examiner* (Canadian Newspaper). https://www.halifaxexaminer.ca/environment/political-manipulation-could-derail-nova-scotias-cap-and-trade-system/.

See: Goldstein, L. (July 23, 2016). "Call it Cap-And-Fraud". *Toronto Sun* (Canadian Newspaper). https://torontosun.com/2016/07/23/call-it-cap-and-fraud/wcm/7635fae3-866b-430c-97b9-24b212458188. This article stated in part: ".........A carbon credit entitles the bearer to emit one tonne of industrial carbon dioxide or equivalent, on the theory another emitter didn't. Since CO2 is a colourless, odourless gas, it's relatively easy to commit fraud. Interpol noted this can include: "........Fraudulent manipulation of measurements to claim more carbon credits from a project than were actually obtained; sale of carbon credits that either do not exist or belong to someone else; false or misleading claims with respect to the environmental or financial benefits of carbon market investments; exploitation of weak regulations in the carbon market to commit financial crimes, such as money laundering, securities fraud or tax fraud; computer hacking/phishing to steal carbon credits and personal information"........The Stockholm Environment Institute reported last year that almost 75% (seventy five percent) of carbon credits generated by Russia and Ukraine could be fraudulent. There have been similar findings with regard to China, India and elsewhere. The public pays the cost because carbon pricing increases the price of most goods and service, since most are made using fossil fuel energy. And if a carbon credit is fraudulent, there's no lowering of emissions because of it.........".

20 See the comments in: Helm (2009); Tanuro (2008); Vlachou & Pantelias (2017); Zeng, Weishaar & Vedder (2018); Antimiani, Costantini, et. al. (2013); Sijm, Neuhoff & Chen (2006); Frondel, Schmidt & Vance (2012); Grubb, Sha, Spencer, et. al. (2015); Goulder & Stavins (2011); Monjon & Quirion (2011); Weishaar (2014); Pang & Duan (2016); Schneider, Kollmuss & Lazarus (2015);

Tynkkynen (2014); Wang, Teng, Zhou & Cai (2017); Berthe & Elie (2015); Romer (1983); Furceri, Loungani & Zdzienicka (2018); and Kerr & Duscha (2014).

21 More specifically, the models and theories in the Paul Romer and William Nordhaus lines of research and related approaches are inaccurate and mis-specified – ie. Nordhaus (2007a;b;c); Nordhaus (2006a;b;c); Nordhaus (1994; 1995; 1998; 1974; 1977; 1992; 1980; 1981; 1998; 2013; 2016); Nordhaus & Moffat (2017); Nordhaus & Boyer (1999); etc..

APPENDIX

The UK FRC's Principles (issued in 2020).
The UK FRC's Principles are as follows:

Audit Board Purpose

P1: The Audit Board should be responsible for providing independent oversight of the audit practice, with a focus on the pursuit of Objective-1. The firm's most senior governance body should be responsible for providing oversight with a focus on the pursuit of Objective-2.

P2: The Audit Board and the management of the audit practice should establish and promote a culture supportive of the public interest.

Audit Board Composition

P3: The Audit Board should be chaired by and have a majority of Audit Non-Executives (ANEs).

Independence Of audit Board from the Firm

P4: At least one of the ANEs should not be a firm INE ('doubly independent'). The Chair of the Audit Board should be an ANE and may also be a firm INE but should not chair any other governance body in the firm.

Skills of Audit Board

P5: At least one ANE on the Audit Board should have experience of audit at an appropriate level of seniority, either as a former auditor or consumer of audit services. Audit Board oversight of Audit CEO and Audit Strategy.

P6: The Audit Board should oversee the firm's audit strategy to ensure that it is consistent with pursuit of the objectives and outcomes set out above. It should be able to require changes where it considers that the strategy is not consistent.

P7: The Audit Board shall be consulted by the Senior Partner of the firm with respect to the appointment of the CEO of Audit and have the opportunity to object to the appointment. The Audit Board may seek the removal of the Audit CEO.

Audit Board Oversight of Partner Promotion and Remuneration

P8: Remuneration of audit partners and audit partner promotion should be overseen by a sub-committee of the Audit Board comprising ANEs only. Admissions of partners will remain a partnership responsibility and subject to the governance procedures of the partnership. However, the selection of candidates to be admitted to the partnership to practice as audit partners will be overseen by the Audit Board.

Other Governance Matters

P9: Appointments of individuals to the Audit Board should be subject to a formal, rigorous and transparent procedure.

P10: The Audit Board should have the authority to commission reviews from Internal Audit to support their oversight role.

Scope of the separate practice.

Services within the "ring-fence":

P11: Statutory audits hould be provided by the audit practice. The audit practice may also provide:

- permitted audit-related and non-audit services to PIE entities audited by the firm;
- audit-related and non-audit services to non-PIE entities audited by the firm which are not prohibited; and
- services to other entities not audited by the firm that are either included on the "white-list" in paragraph-5.40 of the Ethical Standard 2019, or are non-audit assurance engagements where the recipient of the assurance is a third party (e.g. a regulator, government or lender) separate from the client of the audit firm. These assurance engagements should be performed in accordance with a recognized assurance standard (e.g. ISAE 3000; ISAE 3402; SOC1; etc.).

Specialists Supporting Audit

P12: Specialists supporting audit (and other permitted services provided by the audit practice) can be located elsewhere in the firm provided their services are supplied and charged to the audit practice on an arms-length basis.

Other Ring-Fence Matters

P13: Partners and staff in the audit practice should spend the majority of their time on work in the audit practice. This does not preclude the secondment of staff to other areas of the business (in either direction) or the appointment of audit partners to firmwide leadership roles.

P14: Revenues from statutory audit work should make up the majority of the revenue of the audit practice.

Financial

P15: Transactions between the audit practice and the rest of the firm should be conducted and priced on an 'arms-length' basis.

P16: The audit practice should produce a separate profit and loss account with overhead absorption on an equitable basis.

P17: As part of its annual assessment of whether firms are delivering these objectives and outcomes, the FRC will assess whether the overall distribution of profits to the partners in the audit practice and to those in the rest of the firm is consistent with their respective contributions to firm profits, with no material, structural cross subsidy persisting in either direction. This assessment will take account of any non-recurring items and investment to improve audit quality. If the FRC's assessment is that a material, structural cross subsidy persists, the firm should produce an action plan to remove the subsidy over a period to be agreed with the FRC.

Remuneration of Partners

P18: Remuneration policies and practices for audit partners should be designed to reward good audit practice-related behaviours. Good audit quality, along with positive leadership and behaviors should be rewarded and the firm should have measures in place to reduce reward in cases of poor audit quality.

Principles

Transparency:

P19: Firms should publish information about the governance of the audit practice and the terms on which transactions occur between the audit and non-audit business and the nature of these transactions.

P20: Firms should produce annually a separate profit and loss account for the audit practice to a level which is consistent with the firm's own published statutory financial statements. This profit and loss account should be assured by the firm's auditors. Firms should submit more detailed financial information supporting the profit and loss account to the FRC no later than four months after the financial year end. After an agreed transition period, firms should publish the audit practice's profit and loss account described above in their Transparency Reports. Firms should provide to the FRC their budget for the audit practice and sensitivities for the coming year.

Accountability

P21: Firms should appoint one individual (or a small number of individuals with clearly defined and non-overlapping responsibilities) from the Senior Management team to be responsible and accountable for ensuring the outcomes and principles for operational separation are delivered, embedded and monitored.

Transitional Arrangements

P22: Firms should provide a transition timetable to ensure that each of these principles is implemented as soon as practicable and they are met implemented in full by 30 June 2024 at the latest. An implementation plan should be submitted to FRC by 23 October 2020. The FRC will agree a transition timetable including a medium-term plan with a firm. In the first year of submission, the profit and loss account may be done on a 'best efforts' basis. Firms will not be required to publish the profit and loss account during an agreed transition period ending not later than 30 June 2024.

Chapter 6
On Impossibility Theorems, Informal Algorithms, and International Trade:
Allocation Mechanisms for Accounting/Consulting Firms

ABSTRACT

The "Big-Four" accounting firms dominate the global accounting/auditing industry, and the big-seven consulting firms (Bain; McKinsey; Booz; Deloitte; PwC; KPMG and E&Y) dominate the global business/management consulting industry and stifle competition. During 1990-2017, the global auditing/accounting industry and the global management consulting industry experienced significant structural changes that have implications for Financial Stability, systemic risk and the proper functioning of capital markets. Some of the results included the collapses of stock prices and bond prices of firms suspected of earnings management; and substantial litigation against auditing firms, CRAs and board of directors. Accounting/audit firms and consulting firms have always been key elements in the fight against earnings management, securities fraud, corruption and asset quality management because of their unique position as external auditors and advisors. This chapter introduces some efficient Auditor allocation and Compensation Mechanisms. These new "Learning Business Models" and contracts can solve the conflicts of interest, Antitrust, greed, Regret, Deadweight-Losses, complexity and industrial organization problems inherent in the Auditing/consulting industry; and each such model contravenes Myerson-Satterthwaite Impossibility Theorem, Arrow's Impossibility Theorem, Sen's Impossibility Theorem, Gibbard's Theorem, the Gibbard-Satterthwaite Impossibility Theorem, and the Green-Laffont Impossibility Theorem. These issues have implications for international trade and international capital flows given the prevalence of accounting and management consulting in almost all aspects of modern business.

DOI: 10.4018/978-1-7998-7418-8.ch006

INTRODUCTION

This chapter is motivated by various factors. *First*, Accounting is the most global of all professional services, and critically affects how international trade is conducted, recorded and its disputes resolved. Management Consulting is a related field, can have similar effects and is also international. *Second*, during 1990-2016, the global auditing/accounting industry experienced significant structural changes some of which have had un-even effects among large, medium and small auditing firms and their clients. *Third*, there are significant antitrust/competition and structural problems in the global audit/accounting industry which have not been adequately addressed in the literature or by government regulators. *Fourth*, there continues to be substantial earnings management by companies which have had significant and negative effects on capital markets and economic development. In addition, there has been rapid growth of robo-trading (which often heavily depends on which is now questionable accounting data) and increasing reliance on audited financial data by both retail and institutional investors, and suppliers and customers in industries. These problems can be substantially reduced by implementing new allocation mechanisms (ie. allocation of customers; fees; etc.) for accounting firms. *Fifth*, the Global Financial Crisis of 2008-2014 illustrated weaknesses in auditing and in Corporate Governance standards in multinational organizations. There was rapid growth of cross-border trade during 1995-2017 and both individual and institutional investors around the world are increasingly emphasizing the quality and implementation of accounting and corporate governance standards within companies as a major investment criteria. *Sixth*, during 1995-2015 and across the world, there were significant increases in the volume of shareholder activism and associated litigation (and litigation strategies), much of which was directed at, or was handled by or was ultimately influenced by Boards of Directors and external auditing/accounting firms. *Seventh*, the type of, multiplicity and effects of *Regulatory Failure* that were implicit in, and manifested by audit failures, bankruptcies of auditing firms and lawsuits against auditing firms during 1995-2017 and around the world is new and has not been addressed fully in the literature; and are not sufficiently included in analysis of Financial Stability. *Eighth,* the audit failures and the inefficient structure of the global auditing industry and the global management consulting industry created or could have created *Deadweight Losses* in the trading of securities around the world; and *Deadweight Losses* in the demand for auditing and consulting services and Deadweight Losses in the enforcement of accounting, environmental and securities regulations - which have not been fully addressed in the literature. *Ninth*, the existing literature does not address the issue of whether auditing standards (distinct from disclosure standards) are *Public Goods* given the broad geographical scope of their impact and the growing adoption of IASB/IFRS globally. *Tenth*, as auditors that owe duties to several groups, accounting firms can be allocated some liability for their audit-clients' non-compliance or under-compliance with disclosure and other requirements for Climate Finance instruments (such as emissions permits; climate derivatives; climate-linked bonds; etc.). By addressing these issues, this chapter contributes to the algorithmic mechanism design, "learning" algorithms; Group Theory, financial stability, international trade and industrial organization literatures.

EXISTING LITERATURE

There is minimal literature on the economic criteria for allocation of liability to auditing firms; and very minimal literature on the allocation of work to auditing firms; or the allocation of professional fees to auditing firms; or a mechanism-design based comparison of accounting firms and CRAs. Nwogugu

(2010) developed new *Work-Allocation, Liability-Allocation* and *Revenue-Allocation* models for Auditing firms. Liu & Simunic (2005), Ballas & Fafalliou (Nov. 2008), Cox (_____), Ascher (Sept. 2008), Chen, Su & Wu (2007), DeFond, Wong & Li (2000), Lennox & Liu (2012), Gerakos & Syverson (Jan. 2014), Dunn, Kohlbeck & Mayhew (2011), Albrecht (April 2010), Bloom & Schirm (June 2005), Huang, Chang & Chiou (2016) and US GAO (U.S. Government Accounting Office) (2008) discussed oligopoly and competition in the auditing/accounting industry. Nagy (2005) and Gul, Ma & Lai (2017) analyzed audit firm/partner tenure in the industry.

Hogan (1994); Wysocki (Nov. 2009); DeFond, Raghunandan & Subramanyam (2002); DeFond, Wong & Li (2000); Kinney, Palmrose & Scholz (2004); Heibatollah & Ye (Oct. 2005); Ghosh, Kallapaur & Moon (2006); Gul, Sami & Zhou (2009); Habib, Jiang & Zhou (2015); Gordon (2015); and Ke, Lennox & Xin (2015) discussed auditor independence and conflicts-of-interest.

Clinch (2005); Curtis (2012); Geiger, Raghunandan & Riccardi (2014); Ghosh, Kallapaur & Moon (2006); and Heibatollah & Ye (Oct. 2005) discussed capital markets issues.

Lix (2002); European Union (n.d.); Napier (1998); Todea & Stanciu (2009); Dickey (Gibson Dunn) (2008); Cunningham (2004); Maloney (n.d.); Blythe (2014); Grubbs & Ethridge (2007); Davies (2009); European Commission (2008); European Union (2007); and Nahal & Kiesselbach (2009) commented on liability-allocation systems in the audit/accounting industry. Schmidt (2012); Kaplan & Williams (2013); Casterella, Jensen & Knechel (2010); and Boone, Khurana & Raman (2011) conducted empirical analysis of auditors' litigation risks – but omitted liability-allocation regimes and work-allocation mechanisms.

Karpoff, Lee & Martin (2008); Kim, Li & Zhang (2011); and Kim & Zhang (2013; 2014) discussed some negative effects of earnings management on Financial Stability. European Commission (2010); Kothari & Lester (2012); Geiger, Raghunandan & Riccardi (2014); DeHaan (2017); Kwon, Park & Yu (2017); and Tang, Tian & Yan (2015) discussed the impact of accounting/auditing firms and CRAs on financial stability. Nwogugu (2013/2015) introduced new business models for CRAs.

Curtis (2012) found evidence of a structural change in the long-run association between prices and accounting fundamentals. Englund, Gerdin & Abrahamsson (2013), Abidin, Beattie & Goodacre (2010), Payne (Aug. 2016), Abbott, Parker & Peters (2011), Carson, Soo & Wright (2012), and Ferguson, Pinnuck & Skinner (April 2014) analyzed structural changes in the accounting/audit industry.

Using a sample of firms sanctioned by the SEC for fraudulent financial reporting in Accounting and Auditing Enforcement Releases (SEC-sanctioned fraud firms), Markelevich & Rosner (2013) analyzed whether there is a relationship between auditor fee variables and the likelihood of being sanctioned by the SEC for fraud. They found in uni-variate tests, that fraud firms paid significantly higher (total, audit, and NAS) fees; but in multivariate tests, when controlling for other fraud determinants and endogeneity among the fraud, NAS, and audit fee variables, they found that while *NAS fees and total fees* are positively and significantly related to the likelihood of being sanctioned by the SEC for fraud, *audit fees* are not (even after controlling for latent size effects and other rigorous testing).

In the US, the revised Securities and Exchange Commission (SEC) requirements that resulted from the implementation of the Sarbanes-Oxley Act (2002) limited non-audit services (NAS) and require NAS fee disclosure. The general consensus has been that the argument that auditor independence could be impaired (and hence audit quality may be reduced) when auditors become economically dependent on their clients or audit their own work. *Economic bonding* leads to reduced independence, which can reduce audit quality.

Roth & Sotomayor (1992); and Mashayekhy, Nejad & Grosu (2014) studied two-sided matching. Jacobs (2012) discussed coalgebras. Nissam (2007) summarized mechanism design. Mohri & Medina

(2014) and Nazerzadeh, Leme, et. al. (2016) analyzed learning algorithms. Bertsekas (2000) analyzed auctions as algorithms. Thille, Cojocaru, et. al. (2013), Makhdoumi, Malekian & Ozdaglar (2017) and Nakhe (2017) developed dynamic pricing models for various markets.

On *Qualitative Reasoning* in Artificial Intelligence, see Forbus (2019), Halpern (2003), and Bredeweg & Struss (Winter 2003).

Accinelli, Bazzano, et. al. (2015), Sánchez-Sánchez& Vargas-Valencia (2018), Petrohilos-Andrianos & Xepapadeas (2016), Hofer, Jäger & Füllsack (2018), Espinosa-Avila, Longoria & Hernández-Quiroz (2017), Antonio & Coello (2018), Chica, Chiong, et al. (2018) and Deb, Zhu & Kulkarni (2018) discussed models and issues that are relevant to *algorithms*, *Game Theory* and *Dynamical Systems*.

Contract Theory and Mechanism Design

Contract Theory and *Mechanism Design Theory* have been jointly studied from various perspectives including Economics/Finance, Operations Research, Mathematical Psychology, Computer Science, Game Theory and Applied Math - see: Hoppe & Schmitz (2018), Niederhoff & Kouvelis (2019), Hong, Wernz & Stillinger (2016), Wu, Zhao & Tang (2014), Li, Liu & Chen (2018), Lin & Chou (1990), Park & Kim (2014), Goetz, Yatsenko, et. al. (2019), Fang & Yuan (2018), Madureira, Pereira, et. al. (2014), Meneguzzi, Modgil, et. al. (2012), Meneguzzi, Modgil, Oren, et. al. (2011), Zohar & Rosenschein (2008), Terán, Aguilar & Cerrada (2017), Eenmaa-Dimitrieva & Schmidt-Kessen (2019), Drozd & Serrano-Padia (2018) and Wei, Wang, et.al. (2018). However, the models in most of these foregoing articles and literature are static, don't incorporate relevant variables; don't consider varying "states" and often complex "joint" effects of variables; and they don't consider Industrial Organization effects of contracts/ mechanisms - see Nwogugu (2007;b), Nwogugu (2019a;b) and Nwogugu (2006).

Sustainability, Economic Growth, and the Standardization of Contracts

Standardization of contracts can affect economic growth, Sustainability, Inequality and Economic Growth as noted by various academic researchers - see Sussman (1999), Van Assche & Schwartz (2013), Patterson (2010), Engert & Hornuf (2018), Aguirre (2017), Ayotte & Bolton (2011), Baffi (2007; 2012), He, Xue & Zhou (2019), Vo, Nguyen, et.al. (2019), Sheng (2019), Eenmaa-Dimitrieva & Schmidt-Kessen (2019), Dekker, Kawai & Sakaguchi (2018), Iossa & Martimort (2018), and Sprinkle, Williamson & Upton (2008). Sussman (1999) noted that "The main implications of contract standardization are that (i) "financial history matters in the growth process,(ii) early formation of the system may create a drag on economic growth and (iii) the effect may be non-monotonic because the system may be modernized at some point". In the realm of CRAs, CRAs have developed their own standardized contracts for ratings projects and the Big-Three CRAs are dominant.

COMPLEXITY, COMPLEX ADAPTIVE SYSTEMS, AND THE RULE-OF-LAW[1]: THE MECHANISMS INTRODUCED IN THIS CHAPTER ALL VIOLATE THE MYERSON-SATTERTHWAITE IMPOSSIBILITY THEOREM AND ARROW'S IMPOSSIBILITY THEOREM

Complexity pertaining to these issues is or can be manifested in the following ways:

1. Non linearity in relation to rule-of-law development.
2. Non linearity in the growth of regional/national economies and accounting firms.
3. Self organization of institutions and organizations – such as private and public enforcement groups; rule-making; etc..
4. Self organization of accounting firms and their audit clients.
5. Change and theories of change.
6. Non linearity in relation to deadweight loses in the demand for, and enforcement of laws.
7. Non linearity in relation to compliance with statutes and enforcement of laws.
8. Complex Networks – accounting firms; CRAs; audit clients; etc..
9. Network Effects.

The legal and economic environment in which accounting firms and CRAs function (defined by accounting firms; audit clients; expectations; legislatures; regulations; regulators; financial institutions; internet systems; etc.) is a complex adaptive system because it has some or all of the following attributes:

1. The relations between the system and its environment are non-trivial and or non-linear.
2. The system can be influenced by, or can adapt itself to its environment.
3. The system has feedback or memory, and can adapt itself according to its history or feedback.
4. The system is highly sensitive to initial conditions.
5. The number of parts (and types of parts) in the system and the number of relations between the parts is non-trivial.

While, the literature on algorithmic mechanism design is extensive, that on auditing processes as mechanisms is relatively limited (see: Gilpatric, Vossler & McKee (2011); and Kotowski, Weisbach & Zeckhauser (2013)), and most articles have focused on environment-related audits and very few have addressed accounting audits and corporate governance (see: Kofman & Lawarree (1993); Laffont & Martimort (1997); Tirole (1992); Suzuki (2008; 2009)).

Govindan & Wilson (2006); Yoav & Leyton-Brown (2009); and Lutz & Schafke (1985) discussed examples of various uses of Invariants and Game Theory. Telser (1994) and Chiarella, Kopel & Szidarovszky (2010) illustrated the use of *Core Theory*, *Stability* and Invariants in Industrial Organization. Demande, Gale & Sotomayor (1987) and Martínez, Massó, Neme & Oviedo (2012) studied *Matching Games*. Arribillaga, Massó & Neme (2014); Jaume, Masso & Neme (2012) and Sotomayor (2003) analyzed *Assignment Games*. Van den Brink (2012) analyzed efficiency and Collusion Neutrality in Cooperative Games. Bergantiños & Massó (2002) attempted to derive values for NTU Games. Note that Game Strategies and Core Elements are presented as text herein for brevity, although there are equivalent mathematical representations - similar to how *Strategic Complementarity* and *Supermodularity* are mathematically expressed as $\partial^2 f/\partial z_i \partial z_j \geq 0$; for all $i \neq j$; where and z_i and z_j are strategies of participants in the action space and each action is chosen from an interval z_i, z_j ε [a,b]; and the payoff functions f(.), depend on actions/strategies of two or more types of participants z_i and z_j in the action space ($i = 1 \ldots \ldots . n; j = 1 \ldots \ldots \ldots n$).

Colini-Baldeschi, Goldberg, et. al. (Nov. 2017), Deng, Goldberg, Tang & Zhang (2014), Dütting, Roughgarden & Talgam-Cohen (2014), and Gomes (2014) analyzed two-sided auctions. Roth & Sotomayor (1992) and Mashayekhy, Nejad & Grosu (2014) studied two-sided matching. Jacobs (2012) discussed coalgebras. Nissam (2007) summarized mechanism design. Mohri & Medina (2014) and Nazerzadeh, Leme, et. al. (2016) analyzed learning algorithms. Bertsekas (2000) analyzed auctions as algorithms.

Thille, Cojocaru, et. al. (2013); Makhdoumi, Malekian & Ozdaglar (2017); and Nakhe (2017) developed dynamic pricing models for various markets. Accinelli, Bazzano, et. al. (2015), Sánchez-Sánchez& Vargas-Valencia (2018), Petrohilos-Andrianos & Xepapadeas (2016), Hofer, Jäger & Füllsack (2018), Espinosa-Avila, Longoria & Hernández-Quiroz (2017), Antonio & Coello (2018), Chica, Chiong, et al. (2018), Kuehn, Malavolta & Rasmussen (2018), Dmitriev, Tsukanova & Maltseva (2017) and Deb, Zhu & Kulkarni (2018) discussed models and issues that are relevant to algorithms, Game Theory and Dynamical Systems.

The academic mechanism design articles that address accounting audits and corporate governance focus mostly on intra-firm collusion which is only one of the many problems in the global auditing/consulting industry. The main problems with these research studies are as follows:

1. The nature of accounting audits and consulting projects and structure of the auditing industry make it difficult to apply traditional mechanism design theories. The problems and inefficiencies inherent in external audits and consulting projects arise from not only incentive contracts (of auditee-employees, consultants or external-auditors), but also from external factors such as industry structure in the audit/consulting industries, competition among auditing/consulting firms, regulation and inadequate demarcation of the responsibilities and functions of consulting firms.
2. Very few of the studies provide or address *Liability-Allocation Mechanisms*, and none address *Work-Allocation mechanisms* or *fee-allocation mechanisms.*
3. External Auditors and consultants have their own objectives and incentives, which are sometimes not aligned with those of their audit-clients and government regulators. External auditors and consultants often engage in anti-competitive conduct that affects or can affect the efficiency of audits and intra-firm coordination within audit-clients.
4. Adding non-auditor supervisors (employees of the audit-client) to the auditing-process does not necessarily solve the audit-efficiency problem partly because such incremental supervisors face similar constraints, internal politics and incentive-contracts as existing non-auditor supervisors; and such addition increases the risk of collusion especially when the firm and or the industry is in a down-turn. Liability-allocation, Auditor-Work-Allocation and Auditor-Fee-Allocation mechanisms are more likely to be useful.
5. Adding auditor-supervisors (e.g. joint auditing) does not necessarily solve the audit-efficiency problem partly because such incremental supervisors face similar constraints, internal politics and incentive-contracts as existing auditor-supervisors; and such addition increases the risk of collusion especially when the firm and or the industry is in a down-turn. Liability-allocation, Auditor-Work-Allocation and Auditor-Fee-Allocation mechanisms are more likely to be useful.

Each of the new business/compensation mechanisms introduced herein and below violates the *Myerson-Satterthwaite Impossibility Theorem, Arrow's Impossibility Theorem, Sen's Impossibility Theorem, Gibbard's Theorem*, the *Gibbard-Satterthwaite Impossibility Theorem*, and The *Green-Laffont Impossibility Theorem*_because each has the following characteristics of *individual rationality*; *strong budget balance*; *incentive compatibility* of buyers/sellers, *pareto-optimality, feasibility, No-Dictatorship, Pareto-Efficiency* and *Independence of Irrelevant Alternatives* as noted as follows:

1. *Individual Rationality* of buyers (client companies) (*Myerson-Satterthwaite Impossibility Theorem*) - For each buyer, there is a bid such that the buyer always obtains nonnegative utility.
2. *Individual Rationality* of suppliers (auditing firms) (*Myerson-Satterthwaite Impossibility Theorem*).
3. *Strong Budget Balance* (*Myerson-Satterthwaite Impossibility Theorem*) – where not all buyers' payments are given to suppliers, the portion given to suppliers reflects fair value for services rendered.
4. *Dominant-Strategy Incentive Compatibility* of buyers and suppliers (*Myerson-Satterthwaite Impossibility Theorem*) – each buyer and supplier can achieve the best outcome to him/herself by reporting/acting according to his/her true preferences/valuations.
5. *Pareto Optimality* (*Myerson-Satterthwaite Impossibility Theorem*) - there is no other allocation/ matching superior to that provided by the mechanism in all aspects, provided all buyers report their true valuation (its assumed that mechanism structure encourages truth-telling by buyers and suppliers).
6. *Feasibility* (*Myerson-Satterthwaite Impossibility Theorem*) – with respect to real-world constraints.
7. *Privacy* – where bidding is used, the identities of bidders are not disclosed and for each "project" (e.g. an annual audit), only the winning seller-buyer pair are introduced to each other.
8. *Welfare Maximization* (both Exact And Approximate) – the model maximizes welfare with regards to the overall system; and reduces deadweight losses (by reducing consumer surpluses and supplier surpluses).
9. *Regret-positive* – reduces Regret of buyers (client/auditee companies) and sellers (auditing firms).
10. *No-Dictatorship* (*Gibbard's Theorem*; *Arrow's Impossibility Theorem; Gibbard-Satterthwaite Impossibility Theorem*): the outcome should not always be identical to the ranking of one particular alternative.
11. *Non-dictatorial* (*Gibbard's Theorem*; the *Gibbard-Satterthwaite Impossibility Theorem*) - there isn't any distinguished agent who can impose the outcome.
12. *Pareto Efficiency* (*Arrow's Impossibility Theorem*): if every user prefers Outcome-A to Outcome-B, then the outcome should rank A above B.
13. *Independence of Irrelevant Alternatives* (*Arrow's Impossibility Theorem*): the outcome's relative ranking of choices A and B should not change if users change the ranking of other choices but do not change their relative rankings of A and B.
14. *No Two-Option Limit* (*Gibbard's Theorem*; the *Gibbard-Satterthwaite Impossibility Theorem*) - the process doesn't limit the possible outcomes to only two options.
15. *No Strategic-Voting* (*Gibbard's Theorem*, the *Gibbard-Satterthwaite Impossibility Theorem*) - the process isn't open to Strategic-Voting (once an agent has identified their preferences, it isn't possible that they have no action at their disposal that best protects such preferences regardless of the other agents' actions).

A CRITIQUE OF THE EUROPEAN UNION'S (AND US) AUDIT REFORM STATUTES

Nwogugu (2008) critiqued the *Sarbanes Oxley Act* ("SOX"; USA) and also introduced a new model of *Willingness-To-Comply*. Nwogugu (2015a) critiqued FASB, GASB, IASB, ISDA and ICMA, all of which are standards-setting organizations for accounting standards and derivatives standards. Nwogugu (2015a) also critiqued SOX. Nwogugu (2015b;c) critiqued the *Dodd Frank Act* which has collateral effects on audits and the relationships between accounting firms and securities regulatory agencies.

In June 2014, the European Union enacted its Audit Reform statute which officially took effect in June 2016[2]. The EU Audit Reform Statutes imposes mandatory audit firm rotation and significant restrictions on non-audit services for *Public Interest Entities* ("PIEs"). The new laws provide transition arrangements for mandatory audit-firm rotation. The EU Audit Reform Statutes is generally directed at audits of Public Interest Entities (PIEs) which include companies listed on an EU "*regulated market*", EU PIE subsidiaries of companies headquartered outside the EU, and certain other organizations such as banks, insurance companies and other financial entities (in the UK, the regulation applies to companies with listed debt or equities on the main market, but not AIM). The EU Audit Reform Statutes don't address the problems noted in Nwogugu (2015b,c;d)

The other problems inherent in the EU Audit Reform Statutes are as follows:

1. The definition of PIEs is problematic[3] and should be amended to include organizations that have or can have significant economic, social and or psychological impact. PIEs should also include: i) government agencies, ii) large/medium non-profit organizations, iii) small private companies who have many retail customers (e.g. more than 10,000 customers) or a few very-large corporate customers, or a minimum amount of annual revenues (at least Euro20 Million of revenues); iv) large private companies (not traded on stock exchanges).
2. The EU Audit Reform Statutes unnecessarily focuses on, and applies only to PIEs, whereas such audit regulation should apply to both exchange traded companies of all sizes, and private companies whose revenues exceed a specific threshold (eg $20 Million).
3. It does not specify that its auditor "*Rotation*" provisions should also apply to both audit partners and audit staff.
4. It does not specify that its auditor "*Rotation*" provisions should also apply to conglomerates as a whole.
5. The penalties regime/system is vague and has been delegated to member states. Ideally there should be a uniform penalty system across the EU (especially since there is mobility of labor and companies in the EU).
6. There is no liability allocation system. Ideally there should be a uniform liability-allocation system across the EU.
7. It does not specify mandatory quality control by third-party audit firms, especially for large companies, and companies that have many customers (whose failure may have substantial economic, psychological or social effects). See Article-249a)(k)[4].
8. It does not sufficiently address ownership of audit firms and formation of joint ventures among audit firms.
9. It does not sufficiently address sanctions and is vague and leaves sanctions entirely up to member countries. There has to be uniformity and minimum standards for sanctions set at the EU level which all member states must comply with. See Articcle-30a[5] and Article-30b[6].
10. It does not provide sufficient incentives for reporting of breaches; and is vague and leaves it up to member states to deal with the issue. Rather, reporting of breaches should be addressed in detail at the EU level and there should be a centralized repository of such reports (and reports made to the EU Commission)[7].

11. The statutes requirements for Audit Committees are grossly inadequate. See Article-39[8]. First the Independence requirements are inadequate – Audit Committee members should also be independent of the auditee's shareholders and all accounting firms (such person should not have worked at, and should not have had any interest in any accounting firm during the preceding five years. Ideally, all the members of the audit committee shall be independent of the audited entity. Second, the majority of Audit Committee Member should be skilled in auditing and accounting or financial management. Third, all PIEs should have audit Committees.
12. The EU should have a centralized regulatory agency that regulates auditors and monitors the quality of Audits, rather than delegating such tasks to member states. This is because the mobility of labor, capital and companies is a major element of the EU structure
13. The statute does not require mandatory rotation of auditors.
14. Generally, the statute suffers from the same major weakness of most EU statutes, which is inefficient (and perhaps un-constitutional) delegation of the EU's legislative and enforcement duties to its member states.

LIABILITY-ALLOCATION: THE ADVERSE EFFECTS OF OLIGOPOLY IN THE AUDITING INDUSTRY AND LACK OF INDEPENDENCE OF AUDITING FIRMS

The Dodd Frank Act of 2010 (USA) and SOX and similar statutes enacted in the UK and other countries did not solve the primary structural problems in the accounting/auditing profession which have contributed to systemic risk, financial statement fraud, securities fraud and economic stagnation. These problems are as follows.

There has been a continuing Oligopoly in the accounting/auditing industry[9] in most countries wherein the "Big-Four" accounting firms dominate the accounting/auditing industry, and stifle competition. See the comments in: Liu & Simunic (2005); Ballas & Fafalliou (Nov. 2008); Albrecht (April 2010); Cox (n.d.); Ascher (Sept. 2008); Bloom & Schirm (June 2005); Chen, Su & Wu (2007); DeFond, Wong & Li (2000); and Nagy (2005). It's clear from the many corporate scandals that occurred during 1995-2017 that this oligopoly reduces the quality of audits and financial statements, limits innovation and diffusion of knowledge. Long term relationships between accounting firm and their clients breeds complacency, and fosters inertia. Big-Four audit firms have developed an aura of accuracy and stability which investors have come to depend on. Companies often seek the stamp of approval of Big-Four firms, and are willing to pay excessive fees to get such implicit approval. This problem can be solved by: 1) implementing "term limits" for auditing services (e.g. an accounting firm can audit a company only for a maximum of three years during any contiguous Ten-year period); and or 2) statutorily limiting the number of audits that can be performed by an accounting firm in any year; and or 3) statutorily limiting the size of accounting/auditing firms.

Secondly, in most countries, accounting firms are compensated by the companies that they audit – and this is a major conflict interest[10] because auditee-firms can influence auditors and the outcomes of audits, and the expectation of future audit business compromises auditor independence. So long as a company pays an audit firm directly, or pays an audit firm based in part on the stages of completed audit work, the audit firm can never be "independent". See the comments in Bajaj Gunny & Atulya (Feb. 2003); Hogan (1994); Wysocki (Nov. 2009); DeFond, Raghunandan & Subramanyam (2002); Frankel, Johnson & Nelson (2002); Hay, Knechel & Wong (2006); Kinney, Palmrose & Scholz (2004); Larcker,

Richardson (2004); Raghunandan (March 2002); Heibatollah & Ye (Oct. 2005); Ghosh, Kallapaur & Moon (2006); and Clinch (2005).

Under the existing auditor compensation systems in most countries, accounting firms have no incentives to report fraud – in fact, accounting firms have substantial incentives to cover-up fraud in order to obtain repeat business[11]. Any accounting firm that reports fraud will most probably lose future audit/accounting assignments from the auditee company. For the typical accounting firm, repeat audit business is more profitable than new audit projects because it involves low "startup" costs, and the auditing firm is familiar with the auditee company. Because Big-Four firms have developed brand equity and companies seek their services, Big-four firms can afford to shirk due to substantially reduced competition. Also, since the demand for Big-Four auditing services is near in-elastic in some circumstances, and their pricing of audit services may not reflect the quality of their audit services. Audit firms also face substantial reputational penalties for loss of an audit client – which substantially reduces the audit firm's willingness to report fraud or negative information about the auditee company. Auditee-companies typically pay the auditor for audit work in phases, and even if the auditee company cancels the audit, it can retain another auditor at lower costs – and thus, the auditee company can influence the auditor and the auditor's report. Under existing auditor compensation systems, the auditor does not face any penalties for inaccurate audit work – typically it's the auditee company that is sued for mis-statements in financial statements.

SOME PROPERTIES OF EFFICIENT AUDITOR-WORK ALLOCATION MECHANISMS ("AAM")

There is a need for efficient mechanisms for allocating audit work to auditing firms (Auditor-Work Allocation System - "AAS") and for allocating audit fees to audit firms and audit partners (Audit-Fee Allocation System - "AFAS").

Similar problems have arisen in determining an efficient method of allocating work to, and compensating Credit Rating Agencies (ie. Moody's; S&P; Fitch; etc.) – such as *Tie-Breaker Effects*, Platform-Matching; etc.. See Nwogugu (2013/2015). Thus, there is: **i)** a substantial difference between an *Auditor-Work-Allocation Mechanism* and an *Audit-Fee Allocation Mechanism*; **ii)** a substantial difference between a CRA-Work-Allocation mechanism and a CRA-Fee Allocation Mechanism.

In the audit industry, the Fee-allocation system and the Work-allocation system can and should be separated for the foregoing reasons and the following reasons:

1. companies seek multiple ratings in variable period, whereas companies seek only one audit per audit year.
2. the useful-life of a credit rating is shorter and more variable than that of an annual audit report.
3. Credit ratings fees are smaller and can be more variable than audit fees.
4. the CRA industry is highly concentrated and is an oligopoly, whereas the audit industry is more fragmented.
5. audit firms tend to maintain exclusive client relationships for longer periods; whereas each issuer-company typically maintains active contractual relationships with several CRAs.
6. The internal politics of Audits firms are or can be more intense and disruptive than that of CRAs. Audit firm partners often run fiefdoms.

7. The differences between CRAs and Audit-firms described in the table below (that compares Audit reports and credit ratings) also support the separation of auditors' Fee-allocation Mechanism from their Work-allocation Mechanism.

Some properties of an efficient *Auditor-Work Allocation Mechanism* ("**AAM**") are as follows:

1. The AAM reduces auditors' dependence on, and expectations for future audit work from the auditee-company. The AAM expressly requires mandatory Rotation of Audit firms for each auditee-company. The properties of such Auditor Rotation are as follows:
    a. The "*Base Time*" (the maximum number of consecutive audit years that an audit firm can audit a company) must be short enough to avoid formation of detrimental auditor-auditee relationships.
    b. The *Mandatory Rotation* must apply to both audit Partners and Audit Staff, regardless of whether or not they remain with the audit firm.
    c. The "*Exclusion Period*" (the minimum number of audit periods immediately after the Base Time, during which an audit firm cannot audit a company) must be long enough to avoid the formation of detrimental auditor-auditee relationships.
2. The AAM reduces or eliminates the reputational penalties for loss of an auditee client.
3. The AAM provides substantial incentives for audit firms to report fraud and mis-statements.
4. The AAM eliminates the conflicts of interest inherent in auditor compensation.
5. The AAM fosters innovation in auditing.
6. The AAM reduces the adverse effects of the size of the audit firm on the probability of obtaining audit clients (in the auditing industry, the auditing firm's size does not equate to, or guarantee knowledge or accuracy of the auditing firm).
7. The AAM reduces complacency and the negative effects of "relationship auditing" by rotating audit firms and audit partners.
8. *Entrenchment Negative* – the AAM reduces or eliminates entrenchment of any Audit-Firm; and reduces the Audit-Firms' actual or perceived use of market power to retain clients; and minimizes the Audit-Firm's focus on client relationships at the expense of accuracy, timeliness of ratings and pricing of ratings services; and most importantly ensures that any regulations and or business practices that foster entrenchment of Audit-Firm will have minimal effects. The Audit-Firm cannot offer any other fee-based services to Auditee-firms that it rates except the ratings, and the traditional subscription to the Audit-Firm's published ratings of other companies.
9. The AAM ensures fee-neutrality – the auditee-company does not pay audit fees directly to the auditor.
10. The AAM substantially reduces or eliminates the oligopoly in the global auditing industry.
11. The AAM reduces or eliminates fee collusion among audit firms.
12. The AAM prevents the circumvention of audit rules and liability allocation systems, by the dissolution and re-constitution of audit firms, or by the movement of audit partners among audit firms.
13. The AAM reduced audit industry concentration and increases the knowledge of all audit firms (ie. by rotating audit firms).
14. The AAM ensures that the auditee's choice of auditor cannot influence audit outcomes.
15. *Audit Consistency* – The AAM should ensure that Audit-Firms' auditing standards are consistent across industries, Auditee-firms, Audit-Firms, and over time; and the AAM should reduce or

eliminate ratings lags (a ratings lag occurs when the Audit-Firm does not update its post-offering ratings on a timely basis).

16. The AAM reduces the adverse effects of the size of the audit firm on the probability of obtaining audit clients (in the auditing industry, the auditing firm's size does not always equate to, or guarantee knowledge or accuracy of the auditing firm).
17. *Collusion-Neutrality* - The AAM reduces or eliminates fee collusion among audit firms (this can be achieved by have all or most audit-firms use one fee-allocation system or very similar fee-allocation systems).
18. *Information Neutral*: the AAM should ensure that that Audit-Firm can obtain sufficient information from the auditee company. The amount and quality of information that the issuer and its CPA (external auditor) provides to the Audit-Firm shall not be affected by the Audit-Firm's compensation. The AAM should reduce information asymmetry in the capital markets and ensure that the ratings standard of comparison is maintained.
19. *Audit-Decision Neutral* - the Auditee-firm's decisions about the timing of an audit, or about whether to select an Audit-Firm shall not be influenced by the "type" of its CPA.
20. *Positive Penalties Consistency* – the AAM penalize Auditee-firms in a deterrence-consistent manner for providing inaccurate information to the Audit-Firm, and also penalizes Audit-Firms in a deterrence-consistent manner for low-quality audits.
21. *Positive Competition Consistency* – the AAM increases or maintains the consistency of competition in the Audit-Firm industry which in turn, should also increase or maintain the consistency of the quality of the Audit-Firm's audit. The AAM reduces industry concentration.

With regard to allocation of audit fees and given the many problems caused by prior audit-fee schemes, it's imperative that audit fees be allocated directly to <u>both</u> audit firms and audit partners. This is because of the following reasons:

1. Within audit firms, the Partners sometime operate their own fiefdoms.
2. The audit firm's own internal method/formula for sharing *Audit-Fee*s among participating partners and staff is either inefficient, or not internally acceptable among assigned partners/staff and or fosters collusion with auditee-companies to commit fraud. For each audit, typically the following staff participate - the originating Audit-partner that brought in the client; the Audit-Partner that manages the audit; the technical/review Audit-partner that conducts quality control checks; the Senior-Managers, an Audit-Manager and various junior staff and consultants.
3. The differences among audit firms' internal fee-sharing models can become a competitive factor, and can cause some audit firms to be more willing to collude in or cause fraud. Thus, uniformity and transparency of internal fee-sharing models can promote healthy competition, increase audit-quality and reduce financial statement fraud.
4. Traditionally, audit partners are also held personally liable for audit problems. Unless such personal liability is also matched by a more direct and transparent form of fee-allocation, there is likely to be distortions in independence of audit firms and increased propensity for fraud.
5. the current audit-fee allocation schemes can result in conflicts of interest.
6. The current audit-fee allocation schemes create and foster audit-firm dependence on repeat business.
7. The current audit-fee allocation schemes create and foster industry concentration in the audit industry.

SOME PROPERTIES OF EFFICIENT AUDIT-FEE ALLOCATION MECHANISMS ("AFM")

Some properties of an efficient *Audit-Fee Allocation Mechanis*m ("AFM") are as follows; and concepts of *Group Theory* (mathematics), *Game Theory* and *Complex Systems Theory* can be applied to them:

1. The AFM reduces auditors' dependence on, and expectations for future audit work from the auditee company.
2. The AFM reduces or eliminates the *Reputational Penalties* for loss of an auditee client; and provides substantial incentives for audit firms to report fraud and mis-statements.
3. *Entrenchment Negative* – the AFM reduces or eliminates entrenchment of any Audit-Firm; and reduces the Audit-Firms' actual or perceived use of market power to retain clients; and minimizes the Audit-Firm's focus on client relationships at the expense of accuracy, timeliness of audit and pricing of audit services; and most importantly ensures that any regulations and or business practices that foster entrenchment of Audit-Firm will have minimal effects. The Audit-Firm cannot offer any other fee-based services to Auditee-firms that it rates except the audit, and the traditional subscription to the Audit-Firm's published audit of other companies.
4. The AFM eliminates the conflicts of interest inherent in auditor compensation; and fosters innovation in auditing.
5. *Positive Super-Modularity* (and Strategic Complementarity) – the AFM increases positive Super-modularity in the auditing process. *Positive Super-modularity* increases Social Welfare, while *Negative Super-Modularity* reduces Social Welfare.
6. The AFM reduces the adverse effects of the size of the audit firm on the probability of obtaining audit clients (in the auditing industry, the auditing firm's size does not always equate to, or guarantee knowledge or accuracy of the auditing firm).
7. The AFM reduces complacency and the negative effects of "relationship auditing" and also increases the knowledge of all audit firms (e.g. by requiring mandatory rotation of audit firms and audit partners).
8. *Fee-Neutrality* – the auditee-company does not pay audit fees directly to the audit-firm or Audit-partner.
9. *Proportionality* – the audit fee provides sufficient incentives for the Audit-Firm to increase quality, and the fee-structure ensures that the Audit-Firm's efforts are directly proportional to increased audit-quality, and that audit-quality is directly proportional to the AUDIT-FIRM's volume of auditing business.
10. *Collusion-Neutrality* - The AFM reduces or eliminates fee collusion among audit firms (this can be achieved by have all or most audit-firms use one fee-allocation system or very similar fee-allocation systems).
11. The AFM prevents the circumvention of audit rules and liability-allocation systems, by the dissolution and re-constitution of audit firms, or by the movement of audit partners within audit firms and or among audit firms.
12. The AFM ensures that the auditee's choice of auditor cannot influence audit outcomes.
13. *Information Neutral*: the AFM should ensure that that Audit-Firm can obtain sufficient information from the auditee company. The amount and quality of information that the issuer and its CPA provides to the Audit-Firm shall not be affected by the Audit-Firm's compensation. The AFM

should reduce information asymmetry in the capital markets and ensure that the audit standard of comparison is maintained.

14. *Source Neutrality* - The AFM must be source neutral and audit-fees must not be paid directly by the Auditee-firm or the investment bank, both of whom should not influence the AFM.
15. *Audit-Decision Neutral* - the Auditee-firm's decisions about the timing of an audit, or about whether to select an Audit-Firm shall not be influenced by the "type" of its CPA.
16. *Cumulative Fee Independence* – the fee paid by the Auditee-firm for each audit must not be affected by prior fees paid by the same Auditee-firm.
17. *Shock Positive* – the AFM pays extra compensation to the Audit-firm for any substantial downward change in the solvency condition of the auditee-company. This provides substantial incentives for the Auditee-firm to provide adequate and truthful disclosure to the Audit-Firm; and it also compensates the Audit-Firm for any actual or perceived loss of Reputation.
18. *Quality Neutral* – the AFM ensures that the audit-firm's audit-quality does not decline as the Audit-Firm's cost structure changes; and that the audit-firm recovers all of its reasonable costs; and that the audit-firm invests in quality and continually improves its audit processes.
19. *Collusion Proof* – the AFM reduces or eliminates any collusion among the Audit-Firm, investment bank, Auditee-firms and or investors.
20. *Positive Penalties Consistency* – the AFM penalize Auditee-firms in a deterrence-consistent manner for providing inaccurate information to the Audit-Firm, and also penalizes Audit-Firms in a deterrence-consistent manner for low-quality audits.
21. *Volume Neutral* – the AFM should be volume-neutral such that the volume of users, or the volume of trades in the auditee's shares does not affect the Audit-Firm's effort, or the Audit-Firm's fee, or the quality, accuracy and timeliness of the Audit-Firm's audit.
22. *Positive Competition Consistency* – the AFM increases or maintains the consistency of competition in the Audit-Firm industry which in turn, should also increase or maintain the consistency of the quality of the Audit-Firm's audit. The AFM reduces industry concentration.
23. *Audit-Firm Independence* – the AFM ensures that the Audit-Firm is truly independent of the Auditee-firm and the investment bank, and there are no conflicts-of-interest.
24. *Audit Consistency* – the AFM should ensure that Audit-Firms' auditing standards are consistent across industries, Auditee-firms, Audit-Firms, and over time; and the AFM should reduce or eliminate audit lags (an audit lag occurs when the Audit-Firm does not update its audit on a timely basis).

EFFICIENT MODELS OF AUDITOR COMPENSATION MECHANISMS

Each of the new business/compensation models introduced herein and below has all the following properties:

1. *Individual Rationality* of buyers - For each buyer, there is a bid such that the buyer always obtains nonnegative utility.
2. *Individual Rationality* of suppliers.
3. *Strong Budget Balance* – where not all buyers' payments are given to suppliers, the portion given to suppliers reflects fair value for services rendered.

4. *Dominant-Strategy Incentive Compatibility of buyers and suppliers* – each buyer and supplier can achieve the best outcome to him/herself by reporting/acting according to his/her true preferences/ valuations.
5. *Pareto Optimality* - there is no other allocation/matching superior to that provided by the mechanism in all aspects, provided all buyers report their true valuation (its assumed that mechanism structure encourages truth-telling by buyers and suppliers).
6. *Feasibility* – with respect to real-world constraints.
7. *Privacy* – the identities of bidders are not disclosed and for each "project" (e.g. a ratings project), only the winning seller-supplier pair are introduced to each other.
8. *Welfare Maximization* (both *Exact And Approximate*) – the model maximizes welfare with regards to the overall system; and reduces deadweight losses (by reducing consumer surpluses and supplier surpluses).
9. *Regret-positive* – reduces Regret of buyers and sellers.

Thus, each of the new business/compensation models introduced herein and below violates the *Myerson-Satterthwaite Impossibility Theorem* because each has the characteristics of *individual rationality*; *strong budget balance*; *incentive compatibility* of buyers/sellers and *pareto-optimality*. The problem of auditor compensation can be solved in the following ways; and concepts of *group theory* (mathematics), *Game Theory* and *Complex Systems Theory* can be applied to them.

Alternative 1

Auditing firms will be paid from a Special Audit Fund which will be managed by the federal government and some professionals elected by accounting trade associations (such as the AICPA, IMA, etc.). The Special Audit Fund will be funded with: i) proceeds of special graduated monthly/quarterly audit-taxes on all companies (or on companies whose sales revenue, assets and economic impact exceed a certain minimum threshold); and ii) proceeds of prosecutions for fraud and mis-statements in financial statements, and iii) government grants during the first two years of operations; and iv) special taxes on heavy users of financial statements (e.g. banks, insurance companies, pension funds, regulated hedge funds, regulated mutual funds, etc.). Each year, each auditee company will be able to select an auditor from among four to ten auditing firms that will be randomly selected by the Special Audit Fund based on specific criteria. All the auditing firms will be subject to tenure limits (e.g. an audit firm or an Audit Partner cannot audit a company for more than three years in any contiguous ten year period; and an audit firm or an Audit Partner cannot audit more than a specific number of companies in any calendar year). The Special Audit Fund will establish fee rates for auditing firms and their partners/staff. The Special Audit Fund will also establish upfront cash incentive programs for audit firms for identifying specific misconduct or weaknesses such as fraud and misconduct, material weaknesses in internal controls of firms, and collusion among firms.

Alternative 2

The Auditing firm will be paid by the federal government, which in turn will be pre-paid by the subject auditee-company (based on the auditee-company's size, scope of operations, complexity of operations, etc.). Each year, a group of 4-8 accounting firms will be randomly selected by the federal government (and perhaps the subject company) based on known specific criteria and rankings, and then the auditee-company will select an external auditor from among such auditing companies, subject to a tenure limitation (e.g. an audit firm or an Audit Partner cannot audit a company for more than three years in any contiguous ten year period; and an audit firm or an Audit Partner cannot audit more than a specific number of companies in any calendar year). The government will set the fees for auditing firms (and for various staff of auditing firms). All or a substantial portion of the proceeds of government prosecutions for fraud and fines for mis-statements in financial statements will be shared among all audit companies during each calendar quarter.

Auditing firms will be paid from a Special Fund which will be created pursuant to government statutes, and will be managed by a coalition of Accounting/Auditing trade associations (e.g. AICPA, IMA, ACCA). The Special Fund will be funded with: i) the proceeds of government prosecutions for fraud and mis-statements in financial statements; and ii) pre-audit sales of "points" to auditee-companies, iii) special taxes on heavy users of financial statements (such as banks, insurance companies, regulated hedge funds, stock exchanges, mutual funds, pension funds, etc.). Each year, the auditee-company will select an external auditor and prep-pay the auditing firm with its "points". All auditing firms will be, subject to tenure limits (e.g. an audit firm or an Audit Partner cannot audit a company for more than three years in any contiguous ten year period; and an audit firm or an Audit Partner cannot audit more than a specific number of companies in any calendar year). Each year, each audit firm will specify the amount of points that it will charge for providing audit services for companies of various sizes in various industries, and for companies located in 3-4 geographic zones, and for audits performed within certain time frames (this confidential information will made available to designated officers of auditee-companies through the Special Fund's website).

Alternative 3

Auditing firms will be paid from a Special National Audit Fund which will be managed by a coalition of Accounting/Auditing trade associations (e.g. AICPA, IMA, ACCA). The Special Fund will be funded by: i) the proceeds of prosecutions for fraud and mis-statements, and fines for mis-statements, and ii) pre-audit sales of "points" to auditee companies, iii) quarterly or annual special audit taxes that are levied on all companies (or only companies whose sales or economic impact exceed certain minimum thresholds) based on the scope of their activities and the complexity of their operations. Each year, about 5-10 auditing firms will be randomly selected for each company by the Special Audit Fund and the auditee-company based on specific criteria - these audit firms will be subject to tenure limits (e.g. eg. an audit firm or an Audit Partner cannot audit a company for more than three years in any contiguous ten year period; and an audit firm or an Audit Partner cannot audit more than a specific number of companies in any calendar year). The Special Fund will establish fee-rates (upper and lower limits) for audit firms and their Partners/staff. The selected auditing firms will then bid for each company's audit project, and the audit firm that bids the lowest fee will be awarded the auditing project. Auditee-companies that want enhanced audit services (such as a quicker audit or special services) can then use their points to purchase those services. The Special Fund will also create upfront cash incentives for audit firms that report misconduct.

Alternative 4

Auditing firms will be paid from a Special Audit Fund which will be established by government statute and managed by a coalition of Accounting/Auditing trade associations (e.g. AICPA, IMA, ACCA). The Special Fund will be funded with: i) the proceeds of prosecutions for fraud and mis-statements in financial statements; and ii) pre-audit sales of "points" to auditee companies, iii) government grants during the first two years of operations of the Special Audit Fund, iv) special taxes on heavy users of financial statements (such as banks, insurance companies, regulated hedge funds, mutual funds, pension funds, etc.). Each year, the Special Audit Fund will randomly select about 5-10 auditing firms for each company by based on specific criteria. These selected audit firms will be subject to tenure limits (e.g. an audit firm or an Audit Partner cannot audit a company for more than three years in any contiguous ten year period; and an audit firm or an Audit Partner cannot audit more than a specific number of companies in any calendar year). The selected auditing firms (5-10 audit firms) will state their point-fees for auditing companies of various sizes in various industries, and in 3-4 geographic zones in the country, and for performing audits within specific time frames. The Special Fund will establish fee-rates (upper and lower limits) for audit firms and their Partners/staff. The auditee-company will then use its points to select and pre-pay the auditing firm for audit services. The Special Audit Fund will also create upfront cash incentives for audit firms that report actionable misconduct.

Alternative 5

All fees for auditing services must be prepaid or paid into an Escrow Account before the selection of an auditor. Each year, the major accounting trade organization in the country (e.g. AICPA) will select 4-8 auditing firms for the auditee company based on a combination of ranking and bidding. These selected audit firms will be subject to tenure limits (e.g. an audit firm or an Audit Partner cannot audit a company for more than three years in any contiguous ten year period; and an audit firm or an Audit Partner cannot audit more than a specific number of companies in any calendar year).

For each of the foregoing solutions, if there are subsequent re-statements of financial statements due to auditor error, then there should be a mechanism for auditing firms to refund part of the audit fees. While the foregoing auditor selection rules can be limited to large and medium companies in some countries, its recommended that any company that has substantial impact on the economy should be subject to these auditor-selection rules.

Auditing firms are essentially an extension of the government and they perform critical governmental (monitoring and enforcement) functions that have substantial impact on public welfare and financial stability of the economy. Unfortunately, the regulations and institutions (US SEC; AICP; trade associations) that govern accounting firms don't reflect the importance of the external auditing function – and the consequences have been manifested by the Global Financial Crisis, and the sub-prime crisis in the US, and the bankruptcy (or forced sale) of several large financial institutions like Lehman Brothers and Merrill Lynch.

SOME PROPERTIES OF AN EFFICIENT AUDIT LIABILITY-ALLOCATION MECHANISM

The third major problem is allocation of liability for fraud and mis-statement in financial statements and public disclosures issued by organizations. Many parties have suggested various solutions[12]. See the comments in: Lix (2002), European Union (n.d.), Napier (1998), Todea & Stanciu (2009), Dickey (Gibson Dunn) (2008), Cunningham (2004), Maloney (n.d.), Blythe (2014), Grubbs & Ethridge (2007), Davies (2009), European Commission (2008), European Union (2007), and Nahal & Kiesselbach (2009). This issue was not addressed sufficiently by SOX (USA) or the Dodd Frank Act (USA) or similar statutes that were enacted in the UK and other jurisdictions. However, the European Commission[13] has developed the following alternatives for allocation of auditor-liability:

1. Option-1: One single monetary cap at EU level.
2. Option-2: Cap depending on the company's size.
3. Option-3: Cap depending on the audit fees charged to the company.
4. Option-4: Proportionate liability.

Most of the EC's proposals involve capping auditors' liability to specific amounts, which will probably not provide sufficient deterrence effects, particularly where there is an oligopoly in the auditing industry, and the Big-6 accounting firms (the Big-Four firms plus Grant Thornton and BDO Seidman) enjoy substantial and permanent *Reputation Effects*. That is, monetary penalties don't seem to have substantial economic effects or deterrence effects on Big-Six firms; and because of their reputations and size, it's more difficult to obtain court judgments against Big-Six auditing firms, than against a mid-size or small audit firm. Furthermore, judgments against Big-Six firms for financial statement mis-statements are less likely to affect their relationships with other auditee-clients in the same industry, compared to judgments against mid-size or small audit firms. Hence, even for small audit firms, so long as the Liability Cap is less than the present value of the auditor's future fees from than auditee-company (or future fees from other client companies in the same industry) then the punitive and deterrence effects of such capped liability are likely to remain minimal.

Partners of audit firms can re-constitute audit firms, and form new audit firms in order to escape liability. Therefore, any effective liability scheme must permeate the corporate veil of the audit firm, and allocate liability to the audit partners (and perhaps to Senior Managers that report to the Audit Partners). Audit firms Audit-firm Partners often purchase professional liability insurance which reduces or eliminates the punitive and deterrence effects of fines/penalties imposed on them, and thus increases their propensity for risk-taking and collusion. Thus, effective liability allocation schemes must also permeate insurance policies and or limit the ability of audit firms and audit partners to: i) purchase professional liability insurance or apply the proceeds of such insurance to fines/penalties; ii) re-constitute audit firms or create new audit firms in order to avoid liability, or shortly (e.g. within two years) after they have been penalized.

In most instances, the magnitude of audit fees paid to the audit company has no relationship whatsoever to the magnitude of damages caused directly or indirectly by the auditor's negligence when preparing financial statements. The benefits that an auditing firm gains from having a client cannot be measured solely in terms of annual audit fees for one client, but also includes the present value future auditing fees from that client, plus the present value of future audit fees from other clients in the same industry, and present value of fees from ancillary work from clients in the industry. Similarly, in most instances, the size of the auditee-company has no relationship whatsoever to the magnitude of damages/harm caused directly or indirectly by the auditor's negligence when preparing financial statements. Hence, the EC's Option-2 and Option-3 for auditor-liability (which are described above) are meaningless. Another key issue is that of contributory negligence. In most instances, the audit is performed based on data provided by the auditee-company; and the auditee-company physically limits the auditor's search and analysis. Therefore, in most instances, some of the liability for mis-statements should be allocated to the auditee-company. Securities Analysts and brokers employed by securities firms often exacerbate the damages from financial statement mis-statements by knowingly or un-knowingly recommending and aggressively selling shares of auditee-companies whose financial statements are mis-leading. Thus, in certain situations, some liability for financial statement mis-statements should be allocated to brokerage firms. Audit firms and audit partners often purchase professional liability insurance that substantially reduces the punitive and deterrence effects of fines/penalties.

Some Properties of an Efficient Audit Liability-Allocation Mechanism (ALAM)

This section deals strictly with the allocation of liability for audit problems among joint tortfeasors and criminal perpetrators – that is, their respective percentages of total liability (and not the monetary amount of penalties and fines). The properties of an efficient *Audit Liability-Allocation Mechanism* (ALAM) (for allocating liability among audit-firms, auditee-companies; Credit Rating Agencies; banks; and audit staff/partners) are as follows and concepts of group theory (mathematics) and Complex Systems Theory can be applied to them:

1. *Liability-Divisibility And Proportionality* - The ALAM ensures that liability is allocated to both the auditing firm, the auditing firms' senior officers (partners and Senior Managers), and the auditee-company. Liability is divisible.
2. *Fee-neutrality* – the allocation of liability is not based on the magnitude or timing of the audit fees paid to the auditor.
3. *Cumulatively Super-Additive* - that is, the percentage of total liability that is allocated to an audit officer (partner, senior manager) or audit firm or auditee-firm varies with the individual's prior history of audit liability (the greater the amount of prior adverse awards, the more the liability allocated to the officer).
4. *Boundedly insurance-averse* – that is, regardless of the nature of the insurance policy that the auditor officer (partner or senior manager) or audit firm or auditee-firm has, that insurance contract can be applied to reduce audit liability: a) only as a second-loss provision (after the auditor or audit firm or auditee-firm has personally absorbed a first-loss that varies with his/her total wealth, b) as a first-loss provision but up to a capped percentage of the loss.
5. *Contingent Exit* - once an audit officer (partner, senior manager) or audit firm is accrues a minimum amount of liability with respect to one auditee firm, or with respect to an industry, such person/firm will be automatically barred from auditing that company or any company in that industry respectively.
6. *Temporally Positive* – the amount of liability allocated to the audit-firm, auditee-firm and auditors is directly proportional to the amount of time they have been involved in audits in general, and in audits in that specific industry, and in audits of that specific company.

7. *Aggregate Concentration Positive* - the aggregate amount of liability allocated the audit-firm, auditee-firm and auditors is sufficient to reduce industry concentration in the audit industry.
8. *Aggregate Premium Positive* - the aggregate percentages of liability allocated to audit-firms, auditee-firm and auditors as three distinct classes of tortfeasors is publicly disclosed and is sufficient to: 1) increase insurance premiums; ii) reduce industry concentration in the audit industry.
9. *Non-constant proportionality* - For each firm and each targeted audit-year, the proportion of liability allocated to the audit-firm, auditee-firm and auditors is publicly disclosed and differs from that of other audit-years.
10. *Means Positive* – the liability allocation considers the available forms of payment of penalties – e.g. cash vs. real estate vs. intangibles.
11. *Split Insurance Policies*: there should be separate insurance policies for liability-allocation and penalty-allocation.
12. *Aggregate Risk-Propensity Positive* – the allocation of liability to the audit-firm, auditee-firm and auditors in each audit-year is publicly disclosed and is sufficient to reduce the propensity for risk-taking among auditors and auditee firms.
13. *Ancillary-Party Liability*: third parties such as credit rating agencies (CRAs) and banks receive confidential information from borrowers and conduct due diligence on such entities. Banks and CRAs' decisions are based in part on audited financial statements. The key issue is that investors, traders and regulators informally rely on the judgments, internal ratings and lending decisions of these banks and CRAs, such that the banks and CRA function like quasi-auditors and in most jurisdictions are statutorily required to report financial statement fraud to the government. Thus, such banks should bear liability for a financial statement fraud that the overlooked or directly/indirectly participated in.
14. Joint and several liability; and un-limited liability.

Alternatives for Liability Allocation

The often suggested alternative of financial statement insurance will probably not be effective because: i) it substantially reduces incentives for auditee-companies and auditors to comply with accounting regulations, ii) it increases and compounds systemic risk by shifting risk to insurance companies who often also insure loans and financial instruments that are based on such financial statements, iii) risk of financial statement insurance is very difficult to calculate, and thus, the resulting actuarial errors can have disastrous consequences for insurance companies, iv) it nullifies any liability allocation scheme, and without punitive and deterrence measures, compliance becomes a huge issue.

Each of the new models introduced herein and below has all the following properties:

1. *Individual Rationality* of buyers - For each buyer, there is a bid such that the buyer always obtains nonnegative utility.
2. *Individual Rationality* of suppliers.
3. *Strong Budget Balance* – where not all buyers' payments are given to suppliers, the portion given to suppliers reflects fair value for services rendered.
4. *Dominant-Strategy Incentive Compatibility of buyers and suppliers* – each buyer and supplier can achieve the best outcome to him/herself by reporting/acting according to his/her true preferences/valuations.

5. *Pareto Optimality* - there is no other allocation/matching superior to that provided by the mechanism in all aspects, provided all buyers report their true valuation (its assumed that mechanism structure encourages truth-telling by buyers and suppliers).
6. *Feasibility* – with respect to real-world constraints.
7. *Privacy* – the identities of bidders are not disclosed and for each "project" (e.g. a ratings project), only the winning seller-supplier pair are introduced to each other.
8. *Welfare Maximization* (both *Exact And Approximate*) – the model maximizes welfare with regards to the overall system; and reduces deadweight losses (by reducing consumer surpluses and supplier surpluses).
9. *Regret-positive* – reduces Regret of buyers and sellers.
10. No-Dictatorship.
11. Pareto-Efficiency.
12. Independence of Irrelevant Alternatives.

Thus, each of the new business/compensation models introduced herein and below violates the *Myerson-Satterthwaite Impossibility Theorem* and *Arrow's Impossibility Theorem.*

The alternatives for allocating liability among audit-firms, auditee-companies, Credit Rating Agencies, and audit staff/partners for fraud and for mis-statements in financial statements are as follows; and concepts of group theory (mathematics) and Complex Systems Theory can be applied to them.

Alternative 1

For each audit, the Audit firm, the audit Senior Managers and audit Partners will bear full responsibility for their actions and negligence – here won't be any caps or limits on liability. Each Audit Partner and each audit Senior Manager will be required to purchase professional liability insurance.

Alternative 2

Liability for financial statement mis-statements can be allocated to the audit firm, its Partners and its Senior Managers; and to the auditee-company. There will be an *Aggregate Life-time Cumulative Cap* on the monetary liability of each Audit partner, each audit Senior Manager and each audit firm, for all audits; and after the audit partner, Senior Manager or Audit firm exceeds the applicable *Aggregate Life-time Cumulative Cap*, the audit firm will be barred from providing audits; and the audit partner will be barred from serving as an audit Partner (or will not be subject to any *Liability Cap* and will not be able to purchase professional liability insurance); and the audit Senior Manager will not be able to purchase professional liability insurance. Whether or not the audit firm or the Senior Manager or the audit partner obtains professional liability insurance will not affect the *Aggregate Life-time Cumulative Cap.*

Alternative 3

Liability for financial statement mis-statements can be allocated to the audit firm, its Partners and its Senior Managers; and to the auditee-company. A *Special Liability Fund* will be created by government statute, and will pay all penalties assessed against audit firms and their partners/staff for mis-statements in financial statements. This *Special Liability Fund* will be funded with: i) annual pro-rated fees paid by both audit firms and audit partners (depending on the size of the audit firm and number of partners), ii) Audit firms will pay an annual special tax; iii) annual pro-rated payments by audit firms and audit partners that have been fined or penalized for mis-statements in financial statements – such payments will be a pro-rated percentage of such monetary fines/penalties; iv) annual fees paid by auditee-companies.

Alternative 4

Liability for financial statements can be allocated to the audit firm, its Partners and its Senior Managers; and to the auditee-company. A Special Liability Fund will be created by government statute, and will pay all penalties assessed against audit firms and their partners/staff for mis-statements in financial statements. This Special Fund will be funded with: i) annual fees paid by auditee-companies, ii) annual pro-rated payments by only audit firms and audit partners and Senior Managers that have been fined or penalized for mis-statements in financial statements – such payments will be a pro-rated percentage of such monetary fines/penalties; iii) annual pro-rated fees paid by securities brokerage firms.

Alternative 5

There will be an Aggregate Life-time Cumulative Cap on the monetary liability of each Audit partners and each audit firm, for all audits; and after the audit partner or Audit firm exceeds the applicable Aggregate Life-time Cumulative Cap, the audit firm or partner will be subject to full liability for his/her or its negligence and misconduct.

PROPERTIES OF AN EFFICIENT AUDIT PENALTY-ALLOCATION MECHANISM (APAM)

Some properties of an efficient Audit Penalty-Allocation Mechanism (APAM) (for allocating penalties/fines among audit-firms; auditee-companies; Credit Rating Agencies; banks; "Sophisticated Investors" and audit staff/partners) are as follows and concepts of group theory (mathematics), Game Theory and Complex Systems Theory can be applied to them:

1. **Equitable Proportionality**: The APAM ensures that penalties are allocated to both the auditing firm, the auditing firms' senior officers (partners and Senior Managers), and the auditee-company; and applicable Credit Rating Agencies and banks.
2. **Fee-neutrality** – the allocation of penalties is not based on the magnitude or timing of the audit fees paid to the auditor.
3. **Deterrence Positive** - The APAM provides sufficient punitive effect and deterrence effect for the auditee company, the auditor and its staff and associated parties such as banks, CRAs, and securities analysts. The fines/penalties are directly and increasingly proportional to the deterrence effects (for each unit increase in fines/penalties, the deterrence effects increase at a faster rate than the penalties/fines).
4. **Wealth Neutrality** – the penalty can be paid with various types of wealth (e.g. cash; personal property; real property; right to audit other firms; right to issue ratings on other firms; Reputation;

Accounts Receivables; etc.) in such a way that the form of wealth used does not affect the deterrence effect of the penalties/fines.

5. **Wealth Efficiency** – the penalty should be a substantial percentage of the ex-insurance wealth of the audit-firm, auditors and the auditee-firm; and the applicable CRA firm and bank.
6. **Cumulatively Super-Additive** - that is, the percentage of total liability that is allocated to an audit officer (partner, senior manager) or audit firm or auditee-firm varies with the individual's prior history of audit liability (the greater the amount of prior adverse awards, the more the liability allocated to the officer).
7. **Boundedly insurance-averse** – that is, regardless of the nature of the insurance policy that the auditor officer (partner or senior manager) or audit firm or auditee-firm has, that insurance contract can be applied to reduce audit liability: a) only as a second-loss provision (after the auditor or audit firm or auditee-firm has personally absorbed a first-loss that varies with his/her total wealth, b) as a first-loss provision but up to a capped percentage of the loss.
8. **Contingent Exit** - once an audit-officer (partner, senior manager) or audit-firm or CRA accrues a minimum amount of liability with respect to one auditee firm, or with respect to an industry, such person/firm will be automatically barred from auditing that company or any company in that industry respectively.
9. **Aggregate Concentration-Negative** – the aggregate amount of penalties levied against all audit-firms, auditee-companies and auditors in each regulatory period (e.g. one audit year) should be sufficient to cause a reduction of industry-concentration in the audit industry.
10. **Premium Positive** – the premiums charged for auditors' professional liability insurance should be directly proportional to prior liability and penalties imposed on the persons seeking such liability. Thus, regulators should maintain a public database of such liability allocation and penalties.
11. **Ancillary-Party Liability**: third parties such as credit rating agencies (CRAs) and banks receive confidential information from, and conduct due diligence on prospective borrowers. Banks' and CRAs' decisions are based in part on audited financial statements. The key issue is that investors, traders and regulators informally and formally rely on the judgments, internal ratings and lending decisions of these banks and CRAs, such that the banks and CRAs function like quasi-auditors and in most jurisdictions are statutorily required to report financial statement fraud to the government. Thus, such banks and CRAs should bear liability for a financial statement fraud that they overlooked or directly/indirectly participated in.
12. **Non-constant proportionality** - For each firm and each targeted audit-year, the proportion of fines/penalties allocated to the audit-firm, auditee-firm and auditors and applicable CRAs and Banks is publicly disclosed and differs from that of other audit-years.
13. Penalties should be allocated to investors based on their "Sophistication" and knowledge of accounting/finance, and knowledge of such earnings management.
14. The aggregate liability allocated to "Sophisticated Investors" in each year is publicly disclosed, and is sufficient to provide enough incentives to: 1) compel investors to reallocate their portfolios to firms that have good corporate governance; 2) increase the dispersion of shareholders (ie. each sophisticated investor owns lower percentages of each company).

CONCLUSION

Clearly, there are structural problems in the global auditing/accounting industry and the CRA industry which have not been sufficiently addressed by legislation, current industry-structure, industry contracts or industry norms. These structural problems threaten the integrity of audits and advisory-opinions, the functioning of capital markets, and the efficiency of pollution/Climate-Change mechanisms. Specifically, the effects of industry concentration, auditor-tenure, fee competition and auditor-liability need to be addressed quickly.

REFERENCES

Accinelli, E., Bazzano, B., Robledo, F., & Romero, P. (2015). Nash Equilibrium in evolutionary competitive models of firms and workers under external regulation. *Journal Of Dynamics & Games*, *2*(1), 1–32. doi:10.3934/jdg.2015.2.1

Aguirre, A. (2017). Contracting institutions and economic growth. *Review of Economic Dynamics*, *24*, 192–217. doi:10.1016/j.red.2017.01.009

Albrecht, D. (2010). *Audit Fee Competition Threatens Financial Reporting*. Working paper. https://profalbrecht.wordpress.com/2010/04/02/audit-fee-competition-threatens-financial-reporting/

Andrews, M., Pritchett, L., & Woolcock, M. (2017). *Building State Capability: Evidence, Analysis*. Action. doi:10.1093/acprof:oso/9780198747482.001.0001

Antonio, L., & Coello, C. (2018). Coevolutionary Multiobjective Evolutionary Algorithms: Survey of the State-of-the-Art. *IEEE Transactions on Evolutionary Computation*, *22*(6), 851–865. doi:10.1109/TEVC.2017.2767023

Arribillaga, R., Massó, J., & Neme, A. (2014). On the Structure of Cooperative and Competitive Solutions for a Generalized Assignment Game. *Journal of Applied Mathematics*, *2014*, 1–20. doi:10.1155/2014/190614

Arthur, W. (1999). Complexity and the Economy. *Science*, *284*(5411), 107–109. doi:10.1126cience.284.5411.107 PMID:10103172

Ayotte, K., & Bolton, P. (2011). *Covenant lite lending, liquidity, and standardization of financial contracts*. Chapter. In P. Bolon (Ed.), *Research Handbook on the Economics of Property Law" (2011 Edward Elgar Publishing Ltd.)* (pp. 174–189). doi:10.4337/9781849808972.00013

Baffi, E. (2007). *The Economics of Standard Form Contracts*. Working paper. Università degli Studi "Guglielmo Marconi".

Baffi, E. (2012). Contracting in modern world. *Aperta Contrada*. https://www.apertacontrada.it/2012/11/13/contracting-in-modern-world/

Baffi, E. (2000). *Some Characteristic Features of Mass Contracting*. Università degli Studi "Roma Tre" – Faculty of Law".

Bamberger, M., Vaessen, J., & Raimondo, E. (2016). Dealing with Complexity. In *Development Evaluation*. Academic Press.

Bayoumi, T., Pickford, S., & Subacchi, P. (2016). *Managing Complexity: Economic Policy Cooperation after the Crisis*. Brookings Institution Press.

Bernanke, B., & Bertaut, C. (2011). *International Capital Flows and the Returns to Safe Assets in the United States, 2003-2007*. Board of Governors of the Federal Reserve System - International Finance Discussion Papers Number 1014. https://www.federalreserve.gov/pubs/ifdp/2011/1014/ifdp1014.pdf

Bertsekas, D. (2000). *Auction Algorithms*. Working paper, MIT. https://pdfs.semanticscholar.org/c00f/9e12543fff8180b307341fa9c1891eabf727.pdf

Bischi, G., Chiarella, C., Kopel, M., & Szidarovszky, F. (2010). *Nonlinear Oligopolies: Stability and Bifurcations*. Springer. doi:10.1007/978-3-642-02106-0

Bloom, R., & Schirm, D. (2005). Consolidation and Competition in Public Accounting. *CPA Journal*. Available at: http://www.nysscpa.org/cpajournal/2005/605/infocus/p22.htm

Blythe, S. (2014). The In Pari Delicto Defense for Auditors in Professional Negligence Cases: Imputation of Managers' Unlawful Acts to the Client Firm. *Accounting, Economics, and Law Convivium*, *5*(2).

Boone, J., Khurana, I., & Raman, K. (2011). Litigation Risk and Abnormal Accruals. *Auditing*, *30*(2), 231–256. doi:10.2308/ajpt-50003

Bredeweg, B., & Struss, P. (2003, Winter). Current Topics In Qualitative Reasoning. *AI Magazine*, 13–17.

Byrne, D., & Callaghan, G. (2014). *Complexity Theory and The Social Sciences: The State of The Art*. Academic Press.

Casterella, J., Jensen, K., & Knechel, R. (2010). Litigation Risk and Audit Firm Characteristics. *Auditing*, *27*(2), 71–82. doi:10.2308/aud.2010.29.2.71

Chen, C., Su, X., & Wu, X. (2007). Market competitiveness and Big-5 Pricing: Evidence from China's binary market. *The International Journal of Accounting*, *42*(1), 1–24. doi:10.1016/j.intacc.2006.12.001

Chica, M., Chiong, R., Kirley, M., & Ishibuchi, H. (2018). A Networked N-Player Trust Game and Its Evolutionary Dynamics. *IEEE Transactions on Evolutionary Computation*, *22*(6), 866–878. doi:10.1109/TEVC.2017.2769081

Clinch, G. (2005). Discussion of "Market Consequences of Earnings Management in Response to Security Regulations in China". *Contemporary Accounting Research*, *22*(1), 141–143. doi:10.1111/j.1911-3846.2005.tb00081.x

Colini-Baldeschi, R., & Goldberg, P. (2017). Approximately Efficient Two-Sided Combinatorial Auctions. *Proceedings of the 2017 ACM Conference on Economics and Computation*, 591-608.

Cox, J. (2006). The Oligopolistic Gatekeeper: The U.S. Accounting Profession. In After Enron: Improving Corporate Law and Modernizing Securities Regulation in Europe and the U.S. Academic Press.

Cunningham, L. (2004). *Choosing Gatekeepers: The Financial Statement Insurance Alternative to Auditor Liability*. Working Paper. Available at: http://lawdigitalcommons.bc.edu/cgi/viewcontent.cgi?article=1018&context=lsfp

Curtis, A. (2012). A Fundamental-Analysis-Based Test for Speculative Prices. *The Accounting Review*, *87*(1), 121–148. doi:10.2308/accr-10163

Davies, P. (2009). Auditors' Liability: No Need To Detect Fraud? *The Cambridge Law Journal*, *68*(3), 505–507. doi:10.1017/S0008197309990353

Deb, K., Zhu, L., & Kulkarni, S. (2018). Handling Multiple Scenarios in Evolutionary Multiobjective Numerical Optimization. *IEEE Transactions on Evolutionary Computation*, *22*(6), 920–933. doi:10.1109/TEVC.2017.2776921

DeFond, M., Raghunandan, K., & Subramanyam, K. (2002). Do non-audit service fees impair auditor independence? Evidence from going concern audit opinions. *Journal of Accounting Research*, *40*(4), 1247–1274. doi:10.1111/1475-679X.00088

DeFond, M., Wong, T., & Li, S. (2000). The impact of improved auditor independence on audit market concentration in China. *Journal of Accounting and Economics*, *28*(3), 269–305. doi:10.1016/S0165-4101(00)00005-7

DeHaan, E. (2017). The Financial Crisis and Corporate Credit Ratings. *The Accounting Review*, *92*(4), 161–189. doi:10.2308/accr-51659

Dekker, H., Kawai, T., & Sakaguchi, J. (2018). Contracting abroad: A comparative analysis of contract design in host and home country outsourcing relations. *Management Accounting Research*, *40*, 47–61. doi:10.1016/j.mar.2017.09.003

Demange, G., Gale, D., & Sotomayor, M. (1987). A Further Note on the Stable Matching Problem. *Discrete Applied Mathematics*, *16*(3), 217–222. doi:10.1016/0166-218X(87)90059-X

Deng, X., Goldberg, P., Tang, B., & Zhang, J. (2014). Revenue Maximization In A Bayesian Double Auction Market. *Theoretical Computer Science*, *539*(1), 1–12. doi:10.1016/j.tcs.2014.04.013

Dickey, J. (2008). *Auditor Liability "Caps"– The Politics of Catastrophe*. Available at: https://www.gibsondunn.com/publications/Documents/Dickey-AuditorLiabilityCaps.pdf

Drozd, L., & Serrano-Padia, R. (2018). Financial contracting with enforcement externalities. *Journal of Economic Theory*, *178*, 153–189. doi:10.1016/j.jet.2018.09.002

Durlauf, S. (2012). Complexity, Economics And Public Policy. *Politics, Philosophy & Economics*, *11*(1), 45–75. doi:10.1177/1470594X11434625

Dütting, P., Roughgarden, T., & Talgam-Cohen, I. (2014). Modularity and Greed in Double Auctions. *Proceedings of the 15th Conference on Economics and Computation (EC'14)*, 241–258. http://theory.stanford.edu/~italgam/papers/Modular%20Double%20Auctions.pdf

Eenmaa-Dimitrieva, H., & Schmidt-Kessen, M. (2019). Creating markets in no-trust environments: The law and economics of smart contracts. *Computer Law & Security Review*, *35*(1), 69–88. doi:10.1016/j.clsr.2018.09.003

Espinosa-Avila, E., Longoria, P., & Hernández-Quiroz, F. (2017). Game theory and dynamic programming in alternate games. *Journal Of Dynamics & Games*, *4*(3), 205–216. doi:10.3934/jdg.2017013

European Commission. (2008). *Commission Recommendation Concerning The Limitation Of The Civil Liability Of Statutory Auditors And Audit Firms Impact Assessment*. https://ec.europa.eu/internal_market/auditing/docs/liability/impact_assessment_en.pdf

European Commission. (2010). *Green Paper - Audit policy: Lessons from the Crisis*. Available at: https://eurlex.europa.eu/LexUriServ/LexUriServ.do?uri=COM:2010:0561:FIN:EN:PDF

European Union. (2007). *Directorate General For Internal Market And Services Commission Staff Working Paper: Consultation On Auditor's Liability And Its Impact On The European Capital Markets*. Available at: https://ec.europa.eu/internal_market/auditing/docs/liability/consultation-paper_en.pdf

European Union. (n.d.). *Consultation On Auditors' Liability Summary Report*. Available at: https://ec.europa.eu/internal_market/auditing/docs/liability/summary_report_en.pdf

Fang, X., & Yuan, F. (2018). The Coordination and Preference of Supply Chain Contracts Based on Time-Sensitivity Promotional Mechanism. *Journal of Management Science and Engineering*, *3*(3), 158–178. doi:10.3724/SP.J.1383.303009

Finch, J. (Ed.). (2013). *Complexity and the Economy - Implications for Economic Policy*. Edward Elgar.

Forbus, K. (2019). *Qualitative Representations: How People Reason And Learn About The Continuous World*. MIT Press. doi:10.7551/mitpress/11578.001.0001

Geiger, M., Raghunandan, K., & Riccardi, W. (2014). The Global Financial Crisis: U.S. Bankruptcies and Going-Concern Audit Opinions. *Accounting Horizons*, *28*(1), 59–75. doi:10.2308/acch-50659

Gerakos, J., & Syverson, C. (2014). *Competition in the audit market: Policy implications*. Working paper, University of Chicago.

Ghosh, A., Kallapaur, S., & Moon, D. (2006). *Audit And Non-Audit Fees And Capital Market Perceptions Of Auditor Independence*. Working Paper, Center For Analytical Finance, Indian School Of Business.

Gillis, P. (2014). *The Big Four and the Development of the Accounting Profession in China*. Emerald Group.

Gilpatric, S., Vossler, C., & McKee, M. (2011). Regulatory enforcement with competitive endogenous audit mechanisms. *The RAND Journal of Economics*, *42*(2), 292–312. doi:10.1111/j.1756-2171.2011.00134.x

Goetz, R., Yatsenko, Y., Hritonenko, N., Xabadia, A., & Abdulai, A. (2019). The dynamics of productive assets, contract duration and holdup. *Mathematical Social Sciences*, *97*, 24–37. doi:10.1016/j.mathsocsci.2018.10.004

Gomes, R. (2014). Optimal auction design in two-sided markets. *The RAND Journal of Economics*, *45*(2), 248–272. doi:10.1111/1756-2171.12050

Gordon, E. (2015). Discussion of State Ownership and Earnings Management around Initial Public Offerings: Evidence from China. *Journal of International Accounting Research, 14*(2), 117–122. doi:10.2308/jiar-10470

Govindan, S., & Wilson, R. (2006). Sufficient conditions for stable equilibria. *Theoretical Economics, 1*, 167–206. https://econtheory.org/ojs/index.php/te/article/viewFile/20060167/617/25

Grubbs, K., & Ethridge, J. (2007). Auditor negligence liability to third parties revisited. *Journal Of Legal. Ethical & Regulatory Issues, 10*, 75–89.

Gul, F., Ma, S., & Lai, K. (2017). Busy Auditors, Partner-Client Tenure, and Audit Quality: Evidence from an Emerging Market. *Journal of International Accounting Research, 16*(1), 83–105. doi:10.2308/jiar-51706

Gul, F., Sami, H., & Zhou, H. (2009). Auditor Disaffiliation Program in China and Auditor Independence. *Auditing, 28*(1), 29–51. doi:10.2308/aud.2009.28.1.29

Habib, A., Jiang, H., & Zhou, D. (2015). Related-Party Transactions and Audit Fees: Evidence from China. *Journal of International Accounting Research, 14*(1), 59–83. doi:10.2308/jiar-51020

Halpern, J. (2003). *Reasoning about Uncertainty*. MIT Press.

He, Q., Xue, C., & Zhou, S. (2019). Does contracting institution affect the patterns of industrial specialization in China? *China Economic Review, 54*, 191–203. doi:10.1016/j.chieco.2018.11.003

Heibatollah, S., & Ye, Z. (2005, October). Auditor Failure And Market Reactions: Evidence from China. *International Journal Of Accounting, Auditing And. Performance Evaluation, 5*(4), 408–441.

Heinrich, T., & Dai, S. (2016). Diversity Of Firm Sizes, *Complexity*, And Industry Structure In The Chinese Economy. *Structural Change and Economic Dynamics, 37*, 90–106. doi:10.1016/j.strueco.2016.01.001

Hofer, C., Jäger, G., & Füllsack, M. (2018). Critical transitions and Early Warning Signals in repeated Cooperation Games. *Journal Of Dynamics & Games, 5*(3), 223–230. doi:10.3934/jdg.2018014

Hogan, C. (1994). *The Market For Audit Services When Firms Go Public* (PhD Dissertation). Ohio University. http://etd.ohiolink.edu/send-pdf.cgi/Hogan%20Chris.pdf?osu1266927118

Hong, S., Wernz, C., & Stillinger, J. (2016). Optimizing maintenance service contracts through mechanism design theory. *Applied Mathematical Modelling, 40*(21-22), 8849–8861. doi:10.1016/j.apm.2015.07.009

Hoppe, E., & Schmitz, P. (2018). Hidden action and outcome contractibility: An experimental test of moral hazard theory. *Games and Economic Behavior, 109*, 544–564. doi:10.1016/j.geb.2018.02.006

Iossa, E., & Martimort, D. (2018). Corruption in PPPs, incentives and contract incompleteness. *International Journal of Industrial Organization, 44*, 85–100. doi:10.1016/j.ijindorg.2015.10.007

Jacobs, B. (2012). *Introduction to Coalgebra: Towards Mathematics of States and Observations*. Institute for Computing and Information Sciences. http://www.cs.ru.nl/B.Jacobs/CLG/JacobsCoalgebraIntro.pdf

Jaume, D., Masso, J., & Neme, A. (2012). The Multiple-partners Assignment Game with Heterogeneous Sells and Multi-unit Demands: Competitive Equilibria. *Mathematical Methods of Operations Research, 76*(2), 161–187. doi:10.100700186-012-0395-4

Johnson, S. (2007). *PCAOB: The Eleven Things Auditors Need to Fix.* Available at: http://ww2.cfo.com/accounting-tax/2007/10/pcaob-the-11-things-auditors-need-to-fix/

Johnson, S. (2008). *PCAOB to Auditors: Turn Up the Skepticism.* http://ww2.cfo.com/accounting-tax/2008/12/pcaob-to-auditors-turn-up-the-skepticism/

Kaplan, S., & Williams, D. (2013). Do Going Concern Audit Reports Protect Auditors from Litigation? A Simultaneous Equations Approach. *The Accounting Review, 88*(1), 199–232. doi:10.2308/accr-50279

Karpoff, J. M., Lee, D. S., & Martin, G. (2008). The cost to firms of cooking the books. *Journal of Financial and Quantitative Analysis, 43*(3), 581–612. doi:10.1017/S0022109000004221

Ke, B., Lennox, C., & Xin, Q. (2015). The Effect of China's Weak Institutional Environment on the Quality of Big-4 Audits. *The Accounting Review, 90*(4), 1591–1619. doi:10.2308/accr-50943

Kim, J., Li, Y., & Zhang, L. (2011a). Corporate tax avoidance and stock price crash risk: Firm-level analysis. *Journal of Financial Economics, 100*(3), 639–662. doi:10.1016/j.jfineco.2010.07.007

Kim, J., & Zhang, L. (2013). Accounting conservatism and stock price crash risk: Firm-level evidence. *Contemporary Accounting Research, 33*(1), 412–441. doi:10.1111/1911-3846.12112

Kim, J., & Zhang, L. (2014). Financial reporting opacity and expected crash risk: Evidence from implied volatility smirks. *Contemporary Accounting Research, 31*(3), 851–875. doi:10.1111/1911-3846.12048

Kinney, W., Palmrose, Z., & Scholz, S. (2004). Auditor independence, non-audit services, and restatements: Was the U.S. government right? *Journal of Accounting Research, 42*(3), 561–588. doi:10.1111/j.1475-679X.2004.t01-1-00141.x

Kirman, A. (2016). Complexity and Economic Policy: A Paradigm Shift or a Change in Perspective? A Review Essay on David Colander and Roland Kupers's *Complexity and the Art of Public Policy. Journal of Economic Literature, 54*(2), 534–572. doi:10.1257/jel.54.2.534

Kofman, F., & Lawarree, J. (1993). Collusion in Hierarchical Agency. *Econometrica, 61*(3), 629–656. doi:10.2307/2951721

Kothari, S., & Lester, R. (2012). The Role of Accounting in the Financial Crisis: Lessons for the Future. *Accounting Horizons, 26*(2), 335–351. doi:10.2308/acch-50134

Kotowski, M., Weisbach, D., & Zeckhauser, R. (2013). *Audits as signals.* Harvard Kennedy School, Working paper series, RWP13-026, 2013.

Kuhlman, C., & Mortveit, H. (2014). Attractor stability in non-uniform Boolean networks. *Theoretical Computer Science, 559*, 20–33. doi:10.1016/j.tcs.2014.08.010

Kwon, S., Park, J., & Yu, J. (2017). *The Effect of Industry-Specialist Auditors on SEO Under-pricing Before and After the Global Financial Crisis. Auditing: A Journal of Practice & Theory.*

Laffont, J., & Martimort, D. (1997). Collusion under Asymmetric Information. *Econometrica, 65*(4), 875–911. doi:10.2307/2171943

Lennox, C., & Liu, W. (2012). *Does the presence of just a few large audit firms make the audit market un-competitive*? Working Paper. Nanyang Technological University.

Li, W., Liu, Y., & Chen, Y. (2018). Modeling a two-stage supply contract problem in a hybrid uncertain environment. *Computers & Industrial Engineering, 123*, 289–302. doi:10.1016/j.cie.2018.06.031

Lin, E., & Chou, M. (1990). Optimal contracts. *Applied Mathematics Letters, 3*(2), 65–68. doi:10.1016/0893-9659(90)90016-5

Lin, Z., Liu, M., & Wang, Z. (2009). Market Implications of the Audit Quality and Auditor Switches: Evidence from China. *Journal of International Financial Management & Accounting, 20*(1), 35–78. doi:10.1111/j.1467-646X.2009.01026.x

Lix, X. (2002). *Profit Sharing In Audit Partnerships* (PhD Thesis). University Of British Columbia, Canada. Available at: https://circle.ubc.ca/bitstream/handle/2429/13534/ubc_2002-750426.pdf?sequence=1

Lutz, D., & Schafke, R. (1985). On The Identification And Stability Of Formal Invariants For Singular Differential Equations. *Linear Algebra and Its Applications, 7*, 1–46. doi:10.1016/0024-3795(85)90140-5

Madureira, A., Pereira, I., Pereira, P., & Abraham, A. (2014). Negotiation mechanism for self-organized scheduling system with collective intelligence. *Neurocomputing, 132*, 97–110. doi:10.1016/j.neucom.2013.10.032

Makhdoumi, A., Malekian, A., & Ozdaglar, A. (2017). *Strategic Dynamic Pricing with Network Externalities*. https://arxiv.org/pdf/1706.01131.pdf

Maloney, C. (n.d.). *Imputation And The In Pari Delicto Defense In Auditor-Liability Cases: Pennsylvania Declines To Abolish The Traditional Defense, But Limits It As Well*. Available at: https://www.carrmaloney.com/elements/articles/Imputation_In_Pari_Delicto_Defense.pdf

Markelevich, A., & Rosner, R. (2013). Auditor Fees and Fraud Firms. *Contemporary Accounting Research, 30*(4), 1590–1625. doi:10.1111/1911-3846.12013

Martínez, R., Massó, J., Neme, A., & Oviedo, J. (2012). On The Invariance Of The Set Of Core Matchings With Respect To Preference Profiles. *Games and Economic Behavior, 74*(2), 588–600. doi:10.1016/j.geb.2011.08.011

Mashayekhy, L., Nejad, M., & Grosu, D. (2014). A Two-Sided Market Mechanism For Trading Big Data Computing Commodities. *2014 IEEE International Conference On Big Data (Big Data)*. 10.1109/BigData.2014.7004225

Melnik, S., Ward, J., Gleeson, J., & Porter, M. (2013). Multi-stage complex contagions. *Chaos (Woodbury, N.Y.), 23*(1), 013124. doi:10.1063/1.4790836 PMID:23556961

Meneguzzi, F., Modgil, S., & Oren, N. (2011). Algorithms and mechanisms for procuring services with uncertain durations using redundancy. *Artificial Intelligence, 175*(14–15), 2021–2060.

Meneguzzi, F., Modgil, S., Oren, N., Miles, S., Luck, M., & Faci, N. (2012). Applying electronic contracting to the aerospace aftercare domain. *Engineering Applications of Artificial Intelligence*, *25*(7), 1471–1487. doi:10.1016/j.engappai.2012.06.004

Miklashevich, I. (2003). Mathematical Representation Of Social Systems: Uncertainty And Optimization Of Social System Evolution. *Nonlinear Phenomena in Complex Systems*, *6*(2), 678–686.

Mohri, M., & Medina, A. (2014). *Learning Theory And Algorithms For Revenue Optimization In Second-Price Auctions With Reserve*. https://arxiv.org/abs/1310.5665

Nagy, A. (2005). Mandatory Audit firm Turnover, Financial Reporting Quality, and Client Bargaining Power: The Case of Arthur Andersen. *Accounting Horizons*, *19*(2), 51–68. doi:10.2308/acch.2005.19.2.51

Nahal, H. & Kiesselbach, P. (2009). House of Lords Rules on Auditors' Liability in Fraud Case. *International Corporate Rescue*, *6*(5).

Nakhe, P. (2017). *Dynamic Pricing in Competitive Markets*. Working paper. https://arxiv.org/pdf/1709.04960.pdf

Napier, C. (1998). Intersections Of Law And Accountancy: Unlimited auditor liability in the United Kingdom. *Accounting, Organizations and Society*, *23*(1), 105–128. doi:10.1016/S0361-3682(97)00006-8

Nazerzadeh, H., & Leme, R. (2016). *Where to Sell: Simulating Auctions From Learning Algorithms*. https://static.googleusercontent.com/media/research.google.com/en//pubs/archive/45455.pdf

Niederhoff, J., & Kouvelis, P. (2019). Effective and necessary: Individual supplier behavior in revenue sharing and wholesale contracts. *European Journal of Operational Research*, *277*(3), 1060–1071. doi:10.1016/j.ejor.2019.03.038

Nisam, N. (2007). Introduction to Mechanism Design for Computer Scientists. Algorithmic Game Theory, 230–231.

Nwogugu, M. (2006). Employee Stock Options, Production Functions And Game Theory. *Applied Mathematics and Computation*, *181*(1), 552–562. doi:10.1016/j.amc.2005.12.067

Nwogugu, M. (2007a). Issues In Disintermediation In The Real Estate Brokerage Industry. *Applied Mathematics and Computation*, *186*(2), 1054–1064. doi:10.1016/j.amc.2006.08.053

Nwogugu, M. (2007b). Some Issues In Securitization And Disintermediation. *Applied Mathematics and Computation*, *186*(2), 1031–1039. doi:10.1016/j.amc.2006.08.052

Nwogugu, M. (2008). The Efficiency Of Sarbanes-Oxley Act: Willingness To Comply And Agency Problems. *Corporate Control & Ownership*, *5*(1), 449–454. doi:10.22495/cocv5i1c3p5

NwoguguM. (2010). *Structural Changes, Competition And Complexity: Credit Rating Agencies (CRAs) And Allocation Mechanisms For Accounting Firms*. Available at https://ssrn.com/abstract=1762560 doi:10.2139srn.1762560

Nwogugu, M. (2015). *Complex Systems, International Capital Flows and New 'Learning' Business Models for the Credit Rating Agency Industry*. Available at www.ssrn.com

Nwogugu, M. (2015a). *Economic Policy, International Trade And Complexity: The Un-Constitutionality Of Accounting And Derivatives Standards-Setting Organizations; SOX; And Government Bail-Out Programs For Financial Institutions*. Available in www.ssrn.com

Nwogugu, M. (2015b). Failure Of The Dodd-Frank Act. *Journal of Financial Crime*, *22*(4), 520–572. doi:10.1108/JFC-11-2014-0053

Nwogugu, M. (2015c). Un-Constitutionality of The Dodd-Frank Act. *European Journal of Law Reform*, *17*(1), 185–190. doi:10.5553/EJLR/138723702015017001007

Nwogugu, M. (2015d). Goodwill/Intangibles Rules And Earnings Management. *European Journal of Law Reform*, *17*(1). Advance online publication. doi:10.5553/EJLR/138723702015017001006

Nwogugu, M. (2019a). *Human Computer Interaction, Incentive Conflicts And Methods For Eliminating Index Arbitrage, Index-Related Mutual Fund Arbitrage And ETF Arbitrage. In Indices, Index Funds And ETFs HCI: Exploring HCI, Nonlinear Risk And Homomorphisms*. Palgrave MacMillan.

Nwogugu, M. (2019b). Economic Policy, Complex Adaptive Systems, Human-Computer Interaction And Managerial Psychology: Popular-Index Ecosystems. In Indices, Index Funds And ETFs HCI: Exploring HCI, Nonlinear Risk And Homomorphisms. Palgrave MacMillan.

OECD (Ed.). (2016). *New Approaches To Economic Challenges - Insights Into Complexity And Policy*. OECD. https://Www.Oecd.Org/Naec/Insights%20into%20Complexity%20and%20Policy.Pdf

Park, S., & Kim, J. (2014). A mathematical model for a capacity reservation contract. *Applied Mathematical Modelling*, *38*(5-6), 1866–1880. doi:10.1016/j.apm.2013.10.005

Patterson, M. (2010). Standardization Of Standard-Form Contracts: Competition And Contract Implications. *William and Mary Law Review*, *52*(2), 327–340.

Perc, M., Donnay, K., & Helbing, D. (2013). Understanding recurrent crime as system-immanent collective behavior. *PLoS One*, *8*(10), e76063. doi:10.1371/journal.pone.0076063 PMID:24124533

Petrohilos-Andrianos, Y., & Xepapadeas, A. (2016). On the evolution of compliance and regulation with tax evading agents. *Journal Of Dynamics & Games*, *3*(3), 231–260. doi:10.3934/jdg.2016013

Post, D., & Eisen, M. (2000). How Long is the Coastline of the Law? Thoughts on the Fractal Nature of Legal Systems. *The Journal of Legal Studies*, *29*(S1), 545–555. doi:10.1086/468085

Room, G. (2011). *Complexity*. Institutions, and Public Policy.

Ruhl, J., & Ruhl, H. (1997). The Arrow of The Law In Modern Administrative States: Using Complexity Theory to Reveal the Diminishing Returns and Increasing Risks the Burgeoning of Law Poses to Society. *University Of California Davis Law Review*, *30*, 405–426.

Salzano, M., & Colander, D. (2007). *Complexity Hints For Economic Policy*. Springer. doi:10.1007/978-88-470-0534-1

Sánchez-Sánchez, F., & Vargas-Valencia, M. (2018). Games with nested constraints given by a level structure. *Journal Of Dynamics & Games*, *5*(2), 95–107. doi:10.3934/jdg.2018007

Schmidt, J. (2012). Perceived Auditor Independence and Audit Litigation: The Role of Non-audit Services Fees. *The Accounting Review*, *87*(3), 1033–1065. doi:10.2308/accr-10217

Sheng, J. (2019). Neoliberal environmentality and incentive-coordinated REDD+ contracts. *Land Use Policy*, *81*, 400–407. doi:10.1016/j.landusepol.2018.10.055

Singh, H. (2013). Anticompetitive Behavior In The Audit Services Market By The Big Audit Firms: Evidence Over Time. *Corporate Ownership & Control*, *10*(2).

Sprinkle, G., Williamson, M., & Upton, D. (2008). The effort and risk-taking effects of budget-based contracts. *Accounting, Organizations and Society*, *33*(4-5), 436–452. doi:10.1016/j.aos.2007.11.001

Sussman, O. (1999). Economic growth with standardized contracts. *European Economic Review*, *43*(9), 1797–1818. doi:10.1016/S0014-2921(98)00040-3

Suzuki, Y. (2008). Mechanism Design with Collusive Supervision: A Three-tier Agency Model with a Continuum of Types. *Economic Bulletin*, *4*(12), 1–10.

Suzuki, Y. (2009). *Mechanism Design with Collusive Supervision: A Three-tier Agency Model with a Continuum of Types, including Applications to Organizational Design*. Working Paper. Faculty of Economics, Hosei University.

Tang, D., Tian, F., & Yan, H. (2015). Internal Control Quality and Credit Default Swap Spreads. *Accounting Horizons*, *29*(3), 603–629. doi:10.2308/acch-51100

Telser, L. (1994). The Usefulness of Core Theory In Economics. *The Journal of Economic Perspectives*, *8*(2), 151–164. doi:10.1257/jep.8.2.151

Terán, J., Aguilar, J., & Cerrada, M. (2017). Integration in industrial automation based on multi-agent systems using cultural algorithms for optimizing the coordination mechanisms. *Computers in Industry*, *91*, 11–23. doi:10.1016/j.compind.2017.05.002

Thille, H., & Cojocaru, M. (2013). A Dynamic Pricing Game In A Model Of New Product Adoption With Social Influence. *International Conference On Social Computing*. 10.1109/SocialCom.2013.114

Todea, N., & Stanciu, I. (2009). Auditor Liability In Period Of Financial Crisis. *Annales Universitatis Apulensis Series Oeconomica*, *1*(11), 21–25.

US GAO (U.S. Government Accounting Office). (2008). *Audits of public companies: Continued concentration in audit market for large public companies does not call for immediate action*. Available at: https://www.gao.gov/new.items/d08163.pdf

Van Assche, A., & Schwartz, G. (2013). Contracting institutions and ownership structure in international joint ventures. *Journal of Development Economics*, *103*, 124–132. doi:10.1016/j.jdeveco.2013.02.008

Wang, Q., Wong, T., & Xia, L. (2005). *State ownership, institutional environment and Auditor Choice: Evidence From China*. Working Paper. Available at: http://www.baf.cuhk.edu.hk/research/cig/pdf_download/WangWongXia.pdf

Wei, W., Wang, J., Chen, X., Yang, J., & Min, X. (2018). Psychological contract model for knowledge collaboration in virtual community of practice: An analysis based on the game theory. *Applied Mathematics and Computation*, *329*, 175–187. doi:10.1016/j.amc.2018.01.053

Williams, C., & Arrigo, B. (2002). *Law, Psychology And Justice: Chaos Theory And New (Dis)Order*. State University Of New York Press.

WTO (World Trade Organization). (2017). *Accountancy Services*. https://www.wto.org/english/tratop_e/serv_e/accountancy_e/accountancy_e.htm

Wu, Z., Zhao, R., & Tang, W. (2014). Optimal contracts for the agency problem with multiple uncertain information. *Knowledge-Based Systems*, *59*, 161–172. doi:10.1016/j.knosys.2014.01.009

WysockiP. (Nov. 2009). *Corporate Compensation Policies and Audit Fees*. Available at SSRN: http://ssrn.com/abstract=1525016 doi:10.2139srn.1525016

Young, T. (1997). The ABCs OF Crime: Attractors, Bifurcations And Chaotic Dynamics. In D. Milanovic (Ed.), *Chaos, Criminology And Social Justice: The New Orderly (Dis) Order*. Praeger Publishers.

Zohar, A., & Rosenschein, J. (2008). Mechanisms for information elicitation. *Artificial Intelligence*, *172*(16–17), 1917–1939. doi:10.1016/j.artint.2008.08.005

ENDNOTES

1 *See*: Andrews, Pritchett & Woolcock (2017); Byrne & Callaghan (2014); Bamberger, Vaessen & Raimondo (2016); Room (2011); Kirman (2016); Salzano & Colander (2007); OECD, ed. (2016); Finch, ed. (2013); Durlauf (2012); Bayoumi, Pickford & Subacchi (2016); Kuhlman & Mortveit (2014); Melnik, Ward, Gleeson & Porter (2013); Miklashevich (2003); Perc, Donnay & Helbing (2013); Post & Eisen (2000); Ruhl & Ruhl (n.d.); Williams & Arrigo (2002); Young (1997); and Arthur (1999).

2 *See*: *DIRECTIVE 2014/56/EU OF THE EUROPEAN PARLIAMENT AND OF THE COUNCIL of 16 April 2014 amending Directive 2006/43/EC on statutory audits of annual accounts and consolidated accounts*. Available at: https://eur-lex.europa.eu/legal-content/EN/TXT/?uri=CELEX:32014L0056.

3 The statute states in part "*Public-Interest Entities*" means:
(a) entities governed by the law of a Member State whose transferable securities are admitted to trading on a regulated market of any Member State within the meaning of point 14 of Article 4(1) of Directive 2004/39/EC;
(b) credit institutions as defined in point 1 of Article 3(1) of Directive 2013/36/EU of the European Parliament and of the Council (16), other than those referred to in Article 2 of that Directive;
(c) insurance undertakings within the meaning of Article 2(1) of Directive 91/674/EEC; or
(d) entities designated by Member States as public-interest entities, for instance undertakings that are of significant public relevance because of the nature of their business, their size or the number of their employees;......"

4 Article 24(a)(k) states as follows "A statutory auditor or an audit firm shall monitor and evaluate the adequacy and effectiveness of his, her or its systems, internal quality control mechanisms and

arrangements established in accordance with this Directive and, where applicable, Regulation (EU) No 537/2014 and take appropriate measures to address any deficiencies. A statutory auditor or an audit firm shall in particular carry out an annual evaluation of the internal quality control system, referred to in point (g). A statutory auditor or an audit firm shall keep records of the findings of that evaluation and any proposed measure to modify the internal quality control system."

5 Article-30(a) states in part "Article-30(a). Systems of investigations and sanctions.

1. Member States shall ensure that there are effective systems of investigations and sanctions to detect, correct and prevent inadequate execution of the statutory audit.

2. Without prejudice to Member States' civil liability regimes, Member States shall provide for effective, proportionate and dissuasive sanctions in respect of statutory auditors and audit firms, where statutory audits are not carried out in conformity with the provisions adopted in the implementation of this Directive, and, where applicable, Regulation (EU) No 537/2014.
Member States may decide not to lay down rules for administrative sanctions for infringements which are already subject to national criminal law. In that event, they shall communicate to the Commission the relevant criminal law provisions.

3. Member States shall provide that measures taken and sanctions imposed on statutory auditors and audit firms are to be appropriately disclosed to the public. Sanctions shall include the possibility of withdrawal of approval. Member States may decide that such disclosure shall not contain personal data within the meaning of point (a) of Article 2 of Directive 95/46/EC.

4. By 17 June 2016 the Member States shall notify the rules referred to in paragraph 2 to the Commission. They shall notify the Commission without delay of any subsequent amendment thereto…………………"

6 Article-30(b) states in part "Article 30(b) Effective application of sanctions. When laying down rules pursuant to Article 30, Member States shall require that, when determining the type and level of administrative sanctions and measures, competent authorities are to take into account all relevant circumstances, including where appropriate:
(a) the gravity and the duration of the breach;
(b) the degree of responsibility of the responsible person;
(c) the financial strength of the responsible person, for example as indicated by the total turnover of the responsible undertaking or the annual income of the responsible person, if that person is a natural person;
(d) the amounts of the profits gained or losses avoided by the responsible person, in so far as they can be determined;
(e) the level of cooperation of the responsible person with the competent authority;
(f) previous breaches by the responsible legal or natural person.
Additional factors may be taken into account by competent authorities, where such factors are specified in national law.

7 See: Article-30e states in part "Article-30(e): Reporting of breaches.

1. Member States shall ensure that effective mechanisms are established to encourage reporting of breaches of this Directive or of Regulation (EU) No 537/2014 to the competent authorities.

2. The mechanisms referred to in paragraph 1 shall include at least:
(a) specific procedures for the receipt of reports of breaches and their follow-up;

(b) protection of personal data concerning both the person who reports the suspected or actual breach and the person who is suspected of committing, or who has allegedly committed that breach, in compliance with the principles laid down in Directive 95/46/EC;

(c) appropriate procedures to ensure the right of the accused person to a defence and to be heard before the adoption of a decision concerning him or her, and the right to seek an effective remedy before a tribunal against any decision or measure concerning him or her.

3. Member States shall ensure that audit firms establish appropriate procedures for their employees to report potential or actual breaches of this Directive or of Regulation (EU) No 537/2014 internally through a specific channel.

8 Article-39 states in part "Article-39: Audit committee

1. Member States shall ensure that each public-interest entity has an audit committee. The audit committee shall be either a stand-alone committee or a committee of the administrative body or supervisory body of the audited entity. It shall be composed of non-executive members of the administrative body and/or members of the supervisory body of the audited entity and/or members appointed by the general meeting of shareholders of the audited entity or, for entities without shareholders, by an equivalent body. At least one member of the audit committee shall have competence in accounting and/or auditing. The committee members as a whole shall have competence relevant to the sector in which the audited entity is operating. A majority of the members of the audit committee shall be independent of the audited entity. The chairman of the audit committee shall be appointed by its members or by the supervisory body of the audited entity, and shall be independent of the audited entity. Member States may require the chairman of the audit committee to be elected annually by the general meeting of shareholders of the audited entity.

2. By way of derogation from paragraph 1, Member States may decide that in the case of public-interest entities which meet the criteria set out in points (f) and (t) of Article 2(1) of Directive 2003/71/EC of the European Parliament and of the Council (20), the functions assigned to the audit committee may be performed by the administrative or supervisory body as a whole, provided that where the chairman of such a body is an executive member, he or she shall not act as chairman whilst such body is performing the functions of the audit committee.

Where an audit committee forms part of the administrative body or of the supervisory body of the audited entity in accordance with paragraph 1, Member States may permit or require the administrative body or the supervisory body, as appropriate, to perform the functions of the audit committee for the purpose of the obligations set out in this Directive and in Regulation (EU) No 537/2014.

3. By way of derogation from paragraph 1, Member States may decide that the following public-interest entities are not required to have an audit committee:

(a) any public-interest entity which is a subsidiary undertaking within the meaning of point 10 of Article 2 of Directive 2013/34/EU if that entity fulfils the requirements set out in paragraphs 1, 2 and 5 of this chapter, Article 11(1), Article 11(2) and Article 16(5) of Regulation (EU) No 537/2014 at group level;

(b) any public-interest entity which is an UCITS as defined in Article 1(2) of Directive 2009/65/EC of the European Parliament and of the Council (21) or an alternative investment fund (AIF) as defined in Article 4(1)(a) of Directive 2011/61/EU of the European Parliament and of the Council (22);

(c) any public-interest entity the sole business of which is to act as an issuer of asset backed securities as defined in point 5 of Article 2 of Commission Regulation (EC) No 809/2004 (23);

(d) any credit institution within the meaning of point 1 of Article 3(1) of Directive 2013/36/EU whose shares are not admitted to trading on a regulated market of any Member State within the meaning of point 14 of Article 4(1) of Directive 2004/39/EC and which has, in a continuous or repeated manner, issued only debt securities admitted to trading in a regulated market, provided that the total nominal amount of all such debt securities remains below EUR 100 000 000 and that it has not published a prospectus under Directive 2003/71/EC.
The public-interest entities referred to in point (c) shall explain to the public the reasons why they consider that it is not appropriate for them to have either an audit committee or an administrative or supervisory body entrusted to carry out the functions of an audit committee.

4. By way of derogation from paragraph 1, Member States may require or allow a public-interest entity not to have an audit committee provided that it has a body or bodies performing equivalent functions to an audit committee, established and functioning in accordance with provisions in place in the Member State in which the entity to be audited is registered. In such a case the entity shall disclose which body carries out those functions and how that body is composed.

5. Where all members of the audit committee are members of the administrative or supervisory body of the audited entity, the Member State may provide that the audit committee is to be exempt from the independence requirements laid down in the fourth subparagraph of paragraph 1.

6. Without prejudice to the responsibility of the members of the administrative, management or supervisory bodies, or of other members who are appointed by the general meeting of shareholders of the audited entity, the audit committee shall, inter alia:
(a) inform the administrative or supervisory body of the audited entity of the outcome of the statutory audit and explain how the statutory audit contributed to the integrity of financial reporting and what the role of the audit committee was in that process;
(b) monitor the financial reporting process and submit recommendations or proposals to ensure its integrity;
(c) monitor the effectiveness of the undertaking's internal quality control and risk management systems and, where applicable, its internal audit, regarding the financial reporting of the audited entity, without breaching its independence;
(d) monitor the statutory audit of the annual and consolidated financial statements, in particular, its performance, taking into account any findings and conclusions by the competent authority pursuant to Article 26(6) of Regulation (EU) No 537/2014;
(e) review and monitor the independence of the statutory auditors or the audit firms in accordance with Articles 22, 22a, 22b, 24a and 24b of this Directive and Article 6 of Regulation (EU) No 537/2014, and in particular the appropriateness of the provision of non-audit services to the audited entity in accordance with Article 5 of that Regulation;
(f) be responsible for the procedure for the selection of statutory auditor(s) or audit firm(s) and recommend the statutory auditor(s) or the audit firm(s) to be appointed in accordance with Article 16 of Regulation (EU) No 537/2014 except when Article 16(8) of Regulation (EU) No 537/2014 is applied"

9 *See*: *The Audit Oligopoly*. Available at: http://www.oligopolywatch.com/2005/07/13.html.

10 *See*: Lin, Liu & Wang (2009) which states in part "Empirical results show that the quality of an audit and switching to a larger auditor have a positive (negative) impact on earnings response coefficients (ERCs) for firms with positive (negative) abnormal earnings. In contrast, switching to a smaller auditor has a negative (positive) impact on ERCs for firms with positive (negative)

abnormal earnings. These results suggest that large auditing firms (Top 10) in China are perceived as more effective for curbing income-increased earnings management, which leads to higher (lower) ERCs for clients with positive (negative) abnormal earnings. Firms' switching to a larger auditor may signal high-quality earnings. Therefore, investors more often increase stock prices when firms have positive abnormal earnings and less often depreciate prices for negative abnormal earnings. Similarly, switching to a smaller auditor may signal lower earning quality, resulting in opposite market responses. In general, the empirical evidence suggests that audit information is valued by the capital market in China. Large auditing firms have been able to product-differentiate themselves within the Chinese stock market").

See: Wang, Wong & Xia (Sept. 2005) *which* states in part "the information and insurance roles of auditors are less important for State owned enterprises (SOEs) than non-state firms; rather, SOEs prefer to choose, for ease of collusion, small auditors under the same local government's jurisdiction. Our results support this conjecture. However, in regions where governments are less involved with the economy, and credit market and legal environment are more developed, SOEs are more similar to non-state firms in hiring high-quality auditors".

11 *See*: Johnson (December 2008) *which* states in part "In its latest summary of its inspections of the eight largest audit firms — covering four years of reviews — the Public Company Accounting Oversight Board (USA) pings the auditors for failing to use enough professional skepticism in their audits of companies' financial statements. Audit deficiencies have continued to be a problem much in evidence during the series of PCAOB reviews that was mandated by the Sarbanes-Oxley Act of 2002. The firms have frequently strayed from following the PCAOB's standards in issues related to revenue, management's accounting estimates, fair-value measurements, and materiality thresholds. Some of these problems have made the PCAOB question whether the auditors rely too heavily on what their clients tell them. "In some instances, firms did not sufficiently test or challenge management's forecasts, views, or representations that constituted critical support for amounts recorded in the financial statements," the report says. The 28-page document also blames the firms' audit deficiencies on weaknesses in training, supervision, methodologies, monitoring, and enforcement. "Even in recent years, we are seeing deficiencies in the most important and high-risk areas of the audits, where appropriate levels of care and professional skepticism are needed," writes George Diacont, director of the PCAOB registration and inspections division. The PCAOB's summary of the four years' worth of inspections touches upon trends that its auditors have noticed and revealed each year through its auditing of the largest firms: Deloitte & Touche, Ernst & Young, KPMG, PricewaterhouseCoopers, BDO Seidman, Grant Thornton, McGladrey & Pullen, and Crowe Chizek (now called Crowe Horwath). These firms are reviewed annually by the audit firm watchdog. The report does not mention any of the firms by name, but highlights how dominant the larger firms are over public-company auditing. The group audits about 66 percent of all American public companies, and the Big Four's public-company clients represent 98 percent of the total U.S. market capitalization."

See*:* Johnson (Oct. 2007) which *states in part "The Public Company Accounting Oversight Board (USA) on Monday released a report listing eleven problem areas found during its inspections of smaller audit firms. The PCAOB called on the firms to improve their audit quality by focusing on these issues, which include their reviews of business combinations and evaluations of whether a company is a going concern. The PCAOB gathered the information from its nearly 500 inspections of firms that audit fewer than 101 public companies. The five-year-old regulator is entering the* *second round of its small-auditor reviews, which are conducted once every three years. While the report is targeted toward smaller firms, many of the issues noted are found as well at the larger ones, which the PCAOB reviews annually, George Diacont, director of the PCAOB's Division of Registration and Inspections, told CFO.com. Of the 439 inspection reports of small firms conducted so far, 124 didn't list an audit deficiency or a concern about possible defects in the firm's quality-control system. In contrast, each of the Big Four reports so far have listed at least seven audit deficiencies."*

12 *See:* European Union (n.d.) which states in part "The lack of choice in the audit market is recognised by the majority of respondents as an important issue that could jeopardise the efficiency of financial markets. Therefore comprehensive action to reduce barriers of entry to this market should be taken. However, not all respondents agree that limiting auditors' liability would be an appropriate means to address the issue. Several respondents highlight the importance of the future conclusions of a study on ownership rules. Many respondents believe that a limitation would have a positive effect on insurability conditions. Nevertheless, it is highlighted that the main risk of failure arises from United States litigation trends. Some respondents recall that a cap on auditors' liability will result in a shift of liability towards directors and officers, affecting the insurance market for that segment. For those who support a reform, there is no evidence of lower quality in Member States with liability limitations in place. Moreover, the audit profession even considers that maintaining an unlimited liability regime could lead to a decrease in audit quality due to "*defensive auditing*". The audit profession prefers a limitation based on capping (or a combination of proportionate liability and a cap), whereas other respondents that are in general supportive of a reform favor solutions based on proportionate liability. The results do not show a clear preference for a particular option for limiting auditors' liability."

See: Nahal & Kiesselbach (2009) which states in part "In a decision handed down just before the end of term, auditors have won an important House of Lords ruling in *Moore Stephens vs. Stone Rolls Limited* [2009] UKHL 39, limiting their liability in cases where a '*one-man*' company is used as a vehicle for fraud. The law lords dismissed by a majority of three to two a negligence claim brought against an audit firm for failing to detect a massive fraud at Stone & Rolls Limited, a trading company that fell in the late 1990s – holding that the liquidators could not bring a claim for damages when the company itself was responsible for the fraud").

See: European Union (2007) (listing various liability allocation methods such as: a) Option 1: One single monetary cap at EU level, 2) Option 2: Cap depending on the company's size, 3) Option 3: Cap depending on the audit fees charged to the company, 4) Option 4: Proportionate liability).

See: Accounting firms facing rise in negligence claims amid credit crunch fallout. *Available at:* http://business.timesonline.co.uk/tol/business/law/article7079418.ece.

See: Online Bibliographies (2009). *Auditor Liability to Third-Parties*. Available at: https://law.gsu.edu/library/index/bibliographies/view?id=308. The following excerpt from this document contains legislation and summary case laws:

a. Legislation

i. §11 of the Securities Act of 1933:

Subjects an accounting firm to liability to purchasers of securities where the accountant has misstated or omitted a material fact contained in a company's registration statment. 15 U.S.C.A. §77k.

ii. §10b5 of the Securities Exchange Act of 1934:

Rule 10b-5 provides:

"It shall be unlawful for any person, directly or indirectly, by the use of any means or instrumentality of interstate commerce, or of the mails, or of any facility of any national securities exchange- (b) To use or employ, in connection with the purchase or sale of any security registered on a national securities exchange or any security not so registered, or any securities-based swap agreement..., any manipulative or deceptive device or contrivance in contravention of such rules and regulations as the Commission may prescribe as necessary or appropriate in the public interest or for the protection of investors." 15 U.S.C.S. §78j.

iii. State Statutes:

Some States have chosen to codify their own statutory definitions of accountant liability. Most of these statutes simply conform to one of the views expressed under *b. Case Law*, including many states adopting the restatement in their own words.

iv. Sarbanes Oxley:

Section 301(2) provides: "The audit committee of each issuer, in its capacity as a committee of the board of directors, shall be directly responsible for the appointment, compensation, and oversight of the work of any registered public accounting firm employed by that issuer...for the purpose of preparing or issuing an audit report or related work, and each such registered public accounting firm shall report directly to the audit committee."

v. Proposed Legislation:

Senator Arlen Specter has introduced Senate Bill 1551 for the purpose of amending the Securities Exchange Act of 1934 to allow for private party remedies against those who aid and abet companies who violate the Securites Exchange Act of 1934. More information can be found under the **Legislative History** tab or the full text of the bill can be found on **Thomas.gov**.

b. Case Law.

The following cases are organized under the different views that courts have taken on the issue of to whom an accountant owes their duty of care in a standard negligence action. Cases based on actions of fraud and violations of the Securities Acts have been largely excluded in light of overexhasuting this bibliography. The alternative causes-of-actions are well-defined, whereas the scope of duty under a negligence action is the most fragmented issue of third-party liability.

i. Privity or Near Privity View

- *Ultramares Corp vs. Touche*, **255 N.Y. 170, 174 N.E. 441 (1931):** Chief Judge Cardozo ruled there was no cause of action in negligence against an accounting firm who certified inaccurate financial statements which were reiled upon by plaintiff's who had no contractual privity with the defendant accountants. Cardozo warned of the unlimited class of plaintiffs that would arise otherwise.
- *Credit Alliance Corp. vs. Arthur Anderson & Co.*, **65 N.Y.2d 536, 483 N.E.2d 110 (1985):** The Court of Appeals of New York reaffirmed the principles of Ultramares by stating, "[b]efore accountants may be held liable in negligence to noncontractual parties who rely to their detriment on inaccurate financial reports, certain prerequisites must be satisfied: (1) the accountants must have been aware that the financial reports were to be used for a particular purpose or purposes; (2) in the furtherance of which a known party or parties was intended to rely; and (3) there must have been some conduct on the part of the accountants linking them to that party or parties, which evinces the accountants' understanding of that party or parties' reliance." Id. at 551.
- *Parrott vs. Coopers & Lybrand, L.L.P.*, **263 A.D.2d 316, 702 N.Y.S2d 40 (2000):** Relationship between accounting firm and a former officer and shareholder of a privately held

company did not amount to privity, thus firm could not be held liable for negligently valuing the company's stock. *Ultramares* and *Credit Alliance* still held as good law for the proposition that privity or something very near privity is required before a third-party may bring a claim.

• *C5 Investments, Inc. vs. Ernst & Young L.L.P.*, **2007 WL 1381803 (D. Idaho, 2007):** Idaho adopted the three pronged test set forth in *Credit Alliance* in *Idaho Bank & Trust v. First Bancorp of Idaho,* 772 P.2d 720 (Idaho 1989). Here the court reaffirms that accountant liability to third parties is subject to the *Credit Alliance* test of privity.

ii. Forseeability View

• *H. Rosenblum, Inc. vs. Jack F. Adler*, **93 N.J. 324, 461 A.2d 138 (1983):** The New Jersey Supreme Court adopted the forseeability rule. Along with providing excellent policy arguments, the Court stated that an auditor has a duty to all whom they should reasonably foresee would use their statements for business purposes, so long as the third party actually relied on the auditor's statments in making their decision.

• *Citizens State Bank vs. Timm, Schmidt & Co.*, **113 Wis. 2d 376, 335 N.W.2d 361 (1983):** The Supreme Court of WIsconsin reviewed the Restatement approach, concluded its limitations were too restrictive, and stated that "[l]iability will be imposed on...accountants for the forseeable injuries resulting from their negligent acts unless...recovery is deneid on grounds of public policy." Id. at 386. The court listed items to be considered as public policy in light of the facts of the particular case.

• *Chevron Chemical Co. vs. Deloitte & Touch*e, **168 Wis.2d 323, 483 N.W.2d 314 (1992):** The Court of Appeals of Wisconsin dealt with the four elements of negligent misrepresentation: (1) a representation of fact made by defendant, (2) the representation is untrue, (3) the defendant was negligent in making the representation, and (4) the plaintiff's belief that the representation was true and their reliance thereupon to plaintiff's damage. The foreseeability issue was satsified because the defendant knew the plaintiff was using an incorrect statment and failed to notify them. The opinion also contains accounting standards as to notification by an auditor when they learn of a mistake.

iii. Restatement View

• *Bily vs. Arthur Young & Co.*, **3 Cal.4th 370, 834 P.2d 745 (1992):** Landmark decision where the California Supreme Court adopted the Restatement view. The opinion contains a great discussion of all the theories of liability including liabliity under the federal securities acts. This is also a great case to find other cases with the citing references option on Westlaw or LexisNexis.

• McCamish, Martin, Brown & Loeffler vs. F.E. Appling Interests, **42 Tex. Sup. Ct. J. 597, 991 S.W.2d 787 (1999):** The Texas Supreme Court applied §552 of the Restatement to hold a law firm liable to third parties. While similar to the pure foreseeability rule, the Restatement narrows the potential class of plaintiffs by limiting "a section 552 cause of action...only when information is transferred...to a known party for a known purpose." Id. at 794.

• *Raritan River Steel Co. vs. Cherry, Bekaert & Holland*, **322 N.C. 200, 367 S.E.2d 609 (1988):** Holding that a plaintiff must have relied upon the accountant's actual audit opinion. This opinion also provides a good overview of the different approaches in determining the scope of an accountant's duty.

• *PricewaterhouseCoopers, LLP vs. Bassett*, 293 Ga.App. 274, 666 S.E.2d 721 (2008): "Under Georgia law, one who supplies information during the course of his business, profession, employment, or in any transaction in which he has a pecuniary interest has a duty of reasonable care and competence to parties who rely upon the information in circumstances in which the maker was manifestly aware of the use to which the information was intended, either directly or indirectly. In making a determination of whether the reliance by the third party is justifiable, [the factfinder] will look to the purpose for which the report or representation was made. If it can be shown that the representation was made for the purpose of inducing third parties to rely and act upon the reliance, then liability to the third party can attach." at 277, 725.

iv. State Statutes

• *E. Dickerson & Son, Inc. vs. Ernst & Young, L.L.P.*, 179 N.J. 500, 846 A.2d 1237 (2004): New Jersey adopted an accountant liability statute. The adoption of the statute was to scale back the impact of subjecting accountants to liability to "all reasonably foreseeable claimants" including stockholders and public investors." Id. at 504.

v. Other Sources of Liability

• *Blue Bell, Inc. vs. Peat, Marwick, Mitchell & Co.*, 715 S.W.2d 408 (1986): The Court of Appeals of Texas focuses its discussion on negligent misrepresentation, but provides an explanation of fraud, breach of warranty, and breach of fiduciary duty causes of action

See: European Union (2007). Directorate General For Internal Market And Services Commission Staff Working Paper: Consultation On Auditor's Liability And Its Impact On The European Capital Markets. Available at: http://ec.europa.eu/internal_market/auditing/docs/liability/consultation-paper_en.pdf. (listing various liability allocation methods such as: a) Option-1: One single monetary cap at EU level, 2) Option-2: Cap depending on the company's size, 3) Option-3: Cap depending on the audit fees charged to the company, 4) Option-4: Proportionate liability).

Chapter 7
The Existing and Proposed Credit Rating Agency (CRA) Business Models and Compensation Models Are Inefficient

ABSTRACT

Credit ratings agencies (CRAs) are prone to various antitrust and conflict-of-interest problems that arise from their regulation and their business and compensation models. CRAs have played a critical role in global capital markets for the last few decades, and the inefficiencies inherent in the compensation contracts, and business models of CRAs were clearly illustrated during the Global Financial Crisis of 2007-2011, during which ABS trusts and some large companies suddenly defaulted without prior down-grades of their ratings – it's well known that markets often price in potential defaults or down-grades before CRAs revise their ratings downwards. This chapter explores the inefficiencies of the existing and proposed CRA business models and compensation models.

INTRODUCTION

The motivation for and context of this chapter are varied. *First* and unfortunately, the "Big-Three" CRAs (Moodys, Fitch and S&P) now affect the equivalent of more than eighty trillion US dollars of securities, swaps/derivatives and financial instruments globally, and thus have a significant and growing effect on international capital flows. *Second*, the International Organization of Securities Commissions (IOSCO) and the European Commission, the US Government and many governments have debated and issued statements and proposed regulations for CRAs, most of which have been ineffective. *Third*, the business models and compensation contracts of CRAs have symbiotic relationship with antitrust violations and the nature of competition and antitrust in the CRA industry. Becker & Milbourn (2011). Thus, there are

DOI: 10.4018/978-1-7998-7418-8.ch007

sufficient grounds for regulating CRAs through competition law; and that various antitrust problems can be solved or reduced by changing the business models and compensation models of CRAs. *Fourth*, there is a growing consensus in many countries that the big-three CRAs were being used for political and economic-domination purposes. As a result, countries like China and Russia, in their push to de-couple from the US dollar dominated international transactions of 2000-2018, and to ameliorate the effects of Economic Sanctions imposed on them, and to gain more global economic power, have been creating their own CRAs and have developed CRA regulations. Specifically, the number of CRAs in China increased from about one in 2008 to about seventeen in 2015. Given the international scope of investments of Chinese and Japanese government agencies, companies and high-net-worth individuals, that will likely affect many countries. *Fifth*, the bond markets of many countries like China, Brazil, India, Indonesia and Japan grew significantly during 2005-2020 – as of 2020, the Chinese bond market alone was worth more than US$1.7trillion. The exponential growth of cross-border trade during 1995-2020 has led to increases of the numbers and sizes of companies that often subject to conflicting corporate governance standards and continue to rely on credit ratings as one of several measures of trust. Increasing foreign ownership of shares has also highlighted the importance of corporate governance and credit ratings. *Sixth*, the Global Financial Crisis has exposed significant weaknesses in economies and Corporate Governance standards in organizations, and strategic decision-making by Boards of Directors (BODs) and has slowed economic growth in both industrialized and developing countries. Both individual and institutional investors around the world are increasingly emphasizing the quality and implementation of corporate governance standards and Board Dynamics within companies as a major investment criteria. *Seventh*, the enactment of major financial regulations (like the Dodd Frank Act in the US) in many countries during 2008-2014 has changed the uses credit ratings and regulation of CRAs. *Eighth*, the issue of whether credit ratings in various countries are Public Goods has not been addressed in the literature. *Ninth*, the relationship among Credit Rating Agencies (CRAs) and systemic risk and Contagion is somewhat symbiotic and well documented - Sy (2009) summarized some elements of this relationship. However, its widely acknowledged that in most countries, the regulation of CRAs remains woefully inadequate, and despite the significant resultant social-welfare losses, un-regulated CRAs are allowed to operate. *Tenth*, the Global Financial Crisis of 2007-2014 has exposed significant weaknesses in the compensation and business models of CRAs. Many of the CRA business models and compensation schemes developed by governments and individual researchers remain very ineffective. *Eleventh*, the Global Financial Crisis of 2007-2014 has exposed significant weaknesses in the compensation and business models of CRAs. Many of the CRA business models and compensation schemes developed by governments and individual researchers remain very ineffective. The inefficiencies inherent in the compensation contracts for, and business models of CRAs were also clearly illustrated during the Asian Financial Crisis of the 1990s, and the Latin American Debt Crisis of the 1980s and the Global Financial Crisis of 2007-2012 (during which ABS Trusts and some large companies suddenly defaulted without prior downgrades of their ratings).

Twelfth, CRAs have evolved into a type of fintech because they use advanced financial math models, significant data and technology for their analysis, and their ratings products are "consumed" primarily through the internet (ie. computers, cellphones and hand-held devices). In spite of those facts, most analysis of CRAs omit the fintech and "internet-market" elements of the CRA industry.

This chapter provides new insights about, and explain why the existing and proposed business models and compensation of CRAs are ineffective and harmful. Specifically, this article critiques the Alternative Compensation Models for NRSROs developed by the US Government Accountability Office (US GAO), and finds that for each of the models, there is or can be significant *Consumer Surplus* or *Producer Surplus*; which when combined with other mentioned weaknesses, is likely to result in *Deadweight Losses* (and penalty-incentive conflicts; and incentives-welfare incongruence). This article notes that the "*Designation Model*" described in US GAO (2012) can significantly reduce competition among CRAs and ratings-quality.

EXISTING LITERATURE

Nwogugu (2010/2013) explained why existing and proposed non-government-controlled Credit Rating Agency (CRA) Business Models and Compensation Models are inefficient - Nwogugu (2010/2013) also proposed a model for a government-controlled/owned CRA. On CRAs in general, see: Byoun, Han & Shin (2020), Toscano (2020), Hu, Huang, Pan & Shi (2019), Huang & Shen (2019), Chen, Matousek, et. al. (2019), Yalta & Yalta (2018), Park & Lee (2018), Abad, Ferreras & Robles (2020), Ioannou, Wójcik & Pažitka (2020) and Du (2018).

The existing literature on business models and optimal contracts for CRAs is extensive and well defined, and there are six strands of research which are as follows:

1. The first line of research is the economic and financial research which has consisted of variations of the same group of themes, research-methods and topics, but has largely omitted any analysis of some contractual/non-contractual legal issues, Monetary Economics, game theory and behavioral biases that pertain to CRAs. This group includes the following articles: US Dept. of Justice Complaint (Feb. 5, 2013); White (2010); Bannier & Hirsch (2010); Dittrich (2007); Borio (March 2008); Honohan (2001); Pagano & Volpin (2010a;b); Bongaerts (2013); Kashyap & Kovrijnykh (2013); Bongaerts, Cremers & Goetzmann (2012); Galil & Soer (2011); Jiang, Stanford & Xie (2012); Mathis, McAndrews & Rochet (2009); Bonsall (January 2012); Bolton, Freixas & Shapiro (2012); Covitz & Harrison (2003); Fennell & Medvedev (2011); Faure-Grimaud, Peyrachie & Quesada (2009); Fulghieri & Strobl & Xia (2010); Rhee (2013); Hunt (2009); Listokin & Taibleson (2010); Lupica (2009); Manns (2009); Kisgen & Strahan (2010); Kliger & Sarig (2000); Opp, Opp & Harris (2013); Camanho, Deb & Liu (July 2012), United States Government Accountability Office (Jan. 2012); and Faure-Grimaud, Peyrachie & Quesada (2009). Sy (2009) made some useful comments about the relationship between CRAs and systemic risk.
2. The second line of research is the law/regulation articles and books most of which omit any in-depth economic analysis, game theory and behavior analysis, but focus on the history, evolution and current regulation of CRAs and include the following: Rhee (2013), Hemraj (2015), Darbellay (2013), Bai (2010), Coffee (2011), Pendergraft (2012), Schwarcz (2002), Goodhart (June 2008), Hill (2003; 2004; 2008; 2011), Fitzpatrick & Sagers (2009), Flannery, Houston & Partnoy (2010), Hunt (2009), Listokin & Taibleson (2010), Lupica (2009), Lynch (2009), Manns (2013), Manns (2009), Standard & Poors (2013), OECD (2010), Partnoy (2009), Champsaur (May 2005), Land (2007), and Gudzowski (2010).
3. The third line of research is the Antitrust/Competition articles which are relatively more recent and which have focused on possible antitrust violations in the CRA industry and whether to regulate CRAs using antitrust laws. See: Petit & Neyrinck (Aug. 2011), Patterson (2012), Becker & Milbourn (2011), Goodhart (June 2008), Palmigiano & Pieri (Jan 28, 2014), Petit (2002; 2011),

OECD (Oct. 5, 2010), Lannoo (Oct. 2008), Skreta & Veldkamp (2009), Frost (2009), He, Qian & Strahan (2012), Rhee (2013), Mariano (2012), Abrantez-Metz (April 18, 2012), White (2000; 2006; 2010), Doherty, Kartasheva & Phillips (2012), Camanho, Deb & Liu (July 2012), Ki, Nowak & Schumacher (2012), Van Den Brink (2012), and Metz (2012).

4. The fourth line of research is the *Optimal Contracts* strand (Economic Theory and Operations Research). While the existing contracts and regulations for CRA are clearly inefficient and inadequate, most of the proposed CRA contracts and business models are equally inefficient and costly. The federal governments of some countries have enacted regulations and conducted studies of the CRA industry[1] and have filed lawsuits against some CRAs. One problem is that the CRA compensation contract is intricately intertwined with the CRAs' business model which makes it somewhat difficult to compare CRA contracts with contracts in other industries. The optimal-contracts articles include Faure-Grimaud, Peyrachie & Quesada (2009), and Bongaerts (2013).
5. The fifth line of research addresses issues relevant to Monetary Economics and includes Mathis, McAndrews & Rochet (2009), Skreta & Veldkamp (2009), Pagano & Volpin (2010a), Reisen (2010), Roesch (2002), Deb, Manning, Murphy, Penalver & Toth (2011), Honohan (2001), and Tang (2009).
6. The sixth line of research addresses Sustainability/ESG issues and the roles of CRAs in Islamic Finance and Development Finance - and includes Cash (2021;2018; 2020), Mansoor, Ellahi, Hassan, et. al. (2020), Miglionico (2019) and Humphrey (2018).

The Game Theory Literature on CRAs Isn't Detailed or Extensive

Hemraj (2015), Partnoy (2009) and Darbellay (2013) described the history, evolution and regulation of CRAs, but did not analyze behavioral or antitrust issues, and did not develop new business/compensation models for CRAs. White (2010) analyzed the evolution of the credit rating industry and the associated barriers-to-entry; and suggested two possible paths for the credit rating industry: either increase the regulation of the CRAs, or reduce the required centrality of the CRAs.

Jiang, Stanford & Xie (2012) analyzed data from the 1970s when Moody's and S&P were using different compensation models. In particular, from 1971 until June 1974, S&P was charging investors for ratings, while Moody's was charging issuers. During this period, the Moody's ratings systematically exceeded those of S&P. S&P adopted the issuer-pays model in June 1974, and Parton over the next three years their ratings essentially matched Moody's. Becker & Milbourn (2011) analyzed how the rise in market share by Fitch influenced ratings by Moody's and S&P (who had historically dominated the industry), and they found that competition among rating agencies reduces the accuracy of ratings. They also concluded that any given individual bond is more likely to be rated by Fitch when the ratings from the S&P and or Moodys are relatively low; but in the sectors where Fitch issues more ratings, the overall ratings for the sector tend to be higher.

Bolton, Freixas & Shapiro (2012) modelled competition among CRAs with three sources of conflicts: (1) CRAs conflict of understating risk in order to generate business from issuers and investors, (2) issuers' ability to purchase only the most favorable ratings, and (3) the trusting nature of some investor clienteles. Bolton, Freixas & Shapiro (2012) noted that these conflicts create two distortions: i) competition can reduce efficiency because it facilitates ratings-shopping; and ii) ratings are more likely to be inflated during boom periods and when investors are more trusting. Using a new data set of about 2,000 credit rating migrations from Moody's and Standard & Poor's, and matching issuer-level bond prices,

Covitz & Harrison (2003) analyzed whether well-known conflicts of interest at bond rating agencies have a significant influence on their actions and they found that that rating changes do not appear to be importantly influenced by rating agency conflicts of interest and instead CRAs are motivated primarily by reputation-related incentives. Stroble & Xia (2012) concluded that the conflict of interest caused by the issuer-pays rating model leads to inflated corporate credit ratings; and that difference between the issuer-pay and investor-pay models is more pronounced when S&P's conflict of interest is particularly severe: firms with more short-term debt, a newly appointed CEO or CFO, and a lower percentage of past bond issues rated by S&P are significantly more likely to receive a rating from S&P that exceeds their rating from EJR; and these variables are not related to corporate bond yield spreads.

Gromb & Martimort (2007) analyzed the optimal design of incentive contracts for experts in different collusion environments, where a principal relies on experts to gather and report two signals about a project's value; and the principal can have a single expert gather both signals or two experts gather one signal each. Gromb & Martimort (2007) concluded that without collusion, the multi-expert organization dominates the single expert organization, but this ranking is reversed when the experts can collude among themselves (horizontal collusion) and with the principal (vertical collusion). Faure-Grimaud, Peyrachie & Quesada (2009) attempted to develop an optimal contract between an issuer and a CRA, and the conditions under which simple ownership contracts implement this optimal solution; and they concluded that for some distribution functions, a competitive rating market is necessary condition. In this context, competition between rating intermediaries will lead to less information in equilibrium. However, their assumption that the issuer's decision to obtain a rating is endogenous and that the price of a rating is a strategic variable is not always true; and their conclusion that issuers that hide their ratings can be in equilibrium only if they are *ex ante* uncertain of their quality and if the decision to hire the CRA is not observable, is clearly not correct because: a) there are developed markets for low-rated financial instruments; b) investor's ratings criteria may differ substantially from those of the CRA; c) the assigned rating may not be a major investment criteria. Using a theoretical model, Bongaerts (2013) attempted to show that issuer-private benefits of operating induce rating inflation; which may not be reduced or eliminated by investor-paid or investor-produced ratings (ie. these alternatives cannot compete effectively with issuer-paid CRA ratings). Bongaerts (2013) focused on an optimal contracting arrangement where a CRA must be compensated for exerting effort to generate a signal about the quality of project to be funded by outside investors. Fennell & Medvedev (2011) surveyed various CRA business models (issuer-pays model, the investor-pays model, a public model and a platform model).

Bongaerts, Cremers & Goftzmann (2012) analyzed three existing theories about multiple ratings: "Information production", "Rating shopping", and "Regulatory Certification"; and using differences in rating composition, default prediction, and credit-spread changes, they found evidence of only Regulatory Certification; and they noted that additional credit ratings are more likely to occur because of regulatory purposes, but do not provide any incremental information about the issuer's credit quality. Tang (2009) concluded that credit market information asymmetry significantly affects firms' real outcomes. Fulghieri, Strobl & Xia (2010) concluded that under certain economic conditions, a credit rating system that incorporates unsolicited ratings enables the CRA to extract higher ratings fees from issuers; and is beneficial because it leads to more stringent rating standards and improves social welfare. Boot, Milboum & Schmeits (2006) theorized that credit ratings serve as a *coordinating mechanism* in situations where multiple equilibria can occur; and that credit ratings provide a "focal point" for firms and their investors; and Credit ratings can help fix the desired equilibrium which is a major function.

Kisgen & Strahan (2010) notes that after the US SEC officially certified Dominion Bond Rating Service (DBRS) as a CRA in February 2003, bond yields changed in the direction implied by the firm's DBRS rating relative to its ratings from other certified rating agencies (a one-notch-higher DBRS rating corresponds to a 39-basis-point reduction in an issuer's debt cost of capital). Kisgen & Strahan (2010) concluded that the impact on yields is driven by cases where the DBRS rating is better than other ratings and is larger among bonds rated near the investment-grade cutoff; and that these trends indicate that ratings-based regulations on bond investment affect a firms' cost of debt capital. Cheng & Neamtiu (2009) concluded that CRAs improve the timeliness and accuracy of their ratings when their market power is threatened by the risk of increased regulatory intervention and/or reputation concerns. Alp (2013) noted that there were statistically significant changes in ratings standard during 1985-2002, and again during 2002-2007; and that the variation in standards is not completely attributable to changes in the economic climate, but Rating standards affect credit spreads; and lax ratings standards are associated with higher issuer default rates.

Cantor & Packer (1997) noted that while many regulations use private sector credit ratings to determine investment prohibitions and capital requirements for institutional portfolio investments, such regulations implicitly assume that different CRAs have equivalent rating scales, despite the fact that some CRAs assign systematically higher ratings than others. Cantor & Packer (1997) analyzed whether observed rating differences among CRAs reflect different rating scales or simply result from sample *selection bias*; and they found only limited evidence of *selection bias*; and that there was no that firms seek ratings from these CRAs with higher ratings scales/standards in order to surmount specific regulatory hurdles or to reduce ex ante uncertainty about default risk. Opp, Opp & Harris (2012) concluded that introducing rating-contingent regulation that favors highly rated securities may increase or decrease rating informativeness, but unambiguously increases the volume of highly rated securities; and that when the regulatory advantage of highly rated securities is sufficiently large, delegated information acquisition is unsustainable, since the CRA prefers to facilitate regulatory arbitrage by inflating ratings. Beaver, Shakespeare & Soliman (2006) found that Bond ratings from non-certified CRAs are used solely for investment advice; while ratings by Certified CRAs (certified by the US Securities and Exchange Commission (SEC)) are used by a variety of constituents, many of whom write contracts incorporating these ratings; and that the properties of the ratings from the two types of CRAs differ in predictable ways – the non-certified CRAs' ratings are consistent with their role of providing information to investors; and the certified CRA agency is generally more conservative, consistent with their significant role in contracting. Jiang, Stanford & Xie (2012) found that when S&P charges investors and Moody's charges issuers, S&P's ratings are lower than Moody's; and once S&P adopts issuer-pay, its ratings increase and no longer differ from Moody's; and S&P only assigns higher ratings for bonds that are subject to greater conflicts of interest, measured by higher expected rating fees or lower credit quality.

Doherty, Kartasheva & Phillips (2012) studied the effect of competition among CRAs on the information content of ratings, and concluded that a monopolistic CRA pools sellers into multiple rating classes and has partial market coverage, which provides an opportunity for market entry. Doherty, Kartasheva & Phillips (2012) used Standard and Poor's (S&P) entry into the market for insurance ratings (previously provided A.M. Best, a monopolist) to empirically test the impact of market entry on the information content of ratings; and they found that S&P had to implement higher standards in order to assign a rating similar to the one assigned by A.M. Best and that higher-than-average quality insurers in each rating category of A.M. Best chose to receive a second rating from S&P. Thus, a potentially successful CRA-entrant can design a rating scale that differs from that of the incumbent (monopolistic

CRA), and target higher-than-average issuers in each rating grade of the incumbent's rating scale and employ more stringent rating standards. Skreta & Veldkamp (2009) developed an equilibrium model of the market for ratings and use it to examine possible origins of and cures for ratings inflation. In the model, asset issuers can shop for ratings--observe multiple ratings and disclose only the most favorable--before auctioning their assets. When assets are simple, agencies' ratings are similar and the incentive to ratings shop is low. When assets are sufficiently complex, ratings differ enough that an incentive to shop emerges. Thus, an increase in the complexity of recently issued securities could create a systematic bias in disclosed ratings, despite the fact that each ratings agency produces an unbiased estimate of the asset's true quality. Increasing competition among agencies would only worsen this problem. Switching to an investor-initiated ratings system alleviates the bias, but could collapse the market for information.

Mathis, McAndrews & Rochet (2009) stated that the "reputation argument" only works when a large fraction of the CRA income comes from other sources than rating complex products; but when the percentage of the CRA income generated from rating complex products becomes large, the CRA is always too lax with a positive probability and initiates ratings with probability of one when its reputation is good enough. Mathis, McAndrews & Rochet (2009) noted the possibility of "reputation cycles" (wherein a single default provokes a complete loss of reputation of the CRA) and recommended the "platform-pays" business model for CRAs. Using a dataset of corporate bond issuance ratings from 1985 to 2010, Wang (Aug 2012) analyzed whether reputation concerns can discipline CRAs; and concluded that due to CRA's distorted incentives, ratings are more likely to be initiated during recessions when investors are more risk-averse and the slope of corporate bond yield curve is higher. Wang (Aug 2012) suggested that reputation concerns don't always discipline CRAs; and that the sensitivity of credit ratings to the change of macroeconomic conditions is higher for complex issuers, large issuers who contribute more rating fees, and risky issuers. Bar-Isaac & Shapiro (2014) concluded that the value of CRA reputation depends on time-varying economic fundamentals (e.g. competition for analysts, default probabilities, income from fees); and that a CRA is likely to issue less accurate ratings in boom times than it would during recessionary periods; and that competition among CRAs yields similar qualitative results.

Kliger & Sarig (2000) analyzed whether bond ratings contain pricing-relevant information by examining security price reactions to Moody's refinement of its rating system, which were not associated with any fundamental change in issuers' risks, or any prior announcement, and was carried simultaneously for all bonds; ad they concluded that that rating information does not affect firm value, but that: i) when Moody's announces better- (worse-) than-expected ratings, the volatilities implied by prices of options on the fine-rated issuers' shares decline (rise); ii) the issuer's debt value increases (decreases) and equity value falls (rises) when Moody's announces better- (worse-) than-expected ratings. Alissa & Koharki (2013) found that issuers use income-increasing (-decreasing) earnings management activities when they are below (above) their expected ratings; and that firms below or above their expected credit ratings may be able to move toward expected ratings through the use of directional earnings management. Roesch (2002) concluded that default rates vary depending on the information which is incorporated in the underlying rating system; and that default rates which are produced by rating systems that use all available information are constant through time, whereas default rates produced by rating systems which omit relevant Information will exhibit cyclical patterns.

Frost (2009) evaluated important criticisms of the CRAs which were discussed in a US SEC report and found that little rigorously gathered empirical evidence supports the criticisms, many issues remain unresolved; and that tests for potential conflicts of interest and alleged unfair practices are difficult to design, and the alleged deficiencies of CRAs' disclosure practices have not been analyzed; and many criticisms are based on subjective benchmarks that are difficult to quantify and are questionable.

Cantor (2001) stated in part "……by using ratings as a tool of regulation, regulators fundamentally change the nature of the rating agency product. Issuers pay rating fees, not to facilitate access to the capital market, but to purchase a privileged status for their securities from the regulator. As a result, licensed rating agencies will have a product to sell regardless of the analytic quality of their ratings and their credibility with the investor Community……..".

Contract Theory and Mechanism Design

Contract Theory and *Mechanism Design Theory* have been jointly studied from various perspectives including Economics/Finance, Operations Research, Mathematical Psychology, Computer Science, Game Theory and Applied Math - see: Hoppe & Schmitz (2018); Niederhoff & Kouvelis (2019); Hong, Wernz & Stillinger (2016); Wu, Zhao & Tang (2014); Li, Liu & Chen (2018); Lin & Chou (1990); Park & Kim (2014); Goetz, Yatsenko, et. al. (2019); Fang & Yuan (2018); Madureira, Pereira, et. al. (2014); Meneguzzi, Modgil, et. al. (2012); Meneguzzi, Modgil, Oren, et. al. (2011); Zohar & Rosenschein (2008); Terán, Aguilar & Cerrada (2017); Eenmaa-Dimitrieva & Schmidt-Kessen (2019); Drozd & Serrano-Padia (2018); and Wei, Wang, et.al. (2018). However, the models in most of these foregoing articles and literature are static, don't incorporate relevant variables; don't consider varying "states" and often complex "joint" effects of variables; and they don't consider Industrial Organization effects of contracts/mechanisms - see Nwogugu (2007a;b), Nwogugu (2019a;b) and Nwogugu (2006).

Sustainability, Economic Growth, and the Standardization of Contracts

Standardization of contracts can affect economic growth, Sustainability, Inequality and Economic Growth as noted by various academic researchers - see Sussman (1999); Van Assche & Schwartz (2013); Patterson (2010), Engert & Hornuf (2018); Aguirre (2017); Ayotte & Bolton (2011); Baffi (2007; 2012); He, Xue & Zhou (2019); Vo, Nguyen, et.al. (2019); Sheng (2019); Eenmaa-Dimitrieva & Schmidt-Kessen (2019); Dekker, Kawai & Sakaguchi (2018); Iossa & Martimort (2018); and Sprinkle, Williamson & Upton (2008). Sussman (1999) noted that "The main implications of contract standardization are that (i) "financial history matters in the growth process,(ii) early formation of the system may create a drag on economic growth and (iii) the effect may be non-monotonic because the system may be modernized at some point". In the realm of CRAs, CRAs have developed their own standardized contracts for ratings projects and the Big-Three CRAs are dominant.

THE EXISTING AND PROPOSED CRA BUSINESS MODELS AND COMPENSATION MODELS ARE INEFFICIENT, REDUCE COMPETITION AND CAN RESULT IN VIOLATIONS OF ANTITRUST STATUTES

Appendices 1 & 2 summarizes the various existing and proposed CRA business models. More specifically, the models and theories discussed in Bongaerts (2013); Kashyap & Kovrijnykh (2013); Bongaerts, Cremers & Goetzmann (2012); Jiang, Stanford & Xie (2012); Mathis, McAndrews & Rochet (2009); Bonsall (January 2012); Bolton, Freixas & Shapiro (2012); Covitz & Harrison (2003); Fennell & Medvedev (2011); Faure-Grimaud, Peyrachie & Quesada (2009); Fulghieri & Strobl & Xia (2010); Rhee (2013); Hunt (2009); Listokin & Taibleson (2010); Lupica (2009); Manns (2009), Camanho, Deb & Liu (July 2012), United States Government Accountability Office (Jan. 2012), and Faure-Grimaud, Peyrachie & Quesada (2009), are inaccurate and ineffective because of the following reasons.

Contrary to some of the studies (such as Kashyap & Kovrijnykh (2013) and Fulghieri & Strobl & Xia (2010)), the ratings fee cannot be linked to or be contingent on outcomes (such as the ratings offered to the issuer, or the performance of the asset/securities and the quality of the project/company, or whether the issuer raises capital) – because any such linkage constitutes a conflict-of-interest, and will eliminate objectivity and independence from the ratings process, and transform the issuer-CRA relationship into a franchisor-franchisee relationship (subject to state and federal regulations); or a Business Opportunity (subject to state and federal regulations); or a joint venture (ie. in the case of project finance SPVs and Asset Backed Securities Trusts) or a Strategic Alliance; or a partnership; all of which will have significant tax and regulatory consequences. Contrary to some of the studies, having the CRA invest in the issuer as a condition of providing a ratings will eliminate objectivity and independence from the ratings process, and transform the issuer-CRA relationship into a franchisor-franchisee relationship (subject to state and federal regulations); or a Business Opportunity (subject to state and federal regulations); or a joint venture (ie. in the case of project finance SPVs and ABS Trusts); all of which will have significant tax and regulatory consequences. The one-period, two-period and three-period models of CRAs are highly un-realistic and ineffective because of the following: a) the context and purpose of the analysis; b) the actual and perceived duration of the "time period" matters for fixed income instruments; and c) the effects of a ratings last for up to 6-12 semiannual periods during which users/regulators/investors will track the ratings transitions over time.

Contrary to Kashyap & Kovrijnykh (2013), giving a portion of the issuer's surplus to the CRA: a) is illegal in most countries and is a form of kickback; b) alternatively, it will make the relationship a partnership or joint venture with significant tax consequences. The studies also omitted the fact that the relationship between competition and ratings-fees depends on the cost structure of each CRA; and that the relationship between competition and CRA effort depends on the cost structure of each CRA, and the CRA's brand equity; and that the perceived "accuracy" of a rating also depends on many factors that are not controlled by the CRA (and are sometimes not controlled by the issuer) so that post-ratings failure of a project.

The issuer does not have the same knowledge about the project as everyone else ex-ante. Many of the studies didn't address ratings shopping.

Contrary to Bongaerts (2013), requiring CRAs to invest in securities/assets that they rate is wrong and is a conflict of interest. Contrary to Kashyap & Kovrijnykh (2013), and Bolton,Freixas & Shapiro (2012), the rating precision and reputation costs are neither exogenous or chosen by the CRA, but rather, are determined by a complex, dynamic and time-varying combination of factors including skills and motivation of the CRA's staff, non-controllable factors that affect the project; the CRA's policies and procedures; the complexity of the company/project; etc..

In many of the studies, the economic impact of "reputation costs" are omitted from the economic models. Contrary to some of the studies (such as Kashyap & Kovrijnykh (2013)), the sequence of the issuer's pre-ratings and post-ratings actions is not fixed in time or location. Rather, after the rating is issued, the issuer can take one of several steps in any order of sequence depending on its opportunity set, constraints, capital, investor interest and regulations and such steps include but are not limited to the following: a) make the ratings public; b) issue the securities; c) obtain credit enhancement; d) set up a sinking fund –regardless of whether or not such sinking fund is mandatorily required in the terms of the securities. Contrary to some of the studies (such as Kashyap & Kovrijnykh (2013)), the CRA does not have limited liability in all jurisdictions and can be sued.

Contrary to some of the studies (such as Kashyap & Kovrijnykh (2013)), a project can be financed even after the CRA issues a low credit rating, particularly where: a) the issuer can obtain third-party credit enhancement; b) the demand for high yield securities is significant; c) the issuer can enter into joint ventures to finance the project. Contrary to some of the studies (such as Fulghieri & Strobl & Xia (2010), the effects of a rating on firm-value is limited because credit ratings affect debt and cost-of-debt in calculations of the WACC and the debt/capital ratio. Thus, its conjectured that ratings may have a noticeable effect on firm value on when the firm is in the domain of financial distress (ie. when the firm's debt/capital ratio exceeds 60%). Thus, the value of a rated firm is not always an increasing function of the CRA's reputation.

Contrary to some of the studies (such as Fulghieri & Strobl & Xia (2010), and Kashyap & Kovrijnykh (2013)), the firm can and will survive if it does not execute the proposed "project" for which the ratings is sought. Firms also have cash reserves and can borrow short term debt for which ratings are not usually required. Contrary to some of the studies, the outcomes of a "project" is not perfectly observable to investors and event to the subject company because of: a) various associated economic and non-economic multiplier effects of a project; b) the impact of the project on associated contractors who don't disclose their operating reports; and c) the impact of the project on the actual and perceived ratings of other companies in the industry – and such impact is often not transparent. Also, failure of a "project" may be beneficial for the company for various reasons including tax purposes, transfer pricing, depreciation and cost allocation.

Contrary to some of the studies, the possibility of un-solicited ratings dos not always cause the CRA to adopt a more relaxed ratings standard. Many of the studies erroneously assume that the projects are not observable. On the contrary observability is not a very important factor because it occurs ex-post, and many projects are partially observable by consultants, vendors and direct/indirect news releases by the issuer's management. Also, the issuer's employees change jobs and in the case of ABS/MBS/CDOs, the issuer's portfolios are reviewed by institutional investors.

Many of the existing/proposed CRA models in the CRA studies erroneously restrict the level of CRA effort – such restriction does not reflect reality wherein CRA effort varies and can be a function of the size of fees, CRA skill, timing; etc.. The CRA's effort level is determined by several factors including but not limited to the following:

1. The CRA's policies and procedures manual;
2. The estimated importance of the issuer and or associated prospective investors to the CRA;
3. Perceived difficulty of the rating project;
4. Subjective prioritization by the CRA's individual managers;
5. The physical condition of the ratings analysts and their conformance to ethics standards;
6. The Compensation of individual ratings analysts;
7. The internal politics of the CRA's Ratings Committee;
8. The influence of third-party ratings-advisory consultants on both the issuer and the CRA;
9. The estimated ratings of competing CRAs;
10. The nature and tenure of the CRA's relationship with the issuer;
11. The nature of the issuer's industry and whether its regulated.

Contrary to almost all the existing models of CRAs, the CRA's *effort* can be "negative if any of the following conditions exist:

1. the CRA gains extra and incremental monetary and or nonmonetary benefits from third parties by working on the particular ratings project;
2. the CRA's ratings models are inaccurate;
3. The CRA's staff intentionally falsifies inputs into the ratings model;
4. the CRA's effort reduces social welfare.

Contrary to almost all the existing models of CRAs, the CRA's effort can be "economically" costless to the CRA, if any of the following conditions exist:

1. the CRA gains extra and incremental monetary and or non-monetary benefits from third parties by working on the particular ratings project;
2. the CRA's effort increases social welfare which in turn results in more rating business;
3. the CRA's effort alone increases its brand equity (e.g. a greater increase than traditional advertising);
4. there are statutory provisions that reimburse the CRA for its true economic costs for issuing the ratings;
5. the CRA can obtain most of the data and research (needed to issue a ratings) at no or low cost; vi) the CRA decides to adopt the ratings of a competing CRA.

In some of the existing/proposed CRA models, the assumption that the issuer has no assets is wrong – because many issuers have assets and or cash. Even in the case of ABS Trusts, such trusts have assets in the form of contract rights (the right to purchase assets from the sponsor/originator once the ABS Trust raises cash).

Some of the existing/proposed CRA models erroneously assume that the probability of a CRA giving a high rating to a bad-quality project is the same as the probability of the CRA giving a low-rating to a good quality project. This is because the circumstances of issuers differ; an CRA effort and m differs across issuers, fees, industry, CRA-manager and time horizons.

Some of the studies erroneously assume or that it is suboptimal for an issuer to pay a CRA to produce a credit-rating if such ratings not used, and that can be attributed to the following:

1. prospective and actual investors use relative-value approaches as a major investment strategy; ii) un-requested ratings (issuer didn't request) or "un-used" ratings (issuer did not use ratings for any financing transaction) are used for industry analysis and studies of business cycles;
2. even where the issue does not pay for ratings, there are third-parties that can pay monthly subscription fees for such ratings (to get large sets of ratings data cross industries).

Most of the CRA studies and existing/proposed CRA models don't address the legal liability of CRAs for inaccurate ratings. Such liability is becoming an important issue in many jurisdictions, and in the US, S&P and Moodys have been sued in court for inaccurate ratings.

Contrary to many of the existing and proposed models of CRAs, in a static model, an upfront fee can provide the CRA with sufficient incentives not to shirk, if there are also adequate penalties for Shirking, and or the mentioned alternatives to CRA-ratings are sufficiently popular and cheap. Similarly, in a repeated-setting model, an upfront fee can provide the CRA with sufficient incentives not to shirk, if there are also adequate penalties for Shirking, and or the mentioned alternatives to CRA-ratings are sufficiently popular and cheap; and or if the size of the upfront fee depends on the history of the CRA's accuracy; and or if reputation costs are significant and observable ex-ante, and may potentially affect the CRA's ability to continue as a going concern.

Contrary to some of the studies (such as Fulghieri & Strobl & Xia (2010), and Kashyap & Kovrijnykh (2013)), credit ratings don't always reduce information asymmetry because:

1. the CRA's evaluation criteria may differ from those of many investors;
2. the CRA evaluates credit quality but not investment returns, and both can differ substantially; c) in some cases, investors' due diligence can provide them with a sufficient understanding of a project's potential;
3. ratings are typically associated with either a specific financial instrument or with the issuer as a whole;
4. the entire ratings process is subject to the truthfulness of the issuer - the issuer can submit inaccurate information to the CRA (as occurred in the US where ABS trusts submitted wrong information to CRAs);
5. where the size and important of the subject "project" is small or medium relative to the entire operations of the issuer, there can still be substantial information asymmetry;
6. the CRA's effort and inaccuracy may actually increase information asymmetry (as in the case of MBS/CDO/ABS securities issued in the US during 2002-2009);
7. in most instances the ratings pertain to one offering of a specific fixed income instrument, whereas the company typically has several projects; as mentioned in the literature, the CRAs use or can use un-solicited ratings to compel an issuer to request for and pay for a credit rating.

Contrary to some of the studies (such as Fulghieri & Strobl & Xia (2010)), there is a substantial difference between firm-value determined primarily by one or more "projects", and the going-concern value of the company. A company typically has several projects that are simultaneously ongoing. Going-concern value exists even when the company does not have a current "project". There is a substantial distinction between "projects" on one hand, and the going-concern element of a company's business – each company typically has several ongoing projects; and going-concern value exists even when the company does not have any "projects". The effects of a CRA rating on the value of the firm is or can be limited because the ratings usually applies to a specific financial instrument and to the firm's cost-of-debt which is used in calculating WACC; and because investors and regulators begin to focus on ratings when:

1. the firm is in the domain of financial distress;
2. the investor wants to purchase or sell the rated financial instrument;
3. when there is significant bad or good news about the issuer or its industry.

Thus, its conjectured here that the credit ratings begin to have greater than normal effects on firm-value when the firm has a substantial debt/capital ratio or is in the domain of financial/operational distress (even when its financial ratios seem normal).

The Issuer-Pays Compensation/Business Model

The "*Random Selection model*" and the "*Stand-Alone model*" which are described in United States Government Accountability Office (Jan. 2012), are all functional equivalents and variations of the *Issuer-Pays model*. The Issuer-pay model is ineffective because of the following reasons. There is an inherent conflict of interest, because the issuer can influence the CRA's ratings by threatening to cancel future ratings contracts. CRAs have incentive to inflate the ratings of securities/assets of their long term repeat customers (issuers) in order to retain their business. CRA's have less incentives to conduct thorough due diligence or issue adverse ratings because the long-term relationships foster laxness and complacency among CRA staff. Companies/issuers can shop for ratings among several CRAs.

The problem of information asymmetry between investors and the issuer is not completely solved – the CRA often does not have complete information about the company or securities/assets (as was the case for several securitization Trusts rated by S&P and Moodys during 2003-2007); the securities/assets may be too complex for most investors to understand (as in ABS); or the issuer cannot divulge its trade secrets; or there is a "*Ratings Lag*"; or the CRA's staff does not analyze the securities/assets properly (as in during 2003-2008).

There is no implicit or explicit penalty (that can be assessed on CRAs) for low quality; and there are inadequate incentives for the CRA to perform and not shirk. Similarly, the issuer does not face any penalties for fraudulent or inadequate disclosures. This business model exposes the CRA to legal liability – to lawsuits by the issuers, the investors and the government; and other persons who maybe third-party beneficiaries of the CRA-issuer agreement. The *free-riding problem* remains and investors can obtain free ratings and research from sources other than the CRA. This business model does not foster truthful disclosure by issuers – and issuers are not penalized for inadequate disclosure or inaccurate disclosure. The CRA's efforts may not be correlated with the credibility of the assigned ratings.

There can be substantial goal-incongruence and discord between the efforts of the CRA's staff (towards accurate ratings), and the CRA's firm-wide policies that pertain to business development, client retention and updating of ratings. It may not be cost-effective for the CRA to update ratings either frequently (monthly or quarterly) or when there is relevant news. There may be conflicts among the CRA's compensation/incentive system (which may reward employees based on the number of ratings completed, client relations; fees generated; etc.) on one hand, and secondly, the nature and magnitude of effort required to accurately rate assets, and thirdly, the effectiveness of the assigned ratings (timeliness; accuracy; relevance; credibility).

This business model does not ensure or guarantee that increased competition will result in increased effort by CRAs and the opposite may occur when:

1. the CRA charges non-standard fees and discriminatory/personalized fees for services;
2. the CRA has substantial brand equity;
3. the CRA does not face any reputational or monetary penalties for inaccurate ratings;
4. the marginal cost of substitution of a CRA is relatively low;
5. the marginal propensity of an issuer to substitute a CRA is high.

This business model does not ensure or guarantee that increased competition will result in lower prices for ratings services and the opposite may occur when:

1. some CRAs have substantial brand-equity and Reputation Capital;
2. the CRA has expertise in some specific industry/industries;
3. the cost structure of all or most CRAs are similar and are not affected by their pricing schemes and vice versa;
4. the *marginal cost of substitution* of a CRA is relatively low and the *marginal propensity* of an issuer to substitute a CRA is high.

This business model does not always encourage or facilitate revisions of ratings. In the case of ABS and Structured Products (where there is no real company or operations or company officers/CFO), the business model can result in shirking by the CRA. This business model can unfairly discriminate against smaller companies or poor companies, which is not socially optimal (ie. ideally, all companies should be able to afford ratings at least once or twice per year).

This business model fails where the marginal cost of substituting the ratings process is low (including social, economic and psychological costs) – for example:

1. where the company is very well known and perceived to be stable and doesn't need a rating;
2. where financial stability and solvency are not the primary concerns of the company;
3. where the issuer has other verification or reputation mechanisms that are satisfactory to investors;
4. where the issuer is wealthy;
5. where the issuer has a third-party guarantor.

This business model has or can have a substantial effect on the issuer's decision to offer securities. Ideally, the business model and payment systems should not affect the issuer's financing decisions.

The *Stand-Alone Model* is particularly problematic because instead of receiving fees from issuers, the CRAs will be paid through transaction fees for original issuance of securities and secondary market transactions and this compensation structure:

1. provides significant incentives for CRAs to reduce their ratings standards and inflate ratings so that more loans/bonds are issued;
2. provides substantial incentives for CRAs to create "ratings volatility" in specific industries and across industries in order to increase trading volume (ie. the CRA can purposely issue divergent ratings for companies with similar characteristics and in the same industry or in different industries, in order to compel investors – especially "relative value" investors – to execute more trades);
3. provides significant incentives for CRAs to focus more on long term bonds/loans than on short term instruments;
4. adversely affects the buy/sell decisions of investors, particularly investors that have high portfolio turnover (high volume of sales and purchases);
5. can cause investors to engage in derivatives transactions in order to avoid classifying a transaction as a sale;
6. keeps the "CRA Funding Source" within the control or influence of issuers and investors;
7. affects the issuers' corporate financing decisions – issuers are more likely to choose shorter term debt because of this incremental transaction cost.

As a *coordination mechanism*, the *Random Selection Model* is ineffective because it reduces positive Super-modularity and positive Strategic Complementarity (positive Super-modularity and positive Strategic Complementarity both increase Social Welfare; while negative Super-modularity and negative Strategic Complementarity both reduce Social Welfare).

One of the main problems in the *Random Selection Model* described in US GAO (2012) is that the proposed penalties (for shirking or issuance of low-quality ratings) encourage the CRAs to collude, and the penalty mechanisms are unfair aggregation-based penalties that don't distinguish among the quality of specific bonds/loans; and the penalties don't account for market sentiment, and differences in skills and efforts of CRAs. In this industry, the "Peer Comparison review" is susceptible to manipulation and error simply because there are relatively very few CRAs, the barriers to entry are high, and CRA's sources of revenues are limited; and CRAs' true "efforts" are often dampened and "modified" by market forces that are beyond their control (such as general economic fluctuations, competition in industries; bad management; labor problems; new technology; substitute products; etc.). Furthermore, the use of a clearinghouse to set ratings-fees and to functionally influence the cost structure of CRAs may be an adverse restriction of free market force and may be deemed anti-competitive. As a *coordination mechanism*, the *Random Selection Model* is ineffective, because it reduces positive Super-modularity and positive Strategic Complementarity.

Generally, for each of the above-mentioned business models, there is or can be significant *Consumer Surplus* or *Producer Surplus*, which when combined with other mentioned weaknesses is likely to result in *Deadweight Losses*.

The "Investor-Pays" Business/Compensation Model

The "*Alternative-User Pays model*", and the "*User Pays model*" and the "*Stand-Alone model*" which are described in United States Government Accountability Office (Jan. 2012), are all functional equivalents and variations of this "*Investor-Pays*" Business/Compensation model. The Investor-pays business model is not efficient for many reasons including but not limited to the following:

1. CRAs have significant incentives to inflate the credit ratings of securities/financial-instruments that investors like.
2. CRAs will not provide adequate coverage of non-popular securities/assets.
3. The free-riding problem remains and investors can obtain free ratings and research from sources other than the CRA.
4. CRA income/revenues will be tied to success of specific securities.
5. There is or can be an inherent conflict of interest - there can be pressure from investors with strong preferences for specific product ratings.
6. This business model does not completely solve the problem of information asymmetry between investor and issuer – the CRA often does not have complete information about the company or securities/assets (as was the case for several securitization (ABS) Trusts rated by S&P and Moodys during 2003-2007); the securities/assets may be too complex for most investors to understand (as in ABS, or CDOs); or the issuer cannot divulge its trade secrets; or there is a "ratings Lag"; or the CRA's staff does not analyze the securities/assets properly (as in during 2003-2008).
7. Under this business model, the investor can still shop among CRAs.

8. This business model exposes the CRA to legal liability – to lawsuits from the issuers, the investors and the government; and other persons who maybe third-party beneficiaries of the CRA-investor agreement.
9. Under this business model, there is no implicit or explicit penalty (that can be assessed on CRAs) for low quality ratings; and there are inadequate incentives for the CRA to perform its obligations properly (and not shirk). Similarly, the issuer does not face any penalties for fraudulent or inadequate disclosures.

Under this business model, since only high net-worth investors and institutional investors can afford CRAs' services, the securities for which ratings are available will be determined by the preferences of such investors – such arrangement does not maximize social welfare - thus, for securities for which 90% of the outstanding units are owned by small individual investors, it will be unlikely that there will be any ratings from any CRA. Under this business model, Issuers may not cooperate and provide necessary materials to CRAs for ratings analysis. Under this business model, the channels of distribution of the securities can affect the social-value and use-value of the ratings. Under this model, ratings would be kept private (available only to paying investors), but this could hamper the regulatory use of ratings which is facilitated and enhanced by transparency (There can be business models where investors buy ratings separately; or a subscription model).

This business model is problematic in the case of Structured Products which tend to evolve during the ratings process – thus, prospective investors cannot demand for ratings until after the design/terms of the structured product is finalized. CRAs have been accused of conflicts-of-interest for participating in the structuring/revisions of Structured Products). Deb, et. al. (2011) set out some specific ways in which the investor-pay business model could permit free ratings – but the suggested methods don't overcome problems mentioned herein. Under this business model, the free-riding problem remains and investors can obtain free ratings and research from sources other than the CRA. This business model does not foster truthful disclosure by issuers – and issuers are not penalized for inadequate disclosure or inaccurate disclosure.

Under this business model, the CRA's efforts may not be correlated with the credibility of the assigned ratings. Under this business model, there can be substantial goal incongruence and discord between the efforts of the CRA's staff (towards accurate ratings), and the CRA's firm-wide policies that pertain to business development, client retention and updating of ratings - it may not be cost-effective for the CRA to update ratings either frequently (monthly or quarterly) or when there is relevant news. Under this business model, there may be conflicts among the CRA's compensation/incentive system (which may reward employees based on the number of ratings completed, client relations; fees generated; etc.) on one hand, and secondly, the nature and magnitude of effort required to accurately rate assets, and thirdly, the effectiveness of the assigned ratings (timeliness; accuracy; relevance; credibility). The business model does not ensure or guarantee that increased competition will result in increased effort by CRAs – and in fact the opposite may occur when:

1. the CRA charges non-standard fees and discriminatory/personalized fees for services;
2. the CRA has substantial brand equity;
3. the CRA does not face any reputational or monetary penalties for inaccurate ratings;
4. the marginal cost of substitution of a CRA is relatively low;
5. the marginal propensity of an issuer to substitute a CRA is high.

The business model does not ensure or guarantee that increased competition will result in lower prices for ratings services – and the opposite may occur when any of the following exists or occurs:

1. some CRAs have substantial brand equity;
2. the CRA has expertise;
3. the cost-structure of all or most CRAs are similar and are not affected by their pricing schemes and vice versa;
4. the marginal cost of substitution of a CRA is relatively low and the marginal propensity of an issuer to substitute a CRA is high.

This business model does not always encourage or facilitate revisions of ratings. In the case of ABS and Structured Products (where there is no real company or operations or company officers/CFO), the business model can result in shirking by the CRA; and other misconduct. The business model can result in unfair discrimination against smaller companies or poor companies, which is not socially optimal (ie. ideally, all companies should be able to afford ratings at least once or twice per year). This business model fails where the marginal cost of substituting the ratings process is low (including social, economic and psychological costs) – for example:

1. where the company is very well known and perceived to be stable and doesn't need a rating;
2. where financial stability and solvency are not the primary concerns of the company;
3. where the issuer has other verification or reputation mechanisms that are satisfactory to investors;
4. where the issuer is wealthy;
5. where the issuer has a third-party guarantor.

This business model has or can have a substantial effect on the issuer's decision to offer securities. Ideally, the business model and payment systems should not affect the issuer's financing decisions.

The "*User-Pays model*" which is described in United States Government Accountability Office (Jan. 2012), is very inefficient because:

1. it does not consider the CRA's cost structure, and thus exposes the CRA to full market risk wherein the CRA may become insolvent or progressively become unable to function if user-volume declines;
2. the CRA's fee becomes a direct function of the number of "users" and is not related to the CRA's actual cost of providing the ratings and this transforms the CRA-issuer-investor relationship into a strategic alliance or licensing or "Business Opportunity";
3. it provides substantial incentives for CRAs to inflate ratings and to issue ratings that please investors depending on the investor's holdings – ie. to defer or accelerate downgrades of popular and widely held bonds/loans; and or to inflate ratings of new-issue bonds/loans;
4. the model can be cumbersome and can be expensive to implement – however, the model is also a variant of the currently used and loosely enforced subscription-model of CRAs;
5. the model does not completely eliminate the Free-Rider problem – because users that obtain the information can still share it with third parties;
6. provides substantial incentives for CRAs to create "*ratings volatility*" in specific industries and or across industries in order to increase the number of registered "users" (ie. the CRA can purposely

issue divergent credit ratings for companies with similar characteristics and in the same industry, in order to compel more investors – especially "relative value" investors – to execute more trades).

As a *coordination mechanism*, the *User-Pays Model* is ineffective, because it reduces *positive Super-modularity* and *positive Strategic Complementarity* (*positive Super-modularity* and *positive Strategic Complementarity* both increase Social Welfare; while *Negative Super-modularity* and *Negative Strategic Complementarity* both reduce Social welfare).

Generally, for each of the above-mentioned business models, there is or can be significant *Consumer Surplus* or *Producer Surplus*; which when combined with other mentioned weaknesses is likely to result in *Deadweight Losses*.

The Government-Controlled or International Organization Controlled Ratings Agency Model

In this model, the government creates a government agency that will rate some or all bonds/loans and then publicly disclose the ratings – the CRA may charge fees to issuers, and or may charge subscription fees to investors. The pure "government ratings agency" model does not work well because of the following reasons. Under this business model, there is or can be an inherent conflict of interest – e.g. when the CRA is rating government bonds or municipal bonds. Under this business model, the CRA will or can be subject to political influence, which will undermine the CRA's reputation particularly when the CRA wants to rate foreign securities/assets, or companies that are owned by opposing politicians. In the absence of federal statutes that expressly bar lawsuits against such CRAs, this business model exposes the government to legal liability. Under this business model, if the CRA is funded through only national taxes, then it may not be able to cover the costs of its international operations; and if the CRA is funded with fees paid by issuers and or investors, then the above-mentioned limitations/problems may occur. Under this business model, the markets may also be wary of nationalism and protectionism in the CRA's operations and assigned ratings. Under this business model, a government CRA that is insulated from competition may not be efficient – and also the salary/compensation levels in a government CRA will probably be much lower than those of a private CRA. Under this business model, even CRAs that are established at the level of the EBRD, Asian Development Bank, IBRD or the World Bank (IMF or IFC) are subject to the same problems mentioned herein in this section. Under this business model, the *free-riding problem* remains and investors can obtain free ratings and research from sources other than the CRA. Under this business model, there is no implicit or explicit penalty (that can be assessed on CRAs) for low quality; and there is inadequate incentives for the CRA to perform and not shirk. This business model does not foster truthful disclosure by issuers – and issuers are not penalized for inadequate disclosure or inaccurate disclosure.

Under this business model, the CRA's efforts may not be correlated with the credibility of the assigned ratings; and there can be substantial goal incongruence and discord between the efforts of the CRA's staff (towards accurate ratings), and the CRA's firm-wide policies that pertain to business development, client retention and updating of ratings (it may not be cost-effective for the CRA to update ratings either frequently - monthly or quarterly - or when there is relevant news). Under this business model, there may be conflicts among the CRA's compensation/incentive system (which may reward employees based on the number of ratings completed, client relations; fees generated; etc.) on one hand, and secondly, the nature and magnitude of effort required to accurately rate assets, and thirdly, the effectiveness of the assigned ratings (timeliness; accuracy; relevance; credibility). This business model does not ensure or guarantee that increased competition will result in increased effort by CRAs – and the opposite may occur when:

1. the CRA charges non-standard fees and discriminatory/personalized fees for services;
2. the CRA has substantial brand equity;
3. the CRA does not face any reputational or monetary penalties for inaccurate ratings; d) the marginal cost of substitution of a CRA is relatively low;
4. the marginal propensity of an issuer to substitute a CRA is high.

This business model does not ensure or guarantee that increased competition will result in lower prices for ratings services – and the opposite may occur when:

1. some CRAs have substantial brand equity;
2. the CRA has expertise;
3. the cost structure of all or most CRAs are similar and are not affected by their pricing schemes and vice versa;
4. the marginal cost of substitution of a CRA is relatively low and the marginal propensity of an issuer to substitute a CRA is high.

This business model does not always encourage or facilitate revisions of ratings. In the case of ABS and Structured Products (where there is no real company or operations or company officers/CFO), the business model: a) can result in shirking by the CRA; and other misconduct.

This business model can fail where the *Marginal Cost Of Substitution* of the ratings process is low (including social, economic and psychological costs) – for example:

1. where the company is very well known and perceived to be stable and doesn't need a rating;
2. where financial stability and solvency are not the primary concerns of the company;
3. where the issuer has other verification or reputation mechanisms that are satisfactory to investors;
4. where the issuer is wealthy;
5. where the issuer has a third-party guarantor.

This business model can unfairly discriminate against smaller companies or poor companies, which is not socially optimal (ie. ideally, all companies should be able to afford ratings at least once or twice per year). Unless there are subsidies that reduce or eliminate ratings fees, the business model has or can have a substantial effect on the issuer's decision to offer securities. Ideally, the business model and payment systems should not affect the issuer's financing decisions.

Generally, for each of the above-mentioned business models, there is or can be significant *Consumer Surplus* or *Producer Surplus*; which when combined with other mentioned weaknesses is likely to result in *Deadweight Losses*.

The "Pure Platform" Model

The fourth class of business model is the "Pure Platform model" wherein the Platform matches the issuer and one or more CRAs, and the Platform selects the CRA and charges fees to issuers, and also pays fees to the CRAs. The "*Random Selection* model", and the "*Alternative User-Pays* model" and the "*Designation* model" and the "*Issuer And Investor Pays model*" which are described in United States Government Accountability Office (Jan. 2012), are all functional equivalents of this business model. A "platform model" may not work well because of the following reasons. The success of this business model is heavily dependent on the criteria for selecting and matching CRAs with issuers which may be inefficient and may result in misallocation of CRA's efforts and resources. If the selection/matching mechanism is based on an auction, it may result in some CRAs incurring operating losses, and or it may encourage collusion among CRAs. If the Matching Mechanism is based on a group of fixed criteria, it may encourage illegal collusion among CRAs. Under this business model, CRAs still have substantial incentives to inflate ratings of securities that investors like; and the *free-riding problem* remains and investors can obtain free ratings and research from sources other than the CRA. Under this business model, companies/issuers can shop for ratings among several CRAs unless they are specifically or statutorily limited to a specific number of ratings in each period (year or half-year or quarter). Under this business model, the problem of information asymmetry between investors and the issuer is not completely solved – the CRA often does not have complete information about the company or securities/assets (as was the case for several securitization Trusts rated by S&P and Moodys during 2003-2007); the securities/assets may be too complex for most investors to understand (as in ABS); or the issuer cannot divulge its trade secrets; or there is a "ratings Lag"; or the CRA's staff does not analyze the securities/assets properly (as in during 2003-2008). Under this business model, there is no implicit or explicit penalty (that can be assessed on CRAs) for *low quality*; and there are inadequate incentives for the CRA to perform and not shirk; and there is or can be an inherent conflict of interest. Similarly, the issuer does not face any penalties for fraudulent or inadequate disclosures.

This business model exposes the CRA and the Platform to legal liability – to lawsuits (from the issuers, the investors and the government; and other persons who maybe third-party beneficiaries of the CRA-issuer agreement) particularly where the Platform sets ratings-fees and or influences the quality of ratings. Such liability can be eliminated by protective statutes and by contract clauses. Also, depending on how the platform is structured, the CRA-Platform-issuer relationship may be deemed to be a joint venture or strategic alliance or "Business Opportunity".

One of the main problems in the models described in US GAO (2012) is that use of a clearinghouse to set ratings-fees and to functionally influence the cost structure of CRAs may be an adverse restriction of free market forces and may be deemed anti-competitive.

The "*Alternative User Pays model*" which is described in United States Government Accountability Office (Jan. 2012), is very inefficient because:

1. it does not consider the CRA's cost structure, and thus exposes the CRA to full market risk wherein the CRA may become insolvent or progressively become unable to function if user-volume declines;
2. the CRA's fee becomes a direct function of the number of "users" and not the actual cost of providing the ratings and this transforms the CRA-investor-issuer relationship into a strategic alliance or licensing or business opportunity;
3. it provides substantial incentives for CRAs to issue ratings that please investors depending on the investor's holdings (e.g. to defer downgrades of popular and widely held bonds/loans);
4. the model transforms the ratings fee into a transaction cost for the purchasers of securities, and depending on the magnitude of such transaction costs, it may affect investors' investment decisions;

5. the model makes CRAs more susceptible to influence of independent "ratings advisors" (who sometimes function as lobbyists) who can rally or dissuade investors;
6. the model is very cumbersome and can be expensive to implement – however, the model is also a variant of the currently used and loosely enforced subscription model of CRAs;
7. the auction process may become an unjustifiable restriction on market forces (where the auction process does not consider ratings quality, CRA expertise and other relevant factors) and the auction process may cause delays;
8. the proposal to require CRAs to certify on a quarterly basis that they exercised reasonable care in the ratings process, is almost ineffective because ratings processes are standardized and well known, and the two major variables have been and remain the truthfulness of issuers and unforeseen economic shocks.

As a *coordination mechanism*, the *Alternative User Pays Model* is ineffective, because it reduces positive Super-modularity and positive Strategic Complementarity.

Generally, for each of the above-mentioned business models, there is or can be significant *Consumer Surplus* or *Producer Surplus*; which when combined with other mentioned weaknesses is likely to result in *Deadweight Losses*.

The Investor-Owned Business Model

In this model, Institutional investors create and operate an NRSRO; and issuers are required to get two ratings, one from the investor-owned NRSRO and one from an NRSRO of their choice. An "*Investor Owned Model*" may not work well because of the following reasons. First, there is substantial conflict of interest because such CRA has significant incentives to delay downgrades so that investors don't have to recognize losses; and to inflate ratings of "established" companies whose securities are held by many investors; and to tip-off institutional investor-owners about upcoming ratings changes. This business model may also lead to actual or unintentional collusion among various classes of investors – e.g. to boycott a debt offering; or to manipulate securities and markets, etc.. The success of this business model is heavily dependent on the criteria for selecting investors and the amount of equity each investor owns in the CRA; and rights and disclosures that are granted to such investor-owners. Under this business model, CRAs still have substantial incentives to inflate ratings of securities that investors like; and the *free-riding problem* remains and non-owner investors can obtain free ratings and research from sources other than the CRA. Under this business model, companies/issuers can shop for ratings among several CRAs unless they are specifically or statutorily limited to a specific number of ratings in each period (year or half-year or quarter). Under this business model, the problem of information asymmetry between investors and the issuer is not completely solved – the CRA often does not have complete information about the company or securities/assets (as was the case for several securitization Trusts rated by S&P and Moodys during 2003-2007); and the securities/assets may be too complex for most investors to understand (as in ABS); or the issuer cannot divulge its trade secrets; or there is a "*Ratings Lag*"; or the CRA's staff does not analyze the securities/assets properly (as in during 2003-2008). Under this business model, there is no implicit or explicit penalty (that can be assessed on CRAs) for low quality ratings; and there are inadequate incentives for the CRA to perform and not shirk. Similarly, the issuer and investment bank does not face any penalties for fraudulent or inadequate disclosures.

This business model exposes the CRA and the investor-owners to substantial legal liability – to lawsuits (from the issuers, and the government; and other persons who maybe third-party beneficiaries of the CRA-issuer agreement), particularly where the investor-owners have operating control or where majority ownership of such CRA is concentrated in a few investors. Such liability can be eliminated by protective statutes and by contract clauses.

The use of this business model can result in significant *Consumer Surplus* or *Producer Surplus*; which when combined with other mentioned weaknesses is likely to result in *Deadweight Losses.*

Note that in the new European Commission Rules for CRA, in order to reduce the risk of conflicts of interest, CRAs must publicly disclose whether a shareholder that owns more than five percent of shares or votes of the CRA, also holds five percent or more of a rated entity; and the rules expressly bar a CRA from rating an issuer when a shareholder that owns more than ten percent of the CRA's capital or voting rights also holds ten percent or more of the issuer's capital or voting rights. The European Commission's new regulations also prohibits any person from owning five percent or more of the capital or the voting rights of more than one CRA, unless the CRAs are part of the same group (cross-shareholding).

The "Hybrid Model"

The sixth class of business model is the "Hybrid model" wherein the issuer and the investors pay part of the ratings fees either at one time, or over a period of time. The "*Designation* model" and the "*Issuer And Investor Pays model*" which are described in United States Government Accountability Office (Jan. 2012), are all functional equivalents and variations of the *Hybrid Model.* A "*Hybrid Model*" may not work well because of the following reasons. The success of this business model is heavily dependent on the method of allocation of ratings-fees among the issuer and the investors, and thus this model raises major concerns about Fairness of such allocations and timing of the allocated ratings fees which will be sub-consciously or consciously deemed to be transaction costs. The success of this business model is also heavily dependent on the determination of ratings fees – the actual amounts and the party that specifies the fees. Under this model, the CRAs can lose their ability to set their own fees, and such condition may be deemed to be anti-competitive. Under this business model, CRAs still have substantial incentives to inflate ratings of securities that investors like; and the *free-riding problem* remains and investors can obtain free ratings and research from sources other than the CRA. Under this business model, companies/issuers can shop for ratings among several CRAs unless they are specifically or statutorily limited to a specific number of ratings in each period (year or half-year or quarter). Under this business model, the problem of information asymmetry between investors and the issuer is not completely solved – the CRA often does not have complete information about the company or securities/assets (as was the case for several securitization Trusts rated by S&P and Moodys during 2003-2007); the securities/assets may be too complex for most investors to understand (as in ABS); or the issuer cannot divulge its trade secrets; or there is a "ratings Lag"; or the CRA's staff does not analyze the securities/assets properly (as in during 2003-2008). Under this business model, there is no implicit or explicit penalty (that can be assessed on CRAs) for low quality; and there is inadequate incentives for the CRA to perform and not shirk; and there is or can be an inherent conflict of interest. Similarly, the issuer does not face any penalties for fraudulent or inadequate disclosures. Under this business model, the CRA can lose its ability to manage its cost structure effectively.

This business model exposes the CRA and investors to legal liability – to lawsuits from the non-participating investors and the government. Such liability can be eliminated by protective statutes and by contract clauses.

The *Designation Model* (e.g. described in US GAO (2012)) is very problematic because:

1. it significantly reduces competition among CRAs (ie. the probability that a CRA will be paid fees from each offering of rated-debt substantially increases);
2. it reduces or can reduce the quality of each CRA's ratings because each participating CRA has less incentives to be more accurate or to compete based on higher accuracy;
3. the CRA faces no penalties for shirking or inaccuracy; and the issuer is not subject to any penalties for inadequate or fraudulent disclosures to CRAs;
4. it increases the probability of quality-eroding collusion among CRAs;
5. it increases the probability of collusion among prospective investors (e.g. collusion to select favored CRAs; and or collusion to reduce ratings fees; and or collusion to influence loan/bond prices).

As proposed, the *Designation Model* did not specify how ratings fees would be determined or how a third party will allocate fees paid by investors among the designated CRAs, but states that issuers can negotiate fees with the CRAs or the CRA can set its fees. The "*Issuer And Investor Pays model*" which is described in United States GAO (Jan. 2012) is inefficient because of the following reasons:

1. placing CRAs in a queue and assigning ratings projects based on such queue reduces or can reduce competition in the CRA industry;
2. it results in efficient allocation of projects because assignments are not based on CRAs' skill or quality history; and it rewards only those CRAs who complete ratings projects quickly;
3. it reduces or eliminates issuer choice;
4. ratings fees will be funded from a fee levied on issuers of new debt issues and transactional fees charged to investors as parties of secondary market trades – thus the CRA's ratings-fee becomes a direct function of the number of secondary market trades/transactions and the size of the debt offering (and not the actual cost of providing the ratings) and this transforms the CRA-investor-issuer relationship into a strategic alliance or licensing or business opportunity;
5. it does not consider the CRA's cost structure, and thus exposes the CRA to full market risk wherein the CRA may become insolvent or progressively become unable to function if post-ratings trading-volume declines or if the debt offering is small;
6. it provides substantial incentives for CRAs to issue ratings that please investors depending on the investor's holdings (e.g. to defer downgrades of popular and widely held bonds/loans);
7. the model transforms the ratings fee into a transaction cost for the purchasers of securities, and depending on the magnitude of such transaction costs, it may affect investors' investment decisions;
8. the model makes CRAs more susceptible to influence of independent "ratings advisors" (who sometimes function as lobbyists) who can rally or dissuade investors;
9. the model is very cumbersome and can be expensive to implement;
10. the auction process may become an unjustifiable restriction on market forces (where the auction process does not consider ratings quality, CRA expertise and other relevant factors) and the auction process may cause delays;

11. the proposal to require CRAs to certify on a quarterly basis that they exercised reasonable care in the ratings process, is almost ineffective because ratings processes are standardized and well known, and the two major variables have been and remain the truthfulness of issuers and unforeseen economic shocks;
12. the model reduces competition among CRAs because it increases the probability that each licensed CRA will earn ratings-fees within any given time interval – and this may result in quality-erosion.

Generally, for each of the above-mentioned business models, there is or can be significant *Consumer Surplus* or *Producer Surplus*; which when combined with other mentioned weaknesses is likely to result in *Deadweight Losses* (and penalty-incentive conflicts; and incentives-welfare incongruence).

The "Market-Pay Model"

The seventh class of business model is the "*Market Pay model*" which is summarized in United States Government Accountability Office (Jan. 2012). The *Market-Pay Model* is inefficient because:

1. ratings fees will be funded from a fee levied on issuers upon payment of each coupon/dividend – thus, the CRA's ratings-fee becomes a direct function of the size of the offering and the maturity date of the bond/loan (and not the actual cost of providing the ratings) and this transforms the CRA-investor-issuer relationship into a strategic alliance or licensing or business opportunity;
2. it does not consider the CRA's cost structure, and thus exposes the CRA to full market risk wherein the CRA may become insolvent or progressively become unable to function if it rates mostly short-term securities/instruments and or small-volume debt offerings;
3. it provides substantial incentives for CRAs to inflate ratings and to issue ratings that please investors depending on the investor's holdings (e.g. to defer downgrades of popular and widely held bonds/loans);
4. the model transforms the ratings fee into a transaction cost for the issuers of securities, and depending on the magnitude of such transaction costs, it may affect issuers' financing decisions and investors' investment decisions and compel issuers to issue mostly short-term debt or mezzanine equity or regular equity;
5. the model makes CRAs more susceptible to the influence of independent "ratings advisors" (who sometimes function as lobbyists) who can rally or dissuade investors.

The use of this model can result in significant *Consumer Surplus* or *Producer Surplus*; which when combined with other mentioned weaknesses is likely to result in *Deadweight Losses* (and *Penalty-Incentive Conflicts*; and *Incentives-Welfare Incongruence*).

INTERNATIONAL CAPITAL FLOWS AND INTERNATIONAL TRADE

Unfortunately, the "*Big-Three*" CRAs (Moodys, Fitch and S&P) collectively have more than ninety percent market share in the CRA industry; and now affect the equivalent of more than eighty trillion US dollars of securities, swaps/derivatives and financial instruments globally, and thus have a significant and growing effect on international capital flows. A growing percentage of international trade relationships/contracts are based on the credit ratings of foreign trade counter-parties. That is, credit ratings are a critical factor and criteria in the origination, structuring, management and regulation of international strategic alliances, licensing, structured trade financing; international factoring; international long-term supply agreements; off-take agreements; etc.. See: Tomashevskiy & Kono (2015); and Collis, Jarvis & Page (2013). Muuls (2015) discussed the relationship between credit ratings and trade, but some of the models are not entirely correct. Credit ratings also contribute to international financial contagion – e.g. a ratings downgrade of a large US company (e.g. Apple) or a group of smaller companies can result in declines of the credit ratings and or stock prices of their suppliers in Asia or South America. The ratings-based international-investor demand for ABS/MBS, US treasuries and structured securities causes contagion. Also various studies have documented credit ratings contagions in Europe and other regions. Various academic studies have noted that sovereign credit ratings affect international capital flows. The relationship between credit ratings and international capital flows can be significant but is often omitted in academic studies of both phenomena as was the case in Forbes, Warnock & Francis (2012). See: UNCTAD (Nov. 2015), Emara & Said (2015), Bernanke, Bertaut, et. al. (2011), Ntswane (2014) and Fourie & Botha (2015). These factors in turn, affect global systemic risk, trade-deficits, financial stability, and many elements of national economies such as the borrowing costs of governments and companies, FDI, investments in foreign securities, household economics, overall regulatory compliance, consumer-confidence, availability of products/services; excessive consumer/sovereign/municipal/corporate debt; declining productivity; etc. See: Skreta & Veldkamp (2009), de Haan & Amtenbrink (Jan. 2011) and Deb, Manning & Murphy, et. al. (March 2011).

CRA compensation models directly affects the quality of ratings and the psychology of issuers and investors, and perceived/actual compliance with financial regulations that are partly or wholly based on credit ratings. Thus CRA compensation models affect International capital flows, international asset-allocation and trade in several ways including but not limited to the following:

1. The *Issuer-Pays Model* ("IssPM" – issuers pay fees directly to the CRA) encourages ratings shopping by issuers. Ratings shopping tends to delay the issuer's capital raising process and increases uncertainty within institutional investors, which in turn affects capital flows and international trade. The IssPM provides significant incentives for CRAs to inflate ratings in order to generate fees and that has a direct effect on cross-border capital flows and investors' international asset allocation decisions and regulatory compliance – higher ratings encourage cross-border capital flows and trade and increases "apparent compliance" with financial regulations; and vice versa. The IssPM discourages poor countries and small (or cash constrained) issuers from obtaining credit ratings and thus, they are less likely to raise capital in global markets or effect international trade transactions – and thus international capital flow will be lower and FDI investors will generally be less willing to invest in such countries. Given the inherent conflicts of interest, the IssPM also decreases the reliability of credit ratings to investors (especially international investors) and trade counterparties, who then have to commit more resources to credit research and due diligence, which in turn affects their expected returns and asset allocation and thus, affects international capital flows.
2. The "*Issuer Selects Model*" ("IssSM" – the issuer selects the CRA and the fee is paid by the issuer or investor(s)) is a hybrid model that has the same problems as the IssPM.
3. The Investor-Pays Model ("InvPM" - investors pay fees directly to the CRA) provides significant incentives for CRAs to deflate ratings and or to become over-conservative and that has a direct effect on capital flows and investors' international asset allocation decision – it tends to reduce

international capital flows and international trade. The InvPM can create more uncertainty within issuers and trade counterparties (about ratings prospects, investors' reactions; pricing of securities/instruments; etc.), which in turn delays issuers' capital raising processes and trade decisions and thus, reduces international capital flows and trade. The InvPM makes cash-constrained, small or contractually-constrained investors or trade counterparties to become heavily dependent on the decisions and investment patterns of large or un-constrained investors or trade counterparties who can afford (or are contractually permitted) to pay ratings fees – that can increase "herding" in markets and clearly affects capital flows, cross-border trade and international asset allocation decisions. The InvPM is more likely (than IssPM) to make investors become over-reliant on credit ratings and that directly affects international asset allocation decisions and capital flows. As of 2017, FDI accounted for a much larger percentage of total capital flows to developing countries than two decades ago. FDI investors are usually large companies (and not insurance companies, funds or foundations); and under the InvPM, FDI investors are less likely (than institutional investors) to seek ratings from CRAs and that in turn affects FDI investors' due diligence costs and expected returns, and thus affects international capital flows.

4. The "*Investor Selects Model*" ("InvSM" – the issuer selects the CRA and the fee is paid by the issuer or investor(s)) is a hybrid model that has the same problems as the InvPM and IssPM.
5. The "*Hybrid Direct Payment Model*" ("HDPM" – both the issuer and investors pay the ratings fees directly to the CRA) presents the same problems as IssPM and InvPM. Under this HDPM model, the CRAs still have substantial incentives to inflate ratings; and there is a *free-riding problem*; and issuers can shop for ratings among several CRAs unless they are specifically or statutorily limited to a specific number of ratings in each period (year or half-year or quarter); and there is no implicit or explicit penalty (that can be assessed on CRAs) for low quality; and there is inadequate incentives for the CRA to perform and not shirk; and there is or can be an inherent conflict of interest. All these factors directly affect international capital flows, asset allocation and trade.
6. In a substantial portion of international trade (e.g. international strategic alliances and joint ventures; supply agreements; trade financing; etc.) the probability of transactions occurring depends on credit ratings of the parties and the sovereign credit ratings. The payment cycles of such transactions are relatively short. Under IssPM, HDPM and InvPM, often there are significant ratings-lags, and the inherent conflicts-of-interest reduces credibility of corporate ratings all of which affect international capital flows and trade. Thus many trade counterparties conduct more regular credit reviews of their trade and financing counterparties which increases their due diligence costs and "expected"/required returns and affects the volumes of international trade and capital flows.
7. CRAs perform Unsolicited And Un-Compensated Ratings (UURs) without the issuer's permission and with no or very limited information from the issuer. This obviously affects the quality of corporate credit ratings. Various academic and practitioner articles have noted that CRAs use UURs to force issuers to pay for credit ratings; and that UURs are generally lower than paid ratings (paid for by the issuer or investor). Thus, when the volume of UURs exceed that of paid-ratings, international capital flows are likely to decline, and vice versa.
8. Even for institutional investors that are not legally (e.g. pension funds; foundations; etc.) or contractually (e.g. hedge funds; mutual funds; insurance companies; etc.) permitted to invest in foreign securities, CRA compensation models indirectly and significantly affect international capital flows because some of their investee-companies (e.g. large MNEs) invest in, or consider investing in foreign countries and foreign securities/loans.

9. Various academic studies have reported that CRAs' reputation effects support the liquidity, depth and viability of various financial markets (corporate bonds; ABS/MBS; CDS; stocks; currencies; etc.), and thus affect international capital flows and asset allocation. Such reputation effects are likely to be greater in InvPM regimes than in IssPM regimes.
10. During 2000-2017, there was intensive debate in many countries about the liability of CRAs for inaccurate/misleading ratings; and some institutional investors sued CRAs. The liability of CRAs is closely tied to CRA compensation models and the associated conflicts-of-interest – IssPM and HDPM are more likely to result in greater liability for CRAs than InvPM. All else held constant, international investors are more likely to invest in countries where CRAs are more likely to be held liable for inaccurate credit ratings ("high liability countries") and vice versa.

CONCLUSION: SYSTEMIC RISK AND FINANCIAL INSTABILITY

It's clear from the above and from the existing literature that CRAs (and their credit ratings) can cause or increase Systemic Risk and Financial Instability in the following ways. Credit ratings affect bond prices, and ratings downgrades can trigger Contagion in markets and reduce liquidity – ie. the downgrades of any of the major international insurers or international banks. CRA compensation affects or can affect the quality and ranking of credit ratings. There are ratings-lags in many of the ratings of the top three ratings agencies (moody, S&P and Fitch); and many investors still rely on CRAs' ratings.

Banks, insurance companies, investment funds, hedge funds, pension funds and large institutional investors embed credit ratings (provided by Moodys, S&P and Fitch) into their internal risk management systems, trading policies, investment criteria and operational policies. Credit ratings have or can have a significant impact on the liquidity of loans, bonds, Certificates-of-Deposit, guarantees and securities. See comments in: Skreta & Veldkamp (2009), de Haan & Amtenbrink (Jan. 2011), Deb, Manning & Murphy, et. al. (March 2011), Pagano & Volpin (2010a;b), Kuhner (2001) and Sy (December 2009).

Current and proposed CRA compensation models and business models provide significant incentives for regulated and un-regulated CRAs to issue low un-solicited ratings to, or downgrade ratings of companies that don't formally contract with such CRA for a fee-based credit-ratings; and to issue higher-than-justifiable credit-ratings for paid-ratings. Current and proposed CRA compensation models and business models can also amplify/exacerbate the Antitrust problems, the *Excessive Influence* of the Big-3 CRAs, and the "Tie-Breaker Phenomenon in the global CRA industry.

REFERENCES

Abad, P., Ferreras, R., & Robles, D. (2020). Information opacity and corporate bond returns: The dynamics of split ratings. *Journal of International Financial Markets, Institutions and Money*, *68*, 68. doi:10.1016/j.intfin.2020.101239

Abrantes-Metz, R. (2012). *Credit Rating Agencies, the Financial Crisis, and Regulation*. https://www.globaleconomicsgroup.com/financial-regulation/credit-rating-agencies-the-financial-crisis-and-regulation/

Aguirre, A. (2017). Contracting institutions and economic growth. *Review of Economic Dynamics*, *24*, 192–217. doi:10.1016/j.red.2017.01.009

Alissa, W., & Koharki, K. (2013). Firms' use of accounting discretion to influence their credit ratings. *Journal of Accounting and Economics*, *55*(2), 129–147. doi:10.1016/j.jacceco.2013.01.001

Alp, A. (2014). Structural shifts in credit rating standards. *The Journal of Finance*, *68*(6), 2435–2470. doi:10.1111/jofi.12070

Ayotte, K., & Bolton, P. (2011). *Covenant lite lending, liquidity, and standardization of financial contracts*. Chapter. In P. Bolon (Ed.), *Research Handbook on the Economics of Property Law* (pp. 174–189). Edward Elgar Publishing Ltd. doi:10.4337/9781849808972.00013

Baffi, E. (2007). The Economics of Standard Form Contracts. Università degli Studi "Guglielmo Marconi".

Baffi, E. (2012). Contracting in modern world. *Aperta Contrada*. https://www.apertacontrada.it/2012/11/13/contracting-in-modern-world/

Baffi, E. (2000). *Some Characteristic Features of Mass Contracting*. Università degli Studi "Roma Tre" – Faculty of Law".

Bai, L. (2010). On Regulating Conflicts of Interest in the Credit Rating Industry. *NYU Journal Of Legislation And Public Policy*, *13*, 253–263.

Bannier, C., & Hirsch, C. (2010). The economic function of credit CRAs - What does the watchlist tell us. *Journal of Banking & Finance*, *34*(12), 3037–3049. doi:10.1016/j.jbankfin.2010.07.002

Bar-Isaac, H., & Shapiro, J. (2013). Ratings Quality over the Business Cycle. *Journal of Financial Economics*, *108*(1), 62–78. doi:10.1016/j.jfineco.2012.11.004

Beaver, W. H., Shakespeare, C., & Soliman, M. (2006). Differential properties in the ratings of certified versus non-certified bond-CRAs. *Journal of Accounting and Economics*, *42*(3), 303–334. doi:10.1016/j.jacceco.2006.06.002

Becker, B., & Milbourn, T. (2011). How did increased competition affect credit ratings? *Journal of Financial Economics*, *101*(3), 493–514. doi:10.1016/j.jfineco.2011.03.012

Bernanke, B., & Bertaut, C. (2011). *International Capital Flows and the Returns to Safe Assets in the United States, 2003-2007*. Board of Governors of the Federal Reserve System - International Finance Discussion Papers Number 1014. https://www.federalreserve.gov/pubs/ifdp/2011/1014/ifdp1014.pdf

Best, A. M. (2013). *Compensation Disclosure*. Available at: http://www.ambest.com/nrsro/CompensationDisclosure.pdf

Bolton, P., Freixas, X., & Shapiro, J. (2012). The Credit Ratings Game. *The Journal of Finance*, *67*(1), 85–112. doi:10.1111/j.1540-6261.2011.01708.x

Bongaerts, D. (2013). *Can Alternative Business Models Discipline Credit CRAs*? Working Paper.

Bongaerts, D., Cremers, M., & Goetzmann, W. (2012). Tie-Breaker: Certification And Multiple Credit Ratings. *The Journal of Finance*, *67*(1), 113–152. doi:10.1111/j.1540-6261.2011.01709.x

Bonsall, S. (2012). *The Informational Effects of Firm-Funded Certification: Evidence from the Bond CRAs*. The Pennsylvania State University, Smeal College of Business.

Boot, A., Milboum, T., & Schmeits, A. (2006). Credit Ratings as Coordination Mechanisms. *Review of Financial Studies, 19*(1), 81–118. doi:10.1093/rfs/hhj009

Borio, C. (2008). *The financial turmoil of 2007–? A preliminary assessment and some policy considerations*. Monetary and Economic Department, BIS Working Papers No. 251.

Byoun, S., Han, S., & Shin, Y. (2020). Does the Nationally Recognized Statistical Rating Organization certification matter for Japanese credit rating agencies? *Journal of Financial Markets.*

Camanho, N., Deb, P., & Liu, Z. (2012). *Credit Rating and Competition.* Working Paper, Financial Markets Group, London School of Economics and Political Science.

Cantor, R., & Packer, F. (1997). Differences of opinion and selection bias in the credit rating industry. *Journal of Banking & Finance, 21*(10), 1395–1417. doi:10.1016/S0378-4266(97)00024-1

Cash, D. (2018). Sustainable finance ratings as the latest symptom of 'rating addiction'. *Journal of Sustainable Finance & Investment, 8*(3), 242–258. doi:10.1080/20430795.2018.1437996

Cash, D. (2020). Sustainable rating agencies. *Finance and Sustainable Development: Designing Sustainable Financial Systems*, 141.

Cash, D. (2021). Can Regulatory Intervention Save the Sustainability Rating Industry? *Business Law Review.*

Champsaur, A. (2005). *The Regulation Of Credit CRAs In The US And The EU: Recent Initiatives And Proposals* (Un-Published LL.M. Thesis).

Chen, Z., & Matousek, R. (2019). Do rating agencies exhibit herding behaviour? Evidence from sovereign ratings. *International Review of Financial Analysis, 64*, 57–70.

Cheng, M., & Neamtiu, M. (2009). An empirical analysis of changes in credit rating properties: Timeliness, accuracy and volatility. *Journal of Accounting and Economics, 47*(1-2), 108–130. doi:10.1016/j.jacceco.2008.11.001

Coffee, J. (2011). Ratings Reform: The Good, the Bad, and the Ugly. *Harvard. Business Law Review, 1*, 231–234.

Collis, J., Jarvis, R., & Page, M. (2013). *SMEs, Financial Reporting and Trade Credit: An International Study*. The Council of the Association of Chartered Certified Accountants. http://www.accaglobal.com/ab77

Cornaggia, J., & Cornaggia, K. J. (2013). Estimating the Costs of Issuer-Paid Credit Ratings. *Review of Financial Studies, 26*(9), 2270–2310. doi:10.1093/rfs/hht041

Covitz, D., & Harrison, P. (2003). *Testing Conflicts of Interest At Bond CRAs with Market Anticipation: Evidence That Reputation Incentives Dominate*. Finance & Economics Discussion Series 2003-68. Board Of Governors of The Federal Reserve System.

Creighton, A., Gower, L., & Richards, A. (2007). The Impact of Rating Changes in Australian Financial Markets. *Pacific-Basin Finance Journal, 15*(1), 1–17. doi:10.1016/j.pacfin.2006.04.003

Dallocchio, M., Hubler, J., Raimbourg, P., & Salvi, A. (2006). Do Upgradings and Downgradings Convey Information? An Event Study of the French Bond Market. *Economic Notes*, *35*(30), 293–317. doi:10.1111/j.1468-0300.2006.00167.x

Darbellay, A. (2013). *Regulating Credit Rating Agencies*. Edward Elgar. doi:10.4337/9780857939364

de Haan, J., & Amtenbrink, F. (2011). *Credit Rating Agencies*. De Nederlandsche Bank Working Paper No. 278.

Deb, P., Manning, M., Murphy, G., Penalver, A., & Toth, A. (2011). Whither the credit ratings industry? Financial Stability Paper #9, Bank of England.

Dekker, H., Kawai, T., & Sakaguchi, J. (2018). Contracting abroad: A comparative analysis of contract design in host and home country outsourcing relations. *Management Accounting Research*, *40*, 47–61. doi:10.1016/j.mar.2017.09.003

Di Cesare, A. (2006). Do Market-Based Indicators Anticipate Rating Agencies? Evidence for International Banks. *Economic Notes*, *35*(1), 121–150. doi:10.1111/j.0391-5026.2006.00161.x

Diomande, M., Heintz, J., & Pollin, R. (2009). Why U.S. Financial Markets Need a Public Credit CRA. *The Economists' Voice*. www.bepress.com/ev

Dittrich, F. (2007). *The credit rating industry: Competition and regulation* (PhD dissertation). zur Erlangung Des Doktorgrades der Wirtschafts- und Sozialwissenschaftlichen Fakultat der Universitat zu Koln, Germany.

Doherty, N. A., Kartasheva, A. V., & Phillips, R. D. (2012). Information effect of entry into credit ratings market: The case of insurers' ratings. *Journal of Financial Economics*, *106*(2), 308–330. doi:10.1016/j.jfineco.2012.05.012

Drozd, L., & Serrano-Padia, R. (2018). Financial contracting with enforcement externalities. *Journal of Economic Theory*, *178*, 153–189. doi:10.1016/j.jet.2018.09.002

Du, W. (2018). Who carried more credibility?: An analysis of the market responses to news from the Japanese government, the Japanese central bank and international credit rating agencies. *Journal of Economics and Business*, *98*, 32–39. doi:10.1016/j.jeconbus.2018.05.002

Eenmaa-Dimitrieva, H., & Schmidt-Kessen, M. (2019). Creating markets in no-trust environments: The law and economics of smart contracts. *Computer Law & Security Review*, *35*(1), 69–88. doi:10.1016/j.clsr.2018.09.003

Ekins, E., & Calabria, M. (2012). *Regulation, Market Structure, and Role of the Credit Rating Agencies*. Policy Analysis #704. Cato Institute. https://object.cato.org/pubs/pas/PA704.pdf

Ellsworth, L., & Bhabha, I. (2008). *A New Front in Subprime Litigation: Can CRAs Be Held Liable?* LAW360. https://www.law360.com/articles/65936

Emara, N., & Said, A. (2015). *Revisiting Sovereign Ratings, Capital Flows and Financial Contagion in Emerging Markets*. EconWorld2015@Torino, Torino, Italy. https://torino2015.econworld.org/assets/emara_elsaid.pdf

Fang, X., & Yuan, F. (2018). The Coordination and Preference of Supply Chain Contracts Based on Time-Sensitivity Promotional Mechanism. *Journal of Management Science and Engineering*, *3*(3), 158–178. doi:10.3724/SP.J.1383.303009

Faure-Grimaud, A., Peyrachie, E., & Quesada, L. (2009). The ownership Of Ratings. *The RAND Journal of Economics*, *40*(2), 234–257. doi:10.1111/j.1756-2171.2009.00063.x

Fennell, D., & Medvedev, A. (2011). *An Economic Analysis Of Credit CRA Business Models And ratings Accuracy*. Financial Services Occassional Paper #41.

Ferri, G., Liu, L., & Stiglitz, J. (1999). The Pro-cyclical Role of Rating Agencies: Evidence from the East Asian Crisis. *Economic Notes*, *28*(3), 335–355. doi:10.1111/1468-0300.00016

Finch, N. (2004). *International Rating Agencies And Sustainability*. Working Paper, Macquarie University.

Fitzgerald, F. (2002). *The Use of Insurance Credit Scoring In Automobile and Homeowners Insurance: A Report to the Governor, the Legislature and the People of Michigan*. Available at: https://www.michigan.gov/documents/cis_ofis_credit_scoring_report_52885_7.pdf

Fitzpatrick, T., & Sagers, C. (2009). Faith-Based Financial Regulation: A Primer on Oversight of Credit Rating Organizations. *Administrative Law Review*, *61*, 557–587. doi:10.2139srn.1375034

Flannery, M., Houston, J., & Partnoy, F. (2010). Credit Default Swap Spreads as Viable Substitutes for Credit Ratings. *University of Pennsylvania Law Review*, *158*, 2085–2095.

Forbes, K., Warnock, J., & Francis, E. (2012). Capital flow waves: Surges, stops, flight, and retrenchment. *Journal of International Economics*, *88*(2), 235–251. doi:10.1016/j.jinteco.2012.03.006

Fourie, L., & Botha, I. (2015). Sovereign Credit Rating Contagion in the EU. *Procedia Economics and Finance*, *24*, 218–227. doi:10.1016/S2212-5671(15)00651-6

Freifeld, K. (July 10, 2013). *Liquidators of failed Bear Stearns funds sue ratings agencies*. https://www.reuters.com/article/2013/07/10/us-ratings-agency-lawsuitidUSBRE9690QV20130710

Frost, C. (2009). Credit CRAs in Capital Markets: A Review of Research Evidence on Selected Criticisms of the Agencies. *Journal of Accounting, Auditing & Finance*, *22*(3), 469–492. doi:10.1177/0148558X0702200306

FSB. (2010). *Principles for Reducing the Reliance on Ratings*. Available at: www.financialstabilityboard.org/publications/r_101027.pdf

Fulghieri, P., Strobl, L., & Xia, H. (2010). *The Economics Of Solicited And Un-Solicited Credit Ratings*. Working Paper.

Galil, K., & Soer, G. (2011). Good news, bad news and rating announcements: An empirical investigation. *Journal of Banking & Finance*, *35*(11), 3101–3119. doi:10.1016/j.jbankfin.2011.04.010

Garcia, R., & del Pozo, J. (2012). *Credit Rating Agencies on the Watch List: Analysis of European Regulation*. Oxford University Press. doi:10.1093/acprof:oso/9780199608867.001.0001

Goetz, R., Yatsenko, Y., Hritonenko, N., Xabadia, A., & Abdulai, A. (2019). The dynamics of productive assets, contract duration and holdup. *Mathematical Social Sciences*, *97*, 24–37. doi:10.1016/j.mathsocsci.2018.10.004

Gomes, R. (2014). Optimal auction design in two-sided markets. *The RAND Journal of Economics*, *45*(2), 248–272. doi:10.1111/1756-2171.12050

Goodhart, C. (2008). *How, if at all, should Credit Rating s Agencies (CRAs) be Regulated?* LSE Financial Markets Group Paper Series, special paper #181.

Govindan, S., & Wilson, R. (2006). Sufficient conditions for stable equilibria. *Theoretical Economics*, *1*, 167–206. https://econtheory.org/ojs/index.php/te/article/viewFile/20060167/617/25

Grin, J., & Tang, D. (2012). Did subjectivity play a role in CDO Credit Ratings? *The Journal of Finance*, *67*(4), 1293–1328. doi:10.1111/j.1540-6261.2012.01748.x

Gromb, D., & Martimort, D. (2007). Collusion And The Organization Of Delegated Expertise. *Journal of Economic Theory*, *137*(1), 271–299. doi:10.1016/j.jet.2007.01.003

Gudzowski, M. (2010). Mortgage Credit Ratings and the Financial Crisis: The Need for a State-Run Mortgage Securities CRAs. *Columbia Business Law Review*, *10*, 245–255.

He, J., Qian, J., & Strahan, P. E. (2012). Are All Ratings Created Equal? The Impact of Issuer Size on the Pricing of Mortgage-Backed Securities. *The Journal of Finance*, *67*, 2097–2137.

He, Q., Xue, C., & Zhou, S. (2019). Does contracting institution affect the patterns of industrial specialization in China? *China Economic Review*, *54*, 191–203. doi:10.1016/j.chieco.2018.11.003

Hemraj, M. (2015). *Credit Rating Agencies: Self-regulation, Statutory Regulation and Case Law*. Springer. doi:10.1007/978-3-319-17927-8

Hill, C. (2003). CRAs Behaving Badly: The Case of Enron. *Connecticut Law Review*, *35*, 1145–1155.

Hill, C. (2004). Regulating the CRAs. *Washington Law Quarterly*, *82*, 43–53.

Hill, C. (2009). Why Did Anyone Listen to the CRAs After Enron? *Journal of Business & Technology Law*, *4*, 283-293.

Hill, C. (2010). Why Did CRAs Do Such a Bad Job Rating Subprime Securities? *University of Pittsburgh Law Review. University of Pittsburgh. School of Law*, *71*, 585–595.

Hill, C. (2011). Limits of Dodd-Frank's CRA Reform. *Chapman Law Review*, *15*, 133–143.

Hong, S., Wernz, C., & Stillinger, J. (2016). Optimizing maintenance service contracts through mechanism design theory. *Applied Mathematical Modelling*, *40*(21-22), 8849–8861. doi:10.1016/j.apm.2015.07.009

Honohan, P. (2001). Perverse Effects of an External Ratings-Related Capital Adequacy System. *Economic Notes*, *30*(3), 359–372. doi:10.1111/1468-0300.00063

Hoppe, E., & Schmitz, P. (2018). Hidden action and outcome contractibility: An experimental test of moral hazard theory. *Games and Economic Behavior*, *109*, 544–564. doi:10.1016/j.geb.2018.02.006

Hu, X., Huang, H., Pan, Z., & Shi, J. (2019). Information asymmetry and credit rating: A quasi-natural experiment from China. *Journal of Banking & Finance*, *106*, 132–152. doi:10.1016/j.jbankfin.2019.06.003

Huang, Y., & Shen, C. (2019). What role does the investor-paid rating agency play in China? Competitor or information provider. *International Review of Economics & Finance*, *63*, 253–272. doi:10.1016/j.iref.2018.11.007

Humphrey, C. (2018). *The Role of Credit Rating Agencies in Shaping Multilateral Finance: Recent Developments and Policy Options.* Discussion draft, Inter-Governmental Group of, 24.

Hunt, J. (2009). Credit CRAs and the "Worldwide Credit Crisis": The Limits of Reputation, the Insufficiency of Reform, and a Proposal for Improvement. *Columbia Business Law Review*, *2009*, 109–119.

Husisian, G. (1990). What Standard of Care Should Govern the World's shortest Editorials?: An Analysis of Bond CRA Liability. *Cornell Law Review*, *75*, 411–460.

Ioannou, S., Wójcik, D., & Pažitka, D. (2020). Financial centre bias in sub-sovereign credit ratings. *Journal of International Financial Markets, Institutions and Money.*

IOSCO. (2008). *The role of credit CRAs in structured finance markets.* Final Report.

Iossa, E., & Martimort, D. (2018). Corruption in PPPs, incentives and contract incompleteness. *International Journal of Industrial Organization*, *44*, 85–100. doi:10.1016/j.ijindorg.2015.10.007

Ismailescu, I., & Kazemi, H. (2010). The reaction of emerging market credit default swap spreads to sovereign credit rating changes. *Journal of Banking & Finance*, *34*(12), 2861–2873. doi:10.1016/j.jbankfin.2010.05.014

Jiang, J., Stanford, M., & Xie, Y. (2012). Does It Matter Who Pays For Bond Ratings? Historical Evidence. *Journal of Financial Economics*, *105*(3), 607–621. doi:10.1016/j.jfineco.2012.04.001

Kashyap, A., & Kovrijnykh, N. (2013). *Who Should Pay For Credit ratings And How?* Working Paper. University of Chicago.

KerwerD. (2001). Standardization as Governance: The Case of Credit CRAs 3 (MPI Collective Goods, Preprint No. 2001/3, 2001. Available at http://ssrn.com/absract=269311

Kettering, K. (2008). Securitization and Its Discontents: The Dynamics of Financial Product Development. *Cardozo Law Review*, *29*, 1687–1693.

Ki, J., Nowak, S., & Schumacher, L. (2012). *Are CRAs Powerful? An Investigation Into The Impact And Accuracy of Sovereign Ratings.* IMF Working Paper 12/23.

Kisgen, D., & Strahan, P. (2010). Do Regulations Based on Credit Ratings Affect a Firm's Cost of Capital? *Review of Financial Studies*, *23*(12), 4324–4347. doi:10.1093/rfs/hhq077

Kliger, D., & Sarig, O. (2000). The Information Value of Bond Ratings. *The Journal of Finance*, *55*(6), 2879–2902. doi:10.1111/0022-1082.00311

Kohlberg, E., & Mertens, J. (1986). On the Strategic Stability of Equilibria. *Econometrica*, *54*(5), 1003–1037. doi:10.2307/1912320

Kuhner, C. (2001). Financial CRAs: Are they credible? Insights into the reporting incentives of CRAs in times of enhanced systemic risk. *Schmalenbach Business Review*, *53*, 4–20. doi:10.1007/BF03396881

Kultti, K. (2000). A model of random matching and price formation. *European Economic Review*, *44*(10), 1841–1856. doi:10.1016/S0014-2921(99)00027-6

Land, D. M. (2007). Residential Mortgage Securitization and Consumer Welfare. *Consumer Finance Law Quarterly Report*, *61*, 208–218.

Lannoo, K. (2008). *Credit Rating Agencies: Scapegoat or free-riders?* ECMI Commentary No. 20/9.

Lee, J., & Liu, Q. (2013). Gambling Reputation: Repeated Bargaining With Outside Options. *Econometrica*, *81*(4), 1601–1672. doi:10.3982/ECTA9200

Lehmann, A. (2004). Sovereign Credit Ratings and Private Capital Flows to Low-income Countries. *African Development Review*, *16*(2), 252–268. doi:10.1111/j.1017-6772.2004.00091.x

Li, W., Liu, Y., & Chen, Y. (2018). Modeling a two-stage supply contract problem in a hybrid uncertain environment. *Computers & Industrial Engineering*, *123*, 289–302. doi:10.1016/j.cie.2018.06.031

Lin, E., & Chou, M. (1990). Optimal contracts. *Applied Mathematics Letters*, *3*(2), 65–68. doi:10.1016/0893-9659(90)90016-5

Listokin, Y., & Taibleson, B. (2010). If You Misrate, Then You Lose: Improving Credit Rating Accuracy Through Incentive Compensation. *Yale Journal on Regulation*, *27*, 91–100.

Löffler, G. (2004). An Anatomy of Rating Through the Cycle. *Journal of Banking & Finance*, *28*(3), 695–670. doi:10.1016/S0378-4266(03)00041-4

Loffler, G. (2005). Avoiding the Rating Bounce: Why Rating Agencies Are Slow to React to New Information. *Journal of Economic Behavior & Organization*, *56*(3), 365–381. doi:10.1016/j.jebo.2003.09.015

Lupica, L. (2009). Credit CRAs, Structured Securities, and the Way Out of the Abyss. *Review Of Banking & Finance*, *28*, 639–649.

Lynch, T. (2009). Deeply and Persistently Conflicted: Credit CRAs in the Current Regulatory Environment. *Case Western Reserve Law Review*, *59*, 227–237.

Madigan, P. (2009). CRA reform legislation inappropriate and unfair. *Risk Magazine*.

Madureira, A., Pereira, I., Pereira, P., & Abraham, A. (2014). Negotiation mechanism for self-organized scheduling system with collective intelligence. *Neurocomputing*, *132*, 97–110. doi:10.1016/j.neucom.2013.10.032

Makhdoumi, A., Malekian, A., & Ozdaglar, A. (2017). *Strategic Dynamic Pricing with Network Externalities*. https://arxiv.org/pdf/1706.01131.pdf

Manns, J. (2009). Rating Risk After the Subprime Mortgage Crisis: A User Fee Approach for CRA Accountability. *North Carolina Law Review*, *87*, 1011–1021.

Manns, J. (2013). Downgrading CRA Reform. *The George Washington Law Review*, *81*, 749–759.

Mansoor, M., Ellahi, N., Hassan, A., Malik, Q. A., Waheed, A., & Ullah, N. (2020). Corporate Governance, Shariah Governance, and Credit Rating: A Cross-Country Analysis from Asian Islamic Banks. *Journal of Open Innovation*, *6*(4), 170. doi:10.3390/joitmc6040170

Mariano, B. (2012). Market power and reputational concerns in the ratings industry. *Journal of Banking & Finance*, *36*(6), 1616–1626. doi:10.1016/j.jbankfin.2012.01.012

Martínez, R., Massó, J., Neme, A., & Oviedo, J. (2012). On The Invariance Of The Set Of Core Matchings With Respect To Preference Profiles. *Games and Economic Behavior*, *74*(2), 588–600. doi:10.1016/j.geb.2011.08.011

Mason, J., & Rosner, J. (2007). *Where Did the Risk Go? How Misapplied Bond Ratings Cause Mortgage Backed Securities and Collateralized Debt Obligation Market Disruptions*. https://www.hudson.org/files/publications/Hudson_Mortgage_Paper5_3_07.pdf

Mathis, J., McAndrews, J., & Rochet, J. (2009). Rating the raters: Are reputation concerns powerful enough to discipline CRAs? *Journal of Monetary Economics*, *56*(5), 657–674. doi:10.1016/j.jmoneco.2009.04.004

Meneguzzi, F., Modgil, S., & Oren, N. (2011). Algorithms and mechanisms for procuring services with uncertain durations using redundancy. *Artificial Intelligence*, *175*(14–15), 2021–2060.

Meneguzzi, F., Modgil, S., Oren, N., Miles, S., Luck, M., & Faci, N. (2012). Applying electronic contracting to the aerospace aftercare domain. *Engineering Applications of Artificial Intelligence*, *25*(7), 1471–1487. doi:10.1016/j.engappai.2012.06.004

Metz, A. (2012). The Performance of Corporate Credit Ratings. *Antitrust Chronicle*, *4*(1).

Miglionico, A. (2019). *The governance of credit rating agencies: regulatory regimes and liability issues*. Edward Elgar Publishing. doi:10.4337/9781786439949

Muuls, M. (2015). Exporters, importers and credit constraints. *Journal of International Economics*, *95*(2), 333–343. doi:10.1016/j.jinteco.2014.12.003

Nagy, T. (2009). Note: CRAs and the First Amendment: Applying Constitutional Journalistic Protections to Subprime Mortgage Litigation. *Minnesota Law Review*, *94*, 140–150. https://www.minnesotalawreview.org/wp-content/uploads/2011/08/Nagy_MLR.pdf

Niederhoff, J., & Kouvelis, P. (2019). Effective and necessary: Individual supplier behavior in revenue sharing and wholesale contracts. *European Journal of Operational Research*, *277*(3), 1060–1071. doi:10.1016/j.ejor.2019.03.038

Noe, T. (2012). Survey of the Economic Theory of Reputation: Its Logic and Limits. In *The Oxford Handbook of Corporate Reputation*. Oxford University Press.

Ntswane, L. (2014). *The Impact of Sovereign Credit Ratings on Capital Flows and Financial Markets in Africa* (PHD Thesis). Faculty of Commerce, Law and Management, University of the Witwatersrand, Johannesburg, South Africa. www.businessandeconomics.mq.edu.au/our_departments/Economics/Econ_docs/research_papers2/2007_research_papers/Ratings-KimWuFinal.pdf

Nwogugu, M. (2006). Employee Stock Options, Production Functions And Game Theory. *Applied Mathematics and Computation, 181*(1), 552–562. doi:10.1016/j.amc.2005.12.067

Nwogugu, M. (2007a). Issues In Disintermediation In The Real Estate Brokerage Industry. *Applied Mathematics and Computation, 186*(2), 1054–1064. doi:10.1016/j.amc.2006.08.053

Nwogugu, M. (2007b). Some Issues In Securitization And Disintermediation. *Applied Mathematics and Computation, 186*(2), 1031–1039. doi:10.1016/j.amc.2006.08.052

Nwogugu, M. (2019a). *Human Computer Interaction, Incentive Conflicts And Methods For Eliminating Index Arbitrage, Index-Related Mutual Fund Arbitrage And ETF Arbitrage. In Indices, Index Funds And ETFs HCI: Exploring HCI, Nonlinear Risk And Homomorphisms*. Palgrave MacMillan.

Nwogugu, M. (2019b). Economic Policy, Complex Adaptive Systems, Human-Computer Interaction And Managerial Psychology: Popular-Index Ecosystems. In Indices, Index Funds And ETFs HCI: Exploring HCI, Nonlinear Risk And Homomorphisms. New York: Palgrave MacMillan.

NwoguguM. C. I. (2013). *Complex Systems, International Capital Flows and New 'Learning' Business Models for the Credit Rating Agency Industry*. https://ssrn.com/abstract=1761406 doi:10.2139srn.1761406

OECD. (2010). *Competition and Credit Rating Agencies*. DAF/COMP(2010)29. Directorate For Financial And Enterprise Affairs - Competition Committee, OECD. Available at: https://www.oecd.org/regreform/sectors/46825342.pdf

Office of the New York State Attorney General. (2008). *Attorney General Cuomo Announces Landmark Reform agreements With The Nation's Three Principal Credit CRAs*. Available at: http://www.oag.state.ny.us/press/2008/june/june5a_08.html/

Opp, C., Opp, M., & Harris, M. (2013). CRAs In The Face Of Regulation. *Journal of Financial Economics, 108*(1), 46–61. doi:10.1016/j.jfineco.2012.10.011

Ordonez, G. (2013). Fragility Of Reputation And Clustering Of Risk-taking. *Theoretical Economics, 8*(3), 653–700. doi:10.3982/TE1207

Pagano, M., & Volpin, P. (2010a). Credit Ratings Failures And Policy Options. In M. Dewatripont, X. Freixas, & R. Portes (Eds.), *Macroceocomic Stability And Financial Regulation: Key issues For the G20* (pp. 129–148).

Pagano, M., & Volpin, P. (2010b). Credit ratings failures and policy options. *Economic Policy, 25*(April), 401–431. doi:10.1111/j.1468-0327.2010.00245.x

Palmigiano, P., & Pieri, S. (2014). Credit Rating Agencies: Change by Competition Law or Regulation? *Antitrust Chronicle*. https://www.competitionpolicyinternational.com/credit-ratings-agencies-change-by-competition-law-or-regulation/

Park, G., & Lee, H. (2018). Opportunistic behaviors of credit rating agencies and bond issuers. *Pacific-Basin Finance Journal, 47*, 39–59. doi:10.1016/j.pacfin.2017.11.003

Park, S., & Kim, J. (2014). A mathematical model for a capacity reservation contract. *Applied Mathematical Modelling, 38*(5-6), 1866–1880. doi:10.1016/j.apm.2013.10.005

Partnoy, F. (2006). How and why credit ratings are not like other gatekeepers. In *Financial Gatekeepers: Can they protect investors?* Brookings Institution Press. https://papers.ssrn.com/sol3/papers.cfm?abstract_id=900257

Partnoy, F. (2009). Historical Perspectives on the Financial Crisis: Ivar Kreuger, the Credit-CRAs, and Two Theories About the Function and Dysfunction of Markets. *Yale Journal on Regulation*, *26*, 431–440.

Patterson, M. (2010). Standardization Of Standard-Form Contracts: Competition And Contract Implications. *William and Mary Law Review*, *52*(2), 327–340.

Patterson, M. (2012). Manipulation of Product Ratings: Credit-Rating Agencies, Google, and Antitrust. *Antitrust Chronicle*, *4*(1).

Pendergraft, E. (2012). Section 933(b): Nimble Private Regulation of the Capital Market Gatekeepers. *Florida State University Law Review. Florida State University. College of Law*, *39*, 511–515.

Petit, N. (2002). From Formalism to Effects? The Commission's Communication on Enforcement Priorities in Applying Article 82 EC. *World Competition*, *32*, 485–490.

Petit, N. (2011). Credit Rating Agencies, The Sovereign Debt Crisis And Competition Law. *European Competition Journal*, *7*(3).

Petit, N., & Neyrinck, N. (2011). Credit Rating Agencies and Competition Law. *Antitrust Chronicle*, *4*(1).

Reisen, H. (2010). Boom, bust and sovereign ratings: Lessons for the Eurozone from emerging-market ratings. *VOX*. https://www.voxeu.org/article/boom-bustand-sovereign-ratings-lessons-eurozone-emerging-market-ratings

Reiss, D. (2005, September 2). Subprime Standardization: How CRAs Allow Predatory Lending to Flourish in the Secondary Mortgage Market. *Florida State University Law Review. Florida State University. College of Law*, *33*, 2006.

Rhee, R. (2013). On Duopoly and Compensation Games in the Credit Rating Industry. *Northwestern University Law Review*, 108.

Richardson, M., & White, L. (2009). The CRAs: Is Regulation the Answer? In Restoring Financial Stability: How to repair a failed system. John Wiley.

Roesch, D. (2002). The Informational Content of Credit Ratings and Cyclical Patterns of Default Rates. *Central European Journal of Operations Research*, *10*(2), 163–186.

Roth, A., & Sotomayor, M. (1992). Two-Sided Matching: A Study in Game-Theoretic Modeling and Analysis. Academic Press.

Rousseau, S. (2006). Enhancing the Accountability of Credit CRAs: The Case for a Disclosure-Based Approach. *McGill Law Journal. Revue de Droit de McGill*, *51*, 617–621.

Ryan, J. (2012). *The Negative Impact Of Credit Rating Agencies And Propsoals For Better Regulation.* Working Paper – German Institute for International and Security Affairs, Germany. https://www.swp-berlin.org/fileadmin/contents/products/arbeitspapiere/The_Negative_Impact_of_Credit_Rating_Agencies_KS.pdf

Schwarcz, S. (2002). Private Ordering of Public Markets: The CRA Paradox. *University of Illinois Law Review*, *2002*(1), 1–2.

Securities & Exchange Board of India. (2016). *Enhanced Standards for Credit Rating Agencies (CRAs)*. PR No. 150/2016. http://www.sebi.gov.in/cms/sebi_data/attachdocs/1477999985100.pdf

Sheng, J. (2019). Neoliberal environmentality and incentive-coordinated REDD+ contracts. *Land Use Policy*, *81*, 400–407. doi:10.1016/j.landusepol.2018.10.055

Shuermann, T. (2004). *A Review of Recent Books on Credit Risk*. Federal Reserve Bank of New York.

Sinclair, T. (2007). Passing Judgment: Credit Rating Processes as Regulatory Mechanisms of Governance in the Emerging World Order. In P. James & H. Patomäki (Eds.), *Globalization And Economy: Globalizing Finance And The New Global Economy* (pp. 248–253). Sage Publishers.

Skreta, V., & Veldkamp, L. (2009). Ratings Shopping And Asset Complexity: A Theory Of Ratings Inflation. *Journal of Monetary Economics*, *56*(5), 678–695. doi:10.1016/j.jmoneco.2009.04.006

Solovjova, I. (2016). New Approaches to Regulating the Activities of Rating Agencies: A Comparative Analysis. *Procedia: Social and Behavioral Sciences*, *229*, 115–125. doi:10.1016/j.sbspro.2016.07.120

Sotomayor, M. (2003). Some further remark on the core structure of the assignment game. *Mathematical Social Sciences*, *46*(3), 261–265. doi:10.1016/S0165-4896(03)00067-2

Sprinkle, G., Williamson, M., & Upton, D. (2008). The effort and risk-taking effects of budget-based contracts. *Accounting, Organizations and Society*, *33*(4-5), 436–452. doi:10.1016/j.aos.2007.11.001

Standard & Poors. (2013). *What Credit Ratings Are & Are Not*. Available at: http://www.standardandpoors.com/aboutcreditratings/RatingsManual_PrintGuide.html

Sussman, O. (1999). Economic growth with standardized contracts. *European Economic Review*, *43*(9), 1797–1818. doi:10.1016/S0014-2921(98)00040-3

Sy, A. (2009, December). The Systemic Regulation of Credit Rating Agencies And Rated Markets. *World Economy*, *27*(2), 161–174.

Tang, T. (2009). Information asymmetry and firms' credit market access: Evidence from Moody's credit rating format refinement. *Journal of Financial Economics*, *93*(2), 325–351. doi:10.1016/j.jfineco.2008.07.007

Tarashev, N. (2005). *An Empirical Evaluation of Structural Credit Spread Models*. BIS Working Papers, #179.

Telser, L. (1994). The Usefulness of Core Theory In Economics. *The Journal of Economic Perspectives*, *8*(2), 151–164. doi:10.1257/jep.8.2.151

Terán, J., Aguilar, J., & Cerrada, M. (2017). Integration in industrial automation based on multi-agent systems using cultural algorithms for optimizing the coordination mechanisms. *Computers in Industry*, *91*, 11–23. doi:10.1016/j.compind.2017.05.002

Thille, H., & Cojocaru, M. (2013). A Dynamic Pricing Game In A Model Of New Product Adoption With Social Influence. *International Conference On Social Computing*. 10.1109/SocialCom.2013.114

Tomashevskiy, A., & Kono, D. (2015). Extra Credit: Preferential Trade Arrangements and Credit Ratings. *International Studies Quarterly, 59*(2), 291–302. doi:10.1111/isqu.12183

Toscano, F. (2020). Does the Dodd-Frank Act reduce the conflict of interests of credit rating agencies? *Journal of Corporate Finance, 62*, 62. doi:10.1016/j.jcorpfin.2020.101595

UNCTAD. (2015). *Credit Rating Agencies: Junk Status?* https://unctad.org/en/PublicationsLibrary/presspb2015d13_en.pdf

United States Government Accountability Office. (2012). *Credit Rating Agencies: Alternative Compensation Models for Nationally Recognized Statistical Rating Organizations*. Available at: https://www.gao.gov/assets/590/587832.pdf

U.S. Department of Justice. (2009). *Constitutionality of Mandatory Registration of Credit CRAs*. Available at: https://www.justice.gov/olc/2009/opinion-letter-treasury.pdf

US Dept. of Justice Complaint (2013). *Department of Justice Sues Standard & Poors For Fraud In Rating Mortgage Backed Securities In The Years Leading Up To The Financial Crisis*. Author.

U.S. Federal Deposit Insurance Corporation. (2011). *References to Credit Ratings in FDIC Regulations*. Author.

Van Assche, A., & Schwartz, G. (2013). Contracting institutions and ownership structure in international joint ventures. *Journal of Development Economics, 103*, 124–132. doi:10.1016/j.jdeveco.2013.02.008

Van Den Brink, R. (2012). Efficiency and Collusion Neutrality in Cooperative Games and Networks. *Games and Economic Behavior, 76*(1), 344–348. doi:10.1016/j.geb.2012.04.001

Virag, G. (2011). High Profit Equilibria In Directed Search models. *Games and Economic Behavior, 71*(1), 224–234. doi:10.1016/j.geb.2010.08.006

Wang, T. (2012). *Can reputation concerns always discipline credit CRAs? Evidence from corporate bond issuance ratings*. Working Paper.

Wei, W., Wang, J., Chen, X., Yang, J., & Min, X. (2018). Psychological contract model for knowledge collaboration in virtual community of practice: An analysis based on the game theory. *Applied Mathematics and Computation, 329*, 175–187. doi:10.1016/j.amc.2018.01.053

White, L. (2000). *The Credit Rating Industry: An Industrial Organization Analysis*. Stern School of Business, New York University. Prepared for the CIPE project on "Credit Ratings and the International Economy".

White, L. (2006). *Good Intentions Gone Awry: A Policy Analysis of the SEC's Regulation of the Bond Rating Industry*. New York University Law and Economics Research Paper #06-36; Networks Financial Institute Policy Brief, No. 2006-PB-05, April 2006. Available at: https://papers.ssrn.com/sol3/papers.cfm?abstract_id=923566

White, L. (2010). Markets: The Credit CRAs. *The Journal of Economic Perspectives*, *24*(2), 211–226. doi:10.1257/jep.24.2.211

White, L. (2013). Credit Rating Agencies: An Overview. *Annual Review of Financial Economics*, *5*(1), 93–122. doi:10.1146/annurev-financial-110112-120942

Wu, Z., Zhao, R., & Tang, W. (2014). Optimal contracts for the agency problem with multiple uncertain information. *Knowledge-Based Systems*, *59*, 161–172. doi:10.1016/j.knosys.2014.01.009

Yalta, T., & Yalta, Y. (2018). Are credit rating agencies regionally biased? *Economic Systems*, *42*(4), 682–694. doi:10.1016/j.ecosys.2018.08.001

Yoav, S., & Leyton-Brown, K. (2009). *Multiagent Systems: Algorithmic, Game-Theoretic, and Logical Foundations*. Cambridge University Press.

Zohar, A., & Rosenschein, J. (2008). Mechanisms for information elicitation. *Artificial Intelligence*, *172*(16–17), 1917–1939. doi:10.1016/j.artint.2008.08.005

ENDNOTES

1 *See:* U.S. Government Accountability Office (2012). *GAO-12-240, Credit Rating Agencies: Alternative Compensation Models For Nationally Recognized Statistical Rating Organizations (2012). See:* the website of the *European Securities & Markets Authority*. https://www.esma.europa.eu/regulation/credit-rating-agencies.
See: "China rating agency condemns rivals" (2010) at http://www.ft.com/cms/s/0/5632a0b8-94b7-11df-b90e-00144feab49a.html ("the head of China's largest credit rating agency has slammed his western counterparts for causing the global financial crisis and said that as the world's largest creditor nation, China should have a bigger say in how governments and their debt are rated. 'The western rating agencies are politicized and highly ideological and they do not adhere to objective standards,' … Last week, privately-owned Dagong published its own sovereign credit ranking in what it said was a first for a non-western credit rating agency … The results were very different from those published by Moody's, Standard & Poor's and Fitch, with China ranking higher than the United States, Britain, Japan, France and most other major economies, reflecting Dagong's belief that China is more politically and economically stable than all of these countries. 'The US is insolvent and faces bankruptcy as a pure debtor nation but the rating agencies still give it high rankings,' Mr Guan said. 'Actually, the huge military expenditure of the US is not created by themselves but comes from borrowed money, which is not sustainable.' A wildly enthusiastic editorial published by Xinhua, China's official state newswire, lauded Dagong's report as a significant step toward breaking the monopoly of western rating agencies of which it said China has long been a 'victim'. "Compared with the US's conquest of the world by means of force, Moody's has controlled the world through its dominance in credit rating" the editorial said. First established in 1994, Dagong signed a three-year 'technology co-operation' agreement in 1999 with Moody's, which provided the Chinese company with its 'core knowledge' and its first 'systemic understanding'").

See: U.S. Securities & Exchange Commission (2011). *Summary Report Of Commission Staff's Examinations Of Each Nationally Recognized Statistical Rating Organization (as required by Section 15E(p)(3)(C) of the Securities Exchange Act of 1934).*

See: U.S. Securities & Exchange Commission (2011). *Annual Report On Nationally Recognized Statistical Rating Organizations (2011)* (as required by Section 6 of the Credit Rating Agency Reform Act of 2006).

See: *The Credit Rating Agency Reform Act of 2006*, S. 3850 (USA).

See: U.S. Government Accountability Office (2010). *Gao-10-782, Securities And Exchange Commission: Action Needed To Improve Rating Agency Registration Program And Performance-Related Disclosures (2010).*

See: U.S. Securities & Exchange Commission (2003). Report On The Role And Function Of Credit Rating Agencies In The Operation Of The Securities Markets (2003).

See: U.S. Government (2006). *Credit Rating Agency Reform Act*, 109th Congress (2005-2006), www.govtrack.us/congress/bill.xpd?bill=s109-3850 *See:* U.S. Securities and Exchange Commission (June 4, 2003). *Concept Release: Rating Agencies and the Use of Credit Ratings under the Federal Securities Laws.*

See: US Securities & Exchange Commission (January 2003). *Report on the Role and Function of Credit Rating Agencies in the Operation of the Securities Markets - As Required by Section 702(b) of the Sarbanes-Oxley Act of 2002.*

See: US SEC (2013). *Nationally Recognized Statistical Rating Organizations* ("NRSROs"). https://www.sec.gov/divisions/marketreg/ratingagency.htm. There are now eleven Nationally Recognized Statistical Rating Organizations ("NRSROs") in the US; and they are LACE Financial Corp., Rating and Investment Information, Inc.; DBRS Ltd., HR Ratings de México, Japan Credit Rating Agency, Ltd., S.A. de C.V., Egan-Jones Rating Company, Realpoint LLC, A.M. Best Company, Inc., Fitch, Inc., Moody's Investors Service, Inc., and Standard & Poor's Ratings Services.

See: Financial Crisis Inquiry Commission (2011). *Financial Crisis Inquiry Report.* Note 6, at xxv. http://www.gpo.gov/fdsys/pkg/GPO-FCIC/pdf/GPO-FCIC.pdf. (noting that in 2006, Moody's assigned triple-A ratings on an average of thirty mortgage-related securities per day, and 83% - eighty three percent - of these securities were subsequently downgraded).

See: Mary William Walsh & Andrew Ross Sorkin (2013). *"U.S. Accuses S. & P. of Fraud in Suit on Loan Bundles"*, *New York Times*, Feb. 5, 2013, at A1. In 2013, the U.S. Department of Justice sued Standard & Poor's for fraud related to S&P's ratings of mortgage-related bonds during the Global financial crisis. Complaint for Civil Money Penalties and Demand for Jury Trial, *United States v. McGraw-Hill Cos.*, No. CV13-00779 (C.D. Cal. Feb. 4, 2014).

Chapter 8
Complex Systems, Competition/Antitrust, and Legal Problems in the Global Credit Rating Agency Industry

ABSTRACT

This chapter explains how the tie-breaker effect reduces social welfare and distorts equilibria. This chapter introduces new definitions of "equilibrium" in the CRA ratings processes. (This has been one of the major missing elements in the existing literature on the credit ratings industry) It explains why "reputational capital" (of CRAs) is a sub-set of "influence" (which can have more impact on bond-issuers' decisions and investors' decisions than traditional "influence") and critiques the games theorems in Virag and other important papers.

INTRODUCTION

This chapter analyzes various Antitrust/competition and regulatory problems (e.g. liability for credit ratings) within the context of Mechanism Design and "Stability", with the objective of understanding issues surrounding the conflicts-of-interest, Regret, deadweight losses, inefficiency, *Emergence*, Greed and evolution inherent in credit rating agencies. In this context, "*Stability*" refers to the following. First, game-theoretic "*Stability*" in large non-cooperative non-zero-sum NTU finitely-repeated games wherein no player-coalition has any meaningful incentive to deviate from, and is legally required to conform to "*Determined Regulatory Equilibria/equilibrium*" (similar to *Correlated Equilibrium*) which is a non-empty Core regardless of the size (large versus small), scale (single-level versus multi-level games versus multi-stage); tenure and type (cooperative or non-cooperative or mixed) of the games. Second, "*Financial Stability*" wherein the credit ratings process reduces the probability of systemic risk and Contagion and the credit-ratings are more objective and accurate. Third, "*Operational Stability*" wherein both the credit ratings process and the ratings output reduce the probability of the issuer-company becoming financially

DOI: 10.4018/978-1-7998-7418-8.ch008

or operationally distressed. Yoav & Leyton-Brown (2009); Lutz & Schafke (1985); Govindan & Wilson (2006), and Telser (1994) discuss and show examples of various uses of Invariants and Game Theory Strategies in characterizing solutions in Industrial Organization, Games and Dynamical Systems. Govindan, Schemde & Stengel (2004) noted that since *Stability* is a set-valued solution concept, there isnt a unique formulation of some axioms (including symmetry).

EXISTING LITERATURE

See the "Existing Literature" section in Chapter-8 in this book. Byoun, Han & Shin (2020) noted that the Nationally Recognized Statistical Rating Organization (NRSRO) certification increases the market share of new NRSROs in Japan; that newly certified Japanese NRSROs' bond ratings are more informative for predicting yields.

Toscano (2020) concluded that in the USA, the difference between issuer-paid (S&P) and investor-paid credit ratings (EJR) declined after the enactment of the Dodd-Frank Act (even for group of firms that are more exposed to conflicts of interest); and that Issuer-paid CRAs improved their reputation, accuracy and timeliness compared to investor-paid CRAs after the enactment of the Dodd-Frank Act.

Hu, Huang, Pan & Shi (2019) analyzed how Chinese issuer-paid incumbent CRAs changed their rating strategies in response to the 2010 entry of independent CRA named China Bond Rating (CBR) between 2006 and 2015,and found that: i) CBR's business model combined the public utility model and the investor-paid model; ii) CBR's ratings reduced the information asymmetry in the Chinese corporate bond market; iii) after CBR entered the market, there was lower ratings inflation and increased informativeness of ratings-change announcements by incumbent issuer-paid CRAs; iv) CRA credibility is an important channel for incumbent issuer-paid CRAs' strategic ratings.

Huang & Shen (2019) found that: i) the incumbent issuer-paid CRAs in China consider the investor-paid CRA China Bond Rating Company, Ltd. (CBRC), as a competitor; ii) the Chinese incumbent issuer-paid CRAs are more likely to downgrade or less likely to upgrade their credit ratings and the information quality of their ratings improves when the CBRC also rates the same issuer (the improvement in the information quality is consistent for CBRC's solicited and unsolicited ratings); iii) CBRC functions as an information provider; and the differences between CBRC's rating grades and those of issuer-paid rating agencies can explain bond yield spreads.

Chen, Matousek, et. al. (2019) found evidence of Herding (among CRAs) for sovereign credit ratings (and generally towards Standard and Poor's ratings) and there is some degree of heterogeneity over time. Yalta & Yalta (2018) analyzed the degree of bias in sovereign credit ratings issued by Fitch Ratings, Moody's and S&P, and found: i) that there was a strong, robust and statistically significant home bias in favor of the U.S.; ii) that there are no special biases towards or against different country groups; iii) modeling errors increase dispersion in the regional effects, which can cause apparent/perceived bias of CRAs.

Abad, Ferreras & Robles (2020) found that: i) split-rating changes (evidence of information opacity) can explain the response of bonds to downgrades; and also signals higher uncertainty about the credit risk of issues and lessens the credibility of the information disclosed by rating changes; ii) the lower the information opacity the stronger response of excess bond return to downgrades, and the effect of information opacity is stronger for high yield fonds; these results are robust to the measure of CRA's divergence of opinion.

Park & Lee (2018) found that: i) Korean bond issuers tend to fire or switch CRAs that assign lower ratings; ii) when Korean issuers have an additional CRA, the new CRA assigns a higher rating than incumbent CRAs; iii) increased competition among CRAs substantially affects the likelihood of a ratings upgrade.

SOME ACTUAL (AND POTENTIAL) ANTITRUST PROBLEMS IN THE GLOBAL CRA INDUSTRY

Most of the research studies and existing/proposed business models and compensation models for CRAs don't address the significant anti-competitive conduct inherent in CRAs' compensation contracts and business models[1]. These antitrust problems include but are not limited to the following:

1. Price-fixing[2] by CRAs – occurs when CRAs directly or indirectly collude to fix assigned ratings and or ratings fees. The price-fixing can also be done indirectly through investment banks who usually assist issuers in ratings-shopping. CRAs often hire ratings analysts from among themselves and from investment banks and so they know each other. Its conjectured here that in the global financial markets, formally or informally coordinated ratings by CRA is a form of price-fixing because: i) a issuers' cost of funds, trade-credit rates (charged to customer) are often based on widely accepted financial-ratios and the issuer's credit ratings and the information-content of such ratings is a form of "price". ii) banks' main products are loans and bank accounts; iii) when groups of banks in a market engage in earnings management, it directly affects the terms of their borrowing, lending and bank accounts.
2. Oligopoly, *Collective-Dominance*[3] and *concentration* in the global CRA industry – issuers have very limited choice. The big-three CRAs have much bigger influence and dominance than other smaller CRAs. The doctrine of "*Unavoidable Trading Partner*"[4] applies and the Big-Three CRAs are *Unavoidable Trading Partners* in the global fixed income markets, equities markets and commodities markets.
3. Increases in the level of within-industry *Market-Integration* in both the CRA industry and the global fixed income securities market because of the industry practices of CRAs.
4. Collusion among CRAs - to set ratings-fees, assign ratings, determine the nature and structure/terms of securities/assets being rated. CRAs hire ratings analysts from among themselves and from investment banks and so they know each other.
5. Collusion between CRAs and investment banks - to set ratings fees and assigned ratings, and to steer issuers to ratings agencies. The collusion can also be done indirectly through investment banks who usually assist issuers in ratings-shopping.
6. Tying by CRAs – the CRA's ratings may be informally contingent on the duration and type of the ratings contract between the issuer and the CRA. ie. issuers that enter into longer term ratings contracts are more likely to obtain higher ratings from the CRA; compared to issuers that either don't enter into any ratings contract (unsolicited ratings) or enter into one-time or short-term ratings contracts. Most ratings projects use the issuer-pay compensation model, and the fees that such issuers pay for ratings are contingent on the outcome of the ratings. CRAs often actively participate in structuring the securities/interests that they rate (the ratings outcome is tied to CRAs participation in structuring the securities).

7. Tying[5] by investment banks - wherein an investment bank requires that an issuer obtain credit ratings from a specific CRA before it helps an issuer to raise capital or advises the issuer. Many investment banks have an in-house "Ratings Advisory Department" and some investment banks may require issuers to pay for such ratings advisory services as a condition for underwriting the issuer's securities.
8. Price discrimination[6] by CRAs – this occurs when CRAs charge different prices to similarly situated issuers depending on their relationship with the issuer, the type of securities being offered, the type/size of the issuer and the offering, etc..
9. Vertical foreclosure[7] by CRAs and relatively very high costs of entry into the CRA industry – the entry costs are very high because of both the existing regulations (required certifications/licenses, etc.) and the industry practices of CRAs.
10. Increase in the volume of *Exclusive Contracts*[8] offered by CRAs (ratings contracts that include greater than normal exceptions and restrictions).
11. CRAs' improper use of unsolicited ratings recruit new customers or extort customers (by issuing or threatening to issue negative unsolicited ratings – there is empirical evidence that unsolicited ratings are generally lower than solicited ratings).

Petit (2011) noted that several scholarly studies recorded systematic patterns of "*mimetism*", "*inertia*", "*herd behavior*" and "*piggybacking effect*" in the credit rating industry; all of which may be discriminatory and abusive and may constitute violations of antitrust statutes. Also see: Alp (2014). Petit (2011) noted that tacit collusion is inferable from the following characteristics of the CRA industry: i) its an oligopoly; ii) CRAs' activities are similar in range, nature and variety; iii) CRAs have similar business models, v) the "big three" CRAs use the "issuer pays" model; v) CRAs charge similar fees and have similar "list prices"; vi) CRAs have similar cost structures and similar human resources (in size); vii) CRAs use similar rating methodologies; viii) there is high market transparency as to ratings (and the publication of credit ratings); ix) CRAs make contacts with common customers and participate in several professional associations where their staff meet each other. Petit (2011) also noted that the three criteria enumerated in *Laurent Piau vs. Commission* (EU) which indicates that tacit collusion probably exist in the CRA industry are as follows: i) CRAs can easily monitor each other's ratings, ii) CRAs' incentives to copy each other can be facilitated through the threat of price wars or other retaliation mechanisms (e.g. recruitment of key personnel, such as internal analysts); iii) the likelihood of new entrants or expansion in the CRA industry is low because of the high entry costs in the CRA market (confirmed by the persistence of large profit margins in the credit rating industry). Researchers and industry participants have criticized CRAs for repeated type-I errors (erroneous downgrading or under-rating) and type-II errors (erroneous upgrading or over-rating)[9] either of which may be abusive and discriminatory, and may cause the bankruptcy of financial institutions, countries or institutional investors, and thus, may constitute violations of Article 102 TFEU (EU) and US federal antitrust statutes. See comments in Petit & Neyrinck (Aug. 2011); Patterson (2012); Becker & Milbourn (2011); Goodhart (June 2008); Palmigiano & Pieri (Jan 28, 2014); Blaubrock (2007); Petit (2002; 2011); OECD (Oct. 5, 2010); Lannoo (Oct. 2008); Skreta & Veldkamp (2009); Frost (2009); He, Qian & Strahan (2012); Rhee (2013); Manns (2013); Mariano (2012); Abrantez-Metz (April 18, 2012), White (2000); Securities & Exchange Board Of India (Nov. 2016); Ekins & Calabria (Aug. 1, 2012); Camanho, Deb & Liu (July 2012); Gromb & Martimort (2007); Van Den Brink (2012); Pagano & Volpin (2010b); and Metz (2012).

There are also significant conflicts of interest in the operations of CRAs that reduce competition and may have antitrust ramifications. See comments in Lynch (2009); Bai (2010); Bolton, Freixas & Shapiro (2012) and Covitz & Harrison (2003). The existing and proposed compensation and business models of CRAs provide very strong incentives for CRAs to understate issuers' risk in order to generate business from issuers and investors. Most ratings projects use the issuer-pay compensation model, and the fees that such issuers pay for ratings are contingent on the outcome of the ratings. CRAs often actively participate in structuring the securities/interest that they rate. S&P is owned by McGraw-Hill Cos., which has many fee-paying customers in the financial services industry. Berkshire Hathaway and Davis Selected Advisers are the major institutional owners of Moodys. At various times during 2010-2016, Berkshire Hathaway owned at least $29 billion of fixed income securities and at least $2 billion of US government bonds and more than $10 billion of foreign government bonds. Berkshire Hathaway also owns shares in many companies that issue bonds that are rated by Moodys. See Berkshire Hathaway, Inc.'s annual reports for 2010-2016. Davis Selected Advisers is an asset management company that manages various funds including fixed income funds. Funds that are managed by Davis Selected Advisers also own shares in many companies that issue bonds that are rated by Moodys. Some CRA ratings analysts have worked as bankers or research analysts at investment banks who bring issuers to be rated by CRAs (and help issuers in ratings-shopping).

REPUTATIONAL CAPITAL IS A SUB-SET OF "INFLUENCE" WHICH CAN HAVE MORE IMPACT ON ISSUERS' DECISIONS, INVESTORS' DECISIONS AND ANTITRUST/COMPETITION IN THE GLOBAL CRA INDUSTRY

Many empirical and theoretical studies have documented the statistically significant effects of credit ratings on capital markets, which in part accounts for the reputations of CRAs.See: Hunt (2009); Reiss (September 2, 2005); Roesch (2002); Ismailescu & Kazemi (2010); Grin & Tang (2012); Galil & Soer (2011); Afonso, Furceri & Gomes (2012); and Ashcraft, Adam, Goldsmith-Pinkham & Vickery (2010). Various authors have argued that ratings changes lag the market - Covitz & Harrison (2003) stated that seventy five percent of the price adjustment of a typical corporate bond after a ratings downgrade occurs before the CRA's announcement of the downgrade – i.e. ratings typically lags actual price adjustments. Kou & Varetto (2006) concluded that for a set of Eurobonds, the credit spreads often anticipates future changes of CRAs' ratings. Partnoy (2006); Pagano & Olpin (2009) reviewed the recent failures of CRAs in structured finance. Roesch (2002); Dallocchio, Hubler & Raimbourg (n.d.); Salvi (2006); Di Cesare (2006). Cornaggia & Cornaggia (2012) compared Moody's ratings to those of Rapid Ratings, a small rating agency which is funded by subscription fees from investors; and they found that Moody's ratings were slower to react to bad news than those of Rapid Ratings. Löffler (2004) noted that "There is plenty of academic and anecdotal evidence which suggests that agency ratings do not fully reflect available information".

Empirically, various researchers have concluded that public concerns about Reputation are not a sufficient incentive or a self-disciplining mechanism for CRAs – see Wang (2012); Covitz & Harrison (2003); Mathis, McAndrews & Rochet (2009); Fulghieri, Strobl & Xia (2010); Hill (2003); Kerwer (2001); Mariano (2012); Ki, Nowak & Schumacher (2012); Pagano & Volpin (2010); Faure-Grimaud, Peyrachie & Quesada (2009); Covitz & Harrison (2003); Bolton, Freixas & Shapiro (2012); Opp, Opp & Harris (2012); White (2002); Schwarcz (2002); Hill (2004); Kerwer (2001); Kuhner (2001); Husisian (1990);

Hunt (2009), and Rousseau (2006). Theoretically, Reputation concerns are not a sufficient incentive or a self-disciplining mechanism for CRAs because of the following reasons. There are relatively very few rating agencies - the issuers and investors have limited options. For some types of issuers, it can be difficult to find viable substitutes for a credit rating. Investors (especially investors that don't have their own in-house verification systems) do rely on the third party verification provided by ratings agencies. The cost structure of the typical CRA contains substantial fixed costs and substantial regulatory costs, and emphasizes the generation of fees over Reputation-building activities or conduct. CRAs face substantial transaction costs and monitoring costs which do not facilitate Reputation-building activities over profit-generation activities. CRAs are not accountable for the quality of their rating and don't face any penalties for low-quality (inaccurate) ratings – a) no penalties from the government; b) no penalties under ratings contracts with issuers; c) no monetary or non-monetary penalties from investors. The CRAs' internal incentive systems emphasize customer volume and fees; and not quality. CRAs know that politicians and regulators support and require the existence of CRAs. As a result, the CRA's internal valuation of Reputation Capital is very likely to decline as its customer volume increases (volume of actual ratings and not necessary volume of clients, where one client can provide several ratings projects); and as its performance nears or exceeds "average" (when it's more likely than not that the CRA's ratings match issuers' performance during the mid-term horizon of 3-5 years).

Unfortunately the whole empirical and theoretical debate about CRA Reputation Capital has been solely within the context of incentives and payments to CRA, and has glaringly omitted Penalties (and associated deterrence effects) and the *Theory of "Influence"*.

Reputation is distinct from and is a subset of *Influence*, and an entity that has a significant positive Reputation may not have any meaningful Influence; while a CRA that has a negative Reputation may actually command some Influence. Reputation is often built on the direct immediate past performance based on known metrics (ratings quality for an industry or a specific type of financial instrument or for a company that frequently issues bonds/loans). On the other hand, Influence encompasses the foregoing plus other non-performance attributes of the CRA such as its Human Capital, the perceived quality of its ratings models/criteria, the CRA's ancillary businesses (such as sales of monographs, and training programs for executives); the quality and accessibility of the CRA's analysts; the perceived ability of the CRA to obtain information about issuers; the timeliness of the CRA's ratings updates; the CRA's cost structure and profitability; the percentage of publicly-traded securities that are rated by the CRA; the CRA's willingness to disclose the details of its ratings; and the geographical scope of the CRA's ratings operations. Within the context of the CRA industry, its Influence that is more likely to drive investors' decisions and issuers' decisions.

Ordonez (2013) noted that Reputation concerns in credit markets can reduce excessive risk taking by borrowers. Such concerns are affected by other borrowers' behaviors, and thus, reputational discipline is subject to breakdowns without discernible changes in economic fundamentals; and at an aggregate level, breakdowns are clustered among borrowers who have intermediate and good reputations, and that trend magnifies otherwise small economic shocks. Similarly, Reputational Capital of CRAs is hereby: i) conjectured to be concentrated among the big-three CRAs; ii) conjectured to be subject to breakdowns without any noticeable changes in economic fundamentals when trust among market participants (traders; sell-side researchers) declines; or when the average marginal cost of substitution among securities/loans is low or declines substantially, and the average marginal risk of substituting securities/loans also declines or is low; or when the prices in cash markets generally differ substantially from prices inferred by futures contracts and Forward-contracts; or when; iii) conjectured to amplify systemic risk because there is excessive reliance on the big-three CRAs; iv) conjectured to magnify small economic shocks because small shocks that are not incorporated in the ratings of big-three CRAs but are considered by small CRAs or un-licensed CRAs are likely to be considered relevant/significant. Noe (2012), Bonewitz (2010) and Lee & Liu (2013) noted the limitations to Reputation – wherein the CRA is a long-run player and the issuers are short-run players. Thus, the excessive reliance on the reputational Capital of CRAs as a disciplining mechanism, is unjustified.

The key issues are: 1) whether penalties are more effective than incentives for prevention of shirking by CRAs and for eliciting truthful disclosure from issuers; 2) how to structure penalties and incentives in the ratings process such that the CRA is indifferent to the type of business model being used (ie. issuer-pay vs. investor-pay vs. government-pay vs. platform model), and the CRAs' ratings-precision remains constant (or increases) as customer volume increases, and as the number of CRA increases; 3) what elements of Influence are relevant for Equilibrium and for maximizing the value of the typical ratings contract to the CRA, issuer, investors, regulators and the general public.

EQUILIBRIUM, COMPETITION IN THE GLOBAL CRA INDUSTRY AND THE TIE-BREAKER PHENOMENON

In many existing models of CRAs in the literature, "*Equilibrium*" is rarely defined or is rarely defined accurately even though its one of the main elements of both conceptual and analytic solutions forms. Govindan & Wilson (2006) analyzed the sufficient conditions for equilibrium. Kohlberg & Mertens (1986) stated the required properties of a good normal form solution concept and three types of stability (KM stability, full stability and hyperstability) that satisfy some, but not all, of those properties. Goodman & Porter (1988) and Ingo (2003) addressed *Competitive Regulatory Equlibrium* in general.

Although Virag (2011) addresses concepts of Competitive Non-regulatory Equilibrium, most of the theorems in Virag (2011) are wrong; and equations 2,5,4,8,9 & 13 in Virag (2011) are also wrong because: i) Sellers have brand equity and Buyers have individual preferences that evolve (symmetry of Buyers' preferences across Sellers is rara and an unreasonable assumption); ii) zero-utility equilibrium is rare and the paper doesn't state conditions under which it occurs; iii) a Seller's market power is not always inversely proportional to the market-size even in a market that is not an oligopoly/duopoly/monopoly (because of pricing; service/delivery terms; promotions/discounts; complimentary goods; regulation; product quality; lack of substitutes; etc.); iv) the anonymity of buyers varies or can vary across sellers; v) in the equations in which "limits" are mentioned, the formulas don't behave as stated when the variables tend to positive or negative infinity.

Traditional contract theory is not suitable for analysis of CRA contracts and the ratings process because the associated compliance burdens are one-sided (most obligations and regulations applies to CRAs); and Investors are often irrational and thus incentive/compensation systems that are heavily dependent on the volume of trades/transaction or investor-users are inappropriate; issuers and typically subject to managerial controls, and the managers' incentives affect their financing and investment decisions (and hence, the issuers' relationships with CRAs). The parties' ability to contract is statutorily limited. Certification of CRAs and Entrenchment of CRAs imposes artificial price-floors on ratings services; and the nature of the ratings process and the resulting CRA market-power creates natural oligopolies or duopolies. The "*Ratings-Lag*" is a well-known phenomenon and is explained in Loffler (2005), and affects the determination in Equilibrium conditions. See: Skreta & Veldkamp (2009). Boot, Milboum & Schmeits (2006).

Within the context of the CRA industry and credit rating services, the prospective issuer's alternatives to obtaining a traditional pre-offering or supplemental/post-offering ratings from a CRA are as follows. First, the prospective issuer can obtain third-party bond/loan insurance. Secondly, the prospective issuer can include a Loan/bond defeasance clause in the covenants/indentures. Third, the lender and the prospective issuer can reduce the Loan-to-value of the loan/bond. Fourth, the prospective issuer can execute a licensing agreement; or a execute leasing agreement (in lieu of borrowing cash and then purchasing the asset); or execute a joint venture agreement (in which a substantial portion of costs are allocated to, and paid by the JV partner); or execute a Strategic Alliance wherein the prospective issuer uses the excess capacity of the alliance partner who also pays most of the costs; and the prospective-issuer also gets all the benefits of the assets of the alliance partner without actual ownership. Fifth, some or all prospective Institutional Investors (and any individual investor that purchases more than a designated dollar volume of a bond/loan) can be mandatorily/statutorily required to disclose their private ratings and any updates (based on government-provided metrics) on a public portal maintained by the government or a trade association; and they will be required to show evidence that the disclosed ratings are what they use for their investment decisions. Sixth, a government regulator (e.g. the US SEC or the US Treasury Department) can rate all public and private loans and bonds that exceed a minimum size for free, and publicly disclose the ratings. Seventh, Credit (yield) spreads can be used as quasi-ratings. Eighth, Flannery, Houston & Partnoy (2010) concluded that CDS-spreads can be used as quasi-ratings, but that is likely to be inaccurate because of market noise, susceptibility to manipulation of spreads by traders; and market sentiment. Ninth, the government can ban any and all forms of publicly disseminated ratings. Tenth, accounting firms that conduct annual external audits can be required to also provide a quasi-rating of each auditee-company (and not ratings of the company's specific securities/instruments) based on government-provided metrics. Eleventh, the default-probabilities and or the "expected losses given default" of companies can be sued as substitutes for credit ratings. Also, non-certified rating companies can provide credit ratings.

Contrary to many of the studies about CRAs, many "projects" are or can still be financed after a low rating is issued because of the following reasons. First, managers also evaluate projects within the greater context of other existing and proposed "projects" that the issuer is considering; taxation; transfer pricing; etc. (while most CRA ratings processes tend to focus only on one subject "project" for which the CRA has been paid). Secondly, as explained herein, the issuer can obtain third party credit enhancement even after receiving a low credit rating. Thirdly, some investors prefer to arbitrage opportunities inherent in low-rated securities and financial instruments and they will purchase the low-rated securities (ie. high yield securities; and or securities that have been erroneously assigned low ratings by CRAs). Fourth, the issuer may have other profitable projects or subsidiaries. Thus, contrary to many of the studies about CRAs, failure of the rated project may actually be indirectly beneficial for the issuer because of cost allocation, transfer pricing and tax benefits of losses.

Within the context of *Equilibrium* in the credit ratings process, Social welfare can be defined in various ways including but not limited to any of the following: i) Consumer Surplus, Producer Surplus, and Deadweight Losses are minimized; ii) Ratings changes are timely and accurate, such that is no or minimal "Ratings Lags" and the Tie-breaker phenomenon is eliminated; iii) Ratings Standards are consistent across industries, markets, issuers, CRAs and time; iv) Collusion among CRAs, issuers, CPA firms, investment banks and investors is minimized; and the issuer faces penalties for inaccurate disclosure and the CRA faces penalties for inaccuracy and or collusion; v) Market volatility is reduced; vi) Enforcement and investigation costs are minimized; viii) CRAs have substantial incentives and penalties that compel high effort and accuracy; while issuers have substantial incentives and penalties that compel truthful and adequate disclosure.

Bongaerts, Cremers & Goetzmann (2012), and Cantor & Packer (1997) found that Fitch assigns the highest (i.e., most credit-worthy) ratings to corporate bonds, while Moody's ratings are much more conservative than those of both S&P and Fitch; and they also confirmed that Fitch often serves as a "*Tie-Breaker*". Contrary to theories in Bongaerts, Cremers & Goetzmann (2012), the *Tie-Breaker* phenomenon reduces social welfare and can distort analysis of equilibrium conditions because it increases the probability of multiple Equilibria. The *Tie-Breaker phenomenon* creates Consumer Surpluses and Producer Surpluses because the third CRA can charge much higher fees to provide the *Tie-Breaker* ratings and is under pressure to produce ratings demanded by issuer. The Tie-Breaker phenomenon creates *Deadweight Losses* because any "improvement" in the CRA contract will result in a loss by either the CRA or issuer or investor or the general public. The *Tie-Breaker* phenomenon increases the actual and perceived *Entrenchment* of the Big-Three CRAs because it reinforces their dominance as the preferred CRAs. As explained above, given the current structure of the CRA industry, unless a Platform-Matching model allows an issuer to simultaneously (or within a short period of time) obtain ratings from 2-3 CRAs, Platform Matching amplifies the demand for Tie-Breaker Ratings which in turn increases the likelihood of fraud and collusion in the ratings process; and also increases the likelihood that issuers will migrate downwards to non-certified CRAs to obtain Tie-Breaker ratings. In non-Platform-Matching business models, the Tie-Breaker Phenomenon is even more pronounced partly because the Big-three CRA Entrenchment is more severe; and CRA Reputation is correlated with ratings volume.

The demand for Tie-Breaker ratings can be reduced or eliminated only in the following ways:

1. by making it economically feasible/profitable for all or most of the certified CRAs to provide ratings for each debt offering - in the long run (and perhaps even in the short run), this approach can reduce the regulation-driven and market-power-driven reputational disparities between the Big-three CRAs and the smaller CRAs;
2. by statutorily limiting the number of ratings that an issuer can obtain from certified CRAs as a group, for any specific debt obligation within a specific time frame;
3. by implementing *"first-to-downgrade penalties"* for CRAs, wherein all CRAs that rate a company will pay a penalty for a downgrade except the CRA that downgrades the company's debt.

Within the context of the CRA industry and credit rating services, *Equilibrium* can be defined in the following ways, and occurs when any of the following conditions exist:

1. The CRA (effort; accuracy; ratings-fee) is indifferent to the type of payor (ie. investor-pays vs. issuer-pays vs. government-pays vs. platform model); and the CRA's efforts and ratings-quality are neutral to, and not affected by the fee structure (distinct from type of payor), amount of fee and number of ratings projects per year.
2. The issuer's truthfulness is 100% (one hundred percent) and the CRA's effort is at least 100% (one hundred percent) and both the issuer and the CRA face sufficient penalties for inaccurate ratings and inadequate disclosure respectively; and the CRA recovers at least its economic costs (including limited profits).

3. The actual aggregate benefits (to CRA, issuer, investors and the general public) of issuing a credit rating are equal to, or exceed the benefits gained from pursuing any of the above-mentioned alternatives to a rating provided by a CRA.
4. The values of the ratings contract to the CRA, the issuer and the investor and the general public (ie. social welfare) are simultaneously maximized continuously for the time period that ends when the next ratings update is issued.
5. The sum of total effort (exerted by issuer, CRA,CPA firm and investors) plus the negative effect of ratings on social welfare, if any, is less than the sum of total incremental gains (gains that accrue to the issuer, the CRA, investors) plus the positive effects of the CRA's ratings on social welfare, if any.

Aoki & Yoshikawa (2009) critiqued traditional Equilibrium within the context of Search Theory. It is not clear that Nash Equilibrium, Bayesian Nash Equilibrium or similar equilibria are suitable for analysis of optimal contracts for CRAs because of the following reasons. First, as described above, there are several alternatives to traditional credit ratings and the issuer or investor can profitably deviate from any such perceived Nash Equilibrium easily and at low costs. Secondly, the transaction costs inherent in maintaining any Nash Equilibrium, Bayesian Nash Equilibrium or similar equilibria can be prohibitive. Third, the amount and duration of information asymmetry inherent in the ratings process and in maintaining any Nash Equilibrium, Bayesian Nash Equilibrium or similar Equilibria can be prohibitive and precludes any such Equilibria. Fourth, CRAs have or can have different cost structures and very different production costs to ratings.

Rating agencies are prone to various problems that arise from their regulation and the methods by which they are compensated. Seethe comments in: Mason & Rosner (2007), Kerwer (2001), Altman & Saunders (2001), Basel Committee on Bank Supervision (August 2000), White (2002), Reiss (Sept. 2005), Finch (March 2004), Schwarcz (2002), Hill (2004), Bottini (1993) and Hill (2003). The International Organization of Securities Commissions has issued statements and proposed codes for Credit rating Agencies[10]. The European Commission has also debated regulation of Credit Rating Agencies[11].

Unfortunately, rating agencies have a dis-proportionate and major effect on capital markets and on regulation. See: Shuermann (2004) and Tarashev (July 2005). Despite the enactment of new regulations that seek to reduce or eliminate the impact of credit ratings in regulations, in many countries, many securities and capital markets statutes and loan agreements still incorporate credit ratings[12]. See the comments in: Rousseau (2006); Fitzgerald (December 2002); White (2006); Partnoy (2002); U.S. Securities and Exchange Commission (June 4, 2003); Partnoy (May 2006); IOSCO (2008); Madigan (Oct. 2009); Mason & Rosner (May 2007); Husisian (1990); Kuhner (2001); Borio (March 2008); Dittrich (2007); and Beaver, Shakespeare & Soliman (2006). Many regulatory agencies had embedded ratings (by rating agencies) in various statutes and regulations[13], even though there are significant conflicts of interest in the ratings industry; and Ratings were used extensively to determine capital adequacy for financial institutions, and sometimes to determine thresholds for prosecution and investigation by government agencies – but in the US, the US Treasury has limited the use of credit ratings in statutes/regulations. Most governments don't have any control over the quality of the ratings product and over most actions by the rating agencies. Cantor (2001). In the US, the Dodd-Frank Act of 2010 requires some regulation of ratings agencies and their staff, but does not provide adequate regulation.

Table 1. Major International Rating Agencies By Rating Type.

	Insurance	Credit	Mutual Funds	Sovereign	Corporate Governance	Sustainability
A.M. Best Company	Solicited & Un-Solicited	-	-	-	-	-
ASSIRT	-	-	Solicited	-	-	-
Deminor Corporate Governance Rating Service	-	-	-	-	Solicited & Un-Solicited	-
Duff & Phelps	Solicited	-	-	-	-	-
Fitch Ratings - Solicited &	-	Solicited & Un-Solicited	-	-	-	-
Governance Metrics International (GMI)	-	-	-	-	Solicited	-
Investor Responsibility Research Centre (IRCC)	-	-	-	-	Un-Solicited	-
ISS Corporate Governance Quotient	-	-	-	-	Un-Solicited	-
Mercer	-	-	Solicited	-	-	-
Moody's Investor Services	Solicited	Solicited & Un-Solicited	-	Solicited & Un-Solicited	-	-
Morningstar	-	-	Solicited	-	-	-
Rainmaker	-	-	Solicited	-	-	-
RepuTex	-	-	-	-	-	Un-Solicited & Cooperative
Standard & Poor's (S&P)	Solicited	Solicited & Un-Solicited	Solicited	Solicited & Un-Solicited	Solicited	-
Thompson	-	Solicited & Un-Solicited	Solicited	-	-	-
Van Eyck	-	-	Solicited	-	-	-
Weiss Ratings	Solicited & Un-Solicited	-	-	-	-	-
Sources: Finch (2004); Macquarie University; Industry data (2010).						

CRA LIABILITY FOR FAILURE TO INCORPORATE PENSION LIABILITIES, ENVIRONMENTAL LIABILITIES, EARNINGS MANAGEMENT AND CORPORATE GOVERNANCE DEFICIENCIES IN CREDIT RATINGS

The criteria and penalties for CRAs' legal liabilities for such omissions are or should be similar to their legal liabilities for inaccurate credit ratings.

CRA LEGAL LIABILITY FOR INACCURATE RATINGS[14]

Many parties have criticized credit ratings for their inaccuracy and the inherent conflict of interest in ratings[15]; and have sued CRAs for inaccurate ratings and or deception[16] - such as investors (e.g. pension funds that invested in CBOs); the bankrupt Bear Stearns (for losses of $1.12 billion from alleged "fraudulently issuing inflated ratings for securities"); bond insurers and the US government (which sued S&P for $5 billion for "misrepresenting the credit risk of complex financial products").

Although investors and regulators perceive credit ratings as accurate indicators of credit risk, legislators, courts and regulators both in the U.S., the European Union and other jurisdictions consistently define ratings as opinions and believe that there should not be any substantive regulation of credit rating methodologies. U.S. courts have stated that investors' reliance on credit ratings as though they were "guarantees" of a certain level of credit risk was "unreasonable"[17]. Ryan (2012); Rousseau (2006); Ferri, Liu & Stiglitz (1999); Honohan (2001).

Ratings Agencies often actively participate in the structuring of securities, instead of passively rating securities – this represents a major conflict of interest[18] – the conduct of ratings agencies in the ratings process meets the definition of "underwriter"[19].

While several parties have sued CRAs[20] for various types of alleged inaccuracies and fraud in the ratings process, the Courts in the US have not been uniform in applying legal standards. Nagy (2009), Kettering (2008), Sinclair (2007), and Ellsworth & Bhabha (2008) address some of the issues that pertain to legal liability of CRA's for inaccurate ratings and or fraud.

Recent research in finance[21] shows that asset pricing models of the variety used by credit rating agencies fail to explain real world data. Finch (March 2004). For example, observed market spreads typically are much higher than those predicted by structural models, especially at the high quality end of the rating spectrum. These studies suggest that there are significant non-credit components to spreads on fixed-income instruments. Moreover, such models used by CRAs often fail to consider tail risk, and are based on historical measures, which often are not good predictors. Finch (March 2004); Altman & Rijken (2005); Ferri, Liu & Stiglitz (1999). Also, the actual and perceived accuracy of credit ratings are affected by many factors that are beyond the control of investors, issuers and the CRA. Thus, it's difficult to argue or prove that any one CRA is demonstrably 'special' and or worthy of certification by a regulatory body.

Despite, the recent wave of new CRA regulations that were enacted in various countries during 2008-2013 in response to the Global Financial Crisis, some of which expressly reduced or eliminated the use of credit ratings in regulations/statutes, CRAs have continued to exist for the following reasons. First, credit ratings that were embedded in many existing private contracts and company manuals have not been and probably will not be removed until such documents expire – these include leases, derivatives contracts; acquisition agreements, employment contracts; policies and procedures manuals; and corporate governance documents. These documents constitute the majority of the use-volume of credit ratings. Secondly, the "*business judgment*" rule and "*prudent-person rule*" in corporate governance, investment laws and corporation laws in many jurisdictions require or warrant the use of an independent measure such as credit ratings for some transactions and or documentation. Thirdly, the insurance industry, which provides risk management tools for private and government entities is subject to various types of regulations that require independent verification of credit quality such as credit ratings. Fourth, independence and independent verification of credit quality remains a staple requirement for most business transactions in most developed countries. Fifth, global economic activity is concentrated in, and originates from relatively few developed countries where independent credit verification is part of the culture/tradition, and is a business requirement or a statutory requirement. Sixth, under existing case-law in many developed countries, companies face substantial legal liability (from their shareholders, regulators and or business partners) when they don't obtain the independent verification of credit quality that is provided by CRA. Seventh, many of the viable substitutes for credit ratings don't provide the verification element of credit ratings (most involve the use of other types of transactions). During the last fifteen years and especially since the Global financial Crisis of 2007-2012, the monetary cost of loan insurance, CDS and loan guarantees have generally increased; such that it may be cheaper for an issuer to obtain a credit rating than to purchase loan insurance, a CDS or a loan guarantee. Conversely, the non-monetary psychological security provided by loan insurance and loan guarantees has declined during the last fifteen years and the failure of insurance companies and reinsurers in many countries during 2007-2013 has further reduced reliance on such instruments. Furthermore, the use of credit spreads and CDS spreads does not provide a uniformly acceptable standard of comparison of credit risk and is subject to market noise, and manipulation by traders. Eighth, CRAs also serve as a conflict reduction mechanism by establishing and maintaining standards for some types of transactions. The costs of litigation and actual court awards in business litigation can be substantial and can affect not only the profitability of issuers and investment banks, but also the careers and personal lives of their executives and subordinates. Ninth, CRAs serve as a way to reduce transaction costs by centralization of the verification function – rather than having many analysts in many companies doing the same credit research, the CRAs can save costs and increase standardization (at the risk of amplifying errors) by providing ratings. Tenth, CRAs can reduce the cost of capital for issuers because the CRAs provide a generally acceptable system for ranking and comparing companies based on their credit quality. Eleventh, for portfolio managers, CRAs provide independent justification for investment decisions, and a system for developing investment strategies and for maintenance of relationships with their clients (ie. the portfolio managers actions/decisions, objectives, performance and plans can be more easily explained to a broad range of investor types within the framework and system that is offered by CRAs). CRAs also reduce the portfolio managers' operating costs by effectively facilitating the outsourcing of the investment research function. Twelfth, for markets in general, the CRAs reduce the divergences among investor "types" by standardization of comparison metrics and investors' expectations; and by management of investors' expectations. Thirteenth, CRAs reduce or can reduce volatility in bond, equity, currency and commodity markets because credit ratings help to "standardize" and manage investors' expectations, which in the recent past, has been a major cause of liquidity risk (distinct from credit risk) and significant investor loses. Fourteenth, CRAs serve as a provider of "*Confirmation of Trust*", which facilitates transactions between companies in the real sector that did not have any prior business dealings – many issues that pertain to Supply Chains, facilities, inventory and general operations are affected by, and ultimately determined by corporate credit ratings. Fifteenth, the CRA industry has been given a bad name because people and investors confuse credit risk with liquidity risk; and a substantial percentage of the global financial crisis was attributable to liquidity risk (and not credit risk)[22] – many market participants realize this and continue to patronize and depend on CRAs. Sixteenth, CRAs exist because of the "*Regulatory Migration*" phenomenon wherein there has been an un-intended shift of regulatory and enforcement burden (and associated costs) from the government agencies to the CRAs and the investment banks (which is perhaps constitutionally questionable under the *Delegation Doctrine* in most common-law jurisdictions). Execution of CRAs' ratings framework functions as a quasi-investigative and enforcement mechanism that combines elements of the "*suitability*" doctrine of securities laws, with "*prudent-person*" standards and due diligence of audits. Seventeenth, CRAs exist because they help investors to internalize the costs of failure in investments; and help investment banks internalize the differentials between expectations of issuers and investors (especially for new financial instruments) – and such internalization differs from reduction of information asymmetry because it places the CRA in the position of an expert that reduces internal conflicts within the issuer and the investment bank and associated accounting firms. Eighteenth, it's very difficult to successfully sue and win judgments against CRAs in court for publication and or dissemination of their credit ratings - many judges have ruled that a plaintiff suing a CRA has to show that the CRA made false statements with "actual malice" and intent. Nineteenth, up until 2010, in many countries, CRAs were not fully accountable to any government agency (even when licensed) and were not licensed; but now many developed and developing countries require that CRAs obtain government licenses and maintain minimum standards of qualification and training for their ratings analysts and employees. Twentieth, there is a clear *Entrenchment Phenomenon* wherein the actual or perceived market-power of the Big-three CRAs combined with regulation and substantial barriers-to-entry results in an oligopoly or duopoly. This *Entrenchment* phenomenon was not and probably will not be affected by the Global Financial Crisis and the new CRA regulations/statutes that were enacted during 2008-2013 in various jurisdictions. Most of those statutes don't address the key weaknesses in, or change the nature of competition in the CRA industry. It seems that regulators, banks and issuers realize that CRAs can substantially reduce the Consumer Surpluses (issuers pay above-market interest rates; and pay substantial transaction costs), Producer Surpluses (investors accept below-market interest rates; and also pay substantial transaction costs and monitoring costs) and Deadweight-Losses (that ratings contract is not in equilibrium, and cannot be amended without the investor, or issuer or CRA or the investment bank or the general public incurring some additional losses) inherent in the ratings process and the associated pricing of new and seasoned securities/instruments – primarily by issuing ratings, serving as an expert and resolving technical issues. CRAs serve as a conflict-reduction agent that resolves pre-offering and post offering conflicts within and among issuers, investment banks and investors.

From a *Tort Theory* perspective:

1. Imposing liability on CRAs improves social welfare, and will compel CRAs to conduct more thorough due diligence and monitor their client-companies.
2. The benefits of compeling CRAs to monitor companies for earnings management and fraud far outweight the costs of resolving earnings management dispuites or prosecuting perpetrators.
3. The costs of eliminating the possibility of imposing liability on CRAs far outweights the cost of imposing liability on them.
4. CRAs and issuer-companies can become joint tortfeasors and criminal conspirators if the issuer-companies provide sufficient incentives.
5. CRAs have a moral and statutory duty to identify and report inaccurate disclosures, earnings amangement and asset quality management.
6. Failure to impose liability on CRAs may trigger Constitutional-Tort liability for governments.
7. Strict-Liability applies.
8. Public welfare considerations should be priority (ie. investors' losses and corporate failures due to inaccurate disclosures and wrong credit ratings which cause contagion in debt markets; inability of companies and governments to raise capital due to investors' fears; etc.).
9. The compensation structure of CRAs and their analysts combined with the low customer-switching costs and plurality of ratings (most customers simultaneously obtain more than one rating) provides

sufficient incentives for CRAs to issue inflated ratings, downgrade companys' un-solicited ratings and to cover-up earnings management and fraud in order to both retain and obtain new clients. Furthermore, CRAs face significant Reputation Costs if a rated company is subsequently found to have engaged in earnings management – this also provides additional incentives for CRAs to collude in earnings management and fraud. Note that CRAs' liability for inaccurate credit ratings differs substantially from CRAs' liability for earning management and or asset-quality management. In most jurisdictions, CRAs cannot be held liable for inaccurate credit ratings.

Given the foregoing, CRAs should be held liable for credit ratings that in hindsight, prove to be overly wrong (such as the credit ratings assigned by the Big-Three CRAs to many ABS Trusts during 2006-2009). On or around February 3, 2015, the US Justice Department announced that it had reached a settlement agreement with S&P wherein S&P will pay a US$1.375 Billion fine for inaccurate ratings that it issued[23]. As of February 2015, the US Justice Department was investigating Moodys[24].

INDUSTRY STRUCTURE AND THE INTERNATIONAL POLITICAL ECONOMY AND REGULATION DILEMMA: CRAS AS FINANCIAL INSTITUTIONS

CRAs perform or can perform a "*Surplus Balancing*" function wherein CRAs reduce Consumer Surplus (the difference between the market interest rate for the security/instrument and what the investors pay as interest) and the "Producer Surplus" (the difference between the market interest rate for the security/instrument and what the issuers charges as interest) by issuing ratings and revising such ratings. CRAs also function as a check-and-balance mechanism for the accuracy of the audited financial statements that are issued by accounting firms.

Although during 2000-2017, more than eighty-five percent (85%) of CRAs' revenues were derived from issuers who pay for ratings, CRAs rate hundreds or thousands of bond issues annually, and the ratings fee is about $30,000-$600,000 for regular corporate bonds and up to 15bp of the gross offering amount for structured finance securities/instruments; and each CRA's revenues are never concentrated among any particular issuer or group of issuers (e.g. among the big-three CRAs, no single issuer or issuer group represents more than about two percent of the total annual revenues from the CRA's rating business). A. M. Best (2013). He, Qian & Strahan (2012). Garcia & del Pozo (2012).

Complex Systems "Emergence" is a key issue here, and CRAs have emerged as financial institutions for several reasons and should be regulated as such. Partnoy (2006); Schwarcz (2002). Pendergraft (2012). First, the increasing complexity of financial instruments has required more due diligence by CRAs and more deliberation among the issuer, CRA and investment banks. As mentioned above, CRAs often actively participate in the structuring of securities, instead of passively rating securities and – the conduct of ratings agencies in the ratings process meets the definition of "underwriter". Secondly, the sheer volume of financial instruments whose valuations are partly based on credit ratings has exploded during the last decade – the notional volumes of CDS contracts, swaps/derivatives, and structured products has now exceed $500 trillion. Thirdly, up until 2013, credit ratings were embedded in many statutes/regulations in many countries, and hence affected solvency of companies and regulatory compliance. Fourth, as mentioned, many private contracts include credit ratings as part of express contract terms or contingencies – the reasons for this trend are explained herein. Fifth, the volume of financial litigation has increased in many developed countries, and credit ratings are often a major element of such litigation. In many countries, the common law that pertains to financial litigation admits evidence and allocates liability and damages in ways that encourage the use of credit ratings. Sixth, in many countries and during the last decade, new regulations and market trends have encouraged the growth of the intermediation functions of banks (instead of trading or principal transactions) and such activities are heavily dependent on verification provided by credit ratings. Seventh, many of the alternatives to credit ratings also involve financial institutions, so that the public perception and perceived quality of CRAs is now intertwined with these financial institutions.

The issue of the proper regulatory use of credit ratings has been largely determined in many developed countries (the US; European Union; United Kingdom; etc.) and the consensus across countries is that credit ratings should be eliminated or significantly de-emphasized in regulations/statutes.

There are very few CRAs in most countries for several reasons. First legal liability is a major concern for CRAs, and given that CRAs have been sued and that a single award from a lawsuit can bankrupt a CRA, such potential liability is un-attractive to potential entrants. Second, the cost structure of CRAs is not amenable to improvement or realignment and a large percentage of CRA's costs are fixed costs. Due to the implicit quality guarantees and person-specific expertise required in the ratings process, most CRAs cannot outsource their ratings projects, and must pay top dollar to attract professionals. Third, the current and proposed compensation contracts for CRAs are limiting because most expose the CRA to intense competition and or to fluctuations in the volume of users, trading activity, issuers and financial instruments. Most of such contracts are not aligned with the CRA's cost structure. Fourth, the CRA industry is relatively very opaque the CRA's typically don't disclose information about their cost structure and operations, and so it's difficult for new entrants to plan sufficiently. Fifth, existing regulations and required certification for CRAs and the prospect of ever increasing regulation is a major barrier to entry – such certification and regulations exponentially increases the CRA's startup costs and operating costs, and very few individual entrepreneurs have the capital and time to surmount such obstacles. Sixth, the risk-reward ratio for startup CRAs is very low especially when the preceding factors are considered, and for venture capital companies and entrepreneurs, there are other new ventures that offer much higher risk-reward profiles. As a result, new CRAs are usually started by established existing companies, or as joint ventures by or with existing companies who have a long-term view and can afford the initial losses and can provide the substantial capital required for the new startup CRA's operations. Seventh, in many developed countries, many of the alternatives to credit ratings (which are described herein) are well developed, or and have become un-announced but viable alternatives to credit ratings. Eighth, the CRA industry is simply not competitive because for each offering of bonds/loans, most issuers obtain 2-3 ratings from only the Big-Three CRAs, and this "allocation" of ratings assignments based on perceived CRA "market power": a) reduces industry competition and b) ensures that the only the Big-Three CRAs have any significant chance of long term profitability; and c) is a form of un-regulated *refusal-to-deal* or *group boycott* of un-popular or smaller CRAs. Ninth, in the CRA industry, revenues and profits are directly proportional to the CRA's Reputation and Influence, and it takes a relatively long time for new CRAs to build such reputation, during which they must sustain losses – this discourages prospective market entrants. Tenth, in the CRA industry, quality differentiation among the four dominant rating agencies is hard to achieve, but the perceived quality differential between the Big-Three CRAs and the smaller seven CRAs is large and discourages new entrants (it will take large amounts of marketing dollars to overcome such perceptions). Eleventh, the ratings business has become a relationship business wherein the Big-Three CRAs maintain relationship with most existing issuers, and such issuers face the threat of imminent downgrades if they switch to new CRAs that have less Reputation, and this in turn precludes market entry by prospective CRAs. Twelfth, CRA market Power and Influence are significant decision factors for issuers because collusion among the Big-Three CRAs can be hard to detect or investigate (they routinely hire each other staff) and a CRA can downgrade an issuer's ratings or place the issuer on a credit-watch, all of which can suddenly and substantially reduce that issuer's opportunity set. Thirteenth, the Big-Three CRAs routinely hire staff of banks (who have relationships with issuers), and many former CRA ratings analysts are hired by "users" (e.g. banks; pension funds; insurance agencies; bond mutual funds; etc.), and this hiring pattern and symbiotic relationships reinforce the dominance and reputation of the Big-Three CRAs in markets and precludes new or prospective CRAs from hiring reputable ratings analysts that can generate ratings business. Fourteenth, as mentioned, the CRA industry has been given a bad name because people and investors confuse credit risk with liquidity risk – and a substantial percentage of the global financial crisis was attributable to liquidity risk (and not credit risk).

The issue of competition or collusion in the CRA industry is sometimes difficult to address simply because of the opaque nature of CRAs (many are private companies or subsidiaries of large conglomerates and don't release their financial data – only Moodys is an independent exchange-traded company). Also, collusion in the CRA industry is very difficult to detect – CRAs hire staff from each other, use conceptually similar ratings models and sometimes provide the same or similar training for their staff. CRAs have easy access to the ratings of other CRAs, and so collusion can be two-sided (both parties are active participants in collusion) or one-sided (one party is not an active participant) or un-intentional.

CONCLUSION

The regulation and compensation of CRAs remains a major problem because despite the enactment of new financial regulations for CRAs in various countries, and the de-emphasis/removal of credit ratings in regulations, and recommendations of new CRA compensation models, CRAs have substantial potential to undermine national financial systems and to cause or amplify systemic risk. Most if not all recommended business models and compensation arrangement for CRAs are grossly deficient, and or will cause conflicts-of-interest. Many of the economic studies of CRAs almost completely omit analysis of the legal issues that pertain to the ratings process (fraud; conspiracy; freedom-of-speech; extortion; etc.) and competition among CRAs (antitrust; fraud)and the cost structure of CRAs. While there are feasible alternatives to traditional credit-ratings, the associated transaction costs, and susceptibility to market manipulation of such metrics (such as credit spreads and CDS spreads) and the lack of development of some markets (such as leasing, joint ventures and licensing) make them less appealing in the short term. The over-emphasis on Reputational Capital of CRAs is somewhat misplaced and the appropriate solutions to the CRA problem will need to blend compensation with an efficient business model and concern for social welfare and monitoring costs.

REFERENCES

Abad, P., Ferreras, R., & Robles, D. (2020). Information opacity and corporate bond returns: The dynamics of split ratings. *Journal of International Financial Markets, Institutions and Money*, *68*, 68. doi:10.1016/j.intfin.2020.101239

Abrantes-Metz, R. (2012). *Credit Rating Agencies, the Financial Crisis, and Regulation*. https://www.globaleconomicsgroup.com/financial-regulation/credit-rating-agencies-the-financial-crisis-and-regulation/

Afonso, A., Furceri, D., & Gomes, P. (2012). Sovereign credit ratings and financial market linkages: Application to European data. *Journal of International Money and Finance*, *31*(3), 606–638. doi:10.1016/j.jimonfin.2012.01.016

Alp, A. (2014). Structural shifts in credit rating standards. *The Journal of Finance.*

Altman, E., & Rijken, H. (2005). The Impact of the Rating Agencies' Through-the-Cycle Methodology on Rating Dynamics. *Economic Notes*, *34*(2), 127–154. doi:10.1111/j.0391-5026.2005.00147.x

Ashcraft, A., Goldsmith-Pinkham, P. & Vickery, J. (2010). *MBS ratings and the mortgage credit boom.* Federal Reserve Bank of New York Staff Reports no. 449.

Bai, L. (2010). On Regulating Conflicts of Interest in the Credit Rating Industry. *NYU Journal Of Legislation And Public Policy*, *13*, 253–263.

Beaver, W., Shakespeare, C., & Soliman, M. (2006). Differential properties in the ratings of certified versus non-certified bond-CRAs. *Journal of Accounting and Economics*, *42*(3), 303–334. doi:10.1016/j.jacceco.2006.06.002

Becker, B., & Milbourn, T. (2011). How did increased competition affect credit ratings? *Journal of Financial Economics*, *101*(3), 493–514. doi:10.1016/j.jfineco.2011.03.012

Best, A. M. (2013). *Compensation Disclosure*. Available at: http://www.ambest.com/nrsro/CompensationDisclosure.pdf

Blaubrock, U. (2007). Control and Responsibility of Credit Rating Agencies. *Electronic Journal of Comparative Law*, *11*(3), 6.

Bolton, P., Freixas, X., & Shapiro, J. (2012). The Credit Ratings Game. *The Journal of Finance*, *67*(1), 85–112. doi:10.1111/j.1540-6261.2011.01708.x

Bonewitz, P. (2010). Implications of Reputation Economics on Regulatory Reform of the Credit Rating Industry. *William & Mary Business Law Review*, *1*, 391-409. https://scholarship.law.wm.edu/wmblr/vol1/iss2/4

Bongaerts, D. (2013). *Can Alternative Business Models Discipline Credit CRAs*? Working Paper.

Bongaerts, D., Cremers, M., & Goetzmann, W. (2012). Tie-Breaker: Certification And Multiple Credit Ratings. *The Journal of Finance*, *67*(1), 113–152. doi:10.1111/j.1540-6261.2011.01709.x

Boot, A., Milboum, T., & Schmeits, A. (2006). Credit Ratings as Coordination Mechanisms. *Review of Financial Studies*, *19*(1), 81–118. doi:10.1093/rfs/hhj009

Borio, C. (2008). *The financial turmoil of 2007–? A preliminary assessment and some policy considerations*. Monetary and Economic Department, BIS Working Papers No. 251.

Bottini, F. (1993). An Examination of the Current Status of CRAs And Proposals for Limited Oversight of Such Agencies. *The San Diego Law Review*, *30*, 579–589.

Byoun, S., Han, S., & Shin, Y. (2020). Does the Nationally Recognized Statistical Rating Organization certification matter for Japanese credit rating agencies? *Journal of Financial Markets*.

Camanho, N., Deb, P., & Liu, Z. (2012). *Credit Rating and Competition*. Working Paper, Financial Markets Group, London School of Economics and Political Science.

Cantor, R., & Packer, F. (1997). Differences of opinion and selection bias in the credit rating industry. *Journal of Banking & Finance*, *21*(10), 1395–1417. doi:10.1016/S0378-4266(97)00024-1

Cash, D. (2018). Sustainable finance ratings as the latest symptom of 'rating addiction'. *Journal of Sustainable Finance & Investment*, *8*(3), 242–258. doi:10.1080/20430795.2018.1437996

Cash, D. (2020). Sustainable rating agencies. *Finance and Sustainable Development: Designing Sustainable Financial Systems*, 141.

Cash, D. (2021). Can Regulatory Intervention Save the Sustainability Rating Industry? *Business Law Review*.

Chen, Z., Matousek, R., Stewart, C., & Webb, R. (2019). Do rating agencies exhibit herding behaviour? Evidence from sovereign ratings. *International Review of Financial Analysis*, *64*, 57–70. doi:10.1016/j.irfa.2019.04.011

Cornaggia, J., & Cornaggia, K. J. (2013). Estimating the Costs of Issuer-Paid Credit Ratings. *Review of Financial Studies*, *26*(9), 2229–2269. doi:10.1093/rfs/hht041

Covitz, D., & Harrison, P. (2003). *Testing Conflicts of Interest At Bond CRAs with Market Anticipation: Evidence That Reputation Incentives Dominate*. Finance & Economics Discussion Series 2003-68. Board Of Governors of The Federal Reserve System.

DAF/COMP. (2010). *Directorate For Financial And Enterprise Affairs - Competition Committee*. OECD. Available at: https://www.oecd.org/regreform/sectors/46825342.pdf

Dallocchio, M., Hubler, J., Raimbourg, P., & Salvi, A. (2006). Do Upgradings and Downgradings Convey Information? An Event Study of the French Bond Market. *Economic Notes*, *35*(30), 293–317. doi:10.1111/j.1468-0300.2006.00167.x

Darbellay, A. (2013). *Regulating Credit Rating Agencies*. Edward Elgar. doi:10.4337/9780857939364

Di Cesare, A. (2006). Do Market-Based Indicators Anticipate Rating Agencies? Evidence for International Banks. *Economic Notes*, *35*(1), 121–150. doi:10.1111/j.0391-5026.2006.00161.x

Dittrich, F. (2007). *The credit rating industry: Competition and regulation*. Inaugural PHD Dissertation. zur Erlangung Des Doktorgrades der Wirtschafts- und Sozialwissenschaftlichen Fakultat der Universitat zu Koln, Germany.

Du, W. (2018). Who carried more credibility?: An analysis of the market responses to news from the Japanese government, the Japanese central bank and international credit rating agencies. *Journal of Economics and Business*, *98*, 32–39. doi:10.1016/j.jeconbus.2018.05.002

Ekins, E., & Calabria, M. (2012). *Regulation, Market Structure, and Role of the Credit Rating Agencies*. Policy Analysis#704. Cato Institute. https://object.cato.org/pubs/pas/PA704.pdf

Ellsworth, L., & Bhabha, I. (2008). *A New Front in Subprime Litigation: Can CRAs Be Held Liable?* LAW360. https://www.law360.com/articles/65936

Faure-Grimaud, A., Peyrachie, E., & Quesada, L. (2009). The ownership Of Ratings. *The RAND Journal of Economics*, *40*(2), 234–257. doi:10.1111/j.1756-2171.2009.00063.x

Ferri, G., Liu, L., & Stiglitz, J. (1999). The Pro-cyclical Role of Rating Agencies: Evidence from the East Asian Crisis. *Economic Notes*, *28*(3), 335–355. doi:10.1111/1468-0300.00016

Finch, N. (2004). *International Rating Agencies And Sustainability*. Working Paper, Macquarie University.

Fitzgerald, F. (2002). *The Use of Insurance Credit Scoring In Automobile and Homeowners Insurance: A Report to the Governor, the Legislature and the People of Michigan*. Available at: https://www.michigan.gov/documents/cis_ofis_credit_scoring_report_52885_7.pdf

Flannery, M., Houston, J., & Partnoy, F. (2010). Credit Default Swap Spreads as Viable Substitutes for Credit Ratings. *University of Pennsylvania Law Review*, *158*, 2085–2095.

Forbes, K., Warnock, J., & Francis, E. (2012). Capital flow waves: Surges, stops, flight, and retrenchment. *Journal of International Economics*, *88*(2), 235–251. doi:10.1016/j.jinteco.2012.03.006

Frost, C. (2009). Credit CRAs in Capital Markets: A Review of Research Evidence on Selected Criticisms of the Agencies. *Journal of Accounting, Auditing & Finance*, *22*(3), 469–492. doi:10.1177/0148558X0702200306

FSB. (2010). *Principles for Reducing the Reliance on Ratings*. Available at: www.financialstabilityboard.org/publications/r_101027.pdf

Fulghieri, P., Strobl, L., & Xia, H. (2010). *The Economics Of Solicited And Un-Solicited Credit Ratings*. Working Paper.

Galil, K., & Soer, G. (2011). Good news, bad news and rating announcements: An empirical investigation. *Journal of Banking & Finance*, *35*(11), 3101–3119. doi:10.1016/j.jbankfin.2011.04.010

Garcia, R., & del Pozo, J. (2012). *Credit Rating Agencies on the Watch List: Analysis of European Regulation*. Oxford University Press. doi:10.1093/acprof:oso/9780199608867.001.0001

Gomes, R. (2014). Optimal auction design in two-sided markets. *The RAND Journal of Economics*, *45*(2), 248–272. doi:10.1111/1756-2171.12050

Goodhart, C. (2008). *How, if at all, should Credit Rating s Agencies (CRAs) be Regulated?*. LSE Financial Markets Group Paper Series, special paper #181.

Govindan, S., & Wilson, R. (2006). Sufficient conditions for stable equilibria. *Theoretical Economics, 1*, 167–206. https://econtheory.org/ojs/index.php/te/article/viewFile/20060167/617/25

Grin, J. M., & Tang, D. Y. (2012). Did subjectivity play a role in CDO Credit Ratings? *The Journal of Finance, 67*(4), 1293–1328. doi:10.1111/j.1540-6261.2012.01748.x

Gromb, D., & Martimort, D. (2007). Collusion And The Organization Of Delegated Expertise. *Journal of Economic Theory, 137*(1), 271–299. doi:10.1016/j.jet.2007.01.003

He, J., Qian, J., & Strahan, P. E. (2012). Are All Ratings Created Equal? The Impact of Issuer Size on the Pricing of Mortgage-Backed Securities. *The Journal of Finance, 67*(6), 2097–2137. doi:10.1111/j.1540-6261.2012.01782.x

Hemraj, M. (2015). *Credit Rating Agencies: Self-regulation, Statutory Regulation and Case Law*. Springer. doi:10.1007/978-3-319-17927-8

Hill, C. (2003). CRAs Behaving Badly: The Case of Enron. *Connecticut Law Review, 35*, 1145–1155.

Hill, C. (2009). Why Did Anyone Listen to the CRAs After Enron? *Journal of Business & Technology Law, 4*, 283-293.

Hill, C. (2010). Why Did CRAs Do Such a Bad Job Rating Subprime Securities? *University of Pittsburgh Law Review. University of Pittsburgh. School of Law, 71*, 585–595.

Hill, C. (2011). Limits of Dodd-Frank's CRA Reform. *Chapman Law Review, 15*, 133–143.

Hill, C. A. (2004). Regulating the CRAs. *Washington Law Quarterly, 82*, 43–53.

Honohan, P. (2001). Perverse Effects of an External Ratings-Related Capital Adequacy System. *Economic Notes, 30*(3), 359–372. doi:10.1111/1468-0300.00063

Hu, X., Huang, H., Pan, Z., & Shi, J. (2019). Information asymmetry and credit rating: A quasi-natural experiment from China. *Journal of Banking & Finance, 106*, 132–152. doi:10.1016/j.jbankfin.2019.06.003

Huang, Y., & Shen, C. (2019). What role does the investor-paid rating agency play in China? Competitor or information provider. *International Review of Economics & Finance, 63*, 253–272. doi:10.1016/j.iref.2018.11.007

Humphrey, C. (2018). The Role of Credit Rating Agencies in Shaping Multilateral Finance: Recent Developments and Policy Options. *Discussion draft, Inter-Governmental Group of, 24*.

Hunt, J. (2009). Credit CRAs and the "Worldwide Credit Crisis": The Limits of Reputation, the Insufficiency of Reform, and a Proposal for Improvement. *Columbia Business Law Review, 2009*, 109–119.

Husisian, G. (1990). What Standard of Care Should Govern the World's shortest Editorials?: An Analysis of Bond CRA Liability. *Cornell Law Review, 75*, 411–460.

Ioannou, S., Wójcik, D., & Pažitka, D. (2020). Financial centre bias in sub-sovereign credit ratings. *Journal of International Financial Markets, Institutions and Money*.

IOSCO. (2008). *The role of credit CRAs in structured finance markets*. Final Report.

Ismailescu, I., & Kazemi, H. (2010). The reaction of emerging market credit default swap spreads to sovereign credit rating changes. *Journal of Banking & Finance, 34*(12), 2861–2873. doi:10.1016/j.jbankfin.2010.05.014

KerwerD. (2001). *Standardizating as Governance: The Case of Credit CRAs.* MPI Collective Goods, Preprint No. 2001/3, 2001. Available at http://ssrn.com/absract=269311

Kettering, K. (2008). Securitization and Its Discontents: The Dynamics of Financial Product Development. *Cardozo Law Review, 29*, 1687–1693.

Ki, J., Nowak, S., & Schumacher, L. (2012). *Are CRAs Powerful? An Investigation Into The Impact And Accuracy of Sovereign Ratings*. IMF working paper 12/23.

Kohlberg, E., & Mertens, J. (1986). On the Strategic Stability of Equilibria. *Econometrica, 54*(5), 1003–1037. doi:10.2307/1912320

Kuhner, C. (2001). Financial CRAs: Are they credible? Insights into the reporting incentives of CRAs in times of enhanced systemic risk. *Schmalenbach Business Review, 53*, 4–20. doi:10.1007/BF03396881

Land, D. (2007). Residential Mortgage Securitization and Consumer Welfare. *Consumer Finance Law Quarterly Report, 61*, 208–218.

Lannoo, K. (2008). *Credit Rating Agencies: Scapegoat or free-riders?* ECMI Commentary No. 20/9.

Lee, J., & Liu, Q. (2013). Gambling Reputation: Repeated Bargaining With Outside Options. *Econometrica, 81*(4), 1601–1672. doi:10.3982/ECTA9200

Löffler, G. (2004). An Anatomy of Rating Through the Cycle. *Journal of Banking & Finance, 28*(3), 695–670. doi:10.1016/S0378-4266(03)00041-4

Loffler, G. (2005). Avoiding the Rating Bounce: Why Rating Agencies Are Slow to React to New Information. *Journal of Economic Behavior & Organization, 56*(3), 365–381. doi:10.1016/j.jebo.2003.09.015

Lupica, L. (2009). Credit CRAs, Structured Securities, and the Way Out of the Abyss. *Review Of Banking & Finance, 28*, 639–649.

Lutz, D., & Schafke, R. (1985). On The Identification And Stability Of Formal Invariants For Singular Differential Equations. *Linear Algebra and Its Applications, 7*, 1–46. doi:10.1016/0024-3795(85)90140-5

Lynch, T. (2009). Deeply and Persistently Conflicted: Credit CRAs in the Current Regulatory Environment. *Case Western Reserve Law Review, 59*, 227–237.

Madigan, P. (2009). CRA reform legislation 'inappropriate and unfair. *Risk Magazine*.

Manns, J. (2013). Downgrading CRA Reform. *The George Washington Law Review, 81*, 749–759.

Mansoor, M., Ellahi, N., Hassan, A., Malik, Q. A., Waheed, A., & Ullah, N. (2020). Corporate Governance, Shariah Governance, and Credit Rating: A Cross-Country Analysis from Asian Islamic Banks. *Journal of Open Innovation, 6*(4), 170. doi:10.3390/joitmc6040170

Mariano, B. (2012). Market power and reputational concerns in the ratings industry. *Journal of Banking & Finance, 36*(6), 1616–1626. doi:10.1016/j.jbankfin.2012.01.012

Martínez, R., Massó, J., Neme, A., & Oviedo, J. (2012). On The Invariance Of The Set Of Core Matchings With Respect To Preference Profiles. *Games and Economic Behavior, 74*(2), 588–600. doi:10.1016/j.geb.2011.08.011

Mashayekhy, L., Nejad, M., & Grosu, D. (2014). A Two-Sided Market Mechanism For Trading Big Data Computing Commodities. *2014 IEEE International Conference On Big Data*. 10.1109/BigData.2014.7004225

Mason, J., & Rosner, J. (2007). *Where Did the Risk Go? How Misapplied Bond Ratings Cause Mortgage Backed Securities and Collateralized Debt Obligation Market Disruptions*. https://www.hudson.org/files/publications/Hudson_Mortgage_Paper5_3_07.pdf

Mathis, J., McAndrews, J., & Rochet, J. (2009). Rating the raters: Are reputation concerns powerful enough to discipline CRAs? *Journal of Monetary Economics, 56*(5), 657–674. doi:10.1016/j.jmoneco.2009.04.004

Metz, A. (2012). The Performance of Corporate Credit Ratings. *Antitrust Chronicle, 4*(1).

Miglionico, A. (2019). *The governance of credit rating agencies: regulatory regimes and liability issues*. Edward Elgar Publishing. doi:10.4337/9781786439949

Nagy, T. (2009). Note: CRAs and the First Amendment: Applying Constitutional Journalistic Protections to Subprime Mortgage Litigation. *Minnesota Law Review, 94*, 140–150. https://www.minnesotalawreview.org/wp-content/uploads/2011/08/Nagy_MLR.pdf

Noe, T. (2012). Survey of the Economic Theory of Reputation: Its Logic and Limits. In *The Oxford Handbook of Corporate Reputation*. Oxford University Press.

OECD. (2010). *Competition and Credit Rating Agencies*. OECD.

Office Of The New York State Attorney General. (2008). *Attorney General Cuomo Announces Landmark Reform agreements With The Nation's Three Principal Credit CRAs*. Available at: http://www.oag.state.ny.us/press/2008/june/june5a_08.html/

Opp, C., Opp, M., & Harris, M. (2013). CRAs In The Face Of Regulation. *Journal of Financial Economics, 108*(1), 46–61. doi:10.1016/j.jfineco.2012.10.011

Ordonez, G. (2013). Fragility Of Reputation And Clustering Of Risk-taking. *Theoretical Economics, 8*(3), 653–700. doi:10.3982/TE1207

Pagano, M., & Volpin, P. (2010a). Credit Ratings Failures And Policy Options. In M. Dewatripont, X. Freixas, & R. Portes (Eds.), *Macroceocomic Stability And Financial Regulation: Key issues For the G20* (pp. 129–148).

Pagano, M., & Volpin, P. (2010b). Credit ratings failures and policy options. *Economic Policy, 25*(April), 401–431. doi:10.1111/j.1468-0327.2010.00245.x

Palmigiano, P., & Pieri, S. (2014). Credit Rating Agencies: Change by Competition Law or Regulation? *Antitrust Chronicle*. https://www.competitionpolicyinternational.com/credit-ratings-agencies-change-by-competition-law-or-regulation/

Park, G., & Lee, H. (2018). Opportunistic behaviors of credit rating agencies and bond issuers. *Pacific-Basin Finance Journal, 47*, 39–59. doi:10.1016/j.pacfin.2017.11.003

Partnoy, F. (2006). How and why credit ratings are not like other gatekeepers. In Y. Fuchita & R. Litan (Eds.), *Financial Gatekeepers: Can they protect investors?* Brookings Institution Press. https://papers.ssrn.com/sol3/papers.cfm?abstract_id=900257

Partnoy, F. (2009). Historical Perspectives on the Financial Crisis: Ivar Kreuger, the Credit-CRAs, and Two Theories About the Function and Dysfunction of Markets. *Yale Journal on Regulation, 26*, 431–440.

Patterson, M. (2012). Manipulation of Product Ratings: Credit-Rating Agencies, Google, and Antitrust. *Antitrust Chronicle, 4*(1).

Pendergraft, E. (2012). Section 933(b): Nimble Private Regulation of the Capital Market Gatekeepers. *Florida State University Law Review. Florida State University. College of Law, 39*, 511–515.

Petit, N. (2002). From Formalism to Effects? The Commission's Communication on Enforcement Priorities in Applying Article 82 EC. *World Competition, 32*, 485–490.

Petit, N. (2011). Credit Rating Agencies, The Sovereign Debt Crisis And Competition Law. *European Competition Journal, 7*(3).

Petit, N., & Neyrinck, N. (2011). Credit Rating Agencies and Competition Law. *Antitrust Chronicle, 4*(1).

Reiss, D. (2005, September 2). Subprime Standardization: How CRAs Allow Predatory Lending to Flourish in the Secondary Mortgage Market. *Florida State University Law Review. Florida State University. College of Law*, 33.

Rhee, R. (2013). On Duopoly and Compensation Games in the Credit Rating Industry. *Northwestern University Law Review*, 108.

Roesch, D. (2002). The Informational Content of Credit Ratings and Cyclical Patterns of Default Rates. *Central European Journal of Operations Research, 10*(2), 163–186.

Rousseau, S. (2006). Enhancing the Accountability of Credit CRAs: The Case for a Disclosure-Based Approach. *McGill Law Journal. Revue de Droit de McGill, 51*, 617–621.

Ryan, J. (2012). *The Negative Impact Of Credit Rating Agencies And Proposals For Better Regulation.* Working Paper – German Institute for International and Security Affairs, Germany. https://www.swp-berlin.org/fileadmin/contents/products/arbeitspapiere/The_Negative_Impact_of_Credit_Rating_Agencies_KS.pdf

Schwarcz, S. (2002). Private Ordering of Public Markets: The CRA Paradox. *University of Illinois Law Review, 2002*(1), 1–2.

Securities & Exchange Board of India. (2016). *Enhanced Standards for Credit Rating Agencies (CRAs).* PR No. 150/2016. https://www.sebi.gov.in/cms/sebi_data/attachdocs/1477999985100.pdf

Shuermann, T. (2004). *A Review of Recent Books on Credit Risk.* Federal Reserve Bank of New York.

Sinclair, T. (2007). Passing Judgment: Credit Rating Processes as Regulatory Mechanisms of Governance in the Emerging World Order. In P. James & H. Patomäki (Eds.), Globalization And Economy: Globalizing Finance And The New Global Economy (pp. 248–253). Academic Press.

Skreta, V., & Veldkamp, L. (2009). Ratings Shopping And Asset Complexity: A Theory Of Ratings Inflation. *Journal of Monetary Economics*, *56*(5), 678–695. doi:10.1016/j.jmoneco.2009.04.006

Standard & Poors. (2013). *What Credit Ratings Are & Are Not*. Available at: http://www.standardandpoors.com/aboutcreditratings/RatingsManual_PrintGuide.html

Sy, A. (2009, December). The Systemic Regulation of Credit Rating Agencies And Rated Markets. *World Economy*, *27*(2), 161–174.

Tarashev, N. (2005). *An Empirical Evaluation of Structural Credit Spread Models*. BIS Working Papers, #179.

Telser, L. (1994). The Usefulness of Core Theory In Economics. *The Journal of Economic Perspectives*, *8*(2), 151–164. doi:10.1257/jep.8.2.151

Toscano, F. (2020). Does the Dodd-Frank Act reduce the conflict of interests of credit rating agencies? *Journal of Corporate Finance*, *62*, 62. doi:10.1016/j.jcorpfin.2020.101595

United States Government Accountability Office. (2012). *Credit Rating Agencies: Alternative Compensation Models for Nationally Recognized Statistical Rating Organizations*. Available at: https://www.gao.gov/assets/590/587832.pdf

U.S. Department of Justice. (2009). *Constitutionality of Mandatory Registration of Credit CRAs*. Available at: https://www.justice.gov/olc/2009/opinion-letter-treasury.pdf

US Dept. of Justice Complaint. (2013). *Department of Justice Sues Standard & Poors For Fraud In Rating Mortgage Backed Securities In The Years Leading Up To The Financial Crisis*. Author.

U.S. Federal Deposit Insurance Corporation (2011). *References to Credit Ratings in FDIC Regulations*. Author.

Van Den Brink, R. (2012). Efficiency and Collusion Neutrality in Cooperative Games and Networks. *Games and Economic Behavior*, *76*(1), 344–348. doi:10.1016/j.geb.2012.04.001

Virag, G. (2011). High Profit Equilibria In Directed Search models. *Games and Economic Behavior*, *71*(1), 224–234. doi:10.1016/j.geb.2010.08.006

Wang, T. (2012). *Can reputation concerns always discipline credit CRAs? Evidence from corporate bond issuance ratings*. Working Paper.

White, L. (2000). *The Credit Rating Industry: An Industrial Organization Analysis*. Stern School of Business, New York University. Prepared for the CIPE project on "Credit Ratings and the International Economy".

White, L. (2006). *Good Intentions Gone Awry: A Policy Analysis of the SEC's Regulation of the Bond Rating Industry.* New York University Law and Economics Research Paper #06-36; Networks Financial Institute Policy Brief, No. 2006-PB-05, April 2006. Available at: https://papers.ssrn.com/sol3/papers.cfm?abstract_id=923566

White, L. (2010). Markets: The Credit CRAs. *The Journal of Economic Perspectives, 24*(2), 211–226. doi:10.1257/jep.24.2.211

White, L. (2013). Credit Rating Agencies: An Overview. *Annual Review of Financial Economics, 5*(1), 93–122. doi:10.1146/annurev-financial-110112-120942

Yalta, T., & Yalta, Y. (2018). Are credit rating agencies regionally biased? *Economic Systems, 42*(4), 682–694. doi:10.1016/j.ecosys.2018.08.001

Yoav, S., & Leyton-Brown, K. (2009). *Multiagent Systems: Algorithmic, Game-Theoretic, and Logical Foundations.* Cambridge University Press.

ENDNOTES

1 See: Connecticut Attorney General's Office (2008). Press Release - Attorney General Sues Credit Rating Agencies For Illegally Giving Municipalities Lower Ratings, Costing Taxpayers Millions. http://www.ct.gov/ag/cwp/view.asp?A=2795&Q=420390.

2 *See*: *Business Electronics Corp. vs. Sharp Electronics Corp,* 485 U.S. 717 (1988; US Supreme Court); *Copperweld Corp. v Independence Tube*, 467 U.S. 752 (1984; US Supreme Court); *Monsanto Co. v. Spray-Rite Service Corp.*, 465 U.S. 752 (1984; US Supreme Court); *US v. Arnold, Schwinn et. al.*, 388 U.S. 365 (1967; US Supreme Court); *USPS v. Flamingo Industries*, #02-1290 (2004); *Brown v. Pro Football,* 518 U.S. 213 (1996; US Supreme Court); *Federal Trade Commission v. Ticor Title Insurance Company*, 60 U.S.L.W. 4515 (1992; US Supreme Court); *Allied Tube & Conduit Corp. v. Indian head Inc.*, 486 U.S. 492 (1998; US Supreme Court); *Phonetele*, 664 F.2d at 728; *Jacobi v. Bache & Co.*, 520 F.2d 1231 (CA2, 1975).

3 *See*: The doctrine of *Collective Dominance*; and Article-102 TFEU (European Union).

4 *See*: The doctrine of "*Unavoidable Trading Partner*" (European Union) which is applicable to issuer-companies; and see *Hoffmann-La Roche vs. Commission*, E.C.R. 461, para 41 (1979; European Court of Justice).

5 *See*: *Eastman Kodak Co. vs. Image technical Services*, 504 U.S. 451 (1992; US Supreme Court); *Jefferson Parish Hospital vs. Hyde*, 466 U.S. 2 (1984; US Supreme Court); *Zenith Radio Corp. vs. Hazeltine Research*, 395 U.S. 100 (1969; US Supreme Court).

6 *See: Texaco vs. Hasbrouck*, 496 U.S. 543 (1990; US Supreme Court).
See: *J. Truet Payne Co vs. Chrysler Motors*, 451 U.S. 557 (1981; US Supreme Court).
See: Great Atlantic & Pacific Tea Co. vs. Federal Trade Commission, 440 U.S. 69 (1979; US Supreme Court).
See: *US vs. United States Gypsum*, 438 U.S. 422 (1978; US Supreme Court).
See: *FTC vs. Sun Oil Co.*, 371 U.S. 505 (1963; US Supreme Court).

7 *See: Otter Tail Power Co.*, 410 U.S. at 372-75 (US Supreme Court)).

8 *See*: *Standard Oil Co vs. US*, 337 U.S. 293 (1949; US Supreme Court).
See: *US vs. Griffith,* 334 U.S. 100 (1948; US Supreme Court).
See: *Brooke Group Ltd. vs. Brown & Williamson Tobacco,* 509 U.S. 209 (1993; US Supreme Court).

9 *See*: https://www.treasury.gov/connect/blog/Pages/Just-the-Facts-SPs-2-Trillion-Mistake.aspx.
See: https://krugman.blogs.nytimes.com/2011/08/07/i-heard-it-through-the-baseline/.

10 *See*: Proposed Revision Of IOSCO Code (May 2008) - https://www.iosco.org/library/pubdocs/pdf/IOSCOPD270.pdf.
See: IOSCO (December 2004). *Code of Conduct Fundamentals for Credit Rating Agencies.* https://www.iosco.org/library/pubdocs/pdf/IOSCOPD180.pdf.
See: IOSCO: Report on the Sub-prime Crisis – Final Report, Report of the Technical Committee of IOSCO. Available at www.iosco.org.
See: IOSCO: The Role of Credit Rating Agencies in Structured Finance Markets – Final Report. Available at www.iosco.org.
See: https://www.iosco.org/pubdocs/pdf/IOSCOPD153.pdf; https://www.iosco.org/pubdocs/pdf/IOSCOPD151.pdf; https://www.iosco.org/pubdocs/pdf/IOSCOPD180.pdf.
See: IOSCO (Feb. 2007). Review of Implementation of the IOSCO Fundamentals of a Code of Conduct for Credit Rating Agencies, Report of the Technical Committee of IOSCO. Available at www.iosco.org.
See: CFA Institute Center (Feb. 2008). CFA INSTITUTE CENTRE ENCOURAGED BY GLOBAL REGULATORS' FOCUS ON CREDIT RATING AGENCY INDUSTRY REFORM. https://www.cfainstitute.org/aboutus/press/release/08releases/20080205_02.html.

11 *See:* European Commission (June 2013). *Stricter rules for credit rating agencies to enter into force.* https://europa.eu/rapid/press-release_IP-13-555_en.htm?locale=en.
See: European Commission (2013). Regulation 462/2013 of the European Parliament and of the Council of 21 May 2013 amending Regulation (EC) No 1060/2009 on credit rating agencies. https://eur-lex.europa.eu/JOHtml.do?uri=OJ:L:2013:146:SOM:EN:HTML.
See: European Commission (2013). Directive 2013/14/EC of the European Parliament and of the Council of 21 May 2013 amending Directive 2003/41/EC on the activities and supervision of institutions for occupational retirement provision, Directive 2009/65/EC on the coordination of laws, regulations and administrative provisions relating to undertakings for collective investment in transferable securities (UCITS) and Directive 2011/61/EU on Alternative Investment Funds Managers in respect of over-reliance on credit ratings. https://eur-lex.europa.eu/JOHtml.do?uri=OJ:L:2013:145:SOM:EN:HTML.
See: European Commission (March 2006). *Communication On Credit Rating Agencies.* Available at: https://eur-lex.europa.eu/LexUriServ/LexUriServ.do?uri=OJ:C:2006:059:0002:0006:EN:PDF.

12 See: Modification of Treasury Regulations Pursuant to Section 939A of the Dodd-Frank Wall Street Reform and Consumer Protection Act. http://www.gpo.gov/fdsys/pkg/FR-2013-09-06/pdf/2013-21752.pdf.
See: *U.S. Treasury sends credit-rating regulation bill to Congress.* http://blogs.reuters.com/financial-regulatory-forum/2009/07/21/us-treasury-sends-credit-rating-regulation-bill-to-congress/. The new US treasury regulations for credit rating agencies which was submitted to the US Congress in July 2009 are as follows:
"*……….Bar Firms From Consulting With Any Company That They Also Rate……..*
Strengthen Disclosure And Management Of Conflicts Of Interest: **….**

Disclose Fees Paid By An Issuer Along With Each Rating Report: ...
Look-Back Requirement To Address The Conflicts From A "Revolving Door":.....
Designate A Compliance Officer: ......
Require Disclosure Of Preliminary Ratings To Reduce "Ratings Shopping":.....
Require Different Symbols To Be Used To Distinguish The Risks Of Structured Products:.....
Require Qualitative And Quantitative Disclosure Of The Risks Measured In A Rating:......
Establish A Dedicated Office For Supervision Of Rating Agencies: .....
Mandatory Registration: ... ...
SEC Examination Of Internal Controls And Processes: ....
PWG Review of Regulatory Use of Ratings: ...
SEC Recently Requested Public Comment on Whether to Remove References to Ratings in Money Market Mutual Fund Regulation: ......
Require GAO Study On Reducing Reliance: ......
Enable Additional Ratings On Structured Products:... ...
Require Disclosure Of Full Ratings History:......
Strengthen Regulation And Oversight Of Credit Rating Agencies: ...."

13 *See:* Definition of Nationally Recognized Statistical Rating Organization, 70 Fed. Reg. 21,306, 21,307-08 (Apr. 25, 2005) (to be codified at 17 C.F.R. pt. 240).

See: US Securities & Exchange Commission (2003). Report On The Role And Function Of Credit Rating Agencies In The Operation Of The Securities Markets, pp. 10-25 (describing the use of NRSRO ratings in government regulations and legislation).

See: Fons, J. (n.d.). *"Policy Issues Facing Rating Agencies"*. *In* Ratings, Rating Agencies And The Global Financial System, note 141, at 341. ("Historically, the major rating agencies have been against the use of credit ratings in the regulatory process due to potential impact of rating changes on financial markets, incentives to engage in ratings shopping, the accuracy of ratings in reflecting the underlying risks, the use of ratings as 'automatic pilot' substitutes for proper credit analysis by lenders and investors, and the pressure that might be brought to bear on the agencies if they were to become too closely tied to the regulatory process—including regulation of the agencies themselves").

14 *See*: Prieg, P. (25 January 2011). "Credit rating firms are controlling the flow of capital into the developing world - Privately owned credit rating agencies have immense power over the lives of millions of people – but have minimal accountability. This needs to change". *The Guardian (UK).* https://www.theguardian.com/global-development/poverty-matters/2011/jan/25/credit-rating-agencies-poor-countries.

15 *See*: "Financial Crisis Inquiry Commission - Final Report-Conclusions-January 2011". http://www.gpo.gov/fdsys/pkg/GPO-FCIC/pdf/GPO-FCIC.pdf.

See: Casey, K. (Feb. 6, 2009). *"In Search of Transparency, Accountability, and Competition: The Regulation of Credit Rating Agencies". Remarks at "The SEC Speaks in 2009". US SEC.* https://www.sec.gov/news/speech/2009/spch020609klc.htm.

See: "Ratings agencies suffer 'conflict of interest', says former Moody's boss". Rupert Neate. *The Guardian*; 22 August 2011. https://www.theguardian.com/business/2011/aug/22/ratings-agencies-conflict-of-interest.

See: Kerwer, D. (2004). *Holding Global Regulators Accountable The Case of Credit Rating Agencies*. Technical University of Munich, Germany. https://www.ucl.ac.uk/political-science/publications/downloads/spp-wp-11.pdf.

16 See: "Liquidators of failed Bear Stearns funds sue rating agencies". July 10, 2013. Reuters. https://www.reuters.com/article/2013/07/10/us-ratings-agency-lawsuit-idUSBRE9690QV20130710.

See: "*Bond Insurer Sues Credit-Rating Agencies*". July 17, 2013. www.wsj.com. https://www.wsj.com/article/SB10001424127887323993804578612212273026342.html.

See: Wayne, L. (15 July 2009). *"Calpers Sues Over Ratings of Securities". The New York Times*. https://www.nytimes.com/2009/07/15/business/15calpers.html?_r=1&partner=rss&emc=rss.

See: *"S&P Lawsuit First Amendment Defense May Fare Poorly, Experts Say"*. 4 February 2013. Huff Post. https://www.huffingtonpost.com/2013/02/04/sp-lawsuit-first-amendment_n_2618737.html.

See: "*Ohio Jumps On The Rating Agency Lawsuit Bandwagon*". Daniel Indiviglio. theAtlantic.com. Nov 20, 2009. https://www.theatlantic.com/business/archive/2009/11/ohio-jumps-on-the-rating-agency-lawsuit-bandwagon/30602/.

See: *"Credit Rating Agencies Settle 2 Suits Brought by Investors"*. Reuters. April 27, 2013. https://www.nytimes.com/2013/04/28/business/credit-rating-agencies-settle-lawsuits-over-debt-vehicles.html?_r=0.

See: *Reuters (September 3, 2013). "S.&P. Calls Federal Fraud Suit Payback for Credit Downgrade". New York Times.*

See: Snyder, P. (July 18, 2013). *"Federal judge denies credit rating agency's motion to dismiss fraud lawsuit"*. http://jurist.org/paperchase/2013/07/us-district-court-denies-standard-and-poors-motion-to-dismiss-in-fraud-lawsuit.php.

See: "*Corrupted credit ratings: Standard & Poor's lawsuit and the evidence*". Matthias Efing & Harald Hau; 18 June 2013. https://www.voxeu.org/article/corrupted-credit-ratings-standard-poor-s-lawsuit-and-evidence.

See: "*Standard & Poor's Says Civil Lawsuit Threatened By DOJ Is Without Legal Merit And Unjustified*". Reuters.com. 2013/02/04. https://www.reuters.com/article/2013/02/04/ny-sp-doj-lawsuit-idUSnPnNY53856+160+PRN20130204.

See: "Analysis: Credit agencies remain unaccountable". Kathleen Day. *USA Today*. May 19, 2014. https://www.usatoday.com/story/money/business/2014/05/19/credit-rating-agencies-in-limbo/9290143/.

17 *See*: *Quinn v. McGraw-Hill*, 168 F.3d 331 (CA7, 1999).

18 *See*: Riddiough T & Chiang R (2003). *Commercial Mortgage-Backed Securities: An Exploration into Agency, Innovation, Information, and Learning in Financial Markets., Available at:* ([REMOVED HYPERLINK FIELD]https://scholar.google.com/scholar?hl=en&lr=&safe=off&q=cache:tgPHB82FijQJ:www.nchu.edu.tw/Fin/03_research/fin2003/Commercial%2520Mortgage-Backed%2520Securities.pdf+riddiough+chiang+"Commercial+Mortgage-Backed+Securities. (states in part "instead of assuming a passive credit quality certification role, the rating agency actively controls security architecture and are instrumental in determining product design standards").

19 Under the 1933 Securities Act (US), the term "underwriter" includes "any person who… has a direct or indirect participation in any such undertaking, or participates or has a participation in the

direct or indirect underwriting of any such undertaking…" The concept of "collateral participation" encompasses many of the functions of, and services now being rendered by credit rating agencies. Under US federal securities laws, any person who participates in or "takes part in" an underwriting is subject to Section-11 liability.
See: *Naomi O. Harden et al. v. Raffensperger, Hughes & Co., Inc.*, 94 U.S. 2892, *available at* https://caselaw.lp.findlaw.com/cgi-bin/getcase.pl?court=7th&navby=case&no=942892;
Harden vs. Raffensperger, Hughes & Co., Inc., available at
https://caselaw.lp.findlaw.com/scripts/getcase.pl?court=7th&navby=case&no=942892.

20 The following court cases and articles in the US illustrate some of the issues:
See: Jacqueline Bell, *CalPERS Sues Rating Agencies over $1B in Losses*, LAW360, July 15, 2009, https://www.law360.com/articles/111413.
See: Martha Graybow, *Credit Rating Agencies Fending Off Lawsuits from Subprime Meltdown*, INS. J., July 14, 2008, https://www.insurancejournal.com/news/national/2008/07/14/91841.htm (providing an
overview of recent litigation against rating agencies). *See: In re Moody's Corp. Sec. Litig.*, 612 F. Supp. 2d 397 (S.D.N.Y. 2009) (No. 07 CIV 8375) (alleged that Moody's assigned "excessively high ratings to bonds backed by risky subprime mortgages").
See: Reese v. Bahash, 248 F.R.D. 58 (D.D.C. 2008) (No. 1:07-cv-01530-CKK) (charging that S&P assigned misleading ratings to subprime residential mortgage-backed securities and collateralized debt obligations).
See: *Cal. Pub. Employees' Retirement Sys. v. Moody's Corp.*, No. CGC-09-490241 (Cal. App. Dep't Super. Ct. July 9, 2009)
See: Dun & Bradstreet, Inc. v. Greenmoss Builders, Inc., 472 U.S. 749, 751 (1985; US Supreme Court).
See: Jefferson County Sch. Dist. v. Moody's Investor's Servs., Inc., 175 F.3d 848, 850–51 (10th Cir.1999).
See: Quinn v. McGraw-Hill Co., 168 F.3d 331, 336 (7th Cir. 1999) (reliance on ratings was unreasonable).
See: First Equity Corp. v. Standard & Poor's Corp., 869 F.2d 175, 179 (2d Cir. 1989) (parties were not in privity).
See: Sullivan, 376 U.S. at 279–80 (rating agencies not liable absent "actual malice").
See: *In Re Fitch, Inc.*, 330 F.3d at 109–10.
See: In Re Enron Corp. Sec., Derivative & ERISA Litig., 511 F. Supp. 2d 742, 829–30 (S.D. Tex. 2005)

21 *See:* Finch, N (March 2004). *International Rating Agencies And Sustainability.* Working Paper, Macquarie University. (this article concluded that the majority of rating methodologies currently in use are unacceptable, and that the cooperative rating is the superior methodology and states in part "the ratings issued by a rating agency can generally be classified as either a *solicited, unsolicited* or *cooperative*. This classification is used to distinguish the rating methodology upon three key attributes: (1) whether the company being rated has requested the rating; (2) whether the company being rated has paid the agency for the rating; and (3) whether the information source used by the rating agency relies on confidential and non-public information. The *cooperative* rating is a form of unsolicited rating where the rated organization co-operates with the rating agency to provide additional sources of non-public information. This co-operation by the company to provide ad-

ditional information helps to improve the reliability of the rating and therefore its acceptability to users"). Available at: https://papers.ssrn.com/sol3/papers.cfm?abstract_id=658082.

22 See: *The Role of Credit Rating Agencies in the International Financial System* - Prepared remarks by Paul Taylor, President & CEO, Fitch Group. September 10, 2013. United Nations General Assembly Thematic Debate. http://www.fitchratings.com/web_content/corpcomm/press-room/docs/fitch_ptaylor_unga_remarks_2013Sept10.pdf. This article states in part: "Fitch Ratings maintains over 1,300 international public credit ratings on non-financial corporations. Despite bond yields falling to record low levels, our ratings have remained largely stable and well diversified through the rating scale. In practice, a company's rating will typically drift down over a number of years before a default event occurs. Very few companies default while holding an investment grade rating – in fact during the last 25 years less than one quarter of one percent of investment grade companies have defaulted. Each year, we publish extensive rating default and transition data to allow full insight into our performance. With a few notable exceptions, the more-than 3,200 global bank ratings that Fitch maintains have continued to provide important predictive insight into relative credit risk. Global bank credit quality has been under pressure in the face of unprecedented upheaval in the banks' operating environment. Despite the sharp rise in bank failures during 2007-2009, defaults by banks with investment-grade ratings remain extremely low – as we expected and as consistently reflected in our credit views and ratings. Widespread and concerted government intervention has generally limited the magnitude of rating downgrades in the worst affected markets. Failure did not typically turn into default. The prospect and impact of third party support is a key factor in how we assign bank credit ratings. Ratings performance in structured finance markets is a more complex subject with considerable variation between regions and asset classes. Much of the criticism towards the rating agencies has quite rightly been directed at ratings in certain important sectors that, as we have previously acknowledged, performed very poorly and have been too volatile. But the "toxic assets" label sometimes applied to the entire securitization market, particularly straight after the initial onset of the crisis, is inaccurate. Between 2000 and 2011, Fitch rated $9.5 trillion of securitized bonds. To date 1.5% of this amount has been lost through default. We expect the total loss to rise to about 5% over the next several years as assets mature. U.S. residential mortgage-backed securities and repackaging of those securities into collateralized debt obligations account for around 75% of all anticipated losses. Most securitized bonds outside of this troubled sector have held up well in the face of very stressful market conditions."

23 *See:* US Justice Department (Feb 2015). *Justice Department and State Partners Secure $1.375 Billion Settlement with S&P for Defrauding Investors in the Lead Up to the Financial Crisis.* https://www.justice.gov/opa/pr/justice-department-and-state-partners-secure-1375-billion-settlement-sp-defrauding-investors.

24 *See*: Agence Francepresse (Feb 2, 2015). *US probes Moody's rating agency – report.* http://www.abs-cbnnews.com/business/02/02/15/us-probes-moodys-rating-agency-report.

Chapter 9
Informal Algorithms, Impossibility Theorems, and New "Learning" Business/ Compensation Models for the Credit Rating Agency Industry

ABSTRACT

This chapter adopts agent-based and complexity approaches and introduces new "learning business models" and compensation contracts for CRAs that can solve the conflicts of interest, antitrust, greed, regret, deadweight-losses, complexity, and industrial organization problems inherent in the credit rating agency industry, and each model contravenes Myerson-Satterthwaite impossibility theorem, Arrow's impossibility theorem, Sen's impossibility theorem, Gibbard's theorem, the Gibbard-Satterthwaite impossibility theorem, and the Green-Laffont impossibility theorem. The business models include "quasi multi-sided auctions" wherein at any time t several auctions can simultaneously occur, and the payoff functions of any buyer-seller pair in any auction depends on the bidding done by at least another buyer-seller pair either at the same time, or at a different time. This "long-memory bias" of buyers and sellers in auctions is new in the literature.

INTRODUCTION

Credit Ratings Agencies ("CRAs") are prone to various antitrust and conflict-of-interest problems that arise from their regulation and their business and compensation models. CRAs have played a critical role in global capital markets for the last few decades. The many inefficiencies inherent in the compensation contracts for, and business models of CRA were clearly illustrated during the Global Financial Crisis of 2007-2014, during which ABS Trusts and some large companies suddenly defaulted without prior downgrades of their ratings. Its well known that markets often price in potential defaults or down-grades

DOI: 10.4018/978-1-7998-7418-8.ch009

before CRAs revise their ratings downwards. Given significant dependence on CRAs by investors, issuers and regulators, CRA can be a substantial source/cause of Systemic Risk and Financial Instability, and can hamper Sustainable Growth; and thus, the challenge is not only to develop optimal CRA contracts, but also to develop and implement CRA business-models that facilitate such contracts such that social welfare is maximized, and the issuer-CRA relationship cannot be re-characterized as a joint venture, strategic alliance or a franchise/quasi-franchise.

With regards to the motivation for this chapter, see Chapter-8 in this book; and by addressing those issues, this chapter fills several gaps in, contributes to the AI/Learning, financial markets, Antitrust, Mechanism Design, Game Theory, Complex Systems and Complexity literatures.

EXISTING LITERATURE

See literature cited in Chapters 8 & 9 in this book. Nwogugu (2010; 2013) developed new Business Models and Compensation Models for CRAs - Nwogugu (2013) also proposed a model for a government controlled/owned CRA. Roth & Sotomayor (1992); and Mashayekhy, Nejad & Grosu (2014) studied two-sided matching. Jacobs (2012) discussed coalgebras. Nissam (2007) summarized mechanism design.

Thille, Cojocaru, et. al. (2013); Makhdoumi, Malekian & Ozdaglar (2017); and Nakhe (2017) developed dynamic pricing models for various markets.

Govindan & Wilson (2006); Yoav & Leyton-Brown (2009); and Lutz & Schafke (1985) discuss and show examples of various uses of Invariants and Game Theory. Telser (1994) and Bischi, Chiarella, Kopel & Szidarovszky (2010) illustrate the use of *Core Theory*, *Stability* and Invariants in Industrial Organization. Demande, Gale & Sotomayor (1987) and Martínez, Massó, Neme & Oviedo (2012) studied *Matching Games*. Arribillaga, Massó & Neme (2014); Jaume, Masso & Neme (2012); Sotomayor (2003) analyzed *Assignment Games*. Van den Brink (2012) analyzed efficiency and Collusion Neutrality in Cooperative Games. Bergantiños & Massó (2002) attempted to derive values for NTU Games.

Learning and Regret Minimization in Auctions and Dynamic-Pricing

On *Deep Learning* and *Regret Minimization* in Mechanism Design, see: Feng, Narasimhan & Parkes (2018), Dutting, Feng, et. al. (2019) and Sandholm & Likhodedov (2015). On other Artificial Inteligence approaches, see: Zohar & Rosenschein (2008), Jain, Gujar, et. al. (2018), Aziz & Lev (2019), Peng, Al Chami, et. al. (2019), Gondran, Huguet, et. al. (2018), Chassaing, Duhamel & Lacomme (2016), Doshi, Gmytrasiewicz & Durfee (2020), and Mitchell (2006). Mohri & Medina (2014) and Nazerzadeh, Leme, et. al. (2016) analyzed learning algorithms. On algorithms in general, see: Garcia, Berlanga, Molina & Davila (2004). Bertsekas (2000) analyzed auctions as algorithms.

Colini-Baldeschi, Goldberg, et. al. (Nov. 2017); Deng, Goldberg, Tang & Zhang (2014); Satterthwaite & Williams (1989), Dütting, Roughgarden & Talgam-Cohen (2014), Baranwal & Vidyarthi (2015), Wang, Chin & Yin (2011), Scalas, Rapallo & Radivojević (2017), Zhao (2012) and Zhang (2018) analyzed two-sided auctions.

Mashayekhy, Nejad & Grosu (2014) studied two-sided matching. Jacobs (2012) discussed coalgebras. Nissam (2007) summarized mechanism design. Feudel, Pisarchik & Showalter (2018); Wang, Xu & Lai (2018); Anzo-Hernández, Gilardi-Velázquez & Campos-Cantón (2018); and Kwasnioka (2018) analyzed multistability. Levina, Levin, et. al. (2006). Niels & Ten Kate (2000) analyzed Predatory Pricing. Krämer, Schmidt, Spann & Stich (2017) and Levina, Levin, et. al. (2006) studied dynamic pricing.

Contract Theory, Stability, and Mechanism Design

Contract Theory and *Mechanism Design Theory* have been jointly studied from various perspectives including Economics/Finance, Operations Research, Mathematical Psychology, Computer Science, Game Theory and Applied Math - see: Hoppe & Schmitz (2018); Niederhoff & Kouvelis (2019); Hong, Wernz & Stillinger (2016); Wu, Zhao & Tang (2014); Li, Liu & Chen (2018); Lin & Chou (1990); Park & Kim (2014); Goetz, Yatsenko, et. al. (2019); Fang & Yuan (2018); Madureira, Pereira, et. al. (2014); Meneguzzi, Modgil, et. al. (2012); Meneguzzi, Modgil, Oren, et. al. (2011); Zohar & Rosenschein (2008); Terán, Aguilar & Cerrada (2017); Eenmaa-Dimitrieva & Schmidt-Kessen (2019); Drozd & Serrano-Padia (2018); and Wei, Wang, et.al. (2018). However, the models in most of these foregoing articles and literature are static, don't incorporate relevant variables; don't consider varying "states" and often complex "joint" effects of variables; and they don't consider Industrial Organization effects of contracts/mechanisms - see Nwogugu (2007a;b), Nwogugu (2019a;b) and Nwogugu (2006).

This chapter develops new game-theoretic CRA ICS models that use *Platform-Matching* and maintain "*Stability*" among regulated and un-regulated CRAs, and solve the conflicts-of-interest, Regret, deadweight losses, Greed and antitrust problems inherent in credit rating agencies, and can ensure "Stability" as CRAs evolve over time. Again, in this context, "*Stability*" refers to the following. First, game-theoretic "*Stability*" in large non-cooperative non-zero-sum NTU finitely-repeated games wherein no player-coalition has any meaningful incentive to deviate from, and is legally required to conform to "*Determined Regulatory Equilibria/equilibrium*" (similar to *Correlated Equilibrium*) which is a non-empty Core regardless of the size (large versus small), scale (single-level versus multi-level games versus multi-stage); tenure and type (cooperative or non-cooperative or mixed) of the games. Second, "*Financial Stability*" wherein the credit ratings process reduces the probability of systemic risk and Contagion and the credit-ratings are more objective and accurate. Third, "*Operational Stability*" wherein both the credit ratings process and the ratings output reduce the probability of the issuer-company becoming financially or operationally distressed. Yoav & Leyton-Brown (2009); Lutz & Schafke (1985); Govindan & Wilson (2006), and Telser (1994) discuss and show examples of various uses of Invariants and Game Theory Strategies in characterizing solutions in Industrial Organization, Games and Dynamical Systems. Govindan, Schemde & Stengel (2004) noted that since *Stability* is a set-valued solution concept, there isn't a unique formulation of some axioms (including symmetry).

Sustainability, Economic Growth, and the Standardization of Contracts

Standardization of contracts can affect economic growth, Sustainability, Inequality and Economic Growth as noted by various academic researchers - see Sussman (1999); Van Assche & Schwartz (2013); Patterson (2010), Engert & Hornuf (2018); Aguirre (2017); Ayotte & Bolton (2011); Baffi (2007; 2012); He, Xue & Zhou (2019); Vo, Nguyen, et.al. (2019); Sheng (2019); Eenmaa-Dimitrieva & Schmidt-Kessen (2019); Dekker, Kawai & Sakaguchi (2018); Iossa & Martimort (2018); and Sprinkle, Williamson & Upton (2008). Sussman (1999) noted that "The main implications of contract standardization are that (i) "financial history matters in the growth process,(ii) early formation of the system may create a drag on economic growth and (iii) the effect may be non-monotonic because the system may be modernized at some point........". In the realm of CRAs, CRAs have developed their own standardized contracts for ratings projects and the Big-Three CRAs are dominant.

INTERNATIONAL TRADE, INTERNATIONAL CAPITAL FLOWS, AND INTERNATIONAL ORGANIZATION

Unfortunately, the "Big-Three" CRAs (Moodys, Fitch and S&P which control more than 80% market share in the global CRA industry) now significantly affect the equivalent of more than one hundred and twenty trillion US dollars of securities, swaps/derivatives and financial instruments globally, and thus have a significant and growing effect on international capital flows, International Trade and global Financial Stability. A growing percentage of International Trade relationships/contracts are based on the credit ratings of foreign trade counter-parties. That is, credit ratings are a critical factor and criteria in the origination, structuring, management and regulation of international joint ventures, strategic alliances, licensing, structured trade financing; international factoring; international long-term supply agreements; off-take agreements; etc.. See: Tomashevskiy & Kono (2015); and Collis, Jarvis & Page (2013). Muuls (2015) discusses the relationship between credit ratings and trade, but some of the models are not entirely correct. Credit ratings also contribute to international financial contagion – e.g. a ratings downgrade of a large US company (e.g. Apple) or a group of smaller companies can result in declines of the credit ratings and or stock prices of their suppliers in Asia or South America. Studies have noted that sovereign credit ratings affect international capital flows. The ratings-based international-investor demand for ABS/MBS, US treasuries and structured securities causes contagion. Also, various studies have documented credit ratings contagions in Europe and other regions. The relationship between credit ratings and international capital flows can be significant but is often omitted in academic studies of both phenomena as was the case in Forbes, Warnock & Francis (2012). These factors in turn, affect global systemic risk, trade-deficits, financial stability, and many elements of national economies such as the borrowing costs of governments and companies, FDI, investments in foreign securities, household economics, overall regulatory compliance, consumer-confidence, availability of products/services; excessive consumer/sovereign/municipal/corporate debt; declining productivity; etc..See: Skreta & Veldkamp (2009); de Haan & Amtenbrink (Jan. 2011); and Deb, Manning & Murphy, et. al. (March 2011).

International Organizations (such as the WTO, the IFC, EBRD, the International Organization of Securities Commissions (IOSCO), etc.), and the European Commission, the US Government[1] and many governments have debated and issued statements and proposed regulations for CRAs, most of which have been ineffective.

NEW GAME-THEORETIC "LEARNING MODELS" OF PROCESS AND COMPENSATION FOR CREDIT RATING AGENCIES: THE MECHANISMS INTRODUCED IN THIS CHAPTER ALL VIOLATE THE MYERSON-SATTERTHWAITE IMPOSSIBILITY THEOREM AND ARROW'S IMPOSSIBILITY THEOREM

Under most current and proposed compensation and business models for CRAs, CRAs are not independent, whereas the ratings function requires complete independence. See comments in US Securities

& Exchange Commission (January 2003) and Office Of The New York State Attorney General (June 2008). Rating agencies are compensated by issuers and or investment banks, and this creates conflict of interest (before the 1970s, rating agencies were compensated by bond investors). Investment banks and issuers can and often 'shop' for the most favorable ratings. Under the current global CRA industry structure, banks and or issuers pay for the ratings service only after the transaction is closed, and if they can typically ask a second rating agency to rate the securities and all this typically occurs with investors' knowledge. In 2008, the New York State Attorney General's Office entered into binding agreements with most US rating agencies about their compensation[2], although such compensation models are inefficient.

One of the main problems in the CRA business models described in US GAO (2012) is that the proposed penalties for shirking or low-quality credit ratings encourage the CRAs to collude, and the penalty mechanisms are unfair aggregation-based penalties that don't distinguish among the quality of specific bonds/loans; and the penalties don't account for market sentiment, and differences in skills and efforts of CRAs. In this industry, the "Peer Comparison review" is susceptible to manipulation and error simply because there are relatively very few CRAs, the barriers to entry are high, and CRA's sources of revenues are limited; and CRAs' true "efforts" are often dampened and "modified" by market forces that are beyond their control (such as general economic fluctuations, competition in industries; bad management; labor problems; new technology; substitute products; etc.). Furthermore, the use of a clearinghouse to set ratings-fees and to functionally influence the cost structure of CRAs may be an adverse restriction of free market force and may be deemed anti-competitive.

The *Incentive And Compensation Systems* (ICSs) introduced herein are computer-based algorithms that can be built as commercial platforms that can be used by CRAs, investors, issuers, regulators and investment banks. The ICSs are "*learning business models*" because: i) the each ICS is dynamic and the results and incentive effects (of the ratings system/platform) changes with state variables; ii) the parameters of each element of an ICS can be broadened or narrowed based on learning from past performance of the ratings and the ICS; iii) each ICS can learn from past price-setting conditions for ratings fees, and from the performance of actual ratings within the context of ratings-fees charged; iv) the ICS can learn from the disclosed "difficulty" and "analyst effort" of past ratings projects which can be used to set minimum fees for future ratings projects; v) each ICS can learn from actual performance/accuracy of credit ratings which can be used to assign disclosed "accuracy scores" to CRAs and to recommend ratings-fees; vi) the ICS can learn from and adapt to shocks in the economy (such as ratings contagion; default contagions; structural changes in industries; etc.).

Complexity and Properties of an Efficient Incentive and Compensation System (ICS) for CRAs

An *Incentive And Compensation System* (ICS) for CRAs is a learning business model that includes both the ratings-contract between the CRA and other parties (e.g. the issuer or investors), and the CRA's separate subscription-fee programs, and the agreement between the issuer/sponsor and the investment bank, if any (combined business model and compensation model). Branke, Greco, Slowinski & Zielniewicz (2014); Yoav & Leyton-Brown (2009); Kang & Liang (1997); Govindan & Wilson (2006); Kohlberg & Mertens (1986); Lutz & Schafke (1985); and Telser (1994) discussed the use of Invariants and Game-Theory Strategies to characterize solutions in Industrial Organization and Dynamical Systems.

The following properties of CRA ICS models maintain "*Stability*" among regulated and un-regulated CRAs, and solve the conflicts-of-interest and anti-competitive behavior inherent in credit rating processes, and ensure "Stability" as CRAs evolve over time. In this context, "*Stability*" refers to the following:

1. game-theoretic "*Stability*" in large non-cooperative non-zero-sum NTU finitely-repeated games wherein no player-coalition has any meaningful incentive to deviate from, and must conform to "*Determined Regulatory Equilibria/equilibrium*" which is a non-empty Core regardless of the size (large versus small), scale (single-level versus multi-level games); tenure, type (cooperative or non-cooperative or mixed) of the games; and
2. "*Financial Stability*" wherein both the credit ratings process reduce the probability of systemic risk and financial instability and the credit-ratings are more objective and accurate;
3. "*Operational Stability*" wherein both the credit ratings process and the ratings output reduce the probability of the issuer-company becoming financially or operationally distressed (primarily due the inaccuracy of the credit ratings).
4. Stability in Mechanism Design.

Note that Game Strategies, Core Elements and Invariants are presented as text herein for brevity, although there are equivalent mathematical representations - similar to how *Strategic Complementarity* and *Supermodularity* are mathematically expressed as $\partial^2 f/\partial z_i \partial z_j \geq 0$; for all $i \neq j$; where and z_i and z_j are strategies of participants in the action space and each action is chosen from an interval $z_i, z_j \in [a,b]$; and the payoff functions f(.), depend on actions/strategies of two or more types of participants z_i and z_j in the action space ($i = 1 \ldots\ldots. n; j = 1 \ldots\ldots\ldots n$).

The properties of an efficient *Incentive And Compensation System* (ICS) for CRAs are as follows:

1. *Information Neutral*: the ICS should ensure that that CRA can obtain sufficient information from the issuer and its CPA, including the audit work-papers, if any. The amount and quality of information that the issuer and its CPA provides to the CRA shall not be affected by the CRA's compensation. The Incentive & Compensation System (ICS) should reduce information asymmetry in the capital markets and ensure that the ratings standard of comparison is maintained.
2. *Source Neutrality* - The ICS must be source neutral and ratings fees must not be paid directly by the issuer or the investment bank, both of whom should not influence the ICS.
3. *Ratings-Decision Neutral* - the issuer's decisions about the timing of a ratings request, or about whether to rate a financial instrument or to select a CRA shall not be influenced by the "type" of its CPA.
4. *Cumulative Fee Independence* – the fee paid by the issuer for each rating must not be affected by prior fees paid by the same issuer.
5. *Shock Positive* – the ICS pays extra compensation to the ratings agency for any substantial downward change in ratings for the client company. This provides substantial incentives for the issuer to provide adequate and truthful disclosure to the CRA; and incentives for the CRA to provide accurate ratings. It also compensates the CRA for any actual or perceived loss of Reputation.
6. *Quality Neutral* – the ICS ensures that the CRA's ratings-quality does not decline as the CRA's cost structure changes; and that the CRA recovers all of its reasonable costs; and that the CRA invests in quality and continually improves its ratings processes.

7. *Collusion Proof* – the ICS reduces or eliminates any collusion among the CPA, CRA, investment bank, issuers and or investors.
8. *Positive Penalties Consistency* – the ICS penalize issuers in a deterrence-consistent manner for providing inaccurate information to the CRA, and also penalizes CRAs in a deterrence-consistent manner for low-quality ratings and or Ratings-Lags; and such penalties are assessed based on only individual bonds/loans, and only if such errors are persistent over a period of time; or if other CRAs issue sharply divergent ratings.
9. *Volume Neutral* – the ICS should be volume-neutral such that the volume of users, or the volume of trades or the volume of ratings assignments does not affect the CRA's effort, or the CRA's fee, or the quality, accuracy and timeliness of the CRA's ratings.
10. *Liability-Allocation Neutrality* – the allocation of liability between the CPA and the CRA for any ratings shocks (ie. sudden financial distress of an investment grade issuer; or a ratings downgrade by two CRAs) shall be limited/capped and shall not be affected by the type of ratings fee; and shall not reduce the CRA's ratings-quality; and shall not affect the issuer's financing decisions. The ICS limits or favorably modifies the CRA's liability where the CRA relies on the CPA's audited financial statement.
11. *Positive Competition Consistency* – the ICS increases or maintains the consistency of competition in the CRA industry which in turn, should also increase or maintain the consistency of the quality of the CRA's credit ratings.
12. *CRA Independence* – The ICS and the ratings fee ensures that the CRA is independent of the issuer and the investment bank, and there are no conflicts-of-interest.
13. *Un-solicited Ratings Limitations* - The CRA cannot issue un-solicited ratings for any issuer for which it had issued solicited ratings, until the second anniversary of the date of the most recent solicited ratings. Each CRA is permitted to issue up to a maximum number of unsolicited ratings for each issuer in one regulatory time period. All CRA's must first report any pending ratings downgrades to the US SEC, and after an initial rating of an issuer, a CRA cannot formally and publicly announce a downgrade of that issuer's rating unless another reporting CRA also has filed a pending downgrade notice at the US SEC, upon which either CRA can then publicly announce the ratings downgrade.
14. *Solicited Ratings Prohibitions* - The CRA cannot issue solicited ratings for two consecutive years for any issuer for which it has issued ratings for any three consecutive years. Each CRA is permitted to issue up to a maximum number of unsolicited ratings for each issue in one regulatory time period. All CRA's must first report any pending ratings downgrades to the US SEC, and after an initial rating of an issuer, a CRA cannot formally and publicly announce a downgrade of that issuer's rating unless another reporting CRA also has filed a pending downgrade notice at the US SEC, upon which either CRA can then publicly announce the ratings downgrade.
15. Issuers can obtain ratings from no more than two CRAs in each period. Issuers will be statutorily limited to a specific number of solicited ratings per financial instrument in each regulatory time period (year or half-year).
16. *Minimal Ratings Shopping* - The ICS must reduce or eliminate ratings-shopping by issuers and investment banks.
17. *Ratings Consistency* – The ICS should ensure that CRAs' ratings standards are consistent across industries, issuers, CRAs, and over time; and the ICS should reduce or eliminate ratings lags (a ratings lag occurs when the CRA does not update its post-offering ratings on a timely basis).

18. *Entrenchment Negative* – the ICS reduces or eliminates entrenchment of any CRA; and reduces the CRAs' actual or perceived use of market power to retain clients; and minimizes the CRA's focus on client relationships at the expense of accuracy, timeliness of ratings and pricing of ratings services. The ICS ensures that any regulations and or business practices that foster entrenchment of CRA will have minimal effects. The CRA cannot offer any other fee-based services to issuers that it rates except the ratings, and the traditional subscription to the CRA's published ratings of other companies.
19. *Surplus Neutrality* – the ICS contract reduces Consumer Surplus (the difference between the market interest rate for the security/instrument and what the investors pay as interest) and the "Producer Surplus" (the difference between the market interest rate for the security/instrument and what the issuers charges as interest).
20. *Proportionality* – the ratings fee provides sufficient incentives for the CRA to increase quality, and the fee-structure ensures that the CRA's efforts are directly proportional to increased ratings-quality, and that ratings-quality is directly proportional to the CRA's volume of solicited ratings business.
21. *Positive Super-Modularity* (and Strategic Complementarity) – the ICS increases positive Super-modularity in the ratings process. *Positive Super-modularity* increases Social Welfare, while *Negative Super-Modularity* reduces Social Welfare.

Each of the new business/compensation mechanisms introduced herein and below violates the *Myerson-Satterthwaite Impossibility Theorem, Arrow's Impossibility Theorem, Sen's Impossibility Theorem, Gibbard's Theorem*, the *Gibbard-Satterthwaite Impossibility Theorem*, and the *Green-Laffont Impossibility Theorem* because each has the following characteristics:

1. *Individual Rationality* of buyers (client/issuer companies) (*Myerson-Satterthwaite Impossibility Theorem*) - For each buyer, there is a bid such that the buyer always obtains nonnegative utility.
2. *Individual Rationality* of suppliers (CRAs) (*Myerson-Satterthwaite Impossibility Theorem*).
3. *Strong Budget Balance* (*Myerson-Satterthwaite Impossibility Theorem*) – where not all buyers' payments are given to suppliers, the portion given to suppliers reflects fair value for services rendered.
4. *Dominant-Strategy Incentive Compatibility* of buyers and suppliers (*Myerson-Satterthwaite Impossibility Theorem*) – each buyer and supplier can achieve the best outcome to him/herself by reporting/acting according to his/her true preferences/valuations.
5. *Pareto Optimality* (*Myerson-Satterthwaite Impossibility Theorem*) - there is no other allocation/matching superior to that provided by the mechanism in all aspects, provided all buyers report their true valuation (its assumed that mechanism structure encourages truth-telling by buyers and suppliers).
6. *Feasibility* (*Myerson-Satterthwaite Impossibility Theorem*) – with respect to real-world constraints.
7. *Privacy* – where bidding is used, the identities of bidders are not disclosed and for each "project" (e.g. a ratings project), only the winning seller-supplier pair are introduced to each other.
8. *Welfare Maximization* (both Exact And Approximate) – the model maximizes welfare with regards to the overall system; and reduces deadweight losses (by reducing consumer surpluses and supplier surpluses).
9. *Regret-positive* – reduces Regret of buyers (issuer-companies) and sellers (CRAs).

10. *No-Dictatorship* (*Gibbard's Theorem*; *Arrow's Impossibility Theorem; Gibbard-Satterthwaite Impossibility Theorem*): the outcome should not always be identical to the ranking of one particular alternative.
11. *Non-dictatorial* (*Gibbard's Theorem*; the *Gibbard-Satterthwaite Impossibility Theorem*) - there isn't any distinguished agent who can impose the outcome.
12. *Pareto Efficiency* (*Arrow's Impossibility Theorem*): if every user prefers Outcome-A to Outcome-B, then the outcome should rank A above B.
13. *Independence of Irrelevant Alternatives* (*Arrow's Impossibility Theorem*): the outcome's relative ranking of choices A and B should not change if users change the ranking of other choices but do not change their relative rankings of A and B.
14. *No Two-Option Limit* (*Gibbard's Theorem*; the *Gibbard-Satterthwaite Impossibility Theorem*) - the process doesn't limit the possible outcomes to only two options.
15. *No Strategic-Voting* (*Gibbard's Theorem*, the *Gibbard-Satterthwaite Impossibility Theorem*) - the process isn't open to Strategic-Voting (once an agent has identified their preferences, it isnt possible that they have no action at their disposal that best protects such preferences regardless of the other agents' actions).

The following are various alternatives for the compensation of Rating Agencies – the alternatives are designed to reduce conflicts of interest. The models are illustrated using the US government agencies and institutions – but the principles are obviously applicable to other countries.

Definitions

Relevant definitions are as follows:

1. "*Investor Pool*" – The Investor Pool is a proposed Trust fund that will be maintained by a trustee appointed by the government regulator, and will be funded by the following: a) special annual levies on securities accounts based on the amount of assets in the account, b) special levies on each bond transaction, which will be paid by the issuer, c) a fixed fee paid by the "Investor Protection Agency" for every transaction that requires a rating, d) a fee levied on bond insurers for every transaction; special taxes on bond insurers.
2. "*Agency Pool*" – is a type of trust fund that will be maintained by a Trustee appointed by the government regulator (e.g. the US SEC) and will be funded from: a) special taxes on proceeds of rated bond offerings that will be paid to issuers; b) a tax on audit fees (on CPA firms) earned from auditing any issuer of rated bonds or borrower of rated bank loans; c) other sources.
3. The *Incentive & Compensation System* (ICS) – means the ratings agreement between a CRA and an issuer for a specific period of time, and may cover the rating of a single instrument or groups of instruments or the issuer itself.
4. "*Investor Protection Agency*" (e.g. SIPC; FINRA; Municipal Securities Rulemaking Board) – means an investor protection organization such as FINRA or SIPC in the US, whose main goal is to develop and implement programs and policies to protect investors.

The "Learning" Processes

In this context (Mechanism Design, Networks and Network-Decisions), *Learning*/KR&R occurs or can occur in various ways including but not limited to the following:

1. Rate and structure of *Propagation of beliefs* in the Network.
2. Analysis of data on past and current ratings agreements, transaction-types, CRA cost structures and CRA profitability.
3. The degree of *Aggregation* of beliefs and decisions in associated/overlapping Networks.
4. Belief revisions in Networks.
5. The degree of "*Static Interconnectedness*" in the Network (interconnectedness without transactions or major activity).
6. The degree of "*Transactional" Interconnectedness* in the Network (interconnectedness with transactions or major activity and associated variable costs).
7. The degree of "*Dynamic Interconnectedness*" in the Network (interconnectedness without transactions or major activity and associated variable costs; but with social, cultural and political activity).

The specific KR&R types that are implicit in the models introduced herein and below, are as follows:

1. *Structural Knowledge* – problem-solving knowledge that establishes relationships among concepts, contracts, transactions, prices and objects;
2. *Meta Knowledge* – which defines knowledge about other types of Knowledge;
3. *Heuristic Knowledge* – which is expert knowledge in the subject-matter which facilitates the development of "heuristics" and model-inputs;
4. *Declarative Knowledge* – which is objects, facts, events and concepts that are declared in a declarative sentence; and
5. *Procedural Knowledge* – consists of procedures, rules, strategies and methods that are necessary for achieving an objective (e.g. analysis and modelling).

In the models introduced herein and below, *KR&R/Learning* (and Machine Learning) are incorporated in various ways including but not limited to the following:

1. The use of variables that reflect states-of-knowledge over time.
2. The use of variables that reflect the passage of time.
3. "*Relative Evolution*" – changes in variables with respect to both time and other variables.
4. "*Dynamic Conditions*" that reflect changing preferences, beliefs and knowledge over time.
5. The "*Learning*" process is as follows:
    a. Analyze historical data; and continuously gather new data and update the absolute values of the model inputs;
    b. Search for and establish the relationships (if any) among the model variables/inputs over time;
    c. Search for and establish the relationships (if any) between the model variables and "external factors" over time;
    d. Search for and establish reasons for low-relationships (if any) between the model variables and "external factors" over time;

e. Store the absolute values of prior-periods' model-inputs and "relationships";
f. Verify the usefulness of each factor/variable.

One important feature of the Learning process is that it can enable regulators to decide when to switch between CRA Business Models – that is, for any given time period and group of issuers, two or more CRA Business Models can be used.

The foregoing model of *Learning* doesn't have some weaknesses of traditional and new control/optimization methods (e.g. dependence on questionable regressions and probability distributions; inability to identify "turning points" in data series; etc.).

Alternative 1

Each CRA will be able to rate any securities/instruments that it wants and when it wants, without any interference from the issuer but subject to the *Solicited Ratings Prohibition* and the *Un-Solicited Ratings Limitations*. Hence, for un-solicited ratings and solicited ratings, the CRA's revenue will be completely independent and partially independent respectively, of the issuer and or the investment bank; and CRAs can become profitable simply by rating new and seasoned securities/instruments (and earning fees from subscribers in addition to one-time fixed fees paid from the "Investor-Pool" and or the "Agency-Pool" for each ratings assignment). This can solve the *Tie-Breaker Problem* and provides the functional equivalent of *break-ups* and or *divestitures* of the Big-Three CRAs. For solicited ratings, the partial dependence of the CRA's revenue generation process on the issuer provides the CRAs with incentives to compete while reducing reliance on long term client relationships at the expense of quality and timeliness of ratings. The CRA must provide a one-year *Ratings Warrantee* wherein the CRA must pay a pre-determined fee to the issuer (or to a government-managed fund), if there is a significant change in the issuer's financial condition as evidenced by reference to pre-agreed operating performance metrics.

For each solicited or unsolicited rating, the issuer must provide the same amount/quality of information to all licensed CRAs through a website that will be accessible to only such licensed CRAs. Issuers will have the option to select CRAs only for solicited ratings. Each CRA will earn revenues in the following ways:

1. For each new issue of debt or secondary offering, and for only each solicited rating, there will be a fixed one-time *Transaction Fee* paid by the issuer which will be set by the CRA and will cover the CRA's evaluation costs, regardless of whether or not the offering is done or whether the agency's rating is accepted – this fee will not exceed a low fixed percentage (e.g. 20%) of the total fees earned by the CRA from the ratings project, and will be paid to the Administrator that manages the Agency Pool, which will remit same to the CRA; plus
2. For each new issue of debt or secondary offering, and for each solicited or unsolicited rating, there will be a fixed one-time fee paid to the CRA from an "*Agency-Pool*" which will be maintained by the government securities regulator – this Base Fee will be standard and will be set by the government securities regulator and will depend on the dollar amount of the transaction, and the relative complexity of the transaction.
3. The CRA will also earn revenues from subscription fees paid by users of ratings (similar to current subscription fees charged by information providers) including investors, and the CRA will set its

own subscription-fees. The Subscription Fees will be for only details of ratings, but only the CRA's letter-ratings for each company that it rates will be publicly disclosed on a website.

4. Each CRA will be prohibited from providing consulting services to any issuer-company that it rates.

Issuers will be penalized for providing inadequate or fraudulent disclosures to the CRA, if such misconduct is discovered at any time, or if the designated ratings differs substantially from the performance of the issuer within three years after the rating is issued.

The CRA will be penalized for *Low-Quality Ratings* and or *Shirking* in one or more of the following ways:

1. if the CRA's rating of the bond/loan differs substantial from the actual performance of the company or the bond/loan within two years of the rating, then the CRA will pay a fine – where performance is measured by a deterioration of pre-selected metrics (financial ratios and other operating benchmarks of the company);
2. the CRA will provide a one-year warranty of the ratings;
3. if the ratings of a debt instruments of an issuer that is rated by a CRA differs from the ratings issued by any two other CRAs for at least nine months, then the CRA will pay a fine to the Investor Pool or the Agency Pool;
4. if a rated investment grade bond defaults within the first two years of issuance, the CRA must pay a penalty fee, which will be distributed to bond holders;
5. if a rated bond is assigned a two-step negative (downward) ratings transition by any competing CRA within one year of the original rating or a revised rating, then the two or three other CRAs that issued the immediately preceding ratings must pay a penalty fee to bond holders.

The foregoing model is a "*one-sided quasi-auction*" because issuers implicitly "bid" for CRAs' services given the following: i) CRAs have capacity constraints and have an *Opportunity Cost* each time they accept a ratings project; ii) each CRA can service many issuers simultaneously – and presumably the CRA will select the ratings projects that have the highest fees, all-in final-profits, and highest *Reputation-Capital*; iii) each CRA sets its price/fee (the *Transaction Fee*). In another variant of this Business Model (**Alternative-1A**), the CRAs can be required to "bid" for issuer-customers that want a solicited rating. The CRA bidding will be on the basis of only delivery-time and price (*Transaction Fee*) (and perhaps *Reputational Capital* in the form of ratings-scope), and in each country, will be conducted and managed in a government-regulated portal. Thus, for each issuer, there can be several bids from CRAs, and that issuer can make counter-offers to each CRA in two or more rounds until there is one or more issuer-CRA matches. This variant is a "*two-sided quasi-auction*" since both sides of the market directly or implicitly bid in order to set prices. In this variant, "*Learning*" models can be implemented in the CRA bidding system and specifically, to: i) help CRAs and issuers to set prices (e.g. to recommend prices in each bidding round); and ii) to help regulators set prices for the portion of CRAs' fees that are paid from the *Agency Pool* and *Investor Pool*; and iii) to help regulators evaluate and improve the efficiency of the CRA business model. Such *Learning* models will gather, anonymize and use data from prior bidding, descriptions of securities/instruments and actual ratings-contracts and CRAs' reported cost-structures and per-project profitability.

Alternative 2

Each CRA will be able to rate any securities/instruments that it wants and when it wants, without any interference from the issuer but subject to the *Solicited Ratings Prohibition* and the *Un-Solicited Ratings Limitations*. Hence, for un-solicited ratings and solicited ratings, the CRA's revenue generation process will be completely and partially independent respectively, of the issuer and or the investment bank; and CRAs can become profitable simply by rating new and seasoned securities/instruments (and earning fees from subscribers in addition to one-time fixed fees paid from the "Investor-Pool" and or the "Agency-Pool" for each ratings assignment). This can solve the *Tie-Breaker Problem* and can be the functional equivalent of *break-ups* and or *divestitures* of the Big-Three CRAs; and for solicited ratings, the partial dependence of the CRA's revenue generation process on the issuer provides the CRAs with incentives to compete while reducing reliance on long term client relationships at the expense of quality and timeliness of ratings.

The CRA must provide a one-year *Ratings Warrantee* wherein the CRA must pay a pre-determined fee to the issuer, if there is a significant change in the issuer's financial condition as evidences by reference to pre-agreed financial ratios and operating performance metrics.

For each solicited or unsolicited rating, the issuer must provide the same information to all licensed CRAs through a website that will be accessible to only such licensed CRAs. Issuers will have the option to select CRAs only for solicited ratings. Only the CRA's letter-ratings for each company that it rates will be publicly disclosed on a website maintained by the government securities regulator. Each CRA will earn revenues in the following ways:

1. For each new issue of debt or secondary offering, and for only each solicited rating, there will be a fixed one-time *Transaction Fee* paid by the issuer which will be set by the CRA and will cover the CRA's evaluation costs, regardless of whether or not the offering is done or whether the CRA's rating is accepted – this fee will not exceed a low fixed percentage (e.g. 20%) of the total fees earned by the CRA from the ratings project, and will be paid to the Administrator that manages the Agency Pool, which will remit same to the CRA; plus
2. For each new issue of debt or secondary offering, and for each solicited or unsolicited rating, there will be a fixed one-time standard *Base Fee* which will be paid from an *Investor-Pool*, which will cover the CRA's evaluation costs, regardless of whether or not the offering is done or whether the agency's rating is accepted; and this Base Fee will be standard and will be set by the government securities regulator and will depend on the dollar amount of the transaction, and the relative complexity of the transaction.
3. The CRA will be prohibited from charging subscription fees and the CRA will publicly disclose both its letter-ratings and ratings details for each company that it rates.
4. Each CRA will be prohibited from providing fee-based consulting services to any issuer-company that it rates.

Issuers will be penalized for providing inadequate or fraudulent disclosures to the CRA, if such misconduct is discovered at any time, or if the designated ratings differ substantially from the performance of the issuer within three years after the rating is issued.

The CRA will be penalized for *low-quality ratings* and or *shirking* in one or more of the following ways:

1. if the CRA's rating of the bond/loan differs substantial from the actual performance of the company or the bond/loan within two years of the rating, then the CRA will pay a fine – where performance is measured by a deterioration of pre-selected metrics (financial ratios and other operating benchmarks of the company);
2. the CRA will provide a one-year warranty of the ratings;
3. if the ratings of a debt instruments of an issuer that is rated by a CRA differs from the ratings issued by any two other CRAs for at least nine months, then the CRA will pay a fine to the Investor Pool or the Agency Pool;
4. if a rated investment grade bond defaults within the first two years of issuance, the CRA must pay a penalty fee, which will be distributed to bond holders;
5. if a rated bond is assigned a two-step negative (downward) ratings transition by any competing CRA within one year of the original rating or a revised rating, then the two or three other CRAs that issued the immediately preceding ratings must pay a penalty fee to bond holders.

The foregoing model is a "*one-sided quasi-auction*" because issuers implicitly "bid" for CRAs' services given the following: i) CRAs have capacity constraints and have an *Opportunity Cost* each time they accept a ratings project; ii) each CRA can service many issuers simultaneously – and presumably the CRA will select the ratings projects that have the highest fees, all-in final-profits, and highest *Reputation-Capital*; iii) each CRA sets its price/fee (the *Transaction Fee*). In another variant of this Business Model (Alternative-2A), the CRAs can be required to "bid" for issuer-customers that want a solicited rating. The CRA bidding will be on the basis of only delivery-time and price (*Transaction Fee*) (and perhaps *Reputational Capital* in the form of ratings-scope), and in each country, will be conducted and managed in a government-regulated portal. Thus, for each issuer, there can be several bids from CRAs, and that issuer can make counter-offers to each CRA in two or more rounds until there is one or more issuer-CRA matches. This variant is a "*two-sided quasi-auction*" since both sides of the market directly or implicitly bid in order to set prices. In this variant, "*Learning*" models can be implemented in the CRA bidding system and specifically, to: i) help CRAs and issuers to set prices (e.g. to recommend prices in each bidding round); and ii) to help regulators set prices for the portion of CRAs' fees that are paid from the *Agency Pool* and *Investor Pool*; and iii) to help regulators evaluate and improve the efficiency of the CRA business model. Such *Learning* models will gather, anonymize and use data from prior bidding, descriptions of securities/instruments and actual ratings-contracts and CRAs' reported cost-structures and per-project profitability.

Alternative 3

Each CRA will be able to rate any securities/instruments that it wants and when it wants, without any interference from the issuer but subject to the *Solicited Ratings Prohibition* and the *Un-Solicited Ratings Limitations*. Hence, for un-solicited ratings and solicited ratings, the CRA's revenue generation process will be completely and partially independent respectively, of the issuer and or the investment bank; and CRAs can become profitable simply by rating new and seasoned securities/instruments (and earning fees from subscribers in addition to one-time fixed fees paid from the "Investor-Pool" and or the "Agency-Pool" for each ratings assignment). This model can solve the *Tie-Breaker Problem* and can be deemed to be a functional equivalent of a *Break-up* and or *Divestiture* of the Big-Three CRAs and the next three largest CRA. For solicited ratings, the partial dependence of the CRA's revenue generation process on the issuer provides the CRAs with incentives to compete while reducing reliance on long term client relationships at the expense of quality and timeliness of ratings.

The CRA must provide a one-year Ratings Warrantee wherein the CRA must pay a pre-determined fee to the issuer, if there is a significant change in the issuer's financial condition as evidences by reference to pre-agreed financial ratios and operating performance metrics.

For each solicited or unsolicited rating, the issuer must provide the same information to all licensed CRAs through a website that will be accessible to only such licensed CRAs. The government securities regulator can grant ratings licenses to any number of CRAs. Issuers will have the option to select two CRAs only for each solicited rating. Only the CRA's letter-ratings for each company that it rates will be publicly disclosed on a website maintained by the government securities regulator. Each CRA will earn revenues in the following ways:

1. For each new issue of debt or secondary offering, and for only each solicited rating, the issuer will pay a fixed one-time *Transaction Fee* which will be set by the CRA and will cover the CRA's evaluation costs, regardless of whether or not the offering is done or whether the CRA's rating is accepted – this fee will not exceed a low fixed percentage (e.g. 20%) of the total fees earned by the CRA from the ratings project, and will be paid to the Administrator that manages the Agency Pool, which will remit same to the CRA.
2. For each new issue of debt or secondary offering, and for each solicited or unsolicited rating, there will be a fixed one-time standard *Base Fee* which will be paid from an *Agency-Pool*, which will cover the CRA's fixed costs, regardless of whether or not the offering is done or whether the agency's rating is accepted; and this Base Fee will be standard and will be set by the government securities regulator and will be based on the relative complexity of the transaction.
3. For each new issue of debt or secondary offering, and for each solicited or unsolicited rating, there will be a fixed one-time standard *Base Fee* which will be paid from an *Investor-Pool*, which will cover the CRA's direct/variable evaluation costs plus profits, regardless of whether or not the offering is done or whether the agency's rating is accepted; and this Base Fee will be standard and will be set by the government securities regulator and will depend on the dollar amount of the transaction, and the relative complexity of the transaction.
4. The CRA can charge subscription fees (for industry reports; company reports and details of ratings); and the CRA will publicly disclose only it's letter-ratings for free.
5. Each CRA will be prohibited from providing consulting services to any issuer-company that it rates.

Issuers will be penalized for providing inadequate or fraudulent disclosures to the CRA, if such misconduct is discovered at any time, or if the designated ratings differs substantially from the performance of the issuer within three years after the rating is issued.

The CRA will be penalized for low-quality ratings and or shirking in one or more of the following ways:

1. if the CRA's rating of the bond/loan differs substantial from the actual performance of the company or the bond/loan within two years of the rating, then the CRA will pay a fine – where performance is measured by a deterioration of pre-selected metrics (financial ratios and other operating benchmarks of the company);
2. the CRA will provide a one-year warranty of the ratings;

3. if the ratings of a debt instruments of an issuer that is rated by a CRA differs from the ratings issued by any two other CRAs for at least nine months, then the CRA will pay a fine to the Investor Pool or the Agency Pool;
4. if a rated investment grade bond defaults within the first two years of issuance, the CRA must pay a penalty fee, which will be distributed to bond holders;
5. if a rated bond is assigned a two-step negative (downward) ratings transition by any competing CRA within one year of the original rating or a revised rating, then the two or three other CRAs that issued the immediately preceding ratings must pay a penalty fee to bond holders.

The foregoing model is a "*one-sided quasi-auction*" because issuers implicitly "bid" for CRAs' services given the following: i) CRAs have capacity constraints and have an *Opportunity Cost* each time they accept a ratings project; ii) each CRA can service many issuers simultaneously – and presumably the CRA will select the ratings projects that have the highest fees, all-in final-profits, and highest *Reputation-Capital*; iii) each CRA sets its price/fee (the *Transaction Fee*). In another variant of this Business Model (Alternative-3A), the CRAs can be required to "bid" for issuer-customers that want a solicited rating. The CRA bidding will be on the basis of only delivery-time and price (and perhaps *Reputational Capital* in the form of ratings-scope), and in each country, will be conducted and managed in a government-regulated portal. Thus, for each issuer, there can be several bids from CRAs, and that issuer can make counter-offers to each CRA in two or more rounds until there is one or more issuer-CRA matches. This variant is a "*two-sided quasi-auction*" since both sides of the market directly or implicitly bid in order to set prices. In this variant, "*Learning*" models can be implemented in the CRA bidding system and specifically, to: i) help CRAs and issuers to set prices (e.g. to recommend prices in each bidding round); ii) to help regulators set prices for the portion of CRAs' fees that are paid from the *Agency Pool* and *Investor Pool*; and iii) to help regulators evaluate and improve the efficiency of the CRA business model. Such *Learning* models will gather, anonymize and use data from prior bidding, descriptions of securities/instruments and actual ratings-contracts and CRAs' reported cost-structures and per-project profitability.

Alternative 4

Each CRA will be able to rate any securities/instruments that it wants and when it wants, without any interference from the issuer but subject to the *Solicited Ratings Prohibition* and the *Un-Solicited Ratings Limitations*. Hence, for un-solicited ratings and solicited ratings, the CRA's revenue generation process will be completely and partially independent respectively, of the issuer and or the investment bank; and CRAs can become profitable simply by rating new and seasoned securities/instruments (and earning fees from subscribers in addition to one-time fixed fees paid from the "*Investor-Pool*" and or the "*Agency-Pool*" for each ratings assignment). This model can solve the *Tie-Breaker Problem* and is a functional equivalent of *Break-ups* and or *Divestitures* of the Big-Three CRAs; and for solicited ratings, the partial dependence of the CRA's revenue generation process on the issuer provides the CRAs with incentives to compete while reducing reliance on long term client relationships at the expense of quality and timeliness of ratings.

The CRA must provide a one-year Ratings Warrantee wherein the CRA must pay a pre-determined fee to the issuer, if there is a significant change in the issuer's financial condition as evidences by reference to pre-agreed financial ratios and operating performance metrics.

For each solicited or unsolicited rating, the issuer must provide the same information to all licensed CRAs through a website that will be accessible to only such licensed CRAs. The US SEC can grant ratings licenses to any number of CRAs. Issuers will have the option to select two CRAs only for each solicited-rating. Only the CRA's letter-ratings for each company that it rates will be publicly disclosed on a website maintained by the government securities regulator. Each CRA will earn revenues in the following ways:

1. Each licensed CRA is paid a fixed *Base Fee* at the beginning of each quarter or each semi-annual period from the *Agency Pool*, and in exchange the CRA agrees to provide unsolicited ratings for a minimum number of companies. The companies will be allocated among CRAs so that such unsolicited ratings are provided for each company by at least fifty percent (or any specified percentage) of licensed CRAs.
2. Any issuer that wants a "*Solicited Rating*" for an instrument will pay a fixed one-time *Annual Transaction Fee* to the CRA, which will entitle the issuer to obtain Solicited-Ratings for up to eight (or another specified amount) securities/instruments during the one year period; but the *Annual Transaction Fee* will be set by the CRA and will cover the CRA's evaluation costs, regardless of whether or not the offering is done or whether the CRA's rating is accepted – this fee will not exceed a low fixed percentage (e.g. 20%) of the estimated total cost of rating an issuer multiplied by the maximum number of ratings per year. This fee will be paid to the Administrator that manages the Agency Pool, which will remit same to the CRA.
3. The CRA can charge subscription fees (for industry reports; company reports and details of ratings); and the CRA will publicly disclose only it's letter-ratings for free.
4. Each CRA will be prohibited from providing consulting services to any issuer-company that it rates.

Issuers will be penalized for providing inadequate or fraudulent disclosures to the CRA, if such misconduct is discovered at any time, or if the designated ratings differs substantially from the performance of the issuer within three years after the rating is issued.

The CRA will be penalized for low-quality ratings and or shirking in one or more of the following ways:

1. if the CRA's rating of the bond/loan differs substantial from the actual performance of the company or the bond/loan within two years of the rating, then the CRA will pay a fine – where performance is measured by a deterioration of pre-selected metrics (financial ratios and other operating benchmarks of the company);
2. the CRA will provide a one-year warranty of the ratings;
3. if the ratings of a debt instruments of an issuer that is rated by a CRA differs from the ratings issued by any two other CRAs for at least nine months, then the CRA will pay a fine to the Investor Pool or the Agency Pool;
4. if a rated investment grade bond defaults within the first two years of issuance, the CRA must pay a penalty fee, which will be distributed to bond holders;
5. if a rated bond is assigned a two-step negative (downward) ratings transition by any competing CRA within one year of the original rating or a revised rating, then the two or three other CRAs that issued the immediately preceding ratings must pay a penalty fee to bond holders.

The foregoing model is a "*one-sided quasi-auction*" because issuers implicitly "bid" for CRAs' services given the following: i) CRAs have capacity constraints and have an *Opportunity Cost* each time they accept a ratings project; ii) each CRA can service many issuers simultaneously – and presumably the CRA will select the ratings projects that have the highest fees, all-in final-profits, and highest *Reputation-Capital*; iii) each CRA sets its price/fee (the *Transaction Fee*). In another variant of this Business Model (Alternative-4A), the CRAs can be required to "bid" for issuer-customers that want a solicited rating. The CRA bidding will be on the basis of only delivery-time and price (*Transaction Fee*) (and perhaps *Reputational Capital* in the form of ratings-scope). In each country, the CRA bidding will be conducted and managed in a government-regulated portal. Thus, for each issuer, there can be several bids from CRAs, and that issuer can make counter-offers to each CRA in two or more bidding rounds until there is one or more issuer-CRA matches. This variant is a "*two-sided quasi-auction*" since both sides of the market directly or implicitly bid in order to set prices. In this variant, "*Learning*" models can be implemented in the CRA bidding system and specifically, to: i) help CRAs and issuers to set prices (e.g. to recommend prices in each bidding round); ii) to help regulators set prices for the portion of CRAs' fees that are paid from the *Agency Pool* and *Investor Pool*; and iii) to help regulators evaluate and improve the efficiency of the CRA business model. Such *Learning* models will gather, anonymize and use data from prior bidding, descriptions of securities/instruments and actual ratings-contracts and CRAs' reported cost-structures and per-project profitability.

Alternative 5

Each CRA will be able to rate any securities/instruments that it wants and when it wants, without any interference from the issuer but subject to the *Solicited Ratings Prohibition* and the *Un-Solicited Ratings Limitations*. Hence, for un-solicited ratings and solicited ratings, the CRA's revenue generation process will be completely and partially independent respectively, of the issuer and or the investment bank; and CRAs can become profitable simply by rating new and seasoned securities/instruments (and earning fees from subscribers in addition to one-time fixed fees paid from the "*Investor-Pool*" and or the "*Agency-Pool*" for each ratings assignment). This model can solve the *Tie-Breaker Problem* and provides the equivalent of *Divestiture* and or *Break-up* of the Big-Three CRAs (and the next largest three CRAs). For solicited ratings, the partial dependence (of the CRA's revenue generation process) on the issuer provides the CRAs with incentives to compete while reducing reliance on long term client relationships at the expense of quality and timeliness of ratings.

The CRA must provide a one-year *Ratings Warrantee* wherein the CRA must pay a pre-determined fee to the issuer or a government-controlled fund, if there is a significant change in the issuer's financial condition as evidenced by reference to pre-agreed financial ratios and operating performance metrics.

For each solicited or unsolicited rating, the issuer must provide the same information to all licensed CRAs through a website that will be accessible to only such licensed CRAs. The government securities regulator can grant ratings licenses to any number of CRAs. Issuers will have the option to select two CRAs only for each solicited rating. Only the CRA's letter-ratings for each company that it rates will be publicly disclosed on a website maintained by the government securities regulator. Each CRA will earn revenues in the following ways:

1. Each issuer can request for a solicited rating for a financial instrument only if there has not been any type of rating for the prior six months. The number of ratings that can be requested by each issuer for each security/instrument is limited.
2. For each new issue of debt or secondary offering, and for only each solicited rating, the issuer will pay a fixed one-time *Transaction Fee* which will cover the issuer's direct/variable costs and which will be set by the *Investor Pool* Administrator (regardless of whether or not the offering is done or whether the CRA's rating is accepted) and will be subject to the condition that the Transaction Fee will be paid to the CRA only if the CRA industry is not concentrated among any two CRAs (e.g. no two CRAs issue more than sixty percent of the Solicited Ratings in each year). The Investor Pool administrator will publicly disclose *Industry Concentration conditions*, and if the Industry is concentrated, then all the Transaction Fees paid by all issuers will be paid into the *Agency Pool.* Furthermore, this Transaction Fee will be paid only at the end of each calendar year, and it shall not exceed a low fixed percentage (e.g. 20%) of the total fees earned by the CRA from the individual ratings project, and will be paid to the Administrator that manages the *Investor Pool*, which will remit same to the CRA.
3. For each new issue of debt or secondary offering, and for each solicited or unsolicited rating, there will be a fixed one-time standard *Base Fee* which will be paid from an *Agency-Pool*, which will cover the CRA's full costs for the ratings project, regardless of whether or not the offering is done or whether the agency's rating is accepted; and this Base Fee will be standard and will be set by the US SEC and will be based on the relative complexity of the transaction.
4. For each new issue of debt or secondary offering, and for each solicited or unsolicited rating, there will be a fixed one-time standard *Bonus Fee* which will be paid from an *Investor-Pool*, which will cover the CRA's Minimum Profits; and this Bonus Fee will be standard and will be set by the US SEC and will depend on the relative complexity of the transaction. This Bonus Fee will be paid only at the end of each semi-annual period, and only if:
    a. the CRA industry is not concentrated (Industry Concentration will be a function of the number of solicited and unsolicited ratings projects by each licensed CRA, and will be publicly disclosed each week); and
    b. 2 the CRA does not participate in any collusion with other CRAs (the Bonus Fee for any collusive CRA will be paid into the Agency Pool) – and the no-collusion obligation for each period lasts for five years and the SEC will have claw-back rights to any paid bonuses if any collusion is subsequently detected during the subsequent five-year period).
5. The licensed CRA can charge subscription fees (for industry reports; company reports and details of ratings); and the CRA will publicly disclose only it's letter-ratings for each company for free.
6. Each licensed CRA will be prohibited from providing consulting services to any issuer-company that it rates.

Issuers will be penalized for providing inadequate or fraudulent disclosures to the CRA, if such misconduct is discovered at any time, or if the designated ratings differs substantially from the performance of the issuer within three years after the rating is issued.

The CRA will be penalized for low-quality ratings and or shirking in one or more of the following ways:

1. if the CRA's rating of the bond/loan differs substantial from the actual performance of the company or the bond/loan within two years of the rating, then the CRA will pay a fine – where performance

is measured by a deterioration of pre-selected metrics (financial ratios and other operating benchmarks of the company);

2. the CRA will provide a one-year warranty of the ratings;
3. if the ratings of a debt instruments of an issuer that is rated by a CRA differs from the ratings issued by any two other CRAs for at least nine months, then the CRA will pay a fine to the Investor Pool or the Agency Pool;
4. if a rated investment grade bond defaults within the first two years of issuance, the CRA must pay a penalty fee, which will be distributed to bond holders;
5. if a rated bond is assigned a two-step negative (downward) ratings transition by any competing CRA within one year of the original rating or a revised rating, then the two or three other CRAs that issued the immediately preceding ratings must pay a penalty fee to bond holders.

The foregoing model is a "*one-sided quasi-auction*" because issuers implicitly "bid" for CRAs' services given the following: i) CRAs have capacity constraints and have an *Opportunity Cost* each time they accept a ratings project; ii) each CRA can service many issuers simultaneously – and presumably the CRA will select the ratings projects that have the highest fees, all-in final-profits, and highest *Reputation-Capital*; iii) each CRA sets its price/fee (the *Transaction Fee*). In another variant of this Business Model (Alternative-5A), the CRAs can be required to "bid" for issuer-customers that want a solicited rating. The CRA bidding will be on the basis of only delivery-time and price (*Transaction Fee*) (and perhaps *Reputational Capital* in the form of ratings-scope). In each country, the CRA bidding will be conducted and managed in a government-regulated portal. Thus, for each issuer, there can be several bids from CRAs, and that issuer can make counter-offers to each CRA in two or more bidding rounds until there is one or more issuer-CRA matches. This variant is a "*two-sided quasi-auction*" since both sides of the market directly or implicitly bid in order to set prices. In this variant, "*Learning*" models can be implemented in the CRA bidding system and specifically, to: i) help CRAs and issuers to set prices (e.g. to recommend prices in each bidding round); ii) to help regulators set prices for the portion of CRAs' fees that are paid from the *Agency Pool* and *Investor Pool*; and iii) to help regulators evaluate and improve the efficiency of the CRA business model. Such *Learning* models will gather, anonymize and use data from prior bidding, descriptions of securities/instruments and actual ratings-contracts and CRAs' reported cost-structures and per-project profitability.

Alternative 6

Each CRA will be able to rate any securities/instruments that it wants and when it wants, without any interference from the issuer but subject to the *Solicited Ratings Prohibition* and the *Un-Solicited Ratings Limitations*. Hence, for un-solicited ratings and solicited ratings, the CRA's revenue generation process will be completely and partially independent respectively, of the issuer and or the investment bank; and CRAs can become profitable simply by rating new and seasoned securities/instruments (and earning fees from subscribers in addition to one-time fixed fees paid from the "*Investor-Pool*" and or the "*Agency-Pool*" for each ratings assignment). This model can solve the *Tie-Breaker Problem* and can provide the equivalent of *Break-up* and or *Divestitures* of the Big-Three CRAs. For solicited ratings, the partial dependence of the CRA's revenue generation process on the issuer provides the CRAs with incentives to compete while reducing reliance on long term client relationships at the expense of quality and timeliness of ratings.

The CRA must provide a one-year *Ratings Warrantee* wherein the CRA must pay a pre-determined fee to the issuer, if there is a significant change in the issuer's financial condition as evidences by reference to pre-agreed financial ratios and operating performance metrics.

For each solicited or unsolicited rating, the issuer must provide the same information to all licensed CRAs through a website that will be accessible to only such licensed CRAs. The government securities regulator will grant ratings licenses to at least five CRAs. Issuers will have the option to select two CRAs only for each solicited rating. Only the CRA's letter-ratings for each company that it rates will be publicly disclosed on a website maintained by the government securities regulator. Each licensed CRA will earn revenues in the following ways:

1. Each issuer can request for a solicited rating from a CRA for a financial instrument only if there has not been any type of rating for the prior six months by that CRA. The number of ratings that can be requested by each issuer for each security/instrument is limited.
2. For each new issue of debt or secondary offering, and for only each solicited rating, the issuer will pay a fixed one-time *Transaction Fee* which will cover the issuer's direct/variable costs and which will be set by the *Investor Pool* Administrator (regardless of whether or not the offering is done or whether the CRA's rating is accepted) and will be subject to the condition that the Transaction Fee will be paid to the CRA only if the CRA industry is not concentrated among any two CRA (e.g. no two CRAs issue more than sixty percent of the Solicited Ratings in each year). The Investor Pool administrator will publicly disclose *Industry Concentration Conditions*, and if the industry is concentrated, then all the Transaction Fees paid by all issuers will be paid into the *Agency Pool*. Furthermore, this Transaction Fee will be paid only at the end of each calendar year, and it shall not exceed a low fixed percentage (e.g. 20%) of the total fees earned by the CRA from the individual ratings project, and will be paid to the Administrator that manages the *Investor Pool*, which will remit same to the CRA.
3. For each new issue of debt or secondary offering, and for each solicited or unsolicited rating, there will be a fixed one-time standard *Base Fee* which will be paid from an *Agency-Pool*, which will cover the CRA's full costs for the ratings project, regardless of whether or not the offering is done or whether the agency's rating is accepted; and this Base Fee will be set by the government securities regulator and will be based on the relative complexity of each transaction and the issuer.
4. For each new issue of debt or secondary offering, and for each solicited or unsolicited rating, there will be a fixed one-time standard *Bonus Fee* which will be paid from an *Investor-Pool*, which will cover the CRA's Minimum Profits; and this Bonus Fee will be set by the government securities regulator and will depend on the relative complexity of the transaction. This Bonus Fee will be paid only at the end of each semi-annual period, and only if:
    a. the CRA industry is not concentrated (Industry Concentration will be a function of the number of solicited and unsolicited ratings projects by each licensed CRA, and will be publicly disclosed each month/quarter); and
    b. the CRA does not participate in any collusion with other CRAs (the Bonus Fee for any collusive CRA will be paid into the Agency Pool) – and the no-collusion obligation for each period lasts for five years and the government securities regulator will have claw-back rights to any paid bonuses if any collusion is subsequently detected during the subsequent five-year period).

5. The licensed CRA can charge subscription fees (for industry reports; company reports and details of ratings); and the CRA will publicly disclose only it's letter-ratings for each company for free.
6. Each licensed CRA will be prohibited from providing consulting services to any issuer-company that it rates.

Issuers will be penalized for providing inadequate or fraudulent disclosures to the CRA, if such misconduct is discovered at any time, or if the designated ratings differs substantially from the performance of the issuer within three years after the rating is issued.

The CRA will be penalized for low-quality ratings and or shirking in one or more of the following ways:

1. if the CRA's rating of the bond/loan differs substantial from the actual performance of the company or the bond/loan within two years of the rating, then the CRA will pay a fine – where performance is measured by a deterioration of pre-selected metrics (financial ratios and other operating benchmarks of the company);
2. the CRA will provide a one-year warranty of the ratings;
3. if the ratings of a debt instruments of an issuer that is rated by a CRA differs from the ratings issued by any two other CRAs for at least nine months, then the CRA will pay a fine to the Investor Pool or the Agency Pool;
4. if a rated investment grade bond defaults within the first two years of issuance, the CRA must pay a penalty fee, which will be distributed to bond holders;
5. if a rated bond is assigned a two-step negative (downward) ratings transition by any competing CRA within one year of the original rating or a revised rating, then the two or three other CRAs that issued the immediately preceding ratings must pay a penalty fee to bond holders.

Non-licensed CRAs can earn revenues from the following:

1. Providing credit ratings for small companies whose annual revenues don't exceed $100 Million; or companies whose suppliers, customers, bondholders and shareholders don't exceed 5,000 persons.
2. Subscriptions for industry research and company reports.

Alternative 7

The Government (e.g. US Congress) will create and staff a government ratings agency. This CRA will be funded by the following: **i)** special fees levied on all domestic securities accounts, **ii)** special fees levied on each bond transaction (sales, new issues, swaps), **iii)** a fee paid by the SIPC, iv) a fee levied on bond insurers for every transaction, **v)** special fees levied on bank loan transactions; **vi)** special levies on proceeds from rated bond offerings that are paid to issuers, **vii)** special taxes on bond insurers.

This Government ratings agency (GRA) will contract with, and provide ratings services to various private sector-CRAs (PSRA). Hence, all or most of the actual ratings function in the industry will be done by the GRA. That can resolve the issues of industry capacity, ratings redundancy (where different CRAs use the same processes and issue same ratings), and quality differentials. The PSRAs will serve as marketing, customer relations, ratings review and industry research/monitoring entities. The GRA will typically render a ratings opinion to the PSRA, and if the PSRA disagrees with the GRA's ratings, a special panel will determine the rating for the entity (that can help reduce bias and politicization in ratings). In some countries (and depending on the degree of political lobbying and corruption), the GRA's rating on any entity can serve as a "*Ratings Floor*". The PSRA will pay GRA on a cost-plus-profits basis, for the ratings services at the end of each month. The GRA will also be paid a fixed quarterly fee from the *Investor-Pool* and or the Agency Pool. The PSRA will be compensated in the following ways:

1. A Base Fee paid from an *Investor-Pool*, which will cover the CRA's fixed costs, regardless of whether or not the CRA does any ratings project during the year - the fixed costs will include a percentage of employee salaries/benefits, G&A costs, software costs and certain maintenance costs;
2. A Transaction Fee paid from an *Investor-Pool*, which will cover a percentage of the CRA's variable evaluation costs, regardless of whether or not the offering is done or whether the agency's rating is accepted;
3. A *Transaction* Fee paid by the issuer, which will not exceed 30% of the total fees earned by the CRA – the issuer must pay this fee regardless of whether or not the offering is done or whether the agency's rating is accepted by the issuer.

The rationale behind this business model is that: a) the government often bears most of the costs of inaccurate ratings – costs of bankruptcies, government bailouts of financial institutions, tax relief, etc.; b) centralization of the ratings effort can significantly reduce information asymmetry and effects of ratings-dispersion, c) ratings have been incorporated into statutes and regulations worldwide, and hence the governments should review and change the heavy reliance on ratings in regulation. The problem with this alternative is that CRAs are now international – hence, for this model to work, each country's government or a regional government or an economic community (such as the United Nations; the European Union; the African Union, or the Organization Of Latin American State) will have to create a ratings agency.

Alternative 8

There are no CRAs (the government will statutorily bar any operations of CRAs); and the national government in each country will publish a series of analytical ratios and standard ratings methodologies which banks, investors and financial institutions will use in evaluating corporate entities and SPVs. Investment banks will be required to use these ratios in their research reports on companies and SPVs. The national government in each country will also "rate" industries, and publish quarterly reports on each industry. Where any type of ratings is required for regulatory purposes, the government can construct indices based on the above-mentioned analytical ratios. This model can resolve the problems of conflicts-of-interest; Collusion; information-asymmetry, *Tie-Breakers*, ratings-redundancy, CRA-compensation and fraud.

Issuers are specifically or statutorily limited to a specific number of ratings in each period (year or half-year or quarter). Issuers are penalized for providing inadequate or fraudulent disclosures to the CRA, if such misconduct is discovered at any time, or if the designated ratings differ substantially from the performance of the issuer within three years after the rating is issued.

CONCLUSION

The regulation and compensation of CRAs remains a major problem because despite the enactment of new financial regulations for CRAs in various countries, and the de-emphasis/removal of credit ratings in regulations, and recommendations of new CRA compensation models, CRAs have substantial potential to undermine national financial systems and to cause or amplify systemic risk. Most if not all recommended business models and compensation arrangement for CRAs are grossly deficient, and or will cause conflicts-of-interest. Many of the economic studies of CRAs almost completely omit analysis of the legal issues that pertain to the ratings process (fraud; conspiracy; freedom-of-speech; extortion; etc.) and competition among CRAs (antitrust; fraud) and the cost structure of CRAs. While there are feasible alternatives to traditional credit-ratings, the associated transaction costs, and susceptibility to market manipulation of such metrics (such as credit spreads and CDS spreads) and the lack of development of some markets (such as leasing, joint ventures and licensing) make them less appealing in the short term. The over-emphasis on Reputational Capital of CRAs is somewhat misplaced and the appropriate solutions to the CRA problem will need to blend compensation with an efficient business model and concern for social welfare and monitoring costs.

REFERENCES

Abad, P., Ferreras, R., & Robles, D. (2020). Information opacity and corporate bond returns: The dynamics of split ratings. *Journal of International Financial Markets, Institutions and Money*, 68.

Aguirre, A. (2017). Contracting institutions and economic growth. *Review of Economic Dynamics, 24*, 192–217. doi:10.1016/j.red.2017.01.009

Algaba, E., Bilbao, R., van den Brink, A., & Jiménez-Losada, A. (2004). Cooperative Games on Antimatroids. *Discrete Mathematics, 282*(1-3), 1–15. doi:10.1016/j.disc.2003.10.019

Anzo-Hernández, A., Gilardi-Velázquez, H., & Campos-Cantón, E. (2018). On multistability behavior of unstable dissipative systems. *Chaos (Woodbury, N.Y.), 28*(3), 033613. doi:10.1063/1.5016329 PMID:29604643

Arribillaga, R., Massó, J., & Neme, A. (2014). On the Structure of Cooperative and Competitive Solutions for a Generalized Assignment Game. *Journal of Applied Mathematics, 2014*, 1–20. doi:10.1155/2014/190614

Ayotte, K., & Bolton, P. (2011). Covenant lite lending, liquidity, and standardization of financial contracts. Chapter. In P. Bolon (Ed.), *Research Handbook on the Economics of Property Law. Edward Elgar Publishing Ltd*. doi:10.4337/9781849808972.00013

Aziz, H., Lev, O., Mattei, N., Rosenschein, J. S., & Walsh, T. (2019). Strategy-proof peer selection using randomization, partitioning, and apportionment. *Artificial Intelligence, 275*, 295–309. doi:10.1016/j.artint.2019.06.004

Baffi, E. (2007). The Economics of Standard Form Contracts. Università degli Studi "Guglielmo Marconi".

Baffi, E. (2012). Contracting in modern world. *Aperta Contrada*. https://www.apertacontrada.it/2012/11/13/contracting-in-modern-world/

Baffi, E. (2000). *Some Characteristic Features of Mass Contracting.* Università degli Studi "Roma Tre" – Faculty of Law.

Bai, L. (2010). On Regulating Conflicts of Interest in the Credit Rating Industry. *NYU Journal Of Legislation And Public Policy, 13*, 253–263.

Baranwal, G., & Vidyarthi, D. (2015). A fair multi-attribute combinatorial double auction model for resource allocation in cloud computing. *Journal of Systems and Software, 108*, 60–76. doi:10.1016/j.jss.2015.06.025

Becker, B., & Milbourn, T. (2011). How did increased competition affect credit ratings? *Journal of Financial Economics, 101*(3), 493–514. doi:10.1016/j.jfineco.2011.03.012

Bergantiños, G., & Massó, J. (2002). A Compromise Value for NTU-Games. *Mathematical Methods of Operations Research, 56*, 269–286. doi:10.1007001860200193

Bertsekas, D. (2000). *Auction Algorithms.* Working paper, MIT. https://pdfs.semanticscholar.org/c00f/9e12543fff8180b307341fa9c1891eabf727.pdf

Bischi, G., Chiarella, C., Kopel, M., & Szidarovszky, F. (2010). Nonlinear Oligopolies: Stability and Bifurcations. Springer.

Byoun, S., Han, S., & Shin, Y. (2020). Does the Nationally Recognized Statistical Rating Organization certification matter for Japanese credit rating agencies? *Journal of Financial Markets.*

Chassaing, M., Duhamel, C., & Lacomme, P. (2016). An ELS-based approach with dynamic probabilities management in local search for the Dial-A-Ride Problem. *Engineering Applications of Artificial Intelligence, 48*, 119–133. doi:10.1016/j.engappai.2015.10.002

Chen, Z., Matousek, R., Stewart, C., & Webb, R. (2019). Do rating agencies exhibit herding behaviour? Evidence from sovereign ratings. *International Review of Financial Analysis, 64*, 57–70. doi:10.1016/j.irfa.2019.04.011

Colini-Baldeschi, R., & Goldberg, P. (2017). Approximately Efficient Two-Sided Combinatorial Auctions. *Proceedings of the 2017 ACM Conference on Economics and Computation*, 591-608.

de Haan, J., & Amtenbrink, F. (2011). *Credit Rating Agencies.* De Nederlandsche Bank Working Paper No. 278.

Deb, P., Manning, M., Murphy, G., Penalver, A., & Toth, A. (2011). Whither the credit ratings industry? Financial Stability Paper #9, Bank of England.

Dekker, H., Kawai, T., & Sakaguchi, J. (2018). Contracting abroad: A comparative analysis of contract design in host and home country outsourcing relations. *Management Accounting Research, 40*, 47–61. doi:10.1016/j.mar.2017.09.003

Demange, G., Gale, D., & Sotomayor, M. (1987). A Further Note on the Stable Matching Problem. *Discrete Applied Mathematics, 16*(3), 217–222. doi:10.1016/0166-218X(87)90059-X

Deng, X., Goldberg, P., Tang, B., & Zhang, J. (2014). Revenue Maximization In A Bayesian Double Auction Market. *Theoretical Computer Science, 539*(1), 1–12. doi:10.1016/j.tcs.2014.04.013

Dittrich, F. (2007). *The credit rating industry: Competition and regulation*. Inaugural PHD Dissertation. zur Erlangung Des Doktorgrades der Wirtschafts- und Sozialwissenschaftlichen Fakultat der Universitat zu Koln, Germany.

Doshi, P., Gmytrasiewicz, P., & Durfee, E. (2020). Recursively modeling other agents for decision making: A research perspective. *Artificial Intelligence*, *279*, 103202. doi:10.1016/j.artint.2019.103202

Drozd, L., & Serrano-Padia, R. (2018). Financial contracting with enforcement externalities. *Journal of Economic Theory*, *178*, 153–189. doi:10.1016/j.jet.2018.09.002

Du, W. (2018). Who carried more credibility?: An analysis of the market responses to news from the Japanese government, the Japanese central bank and international credit rating agencies. *Journal of Economics and Business*, *98*, 32–39. doi:10.1016/j.jeconbus.2018.05.002

Dutting, P., & Feng, Z. (2019). *Optimal Auctions through Deep Learning*. https://arxiv.org/pdf/1706.03459.pdf

Dütting, P., Roughgarden, T., & Talgam-Cohen, I. (2014). Modularity and Greed in Double Auctions. *Proceedings of the 15th Conference on Economics and Computation (EC'14)*, 241–258. http://theory.stanford.edu/~italgam/papers/Modular%20Double%20Auctions.pdf

Eenmaa-Dimitrieva, H., & Schmidt-Kessen, M. (2019). Creating markets in no-trust environments: The law and economics of smart contracts. *Computer Law & Security Review*, *35*(1), 69–88. doi:10.1016/j.clsr.2018.09.003

Fang, X., & Yuan, F. (2018). The Coordination and Preference of Supply Chain Contracts Based on Time-Sensitivity Promotional Mechanism. *Journal of Management Science and Engineering*, *3*(3), 158–178. doi:10.3724/SP.J.1383.303009

Feng, Z., Narasimhan, H., & Parkes, D. (2018). Deep Learning for Revenue-Optimal Auctions with Budgets. *Proceedings of the 17th International Conference on Autonomous Agents and MultiAgent Systems. International Foundation for Autonomous Agents and Multiagent Systems*, 354–362.

Feudel, F., Pisarchik, A., & Showalter, K. (2018). Multistability and tipping: From mathematics and physics to climate and brain—Minireview and preface to the focus issue. *Chaos (Woodbury, N.Y.)*, *28*(3), 033501. doi:10.1063/1.5027718 PMID:29604626

Forbes, K., Warnock, J., & Francis, E. (2012). Capital flow waves: Surges, stops, flight, and retrenchment. *Journal of International Economics*, *88*(2), 235–251. doi:10.1016/j.jinteco.2012.03.006

FSB. (2010). *Principles for Reducing the Reliance on Ratings*. Available at: www.financialstabilityboard.org/publications/r_101027.pdf

Garcia, A., Berlanga, A., Molina, J., & Davila, J. (2004). Optimization Of Airport Ground Operations Integrating Genetic And Dynamic Flow Management Algorithms. *AI Communications*, *18*(2), 143–164.

Goetz, R., Yatsenko, Y., Hritonenko, N., Xabadia, A., & Abdulai, A. (2019). The dynamics of productive assets, contract duration and holdup. *Mathematical Social Sciences*, *97*, 24–37. doi:10.1016/j.mathsocsci.2018.10.004

Gomes, R. (2014). Optimal auction design in two-sided markets. *The RAND Journal of Economics*, *45*(2), 248–272. doi:10.1111/1756-2171.12050

Govindan, S., & Wilson, R. (2006). Sufficient conditions for stable equilibria. *Theoretical Economics*, *1*, 167–206. https://econtheory.org/ojs/index.php/te/article/viewFile/20060167/617/25

Hong, S., Wernz, C., & Stillinger, J. (2016). Optimizing maintenance service contracts through mechanism design theory. *Applied Mathematical Modelling*, *40*(21-22), 8849–8861. doi:10.1016/j.apm.2015.07.009

Hoppe, E., & Schmitz, P. (2018). Hidden action and outcome contractibility: An experimental test of moral hazard theory. *Games and Economic Behavior*, *109*, 544–564. doi:10.1016/j.geb.2018.02.006

Hu, X., Huang, H., Pan, Z., & Shi, J. (2019). Information asymmetry and credit rating: A quasi-natural experiment from China. *Journal of Banking & Finance*, *106*, 132–152. doi:10.1016/j.jbankfin.2019.06.003

Huang, Y., & Shen, C. (2019). What role does the investor-paid rating agency play in China? Competitor or information provider. *International Review of Economics & Finance*, *63*, 253–272. doi:10.1016/j.iref.2018.11.007

Ioannou, S., Wójcik, D., & Pažitka, D. (2020). Financial centre bias in sub-sovereign credit ratings. *Journal of International Financial Markets, Institutions and Money*.

IOSCO. (2008). *The role of credit CRAs in structured finance markets*. Final Report, May 2008.

Iossa, E., & Martimort, D. (2018). Corruption in PPPs, incentives and contract incompleteness. *International Journal of Industrial Organization*, *44*, 85–100. doi:10.1016/j.ijindorg.2015.10.007

Jacobs, B. (2012). *Introduction to Coalgebra: Towards Mathematics of States and Observations*. Institute for Computing and Information Sciences, Radboud University Nijmegen, Netherlands. http://www.cs.ru.nl/B.Jacobs/CLG/JacobsCoalgebraIntro.pdf

Jain, S., Gujar, S., Bhat, S., Zoeter, O., & Narahari, Y. (2018). A quality assuring, cost optimal multi-armed bandit mechanism for expert-sourcing. *Artificial Intelligence*, *254*, 44–63. doi:10.1016/j.artint.2017.10.001

Jaume, D., Masso, J., & Neme, A. (2012). The Multiple-partners Assignment Game with Heterogeneous Sells and Multi-unit Demands: Competitive Equilibria. *Mathematical Methods of Operations Research*, *76*(2), 161–187. doi:10.100700186-012-0395-4

Kohlberg, E., & Mertens, J. (1986). On the Strategic Stability of Equilibria. *Econometrica*, *54*(5), 1003–1037. doi:10.2307/1912320

Krämer, F., Schmidt, K., Spann, M., & Stich, L. (2017). Delegating pricing power to customers: Pay What You Want or Name Your Own Price? *Journal of Economic Behavior & Organization*, *136*, 125–140. doi:10.1016/j.jebo.2017.01.019

Kwasnioka, F. (2018). Detecting, anticipating, and predicting critical transitions in spatially extended systems. *Chaos (Woodbury, N.Y.)*, *28*(3), 033614. doi:10.1063/1.5022189 PMID:29604649

Lee, J., & Liu, Q. (2013). Gambling Reputation: Repeated Bargaining With Outside Options. *Econometrica*, *81*(4), 1601–1672. doi:10.3982/ECTA9200

Levina, T., & Levin, Y. (2006). Dynamic Pricing With Online Learning Of General Reservation Price Distribution. *IFAC Proceedings*, *39*(3), 461-466.

Li, W., Liu, Y., & Chen, Y. (2018). Modeling a two-stage supply contract problem in a hybrid uncertain environment. *Computers & Industrial Engineering*, *123*, 289–302. doi:10.1016/j.cie.2018.06.031

Lin, E., & Chou, M. (1990). Optimal contracts. *Applied Mathematics Letters*, *3*(2), 65–68. doi:10.1016/0893-9659(90)90016-5

Lutz, D., & Schafke, R. (1985). On The Identification And Stability Of Formal Invariants For Singular Differential Equations. *Linear Algebra and Its Applications*, *7*, 1–46. doi:10.1016/0024-3795(85)90140-5

Madureira, A., Pereira, I., Pereira, P., & Abraham, A. (2014). Negotiation mechanism for self-organized scheduling system with collective intelligence. *Neurocomputing*, *132*, 97–110. doi:10.1016/j.neucom.2013.10.032

Makhdoumi, A., Malekian, A., & Ozdaglar, A. (2017). *Strategic Dynamic Pricing with Network Externalities*. https://arxiv.org/pdf/1706.01131.pdf

Martínez, R., Massó, J., Neme, A., & Oviedo, J. (2012). On The Invariance Of The Set Of Core Matchings With Respect To Preference Profiles. *Games and Economic Behavior*, *74*(2), 588–600. doi:10.1016/j.geb.2011.08.011

Mashayekhy, L., Nejad, M., & Grosu, D. (2014). A Two-Sided Market Mechanism For Trading Big Data Computing Commodities. *2014 IEEE International Conference On Big Data (Big Data)*. 10.1109/BigData.2014.7004225

Meneguzzi, F., Modgil, S., & Oren, N. (2011). Algorithms and mechanisms for procuring services with uncertain durations using redundancy. *Artificial Intelligence*, *175*(14–15), 2021–2060.

Meneguzzi, F., Modgil, S., Oren, N., Miles, S., Luck, M., & Faci, N. (2012). Applying electronic contracting to the aerospace aftercare domain. *Engineering Applications of Artificial Intelligence*, *25*(7), 1471–1487. doi:10.1016/j.engappai.2012.06.004

Mitchell, M. (2006). Complex systems: Network thinking. *Artificial Intelligence*, *170*(18), 1194–1212. doi:10.1016/j.artint.2006.10.002

Mohri, M., & Medina, A. (2014). *Learning Theory And Algorithms For Revenue Optimization In Second-Price Auctions With Reserve*. https://arxiv.org/abs/1310.5665

Muuls, M. (2015). Exporters, importers and credit constraints. *Journal of International Economics*, *95*(2), 333–343. doi:10.1016/j.jinteco.2014.12.003

Nakhe, P. (2017). *Dynamic Pricing in Competitive Markets*. https://arxiv.org/pdf/1709.04960.pdf

Nazerzadeh, H., & Leme, R. (2016). *Where to Sell: Simulating Auctions From Learning Algorithms*. https://static.googleusercontent.com/media/research.google.com/en//pubs/archive/45455.pdf

Niederhoff, J., & Kouvelis, P. (2019). Effective and necessary: Individual supplier behavior in revenue sharing and wholesale contracts. *European Journal of Operational Research*, *277*(3), 1060–1071. doi:10.1016/j.ejor.2019.03.038

Niels, G., & Ten Kate, A. (2000). Predatory Pricing Standards: Is There a Growing International Consensus? *The Antitrust Bulletin, 45*(3), 787–809. doi:10.1177/0003603X0004500309

Nisam, N. (2007). Introduction to Mechanism Design for Computer Scientists. In Algorithmic Game Theory. Academic Press.

Noe, T. (2012). *Survey of the Economic Theory of Reputation: Its Logic and Limits*. The Oxford Handbook of Corporate Reputation.

Nwogugu, M. (2006). Employee Stock Options, Production Functions And Game Theory. *Applied Mathematics and Computation, 181*(1), 552–562. doi:10.1016/j.amc.2005.12.067

Nwogugu, M. (2007a). Issues In Disintermediation In The Real Estate Brokerage Industry. *Applied Mathematics and Computation, 186*(2), 1054–1064. doi:10.1016/j.amc.2006.08.053

Nwogugu, M. (2007b). Some Issues In Securitization And Disintermediation. *Applied Mathematics and Computation, 186*(2), 1031–1039. doi:10.1016/j.amc.2006.08.052

Nwogugu, M. (2019a). *Human Computer Interaction, Incentive Conflicts And Methods For Eliminating Index Arbitrage, Index-Related Mutual Fund Arbitrage And ETF Arbitrage. In Indices, Index Funds And ETFs HCI: Exploring HCI, Nonlinear Risk And Homomorphisms*. Palgrave MacMillan.

Nwogugu, M. (2019b). Economic Policy, Complex Adaptive Systems, Human-Computer Interaction And Managerial Psychology: Popular-Index Ecosystems. In Indices, Index Funds And ETFs HCI: Exploring HCI, Nonlinear Risk And Homomorphisms. Palgrave MacMillan.

NwoguguM. C. I. (2013). *Complex Systems, International Capital Flows and New 'Learning' Business Models for the Credit Rating Agency Industry*. https://ssrn.com/abstract=1761406 doi:10.2139srn.1761406

Office Of The New York State Attorney General. (2008). *Attorney General Cuomo Announces Landmark Reform agreements With The Nation's Three Principal Credit CRAs*. Available at: http://www.oag.state.ny.us/press/2008/june/june5a_08.html/

Park, G., & Lee, H. (2018). Opportunistic behaviors of credit rating agencies and bond issuers. *Pacific-Basin Finance Journal, 47*, 39–59. doi:10.1016/j.pacfin.2017.11.003

Park, S., & Kim, J. (2014). A mathematical model for a capacity reservation contract. *Applied Mathematical Modelling, 38*(5-6), 1866–1880. doi:10.1016/j.apm.2013.10.005

Patterson, M. (2010). Standardization Of Standard-Form Contracts: Competition And Contract Implications. *William and Mary Law Review, 52*(2), 327–340.

Patterson, M. (2012). Manipulation of Product Ratings: Credit-Rating Agencies, Google, and Antitrust. *Antitrust Chronicle, 4*(1).

Roth, A., & Sotomayor, M. (1992). Two-Sided Matching: A Study in Game-Theoretic Modeling and Analysis. Academic Press.

Sandholm, T., & Likhodedov, A. (2015). Automated design of revenue maximizing combinatorial auctions. *Operations Research, 63*(5), 1000–1025. doi:10.1287/opre.2015.1398

Satterthwaite, M., & Williams, S. (1989). The Rate Of Convergence To Efficiency In The Buyer's Bid Double Auction As The Market Becomes Large. *The Review of Economic Studies*, *56*(4), 477–498. doi:10.2307/2297496

Scalas, E., Rapallo, F., & Radivojević, T. (2017). Low-traffic limit and first-passage times for a simple model of the continuous double auction. *Physica A*, *485*, 61–72. doi:10.1016/j.physa.2017.05.020

Securities & Exchange Board of India. (2016). *Enhanced Standards for Credit Rating Agencies (CRAs)*. PR No. 150/2016. https://www.sebi.gov.in/cms/sebi_data/attachdocs/1477999985100.pdf

Sheng, J. (2019). Neoliberal environmentality and incentive-coordinated REDD+ contracts. *Land Use Policy*, *81*, 400–407. doi:10.1016/j.landusepol.2018.10.055

Skreta, V., & Veldkamp, L. (2009). Ratings Shopping And Asset Complexity: A Theory Of Ratings Inflation. *Journal of Monetary Economics*, *56*(5), 678–695. doi:10.1016/j.jmoneco.2009.04.006

Sotomayor, M. (2003). Some further remark on the core structure of the assignment game. *Mathematical Social Sciences*, *46*(3), 261–265. doi:10.1016/S0165-4896(03)00067-2

Sprinkle, G., Williamson, M., & Upton, D. (2008). The effort and risk-taking effects of budget-based contracts. *Accounting, Organizations and Society*, *33*(4-5), 436–452. doi:10.1016/j.aos.2007.11.001

Sussman, O. (1999). Economic growth with standardized contracts. *European Economic Review*, *43*(9), 1797–1818. doi:10.1016/S0014-2921(98)00040-3

Sy, A. (2009, December). The Systemic Regulation of Credit Rating Agencies And Rated Markets. *World Economy*.

Telser, L. (1994). The Usefulness of Core Theory In Economics. *The Journal of Economic Perspectives*, *8*(2), 151–164. doi:10.1257/jep.8.2.151

Terán, J., Aguilar, J., & Cerrada, M. (2017). Integration in industrial automation based on multi-agent systems using cultural algorithms for optimizing the coordination mechanisms. *Computers in Industry*, *91*, 11–23. doi:10.1016/j.compind.2017.05.002

Thille, H., & Cojocaru, M. (2013). A Dynamic Pricing Game In A Model Of New Product Adoption With Social Influence. *International Conference On Social Computing*. 10.1109/SocialCom.2013.114

Tomashevskiy, A., & Kono, D. (2015). Extra Credit: Preferential Trade Arrangements and Credit Ratings. *International Studies Quarterly*, *59*(2), 291–302. doi:10.1111/isqu.12183

Toscano, F. (2020). Does the Dodd-Frank Act reduce the conflict of interests of credit rating agencies? [in-press.]. *Journal of Corporate Finance*, *62*, 62. doi:10.1016/j.jcorpfin.2020.101595

United States Government Accountability Office. (2012). *Credit Rating Agencies: Alternative Compensation Models for Nationally Recognized Statistical Rating Organizations*. Available at: https://www.gao.gov/assets/590/587832.pdf

U.S. Department of Justice. (2009). *Constitutionality of Mandatory Registration of Credit CRAs*. Available at: https://www.justice.gov/olc/2009/opinion-letter-treasury.pdf

US Dept. of Justice Complaint. (2013). *Department of Justice Sues Standard & Poors For Fraud In Rating Mortgage Backed Securities In The Years Leading Up To The Financial Crisis*. Author.

U.S. Federal Deposit Insurance Corporation. (2011). *References to Credit Ratings in FDIC Regulations*. Author.

Van Assche, A., & Schwartz, G. (2013). Contracting institutions and ownership structure in international joint ventures. *Journal of Development Economics*, *103*, 124–132. doi:10.1016/j.jdeveco.2013.02.008

Van Den Brink, R. (2012). Efficiency and Collusion Neutrality in Cooperative Games and Networks. *Games and Economic Behavior*, *76*(1), 344–348. doi:10.1016/j.geb.2012.04.001

Virag, G. (2011). High Profit Equilibria In Directed Search models. *Games and Economic Behavior*, *71*(1), 224–234. doi:10.1016/j.geb.2010.08.006

Wang, G., Xu, H., & Lai, Y. (2018). Emergence, evolution, and control of multistability in a hybrid topological quantum/classical system. *Chaos (Woodbury, N.Y.)*, *28*(3).

Wang, T. (2012). *Can reputation concerns always discipline credit CRAs? Evidence from corporate bond issuance ratings*. Working Paper.

Wei, W., Wang, J., Chen, X., Yang, J., & Min, X. (2018). Psychological contract model for knowledge collaboration in virtual community of practice: An analysis based on the game theory. *Applied Mathematics and Computation*, *329*, 175–187. doi:10.1016/j.amc.2018.01.053

Wu, Z., Zhao, R., & Tang, W. (2014). Optimal contracts for the agency problem with multiple uncertain information. *Knowledge-Based Systems*, *59*, 161–172. doi:10.1016/j.knosys.2014.01.009

Yalta, T., & Yalta, Y. (2018). Are credit rating agencies regionally biased? *Economic Systems*, *42*(4), 682–694. doi:10.1016/j.ecosys.2018.08.001

Yoav, S., & Leyton-Brown, K. (2009). *Multiagent Systems: Algorithmic, Game-Theoretic, and Logical Foundations*. Cambridge University Press.

Zhang, J. (2018). Influence of individual rationality on continuous double auction markets with networked traders. *Physica A*, *495*, 353–392. doi:10.1016/j.physa.2017.12.098

Zhao, D. (2012). *Mechanism Design for Dynamic Double Auctions* (PhD Thesis). University of Western Sydney (Australia) & University Of Toulouse (France). http://dengji-zhao.net/publications/PhD/Dengji%20Zhao_PhD_SCEM_Thesis.pdf

Zohar, A., & Rosenschein, J. (2008). Mechanisms for information elicitation. *Artificial Intelligence*, *172*(16–17), 1917–1939. doi:10.1016/j.artint.2008.08.005

ENDNOTES

1 *See:* US Securities & Exchange Commission (January 2003). *Report on the Role and Function of Credit Rating Agencies in the Operation of the Securities Markets - As Required by Section 702(b) of the Sarbanes-Oxley Act of 2002.*

See: Office Of The New York State Attorney General (June 2008). *Attorney General Cuomo Announces Landmark Reform agreements With The Nation's Three Principal Credit Rating Agencies.* Available at: http://www.oag.state.ny.us/press/2008/june/june5a_08.html/. According to a June 2008 Press Release by the office of the New York State Attorney General "Under the agreements with Attorney General Cuomo, the credit rating agencies will fundamentally alter how they are compensated by investment banks for providing ratings on loan pools. In addition, the ratings firms will all now require for the first time that investment banks provide due diligence data on loan pools for review prior to the issuance of ratings. This will ensure that significant data, which was not previously disclosed to the rating agencies, will be received and reviewed by them before any bonds are rated. "The mortgage crisis currently facing this nation was caused in part by misrepresentations and misunderstanding of the true value of mortgage securities. The tremendous reach of this crisis cannot be understated – our entire economy continues to feel aftershocks from the collapse of the mortgage industry," said Attorney General Cuomo. "By increasing the independence of the rating agencies, ensuring they get adequate information to make their ratings, and increasing industry-wide transparency, these reforms will address one of the central causes of that collapse. The reforms agreed to today by S&P, Moody's, and Fitch should begin to restore investor confidence during what is a very troubling time for the mortgage industry, and I applaud the firms for their cooperation with our investigation".

2 *See*: Office Of The New York State Attorney General (June 2008). *Attorney General Cuomo Announces Landmark Reform agreements With The Nation's Three Principal Credit Rating Agencies.* Available at: http://www.oag.state.ny.us/press/2008/june/june5a_08.html/.

APPENDIX

Table 1. Identified Alternative Compensation Models for NRSROs (Prepared By US GAO)

Name	Description
"Random selection"	***Summary:*** Issuers continue to pay for ratings but payment is made to a ratings board that randomly assigns NRSROs to rate issuances. ***Details:*** A ratings clearinghouse randomly would select NRSROs to rate a new issuance in this proposed model. The clearinghouse could be a nonprofit, a governmental agency such as SEC, or a private-public partnership that would design the criteria by which new entrants could qualify as a credit rating agency. All issuers or sponsors that wanted ratings for their issuances would request them from the clearinghouse, which would use a random number generator to assign an NRSRO registered in the relevant asset class to produce the rating. The clearinghouse would notify the NRSRO of the opportunity to rate the issuance and provide basic information on the type of issuance but not the issuer's name. Not until the NRSRO agreed to complete the rating would the clearinghouse identify the issuer and details of the issuance. If the selected NRSRO agreed to rate the issuance, the issuer would pay a fee to the clearinghouse. The issuer also would pay to cover clearinghouse costs on top of those required to rate the security. Upon completion of the initial and maintenance ratings, the clearinghouse would distribute the fees to the NRSRO. The clearinghouse would set the ratings fees for the NRSRO depending on the type of security issued, but the letter rating would be free of charge to the public. The proposed model incorporates a peer comparison review to create an incentive for NRSROs to produce quality ratings. As part of this review, the clearinghouse would evaluate the performance of all NRSROs on the basis of two empirical tests. For instance, if the default percentage of debt instruments rated by a given NRSRO differed from the default percentage of its peers by a set parameter, then the NRSRO would be subject to sanctions such as losing a percentage of business or rating fees. A second test would compare annual yields of identically rated debt securities from different asset classes. Securities in different asset classes that are rated similarly should have the same yield. An NRSRO would be subject to sanctions if the yields of identically rated securities differed by a certain threshold. According to the author of this proposed model, by eliminating the linkage between the NRSRO and the issuer, this model would eliminate the conflict of interest stemming from the issuer-pays model. Furthermore, the author stated that the peer comparison review coupled with economic sanctions for poor performance would motivate the NRSROs to continually adjust their models and produce quality ratings.
"Investor-owned"	***Summary:*** Institutional investors create and operate an NRSRO. Issuers are required to get two ratings, one from the investor-owned NRSRO and one from an NRSRO of their choice. ***Details:*** Under this model, sophisticated investors—referred to as "highly sophisticated institutional purchasers" in the model—would create and operate an NRSRO that would produce ratings. Issuers would have to obtain two ratings—one from the investor-owned NRSRO and the second from their choice of NRSRO. More specifically, an NRSRO could not publicly release a rating for which an issuer or sponsor paid unless the NRSRO received written notification that the issuer had paid an investor-owned NRSRO to publicly release its rating. The investor-owned NRSRO would publish its rating on or before the date on which the solicited NRSRO published its rating. Institutional investors would have to qualify as highly sophisticated institutional purchasers before forming or joining an investor-owned agency. To qualify, an institutional investor would have to demonstrate that it was large and sophisticated, managed billions of dollars in assets, and could be relied upon to represent the buy-side interest in accurately rating debt market instruments. The investor-purchasers would hold majority voting and operational control over the agency, which could be for-profit or not-for-profit. Market forces would set the agency fees, which likely would be comparable to fees currently charged by dominant NRSROs. The letter rating and the underlying research would be free to the public. Proponents of this model believe that it would improve the rating process by changing incentive structures. They said that investor-owned agencies would introduce new competition to the industry and balance the investors' interests against issuers' interests.
"Stand-alone"	***Summary:*** NRSROs choose which issues to rate. A transaction fee for original issuance and fees from secondary market transactions pay for the ratings. ***Details:*** NRSROs would only be permitted to produce credit ratings in this proposed model. They could interact with and advise organizations being rated, but could not charge fees for advice. Proponents of this model believe that by creating a funding source beyond the influence of both issuers and investors, NRSROs would focus on producing the most accurate and timely credit analysis rather than on satisfying the desires of any other vested interest. Instead of receiving issuer fees, the NRSROs would be compensated through transaction fees for original issuance and secondary market transactions. The issuer or secondary-market seller would pay part of the fee, and the investor purchasing the security (in the primary or secondary market) would pay the other part. The NRSRO would be compensated over the life of the security based on these transaction fees. The letter rating would be free to the public. Proponents of this model believe that by creating a funding source beyond the influence of both issuers and investors, NRSROs would focus on producing the most accurate and timely credit analysis rather than on satisfying the desires of any other vested interest.
"Designation"	***Summary*** :NRSROs choose which issues to rate and securities holders designate which NRSRO(s) would receive the fees they pay for rating(s). A third party collects and distributes fees. ***Details:*** In this proposed model, all NRSROs could opt to rate a new issuance and security holders would direct, or designate, fees to the NRSROs of their choice. When an issuer brought a security to market, it would have to provide all interested NRSROs with the information to rate the issuance and pay rating fees to a third-party administrator, which would manage the designation process. The investors that purchased the debt issuance would each designate one or several NRSROs that rated the security to receive fees, based on their perception of research underlying the ratings. The third-party administrator would disburse the fees in accordance with the designations. If the NRSRO was part of a larger company, interaction between the parent company and the NRSRO would be prohibited. After the initial rating, the issuer would continue to pay maintenance rating fees to the third-party administrator. A final rating fee would be paid in conjunction with the retirement (or repurchase) of the security. The letter rating would be free to the public, while the research underlying it would be distributed to security holders and (at the discretion of the relevant NRSROs) to potential security holders. The authors of this proposed model said it would eliminate conflicts of interest resulting from issuers paying for ratings and increase competition by allowing all NRSROs access to the information necessary to rate any issuance. The authors also stated that this model encourages NRSROs to prepare ratings because each NRSRO that did could profit from its ratings to the extent investors or other users find the ratings useful.
"User-pays"	***Summary:*** Third-party auditors determine who is "using" ratings and require that all "users" pay the NRSROs. ***Details:*** Issuers would not pay for ratings under this proposed model; rather, all users of ratings would enter into a contract with an NRSRO and pay for rating services. The proposal defines "user" as any entity that included a rated security, loan, or contract as an element of its assets or liabilities as recorded in an audited financial statement. For example, users could be holders of long or short positions in a fixed-income instrument, parties that refer to a credit rating in contractual commitments (that is, as parties to a lease), or parties to derivative products that rely on rated securities or entities. A user would have to pay for ratings services supplied during each period in which it booked the related asset or liability. The proposed model relies on third-party auditors to ensure that NRSROs receive payment for their services from users of ratings. The user would have to demonstrate to the auditors that the holder of a rated instrument or contract paid for the rating services. Until auditors were satisfied that NRSROs had been properly compensated, they would not issue audit opinions. The model would require the close cooperation of the auditing community and the Public Company Auditing Oversight Board. The authors of this model stated that, while more cumbersome, the model attempts to capture "free riders"—those users of ratings that do not compensate NRSROs for the use of their intellectual property—and requires them to pay for ratings.
"Alternative user-pays"	***Summary:*** Creditors' resources are pooled and a government agency or independent board uses these resources to solicit ratings. NRSROs bid on the right to rate products. ***Details:*** The alternative user-pays model would pool creditors' resources to secure ratings before debt was issued. A government agency or independent board would administer a user-fee system financed by debt purchasers, which would fund a competitive bidding process for the selection of rating agencies. The agency or board would solicit ratings before the debt issuance and then pay for the expense and related administrative costs through the user fee. NRSROs would bid on the right to issue ratings with the agency or board determining how best to judge the bids and award the right to rate the issuance. For example, the agency or board could weigh factors such as price, extent of diligence the NRSRO proposed to undertake, and the disclosures the NRSRO would demand from issuers as a condition for the rating. The author believes the bidding process would serve to contain the costs for ratings through price competition, level the playing field for smaller competitors and new entrants, and balance the desire for market-based assessments of risk with a greater role for the government agency, such as SEC, or an independent board in defining rating agencies' responsibilities. The user fee could be assessed through a flat fraction of a percentage fee on the initial purchasers of debt offerings. The user fee would allow the agency or board to finance initial ratings on a rolling basis, with the ratings for a given debt issuance being secured before the issuance of the debt. Although the fee could be assessed in many ways, the author of the model suggests a one-time fee at initial sale for administrative ease. NRSROs would bid on the right to issue ratings with the agency or board determining how best to judge the bids and award the right to rate the issuance. For example, the agency or board could weigh factors such as price, extent of diligence the NRSRO proposed to undertake, and the disclosures the NRSRO would demand from issuers as a condition for the rating. The author believes the bidding process would serve to contain the costs for ratings through price competition, level the playing field for smaller competitors and new entrants, and balance the desire for market-based assessments of risk with a greater role for the government agency, such as SEC, or an independent board in defining rating agencies' responsibilities. According to its author, this user-fee model creates additional accountability mechanisms. Users of ratings would be given enforceable rights and would require NRSROs to assume certification and mandatory reporting duties to creditors. The system would set up creditor committees that would serve as a channel for creditors to monitor ratings and assert limited rights against NRSROs. If an NRSRO breached duties owed to the creditors, the committee would serve as the representative in any potential actions and preempt actions brought by individual creditors. The model would require that all contracts with NRSROs detail duties owed to their creditors, to delineate the potential liability exposure for breach of these duties, and channel adjudication of any disputes to an SEC administrative process. For example, NRSROs could be required to certify on a quarterly basis that they exercised reasonable care in conducting due diligence of issuers' financial and nonfinancial disclosures to make accurate assessments of risk exposure. To provide NRSROs with incentives for compliance without jeopardizing their financial viability, the model would limit NRSRO financial liability to cases of gross negligence, coupled with an earnings-based cap on liability and other safeguards
"Issuer and investor-pays"	***Summary:*** Issuers and investors pay a fee on the issuance of new debt and secondary market trades. NRSROs are placed in a continuous queue and assigned to rate issues as their number comes up. Assignment eventually is based on an NRSRO's performance. ***Details:*** This proposed model incorporates characteristics from a number of the models described earlier and leverages an existing structure as the basis for collecting and distributing ratings fees. Under the proposed issuer and investor-pays model, accredited NRSROs would be assigned to rate new issuances. Initially, all NRSROs would be placed in a continuous queue and would receive rating assignments when their respective numbers came up, unless they were unable or unwilling to rate a particular issue. In the future, ratings would be assigned based on the performances of the NRSROs, with those agencies that produced superior performance receiving more assignments. Performance would be measured as the correlation between an NRSRO's ratings and default and recovery rates on issues rated, and tracked using a common, transparent, and defensible methodology. To help ensure rigor and fairness, at least two and possibly three NRSROs would be assigned to rate each issuance. Payments for ratings would come from a fee levied on issuers of new debt issues and investors as parties of secondary market trades. These fees would be deposited in a dedicated fund—the U.S. Ratings Fund—and would be determined and reset periodically. The periodic review would consider the historic and projected volumes of primary issuances and of secondary market trading to determine a fee that would in the aggregate allow the ratings business to attract and retain qualified individuals. This fund would be modeled after the Municipal Securities Rulemaking Board (MSRB), which is authorized to collect fees on new and secondary market municipal issues to fund its activities, and would be overseen by a governing board representing issuers, investors, rating agencies, intermediaries, and independent directors. The fees collected would be used to pay the selected accredited NRSROs for issuing each solicited rating and other necessary administrative activities such as tracking NRSRO's performance and tracking deals to be rated. The authors note that these other activities could be outsourced or performed by the U.S. Ratings Fund. The Fund also would advise SEC on the eligibility and accreditation of the NRSROs. All ratings and related research reports paid for through the U.S. Ratings Fund would be freely available to the public. According to the authors, NRSROs would have incentives to provide accurate ratings and be objective because ratings would be monitored by a regulator and the accreditation of NRSROs would be subject to periodic renewal. The authors also note that legislation likely would be required to set up the new rating agency compensation model. Specifically, the authors said that legislation would need to enumerate the functions and the governance structure of the U.S. Ratings Fund, provide its mandate and methodology for determining the fees to be charged for ratings, and elaborate on how the new rating model would be introduced.
"Market-Pays"	The credit rating agencies would be part of a cooperative overseen by a board made up of individuals representing institutional and retail investor interests. The board's primary functions would be to approve credit rating agencies eligible to rate issuances and collect and distribute fees to the selected credit rating agencies that provided rating services. Implementation of this model would also likely require legislation; such as to enumerate the functions and the governance of the oversight board, as well as to establish the cooperative framework. Unlike the issuer and investor pay model, this variant would generate funds to pay the rating agencies' fees (and potentially board costs) by incorporating a market-wide fee into the issuances' coupon rate, i.e., a payment strip. It also differs by allowing the issuer and investors (as a group) each to select the credit rating agencies in the cooperative they would like to rate the issuances. There would be a limit to the number of rating agencies selected, potentially up to two selected by an issuer and two by the investors. As with the issuer and investor pay model, all ratings and related research would be freely available to the public.

Source: United States Government Accountability Office (2012) - summary of alternative compensation models.

Table 2. The US GAO's Framework for Evaluating Alternative Models for Compensating NRSROs

Factors	Description
Independence	The ability for the compensation model to mitigate conflicts of interest inherent between the entity paying for the rating and the NRSRO. Key questions include: What potential conflicts of interest exist in the alternative compensation model and what controls, if any, would need to be implemented to mitigate these conflicts?
Accountability	The ability of the compensation model to promote NRSROs' responsibility for the accuracy and timeliness of their ratings. Key questions include: How does the compensation model create economic incentives for NRSROs to produce quality ratings over the life of an issuance? How is NRSRO performance evaluated and by whom?
Competition	The extent to which the compensation model creates an environment in which NRSROs compete for customers by producing higher-quality ratings at competitive prices. Key questions include: To what extent does the compensation model encourage competition around the quality of ratings, ratings fees, and product innovation? To what extent does it allow for flexibility in the differing sizes, resources, and specialties of NRSROs?
Transparency	The accessibility, usability, and clarity of the compensation model and the dissemination of information on the model to market participants. Key questions include: How transparent are the model's processes and procedures for determining ratings fees and compensating NRSROs? How would NRSROs obtain ratings business?
Feasibility	The simplicity and ease with which the compensation model can be implemented in the securities market. Key questions include: What are the costs to implement the compensation model and who would fund them? Who would administer the compensation model? What, if any, infrastructure would be needed to implement it?
Market acceptance and choice	The willingness of the securities market to accept the compensation model, the ratings produced under that model, and any new market players established by the compensation model. Key questions include: What role do market participants have in selecting NRSROs to produce ratings, assessing the quality of ratings, and determining NRSRO compensation?
Oversight	The evaluation of the model to ensure it works as intended. Key questions include: Does the model provide for an independent internal control function? What external oversight does the compensation model provide to ensure it is working as intended?

Source: United States Government Accountability Office (2012).

About the Author

Michael C. Nwogugu, is an author, serial entrepreneur and consultant who has held senior management, Board-of-Directors and Advisory Board Member positions in companies in the U.S., Barbados, France, India and Nigeria. Mr. Nwogugu wrote the following books: Risk In the Global Real Estate Market (2012); Illegal File-sharing Networks, Digital Goods Pricing And Decision Analysis (2016); Anomalies In Net Present Value, Returns And Polynomials; And Regret Theory In Decision-Making (2017); Indices, Index Funds And ETFs – Exploring HCI, Nonlinear Risk And Homomorphisms (2019); Complex Systems, Multi-Sided Incentives And Risk Perception In Organizations (2019); Earnings Management, Fintech-Driven Incentives and Sustainable Growth: On Complex Systems, Legal and Mechanism Design Factors (2020); and Geopolitical Risk, Sustainability and "Cross-Border Spillovers" in Emerging Markets (forthcoming 2021). Mr. Nwogugu's research articles have been cited in science journals such as: International Journal of Approximate Reasoning; European Journal of Operational Research; Expert Systems With Applications; Applied Mathematics & Computation; Neural Computing & Applications; Applied Soft Computing; Journal Of Business Research; Information Fusion; Computers & Industrial Engineering; Journal of Experimental Psychology - Learning, Memory & Cognition; Mathematical Methods of Operations Research; Physica-A; Europhysics Letters; International Journal of Project Management; Regional Science & Urban Economics; Journal of Regional Science; the Proceedings Of The National Academy of Sciences of the US (PNAS); Complexity (Wiley + Hindawi); Brain & Cognition; Management Decision; Journal of Grey Systems; Economic Modelling; International Journal of Fuzzy Systems; IEEE Transactions on Software Engineering; Frontiers of Information Technology & Electronic Engineering, and Service Business. Mr. Nwogugu earned degrees from the University of Nigeria (Nigeria); City College Of New York (New York City, USA) and Columbia University (New York City, USA).

Index

Q

R

S

T

V

W

www.ingramcontent.com/pod-product-compliance
Lightning Source LLC
LaVergne TN
LVHW062140300926
849161LV00010B/2584
* 9 7 8 1 7 9 9 8 7 4 1 8 8 *